Light from the Ancient Past

This is a connected account of the background of the Bible and of early Christianity as known through the discoveries of archeology, covering the period 5000 B.C. to A.D. 500. Lucidly written and copiously illustrated, it can be read with delight by the general reader as well as by students of Near East civilization, ancient art, and Hebrew-Christian archeology.

Mr. Finegan traces the history and civilization of the lands in which the Hebrew and Christian religions arose, showing how Biblical history fits into this wider history, and describing and evaluating the Hebrew and Christian monuments which remain from ancient times. His work is founded upon the ancient sources, both literary and monumental, and in the fascinating section on Early Christianity he makes interesting research contributions of his own.

Light from the Ancient Past is notable for its compactness, its sense of continuity and variety of interest. While it was written primarily to illuminate and vivify the history of the Hebrew-Christian religion, it also contains much material relative to other ancient religions, to the history of thought and the development of culture, and to the evolution of art and architecture.

The author is an American scholar who received his Lic. theol. degree *magna cum laude* from the University of Berlin in 1934. He is a minister of the Disciples of Christ and director of religious activities at Iowa State College in Ames.

LIGHT FROM THE ANCIENT PAST

LIGHT FROM
THE ANCIENT PAST

The
Archeological Background
of the
Hebrew-Christian
Religion

By JACK FINEGAN

PRINCETONUNI
VERSITYPRESS
MCMXLVI

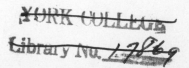

Printed in the United States of America by Princeton
University Press at Princeton, New Jersey

TO THE MEMORY OF

JESSE COBB CALDWELL

AND

HANS LIETZMANN

Preface

THE purpose of this book is to give a connected account of the archeological background of the Hebrew-Christian religion. Within the last century and one-half and largely within the past few decades, oriental archeology has pioneered a new past, in which are revealed more extensive vistas and higher cultures than hitherto were imagined. The account that now can be given of the rise of civilization in the Middle East, of the development of art and of the dawn of conscience, is of fascinating interest in itself. It also is of great significance for an understanding of the Hebrew faith and the Christian movement, both of which in their origin and earlier history were integral parts of the ancient world. To see that world come vividly and startlingly alive is to find Hebrew-Christian history invested with a fresh sense of reality and interest. There are, moreover, many points at which biblical records and archeological discoveries are in direct contact, and increasingly in the later centuries there are many archeological remains which are primary historical monuments of the Hebrew-Christian religion. A knowledge of these facts is now indispensable to all serious study of the history of that religion, and the proper utilization of the abundant new archeological materials may even be said to constitute the next urgent task in that study.

The presentation of this archeological background in the present book is in the form of a continuous account extending, in round numbers, from 5000 B.C. to A.D. 500. After an introduction dealing with the nature of archeological work in general, the narrative begins with the rise of civilization in the valley of the Tigris and Euphrates Rivers where the origins of the Hebrew people traditionally are located and where antecedents of Hebrew mythology and law are found. Then the development of culture in the valley of the Nile is sketched, and the Exodus of the Israelites and their use of Egyptian materials in the Psalms and Proverbs are considered. Moving to Palestine, the "bridge" between these two ancient homes of empire, archeological findings are summarized, illuminating both Canaanitish and Israelitish times. Then the later Assyrian, Neo-Babylonian and Persian empires are described, upon whose imperial policies the fate and future of the kingdoms of Israel and Judah depended. With the world at last under Roman domination, the cities of Palestine are pictured as they were in the time of Jesus, and afterward a glimpse is obtained of the chief places in which the work of the apostle Paul was done. In view of the great importance of Paul's letters and other early Christian documents, a study is made of ancient writing materials and practices and of the transmission of the text to the present time. Then the Roman catacombs are investigated, together with their art and inscriptions, and a brief account is given of characteristic early Christian sarcophagi. Finally, the development of distinctive places of Christian assembly is indicated and the basilicas of Constantinian times are described—basilicas whose successors were the Byzantine churches of the East and the Romanesque and Gothic cathedrals of the West. With the clear emergence of the Christian community, centered in the place where the gospel of Jesus Christ is proclaimed, our story comes to an end.

In the earlier part of the narrative it is the broader background of the general history and civilization which is most illuminated by archeology and to which the major part of the portrayal is devoted. In the later part not only is the general history relatively simpler and more generally known, but there are also many more monuments of the Hebrew-Christian tradition itself. Therefore in the course of the book a steadily diminishing amount of space is apportioned to the general history and a steadily increasing amount given to the specifically biblical and early Christian materials.

In order to give a more vivid sense of direct contact with the living past, frequent quotations are made from the ancient sources, and numerous photographs are presented of actual places and objects. Many of the sites are ones which I have visited and many of the objects are ones which I have studied in the museums of Chicago, Philadelphia, New York, London, Paris, Berlin, Rome, Cairo and Jerusalem. An extensive literature has been consulted and all references cited, both ancient and modern, have been taken from personally used sources. The full title and date of each book are given upon its first appearance, with the exception of those works for which abbreviations are employed and which appear on page 2. The maps and plans have been prepared in detail by myself, and executed and lettered by Mr. William Lane Jones.

In the writing I have thought often of Dean Jesse Cobb Caldwell of the College of the Bible, Drake University, who taught me the importance of history, and of Professor *D.* Hans Lietzmann of *Friedrich-Wilhelms-Universität,* Berlin, who instructed me in early Christian archeology. I should like to dedicate this book to their memory. Also I wish to express appreciation to those who have given encouragement and counsel relative to bringing the work to publication, including Professor William F. Albright of The Johns Hopkins University, Dr. George A. Buttrick of The Madison Avenue Presbyterian Church, New York City; Professor John T. McNeill of Union Theological Seminary, Dr. Charles Clayton Morrison, Editor, *The Christian Century,* and President Charles E. Friley, President Emeritus Raymond M. Hughes, and Dean Harold V. Gaskill of the Iowa State College. Likewise I am very grateful to Mr. Datus C. Smith, Jr., Director of the Princeton University Press, for his deep understanding, constant interest and many courtesies.

JACK FINEGAN

Iowa State College
Ames, Iowa

Acknowledgments

IN addition to the acknowledgments made in the List of Illustrations, thanks are also due to the following for kind permission to make reproductions: to the American Academy of Arts and Sciences, Boston, for Figures 152 and 153; to the American Schools of Oriental Research, New Haven, for Figure 195; to the *Biblioteca Apostolica Vaticana*, Rome, for Figure 145; to the Trustees of the British Museum, London, for Figures 24, 46, 72, 74, 78, 89, 146, 147 and 149; to the Clarendon Press, Oxford, for Figures 64 and 148; to *Les Éditions d'Art et d'Histoire*, Paris, for Figure 82; to *Éditions Albert Morancé*, Paris, for Figures 42 and 49; to the Egypt Exploration Society, London, for Figures 39 and 134; to the Field Press (1930) Ltd., London, for Figures 68 and 69; to the President and Fellows of Harvard College, Cambridge, for Figure 107; to Arthur Upham Pope, Director of the Iranian Institute, New York, for Figure 87; to the Director of the *Istanbul Arkeoloji Müzeleri Müdürlügü*, Istanbul, for Figure 111; to Kirsopp Lake for Figure 148; to Kirsopp and Silva Lake for Figures 152 and 153; to *Librairie Orientaliste Paul Geuthner*, Paris, for Figure 21; to *Librairie Hachette*, Paris, for Figure 97; to Macmillan and Co. Ltd., London, for Figures 4, 5 and 6; to the Director of the National Gallery, London, for Figure 141; to the New York Public Library for Figure 106; to Sir Humphrey Milford, Oxford University Press, Oxford, for Figures 60, 61, 62, 70, 134, 186, 190 and 193; to the Government of Palestine for Figures 190 and 193; to the Palestine Exploration Fund, London, for Figures 59 and 66; to *Presses Universitaires de France*, Paris, for Figure 150; to George Routledge and Sons Ltd., London, for Figure 35; to C. F. A. Schaeffer for Figures 60, 61 and 62; to the *Service des Antiquités de l'Égypte*, Cairo, for Figures 38 and 44; to George Steindorff for Figure 47; to the Studio Limited, London, for Figure 141; to the University of Chicago Press for Figures 30, 40 and 43; to Emery Walker Ltd., London, for Figure 143; and to the Trustees of the late Sir Henry Wellcome, owners of the copyright, for Figure 70. The following pictures are from books whose copyright is vested in the Alien Property Custodian, 1945, pursuant to law, and their reproduction is by permission of the Alien Property Custodian in the public interest under License No. JA-964: Figure 154, Copyright 1919 by *Gesellschaft zur Förderung der Wissenschaft des Juden-*

tums, Berlin; Figure 151, Copyright 1929 by Peter Hanstein, Bonn; Figure 76, Copyright 1938 by J. C. Hinrichs, Leipzig; Figures 84, 85, Copyright 1925 by J. C. Hinrichs, Leipzig; Figure 168, Copyright 1927 by Josef Kösel & Friedrich Pustet K.-G., München; Figures 136, 138, 139, Copyright 1923 by J. C. B. Mohr (Paul Siebeck), Tübingen; Figures 41, 128, Copyright 1936 by *Phaidon Verlag,* Vienna; Figures 75, 129, 142, Copyright 1925 by *Propyläen-Verlag G.m.b.H.,* Berlin; Figures 156, 157, 158, 160, 161, 163, 164, Copyright 1933 by *Verlag für Kunstwissenschaft G.m.b.H.,* Berlin-Friedenau; Figure 120, Copyright 1923 by Ernst Wasmuth A.G., Berlin. Because of the war and other circumstances, it has been impossible to communicate with certain publishers and individuals, and for pictures used under such conditions appreciation is recorded here.

Acknowledgment is also made to the International Council of Religious Education, Chicago, for permission to quote from the American Standard Version of the Bible, and to the University of Chicago Press for permission to quote from *The Bible, An American Translation,* by J. M. Powis Smith and Edgar J. Goodspeed.

Contents

[xiii]

CONTENTS

CONTENTS

[xvi]

CONTENTS

CONTENTS

List of Illustrations

LIST OF ILLUSTRATIONS

[xx]

LIST OF ILLUSTRATIONS

[xxi]

LIST OF ILLUSTRATIONS

[xxiii]

LIST OF ILLUSTRATIONS

LIST OF ILLUSTRATIONS

LIST OF MAPS AND PLANS

MAPS

PLANS

LIGHT FROM THE ANCIENT PAST

LIST OF ABBREVIATIONS

AJA *American Journal of Archaeology.*

ANF Alexander Roberts and James Donaldson, eds., rev. by A. Cleveland Coxe, *The Ante-Nicene Fathers, Translations of the Writings of the Fathers down to A.D. 325.* 10 vols. 1885-87.

ARAB Daniel David Luckenbill, *Ancient Records of Assyria and Babylonia.* 2 vols. 1926-27.

ARE James Henry Breasted, *Ancient Records of Egypt.* 5 vols. 1906-07.

AS *Assyriological Studies.* Oriental Institute.

BA *The Biblical Archaeologist.*

BASOR *Bulletin* of the American Schools of Oriental Research.

CAH J. B. Bury, S. A. Cook, F. E. Adcock, M. P. Charlesworth and N. H. Baynes, eds., *The Cambridge Ancient History.* 12 vols. and 5 vols. of plates, 1923-39.

EB *The Encyclopaedia Britannica.* 14th ed. 24 vols. 1929.

HDB James Hastings, ed., *A Dictionary of the Bible.* 4 vols. 1898-1902.

HERE James Hastings, ed., *Encyclopaedia of Religion and Ethics.* 12 vols. 1910-22.

JBL *Journal of Biblical Literature.*

JE Isidore Singer, ed., *The Jewish Encyclopedia.* 12 vols. 1901-05.

JNES *Journal of Near Eastern Studies.*

KAT J. A. Knudtzon, *Die El-Amarna Tafeln.* 2 vols. 1908-15.

LCL *The Loeb Classical Library.*

LLP Louise Ropes Loomis, *The Book of the Popes (Liber Pontificalis)* I *To the Pontificate of Gregory I.* 1916.

LXX Henry Barclay Swete, ed., *The Old Testament in Greek according to the Septuagint.* ɪ: 4th ed. 1909; ɪɪ: 3d ed. 1907; ɪɪɪ: 3d ed. 1905.

MTAT Samuel A. B. Mercer, *The Tell El-Amarna Tablets.* 2 vols. 1939.

NPNF Philip Schaff, ed., *A Select Library of the Nicene and Post-Nicene Fathers,* First Series. 14 vols. 1886-89.

NPNFss Philip Schaff and Henry Wace, eds., *A Select Library of Nicene and Post-Nicene Fathers of the Christian Church,* Second Series. 14 vols. 1890-1900.

NSH Samuel M. Jackson, ed., *The New Schaff-Herzog Encyclopedia of Religious Knowledge.* 12 vols. 1908-12.

OIC *Oriental Institute Communications.*

OIP *Oriental Institute Publications.*

PATD Samuel B. Platner and Thomas Ashby, *A Topographical Dictionary of Ancient Rome.* 1929.

PEQ *Palestine Exploration Quarterly.*

RBT Michael L. Rodkinson, *New Edition of the Babylonian Talmud.* 10 (xx) vols. 1903, 1916.

SAOC *Studies in Ancient Oriental Civilization.* Oriental Institute.

SRK Paul Styger, *Die römischen Katakomben, archäologische Forschungen über den Ursprung und die Bedeutung der altchristlichen Grabstätten.* 1933.

Introduction

THE ancient Greeks felt themselves to be very modern and hence had a word ἀρχαιολογία which signified the discussion of antiquities. From this term is derived the English word "archeology" which means the scientific study of the material remains of the past.

Archeological interest existed even long before the time of the Greeks. In the seventh century B.C., Ashurbanipal of Assyria was proud of his ability to decipher the writing on ancient tablets, and sent his scribes far and wide to collect copies of early records and documents for his wonderful library at Nineveh. Nabonidus, who ruled at Babylon in the sixth century B.C., made exploratory soundings in the age-old ziggurat which loomed up at Ur, read the foundation records of its earlier builders, and carefully carried out restorations, giving due credit to his ancient predecessors in his own inscriptions. The daughter of Nabonidus, sister of the famous Belshazzar, shared the interest of her father and maintained a small museum in which objects of interest from earlier times were kept.

Unfortunately the "collection" of antiquities was undertaken all too often by persons of less disinterestedness, and untold treasures have been lost to scientific archeology through the depredations of robbers. An early story of papyrus-hunting, for example, concerns Setna-Khaemuast, the fifth and favorite son of Ramesses II. An account written probably in the reign of Ptolemy II tells how this young adventurer of the long ago braved the wrath of the spirits of the departed to enter the tomb of a certain prince. With this prince had been buried a magic roll of papyrus, whose possessor would know what is said by the birds as they fly and by the serpents as they crawl and would be able to enchant anything in heaven or earth. After incredible adventures Setna made away with the papyrus roll, only eventually to be driven to return it to the ghosts of the dead.

Unfortunately the predecessors and successors of the illustrious Setna in the art of tomb-robbing seldom have been constrained by the powers of the spirit world to replace their spoils, and so modern archeologists all too frequently have found themselves anticipated by the unauthorized efforts of plunderers before whose greed and skill not even as mighty monuments as the pyramids were secure. A commission appointed by Ramesses IX to examine into the condition of cemeteries reported in part as follows: "It was found that the thieves had violated them all, that they had torn their occupants away from their coffins and cases, had thrown them into the dust and had stolen all the funeral objects which had been given to them, as well as the gold and silver and the ornaments which were in their coffins." Among the tomb-robbers who rifled so many of the graves of the kings of Ur, special ignominy should attach to those workmen who in the very process of burying Lady Shub-ad managed to loot the grave of her previously deceased husband immediately below, hiding the hole they made in the brick vault by placing over it the lady's great clothes-chest.

In distinction from the foregoing, modern archeology may be said to have had its beginning in 1798, when nearly one hundred French scholars and artists accompanied Napoleon on his invasion of Egypt. They gazed with wonder upon the impressive monuments of that ancient land, wrote out systematic descriptions, copied texts and prepared water-color illustrations.

Early in the nineteenth century Claudius James Rich, the resident of the East India Company at Baghdad, observed in the regions surrounding that place the mounds of ancient cities and found many inscriptions. This aroused widespread interest and when the French vice-consul at Mosul, Paul Émile Botta, found Sargon's palace at Khorsabad, the enthusiasm of a young Englishman, Austen Henry Layard, was stirred. Layard's excavations, begun in 1845, at Nimrod and notably at the mound of Kuyunjik, which was the site of ancient Nineveh, constitute the next great landmark in the history of modern archeology.

The honor of beginning the scientific study of the localities and antiquities of Palestine belonged to an American, Professor Edward Robinson, of Union Theological Seminary in New York City, who on travels through Palestine in 1838 and 1852 made extensive observations and notes. Thereafter the Palestine Exploration Fund was organized in London in 1865, and its first representative, Captain Charles Warren, made a series of sketch maps of the country and, on a second expedition, actually carried out excavations on the temple hill in Jerusalem.

The real archeological work thus initiated in Egypt, Babylonia, Assyria and Palestine, has been continued and extended into related areas by a distinguished international succession of investigators, until modern archeology has become a true science, with most impressive results.

The work involved includes the excavation of far-flung sites, the discovery and decipherment of long-lost inscriptions and manuscripts, and the study of ancient monuments and objects of all kinds. The techniques of the science have been developed slowly through actual practice and experimentation. At first attention naturally was attracted by objects of large size and obvious impressiveness but now even the tiniest pieces of broken pottery are recognized as having their own important story to tell. Early digging sometimes was done without the requisite knowledge and skill to avoid destroying much of value, but today every step is taken with the greatest care and much attention is given to the recording and preservation of the resulting finds.

The difficulties which beset the work are various. The ancient sites may be hidden beneath modern towns or be in the possession of private persons whose interests are quite different from those of the archeologists. In the case of one famous site in Palestine, Tell el-Mutesellim (Fig. 57), the thirteen-acre area was found to be owned privately by no less than ninety separate individuals from whom it had to be leased or purchased. Unexpected discoveries of great value sometimes have provoked national jealousies and led to prolonged litigation concerning the respective rights of those concerned. Again, petty officials have presented formidable impediments to the work. Friction or discontent may arise among the native laborers, while wandering dealers in antiquities sometimes lurk in the neighborhood to buy from the diggers anything which those workmen may manage to steal. Many times the work is done in regions where conditions are hazardous to health, and the malarial mosquito and other scourges often have prostrated archeological staffs. Not infrequently the sites have been in relatively lawless sections where foreigners penetrated only at risk. Even in southern

Palestine as recently as January 10, 1938, an archeologist of the first rank, John Leslie Starkey, was killed by Arab bandits.

The object of investigation is often one of the ancient city-mounds which are so conspicuous a feature of the landscape in the Middle East. Such a mound is usually known as a *tell*, the plural being *tulul*. This word, which occurs in ancient Babylonia and is still in use in modern Arabic, means high, and hence is applicable to a hill or mound.[1] These ancient mounds were built up through the centuries by the accumulation of the debris of the successive cities which occupied the site. The city's own rubbish collected constantly and filled up the streets, while after each time of destruction by war or fire the new city was rebuilt upon the ruins of the old. In Joshua 11:13 there is a picturesque allusion to this situation in the mention of "the cities that stood on their mounds."

When such a *tell* is excavated today, the more recent remains naturally are found toward the top of the mound and the more ancient toward the bottom. Thus in digging from top to bottom one passes through the cultural layers in reverse sequence. While a test pit or trench may be useful as a preliminary survey, or may have to suffice when more extensive excavations cannot be attempted, more effective procedure calls for laying bare a considerable portion of the mound. This is the more necessary because the strata often are not nicely differentiated like the layers of a cake, but are intricately confused. A given stratum may bend down over the edge of the hill just as the town it represents followed the natural slopes or was built on artificial terraces. Hence it is important to clear an adequate area of each stratum and to record it in its proper order. This is known as stratigraphical excavation. Sometimes the entire mound is dug completely but it is regarded as preferable to leave at least a portion where future excavators may check the results.

The process of excavating a city-mound or other ancient site may be very laborious, involving the excavation and disposal of many tons of dirt and debris. The approach to objects of value is made with all care, and not only the pick but also the knife and brush are employed. As the various walls and structures appear they are plotted precisely and all the objects which are found from day to day are

---

[1] Other Arabic words which are frequently encountered include *ain*, spring; *bahr*, lake or canal; *jebel*, mountain; *kalat*, castle; *khirbet*, ruin; *nahr*, river; *shatt*, river or canal; and *wadi*, watercourse or valley.

recorded with the greatest exactitude. Detailed descriptions, drawings and photographs are prepared, and thus the archeologist's conclusions are based upon a comprehensive body of detailed information.[2]

While large numbers of records and documents have been among the finds brought to light in the course of excavations, many other inscriptions have been preserved on monuments above ground. This is notably the case in Egypt where a great body of historical inscriptions provides a major basis for the knowledge of ancient Egyptian history. The transcription of these records, which are slowly perishing under exposure to the elements, and their translation and publication are among the most important parts of the archeological enterprise. Whereas the copying formerly was done entirely by hand, recent epigraphic expeditions have employed more advanced methods. A photograph is taken of the inscription, and this is compared directly with the original by an artist who pencils in any necessary additions and retraces the lines of the whole. The resultant drawing is transformed into a blueprint and it in turn is "proofread" in comparison with the original by an expert in the decipherment and interpretation of ancient inscriptions. Thus the final facsimile combines the accuracy of the camera, the skill of the artist, and the reading ability of the epigrapher.

A great variety of monuments and objects fall under the archeologist's scrutiny. They range in size from the massive pyramids to small bits of jewelry and tiny scraps of papyrus, but none is neglected. Among the modern instruments which have been found useful in the study of the ancient remains is the X-ray. When an Egyptian mummy is to be studied, the X-ray makes it possible, even before the wrappings are opened, to determine the exact position of things such as jewelry which were placed with it; it is even possible to determine facts such as the cause of the individual's death and his approximate age at the time.

While aerial photography has been practiced for some time in connection with archeological work by suspending a camera from a balloon, the more recent employment of the airplane has expanded greatly the possibilities in this field. Not only can the progress of excavations on the ground be recorded from the air but also swift and extensive explorations of unknown areas can be conducted and

[2] cf. W. F. Badè, *A Manual of Excavation in the Near East.* 1934.

pictorial documentation of important sites be secured.[3] Ancient contours invisible on the ground are often seen clearly in such pictures and, if it is desired to heighten the relief effects, stereoscopic photography may be employed.[4] Needless to say, photographs from the air are invaluable to later archeological work on the ground.

Thus through the application of highly scientific techniques and by the cooperative efforts of scholars in many lands, the shattered mosaic of the past is slowly being fitted together again. Some portion of the result will be recounted in the following pages.

[3] Erich F. Schmidt, *Flights over Ancient Cities of Iran*. Special Publication of the Oriental Institute, 1940.
[4] Arthur W. Judge, *Stereoscopic Photography*. 2d ed. 1935, p.284.

I

Mesopotamian Beginnings

THE story begins in Mesopotamia. In the land which is now known as Iraq there flow two great rivers, the Tigris and the Euphrates. So distinctive is the geographical character which they impart to the region that the Greeks coined for it the picturesque name Mesopotamia, meaning "the land between the rivers." Strictly speaking this designation applies only to the upper part of the valley of the two rivers, which in similar fashion the Arabs today call Al Jazira or "The Island." In modern usage, however, the name Mesopotamia includes also the lower part of the valley and describes graphically the entire land.

The Tigris and the Euphrates take their rise in the northern mountains of Armenia where 10,000-foot peaks gather snow and rain sufficient to feed streams destined for the desert. As the Euphrates emerges from the mountains it is flowing in a southwesterly direction as if to empty into the Mediterranean, but it bends in a large circle southward and eastward, swinging toward the course of the Tigris River which is flowing down at the foot of the hills of Kurdistan. The two rivers move in gradually converging courses down across wide and undulating grassy plains which drop 1,000 feet between the foothills and a point somewhat above modern Baghdad. Some 20,000 years ago the Persian Gulf reached this far inland, and here approximately at Samarra and Hit is the old coastline where the Tigris and Euphrates emptied their waters. But the rivers were heavily laden with silt and gradually turned the upper reaches of the Gulf into marsh and finally into an absolutely flat and stoneless alluvial plain. This slow building of the plain has continued until today it stretches for more than 300 miles southeastward to the present head of the Persian Gulf. A curving line drawn somewhere near Eridu, Ur and Lagash probably would indicate the approximate shoreline of 3000

B.C. Today the rivers flow on farther across their own plain and swamps until finally they unite and flow together the last 100 miles into the Gulf. At the mouth of the Shatt-al-Arab, as the united rivers are called, the coastline is still advancing some 72 feet a year or a mile and a half a century.

In this lower part of Mesopotamia, some fifty-five miles south of the present Baghdad, there once stood beside the Euphrates a city which bore the proud name Bab-ilu, "Gate of God." In the Hebrew language the name became Babel, and in the Greek and Latin tongues it took the now familiar form, Babylon. Although the history of the lower valley by no means began with this city, Babylon was so prominent in many later periods that its name is attached permanently to the region, and the plain is known most familiarly as Babylonia.

The Tigris and the Euphrates not only built the plain of Babylonia, their waters have always been indispensable to its productivity. The sun is blazing hot and the average annual rainfall is only six inches, but where the rivers run or irrigation canals are dug from them the soil is very fertile. Wheat, corn, barley, dates, figs and pomegranates are grown. In ancient times an extensive system of canals irrigated the plain and it bore a dense population and was the home of great civilizations. In their inscriptions the kings of those days spoke often, and with justifiable pride, of their works in canal-building. Rim-Sin of Larsa "dug the canal of the plain, the canal of abundance, as far as the sea." Hammurabi of Babylon provided "permanent water of plenty" by a splendid canal to which he gave his own name, "Hammurabi-is-the-prosperity-of-the-folk." Sin-idinnam wrote, "Indeed I have provided waters of everlastingness, unceasing prosperity, for my land of Larsa."

But the onetime fertile gardenland is now a vast desolation. The wonderful system of irrigation which the ancient empires had maintained gradually fell into disrepair and finally, with the coming of the Mohammedans in the seventh century A.D. and the Mongols in the thirteenth, into utter ruin. Under Turkish rule, which lasted until the British took Baghdad in 1917 and were succeeded by the native Iraq government in 1932, the land between the rivers became one of the most desolate areas on earth. Baghdad, which was founded in A.D. 762 and raised to splendor in the ninth century by Harun-al-Rashid, the famous Caliph of the *Arabian Nights,* has shrunk from

MAP 1

MESOPOTAMIA

SCALE OF MILES

0   50   100   150   200

CASPIAN SEA

PERSIAN GULF

ELAM

Susa

Shatt-al-Arab

Basra

SUMER

Ur

Eridu

Tell el-Obeid

Lagash

Larsa

Umma

Uruk

Lagash

Shuruppak

Isin

Adab

Nippur

Tell Obeid

Tendet-Nasr

BABYLON

Kish

Babylon

Agade

AKKAD

Sippar

Esbunna

Baghdad

Samarra

Tigris

Zagros Mts.

Mts. of Nisir

Kirkuk

Nuzu

Tepe Gawra

Nineveh

Tell Billa

Great Zab

Little Zab

Mosul

Tell Arpachiya

Ashur

Tell Hassuna

JAZIRA

AL

MESOPOTAMIA

SYRIA

KURDISTAN

LAKE

Hit

Euphrates

Tigris

Khabour

Tell Chagar Bazar

Tell Halaf

Balikh

Haran

Ain el-Khalil

Urfa

Carchemish

Mari

Abou Kemal

a reputed onetime population of 2,000,000 to 300,000. It is a mud-colored city on the banks of a mud-colored river. The slightest wind blows powdered mud as fine as talcum powder through the streets. Outside the city, roads of beaten mud, where every passing horseman raises clouds of brown dust, lead among such cultivated areas as there are. Beyond this the land stretches away, smooth as a billiard table, brown and barren, to the sky. The city of Ur stood once upon the banks of the Euphrates but now the river has changed its course and from the summit of the ancient city-mound the fringe of palms on the river's bank is visible on the skyline twelve miles eastward. In all other directions, as far as the eye can see, stretches a vast plain of unprofitable sand. Shimmering heat waves dance over the monotonous waste, and mirages feign non-existent waters. Here at Ur a tourist, disgruntled, wrote in the register of the mud hotel, "No wonder Abraham left; even Job would have!" But the scene at Ur was far different, as we shall see, when Abraham saw his native city for the last time.

1. THE EARLY AND PREDYNASTIC PERIODS, c.5000-c.2800 B.C.[1]

EARLY VILLAGES

MESOPOTAMIA was the home of various peoples for thousands of years before the time of Abraham, and if we are to place the Hebrew patriarchs in their true setting we must sketch at least briefly the long historical development of which they were the heirs.

The earliest village settlements which have been discovered belong to the Neolithic Age and are in the northern part of Mesopotamia. Recent excavation by the Iraq Museum at Tell Hassuna, some distance south of modern Mosul, has unearthed the remains of such a village. The first settlers at this place employed only flint or obsidian weapons and tools, and coarse Neolithic pottery. A little later they had rude houses, and their pottery was adorned with incised or painted decorations.[2]

Similar remains have been found at the famous site of Nineveh, the location of which is just across the Tigris from Mosul. Here in 1931-1932, on behalf of the British Museum, M. E. L. Mallowan conducted a prehistoric sounding. A large pit was dug down ninety feet from one of the highest points on the mound to virgin soil. Underlying the later Assyrian levels a series of strata was penetrated, the lowest of which corresponded to the first prehistoric settlement at Nineveh. Here were the remains of a village which once existed on a low mound only slightly above the level of the plain. The huts of the people were represented by debris of decayed wood and ashes. Mingled with this were fragments of their hand-made pottery, which was very coarse and plain. Some of it was incised with deeply cut hatching, notches and punctuations, these illustrating the earliest attempts of the potter at Nineveh to decorate

---

[1] Most dates, it will be noted, are approximate rather than exact, and particularly in the earlier millenniums only the broadest chronological indications can be given. Recent discoveries have necessitated successive revisions in the early chronology of the Middle East, and in general the tendency has been toward the lowering of previously accepted dates. See Sidney Smith, *Alalakh and Chronology*. 1940, p.29; O. Neugebauer in *Journal of the American Oriental Society*. 61 (1941), pp.58-61; Theophile J. Meek in *The Journal of Religion*. 21 (1941), p.404 n.15; William F. Albright in BASOR 69 (Feb. 1938), pp.18-21; 77 (Feb. 1940), pp.25-30; 88 (Dec. 1942), pp.28-36; and in AJA 47 (1943), pp.491f. The dates given here are substantially those of Albright's last revision in BASOR 88, p.32.

[2] AJA 48 (1944), p.371.

his clay vessels. Only later were the first attempts made at painting the pottery.[3]

Another Neolithic village has been discovered a dozen miles northwest of Nineveh at Tepe Gawra, or "The Great Mound." Since 1927 excavations at this site have been conducted by the American Schools of Oriental Research, Dropsie College of Philadelphia and the University Museum of the University of Pennsylvania, under the leadership of Ephraim A. Speiser. A sounding at the edge of the mound has given a sample of what lies at the lowest levels. A burial pit was found in which the bodies evidently had been placed quite at random but with at least the accompaniment of a certain amount of pottery. Both undecorated ware, and brittle orange ware with a wavy red-line ornamentation, were unearthed.[4] Similar pottery has been found in the lowest levels at Tell ej-Judeideh[5] in the Plain of Antioch in Syria, and at Jericho[6] in Palestine.

The Neolithic culture thus represented in the early villages of Mesopotamia as well as of Syria and Palestine must be at least as early as 5000 B.C. and probably is even earlier. Since the introduction of pottery and of building already had taken place, even these remains do not represent an absolute beginning of settled life, and it may be supposed that the first settlements were due to the coming of outsiders.[7]

TELL HALAF

The Neolithic Age, to which the primitive cultures just mentioned belong, was followed by the Chalcolithic or "copper-stone" Period when the peoples were moving out of the age of stone and into the times of the use of metal. To the Chalcolithic Age belongs the first truly great culture of ancient times, which, like its more primitive predecessors, was centered in northern Mesopotamia. This culture is customarily referred to by the name of the site where its evidences were first discovered, Tell Halaf. Tell Halaf is in the northwest, near

[3] M. E. L. Mallowan in *Annals of Archaeology and Anthropology, issued by the Institute of Archaeology, University of Liverpool.* 20 (1933), pp.127-177; and in *Proceedings of the First International Congress of Prehistoric and Protohistoric Sciences, London 1932.* 1934, pp.165-167.

[4] E. A. Speiser in *Asia* 38 (1938), p.543; in *Smithsonian Report for 1939.* 1940, p.444; and in BASOR 66 (Apr. 1937), p.18; 70 (Apr. 1938), pp.6f.

[5] Robert J. Braidwood, *Mounds in the Plain of Antioch, an Archaeological Survey,* OIP XLVIII, 1937, pp.6f.; C. W. McEwan in AJA 41 (1937), pp.10f.

[6] G. Ernest Wright, *The Pottery of Palestine from the Earliest Times to the End of the Early Bronze Age.* 1937, pp.7-11,107.

[7] E. A. Speiser in *Journal of the American Oriental Society.* 59 (1939), No.4 Supplement p.24.

where the Beyrouth-Baghdad railway now swings across the upper part of Al Jazira, and is on the Khabour, the only permanently flowing tributary of the Euphrates in Mesopotamia. Remains of the same culture also have been found at Carchemish over 100 miles west of Tell Halaf, at Tell Chagar Bazar 50 miles to the east and at Tepe Gawra and Tell Arpachiya 175 miles to the east.[8]

The first intimation that Tell Halaf was an ancient site came when native Chechens undertook to bury one of their dead on the hill and were frightened away upon digging up stone statues of animals with human heads. Baron Max von Oppenheim secured the secret from them in 1899 and worked at Tell Halaf in 1911-1913 and again in 1927 and 1929.[9] In the lowest levels were found the remains of a civilization which was much advanced over the life of the primitive Neolithic villages. The most distinctive product of this culture was its superb painted pottery. This was made by hand and among all the handmade wares of antiquity ranks as one of the best on both the technical and the artistic sides. Characteristically it is a fine, thin pottery covered with a smooth cream or buff slip[10] on which are inimitable polychrome designs in black and orange-red paint. Many of the patterns are geometrical in character, while bird, animal and human representations also appear. Several fragments of this remarkable pottery are shown in Fig. 1. A genuine glaze paint was used, and the pottery was fired at an intense heat in closed kilns, which gave it a porcelain-like finish. Kilns of this type, making perfectly controlled temperatures possible, have been found in place at Carchemish, Tell Arpachiya and Tepe Gawra.[11] Among the other technical developments of the time appears to have been the use of wheeled vehicles. On a painted vase found at Tell Halaf there is to be seen what, if its usual interpretation is correct, is the earliest known picture of a chariot. The chariot has great eight-spoked wheels and carries a man.

[8] See e.g. M. E. L. Mallowan and J. Cruikshank Rose, *Prehistoric Assyria, the Excavations at Tall Arpachiyah 1933.* 1935, pp.17,25,104f.

[9] Von Oppenheim, *Tell Halaf, a New Culture in Oldest Mesopotamia* (tr. of *Der Tell Halaf, eine neue Kultur im ältesten Mesopotamien.* 1931).

[10] In pottery-making the "slip" is liquid clay applied to the surface of the vessel as a decoration. It is fired, and serves also to receive whatever painting is done. J. L. Kelso and J. Palin Thorley in *The Annual of the American Schools of Oriental Research.* 21-22 (1941-43), p.106.

[11] See e.g. E. A. Speiser in BASOR 66 (Apr. 1937), pp.15f.; *The New York Times,* May 11, 1937, p.26.

It is thought that the original home of the culture represented at Tell Halaf may have been in North Syria. As far as its date is concerned the Halaf culture certainly must have had its beginnings well back in the fifth millennium B.C.

TELL EL-OBEID

In the ancient times of which we have been speaking, the lower Mesopotamian Valley was not yet settled, but as the marshes dried and areas of solid land came into being, civilization could begin in Babylonia. The first settlement of Babylonia is represented by what is known as the Obeid culture. The name is derived from Tell el-Obeid, a small mound four and one-half miles northwest of the more famous site of Ur. Like Ur, this place once was situated on the Euphrates, but the river has since changed its course and is some distance away.

In 1919 H. R. Hall found early ruins at Tell el-Obeid, and in 1923-1924 the Joint Expedition of the British Museum and the Museum of the University of Pennsylvania, directed by C. Leonard Woolley, began excavations which revealed a primitive settlement of the first immigrants who had come into the Euphrates delta.[12]

The period which takes its name from the findings at Tell el-Obeid is also known from remains at other sites, and plainly represents the earliest culture in this particular region. This was shown, for example, at Ur, where a pit was dug down to virgin soil below present sea level. At the bottom a stiff greenish clay still bearing the marks of plant roots marked the bottom of the original marsh. Above this was a black soil into which a few potsherds had sunk and on which were the remains of huts, flint tools and weapons, and pottery corresponding with that of Tell el-Obeid.

The Tell el-Obeid pottery (Fig. 2) is quite different from that of Tell Halaf, being a fine, pale greenish ware, painted with free geometrical designs in black or dark brown. It was made either entirely by hand or on a slow, hand-turned wheel. While animal motifs were rare in the decoration of the pottery, numerous animal and human figures, hand-modeled in clay, were found.

The houses of the village were necessarily constructed of the materials which were available, and, from first to last in the history of lower Mesopotamia, stone was wholly lacking. Mud, reeds and a

[12] H. R. Hall and C. Leonard Woolley, *Ur Excavations: I, Al-'Ubaid*. 1927.

certain amount of timber were available, so the primitive marsh-dwellers built their huts out of reeds lashed together and plastered with mud. Quite early in the period, as had been the case even earlier in the north, building began to be done with bricks made of mud dried in the sun. The mud-plastered walls sometimes were decorated with most interesting mosaics made of small, slender, pencil-like cones of baked clay, whose ends were left plain, or painted red or black. This usage gave the wall an almost waterproof protection and a permanent decoration, and was practiced for centuries. So the primitive people of Tell el-Obeid made lasting contributions to the building methods of Mesopotamia.

For the most notable architectural achievements of Obeid times, however, we must return to Tepe Gawra. As early as in Level XIX at Tepe Gawra, which corresponds to the beginning of the Obeid period, the remains of a temple are found which thus far is the oldest religious structure known to man. In Level XIII, which is nearer the end of the Obeid period and probably to be dated around the close of the fifth or beginning of the fourth millennium B.C., an extraordinarily impressive acropolis has been discovered. Three monumental temple buildings surrounded a main courtyard. Entering this court the ancient worshiper would have seen on the right the white-plastered façade of what the archeologists now call the Eastern Shrine, on the left the warm reddish-brown brick walls of the Northern Temple, and directly ahead the great niche of the Central Temple whose exterior was white and whose inner rooms and cult chamber were painted in purple. The existence of this acropolis with its imposing places of worship, whose construction was possible only through the combined efforts of a large community, shows that great strides had been taken in social and religious development.[13]

If the culture at Tell Halaf represented the influence of North Syria upon Mesopotamia, the Obeid civilization seems clearly related to the contemporaneous Iranian Highland culture which reached eastward across the plateau of Iran into Baluchistan.[14] It is closely associated with the findings in the lowest levels at Susa, known as Susa I.[15] The famous ancient site of Susa is in Persia, 150 miles north

[13] E. A. Speiser in BASOR 65 (Feb. 1937), p.8; 66 (Apr. 1937), pp.3-9; and in *Asia.* 38 (1938), pp.542f.

[14] Henri Frankfort, *Archaeology and the Sumerian Problem.* SAOC 4, 1932, p.29.

[15] Donald E. McCown, *The Comparative Stratigraphy of Early Iran.* SAOC 23, 1942, p.36 and Fig. 13.

of the head of the Persian Gulf. Susa was explored by the Dieulafoy, Houssaye and Babin Expedition[16] sent out by the French government in 1884-1886, and in 1897 and following years was studied intensively by a series of expeditions under the direction of Jacques de Morgan and R. de Mecquenem.[17] An aerial photograph of the site is shown in Fig. 3. On the principal elevation are the fortlike quarters of the French archeological expedition, while to the left is the modern village of Shush with the traditional "Tomb of Daniel."

Susa was founded about 4000 B.C. and was still a great city in the twelfth century A.D. Outside the earthen rampart of the mud village in which the earliest inhabitants lived were many graves. In them was found an abundance of fragile pottery, painted a glossy black and with decorations including geometrical patterns of triangles, rectangles and zigzags, and human, animal and plant designs reduced to almost geometrical forms. Galloping dogs, goats whose fore and hindquarters are triangles and whose horns are sweeping semicircles, and rows of storks, whose bodies are large triangles and whose heads are small triangles, are among the conventionalized designs represented in the sophisticated art of Susa I.[18] Copper mirrors, beads of black and white limestone or imported turquoise, and little conical vases once containing green mineral paint for the eyelids, were also found. Among tools and weapons buried with the dead were stone-headed clubs and copper-headed tomahawks. Fragments of cloth also remain to indicate that these people had the art of making fine linen.

Beyond Persia lies Baluchistan, the bridge to India, where the Iranian Highland culture may even have come into contact with the culture of the Indus Valley. Baluchistan is now to a great extent desert, but many prehistoric sites have been discovered there which may be links between the civilizations of Mesopotamia and of the Indus Valley.[19] The prehistoric culture of the Indus Valley is known

[16] M. A. Dieulafoy, *L'Acropole de Suse d'après les fouilles exécutées en 1884, 1885, 1886 sous les auspices du Musée du Louvre.* 1890.

[17] See the *Mémoires* of the *Délégation en Perse*, and M. Pézard and E. Pottier, *Les Antiquités de la Susiane.* Musée de Louvre, 1913.

[18] J. de Morgan and R. de Mecquenem, *La Céramique peinte de Suse, Mémoires, Délégation en Perse.* XIII (1912); R. de Mecquenem, *Notes sur la céramique peinte archaïque en Perse, Mémoires,* XX (1928); G. Contenau in Arthur U. Pope, ed., *A Survey of Persian Art from Prehistoric Times to the Present.* 1938, I, pp.171f.

[19] Sir Aurel Stein, *Archaeological Reconnaissances in Northwestern India and Southeastern Iran.* 1937; and in *A Survey of Persian Art.* I, p.168.

through the excavations at Mohenjo-Daro, some 140 miles northeast of Karachi, and at other sites on the Five Streams of the Punjab. At Mohenjo-Daro, "the Place of the Dead," there existed around the middle of the third millennium B.C. a planned city with broad streets, buildings made of fine brick, and an elaborate sanitary system including a bathroom in almost every house.[20]

The indications of early contact between Mesopotamia and India include such facts as the following: In the Tell el-Obeid period the inhabitants of Mesopotamia were making beads out of lapis lazuli, an azure blue stone which comes from Central Asia, and amazonite, a green stone which is found only in Central India and Transbaikalia. Later, in the tombs of Ur, is found the little figure of a squatting monkey precisely similar to figures unearthed at Mohenjo-Daro, while around 2500 B.C. at Tell Asmar other Indian animals—the elephant, rhinoceros, and gharial or fish-eating crocodile—appear on a seal of undoubted Indian workmanship.[21]

URUK

The story of Mesopotamia is continued at Warka, which is the site of the ancient Erech or Uruk[22] and is some 35 miles up the Euphrates valley from Tell el-Obeid. The discoveries at this place indicate a new influence in Mesopotamia. The home of this influence may have been in Anatolia and Transcaucasia; it is therefore referred to as the Northern culture. The Uruk Period probably dates in the latter part of the fourth millennium B.C.

The most distinctive pottery found here is a red ware, running from brick-red to plum-red in color. Black and gray wares were also found; they were baked in a kiln smothered down to make the smoke penetrate and color the clay. Both of these kinds of pottery were made on a genuine spinning potter's wheel, and they were highly polished but left unpainted.[23]

A small pavement of rough limestone blocks at Uruk is the oldest stone construction in Babylonia, and here, too, is found the first ziggurat. The Assyrian-Babylonian word *ziqquratu* means pinnacle

[20] Sir John Marshall, *Mohenjo-Daro and the Indus Civilization.* 3 vols. 1931; *Further Excavations at Mohenjo-Daro.* 2 vols. 1937-38.

[21] Ernest Mackay, *The Indus Civilization.* 1935, pp.170,191-193,199.

[22] Julius Jordan, *Uruk-Warka nach den Ausgrabungen durch die Deutsche Orient-Gesellschaft.* 1928.

[23] T. J. Meek in Elihu Grant, ed., *The Haverford Symposium on Archaeology and the Bible.* 1938, p.164.

or top of a mountain, and the ziggurat was a sort of artificial mountain, built in the flat Mesopotamian plain as a high place for a god, whose shrine stood on its summit. From its first appearance here at Uruk, it was ever afterward the most characteristic feature of temple architecture in Mesopotamia, and the locations of more than two dozen such structures arc known today.[24]

The Uruk ziggurat was simply a vast mass of clay stamped down hard and strengthened with layers of asphalt and unburnt bricks. Rows of pottery jars were embedded in the upper edges to support them and prevent them from crumbling away. Facing outward, their white rims and dark interiors made a striking ornament. The ziggurat measured some 140 by 150 feet and stood about 30 feet high, its corners being oriented toward the points of the compass. On the summit was the actual shrine, oriented similarly, 65 feet long, 50 feet wide, and built about a long narrow court, 14 feet across, and entered by doors at either end and in the center of the southwest side. The outer walls were ornamented with vertical recesses, and this feature together with the system of orientation remained characteristic of later temples. The original whitewash was still preserved on the mud-brick walls, and hence the German archeologists applied to the shrine the name, *der weisse Tempel*, the White Temple. In similar fashion they named a second temple building, to whose walls a plum-red paint had been applied, the Red Temple. Yet another monumental structure was ornamented beautifully with three-colored mosaic work of clay cones in patterns of zigzags, triangles and diamonds. This method of ornamentation already had been developed, it will be remembered, at Tell el-Obeid (p. 17), and the use of the hollow clay cones on the Uruk ziggurat was another adaptation of the same principle.

The most notable achievements of the Uruk culture, however, were the introduction of the cylinder seal and of script. In the White Temple mentioned above, two small square tablets of gypsum plaster were found which bore the impressions of cylinder seals. These are the first instances known of the use of cylinder seals, which appear to have been invented by the people of this period. Such a seal was made in the form of a small stone cylinder which left its impression not by being stamped upon a surface but by being rolled across it.

[24] Jean de Mecquenem in *Gazette des Beaux-Arts*. 6e période 18 (1937), pp.201-214.

The surface of the cylinder was engraved in intaglio, so that when the seal was used it yielded an image in which the design stood out in relief.[25] Such a cylinder seal is shown in Fig. 5 while the impression from the same seal appears in Fig. 6.

The origin of cylinder seals preceded the invention of writing, and at first they were used chiefly to safeguard possessions. A jar or package was sealed with clay, and while this was moist the cylinder was rolled over it. Since each cylinder bore a distinctive design, a permanent proof of personal ownership was left behind. Later, when writing had developed and letters, contracts and other records were inscribed upon clay tablets, these documents were conveniently legalized by similar seal impressions.

From their origin here in the fourth millennium B.C., cylinder seals continued in use until finally supplanted by the stamp seal in Persian times, thus having a demonstrable history of more than 3000 years. From Mesopotamia their manufacture and employment spread to peripheral regions as widely distant as India and Egypt. The decoration of the cylinder seals constituted Mesopotamia's most original contribution to art, and the influence of the seals was felt in all the other branches of decorative art as well.

The excellence of the seals upon their first appearance in the Uruk Period is amazing. Vivid animal studies, ornamental heraldic compositions, abstract religious symbols, and narrative illustrations of ritual practice all are found. In Fig. 4 is shown the impression of a cylinder belonging to this period which was found at Tell Billa northeast of modern Mosul. The scene represented has not been explained fully but seems to be of a ritual character. At the left appears what may be a shrine, and it is approached by three men who are presumably bringing offerings. At the right is a boat which has plants at either end.

Only an intimation of later developments in the glyptic art may be given here. In the Early Dynastic Period (p. 31) a new and distinctive style was achieved. Decoration rather than narration was emphasized. The subject often was reduced to a pattern of lines whose rhythmic recurrence formed a frieze of indefinite extent. The result was a decorative scheme such as a weaver or embroiderer might use, and hence this has been termed the "brocade" style. The long, slender cylinder shown in Fig. 5 comes from this period, and its

[25] cf. Job 38:12-14; Albert E. Bailey, *Daily Life in Bible Times.* 1943, p.27.

impression reproduced in Fig. 6 is characteristic of the style just described. In this instance, the basis of the representation is nothing but two goats, one upright and one upside down, with a few additional strokes completing the design. In the time of Sargon and the Old Akkadian Period (p. 38) another notable change in style took place, and the art of the seal reached perhaps its highest expression. The continuous frieze was supplanted by the heraldic group and the linear figures gave way to wholly modeled figures whose physical characteristics were emphasized realistically. At the center of the composition there was often a panel containing an inscription. A seal impression displaying these characteristic features of the Sargonid style is illustrated in Fig. 7. The bearded hero appears in various ways in Mesopotamian art but here seems to represent a spirit of water. In this capacity he is watering the buffaloes from a vase out of which flow two streams. The water and rock border at the bottom is in harmony with the same theme. The inscription in the panel names a certain scribe, Ibnisharrum, as the owner of the seal and dedicates it to Shargalisharri (p. 41) king of Akkad.[26]

Returning now to Uruk and its culture, it may be noted that the introduction of the cylinder seal was soon followed by the emergence of writing. In the Red Temple at Uruk were found a number of thin flat clay tablets inscribed in a crude pictographic script. This picture-writing represents the earliest stage of Babylonian writing known and is evidently the direct ancestor of cuneiform. The pictographs were gradually reduced for speed in drawing to arbitrary groups of lines and these developed into the wedge-shaped writing which we call cuneiform. As the tablets show, the writing material which was used in Babylonia from the beginning was clay into which the writing signs were pressed with a stylus whose point was formed into a three-sided prism. The clay tablet was held for writing in the left hand, or when larger in size was laid down flat, and the text was written in vertical columns running from left to right. The numerals found on these tablets show that a sexagesimal system of arithmetic, in which the computing was by sixties, was in most common use but that a decimal system also was employed.[27]

[26] Richard A. Martin, *Ancient Seals of the Near East*. Field Museum of Natural History Anthropology Leaflet 34, 1940, No.5. For the basic discussion of the entire subject of cylinder seals see Henri Frankfort, *Cylinder Seals*. 1939.
[27] A. Falkenstein, *Archaische Texte aus Uruk*. 1940, pp.49,62.

JEMDET NASR

A further period in the early history of Mesopotamia is known from the findings at Jemdet Nasr,[28] a site in the Mesopotamian valley not far from where Babylon later was to stand. The date is probably around the end of the fourth or beginning of the third millennium B.C. The characteristic pottery here is a painted ware featuring black and yellow on a deep red ground. Metal was employed more freely, and the first use of bronze indicates the beginning of the Bronze Age in Mesopotamia. Tablets were found written in a semi-pictographic script somewhat more advanced than that of the Uruk Period.

Sculpture in stone was a noteworthy achievement of the people of the Jemdet Nasr Period. Some of the finest examples come from levels at Uruk and Ur contemporary with Jemdet Nasr. At Uruk a block of basalt was found, carved in bas-relief with a hunting scene in which two bearded men are fighting three lions. At Ur the first example of sculpture in the round was discovered. It was the figure of a crouching boar, carved in steatite or soapstone, and executed in the style of a mature art. The conception is on the whole in terms of an abstract balance of mass, but the character of the animal is suggested realistically by the drawing back of the upper lip over the tusks.

During the Jemdet Nasr Period the important cities of Shuruppak (Fara), Eshnunna (Tell Asmar) and Kish were founded. Shuruppak was perhaps 85 miles from Jemdet Nasr down the Mesopotamian Valley in the direction of Tell el-Obeid, Eshnunna was over 50 miles to the north, while Kish was nearer at hand, some 15 miles southwest of Jemdet Nasr. All three of these cities will be mentioned again.

THE FLOOD

At various times great floods devastated Babylonia, or portions of it, as was to be expected from the very nature of the valley. One of these floods is well known from the excavation of Ur by C. Leonard Woolley. An early cemetery was being investigated, where the graves were located in what once had been the rubbish heap of the ancient city. Beneath the level of these graves the modern diggers continued to find the pottery and other objects of the earlier city, the pottery changing from Jemdet Nasr to Uruk to later Obeid forms. Suddenly,

[28] Ernest Mackay and Stephen Langdon, *Report on Excavations at Jemdet Nasr, Iraq.* 1931.

as the shafts went deeper, stratified pottery and rubbish were no longer found but only perfectly clean clay. The workmen thought they had come to the bottom of the original delta but measurements showed this could not be the case. They dug on down through eight feet of clean uniform clay. Beneath this at last they came again upon rubbish full of stone implements and bits of hand-painted pottery such as was found in the earliest levels at Tell el-Obeid. A flood of considerable magnitude must, therefore, have swept over at least a part of Ur sometime in the middle of the Obeid Period.[29]

At the end of the Jemdet Nasr Period, the evidences of a large flood appear at Shuruppak,[30] and at Kish a yet later flood occurred which left a layer of sediment one and one-half feet thick some distance above the Jemdet Nasr stratification.[31] A picture of this flood stratum is shown in Fig. 8.

The tradition of a great flood or floods was well known to the Sumerians who were dominant in lower Mesopotamia in the Early Dynastic Period of which we shall soon speak. It is difficult to say, however, whether any one of the three different floods whose evidences have been mentioned was the basis for these later traditions. It is possible that the flood at Shuruppak or at Kish is the one referred to in the Sumerian King List since it is indicated there that Shuruppak was the last ruling city before the flood and that Kish was the seat of the first Sumerian dynasty after the flood. This Sumerian King List is an interesting chronological list of early rulers, which was written not later than the middle of the famous Third Dynasty of Ur and probably in the slightly earlier reign of Utu-hegal of Uruk.[32] It is obvious that the list is not entirely dependable, however, since it ascribes reigns of the most exaggerated length to the earlier kings. The list begins with the statement, "When kingship was lowered from heaven the kingship was in Eridu," and then continues with the names of the sovereigns who reigned before the flood. Eight such antediluvian kings are listed and it is stated that their rule centered

[29] C. L. Woolley, *Ur of the Chaldees.* 1929, pp. 22-29.

[30] Erich F. Schmidt in *The Museum Journal.* 22 (1931), pp.200f.

[31] S. Langdon in *The Journal of the Royal Asiatic Society.* 1930, p.603; L. C. Watelin, *Excavations at Kish IV 1925-1930.* 1934, pp.40-44.

[32] The Weld-Blundell prism, giving an almost complete text of the King List, was published by S. Langdon, *Oxford Editions of Cuneiform Texts.* II (1923); cf. George A. Barton, *The Royal Inscriptions of Sumer and Akkad.* 1929, pp.346-355. A critical edition of the text, also making use of other tablets now available, is given by Thorkild Jacobsen, *The Sumerian King List,* AS 11, 1939.

in five different cities and lasted for 241,200 years. The last of the eight was Ubar-Tutu who, according to the list, reigned at Shuruppak for 18,600 years. The complete outline of the antediluvian period, according to the cuneiform list, is as follows:

CITY	SOVEREIGN	LENGTH OF RULE	
Eridu	Alulim	28,800	years
	Alalgar	36,000	"
Badtibira	Enmenlu-Anna	43,200	"
	Enmengal-Anna	28,800	"
	divine Dumuzi, a shepherd	36,000	"
Larak	Ensipazi-Anna	28,800	"
Sippar	Enmendur-Anna	21,000	"
Shuruppak	Ubar-Tutu	18,600	"

241,200 years

A later form of the same list has long been known from the writings of Berossos, who was a priest of Marduk at Babylon under Antiochus I (281-261 B.C.). Berossos gives the names quite differently, and a further exaggeration of the length of reigns has taken place:

Alorus	36,000	years
Alaparos	10,800	"
Amelon	46,800	"
Ammenon	43,200	"
Megalaros	64,800	"
Daonos or Daos	36,000	"
Euedorachos	64,800	"
Amempsinos	36,000	"
Otiartes	28,800	"
Xisouthros	64,800	"

432,000 years

Amelon and Ammenon may both be corruptions of the name Enmenlu-Anna, while Xisouthros, the hero of the flood, has been added, thus giving ten names in all. There may be some correspondence between this tradition of ten antediluvian kings, and the Hebrew record of ten patriarchs from Adam to Noah.[33] Then came the flood, apparently wiping out Shuruppak, after which sovereignty again was established from heaven, this time at Kish. The King List states:

[33] George A. Barton, *Archaeology and the Bible*. 7th ed. 1937, p.320.

> After the flood had swept thereover,
> when the kingship was lowered from heaven
> the kingship was in Kish.

After that the King List continues with the First Dynasty of Kish and with other dynasties which we shall mention later.

In addition to the brief allusion in the King List, the Sumerians had an extensive legend concerning a great flood. Like the King List, this legend also, at least in some of its versions, mentions Shuruppak as the particular city upon which the flood came. It is possible, however, that the traditions of other floods such as those at Ur and Kish may have contributed to the development of the story. An early version of this story appears on the fragment of a Sumerian tablet (Fig. 9) found at Nippur, which is a site about midway between Kish and Shuruppak.[34] It is inscribed on both sides, with three columns to the side.

In the first column some deity is speaking who alludes to an earlier destruction of mankind and then tells how men and animals were created. A portion of this reads as follows:

> After Anu, Enlil, Enki, and Ninhursag
> Had created the dark-headed peoples
> Creatures with the breath of life on earth he made plentiful.
> The cattle of the field, them that are four legged, on the plains
>   he called into being as was fitting.

The second column relates how some deity founded five cities, including Eridu, Sippar and Shuruppak. The deity assigned each city to the special care of a guardian god, and also established irrigation canals.

The third column mentions a deluge, which caused the brilliant Ishtar (Ninhursag) to groan on account of her people. At that time, it is explained, Ziusudra (also read Ziusuddu) whose name means, "Life-day prolonged," was king and priest. In his extremity Ziusudra made a wooden idol representing the chief deity and daily prostrated himself before it, seeking guidance. In the fourth column Ziusudra is told to stand beside a wall where some deity will speak to him. In the revelation which now comes to him the full plan of the gods to destroy mankind by a flood is made known:

[34] cf. J. P. Peters, *Nippur, or Explorations on the Euphrates.* 2 vols. 1897; H. V. Hilprecht, *The Excavations in Assyria and Babylonia.* 1903, pp.289-568.

Ziusudra stand thou within and hear.
Beside the wall at my left hand stand . . .
Beside the wall I will speak to the . . .
My instructions hear . . .
By my hand shall a deluge be sent upon the . . .
The seed of mankind shall perish in destruction.
This is the decision, the command of the assembly of the gods.

When column five in its broken form again continues the narrative, the terrific deluge has begun, and Ziusudra is riding it out in a great boat.

The rain storms, mighty winds all of them, they sent all at once.
The Flood came upon the . . .
When for seven days and seven nights,
The Flood had raged over the Land,
And the huge boat had been tossed on the great waters by the
    storms,
The Sun-god arose shedding light in Heaven and on Earth.
Ziusudra made an opening in the side of the great ship.
He let the light of the hero the Sun-god enter in the great ship.
Ziusudra, the king,
Before the Sun-god he bowed his face to the ground.
The king slaughtered an ox, sheep he sacrificed in great numbers.

Thus the terrible storm came to an end, and as column six closes we read how Ziusudra received the gift of immortality and was transferred to live forever in the mountain of Dilmun.

Ziusudra, the king,
Before Enlil bowed his face to the earth.
To him he gave life like a god.
An eternal soul like that of a god he bestowed upon him.
At that time Ziusudra, the king,
Named, "Saviour of living things and the seed of humanity"
They caused to dwell in the inaccessible mountain, mountain of
    Dilmun.[35]

Such is the essential outline of the ancient Sumerian story of the flood as preserved in the fragment from Nippur. This story was ultimately incorporated in the famous epic of Gilgamesh and it is here that it is found in most detailed form. While we are dependent upon

[35] S. Langdon, *Semitic Mythology.* 1931, pp.206-208; S. N. Kramer, *Sumerian Mythology.* 1944, pp.97f. Kramer translates the last line, "They caused him to dwell in the land *of the [sun's] crossing,* in Dilmun, the place where the sun rises," and shows that the land of Dilmun was probably believed to be in southwestern Iran (BASOR 96 [Dec. 1944], pp.18-28).

a copy made for the library of Ashurbanipal at Nineveh in the seventh century B.C. (pp. 181f.), the sources reach back into ancient Babylonia.

Ziusudra appears now in the Babylonian translation of his name as Utnapishtim, "Day of Life." Gilgamesh, a legendary king of Uruk (p. 32), has a friend named Enkidu who is his faithful companion in adventures and difficulties. Enkidu dies and Gilgamesh utters the plaintive cry:

> My friend whom I love has become like clay, Enkidu whom I
>   love has become like clay.
> Shall I not sleep like him?
> Shall I not rise through all eternity?

The sad and desperate Gilgamesh undertakes a hazardous pilgrimage across untraversed mountains and the waters of death to find Utnapishtim, the immortal, and seek from him an answer to the eternal question. On the way he is told by the sun-god,

> The life which thou seekest thou shalt not find,

and from Ishtar he receives advice which Ecclesiastes (9:7-9) will echo:

> O Gilgamesh, whither wilt thou go?
> The life thou seekest thou shalt not find.
> When the gods created mankind,
> Death they prepared for man,
> But life they retained in their hands.
> Fill thou, O Gilgamesh, thy belly.
> Be merry day and night.
> Every day prepare joyfulness.
> Day and night dance and make music.
> Let thy garments be made clean.
> Let thy head be washed, and be thou bathed in water.
> Give heed to the little one that takes hold of thy hand.
> Let a wife rejoice in thy bosom.
> For this is the mission of man.[36]

As these warned him, Gilgamesh was doomed to eventual failure on his mission. Even though at last he reached and conversed with Utnapishtim and at the latter's direction obtained the plant of life, it was stolen from him by a serpent and he returned disconsolate.

It is in the eleventh book of this long epic which occupies twelve

[36] These two passages are found in an old Babylonian version of the epic from around the time of Hammurabi. Bruno Meissner, *Mitteilungen der Vorderasiatischen Gesellschaft.* 1902, Heft 1, p.9.

books that Utnapishtim explains his possession of immortality by relating to Gilgamesh the story of the flood. Utnapishtim begins:

> Shuruppak there is, a city which thou knowest,
> Which on the bank of the Euphrates was founded.
> That city was old and the gods in it
> Were moved in their hearts to send the Deluge, they the great
> gods.

The god Ea participates in the council of the gods, but reveals their plans to Utnapishtim through the wall of a reed hut.

> Ninigikug, the god Ea, sat with them
> And repeated their words to a reed hut:
> "O reed hut, reed hut, O wall, wall,
> Reed hut, hear, wall, understand.
> O man of Shuruppak, son of Ubar-Tutu,
> Destroy the house, build a ship.
> Abandon possessions, seek life.
> Hate property, seek life.
> Bring up the seed of all living things into the ship.
> The ship which thou shalt build,
> Its proportions let be measured.
> Its width and its length shall correspond."

The ark which Utnapishtim obediently constructed was a huge cube, 120 cubits or nearly 200 feet on each side. It was divided into seven stories, each containing nine rooms. Onto the ship he loaded all the silver and gold and all the living things which he had, and embarked with his family and relatives. The appointed time came. At evening a frightful storm took place and the next morning a black thunder cloud advanced from the eastern horizon, darkening the entire land. Even the gods were terrified at the deluge and crouched like dogs by the walls of heaven, or sat dejected and weeping. The climax of the flood and the final grounding of the boat on Mount Nisir (east of Mosul and the Tigris, near the Little Zab River) is described vividly:

> Six days and six nights
> Raged the wind, the Deluge, the hurricane devastated the land.
> When the seventh day arrived, the hurricane, the Deluge, the
> shock of battle was broken,
> Which had smitten like an army.
> The sea became calm, the cyclone died away, the Deluge ceased.
> I looked upon the sea and the sound of voices had ended.
> And all mankind had turned to clay.

Like a roof the hedged park was levelled.
I opened a window and the light fell on my cheek.
I kneeled and sat down to weep,
Tears streaming on my cheeks.
I looked on the quarters of the billowing sea.
A region stood out at a distance of twelve double hour marches.
The boat touched upon Mount Nisir.
Mount Nisir held it fast and allowed it not to move.

On the seventh day Utnapishtim sent forth a dove which came back because it could find no resting place. Likewise a swallow returned, but a raven that was sent out saw that the waters were diminishing, waded about in the mud and did not come back. On top of the mountain peak Utnapishtim offered sacrifice to the gods, who smelled the sweet savor and collected about him like flies. Enlil was angry that anyone had escaped destruction in the flood, but Ea urged that it was not right to have endeavored to destroy the righteous together with the sinful. "On the sinner place his sin," said Ea. Enlil, persuaded, took Utnapishtim by the hand and led him from the boat. With his wife, Utnapishtim knelt before Enlil while the god blessed them:

Formerly Utnapishtim was a man,
But now Utnapishtim and his wife shall be like the gods, even us.
Utnapishtim shall dwell far away at the mouth of the rivers.[37]

Such is the ancient flood story of Babylonia which, purified of its polytheistic elements, survived among the Hebrews in two sources, now woven together into a single moving story in Genesis 6:5 to 9:17.

[37] Langdon, *Semitic Mythology*, pp.210-223; cf. E. A. Wallis Budge, *The Babylonian Story of the Deluge and the Epic of Gilgamesh*. 1920; and for a translation into English hexameters, R. Campbell Thompson, *The Epic of Gilgamish*. 1928.

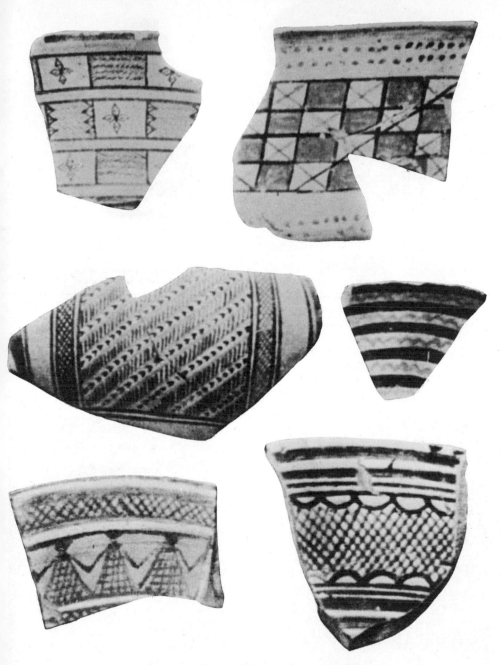

1. Fragments of Painted Pottery from Tell Halaf

2. Pottery from Tell el-Obeid

3. Air View of Susa

4. Impression of Cylinder Seal from the Uruk Period

5. Cylinder Seal from the
Early Dynastic Period

6. Impression of Cylinder Seal from the Early Dynastic Period

7. Impression of Cylinder Seal from the Old Akkadian Period

9. Tablet from Nippur with the Story of the Creation and the Flood

8. The Flood Stratum at Kish

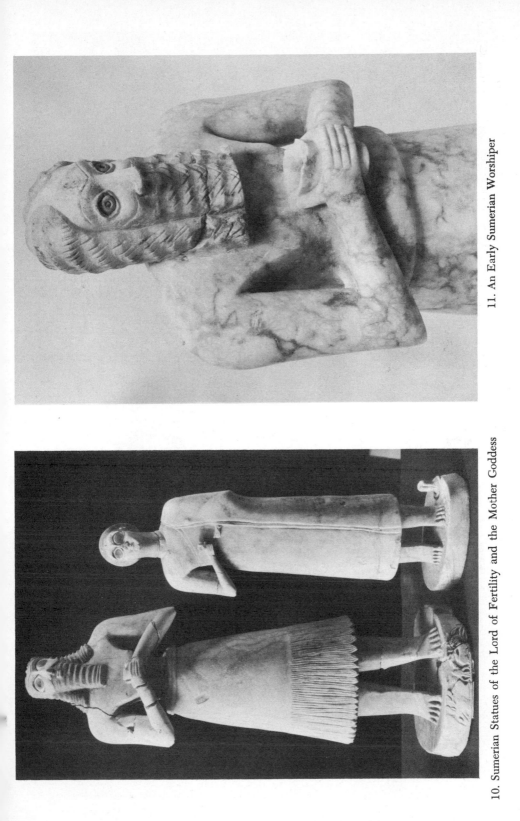

11. An Early Sumerian Worshiper

10. Sumerian Statues of the Lord of Fertility and the Mother Goddess

13. Statue of a Goat and Bush from Ur

12. The Headdress of Lady Shub-ad

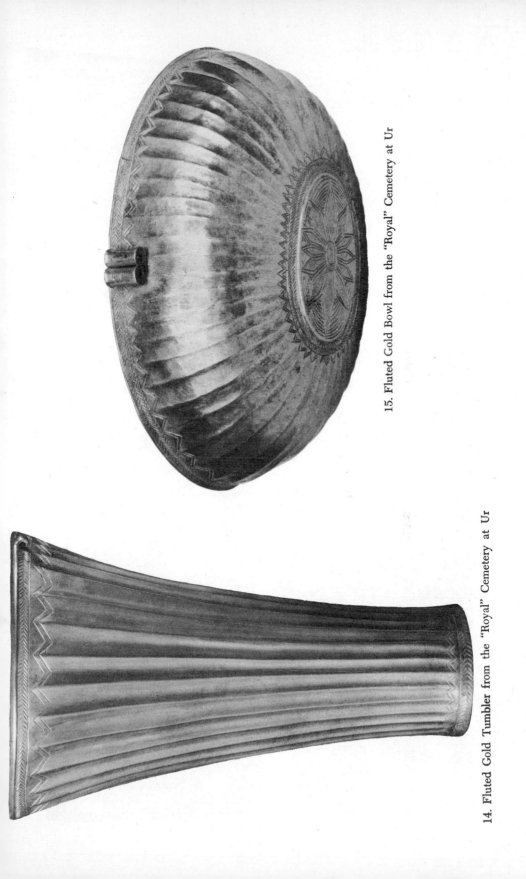

15. Fluted Gold Bowl from the "Royal" Cemetery at Ur

14. Fluted Gold Tumbler from the "Royal" Cemetery at Ur

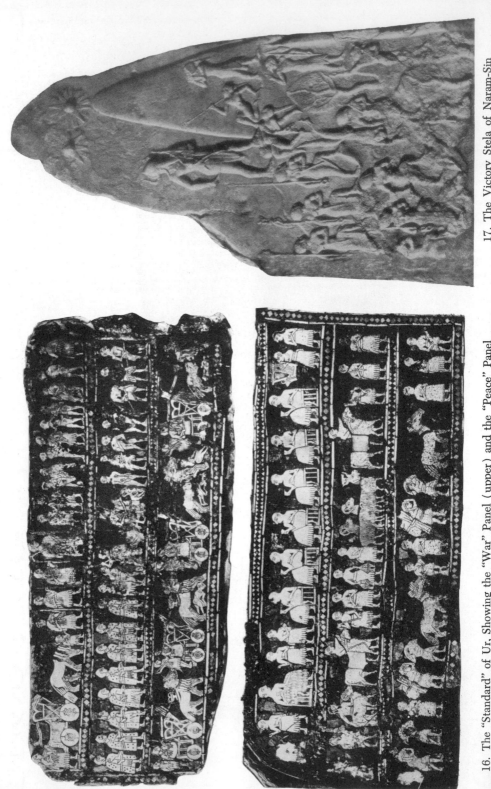

17. The Victory Stela of Naram-Sin

16. The "Standard" of Ur, Showing the "War" Panel (upper) and the "Peace" Panel

18. Statue of Gudea

20. The Stela of Ur-Nammu

19. The Ziggurat at Ur

23. A Business Contract from the Time of Hammurabi

21. A Worshiper Carrying a Kid for Sacrifice

22. Hammurabi Standing before Shamash

25. Camel and Rider from Tell Halaf

24. The Fourth Tablet of the Epic of Creation

2. THE EARLY DYNASTIC PERIOD,
c.2800-c.2360 B.C.

AFTER the mention of the flood the Sumerian King List continues with a series of dynasties which may be summarized as follows:

NAME OF DYNASTY	NUMBER OF KINGS	YEARS OF REIGN
First Dynasty of Kish	23	24,510
First Dynasty of Uruk (E-Anna)	12	2,310
First Dynasty of Ur	4	177
Dynasty of Awan	3	356
Second Dynasty of Kish	8	3,195
Dynasty of Hamazi	1?	360?
Second Dynasty of Uruk	1?	60?
Second Dynasty of Ur	4	116
Dynasty of Adab	1	90
Dynasty of Mari	6	136
Third Dynasty of Kish	1 (queen)	100
Dynasty of Akshak	6	99
Fourth Dynasty of Kish	7	491
Third Dynasty of Uruk	1	25

Whereas the King List treats these dynasties as if they succeeded one another in regular order, it is probable that in actuality some of them were contemporary dynasties which ruled at the same time in various cities. Also it may be noted that in the case of the individual cities there is a tendency to start out with reigns of legendary length and work down to reigns of actual historical length. Evidently the compiler of the King List used as sources a collection of local lists from a number of cities, in most of which the earlier periods were treated with legendary exaggeration while the later times were recorded with historical accuracy. By adding all of these lists together in an uncritical fashion the author of our King List has arrived at a total of over 30,000 years, whereas in all probability the entire period covered by these dynasties was not much more than 500 years.

Among the rulers in the First Dynasty of Kish was Etana "a shepherd, the one who to heaven ascended." A very interesting legend came to be told concerning Etana, as is attested by representations on early Sumerian seals and by fragments of Babylonian and Assyrian literature. Seeking "the plant of birth," Etana rode high into the heavens on the back of an eagle but upon reaching such a height that even the sea could no longer be distinguished grew afraid and fell back to earth. This legend was eventually transferred to Alexander the Great, who was said to have ascended by riding in a basket attached to two great and hungry birds that were attracted upward by a piece of meat held upon a spear above their heads.[1] The next dynasty is described as centering at the temple precinct E-Anna, where later the city of Uruk was built. Twelve kings are said to have reigned here for 2,310 years. Among these kings was Gilgamesh, the hero of the great epic already described.

TELL ASMAR

The art and religion of the middle phase of the Early Dynastic Period are glimpsed in the discoveries made at Tell Asmar, the ancient Eshnunna or Ashnunnak.[2] There was a small square temple here, beneath the floor of which were discovered a number of stone statues. Two of these were idols representing Abu the chief god and lord of fertility and his wife the mother goddess (Fig. 10). The statue of Abu is about 30 inches high and the god is shown with a full black beard, while his consort wears a one-piece cloak passing under the right arm and fastened together on the shoulder. These figures are of great interest both because they are the first known Sumerian cult statues and because of their fine workmanship, the statue of Abu in particular conveying an impression of extraordinary power. Another statue, shown in Fig. 11, represents a worshiper who is holding a cup in connection with his participation in a feast of communion at the temple. The figure is made of gypsum, the eyeballs are of yellow paste set in bitumen and the dark wavy hair and full beard are reproduced with black pitch. It is indeed interesting to have so striking and naturalistic a representation of one of "the blackheaded folk," as they called themselves, the Sumerians of the early third millennium B.C.[3]

THE FIRST DYNASTY OF UR

With the First Dynasty of Ur we find ourselves in the last and culminating phase of the Early Dynastic Period. The information in

[1] Langdon, *Semitic Mythology*, pp.166-174.

[2] H. Frankfort, *Oriental Institute Discoveries in Iraq, 1933/34, Fourth Preliminary Report of the Iraq Expedition.* OIC 19, 1935.

[3] H. Frankfort, *Sculpture of the Third Millennium B.C. from Tell Asmar and Khafajah.* OIP XLIV, 1939.

the King List now agrees with contemporary inscriptions surviving until our day. The King List reads: "Uruk was smitten with weapons; its kingship to Ur was carried. In Ur Mes-Anne-pada became king and reigned 80 years; [A-Anne-pada, son of Mes-Anne-pada reigned . . . years;] Meskiag-Nanna, son of Mes-Anne-pada, became king and reigned 36 years; Elulu reigned 25 years; Balulu reigned 36 years. 4 kings reigned its 177 years. Ur was smitten with weapons."

At Tell el-Obeid a tablet to the goddess Ninhursag was found, bearing the words "A-Anne-pada king of Ur, son of Mes-Anne-pada king of Ur, has built a temple for Ninhursag." This inscription not only verifies the name of Mes-Anne-pada as a ruler of Ur but also makes it possible to explain the one improbability which appears in the King List at this point, namely the ascription of the extraordinarily long reign of 80 years to Mes-Anne-pada. It is of course not impossible that a king might inherit a throne in childhood and reign thereafter for 80 years. But Mes-Anne-pada was the founder of his dynasty which was established only by military victory over Uruk. He is not likely, therefore, to have been only a small child at the time, and the more mature a fighting man he was when he came to the throne the less apt he is to have had yet 80 years to reign. Now it appears, however, that in actuality he was followed in the kingship by a son with the very similar name of A-Anne-pada. Due no doubt to this similarity, the son's name dropped out of the King List. At the same time, the length of the son's reign probably was added to that of the father's, so that Mes-Anne-pada emerged with a reign of 80 years. The King List probably preserved correctly, therefore, the total number of years covered by the dynasty, but needs to be corrected by the addition of the name of A-Anne-pada as in brackets in the quotation just given, and by the distribution of the 80 years between the reigns of the two kings. Concerning A-Anne-pada it is of interest to note that another inscription is in existence in which he calls himself "the god A-Anne-pada."

The high culture which was achieved under the First Dynasty of Ur is shown by the famous "royal" cemetery discovered by C. Leonard Woolley at Ur. This is the burial area deep beneath which were found the evidences of the flood. Outside the walls of the primitive town which stood here after the flood, a great rubbish heap accumulated, into which the graves afterward were dug. The date of this cemetery is probably around 2500 B.C.[4]

The largest number of graves were those of common folk who were buried in rectangular pits, with the bodies wrapped in matting or put in coffins of wood, wickerwork or clay. Often the first sign which showed the excavators that they were coming upon such a grave would be a paper-thin wavy line of white powder remaining from the edge of the reed-mat, or a few small vertical holes left in a line by the decay of the wooden staves which strengthened the sides of the coffin. Personal belongings and other items had been placed in the graves, including bracelets, necklaces, vanity cases, weapons, tools, food and drink. The body always lay on its side, in the attitude of one asleep, and the hands held close to the mouth a cup which probably once contained water. Thus kindly provisions were made for the dead.

The most remarkable graves were those which have become known as the "royal" tombs, although it is now believed by some scholars that they actually belonged not to royal persons but to priests and priestesses sacrificed in fertility rites.[5] The rooms and vaults of these tombs were built of brick and stone—and the stone must have been brought from at least thirty miles away in the higher desert.

In one tomb, which had already been plundered by grave-robbers, a cylinder seal remained to give the name of the deceased, A-bar-gi. Also overlooked against the wall was a silver model of a boat, which was of a type identical with that in use today on the marshes of the lower Euphrates. Above this plundered vault was the untouched grave of a lady, these circumstances suggesting that those who conducted the latter burial were the ones who at the same time contrived to rob the lower tomb. The occupant of the new tomb was identified by a lapis lazuli cylinder as Lady Shub-ad, and her body lay upon the remains of a wooden bier, a gold cup near her hand. Her elaborate

---

[4] Woolley's date of c.3500-3200 B.C. (*Ur Excavations II, The Royal Cemetery* [1934] p.223) was criticized by V. Müller in *Journal of the American Oriental Society*. 55 (1935), pp.206-208; and by H. Frankfort in *The Journal of the Royal Asiatic Society*. 1937, pp.332-341. The most recent chronological correlations point to the date given above (see W. F. Albright in BASOR 88 [Dec. 1942], p.32; and in AJA 47 [1943], p.492).

[5] Sidney Smith in *The Journal of the Royal Asiatic Society*. 1928, pp.862-868; Franz M. Th. Böhl in *Zeitschrift für Assyriologie*. Neue Folge 5 (39) 1930, pp.83-98; H. Frankfort in *Iraq*. 1 (1934), p.12 n.3; and in *The Journal of the Royal Asiatic Society*. 1937, pp.341f.; E. A. Speiser in *Antiquity*. VIII (1934), p.451.

headdress was still in good order, and is shown in Fig. 12 upon a head copied from a Sumerian statuette. The headdress contained nine yards of gold band, and was accompanied by huge crescent shaped earrings and a golden "Spanish comb" whose five points ended in gold flowers with lapis centers.

In a great pit connecting with A-bar-gi's tomb were found the bodies of more than 60 people, while some 25 persons had been buried together with Lady Shub-ad. Other such "death-pits" were found, one containing the remains of as many as 6 men and 68 women. Even chariots were driven down into these death-pits and fine treasures were placed in them. All these people and offerings have the appearance of sacrifices made in honor of the royal or sacred personage who was being buried, yet the indications are that the human victims went willingly to their deaths.

Some magnificent harps or lyres were found in these graves, decorated with heads of animals, including a bearded bull, a cow and a stag, and two statues were recovered each representing a goat standing up in front of a bush from which it is perhaps eating the leaves (Fig. 13).[6]

Another tomb was identified by inscriptions as belonging to "Mes-kalam-dug, Hero of the Good Land." The body lay in a normal way on its right side, between the hands was a bowl of heavy gold, from a broad silver belt hung a dagger of gold and over the fragments of the skull was a helmet of beaten gold. The helmet was made in the form of a wig with the locks of hair hammered up in relief and the individual hairs engraved as delicate lines. Yet other examples of the work of the goldsmiths of Ur are shown in Figs. 14-15. Their achievement approached perfection.

In the largest of the stone-built tombs was found the so-called "Standard" of Ur. This was a wooden panel 22 inches long by 9 inches high, with triangular end pieces, inlaid with mosaic work on both sides, and probably carried on a pole in processions. The wooden background had perished entirely but the tiny pieces of inlay kept their relative positions in the soil, and skillful work made possible the accurate restoration of the mosaics.

The two main panels of the Standard (Fig. 16) illustrate War and Peace respectively, there being in each case three rows filled with

[6] Woolley (*Ur Excavations: II*, p.266) draws an analogy with Genesis 22:13 but there is little likelihood of any actual connection.

figures made of shell and set in a background of lapis lazuli. In the first row of the panel depicting War, stands the king, dismounted from his chariot and distinguished by his greater height, while soldiers bring before him naked captives with arms bound behind their backs. In the second row advances the phalanx of the royal army, the men wearing long cloaks and copper helmets, and carrying axes. Ahead of them are the light-armed infantry, without cloaks, and fighting with axes or short spears. In the third row are the chariots of the javelin throwers, drawn by animals which break into an excited gallop as they encounter the corpses strewn on the ground. Thus the ancient Sumerians anticipated the chariotry which other nations adopted later and the phalanx with which Alexander the Great won his victories. On the other side of the panel, Peace is illustrated with the king and royal family sitting at a feast, entertained by musicians, while servants bring food-supplies for the banquet and spoils captured from the enemy. The people wear the old-fashioned sheepskin kilts, with the upper part of the body left bare.

LAGASH

Another dynasty which flourished during the last phase of the Early Dynastic Period was that founded by Ur-Nanshe at Lagash (Telloh) some fifty miles north of Ur. The inscriptions of Ur-Nanshe make reference to extensive building of temples and digging of canals. A later ruler was Eannatum, who claims victories over Umma, Uruk, Ur, Akshak, Kish and Mari. His battle against nearby Umma is depicted on the Stela[7] of the Vultures, where his soldiers march in a close-packed phalanx with lances protruding from behind huge rectangular shields, and vultures bear heads and limbs away from the field of slaughter.

LUGALZAGESI

Afterward, Lagash fell again to Umma. This was in the days of Urukagina, a king who, under the inspiration of Ningirsu the god of Lagash, carried out commendable reforms including the limitation of the lavish amounts of food and drink hitherto buried with the dead. The new conqueror of Lagash was Lugalzagesi, who was *isag* or governor of Umma. Lugalzagesi ultimately became king of Uruk and Ur and was one of the most important figures in Sumerian his-

---

[7] Stela or stele is a Greek word ($\sigma\tau\acute{\eta}\lambda\eta$) meaning an erect stone and is used in archeology for an ancient monument in the form of an upright stone slab.

tory. His 25-year reign constituted, according to the King List, the Third Dynasty of Uruk.

The extent of the dominion which he achieved is indicated in the following triumphal inscription from Nippur, in which Lugalzagesi prayed Enlil, the wind god, for the permanence of his reign:

"When Enlil king of the countries had granted to Lugalzagesi the kingship of the land; had turned the eyes of the land toward him; had prostrated the countries at his feet: then did he make straight his path for him, from the Lower Sea, by Tigris and Euphrates, to the Upper Sea. From East to West Enlil nowhere allowed him a rival. Lugalzagesi gave the countries to rest in peace; watered the land with water of joy. . . . Then made he Uruk to shine in sheen of countenance; skyward, like a bull's, upraised the head of Ur; Larsa, dear city of the sun-god, watered with waters of joy; nobly exalted Umma, dear city of Shara. . . . May Enlil king of the countries prefer my prayer before his dear father An. May he add life to my life; cause the country to rest at peace with me. Folk as numerous as scented herbs may he bestow on me with open hand; guide for me the flock of An;[8] look benevolently for me upon the land. Let the gods not change the good destiny that they have assigned to me. Shepherd, leader let me be forever!"[9]

The reference to the Upper Sea indicates that the armies of Lugalzagesi marched as far west as the shores of the Mediterranean. So great had become the outreach of Sumerian power.

[8] i.e. mankind.
[9] Patrick Carleton, *Buried Empires, The Earliest Civilizations of the Middle East.* 1939, p.118.

3. THE OLD AKKADIAN PERIOD,
c.2360-c.2180 B.C.

MEANWHILE the strength of Semitic peoples in Mesopotamia had been increasing. They were distinguished from the Sumerians by their language which belonged to the great Semitic family of languages. The Akkadian, Assyrian, and Babylonian dialects constitute the older East Semitic branch of this family, while Hebrew, Aramaic, Phoenician, Syriac, Arabic and Ethiopic are included in the West Semitic.

Semitic names had been appearing for some time in the King List. In the First Dynasty of Kish several of the names were definitely Semitic while the Third Dynasty of Kish consisted of a single ruler "Ku-Baba, a barmaid," whose own name was Sumerian but who bestowed a Semitic name upon her son, Puzur-Sin. The later kings of the Dynasty of Akshak and all the kings of the Fourth Dynasty of Kish bore Semitic names, and excavations both at Mari and at Nuzu show that there were lines of Semitic kings at those places.

SARGON

With Sargon a dynasty of Semitic-speaking kings attained supremacy in all Babylonia. This man was of lowly origin. An inscription makes him say: "Sargon, the mighty king, the king of Akkad, am I. My mother was humble, my father I did not know, the brother of my father lived in the mountains. My city is Azupiranu, on the bank of the Euphrates. My humble mother conceived me; she bore me in secret, placed me in an ark of bulrushes, made fast my door with pitch and gave me to the river which did not overwhelm me. The river lifted me up and carried me to Akki the irrigator. . . . Akki the irrigator hauled me out. . . . Akki the irrigator took me to be his son and brought me up."[1] The story of the baby in the ark of bulrushes reminds one of the similar story concerning Moses.

As a man, Sargon founded the city of Agade from which the narrow northern plain of Babylonia took the name of Akkad and its Semitic peoples the designation of Akkadians. Then he overthrew the powerful Lugalzagesi and conquered the entire Babylonian land, installing his own daughter as high-priestess of the moon-god Nannar at Ur.

[1] Hugo Gressmann, *Altorientalische Texte und Bilder zum Alten Testament.* 1909, I, p.79.

Within a few years the empire wrested from Lugalzagesi was transformed from a Sumerian into a Semitic realm, both linguistically and, at least in part, culturally. Eventually the dominion of Sargon was extended on eastward into Elam and westward as far as Syria and the Mediterranean. An inscription of his gives thanks to "the god Dagan," the chief god of the Semites of northern Syria, for the Syrian coast lands which that deity gave him. Thus Sargon became the most powerful monarch who ever had ruled in Mesopotamia.

A small but important city of the Old Akkadian Period was Gasur, the site of which is known now as Yorgan Tepa and is a dozen miles southwest of modern Kirkuk. Excavations at this place have been conducted through the cooperation of a number of institutions including the American School of Oriental Research at Baghdad, the Iraq Museum, Harvard University and the University Museum of the University of Pennsylvania.[2] In the time of which we are speaking the population of Gasur was overwhelmingly Semitic, but later the city became an important center of the Hurrians at which time it was known as Nuzu (p. 54).[3] Many tablets have been found here which date from the Old Akkadian Period and reveal the prosperity and extensive business activity of those days. Among the business records was an inscribed clay map, prepared perhaps to indicate the location of some estate, and ranking now as the oldest map ever discovered. Other tablets show that buying and selling on the installment plan were practiced, and indicate that the commercial dealings of this one community extended over a very considerable portion of the far-flung empire of Sargon.[4]

Also a rapid development of art took place in this period and reached its climax under Sargon's grandson, the great ruler Naram-Sin, whose full title was, "The divine Naram-Sin, the mighty, god of Agade, king of the Four Quarters." His Victory Stela (Fig. 17), discovered by de Morgan at Susa and now in the Louvre at Paris, "is the most impressive and beautiful work of early western Asiatic art

[2] Richard F. S. Starr, *Nuzi, Report on the Excavations at Yorgan Tepa near Kirkuk, Iraq, conducted by Harvard University in conjunction with the American Schools of Oriental Research and the University Museum of Philadelphia 1927-1931.* 2 vols. 1937-39.

[3] Because the first published documents from this place gave the name in the genitive case, Nuzi, the city frequently is called Nuzi. The nominative Nuzu is correct.

[4] Starr, *Nuzi.* I (1939), p.23; T. J. Meek, *Old Akkadian, Sumerian, and Cappadocian Texts from Nuzi* (Harvard Semitic Series, 10, 1935), p.xv.

which we possess."[5] It celebrates his victorious campaign against the mountain-dwelling Lulubi. The scene is the wooded foothills of a mountain whose conical peak rises to the stars. The king's light-armed soldiers advance up the slope, carrying lances and standards. High in the hill above, from which the bodies of the slain are plunging, the king climbs inexorably upward. He is colossal in size, wearing the horned helmet of a god, and carrying war-axe and bow and arrow. His enemies fall beneath his feet, one with throat transfixed by an arrow. Yet another lifts his hands to beg for his life.

[5] Heinrich Schäfer and Walter Andrae, *Die Kunst des alten Orients.* 1925, p.493.

4. THE GUTIAN PERIOD, c.2180-c.2070 B.C.

BUT Naram-Sin's great empire, stretching from central Persia to the Mediterranean and from northeastern Arabia to the Taurus Mountains, lasted only through the reign of his son Shargalisharri. Thereafter the Gutians, a little-known Caucasian people from the eastern mountain country of Gutium overran Babylonia.

5. THE NEO-SUMERIAN PERIOD, c.2070-c.1960 B.C.

GUDEA

IN THE YEARS when the power of the Gutians was declining, a remarkable Sumerian ruled as governor at Lagash and prepared the way for a renaissance of Sumerian power and culture. His name was Gudea and numerous statues have been found of him, one of which is shown in Fig. 18. Gudea is represented as wearing a turban in the fashion which became very popular in those days, and his face is clean-shaven, grave and kindly.[1]

With true piety Gudea endeavored to be the shepherd of his people and the servant of the gods. Beseeching divine guidance, he prayed in the temple, "I have no mother; my pure mother thou art. I have no father; thou art my pure father." Through a dream it was revealed to him that he should restore Eninnu, "the House of Fifty [gods]," a Lagash temple first mentioned as early as the end of the Jemdet Nasr Period.[2] "In the dream a man that shone like the heaven and was joyful like the earth—from the crown of his head he was a god; by his side was the divine black storm-bird as a companion; below and before him was a storm; on his right and left, lions were standing; he commanded to build his house; his meaning I did not understand." There also appeared in this dream a warrior who held a tablet of lapis lazuli in his hand which contained the plan of a temple. Eventually the goddess Nina made it clear to Gudea that the man at whose side was the storm-bird was the god Ningirsu who wished to command Gudea to build his temple Eninnu, and the warrior with the tablet in his hand was the god Nindub who was bringing the plan for the temple.

---

[1] cf. Gaston Cros, *Nouvelles fouilles de Tello*. II (1911), Pl. I; Simon Harcourt-Smith, *Babylonian Art*. 1928, p.19.
[2] Carleton, *Buried Empires*, p.63.

So Gudea proceeded at once to the task, himself laying the first brick. The work was very extensive, and Gudea's account mentions the bringing of cedar wood all the way from the Amanus Mountains in northern Syria, a part of the same general range as the Lebanon from which Solomon was to cut cedar trees for the temple at Jerusalem (I Kings 5:6). At last the work was finished. "The holy temple rising from earth to heaven . . . shone in the brilliance of heaven with radiant light. . . . It illumined the country."[3]

THE THIRD DYNASTY OF UR

With the final downfall of the Gutians, the great Third Dynasty of Ur arose in splendor. Its first king was Ur-Nammu who took the new title "King of Sumer and Akkad," and whose mightiest work was the erection of a great ziggurat at Ur. The ziggurat which stood at Babylon in the days of Hammurabi and was known as Etemenanki, "the House of the Terrace-platform of Heaven and Earth,"[4] became more famous and was remembered in Hebrew traditions as the Tower of Babel, but the ziggurat at Ur is today the best preserved of all monuments of this type and therefore the best fitted to give a vivid impression of their character (Fig. 19).

As long ago as 1854, J. E. Taylor visited Ur (then only a ruined site known by the Arabs as al Muqayyar, the Mound of Bitumen) and dug down into the corners of the great pile which dominated it. He found cuneiform cylinders of Nabonidus of Babylon (556-539 B.C.), stating that Nabonidus had there restored the ziggurat of Ur, begun by Ur-Nammu. The text reads: "Nabonidus king of Babylon . . . am I. E-lugal-malga-sidi, the ziggurat of E-gish-shir-gal in Ur, which Ur-Nammu, a king before me, had built but not completed, did Dungi his son finish. On the inscription of Ur-Nammu and of his son Dungi saw I that Ur-Nammu had built but not completed that ziggurat and that Dungi his son had finished the work. Now was that ziggurat old. Upon the ancient foundations whereon Ur-Nammu and his son Dungi had built I made good the structure of that ziggurat, as in old times, with mortar and burnt brick. . . ."[5] Then Nabonidus concluded with a dedication to Nannar, lord of the gods of heaven and earth, and a prayer for the life of himself and of his son Belshazzar.

[3] Barton, *Royal Inscriptions of Sumer and Akkad*, pp.206-235.
[4] W. F. Albright in AJA 48 (1944), p.305.
[5] C. L. Woolley, *Abraham, Recent Discoveries and Hebrew Origins*. 1936, p.62.

In 1918 Dr. H. R. Hall cleared part of one end of the mound but the complete excavation requiring the removal of thousands of tons of rubbish was first undertaken by C. L. Woolley in 1922-1923.[6] Ur-Nammu's structure probably was built on top of a smaller ziggurat which may have been as old as the time of Mes-Anne-pada. In its upper part the great artificial mountain clearly was the work of Nabonidus. The bulk of the construction, however, had been carried out by Ur-Nammu himself and his name and title were found stamped on the bricks. The tower was a solid mass of brickwork, 200 feet long, 150 feet wide, and some 70 feet high. The core was of unbaked brick, with a facing about 8 feet thick of baked brick set in bitumen. The whole design was a masterpiece, the lines of the walls all being built on calculated curves to give the appearance of lightness and strength, a principle used long later by the Greeks. Originally the shrine of Nannar, the moon-god, stood on the topmost stage and it is possible that the various terraces were covered with soil and irrigated so that the green of growing plants beautified the whole.[7]

Interestingly enough, we possess a contemporary record of the building of this ziggurat in the Stela of Ur-Nammu, a slab of white limestone nearly 5 feet across and 10 feet high, recovered unfortunately only in fragments (Fig. 20). At the top the king stands in the attitude of prayer while from above come flying angels with vases out of which flow the streams of life. An inscription elsewhere enumerates the canals dug by Ur-Nammu, and here he thanks the gods for the gift of life-bringing water. This is the earliest known representation of an angel in art.[8] At least three panels of the stela are devoted to the building of the ziggurat. In the first of these Ur-Nammu stands at the left in front of the goddess Nin-Gal and again at the right before the god Nannar, receiving the command to build him a house. In the next panel the king is setting forth, bearing on his shoulder the tools of the architect and builder, compasses, mortar-basket, pick and trowel, while in the third panel little remains but one of the ladders of the workmen which leaned against the side of the rising structure.

In the course of time other buildings were erected around the ziggurat, so that the entire sacred area was very extensive. One of

[6] *Ur Excavations: V, The Ziggurat and Its Surroundings.* 1939.
[7] cf. Th. A. Busink, *Sumerische en Babylonische Tempelbouw.* 1940, p.69.
[8] C. L. Woolley, *The Development of Sumerian Art.* 1935, p.112.

these was the square temple known as the Gig-par-ku, which was dedicated to Nin-Gal the moon-goddess and wife of Nannar. The kitchen was an important part of the temple, since worship was by sacrifice and the cooked flesh of the sacrificial animal was shared among the god, the priests and the worshipers. The temple in the Gig-par-ku was equipped with a well for water, fireplaces for boiling the water, a bitumen-covered brick table on which the carcass of the victim was cut up, a flat-topped cooking range and a domed bread oven.

Much business took place within the sacred area. As sacrifices, tithes and taxes were brought in, a receipt was given to each man. The temple scribe then made a notation for himself on a small clay tablet, and eventually these memoranda were incorporated in weekly, monthly and yearly reports. Large numbers of such business tablets and ledgers have been found. Factories and workshops also were to be found there. One such establishment at Ur was a weaving factory which produced twelve sorts of woolen cloth. Tablets still give the names of the women weavers, the amount of rations allotted to them, the quantity of wool issued to each, and the amount of cloth manufactured. The temple area also was the home of the law court. Dublal-mah or "Great House of Tablets" was the name of the building at Ur from whose doorway the judges announced their findings and in whose store chambers the clay documents recording their decisions were kept.

Ur-Nammu was succeeded by his son Dungi (Shulgi), to whom Nabonidus referred as the completer of the ziggurat. This important ruler proclaimed himself "the divine Shulgi, god of his land," and his greatest monument was his own mortuary temple and sepulcher. He was succeeded by his son Bur-Sin who was followed in turn by Gimil-Sin and then by Ibi-Sin.

6. THE PERIOD OF ELAMITE AND AMORITE INVASIONS, c.1960-c.1830 B.C.

IT WAS in the days of Ibi-Sin that disaster came upon the Sumerians. The Elamites stormed down out of the hills, took Ibi-Sin captive and sacked the capital city of Ur. A later poet wrote in lamentation:

O my city attacked and destroyed, my city attacked without
cause,
The strength of the protecting word uttered against the evil,
bitter storm stood not by thee;
O my house of Sin in Ur, bitter is thy destruction.[1]

Among the leaders of the invading Amorites were Ishbi-Irra from Mari, and Naplanum. These two settled respectively at Isin and Larsa. An Elamite ruler, Kirikiri, was established at Eshnunna.

7. THE OLD BABYLONIAN PERIOD, c.1830-c.1550 B.C.

No DOUBT it was the rivalry of these several city-states which made it possible for a little-known man with an Amorite name, Sumu-abu, to become master of an unimportant Akkadian city nine miles west of Kish and carve out a small kingdom for himself in that neighborhood. The name of the city was Bab-ilu or Babylon, and Sumu-abu became the founder of the First Dynasty of Babylon.

THE FIRST DYNASTY OF BABYLON

The struggles among the various city-states were long and complex, but eventually Babylon and Larsa faced each other as the two chief powers in lower Mesopotamia. At Larsa an Elamite, Kudur-Mabug, had placed his son Warad-Sin on the throne and he in turn was followed by his younger brother, Rim-Sin. At Babylon Sumu-abu had been followed by Sumu-la-el, Sabum, Apil-Sin and Sin-muballit. Then Hammurabi came to the throne. When war broke out between Rim-Sin and Hammurabi the outstanding military genius of the latter soon became evident. Rim-Sin and his allies were defeated and Sumer passed into the hands of Hammurabi, Larsa becoming his southern administrative capital. Isin had been cap-

---

[1] S. N. Kramer, *Lamentation Over the Destruction of Ur.* AS 12, 1940, p.57.

tured earlier and Eshnunna soon fell.[2] Mari, the city from which Ishbi-Irra had come, remained as a powerful rival on the northern frontier, athwart the route to the Mediterranean. In the thirty-second year of his reign Hammurabi conquered and partially destroyed this city, too, returning a very few years later to make the destruction complete. Thus was established in full power the Old Babylonian Kingdom.

MARI

Mari is of such importance historically and archeologically that a further word must be said about it at this point. The ancient city was on the Middle Euphrates and is represented today by Tell Hariri 6 or 7 miles north of Abou Kemal. Excavations have been conducted there since 1933 by the *Musée du Louvre* under the leadership of André Parrot.[3] It is revealed that in the third millennium B.C. Mari was one of the most flourishing and brilliant cities of the Mesopotamian world. Among its public edifices were a temple of Ishtar and a ziggurat. Statuettes representing humble worshipers and dedicated to the goddess were found in the temple, and give a vivid picture of the devotion with which Ishtar was regarded. Near the ziggurat another very interesting small statue was found and is shown in Fig. 21. It represents a worshiper carrying in honor in his arms a kid which is doubtless intended for a sacrificial offering.

Most notable of all the buildings in Mari was the palace of the king. This was a tremendous structure covering more than fifteen acres in extent. It contained not only the royal apartments but also administrative offices and even a school for scribes. Furthermore it was adorned with great mural paintings, portions of which are still preserved. Among these were scenes of sacrifice, and a representation of the king of Mari receiving from Ishtar the staff and ring which were the emblems of his authority.[4] The palace bore the marks of two destructions which had been visited upon it in close succession, evidently corresponding to the two times when Mari fell to Hammurabi.

From the archives of the palace over 20,000 tablets were recovered, constituting a discovery of the greatest importance. A large number

[2] H. Frankfort, T. Jacobsen and Conrad Preusser, *Tell Asmar and Khafaje, The First Season's Work in Eshnunna 1930/31.* oic 13, 1932, pp.38,41.

[3] A. Parrot in *Syria, Revue d'Art orientale et d'archéologie.* 16 (1935), pp.1-28, 117-140; 17 (1936), pp.1-31; 18 (1937), pp.54-84; 19 (1938), pp. 1-29; 20 (1939), pp.1-22.

[4] Parrot in *Syria.* 18 (1937), pp.325-354.

of these tablets represent diplomatic correspondence of the last king of Mari, Zimri-Lim, with his ambassadors and agents and with Hammurabi, king of Babylon, himself. Others date from the time of the predecessors of Zimri-Lim. The dynasty of kings ruling at Mari, it is now learned, had been dispossessed temporarily when Shamshi-Adad I of Assyria (p. 168) sent his son Yasmah-Adad to exercise power at Mari. Later Yasmah-Adad had to give way to Zimri-Lim, who was the legitimate heir to the throne. Zimri-Lim then ruled until Mari fell to Hammurabi in the thirty-second year of the latter's reign.[5] The proof given by the Mari documents that Hammurabi was a contemporary of Shamshi-Adad I casts important light on the long-discussed problem of the date of Hammurabi. From the Khorsabad list of Assyrian kings (p. 168 n.5), Shamshi-Adad I can be dated around 1748-1716 B.C. and a detailed examination of the intricate interrelationships leads to fixing the date of Hammurabi at around 1728-1676 B.C.[6]

THE CODE OF HAMMURABI

Hammurabi was not only a great military commander but also an outstanding administrator and law-giver. Relatively little remains today of the Babylon of his time, since the city was reconstructed almost entirely in the sixth century B.C. by Nabopolassar and Nebuchadnezzar, but in one quarter some dwelling houses from Hammurabi's day have been unearthed. The distinctive thing here is the new and planned way in which the streets are laid out in regular straight lines which intersect approximately at right angles. Many letters written by Hammurabi also have been found, revealing his close attention to all the details of his realm and illustrating the terse clarity with which he issued his instructions. But his greatest achievement was represented by his code of laws.

Hammurabi named the second year of his reign the "year when he established justice," and eventually he set forth a compilation and codification of laws, largely based on old Sumerian originals, which continued in force in Babylonia for a thousand years. In 1901 a copy of this code was found by de Morgan at Susa where it had been

---

[5] A. Parrot, *Mari, une ville perdu.* 1935, pp.235f.

[6] François Thureau-Dangin in *Revue d'assyriologie et d'archéologie orientale.* 36 (1939), pp.24f.; W. F. Albright in BASOR 88 (Dec. 1942), pp.28-36; and in AJA 47 (1943), p.492. The date given above for Shamshi-Adad I is that proposed by Albright and differs slightly from that at which A. Poebel arrived, namely 1726-1694 B.C. (JNES 1 [1942], p.285).

carried off by the Elamites. The code was inscribed on a round-topped stela of black diorite, some six feet in height, which now is in the Louvre. At the top is a bas-relief (Fig. 22) showing Hammurabi standing before the enthroned sun-god Shamash, the patron of law and justice. The god wears a pointed headdress with horns, rays are to be seen upon his shoulders, and he holds a ring and staff, the insignia of royalty, in his right hand. Hammurabi, who stands before him to receive his kingly law-giving power,[7] wears a long robe with right arm and shoulder bare, and is shown with beard and clean-shaven upper lip.

Beneath, were carved 51 columns of text, most of which still are preserved, written in the Semitic Babylonian language in beautiful cuneiform characters. In a lengthy prologue it is stated that the gods "called me, Hammurabi, the noble prince who reveres the gods, to make righteousness to shine forth in the land, to destroy the wrong-doer and the wicked man, that the strong should not oppress the weak, to come forth like the sun upon mankind and to illumine the land." The prologue concludes: "When Marduk[8] sent me to rule over men, to grant protection to the land, then I put law and righteousness in the mouth of the people, and brought well-being to my subjects." A long epilogue reaffirms Hammurabi's desire "that the strong might not injure the weak, and that the widow and the orphan might be safe," and says: "Let the oppressed, who has a lawsuit, come before my image as king of righteousness. Let him read the inscription on my monument, and understand my precious words. Let my inscription throw light upon his case, and may he discover his rights, and let his heart be made glad: so that he may say: Hammurabi is a lord, who is a father to his subjects."

The law code itself included nearly 300 paragraphs of legal provisions touching commercial, social, domestic and moral life. Procedure in the law courts had to be taken very seriously for false accusation in a capital case was a ground for death (§3). Theft in certain cases, kidnaping and house-breaking, were punishable by death (§6, 14, 21). In case of stealing at a fire, the thief was to be thrown into the fire (§25). Other laws dealt with the duties of soldiers and tax collectors (§26-41) and regulated farm rentals (§42ff.) deposits and debts (§112ff.). Marriage was legal only when recorded in writ-

[7] T. Fish in E. I. J. Rosenthal, ed., *Judaism and Christianity.* III (1938), p.43.
[8] The god of Babylon, biblical Merodach.

ing (§128) and the woman as well as the man had the right of divorce (§142). Death for both parties was the penalty in case of adultery between a man and another man's wife (§129), but a woman accused of adultery without proof might clear herself by swearing her innocence, or by the ordeal by water (§131f.). This latter consisted of leaping into the sacred river where sinking was proof of guilt and floating of innocence. A married woman might hold property (§150). Inheritance and adoption were regulated (§162-191). Laws covering assault and battery were based largely on the principle of equal retaliation, but with some complications because of the division of society into three classes, patrician, workingman and slave (§195-214).[9] For example (§200f.), "If a man knocks out the tooth of a man of his own rank they shall knock his tooth out. If one knocks out the tooth of a workingman, he shall pay one-third of a mana of silver." One very extreme application of the *lex talionis* was provided for (§209f.): if under certain circumstances a man caused the death of another man's daughter, his own daughter was to be put to death. The fees of physicians were governed and in the case of an operation under which the patient died the doctor's hand might be cut off (§215-225)! Likewise if a builder erected an unsafe house which fell upon its owner and killed him, he himself was liable to death (§229). River navigation (§234-239), rental of cattle (§242ff.), wages of laborers (§257f.) and numerous other matters were covered in the code.

There are a number of similarities between this code and the later laws of the Hebrews which suggest their common background. With the points cited above from the Code of Hammurabi may be compared the following Old Testament laws: According to Deuteronomy 19:18f. a false witness is to be punished with the penalty he had thought to bring upon the other man. Exodus 21:16 makes the stealing and selling of a man a capital offense, and Exodus 22:2 allows the killing of a thief breaking into a house. The biblical law of divorce in Deuteronomy 24:1 permits the man to put away his wife but does not extend the same right to her as the Hammurabi code did. Leviticus 20:10 and Deuteronomy 22:22 agree exactly with Hammurabi's code on the death penalty for both the man and the other

---

[9] *Awilum,* patrician or gentleman; *mushkenum,* workingman or freeman (the modern Arabic *masqin* is derived from this ancient Babylonian term); and *wardum,* chattel-slave.

man's wife in case of adultery. Exodus 21:23-25 and Deuteronomy 19:21 state vividly the same principle of retaliation upon which a number of Hammurabi's laws were based: "life for life, eye for eye, tooth for tooth, hand for hand, foot for foot, burning for burning, wound for wound, stripe for stripe."[10]

In addition to Hammurabi's famous code of laws a great many other written documents remain from the Old Babylonian Period to attest the intense literary activity of those days. Thousands of letters show that a considerable part of the population was literate.[11] Extant texts indicate that a remarkable knowledge of medicine, botany, chemistry, geology and mathematics had been attained.[12] A business document from the time of Hammurabi is shown in Fig. 23. The tablet was found in the region of the Diyala River, and contains a contract concerning a loan of grain on which the borrower paid interest. The date formula on the tablet mentions the year when Shamshi-Adad I died. In the Old Babylonian Period the story of the flood was reedited, as was the epic of creation.

THE EPIC OF CREATION

Like the legend of the flood so, too, an account of creation was at least as ancient as the time of the Sumerians. The fragmentary tablet from Nippur which alluded to the creation as well as narrated the flood has already been mentioned (p. 26), while other Sumerian tablets from around 2000 B.C. have recently been discovered, giving a new version of the creation of the universe and of man. According to the account which they contain, heaven and earth once were united but afterward were separated. This was done in order that the surface of the earth might be the dwelling place for man who himself was fashioned out of clay.[13]

In the First Dynasty of Babylon the epic of creation was given the form in which it was to be told for the next thousand years and the form in which it is most familiar to us. The first tablets containing the Babylonian version of the creation were discovered at Nineveh

[10] W. W. Davies, *The Codes of Hammurabi and Moses* (1905).

[11] G. R. Driver, *Letters of the First Babylonian Dynasty.* Oxford Editions of Cuneiform Texts, 1942; T. Fish in *Bulletin of the John Rylands Library, Manchester.* 16 (1932), p.508.

[12] R. C. Thompson, *Assyrian Medical Texts.* 1923; *A Dictionary of Assyrian Chemistry and Geology.* 1936; O. Neugebauer, *Mathematische Keilschrift-Texte.* 1-3 (1935-37).

[13] *The New York Times,* Nov. 8, 1941, p.17; Dec. 13, 1941, p.23; Kramer, *Sumerian Mythology,* pp.37f.,69f.

in the ruins of the seventh century B.C. library of Ashurbanipal (p. 181), and other tablets and fragments of tablets of the epic have been found at Ashur, Kish and Uruk. Those from Ashur belong to approximately 1000 B.C., while the remaining ones are probably from the sixth century B.C. and later. Despite the relatively late date of the extant tablets, it is almost certain that the epic was composed in substantially its present form in the days of Hammurabi. That was the time when Babylon rose to political supremacy and when Marduk became the national god, and one purpose of the creation epic is to show the preeminence of Babylon over all other cities in the country and especially the supremacy of Marduk over all other Babylonian gods.

The epic, which is written on seven clay tablets and consists in all of about 1000 lines, is known from its two opening words as *Enuma elish* ("When above").[14] The account begins with the time when only the two divine principles, the mythical personalities Apsu and Tiamat, were in existence. These two represented the living, uncreated world-matter, Apsu being the primeval sweet-water ocean and Tiamat the primeval salt-water ocean.[15] It has usually been assumed that the Babylonians thought of Tiamat as a dragon or similar monster, but this now appears doubtful.[16] Tiamat is explicitly called a woman in the myth (Tablet II, line 111) and she and Apsu became the mother and father of the gods. Eventually the doings of these gods became so annoying to their parents that Apsu announced his intention of destroying them. The god Ea, however, perceived the plan and was able to fetter and slay Apsu. Then among the gods the real hero of the myth, Marduk the city-god of Babylon, was born. In the copy of the epic found at Ashur the name of Marduk was replaced by that of the Assyrian god, Ashur. On her side Tiamat created a host of gruesome monsters whose bodies were filled with poison instead of

[14] Alexander Heidel, *The Babylonian Genesis.* 1942.

[15] Jensen in Erich Ebeling and Bruno Meissner, eds., *Reallexikon der Assyriologie.* I (1928), p.123.

[16] Heidel, *The Babylonian Genesis*, pp.72-75. A well-known Assyrian relief from Nimrod (E. A. Wallis Budge, *Assyrian Sculptures in the British Museum, Reign of Ashur-nasir-pal, 885-860 B.C.* 1914. Pl. xxxvii), for example, has often been interpreted as representing the combat of Marduk with Tiamat. It shows a winged god striding forward against a fleeing monster which is half lion and half bird. But this relief comes from the temple of Ninurta and bears an inscription beginning with a prayer to Ninurta, and hence must represent this deity rather than Marduk. Moreover, the monster is a masculine creature of land and air, while Tiamat was a feminine water deity.

blood. One of her own offspring, Kingu, was exalted to be the supreme director of her forces. So much is related in the first tablet of the myth.

Tiamat now was ready to wage war against the gods and avenge Apsu. The gods were afraid when they learned their danger but Marduk volunteered to be their champion. He asked that he should be made the highest god if he should vanquish Tiamat. This is narrated in Tablet II, and Tablet III tells how the gods assembled at a banquet for the council of war. In Tablet IV (Fig. 24) we find Marduk preparing for the struggle. He took bow, arrow and club, and held lightning before his face. He made a net to enclose the body of Tiamat and raised up the hurricane as his mighty weapon. His chariot was the storm, drawn by four steeds, "The Destructive," "The Pitiless," "The Trampler," and "The Fleet." When he came before Tiamat, Marduk uttered his challenge, "Come on and let us, me and thee, do battle!" Then:

> Tiamat and Marduk, the wisest of the gods, took their stands
> opposite each other,
> They pressed on to the battle, they approached in combat.
> The lord spread out his net and enmeshed her,
> The evil wind, following after, he let loose in her face.
> When Tiamat opened her mouth to devour him,
> He drove in the evil wind, so that she could not close her lips.
> As the raging winds filled her belly,
> Her belly was distended, and she opened wide her mouth.
> He shot off an arrow, it tore her belly,
> It cut through her inward parts, it pierced [her] heart.
> When he had subdued her, he destroyed her life;
> He cast down her carcass [and] stood upon it.

The helpers of Tiamat now attempted to flee, but were captured and cast into prison. Then Marduk returned to the corpse of Tiamat.

> The lord rested, to look at her dead body, [to see]
> How he might divide the colossus [and] create wondrous things
> [therewith].
> He split her open like a mussel [?][17] into two parts;
> Half of her he set in place and formed the sky [therewith].

Next Marduk established the earth, which is represented as a great structure in the shape of a canopy over Apsu, and is poetically called Esharra. Then he determined the residences of the gods, Anu being

[17] Sometimes translated "like a flat fish" (Barton, *Archaeology and the Bible*, p.288).

caused to occupy the sky, Enlil the air, and Ea the waters underneath the earth. Here ends Tablet IV. Only a fragment of Tablet V remains, but it tells how Marduk set up the constellations which mark the days and months of the year, and caused the moon to shine forth, entrusting the night to her.

In Tablet VI the creation of man is described. In the assembly of the great gods the guilt for Tiamat's revolt was determined to belong to Kingu, the leader of her hosts. Thereupon, Kingu was slain, and when his arteries were cut open the gods fashioned mankind with his blood. The service of the gods was laid upon mankind, while the gods themselves molded bricks for a year and labored to construct Esagila, the large temple tower of Marduk at Babylon. Then the gods gathered at a festive banquet and joined in singing praises of Marduk. Finally, Marduk's advancement from chief god of Babylon to head of the entire pantheon is signified by the conferring upon him of fifty names which represent the power and attributes of the various Babylonian gods. This is the seventh and last tablet.

Obviously there are some interesting points of comparison between the account of creation given in *Enuma elish* and that in Genesis 1:1-2:3. Both refer to a watery chaos at the beginning of time, and the term *tehom* by which it is designated in Genesis 1:2 may go back to the same Semitic form from which the proper name Tiamat is derived. Genesis 1:7 speaks of a firmament placed to divide the waters beneath it from those above it. The word for firmament means literally "what is spread out" and corresponds in a much more refined way to the crude Babylonian idea of the half of Tiamat used by Marduk to construct the vault of heaven. The sequence of events in the creation also is the same in the two stories, in that the following happenings take place in the same order: the creation of the firmament, the creation of dry land, the creation of the luminaries, and the creation of man. Both accounts begin with the watery chaos and end with the gods or the Lord at rest.

On the whole, however, it must be recognized that the differences between *Enuma elish* and the Old Testament are far more important than the similarities. The Babylonian creation story is mythological and polytheistic while the accounts in Genesis are elevated and strictly monotheistic. Doubtless certain features of the biblical narrative of creation are derived from the Babylonian myth, or at least back of both Hebrew and Babylonian thought are certain common sources. But the dignity and exaltation of the words of the Bible are unparalleled.

NUZU

Other materials which have an important relationship to biblical narratives are found in the tablets from Nuzu. In the second millennium B.C. this city (cf. p. 39) was a provincial center of the Hurrians. The latter were a people who seem to have come into Mesopotamia from the north in the second half of the third millennium and who became a dominant ethnic element throughout the Middle East during the second millennium B.C. They were the biblical Horites (Genesis 14:6, etc.), but aside from the few references to them in the Old Testament have become known only through the archeological discoveries of the last two or three decades.[18] At Nuzu thousands of clay tablets were found which had been written by Hurrian scribes in the Babylonian language but with the occasional employment of native Hurrian words. The bulk of these tablets date in the fifteenth century B.C. or just shortly after the Old Babylonian Period. Since transactions of all kinds are recorded in them, much information is given concerning the life of the people.[19]

Among the customs and laws which the tablets reveal to have prevailed at Nuzu are many which cast light upon incidents recorded in the Bible and particularly upon events of the patriarchal age.[20] Adoption was frequent at Nuzu, and in particular childless couples often adopted a son who would care for them when they were old, bury them when they died, and be heir to their estate. It was specified however that if, after the adoption, they had a son of their own, the adopted son would have to give way to the real son as the chief heir. This provides a legal explanation for Genesis 15:2-4 where the heir of the childless Abraham is expected to be his slave Eliezer, until the promise is given that a son of his own will be born to become his heir.

Marriage contracts at Nuzu contained a provision obliging a childless wife to provide her husband with a handmaid who would bear

[18] W. F. Albright in L. G. Leary, ed., *From the Pyramids to Paul.* 1935, pp.9-13.

[19] For these cuneiform texts see Robert H. Pfeiffer and E. A. Speiser in *The Annual of the American Schools of Oriental Research.* 16 (1935-36); Edward Chiera, *Joint Expedition with the Iraq Museum at Nuzi.* 6 vols. 1927-39; *Harvard Semitic Series.* 5 (1929); 9 (1932); 12 (1942); cf. Cyrus H. Gordon in *Orientalia* 7 (1938), p.32 n.1.

[20] Cyrus H. Gordon, *The Living Past.* 1941, pp.156-178; and in BA III, 1 (Feb. 1940), pp.1-12.

children. This explains the action of Sarah in giving Hagar to Abraham (Genesis 16:1f.) and of Rachel in giving Bilhah to Jacob (Genesis 30:1-3). According to the Nuzu documents the offspring of the handmaid could not be driven out, which shows that there was a legal basis for Abraham's apprehension over the expulsion of Hagar and her child (Genesis 21:11).

Another Nuzu tablet records a relationship between a man named Nashwi and his adopted son called Wullu, which is parallel in some ways to the relationship between Laban and Jacob (Genesis 29-31). Nashwi bestows his daughter upon Wullu, even as Laban promised a daughter to Jacob when he received him into his household. When Nashwi dies, Wullu is to be the heir. If Nashwi begets a son, however, Wullu must share the inheritance with that son, and only the latter shall take Nashwi's gods. Evidently the possession of the household idols implied the leadership of the family. Since Laban had sons of his own when Jacob departed for Canaan, they alone had the right to have their father's gods, and the theft of the teraphim by Rachel (Genesis 31:19, 30-35) was a serious offense.

It will be remembered that Laban searched Jacob's camp in vain for his stolen idols because "Rachel had taken the teraphim, and put them in the camel's saddle, and sat upon them" (Genesis 31:34). In this connection it is of interest to notice a stone slab sculptured in relief, which was found at Tell Halaf and is shown in Fig. 25. It dates from a somewhat later time, probably around the eleventh century B.C., and gives us one of the earliest known representations of the camel.[21] The rider of this camel, moreover, is sitting on a saddle which looks very much like a square box, and is fastened on the animal by crosswise girths. Such a saddle would be exactly the kind in which Rachel could readily have hidden the household idols. Another Tell Halaf sculpture, it may be added, shows a six-winged goddess, the conception of which may have some connection with the description of the seraphim in the Bible (Isaiah 6:2).[22]

HARAN

Other links with patriarchal times appear in northwestern Mesopotamia. The town of Haran (Genesis 11:31f.) is still in existence on the Balikh River sixty miles west of Tell Halaf. Cuneiform sources

[21] William F. Albright, *From the Stone Age to Christianity*. 1940, p.120.
[22] Von Oppenheim, *Tell Halaf*, Pl. xxxii B.

make frequent references to Haran, and show that it was a flourishing city in the nineteenth and eighteenth centuries B.C. The city of Nahor, which was Rebekah's home (Genesis 24:10), is mentioned often in the Mari documents as Nakhur, and seems to have been below Haran in the valley of the Balikh. In the time of Hammurabi, both places were ruled by Amorite princes. It may be noted that Haran and Nahor were the names not only of towns but also of members of Abraham's family (Genesis 11:22-27), and the same situation prevails in relation to several other names, including Terah and Serug. Both were among the ancestors of Abraham, and both names appear as designations of towns near Haran.[23] So persistent is tradition in the East that present-day Mohammedans living in the neighborhood of Haran, particularly at Urfa and at Ain el-Khalil, still relate many legends concerning Abraham, whom they look upon as an Islamic saint. At Urfa, Nimrod is said to have fired glowing charcoal from a catapult against Abraham. Instead of burning the holy man, a pond arose where the charcoal fell, and the glowing bits of charcoal turned into fishes. To this day the fish are holy and not to be eaten. At Ain el-Khalil native Mohammedan peasants still declare themselves to be direct descendants of Father Abraham.[24] It is certain, therefore, particularly in view of the correspondence between the biblical indications and the archeological evidences, that the region of Haran was an important center in the life of the forefathers of the Hebrew people.

THE HABIRU

In the times of which we are speaking, people called Habiru are known in Mesopotamia. The Habiru are mentioned in inscriptions from the days of Rim-Sin, the ruler whom Hammurabi defeated for the mastery of Sumer, and they also figure frequently in the tablets from Nuzu. At Nuzu the Habiru are often found entering voluntarily into positions of slavery. As a matter of fact, the name seems to denote primarily a social status, and the Habiru appear characteristically as relatively footloose people on the fringes of society. In the Tell el-Amarna tablets we will meet them again as marauding raiders (pp. 100f.). The name also occurs in cuneiform as Hapiri which is

[23] Albright, *From the Stone Age to Christianity*, pp.179f.
[24] Von Oppenheim, *Tell Halaf*, pp.65f.

probably the same as the name 'Apiru or 'Aperu which is found in Egyptian texts (p. 142).[25]

Phonetically the word Habiru is practically identical with "Hebrew," and it seems evident that there was some relationship between the two groups. While the many problems involved in this matter are not yet solved, it may be that the Hebrews of the Bible were a smaller group within the larger number of "outsiders" to whom the designation Habiru was applied.

ABRAHAM

The first person in the Bible to bear the name "Hebrew" was Abraham[26] (Genesis 14:13), and he was ever after regarded as the father of the Hebrew people. His migration from Mesopotamia, in response to a divine call and promise (Genesis 12:1-3; cf. Hebrews 11:8-10), was the initial act of faith which made possible the unfolding of all later Hebrew history.

That Abraham's home originally was in Mesopotamia, and specifically at the cities of Ur and Haran, is indicated in several strands of Old Testament narrative. In Joshua 24:2 (E) the Hebrew people are reminded of their polytheistic eastern ancestry in these words: "Your fathers dwelt of old time beyond the River, even Terah, the father of Abraham, and the father of Nahor: and they served other gods." "The River" is a frequent way of referring to the Euphrates,[27] and thus Mesopotamia is clearly indicated. Genesis 11:28-30; 12:1-4a, 6-9; cf. 15:7 (J) identifies the birthplace of Abraham with the city of Ur, and this tradition is echoed in a Levitical prayer of praise in Nehemiah 9:7: "Thou art Jehovah the God who didst choose Abram, and broughtest him forth out of Ur of the Chaldees, and gavest him the name of Abraham."[28] Genesis 11:10-27, 31f.; 12:4b-5 (P) likewise places the original home in Ur but indicates

[25] E. G. Kraeling in BASOR 77 (Feb. 1940), p.32.
[26] Abram (Genesis 11:27, 29, etc.) and Abraham (Genesis 17:5, etc.) probably are only variant spellings of essentially the same name.
[27] HDB IV p.287.
[28] In Genesis 11:28 (J), 31 (P); 15:7 (J), and Nehemiah 9:7 the LXX (I, pp.18f., 23) reads "the land of the Chaldees" instead of "Ur of the Chaldees," but even so the reference is to the same general area, for the home of the Chaldeans was in lower Babylonia. Strictly speaking, the words "of the Chaldees" are an anachronism. The Chaldeans were a Semitic people who first came into southern Babylonia around 1000 B.C. as far as we can tell, and eventually established the Neo-Babylonian or Chaldean empire. It was, of course, quite natural for the Hebrew writers to apply to the city or land the appellation customary in their own day.

that the migration was first to Haran and then, after Terah's death at that place, on to Canaan.[29]

If we seek for indications in the Bible as to the date of Abraham's residence in Mesopotamia, we find it necessary to consider a complex series of chronological notations, most of which are from priestly sources. In some cases they bear not only on the date of Abraham but also on the date of the Exodus, a problem to which attention must be given later.

Priestly notices in Genesis 12:4b; 21:5; 25:26 and 47:9 give a total of 215 years for the period from Abraham's coming into Canaan to Jacob's going down into Egypt. As to the length of time the children of Israel (Jacob) were in the land of Egypt there are two traditions. The first represents this period as covering 430 years, or in round numbers 400 years. The precise figure of 430 years is given in the Hebrew text of Exodus 12:40f. (P), "Now the time that the children of Israel dwelt in Egypt was four hundred and thirty years." The round number, 400 years, is used in Genesis 15:13[30] and also in Acts 7:6. Josephus, likewise, in two passages, represents the Israelites as having been in Egypt for 400 years.[31] The second tradition as to the length of time the Israelites were in Egypt appears in the Septuagint version of Exodus 12:40 which reads, "Now the time that the children of Israel dwelt in Egypt and in the land of Canaan was four hundred and thirty years."[32] Since, as we have seen, the patriarchs were in Canaan for 215 years, this would allow the Israelites only 215 years in Egypt. The statement in Galatians 3:17 evidently was based upon the Septuagint text, for it likewise makes 430 years

[29] There is some ground for believing that Abraham's home originally was at Haran and not at Ur at all. In Genesis 24 (J) Abraham sends his servant (v.10) to the city of Nahor in Aram-naharaim ("Aram of the two rivers"), or northwestern Mesopotamia, calling it "my country" (v.4) and "the land of my nativity" (v.7). If this be taken as the genuine J tradition and be regarded as excluding the possibility that Abraham had been born at Ur, it becomes necessary to suppose that "Ur of the Chaldees" or "land of the Chaldees" (LXX) was an addition to the original J in Genesis 11:28 and 15:7. Then Genesis 11:31 (P) would be a harmonization of the two traditions by representing that Abraham's residence in Haran was the result of a migration from Ur. Nehemiah 9:7 also would represent the secondary tradition. If the localization of Abraham's home at Ur was only a secondary invention, however, it is difficult to explain why that particular city was selected. Therefore it remains preferable to believe that Abraham was born in Ur, moved later to Haran, and went on eventually from there into Canaan. cf. T. J. Meek in *Journal of Religion*. 21 (1941), p.402.

[30] Genesis 15 is largely J and E, but v.13 may be by a later hand.

[31] Josephus (A.D. c.37-c.95), *Antiquities*, II, ix, 1; *War* v, ix, 4 (tr. H. St. J. Thackeray and Ralph Marcus, LCL [1926-], IV, p.253; III, p.321).

[32] Some MSS. read 435 years (LXX I, p.128).

cover the entire period from the call of Abraham to the Exodus and the giving of the law. Josephus also follows this tradition in one passage where he says of the Israelites, "They left Egypt . . . 430 years after the coming of our forefather Abraham to Canaan, Jacob's migration to Egypt having taken place 215 years later."[33]

In this case the Hebrew text of Exodus 12:40 seems more reliable than the reading in the Septuagint. The fortieth verse states that the Israelites were in Egypt 430 years. The forty-first verse continues, "And it came to pass at the end of four hundred and thirty years, even the selfsame day it came to pass, that all the hosts of Jehovah went out from the land of Egypt." In this context, verse 41 is a very impressive affirmation. After 430 long years of life and bondage in Egypt the Israelites finally found deliverance. When verse 40 is rendered according to the Septuagint, however, the point of verse 41 is largely lost. The Israelites left Egypt at the end of a time composed of two periods, one when the patriarchs lived in Canaan and the other when their children sojourned in Egypt, both of which periods when taken together totaled 430 years. Such is the complex and relatively pointless affirmation into which the passage is transformed by the rendering found in the Septuagint. On such grounds of internal evidence, and also because of the support of Genesis 15:13,[34] the tradition represented in the Hebrew text of Exodus 12:40 which describes a 430-year period in Egypt seems stronger than that found in the Septuagint, which refers to a sojourn only 215 years in length.

The statement in Genesis 15:16 (E) must also be taken into consideration, which says that the Exodus will take place "in the fourth generation." Similarly in the priestly genealogies in Exodus 6:16-20 and Numbers 26:57-59 Moses appears as the great-great-grandson of Jacob, that is to say he is a member of the fourth generation after Jacob. Also in Joshua 7:1 (P), Achan is listed as the great-great-great-grandson of Jacob and thus the generation of Joshua's time is represented as the fifth from Jacob. At first sight this appears to support the tradition of a 215 rather than a 430 year sojourn in Egypt. Indeed if a "generation" be reckoned at 40 years, four generations would cover only some 160 years. But in the Hebrew language "gen-

---

[33] *Ant.* II, xv, 2.
[34] In this verse both the Hebrew and the LXX (i, p.23) texts speak of 400 years of affliction.

eration"[35] means a "circle of years" or a "period" rather than a precise 33 or 40 years, and four generations may be taken as four periods each connected with a particular descendant. Also in the keeping of lists and records of this type there is a tendency, as we have seen in the Sumerian King List (p. 33), for individual names to drop out but for the total number of years in a given period to be preserved correctly. For these reasons the genealogies just mentioned can hardly discredit the 430-year figure for the sojourn in Egypt. On the other hand these very genealogies in which not enough names are preserved to cover a 430-year stay in Egypt, may have led to the attempt represented in the Septuagint version of Exodus 12:40 to shorten that period.

It cannot be said that the available evidence is either entirely sufficient or without contradiction, but of the two traditions which represent the Egyptian sojourn as enduring for either 430 or 215 years the former is the more strongly supported. If we accept this view and take the figures as they stand, the patriarchs were 215 years in Canaan and the Israelites were 430 years in Egypt. Abraham entered Canaan, then, 645 years before the Exodus.

As we shall see in the next chapter (pp. 105-108) the most probable date for the Exodus is either around 1441 B.C. or around 1290 B.C., the latter date appearing definitely preferable. Taking the more probable date of 1290 B.C. for the Exodus and adding the figure of 645 years which was just arrived at as the better supported tradition for the period from the Exodus back to Abraham, we arrive at the date of 1935 B.C. for Abraham's entry into Canaan.

Having seen the many complexities and uncertainties involved in these chronological calculations we will not press the figure of 1935 B.C. too far. Nevertheless, it is legitimate to presume that at least an approximate indication of Abraham's place in history was preserved in Hebrew tradition and actually a date around 1935 B.C. seems entirely appropriate. The date means that Abraham left Mesopotamia in the troubled period of the Elamite and Amorite invasions. Surely it was a likely time for a family to depart from its old home.[36]

[35] cf. HDB II, p.142.

[36] Abraham formerly was believed to be a contemporary of Hammurabi, since the latter was identified with "Amraphel king of Shinar" in Genesis 14:1, but this identification now has been generally abandoned.

Interestingly enough, "Abraham" occurs as a personal name at about this time in Babylonia. A clay tablet from the reign of Ammizaduga, tenth king of the First Dynasty of Babylon, deals with the hiring of an ox by a certain Abarama son of Awel-Ishtar. Other similar documents deal with a field leased by Abamrama.[37] While the reference is of course not to Abraham the son of Terah, the name is essentially the same.

Certainly the patriarchal stories fit with thorough congruity and often with surprising relevance of detail into the historical setting of life in Mesopotamia during the early second millennium B.C. Likewise, as we have seen, other portions of the Old Testament reflect intimate connections with both the mythology and the law of Mesopotamia. It may well have been Abraham himself who carried with him upon his historic migration some of the stories and the laws which his descendants were to raise to so high a level and to pass on to the world. If Abraham did come from Mesopotamia sometime in the early second millennium B.C. it is necessary to revise the usual picture of him as a primitive nomad accustomed only to the open spaces of the desert, and to recognize that at least to some extent he was the heir of a complex and age-old civilization.

[37] Barton, *Archaeology and the Bible*, pp.344f.

II

The Panorama of Egypt

W HEN Hecataeus of Miletus called Egypt "the gift of the river" he characterized the land accurately.[1] Similarly an ancient Egyptian oracle said: "Egypt is the land watered by the Nile in its course; and those who dwell below the city Elephantine and drink that river's water are Egyptians."[2] The Nile River upon which Egypt depended for existence was believed by Ptolemy (second century A.D.) to take its rise in farthest Africa at the foot of "the Mountains of the Moon."[3] The ancient geographer was almost correct. In 1888 Henry Stanley for the first time caught sight of a snow-clad mountain towering into the sky at the very Equator. Almost always veiled in mist and clouds and literally invisible, it is small wonder that hitherto it had been known only by rumor. Stanley gave the mountain a new and appropriate name, Ruwenzori, "The Rain-Maker." Early in the twentieth century a mountaineering expedition led by the Duke of the Abruzzi climbed to the 16,791-foot summit of the range and proved that the Nile does rise in the Mountains of the Moon. Their snows and rains drain down to the east and pour into the waters of the lakes, Victoria, Albert and Edward, which in turn are the sources of the famous river of Egypt.[4]

From the Equator to the shores of the Mediterranean is 2,450 miles in a direct line and thither the Nile flows in an estimated 4,000

[1] See Arrian (A.D. c.96-c.180), *Anabasis of Alexander*. v, vi, 5. tr. E. Iliff Robson, LCL (1929-33) II, p.23. Hecataeus lived in the sixth or fifth century B.C. The epigram was quoted later by Herodotus (c.484-425 B.C.) II, 5. tr. A. D. Godley, LCL (1920-24) I, p.281, and then repeatedly by Strabo (c.63 B.C.-after A.D. 21), *Geography*. I, ii, 23, 29; XII, ii, 4 (tr. H. L. Jones, LCL [1917-32] I, pp.111,131; v, p.357). cf. William A. Heidel in *American Academy of Arts and Sciences Memoirs*. XVIII, 2 (1935), p.61.

[2] Quoted by William C. Hayes in *The National Geographic Magazine* 80 (July-Dec. 1941), p.424.

[3] *Geography*. IV, 8. ed. Edward L. Stevenson. 1932, p.109.

[4] James Ramsey Ullman, *High Conquest*. 1941, p.152.

miles of windings, the "greatest single stream on earth," traversing almost one-tenth of the earth's circumference.[5] At Khartoum the White Nile (el Bahr el Abyad), as the upper part of the main river is known, is joined by a tributary, the Blue Nile (el Bahr el Azraq), which descends from the mountains of Ethiopia. One hundred forty miles farther north the only other tributary, the Atbara, flows in from the east. The almost daily tropical rains of the Equator provide the White Nile with a constant volume of water, sufficient to carry it through the thousand miles of rainless Egypt. Ethiopia, on the other hand, has both a dry and a rainy season. During the latter a great flood of turbid water pours down the "Blue" Nile. This accounts for the annual inundation which from time immemorial irrigated and fertilized the lower Nile Valley. As Herodotus said: "The river rises of itself, waters the fields, and then sinks back again; thereupon each man sows his field . . . and waits for the harvest."[6] Herodotus foresaw that the gradual rise in the level of the land would lessen the effectiveness of this natural irrigation system and expressed anxiety for the future of Egypt when it would be neither inundated by the river nor watered by rain—little dreaming of the enormous dam at Aswan which today is capable of giving Egypt a greater cultivable area than it had in the days of the Pharaohs.

Between Khartoum and Aswan there are six cataracts, where the Nile flows over granite ridges. This region was that of ancient Nubia. From the First Cataract at Aswan, which was ancient Elephantine, on down to Memphis, near modern Cairo, is a distance of 500 miles and was known as the land of Upper Egypt. The last 100 miles from Memphis to the Mediterranean, in which the Nile spreads out into the Delta, constituted Lower Egypt. In Nubia and Upper Egypt the valley of the Nile is but a narrow ribbon of green, rarely more than a dozen miles across and strictly bounded on either side by the cliffs and shelves of the desert. In the Delta, however, the fertile land forms a great triangle, traversed by the various mouths of the Nile, of which the most important are the Rosetta and the Damietta.

The archeological situation in Egypt differs somewhat from that in Mesopotamia. Many of Egypt's monumental structures were built of stone, which was naturally far more enduring than the mud brick of Babylonia. In numerous instances pyramids, obelisks, temples and

[5] Emil Ludwig, *The Nile*. 1937, p.vii.
[6] II, 14.

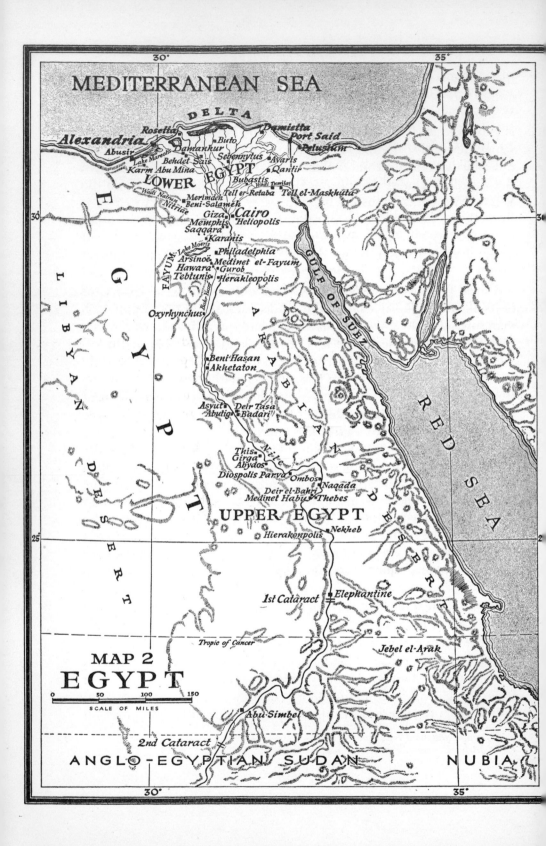

other works stand yet beneath the sky, relatively well preserved, massive and impressive. Immediately upon the beginning of modern archeological investigations, therefore, extensive materials were at hand, and the publications regarding Egyptian monuments issued by the scholars who accompanied Napoleon (p. 4),[7] by Ippolito Rosellini,[8] Jean François Champollion,[9] Karl Richard Lepsius,[10] Auguste Mariette[11] and others, made them known to the world at an early date. To the objects already visible above ground in Egypt have now been added, of course, all the many things which have been discovered in actual excavations and which range from bits of prehistoric pottery to the fabulous treasures of Tutankhamun's tomb.

Probably the most important features of many of the temples and other monuments still standing in Egypt were the inscriptions which appeared on their walls and sides. To a remarkable degree these had endured the ravages of time, yet could not but grow dimmer and less legible as the years went on. It was one of the most urgent tasks in Egyptian archeology, therefore, to make a comprehensive survey of all such records as could be found, and to copy and translate them as accurately as possible. To this undertaking indefatigable labors were devoted by James Henry Breasted (1865-1935), America's most eminent Egyptologist and founder of the Oriental Institute of the University of Chicago. He traveled throughout Egypt, sailing on the Nile, climbing the cliffs on the edge of the desert, entering temples and tombs, seeking out every place where historical documents might have survived.[12] To copy, translate and edit the inscriptions which he found was a task of over a decade, but the resultant publication of the *Ancient Records of Egypt* (5 volumes, 1906-1907) made available a standard compilation of historical sources extending from the First Dynasty to the Persian conquest of Egypt.

In the arrangement of these and other Egyptian materials within a framework of consecutive dynasties, all modern historians are dependent upon an ancient predecessor. This was an Egyptian priest

[7] *Description de l'Égypte, ou Recueil des observations et des recherches qui ont été faites en Égypte pendant l'expédition de l'armée française, publié par les ordres de sa majesté l'empereur Napoléon le Grand.* 21 vols. 1809-28.
[8] *I Monumenti dell' Egitto e della Nubia.* 9 vols. 1832-44.
[9] *Monuments de l'Égypte et de la Nubie.* 4 vols. 1835-45.
[10] *Denkmäler aus Ägypten und Äthiopien.* 12 vols. 1849-56.
[11] *Voyage dans la Haute-Égypte.* 2 vols. 2d ed. 1893.
[12] Charles Breasted, *Pioneer to the Past.* 1943, p.78.

and writer named Manetho who lived under Ptolemy II Philadelphus
(285-246 B.C.). Manetho was born at Sebennytus (now Samannud)
in the Delta. Eventually he rose to be high priest in the temple at
Heliopolis. Berossos of Babylon (p. 25) was practically a contemporary, and the two priests became rivals in the proclamation of the
antiquity and greatness of their respective lands. Manetho's *Egyptian
History*,[13] with which we are concerned here, is preserved only in
fragments, the text of which is often corrupt. Excerpts from the
original work are to be found in Josephus, and Manetho's lists of
dynasties together with brief notes on important kings or events are
preserved in the *Chronicle* (A.D. c.221) of Sextus Julius Africanus,
the *Chronicon* (A.D. 326) of Eusebius, and the history of the world
from Adam to Diocletian written by George Syncellus about A.D.
800. With all of these fragments collected and arranged in order[14] it
is possible to gain a reasonably good view of Manetho's outline, and
the usual division of Egyptian history into thirty dynasties is based
directly upon his work.

Throughout the period covered by these thirty successive houses
of rulers, life in Egypt manifested a notable continuity which was in-
terrupted but not destroyed by such an event as the Hyksos invasion.
While the narrow Nile Valley was by no means isolated from the rest
of the ancient world, it offered its inhabitants sufficient protection to
render incursions of that sort infrequent. Also, in the character of the
people there was a trait of tenacity which may have been exaggerated
in the remark that they "could learn but not forget,"[15] but which
helps to account for the amazing persistence of many things in Egyptian life. In contrast, therefore, with the changing kingdoms which
complicate the scene in Mesopotamia, the drama of Egypt has a
linear quality somewhat akin to that of the land itself which, omitting
the Delta, may be said to have but one dimension—length.[16]

The immediate availability of a large body of historical documents,
the existence of the framework provided by Manetho, and the relative unity of the land and homogeneity of the happenings, have made
it possible to reduce archeological findings to the form of actual
history more quickly in the case of Egypt than in that of some other

13 Αἰγυπτιακὰ ὑπομνήματα.
14 *Manetho*, tr. W. G. Waddell. LCL. 1940.
15 George Foot Moore, *History of Religions*. I (rev. ed. 1920), p.148.
16 Barton, *Archaeology and the Bible*, p.3.

lands. In telling the archeological story of Egypt, therefore, we can follow an historical outline which has already been formulated with considerable definiteness. Before coming to the First Dynasty, however, it is necessary to mention those earlier vistas in Egyptian life which were too remote to be known even to Manetho but which have reappeared within the horizon of our knowledge, thanks to the investigations of modern archeology.

1. THE EARLY AND PREDYNASTIC PERIODS,
c.5000-c.2900 B.C.[1]

As IN Mesopotamia so too in Egypt, we may note that Neolithic settlements were in existence probably at least as early as 5000 B.C. The
culture of this early time is known from discoveries at Deir Tasa
opposite Abutig in Middle Egypt,[2] in the Fayum,[3] and at Merimdeh
Beni-Salameh[4] west of the Rosetta branch of the Nile. A Chalcolithic
culture appears at Badari, twenty miles south of Asyut on the east
bank of the Nile, where the people already had knowledge of copper.
The Badarians were distinguished for their fine pottery and were
accustomed to grind green malachite on slate palettes to use for eye-
paint. Incidentally, this is an excellent germicide, still used by Afri-
cans, and particularly effective when spread around the eyes as a
protection from flies. In their burials the Badarian dead were laid
down as if sleeping, and food offerings as well as other objects were
placed in the graves with them.[5]

Akin to the Badarians were the succeeding Amratians, who belong,
perhaps, to the middle of the fifth millennium B.C., and with whom
the Predynastic Period properly begins. The village sites and cemeteries which represent the Amratian culture are found from Badari
to Lower Nubia. More than the earlier peoples, the Amratians lived
in regular villages as settled communities and they may have been
organized as totemic clans. Copper was used, and boats made out of
bundles of papyrus lashed together facilitated travel on the Nile.
The dead were buried, doubled up, in shallow oval pits and accompanied by food, ornaments and weapons. Statuettes of women and of
servants bearing water-pots on their heads also were placed in the
graves, perhaps as substitutes of magical efficacy for the living wives
and attendants who in earlier times were sent to the grave with their
master. Representations of men and animals on the pottery in the

---

[1] For the dates in early Egyptian history see Albright in BASOR 88 (Dec. 1942),
p.32, where correlations with Mesopotamian and other Middle Eastern chronologies
are indicated. cf. also Meek in *The Journal of Religion* 21 (1941), p.404 n.16.

[2] Guy Brunton in *Antiquity, a Quarterly Review of Archaeology.* 3 (1929), pp.
456-467.

[3] Gertrude Caton-Thompson and E. W. Gardner, *The Desert Fayum.* 2 vols. 1934.

[4] V. Gordon Childe, *New Light on the Most Ancient East.* 1935, pp.58-61; Hermann
Ranke in *Journal of the American Oriental Society.* 59 (1939) No.4, Supplement p.8.

[5] Guy Brunton and Gertrude Caton-Thompson, *The Badarian Civilization.* 1928,
pp.20-42.

grave were also probably intended to be of magical help to the deceased.[6]

The Amratian culture was succeeded by the Gerzean, a culture which originated probably in Lower Egypt but spread into and later dominated Upper Egypt as well. Among the characteristic objects of Gerzean times are wavy-handled jars,[7] pear-shaped maces, vessels of clay or stone in the shape of animals, and amulets representing the bull, the cow, the toad, the fly and the falcon.

The villages were becoming towns and each seems to have recognized an animal or plant as its totem. On decorated pots there are figures of ships which bear totemic standards on their masts. Thus was emerging that structure of society which is known in historic times when the Egyptians lived in independent districts, each designated by a banner or ensign representing an animal or plant. These regional divisions, of which eventually there were twenty-two in Upper Egypt and twenty in the Delta, later were called "nomos" by the Greeks.

Gerzean graves were oblong trenches, on one side of which a ledge accommodated the ever more numerous offerings. Burial places of the rich were lined with mud bricks, and one such has been discovered at the site of Hierakonpolis in which the walls were adorned with a mural painting.[8] Thus the vase-paintings of Amratian times now find a place on the walls of the tomb, where Egyptian paintings are so well known and so important in all later years. The comparative splendor of the tomb just mentioned is an indication, also, of the rise of kingship which led at last to the unification of the land.[9]

Two powerful states came into existence first, one in Upper Egypt, the other in Lower Egypt or the Delta. The capital of southern or Upper Egypt was at Ombos on the left bank of the Nile, near the modern town of Naqada. Its king wore a tall white helmet as a crown, and the symbol of the kingdom was a plant not identified botanically but usually called the lotus. The capital of northern or Lower Egypt was at Behdet, near modern Damanhur and Alexandria.

[6] Brunton in *Antiquity*. 3 (1929), p.460; Childe, *New Light on the Most Ancient East*, pp.69-74.

[7] It was the progressive degeneration of the wavy-ledges which once served as handholds on these jars into mere decorative marks that provided Sir W. M. Flinders Petrie with his clue for the development of "sequence dating" for the Predynastic Period (*Diospolis Parva*. 1901, pp.28-30; *Prehistoric Egypt*. 1920, pp.3f.).

[8] J. E. Quibell, *Hierakonpolis*. II (1902), pp.20f.

[9] Childe, *New Light on the Most Ancient East*, pp. 86-100.

The king's crown here was a red wickerwork diadem, and the kingdom's symbol was the papyrus which grew so abundantly in the swamps and marshes of the Delta. These plants which were the symbols of the two lands are represented on two columns still standing at Karnak (Fig. 26), the lotus of Upper Egypt being at the right and the papyrus of Lower Egypt at the left. Although Egypt ultimately became one united land, the remembrance of the two kingdoms always persisted. The ruler of all Egypt bore the title "King of Upper Egypt and Lower Egypt" and wore a crown which combined the tall helmet of Upper Egypt and the wickerwork diadem of Lower Egypt. The symbol of the united land was a device in which the lotus and the papyrus were knotted together (p. 74).[10] Even in the Old Testament the Hebrew name for Egypt remained literally "the two Egypts."[11]

The earliest Egyptian annals begin with the names of kings in this Predynastic Period. Herodotus remarked that "the Egyptians . . . who dwell in the cultivated country are the most careful of all men to preserve the memory of the past, and none whom I have questioned have so many chronicles."[12] As early as the Fifth Dynasty historical records were inscribed on slabs of stone, fragments of which still survive and constitute "the earliest of all known annals in the history of history."[13] One of these fragments is the famous Palermo Stone, shown in Fig. 27. It is a small piece of hard black diorite, about 17 inches high, 9½ inches wide, and 2½ inches thick. At the top is a simple row of oblong spaces containing hieroglyphic signs. The clue to their meaning is given by the lower section of each oblong space where a figure wearing a red crown and holding a flail appears. This is the sign for the king of Lower Egypt and consequently each symbol in the space above must be the name of a ruler of the Lower Kingdom. Some nine of these names can still be read, and lost portions of the stone doubtless contained more names for Lower Egypt and a list for Upper Egypt too. As a matter of fact, on a Cairo fragment of the annals some Predynastic kings appear wearing the double crown of Lower and Upper Egypt combined.[14]

[10] Sir E. A. Wallis Budge, *The Gods of the Egyptians.* 1904, II, pp.42-48.
[11] Genesis 15:18, etc.
[12] II, 77.
[13] James T. Shotwell, *The History of History.* I. 1939, p.79.
[14] James Henry Breasted, ARE I §76-167; and in *Bulletin de l'Institut Français d'Archéologie Orientale* 30 (1930-31), pp.709-724.

The occurrence of the double crown in Predynastic times, and the domination of Upper Egypt by the Gerzean culture which originated in the Delta, make it probable that a temporary unification of the two lands was accomplished during this period. Evidently this was the work of conquerors from the Delta who were able to establish their supremacy also in Upper Egypt. This union did not endure, however, and the end of the Predynastic Period saw the two lands broken apart again and warring against each other. At this time the capital of Upper Egypt was at Nekheb, a site which later was known as Eileithyiaspolis and is the modern Elkab; and the royal residence was just across the river at Nekhen, which later was called Hierakonpolis. The capital of Lower Egypt was at Buto, with the royal residence in a suburb called Pe. Finally a king of Upper Egypt conquered the Delta and united the two Egypts permanently in a single kingdom under one central rule.[15]

[15] A. Moret, *The Nile and Egyptian Civilization*. 1927, pp.101-113; A. Scharff, *Grundzüge der Ägyptischen Vorgeschichte*. 1927, pp.46-49; Ranke in *Journal of the American Oriental Society* 59 (1939) No.4, Supplement, pp.14f.

2. THE PROTODYNASTIC PERIOD
(FIRST AND SECOND DYNASTIES), c.2900-c.2700 B.C.

MENES

ACCORDING to Manetho the first king of permanently united Egypt was Menes. The statement of the ancient historian as he introduces the First Dynasty runs as follows: "The first royal house numbers eight kings, the first of whom Menes of This reigned for 62 years. He was carried off by a hippopotamus and perished."[1] The native city of Menes was This, not far from the great bend of the Nile below Thebes, and was near where the modern town of Girga stands. This was the capital of the nome of the same name, and was the seat of both the First and the Second Dynasties. The city was known also as Thinis, and from that name the customary designation of the first two dynasties as the Thinite dynasties is derived.

Since This was situated far south in Upper Egypt, the new ruler of all the Egyptians also built a fortress 300 miles to the north, at the apex of the Delta and on the border of the two lands. Herodotus says that the site was gained by building a dam to divert the Nile.[2] In reference to the White Kingdom whose victorious power it represented, the new city was known as "White Wall." From the Sixth Dynasty on it bore the name Men-nefru-Mire or Menfe, from which is derived the familiar Greek name, Memphis.[3]

The cemetery of the Thinite kings was in the desert not far from This and near the site of Abydos. As a result of excavations carried out here in 1899 and following by W. M. Flinders Petrie, the tombs of most of these kings have been discovered.[4] They were in the form of underground pits lined with brick walls, and originally roofed with timber and matting. In the more elaborate examples the burial chamber proper was a wooden hall in the center of the larger pit, surrounded by smaller chambers to hold the offerings. Smaller tombs for the king's servants were ranged about the structure. In the Second Dynasty vaults of brick took the place of the original wooden

---

[1] *Manetho*, tr. Waddell, pp.27-29.   [2] II, 99.

[3] J. H. Breasted, *A History of Egypt*. 1909, p.37. Memphis is mentioned frequently in the Old Testament (Hosea 9:6; Isaiah 19:13; Jeremiah 2:16; 44:1; 46:14, 19; Ezekiel 30:13, 16), the Hebrew name being Noph, which perhaps is a corruption of the middle part of the ancient Egyptian name.

[4] Petrie, *The Royal Tombs of the First Dynasty*. 1900; *The Royal Tombs of the Earliest Dynasties*. 1901.

ceilings for the tombs. In turn a more elaborate superstructure was developed, consisting of a great rectangle of brickwork with sloping sides, distinctive recesses, and a flat top. To this type of tomb it is customary now to apply the Arabic name *mastaba*, meaning platform or bench.

Like so many of the burial places of ancient Egypt, the royal tombs at Abydos had already been plundered by robbers. Enough of their contents remained, however, to show that with the mummies a profusion of jewelry, stone vases, copper vessels and other objects had been buried. Also the names of a number of the kings were found, including Narmer, Aha, Zer and others. These are the "Horus titles" or names of the kings as earthly representatives of the god Horus, rather than their personal names which were used by Manetho. Identifications are not certain, therefore, but it is probable that Narmer is the king who was called Menes by Manetho, and who was founder of the First Dynasty.

The finest monument of Narmer which we possess is a slate palette found at Hierakonpolis and shown in Fig. 28. The palette is like those on which the Egyptians had long ground eye-paint (p. 68), but is of a very large size as befitted a great king. On the obverse side (right) the king and priests walk in triumphal procession while the long necks of two monsters are curved to form a circular recess where the cosmetics may be ground. On the reverse stands the tall figure of the king who lifts a heavy mace with pear-shaped head of white stone to crush the skull of his enemy whom he grasps by the hair. Upon the king's head is the tall, white, helmet-like crown of Upper Egypt, while a long animal tail hangs from the back of his belt. The latter probably was an ancient North African badge of chieftaincy but it remains henceforth a regular attribute of the Egyptian kingship. Behind the king is his servant, carrying the king's sandals and a water-pot or oil-jar. Around the king's belt and also at the top of the palette are heads of Hathor, the cow-goddess. At one side is a very early example of Egyptian hieroglyphics, or writing in picture form. A falcon, as symbol of the king, holds a length of rope which is attached to a man's head. The head is connected with an area of ground out of which grow six papyrus stalks, representing the marshes of Lower Egypt. Below is a single-barbed harpoon head and a rectangle which is the sign of a lake. The entire pictograph means that the falcon king led captive the people of the

Harpoon Lake in Lower Egypt. At the top of the palette, between the heads of Hathor, is the name of the king, Narmer.[5]

Lines two and three of the Palermo Stone (Fig. 27) give annals from the time of the First Dynasty, although the fragment as we have it does not include the beginning of that dynasty. As compared with the bare list of names of the Predynastic kings the record now is fuller, and an entire oblong is devoted to each year of a king's reign, the dividing lines curling over at the top being the hieroglyphic signs for palms, and signifying years. The name of the king is given in the long horizontal space above the yearly records, as may be seen above rows 3 and 4. The vertical line extending up through the horizontal space near the right end of row 2 marks the termination of a reign. The oblong immediately to the right shows six new moons, a sun, and seven strokes, thus indicating six months and seven days which is some detail as to the time when this reign ceased. Continuing to read from right to left, the next oblong gives the date of the new king's accession, the fourth month and thirteenth day, ten being represented by two strokes joined at the top. When a king came to the throne a feast was celebrated called "Union of the Two Lands," and by it the king's first year was characterized and named. This designation appears in the same oblong in the form of the lotus and papyrus tied together. The measurements in the little rectangles below, giving a number of cubits, palms, and fingers, may have registered the height of the Nile inundation that year.

In the early years and reigns most of the events noted are but names of religious feasts. Lines 4 and 5 are devoted to the Second Dynasty, and here we come upon a mention of the "fourth occurrence of the numbering," a reference to a regular census or inventory of some sort. With line 6 and the Third Dynasty the annal becomes yet more detailed and the yearly sections are necessarily much larger. Here there is reference to the building of ships of some size, and the bringing by sea of cedar wood, probably from Lebanon. A double palace was erected whose double name recalled the old kingdoms of South and North: "Exalted-is-the-White-Crown-of-Snefru-upon-the-Southern-Gate. Exalted-is-the-Red-Crown-of-Snefru-upon-the-Northern-Gate." Most of the record of the Fourth Dynasty is missing, but the lines on the back of the Palermo Stone carry the annals on down into the Fifth Dynasty.

[5] Quibell, *Hierakonpolis.* I (1900), p.10.

Before continuing the narrative into later eras it should be indicated that already in the late Predynastic and early Protodynastic Periods Egypt was in contact with the environing world. Indeed the period of about 3000 B.C. constituted the first great epoch of international commerce. This will be remembered as the Jemdet Nasr Period in Mesopotamia (p. 23), and there are definite evidences of Mesopotamian influence in Egypt at the time. In the painted tomb at Hierakonpolis (p. 69) a boat is depicted which is very different from the usual papyrus boats of Egypt but is similar to those represented in Mesopotamia. At Jebel el-Arak a carved ivory knife-handle has been found which not only shows another such foreign-type boat but also reveals a scene whose Mesopotamian character is even more unmistakable. In the latter a hero is shown in combat with two lions which rise against him from either side. Not only is the grouping typically Mesopotamian but the man himself is pictured in Asiatic style with full beard and long robe.[6] Mesopotamian cylinder seals of the Jemdet Nasr Period have also been found in Egypt, and the development of Egyptian cylinder seals was a result of original impact from the land of the Two Rivers.[7] Likewise the sudden appearance in Egypt of an advanced technique and style in the erection of recessed brick buildings evidently was based upon knowledge of architectural achievements in Mesopotamia which had reached a similar level at this time. These facts show that Mesopotamian influences were a stimulus in Egypt during some of the most formative phases of that land's development.[8]

[6] Georges Bénédite in *Académie des inscriptions et belles-lettres, Commission de la fondation Eugène Piot, Monuments et mémoires.* 22 (1916), pp.1-34; René Dussaud in *Syria.* 16 (1935), pp.320-323.

[7] Frankfort, *Cylinder Seals,* pp.292-300.

[8] A. Scharff in *Zeitschrift für ägyptische Sprache und Altertumskunde.* 71 (1935), pp.89-106; H. Frankfort in *The American Journal of Semitic Languages and Literatures* 58 (Jan.-Oct. 1941), pp.329-358; Helene J. Kantor in JNES 3 (1944), pp.110-136.

3. THE OLD KINGDOM (THIRD TO SIXTH DYNASTIES), c.2700-c.2200 B.C.

THE Third to Sixth Dynasties constitute the time of the Old Kingdom or the Pyramid Age, the first great culminating point of Egyptian civilization. Under the rule of Djoser, first king of the Third Dynasty, the remarkable Imhotep attained renown as priest, magician, author of wise proverbs, physician and architect. For his king, Imhotep undertook the construction of a royal mausoleum of a style more impressive than any hitherto known. Starting with a lofty mastaba of stone, and superimposing five successive shells upon it, he built the famous "step pyramid" at Saqqara, a terraced monument 190 feet high, the earliest large structure of stone known in history. From this there developed the great pyramids which have been in all succeeding centuries a wonder of the world.

THE PYRAMIDS

Of all the pyramids the greatest (Fig. 29) was built by Khufu, founder of the Fourth Dynasty. Upon a square base covering some thirteen acres, he heaped up 2,300,000 blocks of yellowish limestone, each weighing on the average two and one-half tons, until the whole pyramid towered originally 481 feet into the sky. According to Herodotus, laborers toiled on the monument in groups of 100,000 men, each group for three months at a time. Ten years were required to make the road whereon the stones were dragged and twenty years more for the pyramid itself. Like a good tourist Herodotus reports that it was written on the pyramid how much was spent on onions and garlic for the workmen and says, "to my sure remembrance the interpreter when he read me the writing said that sixteen hundred talents of silver had been paid."[1] The stonework was done with a precision involving seams of one ten-thousandth of an inch, and the entire exterior was covered with an exquisitely fitted casing of fine white limestone. Such is "the earliest and most impressive witness surviving from the ancient world, to the final emergence of organized society from prehistoric chaos and local conflict, thus coming for the first time completely under the power of a far-reaching and comprehensive centralization effected by one controlling mind."[2]

[1] II, 124f.
[2] J. H. Breasted, A History of the Ancient Egyptians. 1903, p. 110.

Khafre, the successor of Khufu, built the even more spectacular Second Pyramid of Giza. Its present height is 447½ feet, only 1½ feet less than the present height of the Great Pyramid, while its base is smaller, each side of the base now measuring 690½ feet as compared with 746 feet on the Great Pyramid. The angle of the sides of the Second Pyramid (52° 20′) is therefore steeper than that of the Great Pyramid (51° 50′) while the upper one-fourth of the slopes still retains the original casing of smooth limestone and granite slabs.[3] Khafre himself is represented in the head of the great Sphinx which stands to the east of the Second Pyramid. The body of the Sphinx is that of a couchant lion, but the head is that of the king, wearing the usual cloth headdress and with the uraeus or deadly cobra coiled on his forehead. This serpent was symbol of the kingship and coiled itself upon the king's brow to destroy his enemies as once it had annihilated the adversaries of the sun-god Re. The Sphinx was carved out of a spur of natural rock and built up with blocks of stone at the same time that the pyramid of Khafre was built. The monument was gradually half-buried by the ever-drifting sands of the desert but was excavated by Thutmose IV and again by the Egyptian *Service des Antiquités* in 1926-1927.

Kings of the Fifth and Sixth Dynasties caused inscriptions to be carved on the walls of the inner passages and chambers of their pyramids, which are known as the "Pyramid Texts." Their theme is the prospect of a glorious hereafter for the deceased king in the presence of the sun-god. Frequently their form is that of couplets which are parallel in arrangement of words and thought, an early form of poetry which was to be used by the Hebrews 2000 years later.

The composing of proverbs was also begun by the early Egyptians. Imhotep was famous in this regard as we have noted (p. 76) and so were Kagemni and Hardedef. Of all the sages, however, the best known is Ptahhotep, who was grand vizier under a Pharaoh of the Fifth Dynasty. To his son he said, "Be not arrogant because of thy knowledge, and be not puffed up for that thou art a learned man. Take counsel with the ignorant as with the learned. . . . Goodly discourse is more hidden than the precious green-stone, and yet it is found with slave-girls over the millstones." "Covetousness," he warned, "is an incurable malady," but, he promised, "a man shall

---

[3] This is the pyramid from which Rand Herron, member of the 1932 mountaineering expedition to Nanga Parbat, fell to his death. Ullman, *High Conquest*, p. 194.

thrive if he be truly righteous."[4] These maxims of Ptahhotep constitute "the earliest formulation of right conduct to be found in any
literature."[5]

[4] T. Eric Peet, *A Comparative Study of the Literatures of Egypt, Palestine, and Mesopotamia*. 1931, pp.101-103; cf. Adolf Erman, *The Literature of the Ancient Egyptians*. Eng. tr. 1927, p.60.
[5] J. H. Breasted, *The Dawn of Conscience*. 1933, p.129.

4. FIRST INTERMEDIATE PERIOD
(SEVENTH TO ELEVENTH DYNASTIES), c.2200-c.1989 B.C.

As THE glory of the Old Kingdom faded, there ensued a period of disintegration and chaos when weak Pharaohs were unable to maintain a strong, central government. Manetho's Seventh and Eighth Dynasties which continued to rule weakly at Memphis, and the Ninth and Tenth Dynasties which arose at Herakleopolis (77 miles south of Cairo), are included in this Intermediate Period. The upset conditions which were experienced are reflected in "The Admonitions of Ipuwer."

> Behold, he that possessed wealth now spendeth the night athirst;
> He that begged of him his dregs is now a possessor of wine-vats.
> Behold, they that possessed clothes are now in rags;
> He that wove not for himself now possesseth fine linen.[1]

Ipuwer hoped however for the coming of an ideal king whom he described in the following words: "He brings cooling to the flame. It is said he is the shepherd of all men. There is no evil in his heart. When his herds are few, he passes the day to gather them together, their hearts being fevered."[2] Such is one of the earliest expressions of the Messianic hope in history.

Another burdened writer of the same period wistfully longed for death itself as a glad release:

> Death is in my eyes today
> As when a sick man becomes whole,
> As the walking abroad after illness.
>
> Death is in my eyes today
> Like the desire of a man to see his home
> When he hath passed many years in captivity.[3]

In the Eleventh Dynasty the Intefs and Mentuhoteps were able at least partially to restore order and to reestablish a centralized state. Their place of rule was at Thebes, a city which was situated on the

---

[1] Peet, *A Comparative Study of the Literatures of Egypt, Palestine, and Mesopotamia*, p.118; cf. Josephine Mayer and Tom Prideaux, *Never to Die, the Egyptians in Their Own Words*. 1938, p.68.

[2] Breasted, *The Dawn of Conscience*, p.198.

[3] Peet, *A Comparative Study of the Literatures of Egypt, Palestine, and Mesopotamia*, pp.116f.

Nile 440 miles above Memphis, and which was destined later to become Egypt's greatest capital.[4]

[4] The Egyptian name for the town was Weset or more shortly Newt, "the city," whence is derived the biblical No (Jeremiah 46:25; Ezekiel 30:14-16) or No-Amon (Nahum 3:8), "city" or "city of Amun." The Greeks called it Thebes (Θῆβαι) and also Diospolis (Διόσπολις), meaning "city of Zeus" (Amun), or Diospolis Magna in distinction from Diospolis Parva or Hou. The modern villages at this site are Luxor and Karnak.

5. THE MIDDLE KINGDOM
(TWELFTH DYNASTY), c.1989-c.1776 B.C.[1]

WITH the Twelfth Dynasty which was inaugurated by Amenemhet I, Egypt entered the second great period of its history, the Middle Kingdom. The kings of this dynasty were native Thebans but they ruled chiefly from capitals in Memphis and in the Fayum. Their house endured for over 200 years, and their accomplishments included the conquest of Nubia to the Second Cataract, the connecting of the Nile with the Red Sea by canal, and the development of mining in Sinai into a permanent industry. The art and architecture of the age were characterized by refinement. Feminine jewelry was made with unsurpassed beauty of design and microscopic accuracy of execution. A "literature of entertainment" arose for the first time, including such stories as "Baufra's Tale" and "The Eloquent Peasant."[2] In the Fifth and Sixth Dynasties the Pyramid Texts (p. 77) had described a future life to be enjoyed by the king, but now in the Middle Kingdom others besides kings could anticipate the privilege of being buried with texts at hand to guide and protect them in the after-life. These texts were written on the inside of the coffin of the deceased, hence are known as the Coffin Texts.

If Abraham's migration to Palestine and subsequent visit to Egypt[3] fell in the neighborhood of 1935 B.C. (p. 60) then he was in Egypt in the days of the Middle Kingdom. Abraham does not figure in Egyptian records of the time, the earliest occurrence of his name being when Pharaoh Sheshonk I (tenth century B.C.) records capturing a place in Palestine called "The Field of Abram" (p. 113).[4] But it is interesting to have such tangible evidence of communication between Egypt and Palestine and Syria in these very days as appears in the following account.

THE TALE OF SINUHE

When Amenemhet I died, his son, Prince Senwosret I, was campaigning in the western Delta against the Libyans. Word of the old

[1] For the dates in the Twelfth Dynasty see William F. Edgerton in JNES 1 (1942), pp.307-314.

[2] W. M. F. Petrie, *Egyptian Tales*. First Series, 2d ed. 1899, pp.16-22,61-80.

[3] Genesis 12:10-13:1 (J). Genesis 20:1-17 (E) corrects the unfavorable impression created by the story of Sarah in Pharaoh's harem, by transferring the situation to King Abimelech's court at Gerar, and changing many of the details.

[4] ARE IV, §715.

king's death was dispatched to the son who, upon receiving it, kept
the news secret and returned at once to the capital to establish himself firmly as king before any pretender could precede him. This was
quite in accord with the spirit of instructions which Amenemhet had
given his son earlier. The old king, whose life had been attempted
by assassins, had advised:

> Harden thyself against all subordinates. . . .
> Fill not thy heart with a brother,
> Know not a friend,
> Nor make for thyself intimates. . . .
> When thou sleepest, guard for thyself thine own heart;
> For a man has no people
> In the day of evil.[5]

With Senwosret I in the field was a noble of high rank, named
Sinuhe. Accidentally overhearing the message about Amenemhet's
death, he fled the country immediately for political reasons and
returned only in his old age and upon the pardon of Senwosret. The
story of his adventures as he fled overland to Syria is related in
"The Tale of Sinuhe." Hiding in the bushes and fields, he passed
the Egyptian frontier fort at night. In the desert he grew faint
with thirst and his throat was hot with the taste of death but he
was rescued at last by a Bedouin chief. Eventually he came through
Kedem east of the Jordan and arrived in Upper Tenu, or northern
Syria.[6] Of the "goodly land" where he settled, Sinuhe gave a description similar to that later applied to Palestine in the Old Testament
(Exodus 3:8; Deuteronomy 8:8; etc.):

> There were figs in it and vines,
> More plentiful than water was its wine,
> Copious was its honey, plenteous its oil;
> All fruits were upon its trees.
> Barley was there, and spelt,
> Without end all cattle.[7]

[5] ARE I, §479.

[6] Correctly, Upper Retenu, an r having been omitted. Retenu or Khuru (Kharu)
was the usual Egyptian designation of northern Syria, while Palestine and the
Phoenician coastal plain were called Djahi. Amurru (Amor) was the name of the
region between the Lebanon and the Anti-Lebanon, known later as Coelesyria. Naharin
was the name of the land at the upper reaches of the Euphrates. George Steindorff
and Keith C. Seele, *When Egypt Ruled the East.* 1942, pp.35,47.

[7] ARE I, §496.

THE TOMB OF KHNUMHOTEP II

In the days of Senwosret II, fourth king of the Twelfth Dynasty, a powerful noble, Khnumhotep II, lived at Beni Hasan, 169 miles above Cairo. In his tomb a famous scene still depicts a visit paid him by a group of thirty-seven Asiatics of the desert, bringing gifts and desiring trade.[8] Their faces are plainly Semitic, their thick black hair falls to the neck and their beards are pointed. They wear long cloaks and carry spears, bows and throw-sticks. The accompanying inscription reads, "The arrival, bringing eye-paint, which 37 Asiatics bring to him," and their leader bears a good Hebrew name, "Sheik of the highlands, Ibshe."[9] One portion of this very interesting painting is reproduced in Fig. 30. We see a black-bearded nomad walking behind his donkey to the accompaniment of music which he makes upon a lyre. The man carries a water-skin upon his back, while on the donkey's gay saddle-cloth are tied other objects including a spear and throw-stick.

[8] P. E. Newberry, *Beni Hasan*. I (1893), Pl. xxx.
[9] ARE I, p.281,d.

6. SECOND INTERMEDIATE PERIOD
(THIRTEENTH TO SEVENTEENTH DYNASTIES),
c.1776-c.1570 B.C.

IN THE DAYS which followed, Egypt entered again upon a period of disintegration and eventually of rule by foreigners. The Thirteenth and Fourteenth Dynasties were made up of ephemeral and feeble kings, and in the Fifteenth and Sixteenth Dynasties the rulers of Egypt were the Hyksos.

THE HYKSOS

The coming of the Hyksos is described by Manetho in a passage preserved in Josephus. Referring to Tutimaeus, who probably was a king of the Thirteenth Dynasty, Manetho says: "In his reign, for what cause I know not, a blast of God smote us; and unexpectedly, from the regions of the East, invaders of obscure race marched in confidence of victory against our land. By main force they easily seized it without striking a blow; and having overpowered the rulers of the land, they then burned our cities ruthlessly, razed to the ground the temples of the gods, and treated all the natives with a cruel hostility. . . . Finally, they appointed as king one of their number whose name was Salitis."[1] Manetho states further that Salitis ruled from Memphis and that he also rebuilt as a powerful stronghold "a city very favourably situated on the east of the Bubastite branch of the Nile, and called Auaris." The branch of the Nile referred to is the one farthest east, and the city of Auaris or Avaris doubtless is to be identified with Tanis, near the modern fishing village of San el-Hagar. Manetho also explains that the name Hyksos means "'king-shepherds': for hyk in the sacred language means 'king,' and sos in common speech is 'shepherd' or 'shepherds': hence the compound word 'Hyksos.'" It is probable, however, that this is only a late popular etymology and that the name actually was derived from Egyptian words meaning "rulers of foreign lands."[2] In the Eighteenth Dynasty Queen Hatshepsut refers to repairs which she made of damage done by the Hyksos:

I have restored that which was ruins,
I have raised up that which was unfinished,

[1] *Manetho,* tr. Waddell, pp.79-81; Josephus, *Against Apion.* I, 14.
[2] Adolf Erman and Hermann Grapow, *Wörterbuch der ägyptischen Sprache.* III (1929), p.171, 29.

Since the Asiatics were in the midst of Avaris of the Northland,
And the barbarians were in the midst of them.[3]

It is probable that this invasion of the Hyksos took place somewhere around 1700 B.C. and that they ruled Egypt for about a century
and a half. The foreigners may have been of mixed stock but the
preponderant element among them seems to have been Semitic.[4]
As a matter of fact, Josephus identified the Hyksos with the Hebrews.
He introduced his quotations from Manetho concerning the Hyksos
as statements "about us," that is about the Jewish people, and described "the so-called shepherds" as "our ancestors."[5] His purpose
in this identification was that he might adduce the testimony of
Manetho as proving the antiquity of the Jews. While it is hardly
possible to believe from the biblical records that the Hebrews played
any such role of conquest and domination in Egypt as did the Hyksos,
nevertheless there is probably this much truth in the tradition of
Josephus, that the Hebrews were in Egypt at the same time as the
Hyksos. This fact could account for the representation found in
Josephus, and it is antecedently probable that the Hebrews would
find a friendly reception in Egypt at a time when the country was
under rulers who themselves were of Semitic descent.

A papyrus of the Nineteenth Dynasty contains a folk tale relating
how war broke out between Sekenenre, native prince of Thebes, and
King Apophis, Hyksos ruler at Avaris. The story is that Sekenenre
had a hippopotamus pool in Thebes and the bellowing of the hippo-
potami was such that King Apophis sent a complaint from Avaris that
he could not get any sleep day or night.[6] The mummy of Sekenenre,
which shows five terrible wounds in the head, may give more realistic
testimony to the outbreak of conflict between the native Egyptian
princes and their foreign masters. Sekenenre's sons, Kamose and
Ahmose, continued the struggle against the Hyksos. It fell to Ahmose
to drive out the invaders completely. He took Avaris and then pursued the fleeing Hyksos as far as Palestine. There they made a last
stand at Sharuhen (cf. Joshua 19:6) but after a six-year siege Ahmose
destroyed this stronghold too. Of these happenings we can read a
direct account in the biography of one of Ahmose's naval officers.[7]

[3] ARE II, §303.
[4] R. M. Engberg, *The Hyksos Reconsidered.* 1939, pp.9,49.
[5] *Against Apion.* I, 14,16.
[6] Erman, *The Literature of the Ancient Egyptians*, p.166.
[7] ARE II, §1-16.

Whereas Josephus thought that the expulsion of the Hyksos was identical with the Exodus of the Hebrews, it is most probable that the Hebrews still continued to live in Egypt at this time. It is of interest to note that after the expulsion of the Hyksos most of the Egyptian lands and fields, apart from the properties attached to the temples, are found in the possession of the Pharaoh. This is a situation similar to that described in Genesis 47:13-26 as having been instituted by Joseph in time of famine.[8]

[8] Steindorff and Seele, *When Egypt Ruled the East*, p.88.

7. THE NEW KINGDOM
(EIGHTEENTH TO TWENTIETH DYNASTIES),
c.1570-c.1150 B.C.

THE EIGHTEENTH DYNASTY

AHMOSE is usually regarded as the first king of the Eighteenth Dynasty, which was destined to become probably the most brilliant age in all Egyptian history. The horse and chariot became known to the Egyptians during the Hyksos period, and the use of chariotry now facilitated far-flung conquests. An empire soon was to be built which reached from the Fourth Cataract of the Nile to beyond the Euphrates.

HATSHEPSUT

About 1546 B.C. Ahmose was succeeded by his son Amenhotep I, and then (c.1525 B.C.) by his daughter's husband, Thutmose I, who campaigned successfully in Nubia and as far as the Euphrates.[1] The only living child of Thutmose I and his queen was a daughter, the remarkable Hatshepsut (Fig. 31), "the first great woman in history of whom we are informed."[2] Legally, Hatshepsut was the only heir to the throne, yet could not actually reign as "king" but could only convey the crown to her husband by marriage. Thutmose I also had a son who was born by one of his secondary wives. In order to secure the throne for this son, he was married to his half-sister, Hatshepsut, and reigned as Thutmose II. The only son of Thutmose II was born to him by a harem girl and was still a boy when his father died. As Thutmose III he ruled nominally with Hatshepsut, but actually this powerful and brilliant woman now took full control of the government. She had herself proclaimed "king" and appears in a scene representing this proclamation dressed in king's costume and wearing the double crown of Upper and Lower Egypt.[3] As the court official Ineni remarked in his biography, "The God's Wife, Hatshepsut, settled the affairs of the Two Lands according to her own plans. Egypt was made to labor with bowed head for her."[4]

[1] For the dates in the Eighteenth Dynasty see Ludwig Borchardt, *Die Mittel zur zeitlichen Festlegung von Punkten der ägyptischen Geschichte und ihre Anwendung.* 1935, p.87; with revisions by W. F. Edgerton in *The American Journal of Semitic Languages and Literatures* 53 (Oct. 1936-July 1937), pp.188-197.

[2] Breasted, *A History of the Ancient Egyptians,* p.217.

[3] ARE II, §231.

[4] ARE II, §341. For the complicated succession of rulers at this time see W. F. Edgerton, *The Thutmosid Succession.* SAOC 8, 1933, pp.41f.

Part of that labor was directed toward the construction of what remains Hatshepsut's most impressive memorial, her mortuary temple (Fig. 32). This temple rises against the face of an imposing cliff at Deir el-Bahri, near Thebes. It was a beautiful structure of white limestone, built in colonnaded terraces from the plain to the cliff, deep within which the tomb itself was to be found. A major sea expedition to Punt, on the Somali coast, brought back the myrrh trees with which its terraces were planted. Another undertaking on behalf of Hatshepsut was the erection of two great obelisks at Karnak, in a hall built earlier by the queen's father, Thutmose I. The enormous granite shafts were quarried at Aswan and brought down the river on a huge barge drawn by a fleet of galleys. One of these still stands in its place and is the most striking of all known obelisks as well as the largest one now in Egypt. It is 97½ feet high, contains 180 cubic yards of granite and weighs 700,000 pounds. The obelisks were crowned with pyramidions of polished metal and an inscription said concerning them, "Their height pierces to heaven, illuminating the Two Lands like the sun disk. Never was done the like since the beginning."[5]

These great works were carried out for Hatshepsut by the architect Senenmut, her favorite noble to whom she also entrusted the education of her eldest daughter, Princess Nefrure.[6] Senenmut is represented in the statue shown in Fig. 33 holding the little Nefrure protectingly wrapped in his mantle.

THUTMOSE III

After the great queen Hatshepsut was no more, Thutmose III (Fig. 34) reigned as Pharaoh alone. "Pharaoh," it may be explained, is the Hebrew form of the Egyptian title "The Great House," which was pronounced something like *per-o*. Originally a designation of the palace, it was commonly used as the official title of the king from the Eighteenth Dynasty on. Upon emerging as sole ruler, the long-suppressed energies of Pharaoh Thutmose III burst forth in furious activity. He expressed his resentment at having been kept so long in a minor position by hacking out the figure and the name of Hatshepsut wherever these appeared on monuments throughout Egypt. Then he led his armies into battle in Palestine and Syria. His grandfather, Thutmose I, had begun the subjection of Asiatic prov-

---

[5] ARE II, §305.   [6] ARE II, §345-347.

inces for Egypt but among those peoples there was now general revolt. The inhabitants of Palestine, Coelesyria and the coastal plain were Semitic tribes called Canaanites, while the Hyksos also remained there after having been driven out of Egypt. A confederation of these peoples was organized against Egypt and the enemies of the Pharaoh were in control of the strong fortress of Megiddo, commanding the road from Egypt to the Euphrates. Thutmose III acted swiftly and surprised his opponents by approaching through a narrow pass in the Carmel ridge. Battle was joined upon the plain of Esdraelon. "His majesty went forth in a chariot of electrum, arrayed in his weapons of war. . . . His majesty prevailed against them at the head of his army, and when they saw his majesty prevailing against them they fled headlong to Megiddo in fear, abandoning their horses and their chariots of gold and silver."[7] Although the Egyptian troops tarried for a time with the spoils, Megiddo soon was besieged and taken.

In sixteen further campaigns during the next eighteen summers, Thutmose the Great[8] established the absolute power of Egypt as far as the Euphrates,[9] and "built the first real empire." "Never before in history had a single brain wielded the resources of so great a nation and wrought them into such centralized, permanent and at the same time mobile efficiency."[10] In a Hymn of Victory, Amen-Re the god of Thebes was made to address him:

I have given to thee might and victory against all countries,
I have set thy fame, even the fear of thee, in all lands,
Thy terror as far as the four pillars of heaven. . . .
I have felled thine enemies beneath thy sandals.[11]

Coming home each fall from his campaigns, Thutmose III carried out large-scale building projects. Much work was done in enlargement and beautification of the temple of Amun which had stood at

[7] ARE II, §430.
[8] His full name was "Horus: Mighty Bull, Appearing in Thebes; the Two Ladies: Enduring of Kingship; the Horus of Gold: Splendid of Diadems; the King of Upper and Lower Egypt: Enduring of Form Is Re [Menkheperre]; the Son of Re: Thoth Is Born [Thutmose]." The last of these names was the one given him at birth, the others were adopted upon accession to the throne and indicated that the king was the embodiment of the various gods named, such as the Two Ladies who were the tutelary goddesses of Upper and Lower Egypt. So mighty was the name of Thutmose III that for centuries his praenomen Menkheperre was inscribed on amulets as a good-luck charm.
[9] ARE II, §478.
[10] Breasted, A History of the Ancient Egyptians, p.242.   [11] ARE II, §656.

Karnak since the days of the Middle Kingdom[12] and to which many different Pharaohs both before and after Thutmose III made contributions. On the walls of one of the temple's corridors which he built were inscribed the annals of his seventeen military campaigns, from which quotations have just been made. At Karnak and elsewhere he erected great obelisks which have been set up now in places as far distant as Constantinople, the Lateran, London and New York (Fig. 35).[13] Concluding a list of his building works an inscription of Thutmose III said, "He did more than any king who has been since the beginning."[14]

THE TOMB OF REKHMIRE

Many of the building operations of Thutmose III were supervised by his vizier, Rekhmire. The vizier was a sort of prime minister and grand steward who exercised powers as extensive as those ascribed to Joseph in the Old Testament. All administrative business passed through his hands, and he was also a judge and a superintendent of public works. While there was a time beginning in the Fifth Dynasty when the office was hereditary, later it was bestowed by the king upon a noble of his own choosing. One vizier exercised authority over all Egypt until the time of Thutmose III when two appointments were made, one for Upper and one for Lower Egypt. Rekhmire is well known to us from his tomb near Thebes which is covered with scenes and inscriptions depicting and narrating his career. In one of these pictures Rekhmire leans on his staff and inspects stonecutters, sculptors, brickmakers and builders who toil before him. A portion of this painting, showing the labor of the bricklayers, is reproduced in Fig. 36. The making of bricks in ancient Egypt was a process which involved breaking up the Nile mud with mattocks, moistening it with water, and then mixing it with sand and chopped straw (cf. Exodus 5:6-19). After that it was formed in molds and taken out and baked in the sun. Among the makers and layers of bricks pictured in Rekhmire's tomb are Semitic foreigners, and the accompanying inscription refers to the "captives brought by his majesty for the works of the temple of Amun." The bricklayers are quoted as saying, "He

[12] ARE I, §421, 484.
[13] ARE II, §623-636; cf. George A. Zabriskie in *The New York Historical Society Quarterly Bulletin.* 24 (1940), pp.103-112.
[14] ARE II, §158.

supplies us with bread, beer, and every good sort," while the task-master says to the builders, "The rod is in my hand; be not idle."[15]

THE PAPYRUS OF ANI

Some glimpse of Theban religious beliefs in the middle of the Eighteenth Dynasty may be had from the Papyrus of Ani.[16] This papyrus is our finest copy of what is known collectively by the name, "The Egyptian Book of the Dead." The texts which were written in the pyramids of the kings of the Fifth and Sixth Dynasties (p. 77), and the instructions and charms which were inscribed on the interior of coffins in the Middle Kingdom (p. 81), had grown now to be a whole collection of religious compositions relating to the after-life. Written more or less fully on larger or smaller papyrus rolls, every-one might have such a book placed with him in the tomb. The beautiful Papyrus of Ani is no less than 78 feet long and 1 foot 3 inches wide. Chapter 125 is the most important and probably the most ancient part. An illustration of this chapter in the Papyrus of Ani (Fig. 37) shows Ani, followed by his wife Tutu, bowing humbly in the great Hall of Judgment. In the middle is the balance, operated by the jackal-headed Anubis. On the left scalepan is Ani's heart, represented by an Egyptian hieroglyph looking much like a tiny vase, while in the other is a feather symbolizing truth or righteousness. The god of Destiny stands beneath the beam of the balance and two goddesses of Birth are between the scale and Ani. The soul of Ani in the shape of a human-headed hawk hovers at the end of the beam. On the other side stands the ibis-headed god Thoth, performing his function as scribe and recording with pen and writing palette the verdict of the weighing. Behind him is Amemit, the Devourer of the Dead, a monster with the head of a crocodile, the body of a lion, and the hindquarters of a hippopotamus. If Ani's heart is proved unjust by the weighing it will be devoured by this monster, and Ani's hope of immortality will be lost. On the left is written Ani's prayer to his heart not to betray him, above is a panel of twelve gods as judges, and at the right is the sentence of acquittal.

In the text of Chapter 125 the deceased recites a great repudiation of sins in which forty-two sins are denied before forty-two judges. Each judge has a specific crime to consider and the deceased ad-

---

[15] P. E. Newberry, *The Life of Rekhmara*. 1900, p.38; ARE II, §758f.
[16] Sir E. A. Wallis Budge, *The Papyrus of Ani*. 1913.

dresses him by name and denies ever having committed that crime: "O Devourer of Shades . . . I have not stolen." "O Eyes of Flames . . . I have not played the hypocrite." "O Cracker of Bones . . . I have not told falsehoods." "O Swallower . . . I have not blasphemed." "O Eater of Hearts . . . I have not made conspiracies." "O Eye in the Heart . . . I have not defiled the river." Other denials of sins include: "I am not sluggish; I have not made to weep; I am not a land-grabber; I committed not adultery; I am not a slayer of man; I tamper not with the balance; I do not cheat." In a concluding address to the gods the deceased affirms his moral worthiness, here making positive as well as negative statements: "Behold, I come to you without sin, without evil, without wrong. . . . I have done that which men say, and that wherewith the gods are content. I have satisfied the god with that which he desires. I gave bread to the hungry, water to the thirsty, clothing to the naked, and a ferry to him who was without a boat. I made divine offerings for the gods and food-offerings for the dead. Save ye me; protect ye me. Enter no complaint against me before the Great God. For I am one of pure mouth and pure hands. . . ." Having been justified in the hour of judgment, the deceased is led by Horus into the presence of Osiris, where he is welcomed to the joys of paradise. Although the Book of the Dead in most of its parts and in most of its use was a book of magical charms, it reveals a perception of the truth that happiness after death is dependent upon the ethical quality of earthly life.

AMENHOTEP II

Thutmose III died around 1436 B.C. and was followed upon the throne by his son who reigned as Amenhotep II. A statue of this king is shown in Fig. 38, and another interesting representation of him appears in Fig. 39, where he stands beneath the protecting head of the cow-goddess Hathor, a deity fervently worshiped by the sovereigns of the Eighteenth Dynasty. Even in his youth Amenhotep II distinguished himself for strength and valor. In rowing, in horse-manship and in archery he was unsurpassed. A stela recently discovered near the great Sphinx at Giza narrates various exploits of the young prince, among them the following:

"And he came also and did the following, which I wish to call to your attention. He entered his northern garden and found set up for him four targets of Asiatic copper of a span [three inches] in their thickness and

[92]

with twenty cubits [nearly thirty-five feet] between one pole and its fellow. Then his majesty appeared in a chariot like Montu [the god of war] in his power. He seized his bow and grasped four arrows at once. He rode northward, shooting at it [the target] like Montu in his regalia. His arrows came forth from the back of it and struck the other pole. And that is a thing, indeed, which had never been done nor even heard of in story: that an arrow shot at a target of copper came forth from it and dropped to the earth, excepting [at the hand of] the king, rich of glory whom Amun has strengthened, . . . Okheprure [Amenhotep II], heroic like Montu."[17]

When the great warrior's mummy was found in 1898 in the Valley of the Kings at Thebes,[18] his famous bow, which he boasted no other man could draw, was still beside him. It bore the inscription, "Smiter of the Cave-dwellers, overthrower of Kush, hacking up their cities— the Great Wall of Egypt, Protector of his soldiers."[19]

Amenhotep II was followed by his son Thutmose IV. From his time an interesting wall painting survives in the tomb of Sebekhotep at Thebes (Fig. 40). It depicts the arrival of Syrian ambassadors bearing tribute to the Egyptian court. The foremost figures are kneeling and raising their arms in reverence to the sovereign. The bearded faces of the men are typically Semitic, and the shawls which are wound round their bodies from the waist downward are an interesting feature of their costumes.

AMENHOTEP III

The son and successor of Thutmose IV was Amenhotep III who reigned from around 1413 B.C. to around 1377 B.C. Sometimes called "The Magnificent," he was Pharaoh as the empire attained its greatest splendor and Eighteenth Dynasty art reached its zenith. In sculpture, the work of a master is to be seen in the head (Fig. 41) of a gigantic granite statue of the king which once must have stood in his own funerary temple near Thebes. The famous "Colossi of Memnon," each 70 feet high and weighing 700 tons, also were statues of Amenhotep III. It was in Roman times that the northern colossus was believed to be a statue of Memnon, who greeted his mother Eos (Aurora), goddess of the dawn, with a sweet and plaintive note

[17] Steindorff and Seele, *When Egypt Ruled the East*, p.69.

[18] Thutmose I was the first to have his royal tomb excavated in this secluded valley deep among the western cliffs at Thebes, which became the cemetery of the Eighteenth, Nineteenth and Twentieth Dynasties.

[19] *The National Geographic Magazine.* 43 (Jan.-June 1923), p.488.

when she appeared in the morning. This musical phenomenon is mentioned somewhat skeptically by Strabo[20] and described with complete credulity by Philostratus (A.D. c.170-c.245) in connection with the visit of Apollonius and Damis to the statue: "When the sun's rays fell upon the statue, and this happened exactly at dawn, they could not restrain their admiration; for the lips spoke immediately the sun's ray touched them, and the eyes seemed to stand out and gleam against the light."[21]

In architecture the achievements of the time may be illustrated by the great colonnade of Amenhotep III at Luxor (Fig. 42), while in painting the excellence of the work done may be seen in a superb fowling scene from the Theban tomb of Nebamun (Fig. 43). Nebamun, the "scribe who keeps account of the grain," is depicted "taking recreation, seeing pleasant things, and occupying himself with the craft of the Marsh-goddess," as the accompanying inscription states. Accompanied by his wife and little daughter, Nebamun stands upon his light papyrus skiff which is pressing among the lotuses and water-weeds. Three herons are held as decoys, while Nebamun is about to launch his throw-stick at a covey of pintail ducks, geese and other fowl rising from a clump of papyrus. A cat, which already has retrieved three birds, sits precariously upon a few papyrus-stems, while delicately drawn butterflies enhance the gaiety of the scene.

AMENHOTEP IV (AKHNATON)

Amenhotep IV was first co-regent with his father, Amenhotep III, who was very ill in his old age, and then successor to him. Even before the father died there were ominous rumblings of revolt and invasion in Palestine, Syria and the north, but the son's greatness was to lie not in the field of military exploit but in the realm of religious thought. Characterized by his portraits (Fig. 44)[22] as an idealist, an artist and almost a fanatic, Amenhotep IV allowed the empire of his fathers to break apart while he devoted himself to contemplation. Yet so lofty were the ideals which he cherished and so exalted the philosophy which he developed that he became "the first *individual* in human history."[23]

[20] *Geography* xvii, i, 46.
[21] *The Life of Apollonius of Tyana.* vi, 4. tr. F. C. Conybeare. LCL (1912) ii, p.15.
[22] The statues and the mummy of the king indicate that he suffered from an abdominal deformity. M. A. Murray, *Egyptian Sculpture.* 1930, p.135.
[23] Breasted, *A History of the Ancient Egyptians,* p.265.

27. The Palermo Stone

26. The Plants that Were the Symbols of Upper and Lower Egypt

28. Cast of the Slate Palette of King Narmer

29. The Great Pyramid at Giza as Seen from the Summit of the Second Pyramid

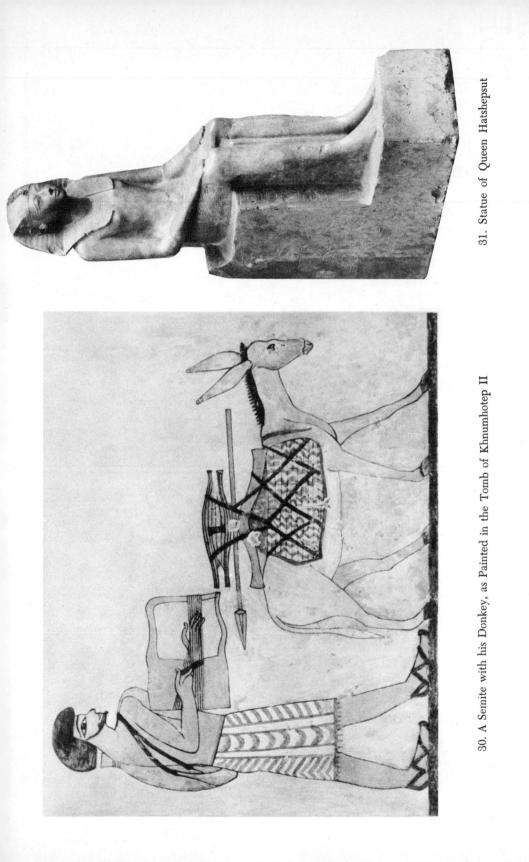

31. Statue of Queen Hatshepsut

30. A Semite with his Donkey, as Painted in the Tomb of Khnumhotep II

29. The Terraced Temple of Hatshepsut at Deir el-Bahri

33. Statue of Senenmut and Nefrure

34. Thutmose III, "The World's First Empire Builder"

35. The Obelisk of Thutmose III now in New York City

36. Bricklayers at Work, a Painting in the Tomb of Rekhmire

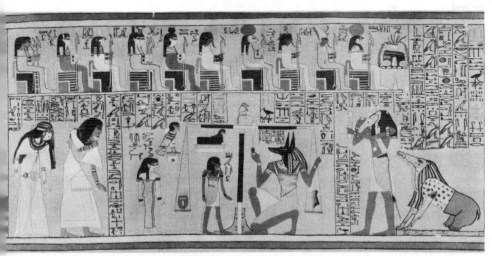

37. The Judgment Scene in the Papyrus of Ani

39. Amenhotep II, Standing under the Protection of the Cow-Goddess, Hathor

38. Statue of Amenhotep II

40. Syrians Bringing Tribute

41. Head of Amenhotep III

42. The Colonnade of Amenhotep III at Luxor
(with the Pylon of Ramesses II in the Background)

43. Fowling in the Marshes

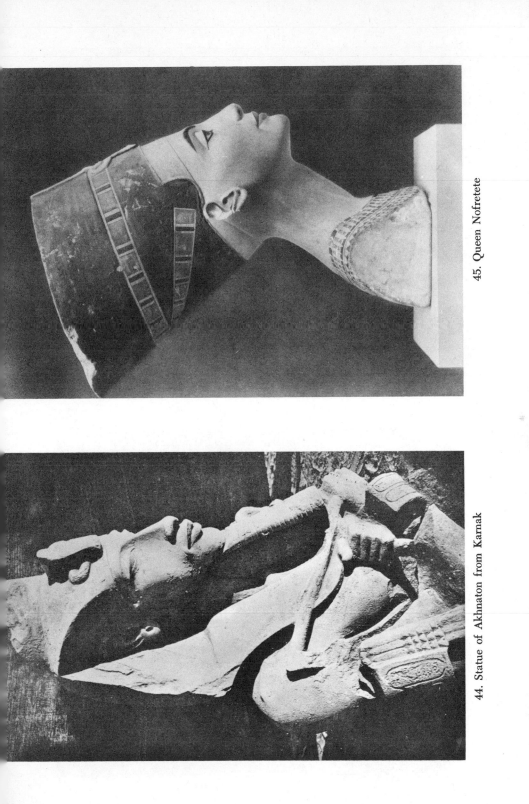

45. Queen Nofretete

44. Statue of Akhnaton from Karnak

47. Portrait Mask of Tutankhamun

46. Obverse of Tell el-Amarna Tablet with Letter
from Rib-Addi to Amenhotep III

49. The Hypostyle Hall in the Temple at Karnak

48. Harmhab as a Royal Scribe, before his Accession as King

53. Temple Relief of Ramesses III at Medinet Habu

52. Philistine Prisoners Being Led into the Presence of Ramesses III

55. The Rosetta Stone

The religion which Amenhotep IV introduced was a solar mono-theism. The sun always was a dominant fact in the Nile Valley and already had been frequently identified as a god and even the supreme god. According to one belief, the sun was the eye of Horus, the falcon-god, who represented the sky; according to another idea he was a calf, born each day of the cow-goddess of the sky, Hathor. Again the sun was a scarabaeus, rolling the solar globe across the sky; or a mariner traversing the sky in a boat, and returning in the night to the east by a subterranean river. At Heliopolis, near Memphis, the sun was worshiped under the name of Re. The priests here, who have been called "the first religious thinkers in Egypt,"[24] taught that Re, or Re-Harakhti ("Re-Horus of the Horizon"), was the greatest of all gods. This was the religion of state in the Fifth Dynasty, and was still highly influential. At Thebes, Amun (or Amen), who originally had been a ram-headed god of life or reproduction, was exalted to the position of chief god of the Egyptian world empire. He, too, was connected with the sun and, united with Re, became the great sun-god Amen-Re, bearing the title, "the father of the gods, the fashioner of men, the creator of cattle, the lord of all being." With Thebes as the capital of the empire, the magnificent temples of Amun at Karnak and Luxor were the center of the state cult and were pre-sided over by a chief priest who claimed to stand at the head of all the priesthoods in the land.

In the exaltation of Re or Amun or Amen-Re to the supreme place in the Egyptian pantheon there was obviously a tendency toward monotheism. Yet the theoretical monotheism of the priests was in most cases accommodated in practice to the practical polytheism of the people. All the other gods were retained in subordinate positions as helpers or as names or forms of the sun-god. Likewise the sun-god himself continued to be represented in all manner of animal and human forms. Amun was connected with the ram, and Re with the falcon, the lion, the cat and the crocodile. A familiar representation of Re was as a man with a falcon's head, on top of which was the solar disk. Amen-Re appeared as a man wearing on his head a disk surmounted by tall ostrich plumes.

Amenhotep IV now endeavored to go all the way in establishing an exclusive solar monotheism as Egypt's religion. An ancient but hitherto neglected name of the solar disk was Aton. Under this name

[24] Moore, *History of Religions.* I, p.152.

the worship of the sun might be set free from its mythological connections and exalted into a purer monotheism. This Amenhotep IV undertook to accomplish. Changing his own name from Amenhotep, "Amun Is Satisfied," to Akhnaton, "He Who Is Beneficial to Aton," the king boldly ousted the powerful priesthood of Amun, suppressed the public worship of Amun, and chiseled the very name of Amun and the other old gods from the monuments throughout the land. Then saying farewell to Thebes, the ancient center of Amun worship, he sailed 300 miles down the Nile to found on an unoccupied site a completely new center for the worship of Aton. The site chosen was where the cliffs retreat from the east side of the river to enclose a plain some three miles wide and five long. At this place Akhnaton built his holy city, devoted to the service of the one god, and named Akhetaton, "Horizon of Aton." Here the king took up his own residence and established the new capital of Egypt. In the sanctuary of the god no idol represented Aton, but only a sun disk from which long rays issued, each ending in a hand, often holding out the hieroglyphic sign for "life," and thus suggesting the celestial power which reached down into the affairs of men.

In the limestone cliffs surrounding the plain of Tell el-Amarna, as Akhetaton's site is now known, are cut a series of tombs of Akhnaton's nobles. Inscriptions in them contain the hymns of the Aton faith. In the great hymn of praise from the tomb of Eye, which may well have been composed by the king himself, the universal and eternal god is hailed in words echoed centuries later by the 104th Psalm:

> Thou dawnest beautifully in the horizon of the sky,
> O living Aton who wast the Beginning of life!
> When thou didst rise in the eastern horizon,
> Thou didst fill every land with thy beauty.
> Thou art beautiful, great, glittering, high over every land,
> Thy rays, they encompass the lands, even to the end of all that
>   thou hast made.
> Though thou art far away, thy rays are upon earth;
> Though thou art in the faces of men, thy footsteps are unseen.
> When thou settest in the western horizon of the sky,
> The earth is in darkness like death.[25]
> They sleep in their chambers,
> Their heads are wrapped up.
> Every lion cometh forth from his den,

[25] cf. Psalm 104:20.

All serpents they sting.[26]
Darkness broods,
The world is in silence,
He that made them resteth in his horizon.
Bright is the earth when thou risest in the horizon;
When thou shinest as Aton by day
Thou drivest away the darkness.
Men waken and stand upon their feet,
Then in all the world they do their work.[27]
How manifold are thy works!
They are hidden before men
O sole God, beside whom there is no other.
Thou didst create the earth according to thy heart.[28]
Thou settest every man into his place,
Thou suppliest their necessities,
Every one has his food,
And his days are reckoned.
The tongues are divers in speech,
Their forms likewise and their skins are distinguished.
How benevolent are thy designs, O lord of eternity!
Thou makest the seasons
In order to make develop all that thou hast made.
Winter to bring them coolness,
And heat that they may taste thee.
Thou makest millions of forms
Through thyself alone;
Cities, villages, and fields, highways and rivers,
All eyes see thee before them,
For thou art Aton of the day over the earth.
When thou hast gone away,
Yet art thou still in my heart.[29]

Thus the king felt that although the darkness fell and men slept, his god still was present in his heart. The life-giving power and fatherly kindness of Aton filled the whole world, he believed. He said, "Thou art the father and the mother of all that thou hast made."

Under the influence of this reformation, art showed an even greater delight than before in lovely natural designs of animals, birds, reeds and plants, and whereas the Pharaoh had always hitherto been depicted in a conventionalized pose of august immobility, Akhnaton allowed himself to be represented in an entirely informal way, often

[26] cf. Psalm 104:21.   [27] cf. Psalm 104:22f.
[28] cf. Psalm 104:24.
[29] Breasted, *The Dawn of Conscience*, pp.281-286.

appearing together with his famously beautiful wife, Queen No-fretete (Fig. 45), and four little daughters.

It is a pathetic fact that Akhnaton did not combine with his great religious insight any corresponding genius for administration and statesmanship. The days of his concentration upon religious reform were days of disintegration of the Egyptian empire. At home resentment and disorder prevailed, abroad in Asia the possessions of the empire were slipping away.

THE TELL EL-AMARNA TABLETS

The state of affairs abroad is very evident in the Tell el-Amarna letters, a group of clay tablets found accidentally by an Egyptian peasant woman at Tell el-Amarna. Written in cuneiform, they represent correspondence from vassal princes and governors in Syria and Palestine with Amenhotep III and with Akhnaton. Although many of the details of the letters remain obscure, it is clear that Syria and Palestine were seething with intrigue within and were under attack from without, while adequate help to maintain Egyptian sovereignty was not forthcoming. Rib-Addi, governor at Gubla or Byblus, 20 miles north of Beyrouth, wrote more than fifty times to Amenhotep III and Akhnaton, the following letter (Fig. 46) probably having been addressed to Amenhotep III:

> Rib-Addi to the king. . . .
> At the feet of my lord, my sun,
> seven times and seven times I fall down. . . .
> The king has let his faithful city
> go out of his hand. . . .
> They have formed a conspiracy with one another,
> and thus have I great fear that there is no man to rescue me
> out of their hand. Like birds that
> lie in a net
> so am I in
> Gubla. Why dost thou hold thyself back in respect to thy land?
> Behold, thus have I written to the palace,
> but thou hast paid no attention to my word. . . .
> May the king care for his land. . . .
> What shall I do in
> my solitude? Behold, thus I ask day
> and night.[30]

[30] C. Bezold and Sir E. A. W. Budge, *The Tell el-Amarna Tablets in the British Museum.* 1892, No.12; KAT No.74 = MTAT No.74.

The governor of a city in northern Syria wrote in similar appeal to Akhnaton:

> To the king of the land of Egypt, our lord. . . .
> At the feet of the lord we fall down. . . .
> Now for twenty years we have been sending to the king, our
>   lord, . . .
> But now Tunip,
> thy city, weeps,
> and her tears are running,
> and there is no help for us.
> We have been sending to the king, the lord, the king of the land
>   of Egypt,
> for twenty years;
> but not one word
> has come to us from our lord.[31]

In Jerusalem, Abdi-Hiba (sometimes Abdi-Heba) was governor, and he wrote repeatedly to Akhnaton, asking for Egyptian troops and stating that unless they were sent the entire country would be lost to Egypt.[32] His letters customarily begin with some salutation of the greatest deference like this:

> To the king, my lord, say.
> Thus saith Abdi-Hiba, thy servant:
> At the feet of the king, my lord,
> seven times and seven times I fall down. . . .[33]

Then he proceeds, as in the following letter, to protest vehemently his own loyalty and to beg urgently for help:

> What have I done to the king, my lord?
> They slander me
> to the king, the lord: "Abdi-Heba
> has become faithless to the king, his lord."
> Behold, neither my father
> nor my mother has put me
> in this place.
> The mighty hand of the king
> has led me into the house of my father.
> Why should I practice
> mischief against the king, the lord?
> As long as the king, my lord, lives
> I will say to the deputy of the king, my lord:

[31] KAT No.59 = MTAT No.59.
[32] H. Winckler, *Keilinschriftliches Textbuch zum Alten Testament.* 3d ed. 1909, pp.4-13.
[33] KAT No.285 = MTAT No.285.

"Why do you love
the Habiru, and hate
the regents?" But therefore
am I slandered before the king, my lord.
Because I say: "The lands of the king,
my lord, are lost," therefore
am I slandered to the king, my lord. . . .
So let the king, the lord, care for his land. . . .
Let the king turn his attention to the archers
so that archers of the king,
my lord, will go forth. No lands of the king remain.
The Habiru plunder all lands of the king.
If archers are here
this year, then the lands of the king,
the lord, will remain; but if archers are not here,
then the lands of the king, my lord, are lost.
To the scribe of the king, my lord, thus saith Abdi-Heba,
thy servant: Bring words,
plainly, before the king, my lord: All the lands
of the king, my lord, are going to ruin.[34]

Other letters of Abdi-Hiba include the following passages:

Verily, this land of Urusalim,
neither my father nor my mother has
given it to me; the mighty hand of the king
gave it to me. . . .
Verily, the king has set his name
upon the land of Urusalim for ever.
Therefore he cannot abandon
the lands of Urusalim.[35]

Let the king care for his land.
The land of the king will be lost. All of it
will be taken from me; there is hostility to me. . . .
But now
the Habiru are taking
the cities of the king. . . .
If there are no archers
this year, then let the king
send a deputy that he may take me
to himself together with my brothers and we
die with the king, our lord.[36]

[34] KAT No.286 = MTAT No.286.
[35] KAT No.287 = MTAT No.287.
[36] KAT No.288 = MTAT No.288.

Behold, Milkilim and Tagi
the deed which they have done is this:
After they have taken Rubuda,
they seek now to take Urusalim. . . .
Shall we then let Urusalim go? . . .
I am very humbly thy servant.[37]

The name Habiru, which figures prominently in the letters of Abdi-Hiba, is the same designation which appeared in Mesopotamia at least as early as the days of Rim-Sin and is as we have seen phonetically similar or equivalent to "Hebrew" (pp. 56f.). There could be, therefore, some connection between these Habiru and the Hebrews of the Old Testament, but the identity of the two groups is not necessarily indicated.[38]

Not even the religious reformation of Akhnaton was permanently successful. Having no son of his own, Akhnaton was followed on the throne, after a period of confusion, by his son-in-law Tutankhaton. He, abandoning the new religion and the new capital, returned to Thebes and Amun worship. His own name was changed back from "Beautiful in Life Is Aton" to Tutankhamun, "Beautiful in Life Is Amun," and the name of Amun was inscribed again on Egypt's monuments. Tutankhamun's reign was not otherwise of great significance and the young king died at the early age of about eighteen. His prominence in the mind of the modern world is due to the circumstance that of all the royal tombs in the Valley of the Kings, his was the first to be found unplundered and intact. Howard Carter's discovery of the tomb in 1922 revealed that the young Pharaoh had gone to his grave amidst an almost unbelievable splendor of golden coffins, thrones and jewels.[39]

For a single example out of this wealth of precious objects we show in Fig. 47 the portrait mask from the head of the king's mummy. This is made of beaten and burnished gold, and the headdress and collar are inlaid with opaque glass of many colors in imitation of semiprecious stones. On the forehead are the royal insignia of vulture and serpent. The mask represents Tutankhamun as he appeared at the time of his death, and it was fashioned by the goldsmiths within the relatively brief period before his burial took place. It is a beautiful

[37] KAT No.289 = MTAT No. 289.
[38] F. H. Hallock in MTAT II, pp.838-845; AJA 46 (1942), p.551.
[39] Howard Carter, *The Tomb of Tut-ankh-Amen*. 2 vols. 1923-27; C. Breasted, *Pioneer to the Past*, pp.327-373.

portrait, and when the actual face of the mummy was exposed it was seen to be a faithful and accurate representation of the young king.[40]

THE NINETEENTH DYNASTY

Tutankhamun was followed briefly by Eye, but soon the government was taken over by a general named Harmhab, who ushered in the Nineteenth Dynasty and another great period of imperial glory. The statue shown in Fig. 48 represents Harmhab as a royal scribe before his accession as king. He sits cross-legged on the floor, holding on his lap a papyrus roll which contains a hymn to Thoth, patron god of scribes. Harmhab was a man of real administrative ability and he gave the kingdom an efficient reorganization. His practical legislation for the abolition of abuses survives as one of the important edicts of ancient Egypt. "Behold," said the king, "his majesty spent the whole time seeking the welfare of Egypt."[41] He was also kind to foreigners and a scene in his tomb shows him receiving fugitive Asiatics who come begging a home in Egypt, as they say, "after the manner of your fathers' fathers since the beginning."[42]

Having no son of his own, Harmhab was succeeded by the son of one of his distinguished army officers. This man, already of an advanced age upon accession to the throne, ruled briefly as Ramesses I, and then around 1319 B.C. was succeeded by his son Sethi I.[43]

Word of the disturbed conditions abroad fell now upon the ear of a man disposed to attempt action. "One came to say to his majesty: ... 'They have taken to cursing and quarreling, each of them slaying his neighbor, and they disregard the laws of the palace.' The heart of his majesty was glad on account of it. Lo, as for the Good God, he rejoices to begin battle."[44] Henceforth the inscriptions of Sethi I speak of campaigns in Palestine and Syria, Pekanan[45] ("the Canaan"),[46] Retenu,[47] and Kadesh[48] being among the places mentioned. One inscription said of his return to Egypt, "His majesty arrived from the countries . . . when he had desolated Retenu and slain their chiefs, causing the Asiatics to say: 'See this! He is like a flame when it goes forth and no water is brought.' "[49]

---

[40] Sir Edward D. Ross, *The Art of Egypt through the Ages.* 1931, pp.43f.

[41] ARE III, §50.   [42] ARE III, §10.

[43] For the dates in the Nineteenth and later dynasties see Borchardt, *Die Mittel zur zeitlichen Festlegung von Punkten der ägyptischen Geschichte und ihre Anwendung,* pp.116-128.

[44] ARE III, §101.   [45] *Pe* is the article.   [46] ARE III, §88.
[47] ARE III, §103, 111, etc.   [48] ARE III, §141.   [49] ARE III, §139.

Actually "the Asiatics" were not as fearful of Egyptian power as Sethi I liked to believe, and his successor, Ramesses II (c.1301-c.1234), had to battle throughout the sixty-seven years of his reign against them. Although his only victory in the famous Kadesh-on-the-Orontes battle with the Hittites was that of escaping complete destruction, the personal heroism of Ramesses II was depicted proudly in numerous Egyptian scenes. Eventually Ramesses II signed a "good treaty of peace and of brotherhood" with the king of the Hittites, which left southern Syria and all of Palestine in the possession of Egypt but relinquished northern Syria and Amurru to the Hittites. This is the earliest extant treaty of international nonaggression. It was sealed by the marriage of Ramesses II and a daughter of the Hittite king.

While the military successes of Ramesses II in Asia were not as glorious as he might have wished, the magnitude of the king's building enterprises left nothing to be desired. These included the erection of his own mortuary temple at Thebes, known as the Ramesseum, the making of additions to the Luxor temple and the completion of the enormous hypostyle hall of the Karnak temple (Fig. 49). In the hypostyle hall, 134 tremendous columns, the tallest 69 feet in height, supported the roof of a room which was part of the largest temple ever erected by man, while six acres of painted relief sculpture decorated the interior of the hall.[50] At Abu Simbel, between the First and Second Cataracts of the Nile, Ramesses II hewed a complete temple in the sandstone cliff above the Nile and carved four colossal 65-foot statues of himself from the rock before it. The upper part of one of these statues is shown in Fig. 50. An ear on the statue measures over three feet in height, yet, enormous as the statues are, they are fine portraits.

While the old capital of Thebes with its great temple of Amun continued to be esteemed most highly, the political center of gravity shifted somewhat in these times to the Delta which was nearer to the Asiatic portions of the Egyptian empire. Early in the Nineteenth Dynasty the seat of government actually was transferred from Thebes to the Delta. The new capital city was Avaris-Tanis (p. 84), which had been forsaken since the expulsion of the Hyksos but was reestablished by Sethi I and enlarged and beautified by Ramesses II.

[50] The National Geographic Magazine 80 (July-Dec. 1941), p.513.

Tanis has been excavated by Pierre Montet, and a large number of statues, sphinxes, stelae and architectural remains have been found which bear the names of Ramesses II and his successors.[51] Some fifteen miles away in the vicinity of modern Qantir, Ramesses II also built a royal residence city with a palace which was adorned with striking glazed tiles and glazed statues.[52]

It is almost certain that Tanis is to be identified with the Per Ramesese Mry-Amun, "House of Ramesses-beloved-of-Amun," which was the Delta residence of the Ramesside kings and which is called Raamses in Exodus 1:11. This identification was proposed by Brugsch as long ago as 1872,[53] and is maintained strongly by Montet on the basis of his excavations.[54] Ramesses II also built or rebuilt a city whose ruins have been found at Tell er-Retaba in the Wadi Tumilat and which was probably known as Pi-Tum, "House of the god Tum," and appears in Exodus 1:11 as Pithom.[55]

THE MERENPTAH STELA

The great Pharaohs of the past had fought campaigns to extend the empire, but those who followed Ramesses II had to struggle to preserve it. Merenptah, the son and successor of Ramesses II, already was advanced in years when he came to the throne. He fought valiantly against Libyans and Mediterranean peoples who were pushing into the western Delta, and also campaigned in Palestine. In the fifth year of his reign (about 1229 B.C.) Merenptah took a large black granite stela set up by Amenhotep III and carved an inscription of victory on it. This stela was found in Merenptah's mortuary temple at Thebes and is shown in Fig. 51. At the top is a double representation of the god Amun and the king. Behind the king on the left stands the goddess Mut, wife of Amun, and behind the king on the right is the moon-god Khonsu, son of Amun and Mut.

[51] P. Montet, *Les nouvelles fouilles de Tanis 1929-1932.* 1933.

[52] William C. Hayes, *Glazed Tiles from a Palace of Ramesses II at Kantir.* The Metropolitan Museum of Art Papers, No.3, 1937.

[53] H. Brugsch in *Zeitschrift für ägyptische Sprache und Alterthumskunde* 10 (1872), p.18.

[54] P. Montet in *Revue Biblique* 39 (1930), pp.15-28. This conclusion now is accepted also by Alan H. Gardiner, who formerly favored an identification with Pelusium. According to Exodus 12:37; 13:20, Raamses was two days' journey from the edge of the wilderness. This agrees exactly with the location of Tanis, whereas Pelusium is itself on the edge of the wilderness. See *The Journal of Egyptian Archaeology* 19 (1933), pp.122-128.

[55] The earlier identification of Pithom with Tell el-Maskhuta, a site 8½ miles farther east, has been abandoned. Albright, *From the Stone Age to Christianity*, p.194.

Below are twenty-eight closely packed lines of inscription, celebrating the triumph over the Libyans and concluding with a strophe in which other defeated foreigners are listed, notably including Israel. This closing portion of the inscription reads as follows:

> The princes are prostrate, while they say, "peace!"
> There is no one who raises his head among the Nine Bows.
>
> Libya is ruined, Khatti is pacified;
> The Canaanite land is despoiled with every evil.
>
> Ascalon is carried captive, Gezer is conquered;
> Yano'am is made as though it did not exist.
>
> The people Israel is desolate, it has no offspring;
> Palestine [Khuru] has become a widow for Egypt.
>
> All lands are united, they are pacified;
> Everyone that is turbulent is bound by King Merenptah, given
>   life like Re, every day.[56]

The foregoing passage is worthy of special attention since it is the only mention in any Egyptian inscription of the name of Israel. The words, "Israel is desolate, it has no offspring," constitute a conventional phrase applicable to any defeated and plundered people; and to say that "Palestine has become a widow for Egypt" means that the land is without a husband, or in other words is without a protector and therefore helpless against Egypt. Thus Israel is clearly listed among other strong and dangerous peoples in the west of Palestine upon whom Merenptah has inflicted defeat. The stela proves, therefore, that Israel was in western Palestine by around 1229 B.C. and provides a convenient point at which to pause to discuss the Exodus.

THE DATE OF THE EXODUS

There are two chief theories as to when the Exodus of the Israelites from Egypt took place.[57] The first is based upon a late notation in I Kings 6:1 which states that Solomon began building the temple in the fourth year of his reign and the 480th[58] year after the Exodus from Egypt. The division of the kingdom under Rehoboam and Jeroboam is probably to be dated around 926 B.C.[59] or slightly later,

---

[56] ARE III, §617; W. F. Albright in BASOR 74 (Apr. 1939), pp.21f.
[57] cf. W. M. F. Petrie, *Palestine and Israel*. 1934, pp.54-58.
[58] The figure is given as 440 instead of 480 in the LXX (I, p.684).
[59] Joachim Begrich, *Die Chronologie der Könige von Israel und Juda und die Quellen des Rahmens der Königsbücher*. 1929, p.155. An earlier date of 931 B.C. is given for this event by Edwin R. Thiele in JNES 3 (1944), pp.147,184.

and since Solomon is said to have reigned for forty years (I Kings 11:42) he must have come to the throne at a time in the neighborhood of 965 B.C. The fourth year of his reign therefore was around 962 B.C., and if this was the 480th year after the departure from Egypt the Exodus must have taken place around 1441 B.C.

The date just mentioned falls within the last few years of the reign of Thutmose III (d. c.1436 B.C.), and if accepted would lead us to consider him as the Pharaoh of the Exodus. The picture of Thutmose III as the oppressor of the Israelites would be quite credible, since we know that he was a great builder and employed Semitic captives on his construction projects (p. 90). Ahmose who expelled the Hyksos might have been the "new king over Egypt, who knew not Joseph" mentioned in Exodus 1:8, and Hatshepsut might even have been the "Pharaoh's daughter" of Exodus 2:5-10. Allowing the traditional forty years in the wilderness (Exodus 16:35; Numbers 14:33; Deuteronomy 2:7; Joshua 5:6; etc.), the Israelites would have arrived in Palestine around 1400 B.C. and might be identified with the Habiru who were pressing into the land at that time (pp. 100f.).[60] Furthermore, according to the archeological evidence, Jericho seems to have fallen sometime between c.1475 and c.1300 (p. 136), which would be quite in harmony with the requirements of this theory.

Attractive as is the hypothesis just outlined, it must be recognized that there are serious objections to it. The identification of the Habiru of the Amarna letters with the biblical Hebrews is improbable, since the frantic correspondence of Abdi-Hiba indicates that Jerusalem was in imminent danger of being taken, and we know that the Israelites did not conquer Jerusalem until in the time of David (II Samuel 5:6f.). Other evidence, moreover, both in Transjordan (p. 132) and in Palestine (p. 140) requires a date considerably later than around 1400 B.C. for the coming of the Israelites to Canaan. As for the original entry of the Israelites into Egypt, if we reckon backward from an Exodus around 1441 B.C. and allow for a sojourn of 430 years in accordance with Exodus 12:40 (pp. 58f.), we arrive at a date around 1870 B.C. This is nearly two centuries before the coming of the Hyksos, however, in whose time it is historically probable that the Israelites first entered Egypt (p. 85). Furthermore, while Thutmose III carried out large building projects, those activities centered as far as we know in Upper Egypt, and it was not until Ramesside times

[60] cf. J. W. Jack, *The Date of the Exodus.* 1925.

that the kings resided in the Delta and directed major attention to building operations there. But it was in the Delta that the Israelites are said to have lived and worked. This brings us to the second and more probable hypothesis as to the date of the Exodus.

The basis of the theory now to be considered is the statement in Exodus 1:11 that the Israelites "built for Pharaoh store-cities, Pithom and Raamses." Raamses hardly can be other than Per Ramesese, the "House of Ramesses [II]," which has been identified with Avaris-Tanis (p. 104). Since Avaris itself was abandoned and allowed to fall into ruins after the expulsion of the Hyksos (c.1570 B.C.) and was reestablished only by Sethi I (c.1319-c.1301), it is not likely that any large construction activities were being conducted in this vicinity in the years just before 1441 B.C. But in the days of Ramesses II the Israelites could have toiled in construction work at Raamses and Pithom as well, both of which cities were rebuilt by this Pharaoh. The only other explanation of Exodus 1:11 would be to say that the Israelites labored at these places at some far earlier time, presumably back in the Hyksos period, and that the use of the name Raamses is an anachronism.

Unless we are to regard Exodus 1:11 as an erroneous or anachronistic statement, we must conclude that Ramesses II was the Pharaoh of the oppression. This is in harmony with our knowledge of his vast building activities and particularly with the fact that he resided in the Delta and devoted the opening years of his reign largely to building operations at Tanis. The general impression given by the book of Exodus is that the Israelites were settled not far from Pharaoh's court, and in Psalm 78:12, 43 they are definitely said to have lived "in the land of Egypt, in the field of Zoan." Zoan is the Hebrew name for Tanis, as the rendering in the Septuagint shows,[61] and thus we have a picture of the Israelites as living in the vicinity of Tanis at a time when Pharaoh's court was there. This situation is fulfilled in the time of Ramesses II but not in the earlier days of Thutmose III.

Ramesses II came to the throne around 1301 B.C., and the Merenptah stela requires that the Israelites have penetrated to western Palestine by around 1229 B.C. If we suppose that the children of Israel toiled for Ramesses II for a decade or so before making their escape, we may date the Exodus in the neighborhood of 1290 B.C.[62] Allowing

[61] LXX II, pp.315,317.
[62] Albright, *From the Stone Age to Christianity*, p.195.

forty years in the wilderness, they would have entered eastern Palestine about 1250 B.C., and over twenty years would remain in which they were to reach western Palestine and be met by Merenptah.

Reckoning backward 430 years from an Exodus around 1290 B.C., we come to around 1720 B.C. as the date for the entry of the Israelites into Egypt. This is approximately the time when the Hyksos came into Egypt and thus we emerge with the very probable conclusion that the Israelites entered Egypt at about the same time as the Hyksos.

The chief objection to this second theory is that it is out of harmony with the 480 years mentioned in I Kings 6:1. The latter appears to be a late addition to the text, however, and may bear the marks of an artificial reckoning in that it amounts to twelve generations of forty years each. It must be admitted that no single theory as to the date of the Exodus is completely conclusive, but best justice is done to the evidence now available if we conclude that the Israelites entered Egypt around 1720 B.C., left that land about 1290 B.C. and entered Palestine in approximately 1250 B.C.

THE TWENTIETH DYNASTY

After the death of Merenptah there ensued a state of confusion in which various usurpers contended for the throne. Order was restored by a certain Sethnakht who founded the Twentieth Dynasty and left a stable throne for his son, Ramesses III.

RAMESSES III

Like his predecessors, Ramesses III had to fight to defend the frontiers of Egypt against invaders who pressed in from the west and the north. Among these enemies were those known as the "peoples of the sea," who included the so-called Peleste. Some of the Peleste settled on the Palestinian coast and became the Philistines of the Bible. In honor of his success in repelling the invaders, Ramesses III erected a large temple to Amun at a point on the western plain of Thebes now called Medinet Habu and adorned its walls with a vast record of his achievements. The earliest known representation of a salt-water naval battle is here,[63] and also realistic representations of the Philistines who had been taken captive. Two of these Philistine prisoners are shown in Fig. 52 being led by an Egyptian officer into

[63] ARE IV, §69; Harold H. Nelson in JNES 2 (1943), pp.40-55.

the presence of the Pharaoh. The unusual manacles which are made in the form of a fish and suspended from the prisoner's neck by a cord are characteristic of this period. In connection with the flight of other enemies, Ramesses III expressed himself poetically as the song of Deborah (Judges 5:20) was to do: "The stars of the *seshed*-constellation were frightful in pursuit of them, while the land of Egypt was glad and rejoiced at the sight of his valor: Ramesses III."[64] The sovereign himself is depicted (Fig. 53) at Medinet Habu in heroic size, with the falcon sun-god hovering with wings protectingly outspread above his head, reminding us of the figure of speech which the Hebrews were to use—"the shadow of thy wings" (Psalms 17:8; 36:7; 57:1; 63:7; cf. Malachi 4:2).

In the later years of the Twentieth Dynasty a series of weak kings, still bearing the name of Ramesses which once had been so great, allowed Egypt to enter a period of decay. The Pharaohs had neither power at home nor prestige abroad. Court documents attest a series of robberies in which most of the royal tombs at Thebes were ransacked,[65] and "The Report of Wenamon" shows the humiliating treatment to which an Egyptian envoy could be subjected in Syria where Egyptian armies once had marched in triumph.[66]

[64] John A. Wilson in *Medinet Habu Studies 1928/29.* oic 7, 1930, p.27.
[65] ARE IV, §499-556.
[66] ARE IV, §557-591.

8. THE DECLINE
(TWENTY-FIRST TO THIRTIETH DYNASTIES),
c.1150-332 B.C.

With the Twenty-first Dynasty the decline of Egypt had set in fully. The Pharaohs ruled feebly at Tanis in the Delta while the high priest of Amun at Thebes was virtually king of Upper Egypt. The intact tomb of the second king of this dynasty, Psusennes I (c.1140 B.C.), was discovered in 1940 at Tanis. The king was buried in a funerary chamber of pink granite and in a series of sarcophagi, the outermost one of which likewise was made of pink granite. The second sarcophagus was sculptured out of black granite in the likeness of the king while the third and fourth were made of silver and of silver overlaid with gold respectively. The other treasures found in the tomb constituted one of the richest discoveries ever made in Egypt, and included a necklace of lapis lazuli and gold which weighed more than 72 pounds.[1]

AMENEMOPE

In these days a certain wise man named Amenemope was moved to profounder reflections. In a way reminiscent of Ptahhotep (p. 77), he offered sound advice to his son on honesty, integrity, self-control and kindliness. The dominant ideal which he held up was that of the truly tranquil man whom he contrasted with the hot-headed man in a figure of two trees:

> As to the passionate man in the temple,
> He is like a tree grown in the forest;
> In a moment comes its loss of foliage;
> Its end is reached in the dock-yard;
> It is floated far from its place,
> The flame is its winding sheet.
>
> The truly tranquil man, he setteth himself aside,
> He is like a tree grown in a plot;
> It grows green, it doubles its yield,
> It stands in front of its lord,
> Its fruit is sweet, its shade is pleasant,
> And its end is reached in the garden.[2]

[1] *The New York Times.* 1940: Feb. 20, p.23; Mar. 6, p.20; May 4, p.6.
[2] F. Ll. Griffith in *The Journal of Egyptian Archaeology.* 12 (1926), p.202.

By reliance on God, Amenemope taught that man could attain this tranquility of mind and consequent freedom from over-anxiety.

> Lay thee not down at night fearing the morrow;
> When day dawns what is the morrow like?
> Man knoweth not how the morrow may be.

> God is ever efficient,
> But man faileth ever.
> The words that men say are one thing,
> The things that God doeth are another.

> There is no success with God,
> Nor is there failure before him;
> If a man turn him to seek success,
> In a moment he destroyeth it.

> Be resolute of heart, make firm thy mind,
> Steer not with thy tongue;
> The tongue of a man is the rudder of the boat
> But the Lord of all is its pilot.[3]

The Wisdom of Amenemope must have been known to the Hebrews, for it is reflected, or even translated, at a number of points in the Old Testament.[4] Both Jeremiah (17:5-8) and Psalm 1 reflect Amenemope's striking picture of the two trees, while freely edited translations from other parts of the Wisdom of Amenemope are recognizable in the book of Proverbs. Here are two parallels:

AMENEMOPE	PROVERBS
Better is poverty in the hand of God, Than riches in the storehouse. Better are loaves when the heart is joyous, Than riches in unhappiness. (IX, 5-8)	Better is little, with the fear of Jehovah, Than great treasure and trouble therewith. Better is a dinner of herbs, where love is, Than a stalled ox and hatred therewith. (15:16f.)
Better is praise as one whom men love, Than riches in the storehouse. (XVI, 11f.)	Better is a dry morsel and quietness therewith, Than a house full of feasting with strife. (17:1)

[3] Peet, *A Comparative Study of the Literatures of Egypt, Palestine, and Mesopotamia,* pp.110f.
[4] H. Grimme in *Orientalistische Literaturzeitung.* 28 (1925), cols. 59-62; D. C. Simpson in *The Journal of Egyptian Archaeology.* 12 (1926), pp.232-239.

Especially does Proverbs 22:17-24:22 seem to be based upon the Wisdom of Amenemope. This may be seen in the following passages.

AMENEMOPE

Incline thine ears to hear my sayings,
And apply thine heart to their comprehension.
For it is a profitable thing to put them in thy heart,
But woe to him who transgresses them.
(III, 9-12)

Fraternize not with the hot-tempered man,
And press not upon him for conversation.
(XI, 13f.)

A scribe skillful in his office,
He shall find himself worthy of being a courtier.
(XXVII, 16f.)

Weary not thyself to seek for more,
When thy need is already secure.
If riches be brought to thee by robbery,
They will not abide the night with thee. . . .
They have made themselves wings like geese,
And they have flown to heaven.
(IX, 14-x, 5)

Remove not the landmark on the boundary of the fields. . . .
Be not greedy for a cubit of land,
And trespass not on the boundary of the widow.
(VII, 12-15)

PROVERBS

Incline thine ear, and hear the words of the wise,
And apply thy heart unto my knowledge.
For it is a pleasant thing if thou keep them within thee,
If they be established together upon thy lips.
(22:17f.)

Make no friendship with a man that is given to anger;
And with a wrathful man thou shalt not go.
(22:24)

Seest thou a man diligent in his business?
He shall stand before kings.
(22:29)

Weary not thyself to be rich; . . .

For riches certainly make themselves wings,
Like an eagle that flieth toward heaven.
(23:4f.)

Remove not the ancient landmark;
And enter not into the fields of the fatherless.
(23:10)

At one point the phrasing of the wise advice may be traced all the way back to Ptahhotep. He had said: "If thou art a man of those who sit at meat by the seat of a man greater than thou, take when he gives to thee what he puts before thee; look not at what is before him; look only at what is before thee, and bombard him not with many glances. . . . Turn thy face downward until he addresses thee, and speak only when he has addressed thee." This counsel from the days of the Fifth Dynasty was echoed by Amenemope and finally adopted by Proverbs.

AMENEMOPE	PROVERBS
Eat not bread in the presence of a great man,	When thou sittest to eat with a ruler,
Nor offer thy mouth in his presence.	Consider diligently what is before thee;
If thou sate thyself with unpermissible food,	And put a knife to thy throat,
It is but pleasure of thy spittle.	If thou be a man given to appetite.
Look only upon the dish that is before thee,	Be not desirous of his dainties;
And let it furnish thy need.	Seeing they are deceitful food.
(xxɪɪɪ, 13-18)	(23:1-3) [5]

SHESHONK I

The Twenty-second Dynasty was founded when a soldier from a Libyan family at Herakleopolis seized the royal authority and proclaimed himself Pharaoh. This new king, Sheshonk I (c.924 B.C.), ruled from a residence at Bubastis[6] in the eastern Delta, and was strong enough to invade Palestine in the fifth year of Rehoboam of Judah (I Kings 14:25, where he is called Shishak). This Palestinian campaign was memorialized in a relief after the style of the earlier Pharaohs on a wall at Karnak. A portion of the relief is shown in Fig. 54 where the god Amun leads forward by cords rows of Semitic captives, doubtless Hebrews. On the entire relief no less than 156 captives are represented, each of whom symbolizes a different Palestinian town which Sheshonk I claims to have taken. In each case the name of the town is enclosed in an oval marked out beneath the head and shoulders of the captive. Of the names which still can be read and identified geographically, many are found in the Old Testament. These include Rabbith, Taanach, Shunem, Beth-shean, Rehob, Hapharaim, Gibeon, Beth-horon, Ajalon, Megiddo, Socoh, and Arad. This is also the list which includes "The Field of Abram" (p. 81).[7] In 1938-1939 the intact burial chamber of Sheshonk I was discovered at Tanis, the body of the king being splendidly arrayed, with a gold mask over his face, and enclosed in a coffin of electrum.[8]

The dynasty founded by Sheshonk I endured for some two cen-

---

[5] Breasted, *The Dawn of Conscience*, pp.372-378.
[6] Called Pi-beseth in Ezekiel 30:17.
[7] ARE ɪv, §712-716. [8] AJA 44 (1940), p.145.

turies, although the country was organized in essentially a feudal way, and Upper Egypt was divided into two principalities dominated respectively by Herakleopolis[9] and Thebes. The Twenty-third and Twenty-fourth Dynasties which followed were short and feeble, and Isaiah was quite correct in his description (Chapter 19) of the divided and hopeless state of Egypt at that time. In the Twenty-fifth Dynasty, Egypt was ruled by Ethiopian kings, including Shabaka (c.711-c.699), Shabataka (c.699-c.689) and Taharka (c. 689-c.663), who endeavored to repel the Assyrian threat which was coming steadily nearer. Taharka suffered defeat by Esarhaddon and after the capture of Memphis was compelled to take refuge in Ethiopia. Tanutamun, the son of Shabaka, succeeded in recovering Egypt for a brief period but was soon defeated and pursued as far as Thebes, where the Assyrians under Ashurbanipal plundered the magnificent capital of Egypt's earlier age of splendor (cf. Nahum 3:8).

Yet a brief period of restoration was at hand. Psamtik I (c.633-c.609) of Saïs took advantage of the preoccupation of the Assyrians in their struggles with Babylon and Elam to establish a new native dynasty, the Twenty-sixth. It was possible for him to set up again a centralized government and to restore a considerable degree of peace and prosperity. It was he who turned back the invading Scythians in Palestine, whether it was by gifts and prayers as Herodotus states,[10] or by his own military power. In this Saïte Period Egypt enjoyed a revival of art, and entered into relations with the rising country of Greece.

NECHO

Psamtik I was succeeded by his son, Nekau or Necho (c.609-c.594), who was able to invade Philistia and take Gaza and Ashkelon.[11] On the historic plain of Megiddo he met the pitifully inadequate forces of Josiah (II Kings 23:29f.), whom he slew and then marched on, as Pharaohs formerly had, to the Euphrates. But the dream of a new Asiatic empire for Egypt was to be shattered quickly. Nebuchadnezzar, son of the king of Babylon and soon himself to take

[9] Called Hanes in Isaiah 30:4. ARE IV, §790.
[10] I, 105.
[11] Jeremiah 47:1 probably refers to this in the statement that "Pharaoh smote Gaza," but the oracle that follows (47:2-7) seems to describe some other invasion which came from the north instead of the south.

the throne, met Necho at Carchemish in 605 B.C. and routed his army completely (cf. Jeremiah 46; II Kings 24:7).

Henceforth Necho confined his attentions chiefly to Egypt, as did his son Psamtik II. The latter's son, Apries (Hophra), dared to challenge, although unsuccessfully, Nebuchadnezzar's invasion of Palestine, in which Jerusalem fell (587 B.C.). Nebuchadnezzar even made some attempt at the invasion of Egypt (cf. Jeremiah 43:8-13; Ezekiel 29-32) in the days of the next king, Amasis. In his closing years Amasis witnessed the rise of Cyrus the Great of Persia. His son Psamtik III had reigned only a few months when he fell at Pelusium (c.525 B.C.) before the invading forces of Cyrus' son and successor, Cambyses II. Henceforth, throughout the Twenty-seventh to Thirtieth Dynasties, Egypt was under Persian rule, although sometimes local kings exercised authority under Persian domination. In 332 B.C. Egypt was conquered by Alexander the Great. After his death (323 B.C.) the land came under the rule of the Ptolemies until the death of Cleopatra (30 B.C.) when it became a Roman province under Octavian.

THE ROSETTA STONE

In 196 B.C. while Alexander's successors were ruling Egypt, the priests at Memphis composed a decree honoring King Ptolemy V Epiphanes (c.203-c.181 B.C.) for numerous benefits which he had conferred upon the temples of Egypt. This decree was ordered engraved on a tablet in three forms, "in the sacred writing, in the native script, and in Greek letters." The "sacred writing" was the ancient picture-writing of Egypt which only the priests then understood, and which the Greeks called *hieroglyphics*, literally "sacred carvings."[12] The "native script" was what the Greeks called *demotic* meaning "common," or "popular," and was a new and simplified form of the Egyptian language and writing that had come into use some hundreds of years before. It was the Greek language which was to provide the clue for the decipherment of the inscription.

A stone inscribed with this decree (Fig. 55) was found in 1798 by an officer of Napoleon's expedition at Rosetta (Rashid) near the westernmost mouth of the Nile. The Greek text at the bottom of the Rosetta Stone was read easily and scholars at once took up the chal-

[12] When hieroglyphics were written on papyrus with a brush-pen, a bolder and more cursive form of writing developed, to which the Greek name *hieratic*, or "priestly," was applied.

lenge to solve the problem of the two Egyptian scripts above. Silvestre de Sacy of France and J. D. Akerblad of Sweden successfully studied the demotic text on the monument, identifying the Greek personal names which it contains—Ptolemy, Berenike, and Arsinoë. Thomas Young of England was then able to identify the name of Ptolemy in the hieroglyphic portion, where groups of signs enclosed in oval frames (called "cartouches") had already been thought to be kings' names. Finally the young French scholar Jean François Champollion (1790-1832) was able to demonstrate the true nature of the hieroglyphic system of writing, to formulate an Egyptian grammar and dictionary, and to read numerous Egyptian texts. Thus the key was found which unlocked the doors to a knowledge of ancient Egypt.[13]

MOSES AND THE CHILDREN OF ISRAEL

In conclusion we may say that Egypt has not afforded us any direct evidence of the sojourn of the Israelites, but it has revealed much which makes that sojourn and the Exodus which followed entirely credible. It was not uncommon for Semitic people to find refuge in Egypt nor for them to be set at heavy labor on the great building projects of the Pharaohs. Without doubt the Hebrews were in Egypt in the days of the Hyksos, and their oppression and Exodus probably fell under Ramesses II. The very name of Moses is clearly Egyptian, being the Egyptian word *mose* meaning "is born." Names like Amenmose ("Amun Is Born") and Thutmose ("Thoth Is Born") were familiar, and it may be presumed that Moses originally bore some fuller name of which only the "Mose" continued in current usage.

In Egypt it has also been possible to trace "the dawn of conscience" which meant so much to the Hebrew prophets and to all mankind. Ideas of the overshadowing care of God, and of ethical demands on earthly life root back here. Actual passages from the wisdom literature of Egypt were taken over by Hebrew writers. Thus the psalms, wisdom books and prophetic works of the Hebrews are connected intimately with Egyptian literature just as the mythology and law of the Old Testament are related closely to that of Babylonia.

[13] Sir E. A. Wallis Budge, *The Rosetta Stone in the British Museum* (1929); H. Hartleben, *Champollion, sein Leben und sein Werk* (2 vols. 1906).

III

Penetrating the Past in Palestine

THE land of Palestine derives its name from the Philistines (Peleste) who settled along the southern coast in the twelfth century B.C. (p. 108). The area where they settled became known as Philistia (Joel 3:4, etc.) and from that in turn came the Greek name Palestine.[1] Josephus refers to the territory which extends from Gaza to Egypt and says that the Greeks call that area Palestine.[2] Herodotus even uses the name to include Phoenicia as well. Referring to the northern part of the coast where the Phoenicians settled, he says, "that part of Syria and as much of it as reaches to Egypt, is all called Palestine."[3] Elsewhere he speaks of "the part of Syria called Palestine,"[4] and "the Palestine part of Syria."[5] The Romans in their turn called the land *Palaestina* and as Palestine it is known most familiarly today.

The older native name of the land was Canaan and by this it is called in the Bible (Genesis 11:31, etc.) and in the Egyptian texts (p. 102). This name may have originally meant "land of the purple," and have had reference to the manufacture of purple dye from the murex shellfish found on the coast.[6] Perhaps applied at first only to the coastal regions, the name Canaan was afterward extended to include all of the country west of the Jordan. The land east of the river was called simply, "beyond the Jordan," or "the other side of the Jordan" (Genesis 50:10, etc.), and to this day is officially known as Transjordan.

Syria, of which as Herodotus said Palestine is a part, includes the entire area of fertile land, bounded by the desert on the east and south, the sea on the west, and extending to the Taurus Mountains

[1] ἡ Παλαιστίνη.　　　[2] *Ant.* I, vi, 2.　　　[3] VII, 89.
[4] I, 105.　　　[5] II, 106.
[6] G. Ernest Wright and Floyd V. Filson, eds., *The Westminster Historical Atlas to the Bible.* 1945, p.33.

on the north. The name Syria was derived by the Greeks from Assyria, but whereas it was at first applicable to the entire Assyrian
Empire from the Caucasus to the Levant, it shrank finally to the
limits just stated.

Palestine proper, meaning the country west of the Jordan and
running from Dan in the north to Beersheba in the south (cf. Judges
20:1, etc.), is 150 miles in length and averages something like 40
miles in breadth. In comparison with the 6,000 square miles of
Palestine proper, Transjordan, running east to the desert, comprises
some 4,000 square miles.

Between the sea and the desert the land of Palestine and Transjordan may be conceived as lying in four parallel strips running north
and south.[7] First, along the coast is the maritime plain, of which the
most famous portion is the Plain of Sharon between Mount Carmel
and Joppa. Secondly, a rugged series of hills runs through the interior
and may be known as the central range. This line of hills descends
from the mountains of Lebanon and Anti-Lebanon far to the north
beyond the bounds of Palestine proper where snowy Mount Hermon
looms up to a height of about 9,100 feet. Between Galilee and
Samaria a spur of the range runs out to the Mediterranean and terminates in 1,810-foot Mount Carmel, to the north of which lies the
Plain of Esdraelon. In Judea the range attains an average elevation
of 2,400 feet, a high point a few miles north of Jerusalem being 3,317
feet in elevation, Jerusalem itself 2,593 feet and Bethlehem 2,550
feet. On the western border between Judea and Philistia the high
central range drops toward the maritime plain in a region of low hills
called the Shephelah or "lowland" (Joshua 15:33, etc.). On the
southern frontier of Judea the range breaks down and spreads out in
the area known as the Negeb, usually translated "the South," but
literally meaning the Dry or Parched Land (Genesis 13:1, etc.).

On its eastern side the central range drops quickly to the Jordan
Valley, whose great depression constitutes the third of the four
parallel bands in which the country may be seen to lie. The Jordan
River has sources at Banias and elsewhere in the neighborhood of
Mount Hermon, where snow and rain provide ample water. Soon
it flows through Lake Hule, where the valley is only seven feet above
sea level. Next, the river flows through the Sea of Galilee, about 685

[7] George Adam Smith, *The Historical Geography of the Holy Land.* 4th ed. 1896,
p.49; Hilaire Belloc, *The Battleground, Syria and Palestine.* 1936, p.23.

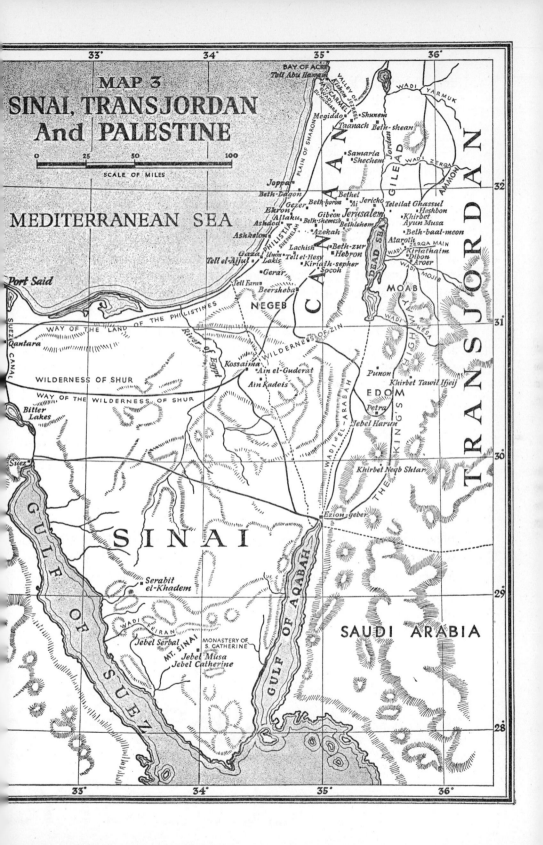

feet below the level of the sea, and then follows an ever deepening valley until it terminates in the Dead Sea about 1,275 feet below sea level.[8] It may be noted that this profound depression represents a geological rift which runs on down along the Wadi el-Arabah to the Gulf of Aqabah and through the Red Sea into Africa. Beyond the Jordan and towering some 4,400 feet above the Dead Sea is an eastern range of barren hills which constitutes the fourth of the parallel bands and beyond which is the desert.

The lower valley of the Jordan is sub-tropical, but the greater part of Palestine lies one or two thousand feet above the level of the sea and enjoys a temperate climate. The year is divided into a dry season and a rainy season, the rains coming from the end of October to the middle of April. During the rainy or winter season, snow is not uncommon in the hills.

Of all the geographical facts that may be adduced about Palestine, the most significant is that it constitutes a "bridge" connecting Mesopotamia and Egypt.[9] With the sea on the one hand and the desert on the other, Palestine was the natural and only highroad between those two great homes of empire, the valley of the Tigris and Euphrates, and the valley of the Nile. Palestine's history was connected intimately, therefore, with that of its powerful neighbors, and it was the fate of the land at most times to be a dependency, a buffer state or a battleground.

A land as often invaded as Palestine, and as perennially dominated by various foreign powers, cannot display an historical development of such homogeneity and directness as was manifest in Egypt. Nor do we find in Palestine, at such ancient periods as in both Egypt and Mesopotamia, powerful rulers and well established dynasties whose records survive to show the course of events. It is only in the time of the Hebrew kings, and then chiefly because of the records preserved in the Bible, that a relatively precise historical framework can be established.[10]

For the earlier Palestinian times we can speak only in terms of broad archeological periods, and it is customary to refer to the Stone,

[8] Félix Marie Abel, *Géographie de la Palestine.* I (1933), Carte VI.

[9] cf. Lewis Browne, *The Graphic Bible.* 1928, p.21.

[10] Begrich, *Die Chronologie der Könige von Israel und Juda und die Quellen des Rahmens der Königsbücher*, p.155.

Chalcolithic, Bronze, and Iron Ages and their respective subdivisions. It will be desirable, therefore, first to sketch briefly the salient characteristics of these successive periods, and then to deal more fully with the archeological discoveries which relate particularly to Hebrew times and happenings.

1. THE ARCHEOLOGICAL PERIODS IN PALESTINE

THE STONE AGE, UP TO c.5000 B.C.

THE traces of the presence of man in Palestine go back into the earliest periods of human life. The famous "Galilee skull" which was found by F. Turville-Petre in 1925 in the "robbers' cave" near the Sea of Galilee, and the fossil human remains which were excavated by Dr. Theodore D. McCown in 1932 in the Wadi el-Mughara or "valley of the cave" at Mount Carmel, belong to Palaeolithic times and represent a primitive type of humanity akin to the Neanderthal.[1] Other discoveries in the Wadi el-Mughara reveal a Mesolithic culture whose people had learned to grow wheat and to carve statuettes and were in the habit of burying their dead, laying the body on its side with legs drawn up and sometimes leaving ornaments with it.[2]

In Neolithic times man had learned to shape and polish his stone implements and before the end of the period pottery was made for the first time in Palestine. The earliest occupation of Jericho (p. 134) belongs to the Neolithic Age and is believed to antedate the fifth millennium, thus being approximately contemporaneous with the first village life of Syria and Mesopotamia (p. 14). In the time represented by the lowest levels, pottery was not yet manufactured but the inhabitants were already living in houses made with walls of beaten earth and with floors of painted and burnished clay. These are the oldest known permanent houses. Agriculture was practiced, and mud figurines of cattle, sheep, goats and pigs show the animals which had been domesticated. One building seems to have been a shrine, and plastic statues occurring in groups representing a man, woman and child suggest that a divine triad of father, mother and son was already worshiped.[3] When the first pottery appears it is a coarse ware mixed with straw, roughly finished and inadequately fired. The oldest examples were undecorated, but in later work geometric designs were used.[4]

---

[1] Sir Arthur Keith, *New Discoveries relating to the Antiquity of Man.* 1931, pp.173-198; Theodore D. McCown and Sir Arthur Keith, *The Stone Age of Mount Carmel: the Fossil Human Remains from the Levalloiso-Mousterian.* II (1939); J. Philip Hyatt in *The Journal of Bible and Religion.* 12 (1944), pp.232-236.

[2] Dorothy A. E. Garrod and D. M. A. Bate, *The Stone Age of Mount Carmel: Excavations at the Wady el-Mughara.* I (1937).

[3] Albright, *From the Stone Age to Christianity,* pp.95,127,187.

[4] Immanuel Ben-Dor in *Annals of Archaeology and Anthropology, issued by the Institute of Archaeology, University of Liverpool.* 23 (1936), pp.77-90.

For the most part throughout the Stone Age in Palestine the caves in which the land abounds were the chief dwelling places. As a matter of fact many of the inhabitants of Palestine live in such caverns even today. At Gezer a number of caves in which people of the Stone Age dwelt were explored by R. A. S. Macalister.[5] Some of these were natural, some had been enlarged, and others had been cut out of the soft limestone. In size they varied from 18 to 40 feet in diameter and the roofs usually were very low, the entrance in most cases being through a hole in the roof. Rude drawings on the walls show an animal among reeds, shot by an arrow, and a man plowing with a pair of oxen or buffaloes. At Jerusalem under ancient Zion there is a large natural cave which originally was entered through a sort of rock funnel. Those who dwelt in it lived at one end and buried their dead at the other, while a rough pit in the floor served as the place where pottery was made.[6]

Across in Transjordan we find prehistoric rock-drawings, including representations of the ox and the ibex, which probably come from the Middle Stone Age,[7] and also menhirs and dolmens, which quite likely date from the Late Stone Age. The latter are megalithic monuments in which huge stones are placed in an upright position as monoliths or arranged to form a chamber covered by a flat capstone. These are believed to have been burial monuments in most cases and to have belonged to pastoral peoples who ranged across these regions.[8]

THE CHALCOLITHIC AGE, c.4500-c.3000 B.C.

As in the countries hitherto studied, so also in Palestine the Stone Age was followed by a period in which flint still was used extensively but in which copper also was employed. This was the Chalcolithic Period to which it will be remembered the cultures of Tell Halaf in Mesopotamia (p. 14) and Badari in Egypt (p. 68) belonged. The Palestinian culture which corresponds approximately in time to the Halafian and the Badarian is known as the Ghassulian. It takes its name from the site of its first discovery, Teleilat Ghassul, just north of the Dead Sea and not far from Jericho. The pottery of this period was improved in technique and more varied in form, simple painted

---

[5] Macalister, The Excavation of Gezer. i (1912), pp.72-152.
[6] J. Garrow Duncan, Digging Up Biblical History. 1931, i, pp.14-17.
[7] Nelson Glueck, The Other Side of the Jordan. 1940, pp.45-49.
[8] Albright, From the Stone Age to Christianity, pp.95f.; Edwin C. Broome, Jr. in JBL 59 (1940), pp.479-497.

designs being common. At Teleilat Ghassul the houses were made of mud brick and their plastered inner surfaces were adorned with amazing mural paintings. Among the frescoes which survive are intricate and elaborate geometric patterns, figures now almost destroyed but apparently representing a seated god and goddess, and a well preserved painting of a bird executed in a most naturalistic and lifelike way.[9]

THE EARLY BRONZE AGE, c.3000-c.2000 B.C.

By somewhere around 3000 B.C. metal had displaced stone as the dominant material for tools and weapons in Palestine and the Bronze Age was ushered in. It is customary to divide this era into three periods of which the Early Bronze Age is dated from around 3000 to around 2000 B.C. This corresponds approximately to the Early Dynastic Period in Sumer and the succeeding empire of Sargon I in Akkad and to the time of the first half-dozen or more dynasties in Egypt. As far as material culture is concerned, Palestine at this time was but an outlying and destitute part of Syria, and nothing like the magnificence of the First Dynasty of Ur or of the Pyramid Age is to be found. The cities were often on low hills and fortified with strong walls, but their buildings were usually constructed rather crudely as compared with the architecture of Mesopotamia and Egypt. The pottery likewise is poorer than that of the neighboring lands, although made in some cases with considerable excellence. The first clay lamps appear, being simply small bowls with a pinched place in the rim to hold the wick. No writing has been found as yet in the Early Bronze Age in Palestine proper, but at Byblus on the Syrian coast a number of syllabic inscriptions on copper have been discovered which date probably from the late third millennium B.C.[10]

The earliest Canaanite sanctuaries that have been discovered belong to this age and include examples at Megiddo, Jericho, and Ai. In the case of the temple at Ai there were two main rooms, the first of which was approached by a ramp, and contained ledges perhaps for the purpose of holding offerings. Through a narrow door access was gained to the inner room, where behind a partition stood

[9] A. Mallon, R. Koeppel and Rene Neuville, *Teleilat Ghassul* I, *Compte rendu des fouilles de l'Institut Biblique Pontifical 1929-1932.* 1934. cf. Nelson Glueck in BASOR 97 (Feb. 1945), pp.10f.

[10] W. F. Albright in *The Haverford Symposium on Archaeology and the Bible*, p.13.

the altar. Bones of birds, fowls and lambs were found in the ashes on the ground.[11]

Semitic Amorites probably were in Palestine in this period and according to the Old Testament were there when Abraham came (Genesis 14:13) as well as when the children of Israel invaded the land (Amos 2:9).

In Transjordan an important civilization flourished between the twenty-third and twentieth centuries B.C. A long line of settlements existed along the main north-south track through central Transjordan and the fertile plateau lands of the country were employed for agriculture.[12]

THE MIDDLE BRONZE AGE, c.2000-c.1500 B.C.

The Middle Bronze Age is dated in Palestine from around 2000 to around 1500 B.C. and includes, according to our reckoning, the time of Abraham's migration as well as the period of Hammurabi and his predecessors and successors in Mesopotamia and the time of the Hyksos invasion of Egypt. The Hyksos must have moved through Palestine and Transjordan on their way into Egypt, and after their expulsion from that land they remained in Palestine at least until the time of Thutmose III. Their presence in Palestine is indicated by the appearance of a new type of fortification, namely great rectangular camps surrounded by massive sloping ramparts of packed earth, and doubtless used to shelter the horses and chariots which were introduced into Palestine as well as Egypt at this time.

It is probable that Hittites settled in Palestine during the Middle Bronze Age, perhaps in some connection with the Hyksos. In Genesis 23, Hebron is described as in possession of the "children of Heth," or Hittites, when Abraham purchased the cave of Machpelah there as a burial place; and in Ezekiel 16:3, 45 Jerusalem is described as a Canaanite city founded and built by a combination of the Amorites and Hittites: "By origin and birth you belong to the land of the Canaanites, your father was an Amorite, and your mother a Hittite."[13]

In general the cities of the Middle Bronze Age were powerfully fortified—walls, towers and moats being employed. Some of the walls were constructed in a type of masonry known as Cyclopean which employed huge irregularly shaped blocks of stone and filled the

[11] Millar Burrows, *What Mean These Stones?* 1941, p.200.
[12] Glueck, *The Other Side of the Jordan*, pp.114-125.
[13] *An American Translation.*

spaces between them with small stones. The potter's wheel, which had been introduced in the Early Bronze Age, was in general use, and good pottery is characteristic of the time.

We know a Canaanite shrine of this period which stood on the slope of Mount Gerizim above Shechem, and consisted of a small central court surrounded on all four sides by chambers. Also three buildings were found at Megiddo which are to be dated around 1900 B.C. and probably were used for sacred purposes. In each of these a porch with end walls gave access to a single large room, off which in at least two instances a smaller room opened. The three buildings stood in connection with a circular structure ascended by a flight of steps, which evidently was a sacrificial altar of unique form.[14]

Presumably it was around 1900 B.C. that the catastrophic destruction of Sodom and Gomorrah (Genesis 19:24-28) took place. A careful survey of the literary, geological and archeological evidence points to the conclusion that the infamous "cities of the Plain" (Genesis 19:29) were in the area which now is submerged beneath the slowly rising waters of the southern part of the Dead Sea, and that their ruin was accomplished by a great earthquake, probably accompanied by explosions, lightning, ignition of natural gas and general conflagration.[15]

In Transjordan about 1900 B.C. the formerly flourishing settlements and fortresses fell into disuse as the people for some unknown reason ceased living in towns and returned again to nomadic life.

Down in the peninsula of Sinai at about this time appear what are believed to be the earliest known attempts at a purely alphabetic form of writing. These are fragmentary inscriptions which were first discovered in 1904-1905 by Flinders Petrie on monuments and rocks at Serabit el-Khadem, only about 50 miles from the traditional site of Mount Sinai.[16] In this region there are ancient turquoise mines which were worked by the Egyptians, and the inscriptions were probably written by Semitic people whose home was in the country between the Red Sea and the Dead Sea and who were laborers in the Egyptian mines. The date of the writings is thought to be in the period of the Twelfth Egyptian Dynasty (c.1989-c.1776 B.C.). In distinction

[14] Gordon Loud in *The Illustrated London News*, Nov. 25, 1939, p.794.
[15] J. Penrose Harland in BA v, 2 (May 1942); vi, 3 (Sept. 1943).
[16] Petrie, *Researches in Sinai*. 1906, pp.129-132.

from the properly so-called Sinaitic inscriptions which consist of a large number of Nabatean inscriptions dating from the first several centuries A.D., these are known as the proto-Sinaitic inscriptions. The script seems to be founded upon Egyptian hieroglyphic, but is properly described as paleo-Semitic, and represents for the first time within the scope of our knowledge the emergence of a true alphabet. This alphabet was the progenitor of the Hebrew alphabet, and ultimately of the Phoenician, out of which in turn grew the Greek, Latin, and English alphabets.[17]

THE LATE BRONZE AGE, c.1500-c.1200 B.C.

The Late Bronze Age in Palestine covers the years from around 1500 to around 1200 B.C. and corresponds to the days of the Kassites in Babylonia and the Hittites at Boghaz-keui and the time of Thutmose III, Amenhotep IV and Ramesses II in Egypt. One of the interesting discoveries belonging to this period is that of an actual potter's workshop, which was found in a cave at Lachish (Tell ed-Duweir). The workshop still contained the stone seat on which the potter sat, a limestone pivot on which no doubt the potter's wheel turned, and sherds, pebbles, shells and a bone point, all of which had been used for smoothing, burnishing and incising the vessels.[18] The pottery now was decorated much more frequently with geometric designs and with pictures of birds, fishes and animals. The most notable artistic work was that done by an unknown vase-painter of about the sixteenth century whose products were found by Flinders Petrie at Tell el-'Ajjul, the "Mound of the Little Calf," four miles southwest of modern Gaza. Extraordinary talent was manifest in his animal paintings which were executed in a sensitive and beautiful way.[19]

Mycenaean pottery also was imported into Palestine by sea at this time. Excavations in 1932-1933 at Tell Abu Hawam, near modern

---

[17] Martin Sprengling, *The Alphabet, Its Rise and Development from the Sinai Inscriptions*. OIC 12, 1931; John W. Flight in *The Haverford Symposium on Archaeology and the Bible*, pp.115-118.

[18] Burrows, *What Mean These Stones?* p.163.

[19] Petrie, *Ancient Gaza, Tell El Ajjul*. 4 vols. 1931-34; W. F. Albright in *The American Journal of Semitic Languages and Literatures*. 55 (1938), pp.337-359; W. A. Heurtley in *The Quarterly of the Department of Antiquities in Palestine*. 8 (1939), pp.21-37.

Haifa, have shown that at the end of the Late Bronze Age this place probably was an important port for the reception of such wares.[20]

THE EARLY IRON AGE, c.1200-c.900 B.C.

The beginning of the Iron Age in Palestine is dated around 1200 B.C. Iron was known before this, as is shown by a steel battle-axe of about 1400 B.C. found at Ras Shamra, but it took the place of bronze only gradually.[21] As far as the Hebrews were concerned, the Philistines managed to maintain a monopoly of the importing and forging of iron until the reign of Saul (I Samuel 13:19-22).[22]

It is customary to divide the Iron Age into three periods of which the first is that of the Early Iron Age from around 1200 to around 900 B.C. This period includes the time when Tiglath-pileser I was beginning to raise Assyria toward world power and when the kings of the Twentieth and Twenty-first Dynasties were allowing Egypt to slip into decline.

THE MIDDLE IRON AGE, c.900-c.600 B.C.

The second period is that of the Middle Iron Age around 900 to around 600 B.C. In these years the world trembled before the power of Assyria, and Palestine felt the tramp of the armies of Shalmaneser III, Sargon II and Sennacherib, while the continuing decline of Egyptian power was only slightly relieved by the exploits of such kings as Sheshonk I and Taharka.

THE LATE IRON AGE, c.600-c.300 B.C.

The third period is known as the Late Iron Age and is dated from around 600 to around 300 B.C. During these centuries the New Babylonian and Persian Empires succeeded each other swiftly on the stage of world history, while Egypt enjoyed a brief renaissance under Psamtik I and his followers and then bowed to Persian power. But before the close of the period all the world was ruled by Alexander the Great.[23]

[20] R. W. Hamilton in *The Quarterly of the Department of Antiquities in Palestine.* 3 (1934), pp.74-80; 4 (1935), pp.1-69.

[21] Burrows, *What Mean These Stones?* p.158.

[22] W. F. Albright in *The Annual of the American Schools of Oriental Research.* 4 (1922-23), p.17.

[23] The later archeological periods in Palestine are the Hellenistic (c.300-63 B.C.), Roman (63 B.C.-A.D. 323), Byzantine (323-636), Arabic (636-1517) and Turkish (1517-1918).

2. EXCAVATIONS AND DISCOVERIES RELATING TO HEBREW TIMES

THE COMING OF THE ISRAELITES

IF OUR earlier reckoning (p. 108) was correct it was around 1250 B.C. or approximately at the beginning of the Early Iron Age that the children of Israel came into the promised land. Is any light cast upon their coming by archeological evidences in Transjordan and Palestine?

To some extent we can trace the probable course of the Israelites in their journey from Egypt to Palestine. The name of the wilderness and the mount where the law was given was Sinai according to J (Exodus 19:18, 20, etc.) and P (Exodus 19:1, etc.; Numbers 10:12; 33:16) although in other sources (Exodus 3:1; 33:6 [E]; Deuteronomy 1:2, 6, 19; 4:10, etc.) "the mountain of God" is called Horeb. At least since Byzantine times Christian tradition has placed the giving of the law somewhere in the lofty granite range of Sinai in the south central part of the peninsula of Sinai (cf. p. 342), and this tradition may well be correct. The range of Sinai is an impressive mass of mountains, dominated by three peaks, all of which might be enclosed within a circle twenty-five miles in diameter. The three peaks are known today as Jebel Serbal (6,759 feet), Jebel Musa or "Mountain of Moses" (7,519 feet) and Jebel Catherine (Katerina) (8,551 feet), the latter two being side by side and the first named farther distant. Geologically speaking, the crystalline masses of these mountains appear to have loomed up here practically unchanged since the oldest times. Encircled by the desert, their towering cliffs, stupendous precipices and magnificent summits form a wild and imposing scene.[1]

From the wilderness of Sinai the Israelites journeyed by many stages to Ezion-geber (Numbers 33:16-35 [P]). Ezion-geber probably is to be identified with Tell Kheleifeh at the head of the Gulf of Aqabah, which is the site where Solomon later built a port city and factory town (p. 152). As far as is known from excavations there, no city existed at Tell Kheleifeh at the time of the Exodus, but what

[1] F. E. Hoskins in *The National Geographic Magazine*. 20 (1909), pp.1021f.; Karl Baedeker, *Palestine and Syria*. 5th ed. 1912, pp.196,206,208.

is meant is that the Israelites stopped at the place where the city later was established.[2]

From Ezion-geber the Israelites came to Kadesh or Kadesh-barnea in the wilderness of Zin (Numbers 20:1; 33:36f.; Deuteronomy 1:19) and apparently made their headquarters there for some considerable time.[3] Miriam died and was buried there (Numbers 20:1b) and from there the spies were sent to view the promised land (Numbers 13:21-26; Deuteronomy 1:19-25). The wilderness of Zin has been explored by C. Leonard Woolley and T. E. Lawrence and the probable location of Kadesh-barnea discussed in the light of their experiences. Largely because of the similarity of names, Kadesh-barnea has been traditionally identified with Ain Kadeis. But Woolley and Lawrence found Ain Kadeis only an obscure water-hole, "too small to water the flocks of other than the few poor families who live near it, and . . . too remote from all roads to come to the notice of such Arab guides as live at any distance." They think, however, that the Israelites may have come upon the valley of Kadeis first and have extended its name to the whole district as far as Kossaima. This larger area would have been a very likely place for the Israelites to abide. The Kossaima Plain is relatively extensive and fertile, and enjoys the proximity of a strong though not easily found spring known as Ain el-Guderat, "The Spring of the Earthenware Kettles." Strategically, this district agrees well with what is known of Kadesh-barnea, for roads run out to north, south, east and west. The road to the south runs to Elath or Ezion-geber. The Darb el-Shur or "Way of the Wilderness of Shur" runs westward directly to Egypt and may have accentuated the longings for a return thither (cf. Numbers 14:4). Northward the same road runs to Hebron, whither the men went to spy out the land. Eastward other roads lead into the Wadi el-Arabah, the great valley which runs from the Gulf of Aqabah to the Dead Sea, and to Jebel Harun, the traditional Mount Hor, "by the border of the land of Edom," where Aaron died (Numbers 20:

---

[2] Ezion-geber is connected with Elath in Deuteronomy 2:8 and is said to be beside Eloth in I Kings 9:26. The exact connection between the two is obscure but perhaps in its later history Ezion-geber was called Elath or Eloth.

[3] According to Numbers 20:14 (JE) they still were encamped at Kadesh in their fortieth year, just previous to making the circuit of Edom. Deuteronomy 1:46 says that they "abode in Kadesh many days" but seems to imply that they spent the last 38 years of their wanderings in compassing Mount Seir and coming to the brook Zered (Deuteronomy 2:1, 14).

22-29; 33:38f.).[4] In the Wadi el-Arabah it has been possible to identify one of the points mentioned in the route of the Exodus, namely
Punon (Numbers 33:42f.). The Arabs, who cannot pronounce the
letter "P" and change it into either "B" or "F," still call the place
Feinan.[5]

From Kadesh, Moses sent messengers to the king of Edom request-
ing permission for the Israelites to pass through the land: "Thus
saith thy brother Israel . . . behold we are in Kadesh, a city in the
uttermost of thy border. Let us pass, I pray thee, through thy land . . .
we will go along the king's highway; we will not turn aside to the
right hand nor to the left, until we have passed thy border" (Numbers
20:14, 16f.). These words presuppose that at that time a strong
kingdom existed in Edom and that the land was traversed by the
"king's highway." As we have noted (p. 125) there was a flourishing
civilization in Transjordan in the Early Bronze Age. A main central
highway ran from north to south through the land at that time and
is clearly traceable by the ruins of sites dated from the twenty-third
to the twentieth centuries B.C. This was probably the line along which
the eastern kings of Genesis 14 moved when they pushed the length
of Transjordan and as far as El-paran, which may have been on the
north shore of the Gulf of Aqabah. The same route was followed by
the famous Trajan highway built by the Romans in the first part
of the second century A.D. The Roman road was paved all the way
from Aqabah to Bosrah and many sections of it still are comparatively intact. It was divided into two lanes with the middle line and
the sides marked by raised stones. The modern highway constructed
by the Government of Transjordan and known as the Sultan's Road
follows the old Roman road almost exactly. Thus the "king's highway" has a history from before the twentieth century B.C. to the twentieth century A.D.

But the Early Bronze Age civilization of Transjordan disappeared
about 1900 B.C. (p. 126) and from then until upon the eve of the
Early Iron Age there is a gap in the history of permanent sedentary
occupation in that land. Not until the beginning of the thirteenth
century did a new agricultural civilization appear belonging to the
Edomites, Moabites, Ammonites and Amorites.[6] Therefore the situ-

[4] Woolley and Lawrence, *The Wilderness of Zin.* 1936, pp.70-88.
[5] Glueck, *The Other Side of the Jordan,* p.27.
[6] ibid., pp.125-147.

ation presupposed in Numbers 20:14-17 did not exist before the thirteenth century B.C. but did prevail from that time on exactly as reflected in the Bible. If the Israelites had come through southern Transjordan at any time within the preceding 600 years they would have found neither the Edomite nor the Moabite kingdoms in existence and only scattered nomads would have disputed their passage. But coming sometime in the thirteenth century as we have reason for believing they did, they found their way blocked at the outset by the well organized and well fortified kingdom of Edom. The high, comparatively fertile and well watered plateau of Edom drops off precipitously on the south. At Khirbet Neqb Shtar on the southwestern corner of the plateau, at Khirbet Tawil Ifjeij on the eastern side, and at a series of other strategic points, the frontiers were guarded by fortresses whose ruins still are impressive. Many of them were so well located that their sites serve as major triangulation points for modern government surveys.

Thus when the ruler of Edom refused permission for the Israelites to traverse the land by the "king's highway" it became necessary for them to make their weary way around through the wilderness. It is written that when "they journeyed . . . to compass the land of Edom, . . . the soul of the people was much discouraged because of the way" (Numbers 21:4).

North of Edom was Moab. The boundary between the two countries was the Wadi Hesa, which runs into the lower corner of the Dead Sea. It is known in the Bible as the valley of Zered or the brook Zered, and the arrival of the Israelites at it is mentioned in Numbers 21:12. Moab stretched eastward from the Dead Sea to the desert and extended northward to the Wadi Mojib which is the biblical river Arnon. Like Edom, Moab was strongly fortified at strategic sites on the borders and in the interior. Therefore the Israelites had to continue to march "in the wilderness which is before Moab, toward the sunrising" (Numbers 21:11) until they reached "the other side of the Arnon" (Numbers 21:13). Beyond the Arnon (Wadi Mojib) lay the land of Gilead which was the territory of the Amorites. The king of the Amorites was Sihon, who had taken or retaken land from Moab and made Heshbon his capital city. From the River Arnon his land extended north to the River Jabbok (Judges 11:22) which is now the Wadi Zerqa. This wadi runs east from the Jordan and then turns south. The latter portion of the Wadi Zerqa, running approximately north and south, constituted the eastern border of Sihon's territory, beyond which was the kingdom of Ammon. North of the east-west stretch of the River Jabbok was the territory of King Og, which extended to the Wadi Yarmuk, not far below the Sea of Galilee. While the Israelites had laboriously to make the circuit of Edom and Moab they were able successfully to challenge Sihon and Og in battle and so to arrive at the Jordan Valley opposite Jericho (Numbers 21:21-35; 22:1; Deuteronomy 2:26-3:11).[7] Incidentally, Balaam who figures in the story at this point (Numbers 22:2-24:25) seems to have been a typical Babylonian diviner, and has been shown from parallels in Mesopotamian ritual to have proceeded with what was at the time quite an approved ceremony of divination.[8]

From the heights of Pisgah, or Mount Nebo, Moses looked upon the promised land and then died and was buried in the valley in the land of Moab (Deuteronomy 3:27; 34:1-8). Today the towers of Jerusalem and of Bethlehem are seen plainly with the naked eye when one looks westward from the high vantage points east of the Jordan River valley. Mount Nebo itself is known now as Jebel Siyaghah and on its top are the remains of a Byzantine church. A steep trail leads down from the mount to the Ayun Musa or "Springs of Moses," overlooking which are the ruins of a fortress, the Khirbet Ayun Musa, that may have been in existence in the time of Moses.[9]

JERICHO

The chief city of strategic importance commanding the entrance to Canaan from the east was Jericho. The mound which represents the Old Testament site is known now as Kom el-Sultan and rises above an oasis and a spring called Ain el-Sultan, which is the most abundant water supply in the vicinity. In the background the hills of the western highlands rise very sharply, and only a mile away the bold, 1,500-foot-high ridge called Jebel Kuruntul casts its shadow

[7] In view of our date for these events at the end of the Late Bronze Age and near the beginning of the Early Iron Age it is interesting to note that King Og is reported to have had a bedstead of iron (Deuteronomy 3:11). The term used is believed by some, however, to refer instead to a sarcophagus made of black basalt which has an iron content of about 20 per cent. S. R. Driver, *Deuteronomy* in *The International Critical Commentary*. 1895, pp.53f.
[8] Samuel Daiches in *Hilprecht Anniversary Volume*. 1909, pp.60-70; cf. W. F. Albright in JBL 63 (1944), p.231 n.141.
[9] Glueck, *The Other Side of the Jordan*, pp.143f.

upon the city in the early afternoon. This was "the mountain" to which Joshua's spies fled from Rahab's house (Joshua 2:22). Forbidding as the western barrier of the hills appears, it is actually cut by gorges which give access to the interior plateau of Palestine. Jericho's strategic significance lay in the fact that it guarded these passes.

The excavation of Jericho was first attempted by Professor Ernst Sellin and the *Deutsche Orientgesellschaft* in 1907-1909,[10] and was continued by Professor John Garstang in 1930-1936.[11] A portion of the excavated mound is shown in the foreground of Fig. 56, while in the background is the nearby oasis. The site of Jericho was occupied as early as in Neolithic times (p. 122), and in the Chalcolithic and following periods a series of successive cities stood there. The later cities are known by the alphabetical designations assigned them by Professor Garstang. City A, with a brick wall, belongs to the Early Bronze Age about 3000 B.C. City B, also protected by a wall of brick, was founded in the neighborhood of 2500, was in existence in the days of the patriarchs, and fell about 1700. City C was larger than its predecessors and boasted an important palace as well as tremendous city walls with stone glacis and outer moat. This city existed in Hyksos times and many scarabs of the Hyksos period were found in its ruins. It dates probably from around 1700 and suffered a violent destruction sometime near 1500.

City D was built probably around 1500, and is the one with which we are concerned chiefly. At this time the old palace of City C was rebuilt and the summit of the mound was refortified with a double wall of sun-dried brick. An outer wall six feet thick stood on the edge of the mound. Separated from it by a space of from twelve to fifteen feet, was the inner wall, itself twelve feet thick. The greatest preserved height of the wall is eighteen feet, and it may be thought of as having risen originally to a height of twenty-five or thirty feet. The area of the city at this time was less than six acres, and the pressure of the population led to bridging the space between the inner and outer walls with timbers and building houses upon them, as Rahab's house is said to have been located (Joshua 2:15). Actually the outer wall, which stood upon a footing of debris and bore the

---

[10] Ernst Sellin and Carl Watzinger, *Jericho*. 1913.

[11] J. Garstang in *Annals of Archaeology and Anthropology, issued by the Institute of Archaeology, University of Liverpool*. 19 (1932), pp.3-22; 20 (1933), pp.3-42; 21 (1934), pp.99-136; 22 (1935), pp.143-168; 23 (1936), pp.67-76; J. and J. B. E. Garstang, *The Story of Jericho*. 1940.

weight of the houses which rested upon it, was relatively weak and a source of danger to the city. Such was the Canaanite city of Jericho in the years of the Late Bronze Age.

Inside City D there are evidences of two destructions. The first is marked by the fall of the palace, which is believed to have taken place sometime during the fifteenth century. Over the ruins of the palace storerooms there was then erected the so-called Middle Building, whose downfall indicates the second destruction. The latter building contained fragments of painted pottery which appear to be earlier than the thirteenth century and suggest that this second destruction took place not later than around 1300.

As for the city walls, they too suffered a terrific destruction. The excavators found that the outer wall had tumbled forward down the slope of the mound, and the inner one had fallen, together with the buildings upon it, into the original space between the walls. Reddened masses of brick, cracked stones, charred timbers and ashes, showed that an intense fire had accompanied the destruction of the city. It is possible that an earthquake was the cause of the catastrophe.[12]

It is natural to conclude that this destruction of the walls of Jericho is the same as that to which reference is made in Joshua 6. Such an identification is the more probable inasmuch as the excavations indicated that after this demolition Jericho lay in ruins with no appreciable population and was not again rebuilt until the time of City E which belongs to the Iron Age. The construction of City E may well be connected with the statement in I Kings 16:34 that a man from Bethel named Hiel built Jericho in the days of Ahab.

Unfortunately, however, the date of the catastrophic destruction of the walls of the Late Bronze Age city cannot now be determined with exactitude. Father Hugues Vincent, formerly of the Dominican Biblical School in Jerusalem, has argued that Jericho fell around 1250,[13] but this is not substantiated by the latest ceramic correlations. Professor Garstang, on the other hand, has pointed to a date about 1400, because the latest scarabs found at Jericho bear the name of

---

[12] J. Garstang, *Joshua Judges, The Foundations of Bible History.* 1931, pp.144f., 404. Garstang (ibid., pp.136f.) also reckons seriously with the possibility that an earthquake was responsible for damming the Jordan temporarily at the time of the crossing by the Israelites (Joshua 3:7-17). Such an occurrence actually shut off the flow of the Jordan for over 20 hours as recently as 1927.

[13] H. Vincent in *Revue Biblique.* 44 (1935), pp.583-605.

Amenhotep III who reigned c.1413-c.1377.[14] Very few scarabs of Pharaohs between Amenhotep III and Ramesses II (c.1301-c.1234) have been found in Palestine, however, so this argument is not conclusive. Actually it is to be presumed that the walls fell either at the time of the destruction of the palace in the fifteenth century or at the time of the downfall of the Middle Building in the fourteenth century. Thus it is only the broadest limits which can be fixed with confidence for the date of the decisive destruction of the city. After going over the materials with Professor Garstang, Professor G. Ernest Wright concludes a recent study of the entire matter with the belief that the question of Jericho is more of a problem than ever, and that all that can be said about it with certainty is that the fall of the city to the Hebrews took place sometime between around 1475 and around 1300.[15]

This date would be in general agreement with the theory that the Israelites arrived in Palestine around 1400 B.C. (p. 106), but since on many other grounds it seems necessary to date their entry around 1250 B.C. we are faced by an unresolved difficulty. The only solution at present seems to be to admit that the conquest of Canaan did not proceed with quite the swiftness and uniformity with which it is represented in the book of Joshua but was the result of successive waves of invasion.[16]

In the case of the cities of Bethel, Lachish and Debir, however, we have evidence of their destruction within the thirteenth century B.C., which is in agreement with the hypothesis that the Israelite conquest was in progress at that time. These cities will be among those next to be considered.

AI AND BETHEL

The capture of Ai is described in Joshua chapters 7-8. Ai is identified with et-Tell, a site 13 miles west and somewhat north of Jericho, and 3,200 feet higher in the hill country. The place was excavated in 1933 and 1934 by Mme. Judith Marquet-Krause and the remains of an important city of the Early Bronze Age were uncovered. This city was completely destroyed and abandoned

[14] Garstang in PEQ 1941, p.170.
[15] G. E. Wright in BASOR 86 (Apr. 1942), pp.32-34; cf. BA III, 3 (Sept. 1940), pp.32-36.
[16] J. Garstang (The Heritage of Solomon. 1934, pp.222,261) supposes that the children of Israel took Jericho and entered the land about 1400 B.C. but won no further decisive victories over the Canaanites until around 1200 B.C.

about 2200 B.C. and the site was not occupied again except by a brief village settlement sometime between 1200 and 1000 B.C.[17] At the time of the Hebrew conquest, therefore, no city existed at this place. As a matter of fact, the Hebrew name Ai means "the Ruin."

The most probable explanation of the difficulty at this point lies in a confusion between Ai and Bethel. The site of the latter city is less than one and one-half miles distant from Ai, and was excavated in 1934 by a joint expedition of the American School of Oriental Research in Jerusalem and the Pittsburgh-Xenia Theological Seminary under the leadership of Professor W. F. Albright. Bethel was found to have first been occupied after the destruction of the Early Bronze Age city of Ai and to have existed as a well-built town in the Middle and Late Bronze Ages. Sometime in the thirteenth century B.C. the city was consumed by a tremendous conflagration which left behind a solid mass of burned brick, ashes and charred debris. There can be little doubt but that this destruction represents the conquest of the city by the children of Israel. In the Early Iron Age the town was rebuilt, presumably by the Israelites, and in a rude fashion as compared with the earlier Canaanite city. In the sixth century B.C. Bethel was again destroyed by fire, probably by the Chaldeans, and afterward reoccupied in the Persian and Hellenistic periods.[18]

It may be noted that in the book of Joshua no account is given of the capture of Bethel while, on the other hand, in the probably older account of Judges 1 the taking of Bethel by the house of Joseph is narrated (vv. 22-25) but nothing is said of Ai. Therefore it must be assumed that at a later date the tradition of the sack of Bethel was attached, erroneously but naturally, to the nearby and impressive ruins of Ai.[19]

LACHISH

One of the next cities to fall to the Israelites was Lachish as is told in Joshua 10:31f. The site of Lachish was sought first at Umm Lakis and then at Tell el-Hesy,[20] but finally was identified at Tell ed-Duweir.[21] Excavations were begun here by the Wellcome-Marston

[17] AJA 40 (1936), p.158.
[18] W. F. Albright in BASOR 56 (Dec. 1934), pp.2-15.
[19] W. F. Albright in BASOR 74 (Apr. 1939), pp.15-17; G. E. Wright in BA III, 3 (Sept. 1940), p.36.
[20] W. M. F. Petrie, *Tell el-Hesy (Lachish)*. 1891; F. J. Bliss, *A Mound of Many Cities*. 1894.
[21] W. F. Albright in *Zeitschrift für die alttestamentliche Wissenschaft.* 6 (1929), p.3.

Archaeological Expedition in 1933, the work being directed by J. L. Starkey until his murder by brigands January 10, 1938 (p. 6), and continued thereafter by Charles H. Inge and Lankester Harding. It was found that the site had been occupied by a cave dwellers' settlement in the Early Bronze Age and thereafter by a whole series of cities. The city with which we are concerned at this point is the Lachish of the Late Bronze Age which was standing when the Israelites came.

One of the important features of Lachish at this time was the temple, which probably was constructed in its earliest form in the first part of the fifteenth century B.C. and was rebuilt at least twice thereafter.[22] The temple had walls of stone plastered with lime, the floor was of hard clay, and the roof was supported by wooden columns. A small vestibule gave access to the sanctuary proper, where there was a raised shrine on top of which presumably the cult statue or statues stood. At the base of the shrine was a small hearth, beside it was a pottery stand to hold a bowl for libation, and near-by was a niche for lamps. Benches running around three sides of the room provided a place for the laying of offerings, for the storage of which there was also a large bin and a back storeroom. Around the shrine and in the rubbish pits connected with the building were large quantities of bones of sheep, oxen and other animals. Most of the bones were from the right foreleg, which corresponds to the prescription for Hebrew sacrifice in Leviticus 7:32.[23]

One of the lion-hunt scarabs of Amenhotep III, commemorating his feat of killing 102 lions with his own hand during the first ten years of his reign, was found at Lachish and the continuation of Egyptian dominance until in the thirteenth century was indicated by the presence of a scarab of Ramesses II. But the most important discovery for the fixing of the date when the Late Bronze Age city was destroyed, was that of a broken bowl on which had been written in Egyptian and apparently by an Egyptian tax collector a record of certain wheat deliveries. All of these were dated in the "year four"

[22] Olga Tufnell, C. H. Inge and L. Harding, *Lachish II (Tell Ed Duweir), The Fosse Temple.* 1940.

[23] G. Ernest Wright points out that such similarity between early Canaanite ritual and late priestly legislation in the Old Testament tends to support the claim that the substance of much of the ritual contained in the priestly document is very old and reflects practices of the Solomonic temple perhaps ultimately borrowed from the Canaanites (AJA 45 [1941], p.634).

of a certain Pharaoh. The character of the script points to the time of Merenptah, and it is believed almost certain that he is the Pharaoh in question. The "year four," therefore, is to be referred to his reign and is equivalent to about 1230 B.C. Since the fragments of the bowl were found, all together, in the debris of the burned city, the bowl was doubtless broken at the very time when the city fell. The destruction of Lachish thus must have taken place closely around 1230 B.C. and doubtless was the work of the Israelites just as it is stated in the Old Testament.[24]

There must be mentioned also the discovery, in the Late Bronze Age temple at Lachish, of a bowl and a jar on which were inscriptions written in an early type of Canaanite script. This script is identical with that of the proto-Sinaitic or paleo-Semitic inscriptions found at Serabit el-Khadem (p. 126). Other specimens of similar script also have come to light in Middle and Late Bronze Age levels at such Palestinian sites as Shechem (p. 140), Gezer, Tell el-Hesy, and Beth-shemesh. The Lachish inscriptions together with these others constitute very important connecting links between the proto-Sinaitic and the earliest known Phoenician forms of the alphabet.[25]

DEBIR

Debir, earlier known as Kiriath-sepher, was another city taken by the Israelites. The older narrative (Joshua 15:15-17; Judges 1:11-13) relates that it was captured for the tribe of Judah by Caleb's nephew, Othniel, while a later version of the event (Joshua 10:38f.) ascribes the conquest directly to Joshua and all Israel. Kiriath-sepher is thought to be the mound now called Tell Beit Mirsim, 13 miles southwest of Hebron. The excavation of Tell Beit Mirsim was carried out in 1926 and following years by a joint expedition of the Pittsburgh-Xenia Theological Seminary and the American School of Oriental Research at Jerusalem under the leadership of Melvin G. Kyle and William F. Albright.[26] A beautiful royal scarab of Amenhotep III

[24] W. F. Albright in BASOR 68 (Dec. 1937), pp.23f.; 74 (Apr. 1939), pp.20-22; Raymond S. Haupert in BA I, 4 (Dec. 1938), p.26.

[25] Tufnell, Inge and Harding, Lachish II (Tell Ed Duweir), The Fosse Temple, pp.47-57; W. F. Albright in BASOR 58 (Apr. 1935), pp.28f.; 63 (Oct. 1936), pp.8-12; S. Yeivin in PEQ 1937, pp.180-193; Chester C. McCown, The Ladder of Progress in Palestine. 1943, pp.100-117.

[26] Albright in Zeitschrift für die alttestamentliche Wissenschaft. 6 (1929), pp.1-17; and in The Annual of the American Schools of Oriental Research. 12 (1930-31); 13 (1931-32), pp.55-128; 17 (1936-37); 21-22 (1941-43); M. G. Kyle, Excavating Kirjath-Sepher's Ten Cities. 1934.

was found which doubtless was used by the Egyptian official at Kiriath-sepher. This is clear evidence that in the reign of Amenhotep III Egypt was still in power here and the Israelites had not yet taken possession of the land. At the end of the Late Bronze Age there is a great burned layer and above it are Israelite remains. Thus the evidences here, too, point to the arrival of the Israelites and the destruction of the Canaanite city shortly before 1200 B.C.[27]

Among the interesting discoveries made at Tell Beit Mirsim was a household stela showing a Canaanite serpent goddess. She appears as a woman clad in a long robe and with a large snake coiling around her. Exactly the same kind of representation was found on a small limestone plaque at Shechem (Balatah) in 1934 by Dr. H. Steckeweh. This plaque also carried an inscription written in the early alphabetic script of Canaan.[28]

Yet another city occupied by the Israelites was Beth-zur, according to Joshua 15:58, although no description of its capture is given. Partial excavation at Beth-zur in 1931 pointed to the conclusion that it had been destroyed and abandoned at approximately the time when the Hyksos were expelled from Egypt, and was reoccupied only at the beginning of the Iron Age, or around 1200 B.C.[29] Also mentioned in Joshua 15:27 is the city of Beth-pelet. Petrie believed that he found Beth-pelet at Tell Fara, southeast of Gaza,[30] but Albright thinks that this is more probably ancient Sharuhen.[31]

In the case, therefore, of at least some cities which the Israelites are said in the Bible to have captured, notably including Lachish and Debir, there is evidence upon the site of a destruction of the city at the end of the Late Bronze Age or shortly before 1200 B.C. The identification of this event with the conquest by the children of Israel is almost certain.

It is significant, also, to note that at the beginning of the Early Iron Age the houses and fortifications of Palestine are considerably poorer than before. Likewise the pottery shows in general a great deterioration in quality, and is little ornamental. This sudden drop in the cultural level fits well with the invasion of the Israelites from

[27] Kyle, *Excavating Kirjath-Sepher's Ten Cities*, p.192; Albright in *The Annual of the American Schools of Oriental Research*. 17 (1936-37), p.79.

[28] Albright in *The Annual of the American Schools of Oriental Research*. 17 (1936-37), Plates 21a, 22; pp.42f.

[29] Burrows, *What Mean These Stones?* p.77.

[30] W. M. F. Petrie, *Beth-pelet I (Tell Fara)*. 1930.

[31] W. F. Albright, *The Archaeology of Palestine and the Bible*. 2d ed. 1933, p.53.

the desert, any cultivation of the arts among whom would have suffered during the long years in the wilderness. The characteristic city walls as built by the Israelites were only five, six or seven feet in width, because with their looser patriarchal form of society there was no systematic coercion of the individual and it was not possible to make the people submit to the prolonged and difficult labor of constructing a massive city wall.[32]

Remembering, however, that Jericho must have fallen in an earlier wave of conquest (p. 136) than this in which Lachish and Debir were destroyed, we must guard against oversimplifying the picture of the invasion. As a matter of fact there are indications in the Old Testament that the subjugation of the entire land was not immediate and complete. Certain later summaries of the conquest, to be sure, picture it as a swift, united effort of all Israel under the leadership of Joshua and state that Joshua himself "took the whole land" (Joshua 11:16-23; cf. 10:40-43). Fragments of earlier records survive, however, to indicate that the invasion and settlement of Palestine by the Israelites actually was a slower, more difficult and more scattering enterprise. In Judges 1:1-2:5 there are portions of an old account of the conquest of Canaan by the individual efforts of the separate tribes where the positive successes of the tribes of Judah and Simeon (1:1-20) and of the house of Joseph (1:22-26) are narrated but where the failures of other tribes, including Manasseh, Ephraim, Zebulun, Asher, Naphtali and Dan (1:27-36), to dispossess the native inhabitants are frankly admitted.[33] Among the cities here listed as not taken by the Hebrews are to be recognized some of the well-known and powerful forts of the Canaanites, such as Beth-shean, Taanach, Megiddo (Judges 1:27), Gezer (Judges 1:29) and Beth-shemesh (Judges 1:33). From discoveries at these sites we may learn

---

[32] ibid., p.102.

[33] Even here the more ancient account may have been edited to some extent. The words, "And it came to pass after the death of Joshua," are an introduction to the book of Judges. Judah has been substituted for Caleb in 1:10, contrast 1:20b; Joshua 15: 13-19; and Benjamin for Judah in 1:21, contrast Joshua 15:63. The attribution to Judah of the conquest of Jerusalem (1:8) is incorrect (contrast 1:21), for Jerusalem was first taken by David (II Samuel 5:6-10). The statement concerning the conquest of the Philistine cities, Gaza, Ashkelon and Ekron (1:18) is also incorrect and contradicted by 1:19. Finally, the explanation of the name Bochim, i.e. "Weepers," in 2:1-5, may be an expression of the editor's indignation at the failure of the Israelites to exterminate the Canaanites. S. R. Driver, An Introduction to the Literature of the Old Testament. 1913, p.162; Robert H. Pfeiffer, Introduction to the Old Testament. 1941, pp.316f.

more of the Canaanite culture into the midst of which the Israelites had come.

BETH-SHEAN

Beth-shean, also known as Beth-shan or Beisan, and later the Hellenistic city of Scythopolis, is identified with the imposing mound Tell el-Husn above the Jordan in the valley of Jezreel. Excavations have been conducted on the site by the University Museum of the University of Pennsylvania under the leadership of Clarence S. Fisher, Alan Rowe and G. M. Fitzgerald. The Canaanite city here was found to have been fortified with double walls, as was Jericho, and the inner and outer walls were connected with cross walls which formed small rooms. The fortifications included a strong tower, built with large unbaked bricks on a foundation of basalt blocks. Beth-shean was occupied by Egyptian garrisons down at least to the time of Ramesses III. An Egyptian stela of Sethi I (c.1319-c.1301 B.C.) was found there which refers to the 'Apiru of some mountain district with a Semitic name. As we have noted (p. 57) the supposed relationship of the Habiru, the 'Apiru and the Hebrews is not yet clear and therefore it cannot be said with confidence whether this means that pre-Israelite Hebrews already were in the highlands.[34]

No less than four Canaanite temples have been excavated at Beth-shean: one, of the seventh city level which is ascribed to the thirteenth century B.C.; another, of the sixth level which dates in the twelfth and early eleventh centuries; and two of the fifth level belonging to the eleventh and tenth centuries. Since the last two temples continued in use until approximately the tenth century it has been suggested that the Southern Temple may have been the Temple of Dagon of I Chronicles 10:10, and the Northern Temple may have been the House of Ashtaroth of I Samuel 31:10. Serpents played an important part in the cult here too (cf. p. 140) and plaques with serpents and shrine-houses with serpents on them were found in the temples.[35]

TAANACH

Taanach still bears the name Tell Taanak and attracted the attention of Professor Ernst Sellin of Vienna on a visit to Palestine as

---

[34] Albright, *From the Stone Age to Christianity*, p.211.
[35] Alan Rowe, *The Four Canaanite Temples of Beth-shan.* I (1940); G. E. Wright in AJA 45 (1941), pp.483-485.

early as 1899. His excavations there in 1902 and 1903 were the first to be carried out in northern Palestine.[36] Taanach was found to have been fortified with stone walls built in the so-called Cyclopean style of masonry (p. 125) and the remains of a fourteenth century B.C. palace of a Canaanite king were uncovered. Tablets unearthed at Taanach contain the interesting expression, "If the finger of Ashirat points," which is interpreted as meaning that oracles were given in the name of a goddess Ashirat, who probably is the same as the goddess Asherat known from Ras Shamra (pp. 147f.). The Asherim mentioned in the Old Testament may have been wooden symbols, perhaps trees or poles, of this goddess (Exodus 34:13; Deuteronomy 16:21; I Kings 14:23; II Kings 17:10; 18:4; 23:14), while she herself probably is referred to in other passages (Judges 3:7; I Kings 15:13; 18:19; II Kings 21:7; 23:4, 6, 7).[37] Later brick houses whose ruins were found at Taanach may represent the eventual Israelite settlement there.[38] In a building which may have been a private house of Hebrew times was found a terra-cotta incense altar possibly used by the Israelites in worship.[39]

MEGIDDO

Commanding the best pass from the Mediterranean coastal plain to the Valley of Esdraelon and on north to Galilee and Damascus, Megiddo always has been a point of great strategic importance. This was where Thutmose III met the Asiatics (p. 89) and where Josiah was slain by Necho (p. 114). It was through the same pass that Allenby's cavalry surprised the Turkish armies in 1918,[40] and it is here that the book of Revelation expects "the war of the great day of God, the Almighty" (16:14, 16).

The modern name of the site of Megiddo is Tell el-Mutesellim (Fig. 57), and Dr. G. Schumacher of the *Deutsche Orientgesell-*

[36] E. Sellin, *Tell Ta 'annek*. 1904.

[37] Burrows, *What Mean These Stones?* p.231. Numerous nude female figurines have been found in most Palestinian excavations of the second and first millenniums B.C., and it is possible that they are representations of Asherah or of other similar Canaanite goddesses such as Ashtart or Anat (James B. Pritchard, *Palestinian Figurines in Relation to Certain Goddesses Known through Literature*. 1943; cf. G. E. Wright in JBL 63 [1944], pp.426-430).

[38] Duncan, *Digging Up Biblical History*. I, p.181.

[39] Barton, *Archaeology and the Bible*, p.221.

[40] It is a well-known fact that Allenby depended chiefly upon the Bible and upon *The Historical Geography of the Holy Land* by George Adam Smith for information concerning the topography of Palestine. cf. David S. Cairns in *Religion in Life*. 11 (1942), pp.532f.

schaft first drove an exploratory trench into it in 1903-1905.[41] Large-scale systematic horizontal clearance of the site was begun by the Oriental Institute of the University of Chicago under the direction of Clarence S. Fisher in 1925 and continued in succeeding years by P. L. O. Guy and by Gordon Loud. It appears that in the Early Bronze Age, Megiddo was surrounded by a massive city wall, originally some 13 feet thick and later strengthened to twice that thickness. A mud brick wall and gate of about 1800 B.C. are known, and the present indications are that the Canaanite city was destroyed near the end of the twelfth century, while the Israelite occupation, represented for example by the mud brick wall of Level V, began about a half century later.

In 1937 Gordon Loud explored the palace of the princes who ruled at Megiddo as vassals of the Pharaohs of Egypt. The palace showed five building periods, running from the sixteenth into the twelfth century B.C., and the fifth palace had a subterranean treasury in which a wonderful find of more than 200 carved and incised ivories was made. One of these was an ivory pen case belonging to an Egyptian who bore the title, "Royal Envoy to every Foreign Country." It is to be dated just after 1200 B.C. since it carries the cartouche of Ramesses III. Another is an ivory plaque which shows the prince of Megiddo probably celebrating a victory (Fig. 58). At the right he drives naked captives before his chariot. At the left he sits upon his sphinx-sided throne and drinks from a bowl while a musician, "a David of his court," plays upon the harp. At the extreme left is a large jar, with animal heads.[42]

GEZER

The site of Gezer was identified at Tell Jezer by Professor Clermont-Ganneau in the nineteenth century, and the city was excavated for the Palestine Exploration Fund by Professor R. A. S. Macalister in 1902-1908.[43] Gezer is well situated on the lower slope of hills above the maritime plain to guard the western frontier. Cave dwellers lived here at an early time in natural rock caverns, and apparently practiced the cremation of their dead. In the Early Bronze Age several of the caves were used for interments as the

[41] G. Schumacher and C. Steuernagel, *Tell El-Mutesellim.* 1908.

[42] Loud, *The Megiddo Ivories.* 1939; C. De Mertzenfeld in *Syria.* 19 (1938), pp.345-354.

[43] Macalister, *The Excavation of Gezer.* 3 vols. 1912.

inhabitants gradually shifted to homes on the rock surface above.[44] Later the city was fortified with a brick wall, and still later with a 13-foot-thick stone wall. After the destruction of the latter, its materials were employed in the construction of what is now known as the outer wall, 14 feet thick and enclosing an area of 27 acres. One hundred and twenty feet below the present surface of the ground and 94 feet below the surface of the rock is a spring in a cave to which a tunnel was cut to enable the people of the city to obtain water in time of siege.

In the northern part of the city and above one of the caves in which early burials were made is a row of standing stones (Fig. 59) which have elicited much interest. Originally the series consisted of ten rough stone pillars varying in height from five to ten feet, and standing in a slightly curved line from north to south. At the time of discovery one was fallen and two were broken off at the bottom, but the remainder still stood upright. At a point near the middle of the row and just to one side was a stone base with a rectangular depression in which doubtless yet another stela once stood. The area containing these standing stones has been regarded as of cultic significance and interpreted as a Canaanite "high place,"[45] but it now appears more probable that the pillars were simply memorial stones of the kings of the city.[46]

BETH-SHEMESH

Beth-shemesh, now known as Ain Shems or Tell er-Rumeileh, and lying southeast of Gezer in the Shephelah, was the next site after Gezer whose excavation was undertaken by the Palestine Exploration Fund. The work was directed by Dr. Duncan Mackenzie during the years 1911-1912 and was the last Palestinian excavation just before the First World War.[47] Further excavations have been carried out since 1928 by Professor Elihu Grant of Haverford College.[48] It appears that the site was occupied by a series of cities between 2000 and 600 B.C., final destruction having probably come from the army of Nebuchadnezzar II of Babylon. Fine pottery, weapons, jewelry and scarabs were uncovered from the late Canaanite and early

[44] G. E. Wright in PEQ 1937, pp.67-78.
[45] R. A. S. Macalister, *Bible Side-Lights from the Mound of Gezer*. 1906, pp.57-65.
[46] Carl Watzinger, *Denkmäler Palästinas*. I (1933), pp.63f.
[47] R. A. S. Macalister, *A Century of Excavation in Palestine*. 1930, p.69.
[48] E. Grant, *Beth Shemesh* (1929); *Ains Shems Excavations*. 5 vols. 1931-39.

Israelite periods and further illustration of Canaanite religion appeared in a plaque with a serpent goddess.

RAS SHAMRA

The insights which Palestinian archeology has been giving as to Canaanitish culture and religion have been greatly supplemented by recent discoveries in Syria, particularly at Ras Shamra. This is a site on the northern coast of Syria, opposite the island of Cyprus, which was discovered almost by chance in 1929 and studied since that date in a series of campaigns conducted by C. F. A. Schaeffer.[49] The site was already occupied in the Neolithic Age, to which time the plain pottery of the lowest level belongs.[50] As early as the second millennium B.C. the city is called by the name Ugarit and it is mentioned in Egyptian inscriptions, in the Tell el-Amarna letters and in Hittite documents. In the days of the Twelfth Dynasty, Egyptian influence was strong, as is shown by the finding of a statue of the wife of Senwosret II and two sphinxes sent by Amenemhet III. In the fifteenth and fourteenth centuries Ugarit flourished greatly but was overwhelmed by an earthquake about the middle of the fourteenth century. After the earthquake the city again prospered, being first under the dominance of the Hittites but coming again under Egyptian authority with Ramesses II. Toward the close of the thirteenth or beginning of the twelfth century the city suffered invasion from the peoples of the north and from the sea, and after the twelfth century Ugarit ceased to exist.

The discovery of revolutionary importance at Ras Shamra was that of documents in a library which had been housed in a building situated between the city's two great temples, one dedicated to Baal and the other to Dagon. Hundreds of clay tablets were uncovered, dating from the fifteenth and early fourteenth centuries, and bearing texts in a cuneiform alphabet which is the earliest known alphabet written with wedge-shaped signs. The language was recognized by Professor H. Bauer of the University of Halle to be of Semitic

[49] C. F. A. Schaeffer in *Syria* 10 (1929), pp.285-297; 12 (1931), pp.1-14; 13 (1932), pp.1-27; 14 (1933), pp.93-127; 15 (1934), pp.105-131; 16 (1935), pp.141-176; 17 (1936), pp.105-149; 18 (1937), pp.125-154; 19 (1938), pp.193-255,313-334; 20 (1939), pp.277-292; *The Cuneiform Texts of Ras Shamra-Ugarit* (1939); Johannes Friedrich, *Ras Schamra, ein Überblick über Funde und Forschungen* (*Der Alte Orient* 33, 1/2, 1933).

[50] C. F. A. Schaeffer, *Ugaritica, études relatives aux découvertes de Ras Shamra.* Première Série, 1939, pp.3-8; T. H. Gaster in *Antiquity.* 13 (1939), p.306.

origin and its decipherment was finally accomplished by Bauer and the French scholars É. Dhorme and C. Virolleaud. Known as Ugaritic, this language is closely related both to biblical Hebrew and to Phoenician. Most of the Ras Shamra texts are poetic in form, and the Ugaritic poetry exhibits exactly the same characteristic feature of parallelism as does Hebrew poetry. This may be seen in an example such as the following:

> The heavens rain oil
> The wadies run with honey.[51]

The majority of the documents under consideration are in the nature of mythological poems concerning Canaanite gods and heroes, but some of the texts deal with other subjects including even the treatment of sick and infirm horses. Incidentally, one of the remedies mentioned in this "veterinary manual" is a sort of pressed fig-cake which is similar to what Isaiah ordered for Hezekiah's boil (II Kings 20:1-8). The early Canaanitish beliefs which are reflected in the religious and mythological texts are of the greatest interest, and the discussion of them and their evident relationship with many of the religious beliefs and practices reflected in the Old Testament has already elicited an extensive literature.[52] The supreme god is known as El, a name by which God is called in the Old Testament.[53] On a stela found at Ras Shamra the god El is shown seated upon a throne with the king of Ugarit presenting an offering before him (Fig. 60). The god is represented as mature in age and paternal and majestic in appearance. The wife of El is Asherat-of-the-Sea, the counselor of the gods, and their son is the god Baal. Baal is a god of the rain and storm and is represented on a Ras Shamra stela brandishing a mace in his right hand and holding in his left hand a stylized thunderbolt ending in a spear-head (Fig. 61). One of his titles is "Zabul [Prince],

[51] Cyrus H. Gordon, *The Loves and Wars of Baal and Anat and Other Poems from Ugarit.* 1943, pp.xi,10.

[52] Charles Virolleaud in *Antiquity* 5 (1931), pp.405-414; William C. Graham in *The Journal of Religion* 14 (1934), pp.306-329; Walter G. Williams in *The American Journal of Semitic Languages and Literatures* 51 (1934-35), pp.233-246; J. W. Jack, *The Ras Shamra Tablets, Their Bearing on the Old Testament.* 1935; Ditlef Nielsen, *Ras Šamra Mythologie und biblische Theologie (Abhandlungen für die Kunde des Morgenlandes, Deutsche morgenländische Gesellschaft.* 21 [1936] No.4); René Dussaud, *Les découvertes de Ras Shamra (Ugarit) et l'Ancien Testament.* 1937; Samuel H. Hooke, *The Origins of Early Semitic Ritual.* 1938, pp.28-38; J. Philip Hyatt in BA II, 1 (Feb. 1939), pp.2-8; John H. Patton, *Canaanite Parallels in the Book of Psalms.* 1944; H. L. Ginsberg in BA VIII, 2 (May, 1945).

[53] Genesis 33:20, and frequently in the plural of majesty, *Elohim.*

Lord of the Earth," and this doubtless has survived in the name of the god Baal-zebub in II Kings (1:2, etc.) and of Beelzebub in the New Testament (Mark 3:22, etc.). Asherat probably is to be identified with Asherah in the Old Testament (p. 143), and Baal of course figures prominently there. Asherat is mentioned regularly after Baal in the Ras Shamra texts and the similar and close connection of the two is likewise reflected in I Kings 18:19 and II Kings 23:4.[54] Among the adventures related of Baal in the Ras Shamra tablets is a conflict with Lotan, "the nimble serpent . . . the sinuous serpent, the mighty one with seven heads." Lotan is the same as the Hebrew Leviathan that is described in similar terms in Isaiah 27:1 (cf. Job 26:12f.).

Baal or Aliyan Baal figures prominently in the mythology made known by the Ras Shamra tablets. Aliyan represents the growth of plants, and fights against Mot, the god of the dried-up summer soil, but is slain by him. Thereupon the goddess Anat, the sister and lover of Aliyan, goes in search of him, recovers his body and slays his enemy, Mot. Aliyan is then brought back to life and placed on Mot's throne so that he may ensure the revival of vegetation in another season.[55]

An interesting legend is written on four large tablets found at Ras Shamra, one of which is shown in Fig. 62. This is the Legend of Keret and tells of the time when El entrusted Keret with the command of "the army of the Negeb."

One rite is mentioned in the Ras Shamra texts in which the seething of a kid in milk is prescribed as an item in the magical technique for producing the early rains. This procedure is practically what the Israelites are forbidden to carry out, in Exodus 23:19; 34:26. A wise hero Daniel is mentioned who is identified by some with the Daniel mentioned in Ezekiel 14:14. Such biblical words occur as "anoint" from which "Messiah" is derived, and also the expression for "bring good tidings." The *rpem* or *rpum* are mentioned frequently, these probably being the same as the Old Testament *rephaim*, the "shades" or inhabitants of the world of the dead (Job 26:5, etc.).

Such are a few of the glimpses given us by the Ras Shamra tablets of the religion which prevailed among the Canaanites of Ugarit at a time only shortly before the period when the Israelites entered Palestine. This religion was polytheistic, mythological and ritualistic,

[54] H. Bauer in *Zeitschrift für die alttestamentliche Wissenschaft*. 10 (1933), p.89.
[55] W. F. Albright, *Archaeology and the Religion of Israel*. 1942, pp.84-90.

and was centered to a large degree in interest in the fertility of the soil. When the Hebrews came in contact with this environment they evidently adopted some of the customs and beliefs of their neighbors, but through the leadership of the prophets were able to rise superior to the grosser features of the Canaanite fertility religion.

JERUSALEM

Jerusalem was captured by the Israelites under David and made the capital of the Hebrew kingdom (II Samuel 5:6-10; I Chronicles 11:4-9). The city has a strategic location of exceptional strength. Its site is a rocky plateau with two promontories running south from it. Between these two rocky ridges is the valley El-Wad, which in Roman times was known as the Tyropoeon. On the east is the valley of the Kidron, and on the south and west the valley of Hinnom. Two springs provide water. One, an intermittent spring known as Gihon (now Ain Sitti Maryam or "Fountain of the Virgin"), is at the foot of the eastern hill in the Kidron Valley. The other, known as En-rogel (now Bir Aiyub or "Job's Well") is farther distant, at the point where the valleys of Kidron and Hinnom join, and beneath the hill where the modern village of Silwan (Siloah) stands.[56] An interesting discovery in connection with the Gihon spring was made by Charles Warren in the earliest explorations at Jerusalem by the Palestine Exploration Fund. He found that the early inhabitants of Jerusalem had made a rock-cut passage, similar to the one at Gezer (p. 145), to enable them to secure water from the spring without going outside the city walls. From the cave in which the Gihon spring empties,[57] a horizontal tunnel was driven back into the hill, some 36 feet west and 25 feet north. This led the spring waters back into an old cave, which thus served as a reservoir. Running up from this was a vertical shaft perhaps 40 feet high, at the top of which was a platform on which the women could stand to lower and lift their water vessels. From this a sloping passage ran on up to open within the city walls. This probably constituted the water system which was in use by the Jebusites who occupied Jerusalem through the period of the Judges (Judges 19:10f.) and in the time of David. The account of David's

[56] Baedeker, *Palestine and Syria*, pp.83f.
[57] Actually its source is a great crack in the rock at the bottom of the valley, at the eastern end of which a wall was built by some of the earliest inhabitants of the place which compels the water to flow into the cave rather than emptying into the valley.

capture of the city includes the words (II Samuel 5:8), "Whosoever smiteth the Jebusites, let him get up to the water course," which makes it seem possible that access to the city was first gained when Joab (I Chronicles 11:6) penetrated this tunnel.[58]

Thus "the stronghold of Zion," as the city of the Jebusites was called became "the city of David" (II Samuel 5:7, 9), and the capital of the Hebrew nation. It is quite certain that Zion was the lower eastern hill at Jerusalem and that David's city was situated on the portion of the hill known as Ophel or "hump" (II Chronicles 27:3, etc.) above the Virgin's Spring.[59] Excavations at Zion have revealed a strong stone wall which was broken through violently, and it may be that this is the breach made by David in his assault on the city. Behind the breach a lighter wall was built which perhaps was put there by David as a temporary barricade, and may have been the work referred to in II Samuel 5:9. Above the breach a fortress tower was finally built, which filled the gap in the wall and used the fallen stones of the breach as a foundation. This may have been the "Millo" which was built by Solomon (I Kings 9:15, 24; 11:27).[60]

Solomon may also have included the western hill inside "the wall of Jerusalem round about" which he constructed (I Kings 3:1; cf. 9:15). In early excavations on the western hill, walls were found which may have been the work of Solomon. The most famous building of Solomon, of course, was the temple,[61] which he began to construct in the fourth year of his reign (I Kings 6:1). According to II Chronicles 3:1 this was on Mount Moriah at a place where Ornan (or Araunah) the Jebusite had had a threshing floor. The threshing

[58] Macalister, A Century of Excavation in Palestine, pp.173-178; and in CAH III, p.343. This interpretation rests upon the usual translation in II Samuel 5:8 as "water course" or "water shaft." Since the meaning of this Hebrew word is much debated, however, the theory must be held only tentatively. Duncan (Digging Up Biblical History. I, p.15) thinks that the word refers to the funnel entrance from within the city to a large cave which also has an eastern exit in the hill above the Gihon spring.

[59] George Adam Smith, Jerusalem. 1908, I, pp.134f.,161f.; II, p.39. Josephus (War. v, iv, 1; Ant. VII, iii, 2) and later tradition erroneously located the city of David on the western hill and this error is preserved in modern names like that of "David's Tower" near the Jaffa Gate which probably actually stands on the base of Herod's Tower of Phasael.

[60] If Millo was built first by Solomon, its mention in II Samuel 5:9 must be regarded as meaning that David built from the point where later Millo stood. On the other hand, Solomon's work might have been that of rebuilding an earlier structure, known already in David's time as Millo.

[61] G. E. Wright in BA IV, 2 (May 1941), pp.17-31; VII, 4 (Dec. 1944), pp.73-77.

floor had been purchased earlier by David for the erection of an altar at the time of pestilence (II Samuel 24:15-25). Moriah is also named in Genesis 22:2 as the place where Abraham went to offer Isaac.

The site lies today within the sacred enclosure of the Moslems known as the Haram esh-Sherif, "the Noble Sanctuary." The most striking natural feature is a great outcropping of rock some 58 feet long, 51 feet broad and 4 to 6½ feet high. This is known as es-Sakhra or the sacred Rock, and today is covered by a structure called the Kubbet es-Sakhra ("Dome of the Rock"). The Dome of the Rock is shown in Fig. 63 and in Fig. 64 we look down from within the balcony of the Dome upon the sacred rock enclosed as it now is by a wooden screen. Evidently the rock was used as an altar in very ancient times, since channels can still be traced on it; they may have conducted the blood of the sacrificial animals to an opening and on down to a cavity below. The rock itself most likely served as Araunah's threshing floor, since presumably the strongest breeze for the threshing was found on it. Therefore David's altar probably was erected on the very rock.[62] On the other hand, it is possible to suppose that the relatively large and level area directly east of the rock provided a better surface for the work of threshing, and became the site of the altar. In the latter and somewhat less probable case it was the Holy of Holies which eventually arose over the sacred rock itself.[63]

The building of the temple required seven years, while thirteen years were spent by Solomon in the building of his own palace (I Kings 6:38; 7:1). Phoenician craftsmen and workers were supplied for these enterprises by Hiram of Tyre (I Kings 5:1-12) and doubtless the work was of a character unusually imposing in Palestine. The buildings are described in detail in the Old Testament[64] but, save for the great ancient rock, almost everything connected with them has been lost to us.

[62] A. T. Olmstead, *Jesus in the Light of History.* 1942, p.85; G. Dalman, *Neue Petra-Forschungen und Der heilige Felsen von Jerusalem.* 1912, pp.133-145; Floyd V. Filson in BA VII, 4 (Dec. 1944), p.81.

[63] F. J. Hollis, *The Archaeology of Herod's Temple, with a Commentary on the Tractate "Middoth."* 1934, pp.84-86,99; Hans Schmidt, *Der Heilige Fels in Jerusalem.* 1933, pp.26,55. cf. below p.247.

[64] I Kings 6:1-7:51; II Chronicles 3:1-5:1. Ezekiel's vision of the future temple (40:1-44:3) probably was based on his memories of the first temple before its destruction in 587 B.C. cf. Watzinger, *Denkmäler Palästinas.* I, pp.88-95. A description of Solomon's temple, in which the biblical account is amplified somewhat, is given by Josephus, *Ant.* VIII, iii.

THE STABLES AT MEGIDDO

Solomon is also known to have rebuilt the city of Megiddo (I Kings 9:15). In view of the king's well-known interest in horses and chariots (I Kings 10:26-29; II Chronicles 1:14-17) it was a matter of great interest to discover extensive stables in the excavation of Megiddo. A photograph of them is shown in Fig. 65. It is evident that they were composed of units built on a standard plan. Stone pillars, with holes in their corners, separated the horses and served as hitching-posts. Stone mangers were provided, and the ground on which the horses stood was paved with rough stones to prevent hoofs from slipping.

The date of these stables has not been determined with certainty, and it is believed by some that they were the work of the warrior king Ahab (cf. p. 172) rather than of Solomon.[65] The most authoritative study of the chronology of Megiddo, however, places Stratum IV in which the stables were found, at least partly within the reign of Solomon, and it remains probable that these famous structures really belonged to that king.[66]

EZION-GEBER

In I Kings 9:26 (cf. 9:27f.; 10:11, 22) it is recorded that Solomon furthermore built a fleet of ships at Ezion-geber, beside Eloth, on the shore of the Red Sea. This seaport city of the king has been discovered and excavated at Tell Kheleifeh at the head of the Gulf of Aqabah (cf. p. 129).[67] The city was built on a carefully chosen and hitherto unoccupied site, according to plans which had been worked out in advance. The site selected was between the hills of Edom on the east and the hills of Palestine on the west, where the north winds blow most steadily and strongly down the center of the Wadi el-Arabah. This was because Ezion-geber was to be not only a seaport but also an important industrial city. An elaborate complex of industrial plants, devoted to the smelting and refining of copper and iron and the manufacturing of metal articles for markets at home and abroad, was uncovered there. The furnace rooms were set at an angle

[65] J. W. Crowfoot in PEQ 1940, pp.143-147.

[66] W. F. Albright in AJA 44 (1940), pp.546-550; and in *The Annual of the American Schools of Oriental Research.* 21-22 (1941-43), p.2 n.1; Robert M. Engberg in BA IV, 1 (Feb. 1941), pp.12f.

[67] Glueck, *The Other Side of the Jordan,* pp.50-113; and in *The National Geographic Magazine* 85 (Jan.-June 1944), pp.233-256.

carefully calculated to get the full benefit of the winds from the north and to utilize these to furnish the draft for the fires. Ezion-geber was able to draw upon the important mineral deposits which are found in the Wadi el-Arabah all the way from the Gulf of Aqabah to the Dead Sea, and a series of mining centers of Solomon's time is known where these ores were dug and subjected to an initial smelting process. The mines of the Wadi el-Arabah were probably used first by the Kenites, whose name means "smiths,"[68] and the related Kenizzites, from whom in turn the Edomites learned mining and metallurgy. When David subjugated the Edomites (II Samuel 8:13f.; I Kings 11:15f.; I Chronicles 18:11f.) he may well have continued to exploit these mines, but it was Solomon who had the ability and power to put the mining industry in the Wadi el-Arabah on a truly national scale. Ezion-geber still belonged to the domain of Judah in the days of King Jotham, and a signet seal ring inscribed with the name of the latter was found there recently in the stratum belonging to the eighth century B.C.[69]

THE GEZER CALENDAR

In Canaan itself agriculture, of course, always remained far more important than industry. A side-light on Palestinian agriculture comes from the Gezer calendar. This is a small limestone tablet which was found at Gezer and comes probably from a time around 925 B.C. It seems to be simply a schoolboy's exercise, but it contains a list of the various months and the agricultural work done in them:

> His two months are [olive] harvest; his two months are
> grain-planting; his two months are late planting;
> his month is hoeing up of flax;
> his month is barley harvest;
> his month is harvest and festivity;
> his two months are vine-tending;
> his month is summer-fruit.[70]

In view of the oppression which the peasantry endured at the hands of Solomon and which contributed to the division of the kingdom after his death, some interest attaches to an inscription on an Aramean stela of King Kilamuwa which reads: "Before the former

[68] A. H. Sayce in HDB II, p.834.
[69] AJA 45 (1941), p.117.
[70] W. F. Albright in BASOR 92 (Dec. 1943), pp.16-26.

kings the Muskabim [peasant farmers] crawled like dogs, but I [Kilamuwa] was a father to one, a mother to another."[71]

Unfortunately Rehoboam was not as wise as this Kilamuwa, and the great kingdom of Solomon broke into two parts (I Kings 12:1-20). Jeroboam, a political exile in Egypt in Solomon's time (I Kings 12:2), returned to lead the revolt of the northern tribes. Egypt itself, which had entered into an alliance with Solomon (I Kings 3:1), now took advantage of the divided and weakened kingdom, and invaded Palestine. Shishak (Sheshonk I), founder of the Twenty-second Dynasty, plundered Jerusalem in the fifth year of King Rehoboam (I Kings 14:25f.) and also conquered other cities both in Judah and Israel, a record of which exploits was duly inscribed at Karnak (p. 113). Among the cities mentioned in the Karnak inscription was Megiddo, and in the excavation of Megiddo a fragment of a stela of Shishak was found.[72]

SAMARIA

While Jeroboam lived first at Shechem (I Kings 12:25) and then at Tirzah (I Kings 14:17), his fifth successor, Omri, built a new capital on the hill Samaria. This hill, whose name probably means "Watch-Mountain," rises 300 or 400 feet above the valley and provided a strong strategic site for the capital of northern Israel. Excavations were carried out at Samaria in 1908-1910 by Harvard University under the leadership of G. A. Reisner, C. S. Fisher and D. G. Lyon,[73] and this work was continued in 1931-1933 under the direction of J. W. Crowfoot in a joint expedition in which Harvard University, the Hebrew University in Jerusalem, the Palestine Exploration Fund, the British Academy, and the British School of Archaeology in Jerusalem participated. Yet further work was done in 1935 by the three last-named institutions.[74]

The stratigraphy of Israelite times has been clarified by the recent excavations, and the following periods are now recognized: I and II, the Omri-Ahab Dynasty; III, the time of Jehu, who wrought havoc

---

[71] Duncan, *Digging Up Biblical History*. II, p.132.

[72] R. S. Lamon and G. M. Shipton, *Megiddo I, Seasons of 1925-34, Strata I-V*. 1939, p.61.

[73] Reisner, Fisher and Lyon, *Harvard Excavations at Samaria 1908-1910*. 2 vols. 1924.

[74] J. W. Crowfoot, Kathleen M. Kenyon and E. L. Sukenik, *The Buildings at Samaria*. 1942.

thcrc (II Kings 10:17); and IV to VI, the time of the eighth century when the city was most prosperous.

Omri and Ahab evidently levelled the top of the hill, banked its sides, and built inner and outer walls with geomètrical precision around the summit. Later walls were built on the middle terraces and also on the lower slopes of the hill, thus rendering the city exceedingly well fortified. These walls constitute a graphic commentary on the two sieges which Samaria underwent, the first when the city held out against the Syrians to the terrible lengths described in II Kings 6:24-30, and the second when Samaria withstood the mighty Assyrians for so long before succumbing (II Kings 17:5). The city has also been found to have been provided with a number of large cisterns which were very important in time of siege since there is no natural water supply.

The Hebrew kings built their palaces within the walls on the western brow of the hill. The first palace was relatively simple but served as a core for later and more splendid structures. The palace which hitherto has been ascribed to Ahab, but perhaps belonged to Jeroboam II instead, was built from large blocks of limestone, and boasted a strong rectangular tower and an extensive outer court. At the north end of the palace courtyard was a cemented water pool, which may even have been the "pool of Samaria" in which the blood-stained chariot of Ahab was washed (I Kings 22:38).

It is probably from the time of the reign of Jeroboam II in the first part of the eighth century that the famous Samaritan ostraca come.[75] These are potsherds with writing on them, which were found in a storehouse in one of the palaces. They contain notes or accounts of oil and wine received as royal revenue for the king. A typical one reads:

> In the tenth year.
> To Gaddiyau.
> From Azah.
> Abi-ba'al 2
> Ahaz 2
> Sheba 1
> Meriba'al 1

In this case Gaddiyau was the steward of the treasury to whom the wine was sent, Azah the name of the village or district, and the other

[75] J. W. Jack, *Samaria in Ahab's Time*. 1929, pp.37-105; McCown, *The Ladder of Progress in Palestine*, p.199.

names those of the peasant farmers who paid their taxes in the form
of so many jars of wine. The stewards frequently have names which
are used also in the Bible, such as Ahinoam, Gamar (Gomer), and
Nimshi. Too, the senders of contributions often have biblical names,
as do Ahaz, Sheba and Meribaal in the ostracon quoted above. The
name Meribaal and many other names compounded with Baal testify
to the prevalence of Baal-worship. It will be remembered that
Meribbaal is the name borne by Jonathan's son, for which Mephi-
bosheth (*bosheth* meaning "shame") later was substituted when it
came to be felt wrong to use the title Baal (lord) in connection with
the God of Israel.[76] On the other hand many of the names have *Yahu*
as an element, thus suggesting that the divine name Yahweh
(Jehovah) was often used in personal names at this time. The
ostraca also mention over twenty place-names in the northern kingdom, six of which—Abiezer, Helek, Shechem, Shemida, Noah and
Hoglah—appear as names of clans in the Old Testament (Joshua
17:2; Numbers 26:30-33). Two more of the ostraca may be quoted
since they provide a commentary on Amos 6:6:

> In the tenth year.
> From Abiezer to Shemariyo.
> A jar of old wine.
> To Ish-Ba'al [?].
> A jar of old wine.
> From Tetel.

> In the tenth year. From Azzah.
> To Gaddiyo. A jar of fine
> oil.

The old wine or "pure clarified wine," and the fine oil used probably
for anointing the body, which are specified here, are exactly the
things whose use by the luxurious and selfish rich people of Samaria
is mentioned and condemned by the prophet.[77]

In view of the similar denunciation by Amos (6:4; 3:15) of the
"beds of ivory" and "houses of ivory" of the rich people of Samaria
and the mention in I Kings 22:39 of the "ivory house" which Ahab
(871-852 B.C.) built, it is of much interest that numerous ivories
were found in the excavation of Samaria. These are mostly in the

---

[76] I Chronicles 8:34; 9:40; II Samuel 4:4; 9:6, 10, etc.; cf. HDB II, pp.501f.
[77] René Dussaud in *Syria* 7 (1926), pp.9-29.

form of plaques or small panels in relief and presumably were once attached to furniture and inlaid in wall paneling. The subjects depicted in the ivories include lotus, lilies, papyrus, palmettes, lions, bulls, deer, winged figures in human form, sphinxes and figures of Egyptian gods such as Isis and Horus. A richly decorated ivory medallion in relief showing the infant Horus sitting upon a lotus, holding a flail in the right hand and raising the forefinger of the left hand to his lips in typical gesture, is shown in Fig. 66. This and other subjects as well as the technique of execution of the ivories indicate that Egyptian influence was strong in Palestine at this time.[78]

THE MOABITE STONE

In the days of Ahab the kingdom of Moab was tributary to Israel and sent annual payments of "the wool of a hundred thousand lambs, and of a hundred thousand rams," but "when Ahab was dead . . . the king of Moab rebelled against the king of Israel" (II Kings 3:4f.). Ahab's immediate successor Ahaziah reigned but briefly and it was Jehoram who went out to do battle with Mesha king of Moab. In the midst of the battle Mesha offered his oldest son as a burnt-offering upon the wall and "there was great wrath against Israel" (II Kings 3:27).

A contemporary record of the relations between Israel and Moab exists in the famous Moabite Stone (Fig. 67). It was erected, with a long inscription, by King Mesha at Dibon (the modern Diban), north of the Arnon. Reports of its existence came to the French scholar Clermont-Ganneau in Jerusalem, and a Prussian traveler, the Reverend F. A. Klein, saw it for the first time in 1868. A squeeze[79] was taken of it, but before the stone itself could be obtained it was broken into pieces by the Arabs. Finally two large fragments and eighteen small pieces were recovered and a restoration and reconstruction was made and the monument placed in the Louvre.[80] In the inscription Mesha says in part: "I am Mesha, son of Chemosh . . . , king of Moab, the Dibonite. . . . Omri, king of Israel . . . oppressed Moab many days because Chemosh was angry with his land. And his son succeeded him, and he also said, I will oppress Moab. In my days, he spoke. But I saw my desire upon him and upon his house, and Israel

---

[78] J. W. and Grace M. Crowfoot, *Early Ivories from Samaria.* 1938.

[79] A squeeze is a facsimile impression made by forcing a plastic substance into the depressions.

[80] C. S. Clermont-Ganneau, *La Stèle de Mésa.* 1887.

perished forever. Now Omri annexed all the land of Madeba, and Israel occupied it, his days and half his sons' days, forty years, and Chemosh restored it in my days."[81]

Obviously there are differences between this and II Kings 3:4-27 and it is not certain whether the two accounts relate to the same or different campaigns. According to the Bible the total reigns of Omri and his son Ahab amounted to only thirty-four years,[82] but Mesha's "forty years" could be a round number. Also he claims that "Israel perished forever" in the days of Ahab, while it was under Jehoram that Israel suffered the defeat which probably is referred to in the cryptic statement of II Kings 3:27. In general it is apparent that on each side the writers selected that part of the history of the two lands to record which was most pleasing to them. Also it is noteworthy that Israel ascribed its victory to Jehovah (II Kings 3:18) while Mesha thanked his god Chemosh for his. Modern statesmen and dictators have been known to do likewise. In the entire inscription the following places are mentioned which are also named in the Bible: the Arnon (Numbers 21:13, etc.; Deuteronomy 2:24; 3:16, etc.), Aroer (Joshua 13:16), Ataroth (Numbers 32:34), Baalmeon or Beth-baal-meon (Joshua 13:17; Numbers 32:38), Bethbamoth (Bamoth-baal, Joshua 13:17), Beth-diblathaim (Jeremiah 48:22), Bezer (Joshua 20:8), Dibon (Numbers 32:34; Joshua 13:17; Isaiah 15:2), Horonaim (Isaiah 15:5), Jahaz (Joshua 13:18; Isaiah 15:4), Kerioth (Jeremiah 48:24), Kiriathaim (Joshua 13:19; Jeremiah 48:23), Madeba (Medeba, Joshua 13:9, 16; Isaiah 15:2), and Nebo (Numbers 32:38; Deuteronomy 34:1; Isaiah 15:2).

THE SILOAM TUNNEL

In 721 B.C. Samaria fell to Sargon of Assyria. In 701 B.C. Sargon's successor, Sennacherib, invaded Palestine and besieged Jerusalem itself. Hezekiah was king of Judah at this time, and he seems to have taken a far-sighted measure to strengthen the city against siege. II Kings 20:20 states that "he made the pool, and the conduit, and brought water into the city." The same achievement is narrated in II Chronicles 32:30: "This same Hezekiah also stopped the upper spring of the waters of Gihon and brought them straight down on the west side of the city of David." Thus the attackers were deprived

[81] W. H. Bennett in HDB III, p.407.
[82] I Kings 16:23—Omri, 12 years; 16:29—Ahab, 22 years.

56. Jericho

57. Tell el-Mutesellim, the Site of Megiddo (Armageddon)

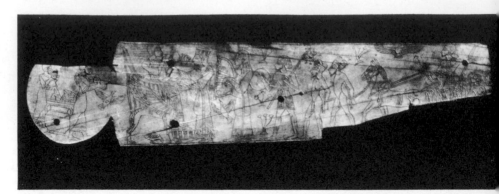

58. Ivory Plaque of the Prince of Megiddo

59. Standing Stones at Gezer

60. Ras Shamra Stela with the God El

61. Ras Shamra Stela with the God Baal

62. Ras Shamra Tablet with the Legend of Keret

64. The Sacred Rock beneath the Dome of the Rock

63. The Dome of the Rock

65. The Great Stables at Megiddo

66. Ivory Medallion with the Child Horus

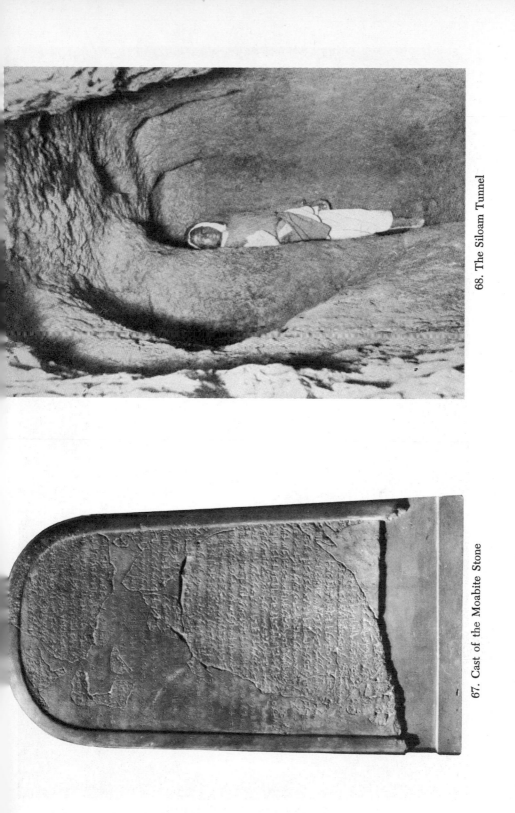

67. Cast of the Moabite Stone

68. The Siloam Tunnel

69. The Siloam Inscription

70. One of the Lachish Letters

of water at the same time that the besieged city was assured of an unfailing supply. "Why should the kings of Assyria come, and find much water?" they asked as they stopped the waters that were without the city (II Chronicles 32:2-4).

It will be remembered (p. 149) that Jerusalem's main source of fresh water was the Gihon spring, outside the city wall on the edge of the Kidron Valley, and that the Jebusites had somewhat difficult access to these waters through a vertical shaft and connecting tunnel. The entire system of tunnels related to the Gihon spring was cleared by Captain Parker in 1909-1911 and studied, measured and photographed by Father Vincent at that time. The Jebusite water system was found to have been walled off near the cave at the foot of the vertical shaft, and from this point a new rock tunnel was cut west and southwest for around 1,777 feet to empty into the Pool of Siloam (Ain Silwan). The ancient wall of Jerusalem used to cross the Tyropoeon Valley just below this point, so at that time this pool was within the walls and safe from attackers in time of siege. It is natural to conclude that the cutting of this tunnel was the work of Hezekiah as referred to in II Kings 20:20 and II Chronicles 32:30.

Another tunnel also remains which runs south from the spring of Gihon near the outside edge of the rock and probably emptied into the old Pool of Siloam or a similar reservoir within the city. It may be that this tunnel was cut by one of the earlier kings, perhaps David or Solomon, and afterward repaired by Hezekiah. This would provide a possible explanation of the difficult passage in which Isaiah (22:11) reproaches Hezekiah: "Ye made also a reservoir between the two walls for the water of the old pool. But ye looked not unto the maker thereof, neither had ye respect unto him that purposed it long ago." This would mean that Hezekiah took the entire credit for the conduit to himself, and also failed to follow David's example in faithfulness to God. Even if this is the correct explanation of its character, this tunnel must have proved insufficient, for ultimately it was supplanted by the more efficient tunnel cut right back through the heart of the rock and identified with Hezekiah's work as described in II Kings and II Chronicles.[83]

The great tunnel of Hezekiah was excavated in the solid rock with wedge, hammer and pick, and the marks of the expertly wielded pickaxes are still to be seen on the walls. The excavators worked from

[83] Duncan, *Digging Up Biblical History.* II, pp.126f.,201-215.

both ends, and after many windings and turnings met in the middle. The average height of the tunnel is about six feet, but later cutting has made it much higher at the Siloam end. A photograph of the tunnel at the point where the workers met is shown in Fig. 68. On the right wall of the tunnel, about nineteen feet in from the Siloam entrance, an inscription was discovered in 1880 by a boy who had been wading in the pool.[84] This inscription (Fig. 69) was later cut out and taken by the Turkish government to the Imperial Ottoman Museum in Constantinople. It is translated as follows: "The boring through is completed. And this is the story of the boring through: while yet they plied the drill, each toward his fellow, and while yet there were three cubits to be bored through, there was heard the voice of one calling unto another, for there was a crevice in the rock on the right hand. And on the day of the boring through the stone-cutters struck, each to meet his fellow, drill upon drill; and the water flowed from the source to the pool for a thousand and two hundred cubits, and a hundred cubits was the height of the rock above the heads of the stone-cutters."[85] Such was the conclusion of a truly notable engineering feat.

THE LACHISH LETTERS

Although Jerusalem was wonderfully delivered from Sennacherib as Isaiah promised (Isaiah 36-37; II Kings 19:20, 32-36; II Chronicles 32:20-22), its downfall came at last. In succession to the Assyrians, the Neo-Babylonian Empire dominated western Asia. When King Jehoiakim of Judah ventured to rebel, he and his son Jehoiachin who succeeded him were punished speedily by the invasion of Judah and the taking of Jerusalem in 598 B.C. (II Kings 24:1-17). Zedekiah was installed at Jerusalem as puppet king and when he, too, broke faith with his Babylonian master the city's final doom was sealed. Nebuchadnezzar II advanced for the last time upon Judah, and after an eighteen-month siege Jerusalem fell (587 B.C.), its walls were broken down, its houses and great temple burned with fire, and its people, save for the very poorest of the land, carried into exile (II Kings 25:1-12).

Jeremiah the prophet lived through these terrible events and in the introduction to one of the prophecies which he addressed to

[84] A. H. Sayce, *Records of the Past.* New Series, I, pp.168-175; Gesenius-Kautzsch, *Hebrew Grammar.* ed. Collins and Cowley, 1898, p.xix.
[85] Barton, *Archaeology and the Bible,* p.476.

Zedekiah there is a striking reference to the time "when the king of Babylon's army was fighting against Jerusalem, and against all the cities of Judah that were left, against Lachish and against Azekah; for these alone remained of the cities of Judah as fortified cities" (Jeremiah 34:7). Both of these cities have been excavated. Azekah is identified with Tell Zakariya in the Shephelah. It was excavated in 1898 by Dr. Frederick J. Bliss of the Palestine Exploration Fund and revealed a strong inner citadel fortified with eight large towers. This may have been built by Rehoboam, who is reported to have fortified this city, as well as Lachish (II Chronicles 11:9).[86] The identification of Lachish with Tell ed-Duweir and the excavations at this site have already been mentioned (pp. 137f.). Some of the most important finds at Lachish relate to the very time we are now discussing, that of Nebuchadnezzar's invasions of Palestine.

It appears that Lachish was destroyed by fire twice within a few years at about this time, doubtless when Nebuchadnezzar came in 598 and again in 588 B.C. A clay seal was found, the back of which still showed the mark of the fibers of the papyrus document to which it had been affixed, and on which was the inscription, "The property of Gedaliah who is over the house." This is the same name as that of the man who was made governor of Judah by Nebuchadnezzar after 587 B.C. (II Kings 25:22; Jeremiah 40:5f.; 41:2) and his title "who is over the house" is elsewhere known in the Old Testament (Isaiah 22:15; 36:3).[87]

Most striking of all was the discovery made in 1935 by J. L. Starkey. In a small room, believed to be the guard room, adjoining the outer gate of the city of Lachish and lying buried in a burnt layer of charcoal and ashes were eighteen ostraca with Hebrew writing in the ancient Phoenician script.[88] Almost all of them were dispatches or letters which had been written by a certain Hoshaiah, who was at some military outpost, to a man named Jaosh, who must have been a high commanding officer at Lachish. While Nebuchadnezzar had attacked and partly burned Lachish some ten years before in the reign of Jehoiakim, these letters belong to the layer of ashes which

[86] Macalister, *A Century of Excavation in Palestine*, pp.55f.
[87] *Palestine Exploration Fund Quarterly Statement for 1935*, pp.195f.
[88] Harry Torczyner, *Lachish I, The Lachish Letters.* 1938; W. F. Albright in BASOR 70 (Apr. 1938), pp.11-17. Three additional ostraca, bringing the total number up to twenty-one, were found in the last campaign at Lachish in 1938 (BASOR 80 [Dec. 1940], pp.11-13; 82 [Apr. 1941], p.24).

represents the final destruction of the city. Therefore they are to be dated early in 588 B.C. when Nebuchadnezzar was beginning the final siege of Jerusalem together with that of Lachish and Azekah. Azekah may even have fallen already at this time, since one of the letters says, "We are watching for the signal-stations of Lachish, according to all the signals you are giving, because we cannot see the signals of Azekah." Lachish itself appears to have held out until after the autumn olive harvest in the next November or December since many carbonized olive stones were found in the embers of the burned city. Jerusalem fell during the middle of the next summer, 587 B.C.

One of the letters (No. III) reads as follows:

"Thy servant Hoshaiah hath sent to inform my lord Ya'osh: May the Lord [Yhwh] cause my lord to hear tidings of peace! And now thou hast sent a letter but my lord hath not enlightened thy servant concerning the letter which thou didst send to thy servant yesterday evening, for the heart of thy servant hath been sick since thou didst write to thy servant. And as for what my lord hath said, 'Thou dost not know it!—read [any] letter,' as the Lord liveth no one hath undertaken to read me a letter at any time, nor have I read any letter that may have come to me nor would I give anything for it!—And it hath been reported to thy servant saying, 'The commander of the host, Coniah son of Elnathan, hath come down in order to go into Egypt and unto Hodaviah son of Ahijah and his men hath he sent to obtain [supplies] from him.'—And as for the letter of Tobiah, servant of the king, which came to Shallum son of Jaddua through [the instrumentality of] the prophet, saying, 'Beware,' thy servant hath sent it to my lord."[89]

Hoshaiah is a biblical name and appears in Jeremiah 42:1 and Nehemiah 12:32. God is referred to by the four letters *Yhwh*, which are the consonants of the name Yahweh or Jehovah and in this and other of the letters many of the men's names have Yahweh endings. The prophet who is mentioned in this letter has been believed by some to be Jeremiah himself,[90] but this is not necessarily or even probably true.[91]

Another of the Lachish letters (No. VI) is illustrated in Fig. 70 and translated as follows:

> To my lord Ya'osh: May the Lord cause my lord to see
> this season in good health! Who

[89] W. F. Albright in BASOR 82 (Apr. 1941), pp.20f.
[90] J. W. Jack in PEQ 1938, pp.165-187.
[91] Gordon, *The Living Past*, p.189.

is thy servant [but] a dog that my lord hath sent the letter
of the king and the letters of the prince[s, say]ing,
"Pray, read them"? And behold the words of the pr[inces]
are not good, but to weaken you[r] hands [and to sl]acken
the hands of the men who are informed
about them [?] [. . . . And now,] my lord, wilt thou not write
to th[em,] say[ing,] "Why do ye do
thus even [?] in Je[ru]salem? Be[hol]d
unto the king [and] unto his [house (?)] are ye doing this
[th]ing! [And] as the Lord thy God liveth
[it is true that] since thy servant read
the letters there hath been no
[peace (?)] for [thy] servant. . . ."[92]

The mention in this letter of words which are weakening the hands
of the people, reminds us again of Jeremiah against whom it was
charged: "he weakeneth the hands of the men of war that remain
in this city, and the hands of all the people, in speaking such words
unto them" (Jeremiah 38:4). In the letter, however, the discourag-
ing words appear to have come from princes rather than from a
prophet, and so Jeremiah probably is not referred to here either.
Nevertheless, despite the enigmatical language of the letters we can
discern conditions very comparable to those which are known from
the biblical records to have prevailed at this time.

The ravages of the conquest of Palestine by Nebuchadnezzar were
very terrible. The land was devastated and laid waste, and the best
of the population was carried off into captivity. From this awful time
Judah did not recover for two or three hundred years. The exiles were
allowed to return to their homeland at last but the population remained small and poor, while the temple which Zerubbabel rebuilt
was as nothing in the eyes of those who had seen it in its former
glory (Haggai 2:3). This pitiful state of affairs is reflected only too
clearly in the archeological realm by the paucity of important materials. We know that the small Jewish state stamped official jar
handles and also silver coins with the legend Yehud, that is "Judah,"[93]
but it is not until in the Hellenistic Period (c.300-63 B.C.) that solidly
constructed buildings and abundant pottery again appear. Even then
the archeological monuments thus far discovered in Palestine are
relatively scant.

[92] W. F. Albright in BASOR 82 (Apr. 1941), pp.22f.
[93] E. L. Sukenik in *The Journal of the Palestine Oriental Society* 14 (1934),
pp.178-184.

IV

Empires of Western Asia: Assyria, Chaldea and Persia

IN ITS later Old Testament days the fate of the Hebrew people was connected closely, as we have just seen, with the great powers to the north and east.

1. THE KASSITES, c.1650-c.1175 B.C.

THE beginnings of civilization in the valley of the Tigris and Euphrates have already been traced and Mesopotamia has been described as it was in the time of Abraham and of Hammurabi (Chapter I). In the days that followed, the entire northern boundary of the Fertile Crescent felt the pressure of advancing Indo-European hordes[1] and the kings who came after Hammurabi on the throne of Babylon had to struggle against Kassites from the eastern mountains and Hittites from the west. Samsuiluna, Hammurabi's immediate successor, repelled a wholesale invasion of Kassites but the latter continued to make a peaceful penetration of the country, and for almost 150 years Kassite names appear in Babylonian business documents as laborers, harvesters and hostlers. Finally the Kassites attained power and established a dynasty which ruled in Babylon for half a millennium. On the whole the Kassite Period is obscure historically but it is thought that the main outlines of the social order as established by Hammurabi continued to exist. It is known that the horse, which was a divine symbol to the Kassites, became common in Babylonia only after their entry.[2]

Eventually the Kassite Dynasty gave way to the Pashe Dynasty which ruled Babylonia for perhaps a century and a quarter. The

[1] Albrecht Götze, *Hethiter, Churriter und Assyrer.* 1936, p.27.
[2] George G. Cameron, *History of Early Iran.* 1936, pp.89-95.

greatest king was Nebuchadnezzar I who reigned probably around the middle of the twelfth century B.C. In the middle of the next century the country was overrun by Elamites, and for the next 450 years Babylonia was of little importance politically.

2. THE HITTITES, c.1900-c.1200 B.C.[1]

THE center of the Hittites' power was in Asia Minor, where an empire that was once great but had been long forgotten was rediscovered by modern archeology. William Wright, a missionary at Damascus, and Professor A. H. Sayce were among the first to reconstruct from scattered monuments the picture of this empire.[2] Then in 1906 excavations were begun by Professor Hugo Winckler at Boghaz-keui, a site which lies 90 miles east of Angora in a great bend of the Halys River.[3] It was found in this and following work that Boghaz-keui had been an important Hittite capital and a large number of clay tablets were unearthed containing texts in a half-dozen different languages. Among these were a large number written with cuneiform characters in the Hittite language. Through the labors of many men and particularly of the Bohemian scholar Friedrich Hrozny this language was eventually deciphered.[4]

There are two chief periods of Hittite power, the first that of the old Hittite kingdom which goes back into the time of the First Dynasty of Babylon, and the second that of the new Hittite kingdom which flourished in the years around 1400 to 1200 B.C.[5] The latter kingdom was consolidated by a great ruler at Boghaz-keui named Subbiluliuma, who conquered and incorporated in his empire the Mesopotamian kingdoms of Mitanni and the Hurri and also sent his armies southward into Syria and to the confines of Palestine. The ruler of Mitanni whom he conquered was Tushratta, who is known to us from his correspondence with Amenhotep III and Amenhotep IV of Egypt.[6] Tushratta gave his daughter Taduhepa to be the wife

---

[1] Götze, Hethiter, Churriter und Assyrer, p.80.

[2] Wright, The Empire of the Hittites. 1884; Sayce, The Hittites, The Story of a Forgotten Empire (rev. ed. 1925).

[3] Winckler, Die im Sommer 1906 in Kleinasien ausgeführten Ausgrabungen (Sonderabzug aus der Orientalistischen Litteratur-Zeitung. Dec. 15, 1906).

[4] Hrozny, Die Sprache der Hethiter. 1917.

[5] cf. Kurt Bittel, Die Ruinen von Bogazköy, der Hauptstadt des Hethiterreiches. 1937, table following p.102.

[6] KAT Nos.17-25,27-29 = MTAT Nos.17-25,27-29.

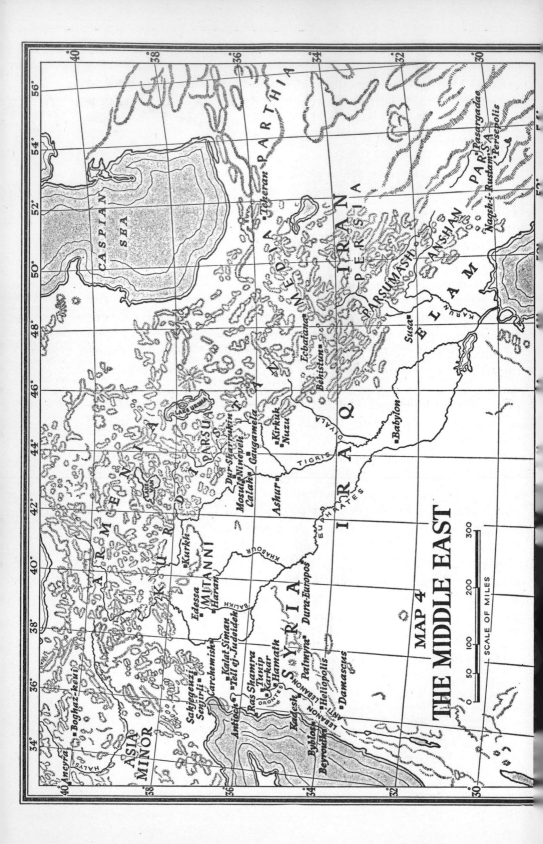

MAP 4

THE MIDDLE EAST

SCALE OF MILES

0   50   100   200   300

of Amenhotep III. Subbiluliuma also corresponded with Amenhotep IV, whom he called Huria, and the following is one of the letters which has been preserved:

> Thus hath Subbiluliuma, the great king,
> king of Hatti-land, to Huria,
> king of Egypt, my brother, spoken:
> I am well. With thee may it be well.
> With thy wives, thy sons, thy house, thy warriors, thy chariots,
> and in thy land, may it be very well.
>
> Now, thou, my brother, hast ascended the throne of thy father,
> and, just as thy father and I
> mutually requested presents,
> so wilt also thou and I now be mutually
> good friends.[7]

Subbiluliuma was succeeded by Arandash and then by the latter's brother, Murshilish. Murshilish was followed by his son Muwatallish who almost defeated Ramesses II and the Egyptians in the famous battle of Kadesh. The brother and second king after Muwatallish was Hattushilish, who signed a nonaggression pact with Ramesses II in the twenty-first year of the latter's reign. The agreement was confirmed by the marriage of the daughter of Hattushilish to Ramesses II (p. 103).

By this time, however, both the Hittites and the Egyptians were weakened greatly and around 1200 B.C. the Hittite Empire reached its end.[8] The "Hittite City," as Boghaz-keui was called, fell, and such Hittite kingdoms as continued to exist at Carchemish, Senjirli, Sakjegeuzi, Hamath and other places were relatively small and impotent. Thus the old balance of power was destroyed and Assyria's opportunity had come to emerge in international affairs as the dominant world power.

[7] KAT No.41 = MTAT No.41.
[8] K. Bittel and R. Naumann, *Bogazköy.* 1938, p.5.

3. ASSYRIAN BEGINNINGS, c.3000-c.1700 B.C.

THE homeland of Assyria was in the northeast corner of the Fertile Crescent where the Tigris River flows southward across the plains, and the mountains of Kurdistan loom up in the background. The country has a length of about 350 miles and a width of from 200 to 300 miles, with a total area of some 75,000 square miles or somewhat smaller, for example, than the state of Nebraska. In contrast with stoneless Babylonia, Assyria was supplied abundantly with limestone, alabaster and, in the Kurdistan hills, marble.[1]

The city which gave its name to the country and empire, even as it took its own name from the national god, was Ashur.[2] It was located strategically on a low bluff on the right bank of the Tigris at a place now called Qalat Sharqat. After some earlier digging done there by Layard, Rassam and Place, Ashur was excavated in 1903-1914 by a German expedition under the direction of Walter Andrae.[3] It appears that the site was occupied from the early part of the third millennium B.C., while the earliest literary references to the city of Ashur occur in texts which were found at Nuzu and which date from the Old Akkadian Period.[4]

Under Shamshi-Adad I (c.1748-c.1716 B.C.)[5] Assyria enjoyed a period of independence and Ashur began to be a great city, well fortified and with a fine temple to house its god.[6]

[1] Morris Jastrow, *The Civilization of Babylonia and Assyria.* 1915, p.6.
[2] A. T. Olmstead, *History of Assyria.* 1923, p.1.
[3] Andrae, *Das wiedererstandene Assur.* 1938.
[4] Meek, *Old Akkadian, Sumerian and Cappadocian Texts from Nuzi,* p.xi.
[5] The dates of the kings are based now upon a list of Assyrian rulers discovered in the palace of Sargon III at Khorsabad by the Oriental Institute of the University of Chicago in 1932-33 and published by A. Poebel in JNES 1 (1942), pp.247-306,460-492; 2 (1943), pp.56-90. Albright's revision of Poebel's date for Shamshi-Adad I is that which is given here (cf. p.47 n.7).
[6] ARAB I, §43A.

4. THE ASSYRIAN KINGDOM, c.1700-c.1100 B.C.

As THE First Dynasty of Babylon declined the power of Assyria increased. Doubtless there was also stimulus at this time from the presence of the Hurrians, whose important city of Nuzu has already been mentioned (p. 54).

Some light is cast on the life of this period by the Assyrian laws which were discovered at Ashur. The Babylonian code, or a body of laws of closely related character, was still the law of the land. However, in cases where the Babylonian code was inadequate to Assyrian requirements and customs or in need of amendment to suit Assyrian conditions, further regulations were necessary and these are represented by the laws just mentioned.[1]

In the days of Subbiluliuma of the Hittites and Amenhotep IV of Egypt, Ashur-uballit I, "Ashur-has-given-life" (c.1362-c.1327) was king of Assyria. Among the Tell el-Amarna tablets are letters which he addressed to Amenhotep IV. In one he wrote:

> To the king of Egypt,
> say.
> Thus saith Ashur-uballit, king of Assyria:
> With thee, thy house, thy wives,
> thy chariots, and thy chief men
> may it be well!

In another he told of the gifts he was sending:

> A beautiful royal chariot, with my span,
> and two white horses, with my span, also
> one chariot without a span, and one seal of beautiful lapis lazuli.

But he expected gifts in return:

> If thou art very friendly disposed,
> then send much gold.[2]

His proud assumption of equality with the Egyptian Pharaoh was not entirely unjustified, for Ashur-uballit I was one of the men who by conquest and political strategy began to make the kingdom of Assyria into the great Assyrian Empire.

[1] G. R. Driver and J. C. Miles, *The Assyrian Laws*. 1935, pp.14f.
[2] KAT Nos.15f. = MTAT Nos.15f.

5. THE ASSYRIAN EMPIRE, c.1100-633 B.C.

WITH Tukulti-apil-Esharra I, better known as Tiglath-pileser I (c.1114-c.1076), we enter the period that may properly be called that of the Assyrian Empire. This was the time described above (p. 167) when the stage was clearly set for the emergence of Assyria as the greatest power in the Middle East. Amidst the confusion of small, hostile states which had taken the place of the old balance of power, Tiglath-pileser I was able to extend the conquests of Assyria westward to the Mediterranean Sea and northward to the region of Lake Van. Now, too, for the first time in Assyrian history, detailed annals are available describing many of the campaigns in which Tiglath-pileser I strove for the mastery of the world.[1] He said: "Ashur and the great gods, who have made my kingdom great, and who have bestowed might and power as a gift, commanded that I should extend the boundary of their land, and they entrusted to my hand their mighty weapons, the storm of battle. Lands, mountains, cities, and princes, the enemies of Ashur, I have brought under my sway, and have subdued their territories. . . . Unto Assyria I added land, unto her peoples, peoples. I enlarged the frontier of my land, and all of their lands I brought under my sway."[2]

ASHUR-NASIR-PAL II

The next two centuries, however, were ones of relative darkness for Assyria, and it remained for Ashur-nasir-pal II (883-859) to make Assyria the ruthless fighting machine whose calculated frightfulness was the terror of its enemies. The merciless cruelty of his campaigns is the constant boast of Ashur-nasir-pal II:

"I stormed the mountain peaks and took them. In the midst of the mighty mountain I slaughtered them, with their blood I dyed the mountain red like wool. With the rest of them I darkened the gullies and precipices of the mountains. I carried off their spoil and their possessions. The heads of their warriors I cut off, and I formed them into a pillar over against their city, their young men and their maidens I burned in the fire."

"I built a pillar over against the city gate, and I flayed all the chief men who had revolted, and I covered the pillar with their skins; some I walled up within the pillar, some I impaled upon the pillar on stakes, and others I bound to stakes round about the pillar; many within the border of my

---

[1] A. T. Olmstead, *Assyrian Historiography* (*The University of Missouri Studies, Social Science Series.* III, 1). 1916, p.10.
[2] ARAB I, §219.

own land I flayed, and I spread their skins upon the walls; and I cut off the limbs of the officers, of the royal officers who had rebelled."[3]

The quotations just given are typical of many more which can be read in the annals of this king. The final edition of these annals was inscribed on the pavement slabs of the entrance to the temple of Ninurta at Calah. It was characteristic of some of the most energetic rulers of Assyria to move the royal residence to a new center, and the already ancient and ruined city of Calah (cf. Genesis 10:11) was that chosen by Ashur-nasir-pal II for his new capital. Calah is now represented by the mound of Nimrod and that is where the young Englishman, Austen Henry Layard, began his Assyrian excavations in 1845. At the very outset the palace of Ashur-nasir-pal II was uncovered. When the first colossal winged man-headed lion (Fig. 71) which guarded the palace entrance came into view the Arab chief cried, "This is not the work of men's hands, but of those infidel giants of whom the Prophet (peace be with him!) has said that they were higher than the tallest date-tree. This is one of the idols which Noah (peace be with him!) cursed before the Flood."[4] In a small temple near by, a statue of Ashur-nasir-pal II, about half life-size, was found which is the only perfect statue in the round of an Assyrian king that is extant. This statue is shown in Fig. 72. The king holds in each hand a symbol of sovereignty, that in the right hand resembling an Egyptian scepter and that in the left is a mace. On the breast are eight lines of inscription, giving the king's name and titles and stating that he had conquered the whole region from the Tigris to Mount Lebanon and the Great Sea, meaning the Mediterranean.

SHALMANESER III

The ruthless Assyrian fighting machine which Ashur-nasir-pal II had developed was directed by his son Shulmanu-ashared III or Shalmaneser III (858-824) in repeated campaigns against Syria and Palestine. "In my first year of reign," states Shalmaneser III, "I crossed the Euphrates at its flood. To the shore of the sea of the setting sun I advanced. I washed my weapons in the sea."[5] A few years later a great battle was fought at Karkar on the Orontes River against a formidable Syrian coalition of twelve kings. The "Monolith Inscription" of Shalmaneser III, which came to the British Museum

[3] ARAB I, §447, 443.
[4] Sir Frederic Kenyon, *The Bible and Archaeology.* 1940, p.38.
[5] ARAB I, §558.

from Kurkh, records the military activities of the king up to his sixth year and includes in its annals a description of this battle. Among the allied leaders who opposed Shalmaneser III, the king of Damascus, "Hadad-ezer of Aram," is named first. Then Irhuleni of Hamath is mentioned and in third place stands "Ahab, the Israelite."[6] While the Bible does not mention this incident, the Assyrian inscription testifies to the prominence of Ahab among the rulers of the time. The inscription gives statistics on the fighting forces involved and describes Ahab as commanding 2,000 chariots and 10,000 soldiers. In chariotry, Ahab's forces were much larger than those of any other king, Hadad-ezer being credited with 1,200 and Irhuleni with 700. The mention of Ahab is of importance also in giving an entirely independent confirmation of the fact that this king was on the throne of Israel just before the middle of the ninth century B.C. In this battle Shalmaneser III claimed an overwhelming triumph in which he made the blood of his enemies flow down the valleys and scattered their corpses far and wide, yet the fact that he avoided Syria thereafter for several years may mean that the victory was not as decisive as his boasts would indicate.

On one of the later campaigns of Shalmaneser III, Jehu of Israel paid heavy tribute to him. This is known to us from the famous Black Obelisk which Layard found in 1846 in the palace of Shalmaneser at Nimrod.[7] This is a four-sided pillar of black limestone six and one-half feet in height with five rows of roughly executed bas-reliefs extending around it and with texts between and below them. The inscriptions record the military achievements of Shalmaneser III from the first 31 years of his reign and the reliefs illustrate the payment of tribute from five different regions. A reproduction of the Black Obelisk is seen in Fig. 73 where, on the front of the monument in the second row of reliefs, Jehu is actually pictured kneeling before Shalmaneser III. The Assyrian king accompanied by two attendants, one of whom holds a sun-shade above him, stands proudly, with the symbols of Ashur and Ishtar in the field above. At his feet kneels Jehu in all humility. The Israelite king is shown with a short, rounded beard and wears a soft cap on his head. He is clothed in a sleeveless

---

[6] ARAB I, §611.

[7] A. H. Layard, *Nineveh and Its Remains*. 1849, I, p.282. The Black Obelisk was nearly lost at sea when the sailing-ship on which it was being transported to England came close to foundering in a great storm in the Indian Ocean. C. J. Gadd, *The Stones of Assyria*. 1936, p.48.

jacket and long fringed skirt with girdle. Following him come Israelites in long robes, carrying precious metals and other tribute. The inscription reads: "Tribute of Jehu, son of Omri. Silver, gold, a golden bowl, a golden beaker, golden goblets, pitchers of gold, lead, staves for the hand of the king, javelins, I received from him."[8]

Shalmaneser III liked to call himself "the mighty king, king of the universe, the king without a rival, the autocrat, the powerful one of the four regions of the world, who shatters the might of the princes of the whole world, who has smashed all of his foes like pots,"[9] but despite his boasts, he died amidst revolts with which his son Shamshi-Adad V (823-811) had to contend. Shamshi-Adad V, Sammuramat or Semiramis the famous queen, and her son Adad-nirari III (810-783), were fairly successful in maintaining the power of Assyria but under Shalmaneser IV (782-773), Ashur-dan III (772-755) and Ashur-nirari V (754-745) came decline.

TIGLATH-PILESER III

Then the throne was usurped by a great warrior and statesman who took the famous name of Tiglath-pileser (p. 170). Tiglath-pileser III (744-727), a sculptured representation of whose head is shown in Fig. 74, brought the moribund Assyrian Empire back to vigorous life. He carried out conquests to the east and west and in Babylon itself was recognized as king. There they called him Pulu, and it is by this name, Pul, that he is referred to in II Kings 15:19 where his taking of tribute from Menahem, king of Israel, is recorded. It is interesting to find this very event mentioned also in the annals of Tiglath-pileser III: "As for Menahem, terror overwhelmed him, like a bird, alone he fled and submitted to me. To his place I brought him back and ... silver, colored woolen garments, linen garments ... I received as his tribute."[10]

A few years later, however, Pekah of Israel and Rezin of Damascus allied themselves against Assyria and provoked another advance of Tiglath-pileser III into the west. He overran the kingdom of Israel and deported many of the inhabitants as is stated in II Kings 15:29. In Tiglath-pileser's own inscriptions this is referred to in the words, "The land of Bit-Humria . . . all of its people, together with their goods I carried off to Assyria."[11] Bit-Humria or "House of Omri" had

[8] ARAB I, §590.
[9] ARAB I, §674.
[10] ARAB I, §815.
[11] ARAB I, §816.

been the regular Assyrian designation for the land of Israel ever since the days of King Omri more than one hundred years before. That such a ruthless deportation of peoples in order to prevent future rebellions was a usual feature of Tiglath-pileser's policy we know from other of his inscriptions. Elsewhere he says, for example, "30,000 people I carried off from their cities and placed them in the province of the city of .... 1,223 people I settled in the province of the land of Ulluba."[12] By treachery Pekah himself was slain and Tiglath-pileser III made Hoshea ruler of Israel (II Kings 15:30), expecting him to pay heavy tribute to Assyria. This was also duly recorded in Tiglath-pileser's inscriptions. "Paqaha [Pekah] their king they deposed and I placed Ausi' [Hoshea] over them as king. Ten talents of gold, ... talents of silver, as their tribute I received from them and to Assyria I carried them."[13] Then the Assyrian king turned against Damascus and took it, and Ahaz of Judah also came thither to become his vassal (II Kings 16:9f.) and eventually to appear as "Iauhazi of Judah"[14] in Tiglath-pileser's lists of those from whom he received tribute.

Soon after the death of Tiglath-pileser III, Hoshea ventured to rebel against Assyria. The new ruler of Assyria, Shalmaneser V (726-722) thereupon laid siege to the Israelite capital. Samaria held out stubbornly for three years (II Kings 17:5), and before the collapse came Shalmaneser V had been succeeded by Sharrukin II or Sargon II (721-705).

SARGON II

This man was a general who usurped the throne to found a new dynasty and who took the ancient and great name of Sargon (p. 38). Sargon II is mentioned in Isaiah 20:1 in connection with his capture of Ashdod[15] and for a long time this was the only place in extant literature where his name was known. In 1843 the French consular agent at Mosul, Paul Émile Botta, began to dig at Khorsabad (Dur-Sharrukin) and discovered the palace of Sargon II. Sargon had made his capital successively at Ashur, Calah and Nineveh and then finally here at this place. He called the new capital after himself, Dur-Sharrukin or Sargonsburg, but eventually the ruin was ascribed to

---

[12] ARAB I, §770.   [13] ARAB I, §816.

[14] ARAB I, §801. The way the name is written in the Assyrian inscription makes it probable that Ahaz actually was an abbreviated form of Jehoahaz.

[15] cf. ARAB II, §30.

a Sassanid hero, Chosroes, and called Khorsabad, "town of Chosroes." The large palace which Botta discovered and which has been reexplored more intensively in recent years by the Oriental Institute of the University of Chicago, was built by Sargon II in the closing years of his reign and was adorned on the walls with texts describing the events of his reign.[16]

In these Khorsabad annals of his reign, Sargon II lists the fall of Samaria as the outstanding event of the first year of his reign. The text is fragmentary at this point but is reconstructed and translated as follows: "At the beginning of my rule, in my first year of reign . . . Samerinai [the people of Samaria] . . . of Shamash who causes me to attain victory . . . 27,290 people, who lived therein I carried away; 50 chariots for my royal equipment, I selected from among them. . . . The city I rebuilt, I made it greater than it was before; people of the lands my hand had conquered, I settled therein. My official I placed over them as governor. Tribute, tax, I imposed upon them as upon the Assyrians. . . . I mixed together, made the price to be. . . ."[17]

Again in Sargon's so-called "Display Inscription" at Khorsabad, which is a résumé of the events from the first to the fifteenth years of his reign, he says: "I besieged and captured Samaria, carrying off 27,290 of the people who dwelt therein. 50 chariots I gathered from among them, I caused others to take their [the deported inhabitants'] portion, I set my officers over them and imposed upon them the tribute of the former king."[18]

An alabaster relief from Khorsabad gives us an impressive picture of the kind of fighting man Sargon II could send against Samaria (Fig. 75). Carrying bow and arrow, short sword and short club, this powerfully muscled warrior stands in calm confidence, a symbol of the overwhelming military might of Assyria. Yet sometimes even the Assyrians faced enemies against which the bowsman could not avail and terrible plagues of locusts devastated the land as they did in Judah in the days of Joel. An enameled tile painting (Fig. 76) from the time of Sargon II shows some great man of Assyria standing in front of the all-seeing sun-god Shamash to ask for deliverance from

[16] Gordon Loud, *Khorsabad I, Excavations in the Palace and at a City Gate.* OIP XXXVIII, 1936; G. Loud and Charles B. Altman, *Khorsabad II, The Citadel and the Town.* OIP XL, 1938.

[17] ARAB II, §4; cf. A. G. Lie, *The Inscriptions of Sargon II, Part I The Annals.* 1929, p.5.

[18] ARAB II, §55.

a plague of locusts, or possibly to give thanks for the deliverance which has already taken place. The theme of his prayer is made unmistakable by the representation of the locust above his head.

SENNACHERIB

Sargon II fell in battle and was succeeded in 704 B.C. by his son, Sennacherib, who ruled until 681 B.C. The capital of Sennacherib was the famous city of Nineveh on the east bank of the Tigris, across from where the modern city of Mosul now stands. Sennacherib planned the fortifications of this city, gave it a system of waterworks, restored its temples and built its most magnificent palaces. The ancient city is represented by two large mounds known as Kuyunjik and Nebi Yunus, the latter being so named because it is the site of the reputed tomb of the prophet Jonah. In 1820 Claudius James Rich, the British resident at Baghdad, visited Mosul. Although he died of cholera the next year, the posthumous publication in 1836 of his *Narrative of a Residence in Koordistan* awakened much interest in the possibilities of archeological work in Assyria. In 1842 Paul Émile Botta was sent to Mosul by the French government as consular agent. He made brief and unsuccessful attempts to dig at Nebi Yunus and Kuyunjik before transferring his efforts to Khorsabad where he made the brilliant discovery mentioned above (p. 174). He was followed in work both at Khorsabad and at Kuyunjik by Victor Place. Austen Henry Layard, the English archeologist, concerned himself first with Nimrod, as we have seen (p. 171), but also did some digging at Kuyunjik and in 1847 discovered there the great palace of Sennacherib. During Layard's second expedition, which lasted from 1849 to 1851, this palace was largely unearthed. No less than 71 rooms were found, and it was computed that the palace had contained approximately 9,880 feet of walls lined with sculptured slabs.[19]

Early in the reign of Sennacherib, Hezekiah of Judah revolted against Assyria and in 701 B.C. the Assyrian king moved west and south. The campaign is described in the annals of Sennacherib which were recorded on clay cylinders or "prisms." The final edition of these annals appears on the Taylor Prism of the British Museum and in an even better copy on a prism now in the Oriental Institute of the

[19] Layard, *Nineveh and Its Remains*. 1849; *Discoveries among the Ruins of Nineveh and Babylon*. 1875; *The Monuments of Nineveh*. 1853; *A Second Series of the Monuments of Nineveh*. 1853.

University of Chicago (Fig. 77). The prism is hexagonal in form, and the middle column in the photograph contains the reference to Hezekiah quoted below.

Sennacherib names Sidon, Beth-Dagon, Joppa and other cities as having fallen before him and tells of his victory in a great battle fought in the neighborhood of the city of Altaku or Eltekeh[20] in which the Palestinian forces were assisted by Egyptian bowmen and chariotry. Then Sennacherib continues:

"As for Hezekiah, the Jew, who did not submit to my yoke, 46 of his strong, walled cities, as well as the small cities in their neighborhood, which were without number,—by escalade and by bringing up siege engines, by attacking and storming on foot, by mines, tunnels and breaches, I besieged and took. 200,150 people, great and small, male and female, horses, mules, asses, camels, cattle and sheep, without number, I brought away from them and counted as spoil. Himself, like a caged bird, I shut up in Jerusalem, his royal city. Earthworks I threw up against him,—the one coming out of his city gate I turned back to his misery. The cities of his, which I had despoiled, I cut off from his land and to Mitinti, king of Ashdod, Padi, king of Ekron, and Silli-bel, king of Gaza, I gave them. And thus I diminished his land. I added to the former tribute, and laid upon him as their yearly payment, a tax in the form of gifts for my majesty. As for Hezekiah, the terrifying splendor of my majesty overcame him, and the Urbi and his mercenary troops which he had brought in to strengthen Jerusalem, his royal city, deserted him. In addition to 30 talents of gold and 800 talents of silver, there were gems, antimony, jewels, large sandu-stones, couches of ivory, house chairs of ivory, elephant's hide, ivory, maple, boxwood, all kinds of valuable treasures, as well as his daughters, his harem, his male and female musicians, which he had them bring after me to Nineveh, my royal city. To pay tribute and to accept servitude he dispatched his messengers."[21]

Presumably this inscription refers to the same invasion that is described in II Kings 18:13-19:37; II Chronicles 32:1-22; Isaiah 36:1-37:38. In comparing the Old Testament account with Sennacherib's record we note that Hezekiah's tribute is placed at 30 talents of gold in both sources but at only 300 talents of silver in II Kings 18:14 as compared with 800 talents of silver which the Assyrian king claims to have received.

In II Kings 19:9 = Isaiah 37:9 it is stated that "Tirhakah king of Ethiopia" came out to fight against Sennacherib. As we have seen (p. 114), an Ethiopian dynasty was ruling Egypt at this time but

---

[20] Probably the same city mentioned in Joshua 19:44; 21:23 (HDB I, p.698).
[21] ARAB II, §240.

Taharka (Tirhakah) did not come to the throne until about 689 B.C., some dozen years later than the date of Sennacherib's invasion. Two explanations are possible. First, we may assume that Taharka actually opposed Sennacherib in battle in 701 B.C. but that he was still in the position of a military commander only, while his uncle, Shabaka, was king.[22] The mention of Taharka as "king" at this time is, then, a mistake, which is not too surprising since he did come to the throne a comparatively few years later. The second explanation which may be offered, however, is that Sennacherib made a second invasion after Taharka actually was ruling as king, that is between about 689 B.C. and his own death in 681 B.C. In this case we might consider II Kings 18:13-19:8 as describing Sennacherib's first invasion when Hezekiah paid heavy tribute, and II Kings 19:9-37 with its mention of Tirhakah as king as referring to Sennacherib's second campaign. Some support is gained for this view if II Kings 19:37 is interpreted as giving the impression that Sennacherib's death ensued shortly after his return from the disaster at Jerusalem. It is true that such a second and later Palestinian campaign on the part of Sennacherib cannot be verified in his own annals but inscriptions referring to the last eight years of his reign are lacking.

At all events we must acknowledge that Sennacherib says nothing of the disaster which overwhelmed his armies at Jerusalem according to II Kings 19:35f. = Isaiah 37:36f. In view of the general note of boasting which pervades the inscriptions of the Assyrian kings, however, it is hardly to be expected that Sennacherib would record such a defeat. Perhaps the fact that he claims to have shut up Hezekiah in Jerusalem "like a caged bird" but does not claim to have taken the city is evidence that he did suffer discomfiture there. Incidentally, the Old Testament account finds support in a somewhat enigmatic story recorded by Herodotus and running as follows:

"The next king was the priest of Hephaestus, whose name was Sethos. He despised and took no account of the warrior Egyptians, thinking he would never need them; besides otherwise dishonouring them, he took away the chosen lands which had been given to them, twelve fields to each man, in the reign of former kings. So presently came king Sanacharib against Egypt, with a great host of Arabians and Assyrians; and the warrior Egyptians would not march against him. The priest, in this quandary, went into the temple shrine and there bewailed to the god's image the peril which threatened him. In his lamentation he fell asleep,

22 L. L. Honor, *Sennacherib's Invasion of Palestine.* 1926, p.34 n.112.

and dreamt that he saw the god standing over him and bidding him take courage, for he should suffer no ill by encountering the host of Arabia: 'Myself,' said the god, 'will send you champions.' So he trusted the vision, and encamped at Pelusium with such Egyptians as would follow him, for here is the road into Egypt; and none of the warriors would go with him, but only hucksters and artificers and traders. Their enemies too came thither, and one night a multitude of field-mice swarmed over the Assyrian camp and devoured their quivers and their bows and the handles of their shields likewise, insomuch that they fled the next day unarmed and many fell. And at this day a stone statue of the Egyptian king stands in Hephaestus' temple, with a mouse in his hand and an inscription to this effect: 'Look on me, and fear the gods.' "[23]

The mention of mice may well indicate that it was plague which struck Sennacherib's army, since mice are a Greek symbol of pestilence and since rats are carriers of the plague. Perhaps this is the real explanation of the disaster referred to in II Kings 19:35 as a smiting of the army by an angel of Jehovah, for plague and disease elsewhere in the Bible are regarded as a smiting by an angel of God (II Samuel 24:15-17; Acts 12:23).

In Fig. 78 we see a portion of a frieze illustrating one of Sennacherib's wars in the west. His soldiers are advancing to the attack in relentless procession. At the left are auxiliaries in crested helmets, carrying round shields and long spears, and wearing knee-coverings. In the center are spearsmen of a different type and in front are slingers. Another sculpture (Fig. 79) shows Sennacherib seated upon his throne before the captured city of Lachish (cf. II Kings 18:14, 17; 19:8, etc.) and receiving the spoils of the city to the accompaniment of the torture of hapless prisoners.[24] The inscription states: "Sennacherib, king of the universe, king of Assyria, sat upon a house chair while the booty of Lachish passed before him."[25]

ESARHADDON

Sennacherib was assassinated in 681 B.C. He had named his favorite son Esarhaddon to be his successor, although the latter was not the eldest son. The other sons, hoping to gain the kingship, slew Sennacherib their father, but Esarhaddon swiftly attacked the rebels and secured the crown.[26] The most important achievements of Esarhaddon's reign (680-669) were the restoration of the city of Babylon,

[23] II, 141.
[24] Layard, *Discoveries among the Ruins of Nineveh and Babylon*, pp.126-128.
[25] ARAB II, §489.   [26] ARAB II, §500-506.

which had been destroyed by his father, and the defeat of Taharka, now upon the throne of Egypt, at whose border Sennacherib had been turned back.

The victory over Taharka was commemorated with a victory stela (Fig. 80) set up at Senjirli in northern Syria, and discovered in 1888 by a German expedition. It shows the king with a mace in his left hand, and in his right a cup from which he has poured a libation to the gods symbolized at the top of the stela. From the left hand extend ropes which pass through the lips of the two figures at his feet. The first is doubtless Taharka, represented with strongly marked Negroid features. He is on his knees with hands lifted in supplication and both hands and feet are shackled. The other figure, standing, may be Ba'alu of Tyre, although the inscription does not claim his surrender. The inscription says concerning the conquest of Egypt: "Of Tirhakah, king of Egypt and Ethiopia, . . . daily without cessation I slew multitudes of his men, and him I smote five times with the point of my javelin, with wounds from which there was no recovery. Memphis, his royal city, in half a day, with mines, tunnels, assaults, I besieged, I captured, I destroyed, I devastated, I burned with fire."[27] Proudly Esarhaddon says of himself, "I am powerful, I am all powerful, I am a hero, I am gigantic, I am colossal," and for the first time an Assyrian ruler takes the new title, "King of the kings of Egypt."[28]

ASHURBANIPAL

Taharka may have been wounded grievously, but he survived to fight again, while Esarhaddon died on his next march toward Egypt. Esarhaddon was succeeded by his son Ashurbanipal (669-633), the great king who was called Osnapper in the Old Testament (Ezra 4:10) and Sardanapalus by the Greeks. Ashurbanipal campaigned in Egypt, defeating both Taharka and Tanutamun and taking both Memphis and Thebes (p. 114). Concerning the plundering of Thebes and the triumphs in Egypt Ashurbanipal wrote: "Silver, gold, precious stones, the goods of the palace, all there was, brightly colored and linen garments, great horses, the people, men and women, two tall obelisks, fashioned of glittering electrum, whose weight was 2,500 talents, placed at the gate of the temple, I removed from their positions and took off to Assyria. Booty, heavy and countless, I carried

[27] ARAB II, §580. [28] ARAB II, §577, 583.

away from Thebes. Against Egypt and Ethiopia I waged bitter war-
fare and established my authority. With a full hand I returned safely
to Nineveh, the city of my lordship."[29]

Ashurbanipal's wars were numerous and his conduct often ruthlessly cruel, yet he is remembered most of all for his culture. The
paradox of his culture and his cruelty is well represented in the relief
which shows him at a banquet in the royal pleasure garden with his
queen Ashur-sharrat (Fig. 81). The scene is one of peaceful beauty
until it is noted that the head of the leader of the Elamites, whom
Ashurbanipal has just conquered, hangs like ghastly fruit from the
coniferous tree at the left.

In his inscriptions Ashurbanipal refers frequently to the education
which he received in the days of his youth and to his intellectual as
well as military and sporting achievements.

"I, Ashurbanipal, learned the wisdom of Nabu,[30] the entire art of writing on clay tablets. . . . I learned to shoot the bow, to ride, to drive and to
seize the reins.

"I received the revelation of the wise Adapa, the hidden treasure of the
art of writing. . . . I considered the heavens with the learned masters.
. . . I read the beautiful clay tablets from Sumer and the obscure Akkadian
writing which is hard to master. I had my joy in the reading of inscriptions
on stone from the time before the flood. . . . The following were my daily
activities: I mounted my horse, I rode joyfully . . . I held the bow . . . I
drove my chariot, holding the reins like a charioteer. I made the wheels
go round. . . . At the same time I learned royal decorum and walked in
kingly ways."[31]

The interest of Ashurbanipal in education resulted ultimately in
the establishment of a great royal library. In the Temple of Nabu at
Nineveh one library had already been in existence at least since the
time of Sargon II, but the collection of Ashurbanipal was to surpass
all others in size and importance. He sent scribes throughout Assyria
and Babylonia with authority to copy and translate the writings they
found, and tens of thousands of clay tablets were brought together,
containing historical, scientific and religious literature, official dispatches and archives, business documents and letters. Ashurbanipal's
royal palace containing this library was discovered in 1853 by

[29] Arthur C. Piepkorn, *Historical Prism Inscriptions of Ashurbanipal.* I (AS 5, 1933),
pp.39-41.

[30] The patron god of the art of writing (A. H. Sayce in HDB III, pp.501f.).

[31] Maximilian Streck, *Assurbanipal und die letzten assyrischen Könige bis zum
Untergang Ninevehs.* 1916, II, pp.5,255,257.

Hormuzd Rassam, the brother of the British vice-consul at Mosul, who was continuing Layard's work at Kuyunjik.

Among the tablets which Rassam unearthed and sent to the British Museum were the ones which were later found to contain Assyrian copies of the Babylonian flood and creation stories (pp. 28, 50). The identification and decipherment of these particular tablets was the work of George Smith, then a young assistant in the British Museum. In 1872, while engaged in the sorting and classification of the Kuyunjik tablets, he noticed pieces containing portions of mythical stories. "Commencing a steady search among these fragments," Smith afterward related, "I soon found half of a curious tablet which had evidently contained originally six columns. . . . On looking down the third column, my eye caught the statement that the ship rested on the mountains of Nizir, followed by the account of the sending forth of the dove, and its finding no resting-place and returning. I saw at once that I had here discovered a portion at least of the Chaldean account of the Deluge."[32]

In the royal palace were also found the magnificent reliefs of the lion hunts of Ashurbanipal, one section of which is reproduced in Fig. 82. With their close attention to animal forms, their thrilling realism and unmistakable atmosphere of the excitement of the chase, these sculptures represent the climax of Assyrian art.

[32] R. C. Thompson, *A Century of Exploration at Nineveh.* 1929, p.49. Quoted by permission of the publishers, Luzac and Co., London.

6. THE DECLINE AND FALL OF ASSYRIA,
633-612 B.C.

FOLLOWING Ashurbanipal with Assyria at the height of its glory, three undistinguished rulers, Ashur-etil-ilani, Sin-shum-lishir and Sin-shar-ishkun occupied the throne, and then the end came with startling suddenness and Assyrian civilization was snuffed out.

For the story of Nineveh's fall and the end of the Assyrian Empire, we can now turn to a contemporary record of events. Assyrian records are largely lacking during the last twenty-five years before the end, perhaps because Oriental kings are reluctant to record their reverses, but a Babylonian clay tablet which chronicles the fall of Nineveh has been discovered and is in the British Museum.[1] The tablet is inscribed with a summary of the chief events during eight years of the reign of Nabopolassar, king of Babylon (625-605).[2] Nabu-apal-usur, or Nabopolassar in the Greek form of the name, was a Chaldean. The Chaldeans, whom Jeremiah (5:15) called "an ancient nation," were a Semitic people who entered Babylonia around 1000 B.C.[3] They stirred up disaffection against Assyrian rule of Babylonia, and in the days of Sargon II one of their chiefs, Merodach-baladan, was able to rule Babylon for a time. The persistent rebelliousness of Babylon was finally punished by Sennacherib, who destroyed the city completely. Esarhaddon restored Babylon, hoping to gain the support of the south, and when he died left Ashurbanipal's younger brother, Shamash-shum-ukin, as king of Babylon. After the rebellion and death of Shamash-shum-ukin, Ashurbanipal was himself king of Babylon. But when he died, Nabopolassar, a Chaldean and a descendant of Merodach-baladan, seized the kingship of Babylon and established an independent Chaldean or New Babylonian empire.

The Babylonian chronicle states that Nineveh fell in the fourteenth year of Nabopolassar, or 612 B.C. Nabopolassar of Babylon was joined in the destruction of Nineveh by Cyaxares the Mede (p. 192) and by the king of the Scythians. As a matter of fact, the Median king was the most important figure in the enterprise. He had begun operations against Nineveh a few years earlier, and although he did not take

[1] C. J. Gadd, *The Fall of Nineveh*.

[2] For most of the dates in the remainder of this chapter see Richard A. Parker and Waldo H. Dubberstein, *Babylonian Chronology 626 B.C.-A.D. 45*. SAOC 24, 1942; and cf. Dubberstein in JNES 3 (1944), pp.38-42.

[3] Olmstead, *History of Assyria*, p.250.

the capital at that time did capture the city of Ashur. In 613 B.C. the siege of Nineveh seems to have been lifted, and this may have been due to a Scythian attack upon the Medes, which is mentioned by Herodotus.[4] But in 612 B.C. the Babylonians, Medes and Scythians all combined for the final and successful attack upon the Assyrian capital. The siege lasted from June to August, but eventually Nineveh fell and its last king, Sin-shar-ishkun, died. Yet one more man, a certain Ashur-uballit II (c.612-c.606), reigned for a few years as king of Assyria in the western city of Haran, but this last capital of a great empire soon was also taken by the Scythians. Nineveh the Great had fallen. The destruction predicted by Zephaniah (2:13-15) had taken place. As he saw the end come Nahum cried (3:1-3):

> Woe to the city, bloody throughout,
> Full of lies and booty!
> Prey ceases not.
> The crack of the whip, and the noise of the rumbling wheel,
> And the galloping horse, and the jolting chariot;
> The charging horseman, and the flashing sword,
> And the glittering spear, and a multitude of slain,
> And a mass of bodies, and no end to the corpses!
> . They stumble over the corpses![5]

The spoils were divided equally, the Medes taking the regions east and north of the Tigris, and the king of Babylon taking those to the west and south of that natural dividing line.[6] The agreement was sealed by the marriage of Amytis, daughter of Cyaxares's son Astyages, to Nebuchadnezzar II, son of Nabopolassar.

[4] I, 103-106.
[5] *An American Translation.*
[6] George Stephen Goodspeed, *A History of the Babylonians and Assyrians.* 1902, p.333.

7. THE NEW BABYLONIAN EMPIRE, 612-539 B.C.

THE New Babylonian Empire soon had to face a challenge from Egypt. In 605 B.C. Pharaoh Necho marched as far as the Euphrates (p. 114). Nabopolassar sent his son, Nebuchadnezzar II, to meet him and the decisive battle was fought at Carchemish. Necho was defeated and Nebuchadnezzar II pursued him across Palestine and to the border of Egypt (cf. Jeremiah 46). There word reached Nebuchadnezzar of the death of his father and he hastened home to ascend the throne (605-562).

NEBUCHADNEZZAR II

Jehoiakim, whom Necho had placed on the throne of Judah (II Kings 23:34), soon became vassal to Nebuchadnezzar (II Kings 24:1), and ere long all the Asiatic possessions of Egypt were in the hands of the new and powerful king of Babylon (II Kings 24:7). When Jehoiakim later ventured to rebel against Nebuchadnezzar II, he suffered swift ruin. The Chaldean armies invaded Judah, and Jehoiakim was killed, perhaps in an uprising at court, since his dead body was cast forth outside the city gate and left to lie there like the carcass of an animal (Jeremiah 22:18f.; 36:30). His son Jehoiachin (Coniah) succeeded to the throne as a youth of eighteen, but had reigned only three months when Nebuchadnezzar laid siege to Jerusalem. Jehoiachin surrendered and was carried off to Babylon together with the finest of the population and the royal and temple treasures. This was in the eighth year of Nebuchadnezzar (II Kings 24:12), or 598 B.C. Jehoiachin's uncle, Mattaniah, was made puppet king of Judah, his name being changed to Zedekiah (II Kings 24:17). When he, too, rebelled against his Babylonian master, Nebuchadnezzar II returned again to besiege Jerusalem. The city held out stubbornly for a year and one-half, but succumbed at last in the eleventh year of Zedekiah and the nineteenth year of Nebuchadnezzar (II Kings 25:2, 8), or 587 B.C. Jerusalem now was destroyed utterly, and all the population save only the poorest of the land were carried captive to Babylon.

Of these events, Nebuchadnezzar II tells us nothing in his inscriptions, but describes his conquests only in general terms: "In exalted trust in him [Marduk] distant countries, remote mountains from the upper sea [Mediterranean] to the lower sea [Persian Gulf], steep paths, blockaded roads, where the step is impeded, where was no footing, difficult roads, desert paths, I traversed, and the disobedient I destroyed; I captured the enemies, established justice in the lands; the people I exalted; the bad and evil I separated from the people."[1]

Concerning Babylon itself and its splendor under Nebuchadnezzar II much is known. The king's own inscriptions deal largely with his extensive building operations, and his capital city was excavated thoroughly by the *Deutsche Orientgesellschaft* under the direction of Robert Koldewey from 1899 onward.[2] Nebuchadnezzar's work included the design and construction of a vast system of fortifications, and the building of streets, canals, temples and palaces. The king could well have uttered the words which are put in his mouth in Daniel 4:30, "Is not this great Babylon, which I have built for the royal dwelling-place, by the might of my power and for the glory of my majesty?"

A general view of the tremendous complex of ruins that is Babylon today is shown in Fig. 83. Most prominent is the Ishtar Gate, a double gate leading through the double wall of fortifications and adorned with rows of bulls and dragons in enameled, colored brick.[3] The gate gave access to the city's processional street whose walls were lined with enameled lions like the one shown in Fig. 84. The throne room in the palace of Nebuchadnezzar II likewise was adorned with enameled bricks in patterns such as are shown in Fig. 85. In the temple area the most conspicuous structure was the ziggurat which Nebuchadnezzar rebuilt (cf. p. 42). Only the ground plan now remains but Herodotus says that it rose to a height of eight stages, with an ascent to the top running spirally around the successive towers.[4] Not far away was Esagila ("House whose Top is Lofty"), the temple of Marduk or Bel, which the king also restored, a tremendous pile, built with step-backs like a skyscraper in a modern city.[5] Most famous of all Nebuchadnezzar's works at Babylon were the hanging gardens which the king built in terraces to compensate his Median queen for the absence of her beloved mountains, and which were known to the Greeks as constituting one

[1] Barton, *Archaeology and the Bible*, p.478.
[2] Koldewey, *Das wieder erstehende Babylon*. 4th ed. 1925.
[3] R. Koldewey, *Das Ischtar-Tor in Babylon*. 1918.
[4] i, 181. For a reconstruction of the Tower of Babel according to a description on a cuneiform tablet of the third century B.C. see E. Unger, *Assyrische und babylonische Kunst*. 1927, Fig. 104.
[5] Wilfred J. Funk, *"So You Think It's New."* 1937, p.126.

of the seven wonders of the world. The gardens can no longer be identified with any certainty. The ruins of a series of vaulted rooms found near the Ishtar Gate were believed by the excavators to represent their substructure, but now appear more probably to have been a part of some other important public building, perhaps a distribution depot for the royal storehouses.

Nebuchadnezzar II was indeed a man more of peace and of construction than of war and of destruction, and the arts of civilization flourished under his rule. The typical Babylonian gentleman, as described by Herodotus little more than a century later, was obviously a man of culture: "For clothing, they wear a linen tunic, reaching to the feet; over this the Babylonian puts on another tunic, of wool, and wraps himself in a white mantle; he wears the shoes of his country, which are like Boeotian sandals. Their hair is worn long, and covered by caps; the whole body is perfumed. Every man has a seal and a carven staff, and on every staff is some image, such as that of an apple or a rose or a lily or an eagle: no one carries a staff without a device."[6]

In religion, also, lofty sentiments were expressed in the name of Nebuchadnezzar:

> O eternal prince! Lord of all being!
> As for the king whom thou lovest, and
> Whose name thou hast proclaimed
> As was pleasing to thee,
> Do thou lead aright his life,
> Guide him in a straight path.
> I am the prince, obedient to thee,
> The creature of thy hand;
> Thou hast created me, and
> With dominion over all people
> Thou hast entrusted me.
> According to thy grace, O Lord,
> Which thou dost bestow on
> All people,
> Cause me to love thy supreme dominion,
> And create in my heart
> The worship of thy god-head,
> And grant whatever is pleasing to thee,
> Because thou hast fashioned my life.[7]

[6] I, 195; cf. Ezekiel 23:14f.
[7] Goodspeed, A History of the Babylonians and Assyrians, p.348.

THE CAPTIVITY OF JEHOIACHIN

Amidst the splendors of Babylon, however, our greatest interest lies in the inquiry as to whether any traces of the Jewish exiles remain. A discovery of much importance to the biblical archeologist now makes it possible to give an affirmative answer to this question.[8] In the ruins of the vaulted building near the Ishtar Gate which was mentioned above (p. 187), some 300 cuneiform tablets were unearthed. Upon study these have been found to date from between 595 and 570 B.C., and to contain lists of rations such as barley and oil paid to craftsmen and captives who lived in and near Babylon at that time. Among the recipients of these rations are persons from Egypt, Philistia, Phoenicia, Asia Minor, Elam, Media, Persia, and Judah. The Jews who are mentioned include some with such biblical names as Gaddiel, Semachiah and Shelemiah, the last named being called a "gardener." But the name of most significance to us is none other than that of Yaukin, king of Judah, with whom also five royal princes are listed.

The name of this king is written in several ways on the tablets, but clearly was pronounced something like "Yow-keen." The same name had already been found stamped on some jar handles in Palestine and had been recognized as an abbreviated form of Jehoiachin. On the tablets from Babylon, Yaukin is explicitly called "king of the land of Yahud." Yahud is simply a shortened form of the name of Judah such as is perfectly familiar in the time after the exile (cf. p. 163). Since the date of the tablets in general corresponds to the time when the first Jewish exiles were in Babylon, and since one of the documents which mentions Yaukin is specifically dated in 592 B.C., there can be little doubt that the reference is to the biblical Jehoiachin himself, who at that time was residing with his family in the land of his banishment.

Immediately after the name of Yaukin, the tablets three times refer to his five sons who are described as in the hands of an attendant with the Jewish name of Kenaiah. Doubtless several or all of these young sons lived to be included in the list of seven sons of Jehoiachin (Jeconiah) given in I Chronicles 3:17f., where Shealtiel is named as the oldest (cf. Matthew 1:12; Luke 3:27).

It is evident from these tablets that the Babylonians themselves

---

[8] Ernst F. Weidner in *Mélanges Syriens offerts a Monsieur René Dussaud* II (1939), pp.923-927; W. F. Albright in BA V, 4 (Dec. 1942), pp.49-55.

continued to regard Jehoiachin as the legitimate claimant to the throne of Judah, although they did not see fit to restore him to actual rule. At this time he seems to have been free, moreover, to move about in the city, as is suggested by the distribution of rations to him. Presumably it was only at a later date, therefore, that he was cast into the prison out of which in the thirty-seventh year of his captivity we find him being lifted up and restored to favorable and even preferential treatment (II Kings 25:27-30).

In view of this understanding of Jehoiachin's position in Babylon, the dating of events by Jewish writers according to the years of his captivity is thoroughly understandable. He was the lawful but exiled king of Judah. The Jews wished to recognize their rightful king, yet did not dare to date events by the years of his reign since that actual rulership had been terminated by the Babylonians. Hence Jews in the exile dated by the years of their king's captivity. It is well known that Ezekiel's prophecies are dated by this system (Ezekiel 1:2; 8:1; 20:1, etc.), and it is interesting to find that his vision of abominations in Chapter 8 belongs to exactly the same year as our dated tablet mentioning Jehoiachin, 592 B.C.

NABUNAID AND BELSHAZZAR

The New Babylonian empire also was destined to fall, and the decline came rapidly. Nebuchadnezzar II was followed on the throne by his son Amel-Marduk (562-560), or Evil-Merodach as he is called in II Kings 25:27. This man was soon slain by his brother-in-law, Nergal-shar-usur (Neriglisar). The latter ruled but four years (560-556) and his son, Labashi-Marduk (Laborosoardoch), was on the throne only a few months (556) when conspirators made away with him. One of the conspirators, a Babylonian noble named Nabunaid (Nabonidus), then ruled (556-539) as the last king of New Babylonia.[9]

In practice, however, Nabunaid shared the kingship with his own eldest son Belshazzar. Belshazzar is named as the first-born son of Nabunaid in Babylonian inscriptions, and in one cuneiform text we read the following statement concerning Nabunaid:

"He entrusted a camp to his eldest, first-born son; the troops of the land he sent with him. He freed his hand; he entrusted the kingship to him. Then he himself undertook a distant campaign, the power of the land of

[9] cf. Berossos quoted by Josephus, *Against Apion*. i, 20.

Akkad advanced with him; towards Tema in the midst of the Westland he set his face. He undertook a distant campaign on a road not within reach of old. He slew the prince of Tema with the sword; the dwellers in his city and country, all of them they slaughtered. Then he himself established his dwelling in Tema; the power of the land of Akkad. . . . That city he made glorious; he made . . . ; they made it like the palace of Babylon. . . ."

This passage plainly states that before Nabunaid started on an expedition to Tema in Arabia he divided the rule of the empire between himself and his son, entrusting actual kingship to Belshazzar. Then he undertook the distant campaign, conquered Tema, established his residence there and built that city with the glory of Babylon. Again the Nabunaid chronicle contains the following statements:

"In the seventh year the king was in the city of Tema. The son of the king, the princes and his troops were in the land of Akkad. . . .

"In the ninth year Nabunaid, the king, was in the city of Tema. The son of the king, the princes and the troops were in the land of Akkad. . . .

"In the tenth year the king was in the city of Tema. The son of the king, the princes and his troops were in the land of Akkad. . . .

"In the eleventh year the king was in the city of Tema. The son of the king, the princes and his army were in the land of Akkad."

Each of these initial statements for the seventh, ninth, tenth and eleventh years of the king is supplemented by this comment: "The king for the month Nisan did not come to Babylon; Nabu did not come to Babylon; Bel did not go forth [from Esagila]; the New Year's festival ceased [i.e. was not celebrated]." This means that during the years mentioned Nabunaid was in Arabia and Belshazzar was in Babylon and that owing to the absence of Nabunaid the usual New Year's festival was not observed. Since, therefore, Belshazzar actually exercised the co-regency at Babylon, and doubtless continued to do so unto the end, the book of Daniel (5:30) is not wrong in representing him as the last king of Babylon. Probably Belshazzar was a grandson of Nebuchadnezzar and therefore to call Nebuchadnezzar his father (Daniel 5:18) was quite in harmony with Semitic usage.[10]

THE FALL OF BABYLON

On October 13, 539 B.C. Babylon fell to Cyrus the Persian. The date is given by the Nabunaid chronicle which also tells that Sippar fell to the Persian forces on October 11 and that Cyrus first entered

[10] R. P. Dougherty, *Nabonidus and Belshazzar*. 1929, pp.105-200.

71. Man-headed Lion from the Palace of Ashur-nasir-pal II

72. Ashur-nasir-pal II

74. Head of Tiglath-pileser III

77. The Prism of Sennacherib

76. An Assyrian Prays to Shamash Concerning a Plague of Locusts

75. A Warrior of Sargon II

78. The Army of Sennacherib Advances to the Attack

79. Sennacherib at Lachish

80. The Senjirli Stela of Esarhaddon

81. Victory Banquet of Ashurbanipal and his Queen

82. Ashurbanipal on the Lion Hunt

83. The Ruins of Babylon

84. Enameled Lion from the Processional Street in Babylon

85. Enameled Bricks from the Throne Room of Nebuchadnezzar II

86. The Cyrus Cylinder

87. Relief from the Palace of Cyrus at Pasargadae

88. The Tomb of Cyrus the Great

90. Darius Triumphs over the Rebels

91. The Rock-hewn Tomb of Darius I the Great

92. The Palace of Darius (Tachara) at Persepolis

93. Tripylon Relief at Persepolis Showing Darius I and Xerxes

94. Standing Columns of the Hall of Xerxes (Apadana) at Persepolis

95. Relief from the Apadana Stairway at Persepolis

96. Eastern Portal of the Gate of Xerxes at Persepolis

97. Enameled Brick Panels from Susa Showing Spearmen of the Achaemenid Period

the city of Babylon in person on October 29.[11] The fall of Babylon is narrated not only in the Nabunaid chronicle but also in the inscription on the famous cylinder of Cyrus (Fig. 86). The latter reads in part as follows:

"Marduk . . . sought a righteous prince, after his own heart, whom he took by the hand. Cyrus, king of Anshan, he called by name, to lordship over the whole world he appointed him. . . . To his city Babylon he caused him to go, he made him take the road to Babylon, going as a friend and companion at his side. His numerous troops, in number unknown, like the water of a river, marched armed at his side. Without battle and conflict he permitted him to enter Babylon. He spared his city Babylon a calamity. Nabunaid, the king, who did not fear him, he delivered into his hand."[12]

If Cyrus claimed to be sent by Marduk, the Second Isaiah felt that the conqueror was anointed by Jehovah himself for the task of releasing the Jewish exiles and returning them to their home (Isaiah 45:1; cf. 44:28). The spirit of Cyrus's decree of release which is quoted in the Old Testament (II Chronicles 36:23; Ezra 1:2-4) is confirmed by the Cyrus cylinder, where the king relates that he allowed the captives to return to their various countries and rebuild their temples:

"From . . . to Ashur and Susa, Agade, Ashnunnak, Zamban, Meturnu, Deri, with the territory of the land of Gutium, the cities on the other side of the Tigris, whose sites were of ancient foundation—the gods, who dwelt in them, I brought back to their places, and caused them to dwell in a habitation for all time. All their inhabitants I collected and restored them to their dwelling places. And the gods of Sumer and Akkad, whom Nabunaid, to the anger of the lord of the gods, had brought into Babylon, by command of Marduk, the great lord, I caused them peacefully to take up their dwelling in habitations that rejoiced the heart. May all the gods, whom I brought into their cities, pray daily before Bel and Nabu for long life for me, and may they speak a gracious word for me and say to Marduk, my lord, 'May Cyrus, the king who worships thee, and Cambyses, his son, their . . . I permitted all to dwell in peace. . . .' "[13]

[11] Parker and Dubberstein, *Babylonian Chronology 626 B.C.-A.D. 45*, p.11.
[12] Robert William Rogers, *Cuneiform Parallels to the Old Testament*. 1912, p.381; cf. *A Guide to the Babylonian and Assyrian Antiquities, British Museum*. 3d ed. 1922, p.144.
[13] Rogers, *Cuneiform Parallels to the Old Testament*, p.383.

8. THE PERSIAN EMPIRE, 539-331 B.C.

CYRUS THE GREAT, conqueror of Babylon and king in that city from 539 until his death in 530 B.C., was the founder of the Persian Empire. In order to understand his place in history it is necessary to indicate briefly the earlier happenings in the land of Persia.

THE EARLIER HISTORY OF PERSIA

The homeland of Persia was the western and larger part of the Iranian plateau, which stretches from the Indus on the east to the Tigris and Euphrates on the west. It is a high, arid plateau overlooked by vast barren mountain ranges. The native name of the land, and the name to which the Persian government officially returned in 1935, is Iran. This name, Airyana or Iran, means "the [land] of the Aryans,"[1] and refers to the Aryan-speaking people who settled on the highland. Before the Aryans came, aboriginal Caspians had lived on the plateau and perhaps were the first people to develop agriculture and metallurgy. Then, around 1500 B.C., the Aryans entered the country.[2]

The two Aryan tribes which were to attain the greatest importance were the Amadai or Medes and the people from the land of Parsua (west of Lake Urmia) or Persians. Both are mentioned for the first time in annals of Shalmaneser III concerning Assyrian campaigns in the region of the Caspian plateau.[3] The Medes occupied the northwestern part of the country, now Iraq-i-ajam, with their capital at Hagmatana, known later as Ecbatana and now as Hamadan. According to Herodotus[4] Ecbatana was founded by "a clever man called Deioces" who for the first time united the nomadic Median tribes into one nation and ruled as king. Deioces was succeeded by his son Phraortes, as Herodotus further states, and he in turn by his son Cyaxares. Cyaxares (or Uvakhshatra) we have already seen cooperating with Nabopolassar in the overthrow of Nineveh in 612 B.C. (p. 183).

The Persians moved on southward and settled not far from the Elamite land Anzan or Anshan in a region to which they gave the name Parsamash or Parsumash in memory of their old homeland of Parsua. By about 700 B.C. their leader was Hakhamanish or Achae-

---

[1] Old Persian, *Aryanam khshathram*; Middle Persian, *Eran*. Ernst Herzfeld and Sir Arthur Keith in *A Survey of Persian Art*. I, p.42 n.1.
[2] Ernst Herzfeld, *Archaeological History of Iran*. 1935, p.8.
[3] ARAB I, §581.   [4] I, 96-103.

menes whose name was preserved by the later Persian kings. Around 675 to around 640 B.C. Teispes was king of Parsumash, and he was able to extend the Persian holdings to include a region east of Anshan and north of what we call the Persian Gulf. This area became known as Parsa or Persian land. Teispes divided his empire between his two sons, Ariaramna (c.640-c.615) receiving Parsa and Cyrus I (c.640-c.600) receiving Parsumash.

In the land of Elam, it may be explained, a series of kingdoms had been in existence for many centuries but mostly under domination by Mesopotamian rulers from Sargon (p. 39) to the Kassites. In the first quarter of the twelfth century Kutir-Nahhunte of Elam ended Kassite control and established a true Elamite Empire but by the middle of the century Elam succumbed again to Nebuchadnezzar I. Elam enjoyed other periods of dominance but finally about 646 B.C. was destroyed and depopulated by the Assyrians.[5] Thus it was possible for the Persians to acquire much Elamite territory and we find Cambyses I (c.600-c.559), the successor of Cyrus I, bearing the title "king of the city Anshan."

Up to this time the Persians had been under the domination of the Medes. Nominally Cambyses I was a king in his own right, yet actually he was subordinate to the Median king Astyages (p. 184) to whose daughter Mandane he was married. The subserviency was not to last much longer. The son of Cambyses I and Mandane was Cyrus the Great.[6]

CYRUS II THE GREAT

Cyrus II came to the throne of Anshan around 559 B.C., and Astyages soon recognized that revolt was intended. Astyages therefore marched against Cyrus, but the Median army rebelled and Cyrus was able to proceed to Ecbatana, the capital of his former master, in triumph. Parsa henceforth was the first ranking satrapy in the entire land, Media the second and Elam the third. The sovereignty of the Persians was definitely established although the Medes continued to have equal honor with the Persians and foreigners spoke of either "the Persians and the Medes" (Esther 1:19) or "the Medes and Persians" (Daniel 5:28, etc.).[7]

Cyrus II extended his conquests swiftly and far. He challenged

[5] René Grousset in *A Survey of Persian Art*. I, pp.61,64.
[6] Herodotus. I, 107-130.
[7] Cameron, *History of Early Iran*, pp.179-226.

Croesus, the famously rich king of Lydia, who held sway as far eastward as the Halys River, and defeated him (c.546 B.C.). Finally he completed his task by conquering Babylon itself (539 B.C.) as we have already seen. Thus was established the mighty Persian Empire in which Judea for the next two centuries remained a province. The new king wrote proudly: "I am Cyrus, king of the world, the great king, the mighty king, king of Babylon, king of Sumer and Akkad, king of the four quarters of the world, son of Cambyses, the great king, king of Anshan, grandson of Cyrus, the great king, king of Anshan, great-grandson of Teispes, the great king, king of Anshan; an everlasting seed of royalty."[8]

Throughout his extensive campaigns, and in contrast with other ancient oriental conquerors, Cyrus always was humane. The lives of Astyages and Croesus were spared and each was allotted a royal train. Babylon was not destroyed but its people won over by his mercy and the Jews were reestablished in their homeland as we have seen.

Cyrus made his capital at Pasargadae in the land of Parsa. Here he built a palace on whose ruins the repeated inscription is still to be read, "I, Cyrus, the king, the Achaemenid."[9] The royal buildings seem to have formed a group consisting of scattered individual pavilions set amidst gardens, and surrounded by a masonry wall some 13 feet in thickness.[10] The carving shown in Fig 87 adorned a doorway at Pasargadae and is our earliest extant Persian relief. The strange four-winged genius is believed by some to represent the deified Cyrus.

Nine years after the surrender of Babylon, Cyrus marched eastward to meet enemies and was killed in battle (530 B.C.). His body was brought back to Pasargadae and buried in a tomb which still exists and which consists of only a single small room on a foundation course of six steps (Fig. 88). Arrian (A.D. c.96-c.180) describes the tomb as follows: "The tomb itself was built, at the base, with stones cut square and raised into rectangular form. Above, there was a chamber with a stone roof and with a door leading into it so narrow that with difficulty, and after great trouble, one man, and he a small one, could enter. And in the chamber was placed a golden sar-

[8] Barton, *Archaeology and the Bible*, p.484.
[9] E. Herzfeld, *Archaeologische Mitteilungen aus Iran.* I (1929-30), p.10.
[10] Friedrich Wachtsmuth in *A Survey of Persian Art.* I, p.309.

cophagus, in which Cyrus' body had been buried."[11] Plutarch (A.D. c.46-c.120) says that the tomb had this inscription: "O, man, whosoever thou art and whencesoever thou comest, for I know that thou wilt come, I am Cyrus, and I won for the Persians their empire. Do not, therefore, begrudge me this little earth which covers my body."[12]

CAMBYSES II

Cyrus was followed on the throne by his son Cambyses II (530-522) who defeated the Egyptians at Pelusium (p. 115) and added Egypt to the Persian dominions. The Persian Empire was now the greatest the world had ever seen. Not long after his Egyptian victories, however, Cambyses went mad and committed suicide. The new empire nearly broke up in the confusion which followed. Gaumata, a Magian, declared himself to be Smerdis, the younger brother of Cambyses (who actually had been murdered), and seized the throne. Also national kings of Babylonia, Media, Armenia and other provinces which had been annexed by Cyrus, attempted to break away.

DARIUS I THE GREAT

It was an Achaemenid prince of a younger line, Darius I the Great (522-486), son of Hystaspes,[13] who saved the empire. The name of the father of Darius, Hystaspes or Vishtaspa, is the same as that of the traditional royal convert and patron of Zoroaster. The traditional dates for Zoroaster (c.660-c.583) are too early to allow for the identification of the father of Darius with the patron of the prophet, however, and either it must be supposed that the latter was an earlier Vishtaspa or else the date of Zoroaster's birth must be brought down to a later date, perhaps around 570 B.C.[14] At any rate it is well known that Darius I was an ardent Zoroastrian and zealous worshiper of Ahura Mazda, and so were Xerxes and Artaxerxes as well.

In the Old Testament the appearance of the prophet Haggai in Jerusalem is dated (Haggai 1:1) on the first day of the sixth month of the second year of Darius, which would be August 29, 520 B.C.; and the first sermon of Zechariah is placed (Zechariah 1:1) in the eighth month of the same year or in October-November 520 B.C. Likewise

---

[11] *Anabasis of Alexander.* vi, xxix, 5. tr. E. I. Robson, LCL (1929-33) ii, p.197.
[12] *Life of Alexander.* LXIX, 2. tr. B. Perrin, LCL (1914-26) vii, p.417.
[13] Herodotus. i, 209.
[14] Herzfeld, *Archaeologische Mitteilungen aus Iran.* ii (1930), p.47.

the completion of the rebuilt Jewish temple is dated on the third day of the month Adar in the sixth year of Darius (Ezra 6:15). The Jewish month Adar corresponded to the Babylonian Addaru, and the date indicated is March 12, 515 B.C.

THE ROCK OF BEHISTUN

Returning now to the rebellion with which Darius I was confronted, it may be said that the new king acted swiftly. Gaumata was defeated, seized and killed, and the various provincial uprisings were suppressed. An impressive memorial of the victory over the rebels was left on the famous Rock of Behistun. This great rock looms up above a spring-fed pool of water on the old caravan-road from Ecbatana to Babylon. The rock is really the last peak (3,800 feet high) of a long narrow range of mountains which skirts the plain of Karmanshah on the east. The name by which we customarily refer to it is derived from the small village of Bisitun or Behistun which is now located at its foot. High upon the face of the rock, perhaps 500 feet above the level of the plain, Darius I carved a large relief panel and accompanied it with many columns of inscription (Fig. 89).[15] The scene represents the king receiving the submission of the rebels. At the left (Fig. 90) we see the life-sized figure of Darius I, accompanied by two attendants. The king's left foot is placed upon the prostrate form of Gaumata, the leading rebel. In his left hand the king grasps a bow while he lifts his right hand toward the winged disk with anthropomorphic head which is the symbol of Ahura Mazda. Behind Gaumata is a procession of rebel leaders, roped together by their necks. The last one, Skunkha the Scythian, wearing a high pointed cap, was a later addition to the group. Beside and beneath the sculptured panel are many columns of inscription relating how Darius gained the crown and put down the rebellion. The inscription is composed in three languages, Old Persian, Elamite and Akkadian (formerly known as Old Persian, Susian and Babylonian), all written in cuneiform characters. Copies of the inscription were also circulated in distant provinces of the Persian Empire, as is known from the discovery of an Aramaic version of it among papyri at Elephantine in Upper Egypt (p. 201).

The great carving at Behistun was indestructible and unconceala-

---

[15] cf. E. Herzfeld, *Am Tor von Asien, Felsendenkmale aus Irans Heldenzeit.* 1920, Pl. IX.

ble and hence early became known to travelers in that region. The Arabian geographical writer Ibn Hawkal, who was born at Mosul in the tenth century A.D., described it and supposed that the scene represented "a schoolhouse, with the master and the boys; further in the schoolmaster's hand is an instrument like a strap wherewith to beat."[16] In the early nineteenth century another traveler saw the monument and thought that the winged figure of Ahura Mazda was a cross, and that Darius and his officers and prisoners were the Twelve Apostles![17]

Then in 1835 and following, Henry C. Rawlinson, a British official in the Middle East, made the difficult climb up to the inscription and made copies and squeezes. He said, "The climbing of the rock to arrive at the inscriptions, if not positively dangerous, is a feat at any rate which an antiquary alone could be expected to undertake."[18] Fresh copies were made from the original in 1904 by L. W. King and R. Campbell Thompson, who were sent out by the British Museum,[19] and new photographs of the monument have been taken recently by Dr. George G. Cameron of the Oriental Institute of the University of Chicago (see Fig. 89).[20]

Efforts had already been made to read cuneiform, or wedge-shaped writing, particularly by G. F. Grotefend of Germany who was able to identify in other inscriptions the names of Darius and his son Xerxes as well as the title "King of Kings." Rawlinson was finally able to decipher the Persian part of the Behistun inscription and this victory at last led to the reading of the other two languages.[21] Such was the Rosetta Stone of cuneiform decipherment.

Darius I not only dealt effectively with the rebellion which he faced at the beginning of his reign but also continued to rule well the far-flung Persian territories. Indeed his genius lay most of all in the field of administration, and one of his outstanding achievements was the completion of the organization of the empire into twenty satrapies.[22] Furthermore, he undertook extensive works of

[16] G. LeStrange, *The Lands of the Eastern Caliphate.* 1905, p.187.
[17] E. A. W. Budge, *The Rise and Progress of Assyriology.* 1925, p.30.
[18] A. V. W. Jackson in *Journal of the American Oriental Society.* 24 (1903), p.81.
[19] King and Thompson, *The Sculptures and Inscription of Darius the Great on the Rock of Behistun in Persia.* 1907.
[20] JNES 2 (1943), pp.115f. and Pl. II.
[21] Sir Henry C. Rawlinson, *The Persian Cuneiform Inscription at Behistun.* 1846.
[22] CAH IV, pp.194f.

construction which ranged from the digging of a canal from the Nile to the Red Sea,[23] to the erection of a new capital at Persepolis (p. 202).

Despite the fact that in so many ways Darius I deserved the title "the Great," which has been given him, the closing years of his reign saw the outbreak of the Greco-Persian wars which were to be disastrous for Persia. This conflict grew ultimately out of the fact that the conquests of Cyrus in Asia Minor had included Greek colonies, but the wars now were begun by the Greeks themselves. During the reign of Darius I, Persian armies suffered defeat at Marathon (491 B.C.) and again a few years after his death the Persian fleet was beaten at Salamis (480 B.C.). Thereafter the future belonged to Europe instead of Asia.

NAQSH-I-RUSTAM

Darius I died in 486 B.C. and was buried in a rock-hewn tomb at Naqsh-i-Rustam (Fig. 91) a few miles northeast of Persepolis.[24] The name of this place means "Pictures of Rustam," for the rock sculptures have been associated by the local inhabitants with the legendary Persian hero, Rustam. The tomb of Darius bears trilingual inscriptions which give the king's own account of his achievements and of his character. His words include the following: "Says Darius the king: By the favor of Ahuramazda I am of such a sort that I am a friend to right, I am not a friend to wrong; it is not my desire that the weak man should have wrong done to him by the mighty; nor is that my desire, that the mighty man should have wrong done to him by the weak."[25]

Similar tombs were later cut from the same cliff for the three successors of Darius—Xerxes, Artaxerxes I and Darius II—and are to the right and to the left of the tomb of Darius. These tombs do not appear in Fig. 91. The carving which is seen in the lower left hand corner of the illustration is a yet later representation of the Sassanian king Shapur I (A.D. 241-272) receiving the submission of the Emperor Valerian. Not far away and facing the cliff of the royal tombs is a strange structure of stone to which the name Ka'bah-i-Zardusht ("Square [Tomb] of Zoroaster") has been attached. It is thought

23 Roland G. Kent in JNES 1 (1942), pp.415-421.
24 cf. E. Herzfeld and F. Sarre, *Iranische Felsreliefs.* 1910, Pl. IV.
25 Roland G. Kent in JNES 4 (1945), pp.39-52.

perhaps to have been a very early Achaemenian tomb, and later may have served as the shrine where the Sassanian kings were crowned and the crown jewels were kept.

XERXES

Darius was followed on the throne of Persia by his son Xerxes (486-465 B.C.). An important historical inscription of Xerxes recently discovered at Persepolis lists the numerous subject nations over which he ruled, tells of uprisings with which he had to contend at the time of his accession to the throne, and reveals his devotion to the worship of Ahura Mazda. This record reads as follows:

"A great god is Ahuramazda, who created the earth here, who created the heaven yonder, who created man, who created peace for man, who made Xerxes king, one king of a multitude, one lawgiver of a multitude.

"I [am] Xerxes, the great king, the king of kings, the king of the land of many tribes, the king on this wide, far-stretching earth, the son of Darius the king, an Achaemenid, a Persian, son of a Persian, an Aryan, of Aryan lineage.

"Speaks Xerxes the king: By the will of Ahuramazda these are the lands outside of Fars over which I was king; I ruled over them; they brought me tribute; what was ordered them by me, that they did; my law held them: Media, Elam, Arachosia, Armenia, Drangiana, Parthia, Aria, Bactria, Sogdia, Chorasmia, Babylonia, Assyria, Sattagydia, Sardis, Egypt, the Ionians that dwell in the sea and those that dwell beyond the sea, the people of Maka, Arabia, Gandara, the Indus land, Cappadocia, the Dahae, the Amyrgian Scythians, the Pointed-capped Scythians, Skudra, the people of Akaufaka, the Putites, the Carians, the Cushites.

"Speaks Xerxes the king: When I became king there were among those lands which are written above [some which] rebelled. Then Ahuramazda helped me. By Ahuramazda's will such lands I defeated, and to their place I restored them. And among those lands were some where previously the Daivas were worshiped. Then by Ahuramazda's will of such temples of the Daivas I sapped the foundations, and I ordained: the Daivas shall not be worshiped. Where the Daivas had been worshiped before, there I worshiped Ahuramazda with Arta the exalted; and whatever else had been done wrongfully, that I righted. This which I did, I did it all by the will of Ahuramazda; Ahuramazda helped me until I had completed the task.

"Thou who art of an after age, if thou thinkest, 'I wish to be happy in life, and in death I wish to belong to Arta,' abide in those laws which Ahuramazda has established and worship Ahuramazda together with Arta the exalted. The man who abides in the laws which Ahuramazda has established and worships Ahuramazda together with Arta the exalted, that one shall be happy in life, and in death he shall belong to Arta.

"Speaks Xerxes the king: May Ahuramazda guard from evil me and my house and this land. This I implore of Ahuramazda; this may Ahuramazda grant me."[26]

Xerxes is no doubt the Ahasuerus[27] who is mentioned in Ezra 4:6 between Darius and Artaxerxes and who also figures prominently in the book of Esther (1:1, etc.).

ARTAXERXES I

The successor of Xerxes was Artaxerxes I Longimanus (465-423 B.C.). According to Nehemiah 2:1 the request of Nehemiah to visit Jerusalem was made in the month Nisan in the twentieth year of Artaxerxes. The Hebrew month Nisan was equivalent to the Babylonian Nisanu; assuming, as is very probable, that the reference is to Artaxerxes I, the date indicated is in April-May, 445 B.C.

General confirmation of a date around this time for Nehemiah is found in the Elephantine papyri, which belong toward the end of this same century and mention by name two persons connected in the Old Testament with Nehemiah. The first is Sanballat, whose two sons are referred to as governors of Samaria in 408 B.C. Doubtless this is the same man who years before was the leading opponent of Nehemiah (Nehemiah 2:19, etc.). The second is Johanan or Jehohanan who, according to the papyri, was high priest in Jerusalem in 408 B.C. Since Nehemiah is said (Nehemiah 3:1) to have been in Jerusalem when Johanan's father Eliashib (Nehemiah 12:23) was high priest, this also agrees well with the date given above for Nehemiah.

In Ezra 7:1, 8 it is stated that Ezra came to Jerusalem in the seventh year of Artaxerxes. If this means Artaxerxes I the date was 458 B.C. and Ezra preceded Nehemiah. Since Jehohanan the son of Eliashib is mentioned in connection with the work of Ezra (Ezra 10:6), however, it seems probable that Ezra followed Nehemiah. In this case Ezra's mission may have fallen under Artaxerxes II, the seventh year of whose reign was 398 B.C.[28]

---

[26] Erich F. Schmidt, *The Treasury of Persepolis and Other Discoveries in the Homeland of the Achaemenians.* OIC 21, 1939, pp.14f.

[27] The Hebrew represents the Persian Khshayarsha of which the Greek form is Xerxes. In Esther the LXX (II, p.755) renders the name as Artaxerxes and is followed in this by Josephus (*Ant.* XI, vi) who names Artaxerxes I as king in the days of Esther.

[28] Albright, *The Archaeology of Palestine and the Bible,* pp.169f.; Pfeiffer, *Introduction to the Old Testament,* pp.819f.,827.

THE ELEPHANTINE PAPYRI

The Elephantine papyri referred to above give us an interesting glimpse of one of the outlying regions of the Persian empire at this time. These documents were discovered in 1903 on the island of Elephantine at the First Cataract in Egypt.[29] They date from toward the end of the fifth century B.C. and come from a Jewish military colony which was settled here. The papyri are written in Aramaic, which was the language of diplomacy and of trade throughout western Asia in the Persian period, and which was gradually replacing Hebrew as the everyday tongue of the Jewish people not only abroad but also at home in Palestine.

The contents of the Elephantine papyri are varied, ranging from the copy of the Behistun inscription of Darius mentioned above (p. 196), to such a document as a Jewish marriage contract. In one letter, dated about 419 B.C., the Jews of Elephantine are instructed by the authority of the Persian government to celebrate the Passover according to the official practice of the Jerusalem temple as embodied in the priestly code (Exodus 12:1-20). Again we learn that there was a Jewish temple at Elephantine which had just been sacked in an anti-Jewish pogrom of around 411 B.C. As their national God, the Jews of this colony worshiped Yahweh, whom they referred to by the name Yahu. Also three other divine names appear, Eshem-bethel, Herem-bethel and 'Anath-bethel or 'Anath-Yahu. These usually have been interpreted as polytheistic borrowings on the part of the Elephantine Jews from their pagan surroundings. It is possible, however, that they represent hypostatized aspects of Yahweh under the respective titles, "Name of the House of God," "Sacredness of the House of God," and "Sign of the House of God."[30]

As both the Elephantine papyri and the biblical records show, the Persian kings took an interest in the welfare and religious life of their subjects. Despite some exceptions, it may be said in general that the Achaemenids exercised a more liberal rule than any other oriental despots of the ancient world. They manifested a great capacity for administration and adhered to relatively high ethical conceptions. Under their sway peace was maintained throughout the Orient for approximately two centuries. The different civilizations which fell

---

[29] E. Sachau, *Aramäische Papyrus und Ostraka aus einer jüdischen Militär-Kolonie zu Elephantine.* 2 vols. 1911; A. Ungnad, *Aramäische Papyrus aus Elephantine.* 1911; A. Cowley, *Aramaic Papyri of the Fifth Century B.C.* 1923.

[30] Albright, *From the Stone Age to Christianity*, p.286.

under their dominion were allowed to continue in existence, and the various religions were tolerated. Instead of sudden, random exactions of tribute, systematic taxation was introduced and with it civil progress was supported in many ways. Roads were repaired carefully, agriculture was protected and justice was administered systematically and well. The attitude of the Jews is significant in this regard, for we find them, although still a subject people, displaying an appreciation of their Achaemenid masters which contrasts strongly with their resentment against all of their other conquerors, Egyptian, Assyrian, Chaldean, Seleucid and Roman.[31]

PERSEPOLIS

The most impressive evidence of the height which Persian culture attained is to be found in the ruins of Persepolis. This was the place to which Darius I transferred the main capital of Persia from Pasargadae (pp. 194, 198), and it remained from that time on the chief home of the Achaemenian dynasty. Archeological excavations have been conducted at Persepolis by the Oriental Institute of the University of Chicago under the direction of Ernst Herzfeld in 1931-1934 and of Erich F. Schmidt in 1935-1939. The location of the new capital was some 25 miles southwest of Pasargadae, on a spur of what is now known as the Kuh-i-Rahmat or "Mountain of Mercy," overlooking the plain now called Marv Dasht.

Persepolis was surrounded by a triple fortification system with one row of towers and walls running over the crest of the mountain itself. The chief buildings were erected upon a large, roughly rectangular, terrace. Here stood the palace of Darius, known as the Tachara (Fig. 92). It had an entrance hall opening across the entire width of the building, and a main hall some 50 feet square. It was adorned with relief sculptures which are still well preserved, and bears the repeated inscription, "I am Darius, great king, king of kings, king of lands, son of Hystaspes, the Achaemenid, who constructed this palace."[32]

A building known today as the Tripylon probably was the first reception hall of Persepolis. In its stairway reliefs, rows of dignitaries are shown ascending, and on its eastern gate jambs Darius I is shown on the throne, with Xerxes, the crown prince, standing behind him

[31] René Grousset in A Survey of Persian Art. I, pp.66f.
[32] F. H. Weissbach, Die Keilinschriften der Achämeniden. 1911, pp.80f.

(Fig. 93). The later and greater audience halls at Persepolis were the so-called Apadana, begun by Darius I and completed by Xerxes, and the Hall of One Hundred Columns started by Xerxes and finished by Artaxerxes I. The Apadana or Hall of Xerxes was a huge room approximately 195 feet square and surrounded by vestibules on three sides. The wooden roof was supported by 72 stone columns of which 13 still stand. Several of these are shown in their classic beauty in Fig. 94. The building stood upon an elevated platform which was ascended by two monumental sculptured stairways. Of these the northern one has always been partially exposed and is badly weathered, but the eastern was discovered and excavated first by Professor Herzfeld. The reliefs on the latter are very well preserved and show the opposite side of the same procession which is sculptured on the northern stairway. The chief figures are those of envoys from twenty-three subject nations who are bringing New Year's gifts to the Persian emperor. A portion of these reliefs is illustrated in Fig. 95. In the upper panel we see Parthians bringing vessels and leading a camel, in the center are Gandarans from the region of Afghanistan with a humped bull, shields and lances, and in the lower panel are Bactrians with gold vessels and another camel. The reliefs are regarded as the greatest monument of Achaemenian art, and the rhythmical arrangement of the figures in the procession and the excellent delineation of the animal forms are particularly noteworthy.[33]

The central unit of the Hall of One Hundred Columns was even more immense than that of the Apadana, being a room over 229 feet square. The roof was once supported by 100 columns, the northern portico was flanked by huge stone bulls, and eight stone gateways were ornamented with throne scenes and representations of the king's combat with demons.

Another impressive structure on the royal terrace was the Gate of Xerxes, which stood above the stairway leading up from the plain. As in the Assyrian palaces, colossal bulls guarded the entrances of this gate. Those on the eastern side, shown in Fig. 96, are human headed, bearded and crowned. The accompanying inscription reads, "King Xerxes says: By the grace of Ahura Mazda I constructed this gateway called All-Countries."[34]

Other buildings at Persepolis include the Harem of Darius and

[33] Stanley Casson in A Survey of Persian Art. i, p.349.
[34] Weissbach, Die Keilinschriften der Achämeniden, pp.108f.

Xerxes, the residence of Xerxes known as the Hadish, a badly weathered palace which may have been begun by Xerxes and completed by Artaxerxes I, and the royal treasury which contains fine reliefs of Darius and Xerxes like those on the Tripylon.[35]

ECBATANA AND SUSA

Both Ecbatana and Susa were also important centers of the Persian Empire, the former serving as a summer residence of the kings and the latter as a winter capital. Ecbatana, as we have seen (p. 192), was the former Median capital. Polybius (c.208-c.126 B.C.) says that the citadel of the city was strongly fortified, and he gives a description of the palace of the Persian kings in which he says that "the woodwork was all of cedar and cypress, but no part of it was left exposed, and the rafters, the compartments of the ceiling, and the columns in the porticoes and colonnades were plated with either silver or gold, and all the tiles were silver."[36] Little now remains of the ancient city, but an inscription has been found there in which Artaxerxes II Mnemon (404-359) celebrated the erection of a palace.[37]

Susa became a part of the Achaemenid empire when Cyrus took Babylon and all of its provinces. The city is called Shushan in the Old Testament (Nehemiah 1:1; Esther 1:2, etc.; Daniel 8:2), just as the natives there today call it Shush (p. 18) which was probably the ancient name. The greatest monument of Persian Susa is the royal palace which was begun by Darius I and enlarged and further beautified by the later kings.[38] The foundation of the building was commemorated by Darius I in an inscription in which he tells of bringing materials for its decoration from afar, including columns of stone from a town called Aphrodisias of Ogia, cedar wood from Lebanon, silver from Egypt, gold from Bactria and ivory from India.[39]

The outline of the palace can still be traced by some rows of bricks, and bits of brick and lime remain from the pavements. The main plan included three courts of varying size, surrounded by large halls and

[35] Schmidt, *The Treasury of Persepolis and Other Discoveries in the Homeland of the Achaemenians.*
[36] *The Histories.* x, xxvii, 10. tr. W. R. Paton, LCL (1922-27) IV, p.167.
[37] Georges Perrot and Charles Chipiez, *Histoire de l'art dans l'antiquité.* v (1890), p.501; Oscar Reuther in Gunther Wasmuth, ed., *Lexikon der Baukunst.* II (1930), p.328.
[38] R. de Mecquenem in *A Survey of Persian Art.* I, pp.321-326.
[39] J. M. Unvala in *A Survey of Persian Art.* I, p.339.

apartments, while a great hypostyle hall stood near-by. The walls were of sun-dried brick covered with whitewash on the inside, and the paving was coated throughout with polished red ochre.

Panels of beautifully colored glazed bricks, which served in the same role as tapestries, constituted the most notable feature in the decoration of the palace. Many of the designs were executed in relief, and included winged bulls, winged griffins, and the famous spearmen of the guard—of whom two are shown in Fig. 97. Most of the extant examples of this type of decoration at Susa come probably from the reign of Artaxerxes II Mnemon, mentioned above.[40]

The splendid capitals of the Achaemenid kings were destined to be looted and destroyed by Alexander the Great. Following Artaxerxes I the Persian throne was occupied by Darius II (423-404 B.C.), Artaxerxes II Mnemon (404-359), Artaxerxes III Ochus (359-338), Arses (338-335) and Darius III (335-331).[41] Then came the end.

[40] Stanley Casson in *A Survey of Persian Art.* I, p.351.

[41] It was in the reign of either Artaxerxes II or Artaxerxes III that a rebellion of the Jews was put down with great severity by the king's general Bagoses (Josephus, *Ant.* xi, vii, 1).

9. ALEXANDER THE GREAT, 336-323 B.C.

In 331 B.C. Alexander the Great invaded Persia after having made himself master of the entire eastern Mediterranean world including Egypt. Beyond the Tigris by the village of Gaugamela, Alexander met and defeated the armies of Darius III. Then he advanced to Susa, Persepolis and Ecbatana, at each of which places he seized fabulous treasures. At Persepolis, according to Plutarch, 10,000 pairs of mules and 5,000 camels were required to carry away the loot.[1] There at the main capital, with 3,000 of his soldiers occupying the royal terrace, Alexander sealed the conquest of Persia by putting to the torch the palaces which symbolized the power of the Achaemenids.

In 324 B.C. the youthful conqueror of the world returned from India and stopped to visit the tomb of Cyrus at Pasargadae, which he found already despoiled. The man who had committed the outrage was slain, and Plutarch adds that the sight of the inscription on the tomb (p. 195) "deeply affected Alexander, who was reminded of the uncertainty and mutability of life."[2] If this is true, Alexander's forebodings were not unfounded, for he died not long after (323 B.C.) at the early age of thirty-three.

[1] *Life of Alexander.* xxxvii, 2.
[2] ibid., lxix, 3.

10. THE SUCCESSORS OF ALEXANDER, 323-30 B.C.

AFTER the death of Alexander the Great, his empire fell to his gen-erals who are known as the Diadochi or "Successors." In Egypt, Ptolemy I Soter I (323-285), son of Lagus, carried on the government at first for Philip Arrhidaeus, the feeble-minded half-brother of Alexander the Great, and Alexander (II), the young son of Alexander the Great, and then for the latter alone after Philip Arrhidaeus was killed around 317. About 310 Alexander II was killed and Ptolemy assumed the title of king. His successors, the dynasty of the Ptolemies or the Lagidae, ruled Egypt until it became a Roman province in 30 B.C.[1] In the eastern provinces, Seleucus I Nicator (312-281) emerged eventually as master. He took Babylon and began his official reign in Syria in the autumn of 312. The founding of the Seleucid Kingdom was taken as the beginning of the Seleucid era, a chronological system which was long used in western Asia and among the scattered Jews.[2] The successors of Seleucus I, comprising the Seleucid Dynasty, continued to rule Syria until Pompey made it a Roman province in 64 B.C.[3]

[1] The kings who followed the first Ptolemy, with their approximate dates, were: Ptolemy II Philadelphus (285-246), Ptolemy III Euergetes I (246-222), Ptolemy IV Philopator (222-203), Ptolemy V Epiphanes (203-181), Ptolemy VI Philometor (181-146), Ptolemy VII Eupator, Ptolemy VIII Neos Philopator, Ptolemy IX Euergetes II (Physkon), Ptolemy X Soter II (Lathyrus), Ptolemy XI Alexander I, Ptolemy XII Alexander II, Ptolemy XIII Neos Dionysos (Auletes) (80-51), Ptolemy XIV (51-47), Ptolemy XV (47-45), Ptolemy XVI Caesar or Caesarion (45-44). Cleopatra became queen jointly with Ptolemy XIV and dominated the closing part of this period until her death in 30 B.C. George Steindorff in Karl Baedeker, *Egypt and the Sudan.* 8th ed. 1929, pp.cxi-cxiii.
[2] The Seleucid era began in the Macedonian calendar with October 7, 312 B.C., and in the Babylonian with April 3, 311 B.C. Parker and Dubberstein, *Babylonian Chronology 626 B.C.-A.D. 45*, p.18; cf. Wilhelm Kubitschek, *Grundriss der antiken Zeitrechnung* (in Walter Otto, ed., *Handbuch der Altertumswissenschaft.* I, 7 [1928]), p.70.
[3] The kings who followed Seleucus I, with their approximate dates, were: Antiochus I Soter (281-261), Antiochus II Theos (261-246), Seleucus II Callinicus (246-227), Seleucus III Soter (227-223), Antiochus III the Great (223-187), Seleucus IV Philopator (187-175), Antiochus IV Epiphanes (175-164), Antiochus V Eupator (164-162), Demetrius I Soter (162-150), Alexander I Balas (150-145), Demetrius II Nicator (145-139/38, 129-125), Antiochus VI Epiphanes (145-142/41), Antiochus VII Sidetes (139/38-129), Alexander II Zabinas (128-123), Antiochus VIII Grypus and Cleopatra Thea (125-121), Seleucus V (125), Antiochus VIII Grypus (121-96), Antiochus IX Cyzicenus (115-95), Seleucus VI Epiphanes Nicator (96-95), Antiochus X Eusebes Philopator (95-83), Demetrius III Eucaerus Philopator Soter (95-88), Antiochus XI Philadelphus (92), Philippus I Philadelphus (92-83), Antiochus XII

As far as Judea was concerned, the land was ruled for a time by the Ptolemies, but around 198 B.C. was taken by Antiochus III and made a part of Syria, where the Seleucids had established their capital at Antioch. In general the rule of the Ptolemies was favorable to the Jews, and Ptolemy II Philadelphus is remembered favorably for having encouraged the beginning of work by the Seventy at Alexandria on the famous Greek version of the Old Testament. The Seleucids, however, soon laid a heavy hand upon the Jews and the persecution by Antiochus IV Epiphanes (c.168 B.C.) led to the Maccabean war and the temporary freedom of Judea. This independence lasted until Jerusalem fell to Pompey (63 B.C.) and Palestine passed under the sway of Roman power.

Dionysus (87-84), Tigranes of Armenia (83-69), Antiochus XIII Asiaticus (69-64), Philippus II (65-64).

When the Seleucids neglected their Iranian possessions in favor of their Syrian territory, Persia fell into the power of the Parthians, an Iranian people whose leader Arsaces (c.250-c.248 B.C.) founded the Arsacid Dynasty which endured from c.250 B.C. to A.D. c.229. The Parthian Empire was overthrown by Ardashir I (the name is the modern form of Artaxerxes), who ruled A.D. c.224-241. He was the descendant of Sasan, and thus the Sassanian or Neo-Persian Empire was established which endured until the victory of the Arabs in A.D. 651. Parker and Dubberstein give a list of the Parthian kings in *Babylonian Chronology 626 B.C.-A.D. 45*, p.22, and Eduard Meyer gives a list of the Sassanid kings in EB XVII, p.583.

V

The Holy Land in the Time of Jesus

1. THE RISE OF ROME AND THE ROMAN EMPIRE, c.753 B.C.-A.D. 476

IN EARLY Christian times the Mediterranean world was ruled by Rome. Stone Age remains in the neighborhood of Rome attest the great antiquity of human settlement in that vicinity. The actual founding of the city was supposed, according to Roman traditions, to have occurred in 753 B.C., and that date was taken as the initial point in the usual chronological system which reckoned *ab urbe condita*, from the founded city.

The early kings gave way in 509 B.C., according to the traditional chronology, to a republican form of government which endured until 27 B.C. Rome was the natural center of the Mediterranean, and her supremacy in the West was established indisputably by the defeat of Hannibal of Carthage in the battle of Zama in 202 B.C. In the East, Greece and western Asia Minor were conquered by the middle and end respectively of the second century B.C., but it remained for the Roman general Pompey (106-48 B.C.), whose bust is shown in Fig. 98, to close the circle of empire around the eastern end of the Mediterranean.

The opposition to Rome in the East was headed by King Mithradates VI Eupator of Pontus, member of a dynasty which belonged to the highest Persian nobility, who warred with the Romans in Asia Minor for 25 years, and by his son-in-law King Tigranes of Armenia, member of a dynasty founded by Artaxias, a general of Antiochus III. Tigranes was for a time the most powerful ruler in western Asia, and used Antioch in Syria as one of his residential cities. The defeat of Mithradates and Tigranes by Pompey led to the consolidation of Roman power in the eastern Mediterranean, to the establishment of Syria as a Roman province and to the inclusion of Palestine in the empire (cf. p. 208).

While Pompey was winning the East, Gaius Julius Caesar (c.102-44 B.C.) was rising to political importance in Rome. For a time the two men shared power, then faced each other in civil war. Pompey was defeated at Pharsalus in 48 B.C. and afterward was murdered in Egypt, whither he fled for refuge, while the last of his forces were crushed at Munda in Spain in 45 B.C. Thereafter Caesar was undisputed master of the Roman world, a glory which he enjoyed for only a brief six months before being assassinated on March 15, 44 B.C.

Two relatives of Julius Caesar were then the chief claimants to his empire. The first was Marcus Antonius, commonly called Mark Antony, who was related on his mother's side to Julius Caesar, and who was consul with Caesar in 44 B.C. The second was Gaius Octavius, whose grandmother was Caesar's sister, and who was adopted and made heir by Caesar, thereby acquiring the designation of Gaius Julius Caesar Octavianus. Associating himself with Cleopatra, the heiress of the Ptolemies in Egypt, Mark Antony was dominant in the East, while Octavian appropriated Italy and the West. The final trial of strength between the two rivals came in the naval battle of Actium (September 2, 31 B.C.), where Antony was decisively defeated. In the following year Alexandria was taken and Antony and Cleopatra committed suicide.

From 31 B.C. on, Octavian was the real master of the empire, and two years later the restoration of peace was marked by the closing of the doors of the temple of Janus for the first time in 200 years. In recognition of Octavian's distinguished services to the state, the Roman Senate in 27 B.C. conferred upon him the title Augustus, meaning august or majestic. This appellation of dignity was borne by him as the first Roman emperor, and was adopted by all the later Caesars or emperors of Rome.

Under the rule of Augustus (d. A.D. 14) and his successors, for two centuries the Mediterranean world as a whole enjoyed an internal peace, the *Pax Romana*, which it never before had had and which for so long a period it has never since possessed. The author of this outstanding achievement is portrayed in the statue shown

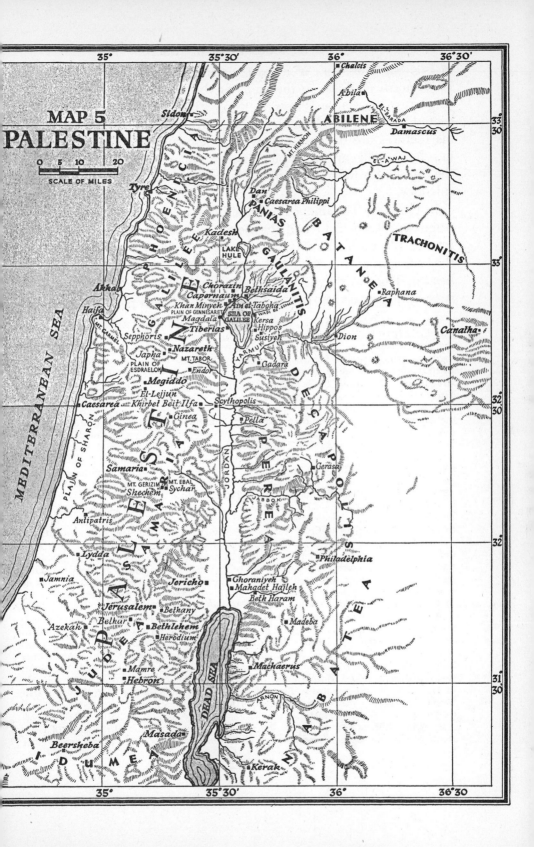

MAP 5
PALESTINE

0   5   10   20
SCALE OF MILES

in Fig. 99. This work of a master sculptor[1] was found near Prima Porta north of Rome in the ruins of the villa of Livia, the wife of Augustus; the statue is now in the Vatican. The emperor is represented in the prime of manhood and at the height of his power, and his features are delicate and refined. On his breastplate is carved in relief an allegory of empire. Beneath Caelus, the Sky, drives Sol, the Sun, in his four-horse chariot—symbol of the new order in all its splendor.

In the New Testament the birth of Jesus is dated in the reign of Augustus (Luke 2:1) and the beginning of the public ministry of Jesus is placed in the reign of Tiberius (Luke 3:1). The latter was the successor of Augustus, and reigned from A.D. 14 to 37. The marble head of Tiberius shown in Fig. 100 is in the Boston Museum of Fine Arts, and portrays him as yet a lad with fresh and pleasing features.[2]

[1] Gerhart Rodenwaldt in *Die Antike, Zeitschrift für Kunst und Kultur des klassischen Altertums.* 13 (1937), pp.160-163.

[2] The successors of Augustus and Tiberius in the Julio-Claudian line were Gaius (A.D. 37-41), generally known as Caligula, Claudius (41-54), and Nero (54-68). In 68 Galba, Otho and Vitellius all claimed the throne, but the final winner in the struggle was Vespasian (69-79). The Flavian Dynasty which he founded included also Titus (79-81) and Domitian (81-96). The rulers who followed belonged to the house of Nerva and included Nerva (96-98), Trajan (98-117), and Hadrian (117-138). Then the Antonines came to the throne, including Antoninus Pius (138-161), Marcus Aurelius (161-180), and Commodus (180-192). The Severan house embraced Septimus Severus (193-211), Caracalla (211-217), Elagabalus (218-222), and Severus Alexander (222-235). The succeeding military emperors were Maximinus Thrax (235-238), Philip the Arab (244-249), Decius (249-251), Gallus (251-253), Valerian (253-260), and Gallienus (260-268). After Gallienus was murdered, Claudius II reigned briefly (268-270), but it remained for Aurelian (270-275) to restore unity. He was followed by Tacitus (275), Probus (276-282), Carus (282), Carinus and Numerian (283), and Diocletian (284-305). Diocletian reorganized the empire in 286 by entrusting the West to his friend Maximian while he retained the East for himself. This arrangement was modified further in 292 when the two Augusti each recognized a Caesar as a subordinate colleague. Thus Galerius Caesar was associated with Diocletian Augustus in the East and Constantius Chlorus Caesar with Maximian Augustus in the West. Diocletian and Maximian abdicated in 305, leaving Galerius and Constantius Chlorus as Augusti in control of the empire. Galerius was able to secure the promotion to the rank of Caesar of his faithful servant Flavius Valerius Severus and of his nephew Daia Maximinus, hoping thus on the death of Constantius Chlorus to become the sole master of the empire. Constantius Chlorus died in 306, but his soldiers continued to be loyal to Constantine, son of Constantius Chlorus and Helena. Maximian now reassumed the dignity which he had relinquished in 305, and with his son Maxentius brought the number of Roman rulers to six. In the struggle that followed, Maximian was killed in 310, and Maxentius was defeated by Constantine at the decisive battle of the Milvian bridge outside Rome in 312. Meanwhile in the East Licinius had become co-regent with Galerius and, upon the latter's death in 311, succeeded him on the throne. Constantine and Licinius now (313-323) exercised authority jointly as colleagues in the West and the East respectively, and Licinius married the sister of Constantine. The two rulers warred however in 314 and again in 323. In the second conflict

In connection with the birth and the public appearance of Jesus, Luke not only refers to the Roman emperors Augustus and Tiberius, but also gives more detailed mention of a number of lesser governors and officials. The passages (Luke 2:1f.; 3:1f.) are as follows:

"Now it came to pass in those days, there went out a decree from Caesar Augustus, that all the world should be enrolled. This was the first enrolment made when Quirinius was governor of Syria."

"Now in the fifteenth year of the reign of Tiberius Caesar, Pontius Pilate being governor of Judea, and Herod being tetrarch of Galilee, and his brother Philip tetrarch of the region of Iturea and Trachonitis, and Lysanias tetrarch of Abilene, in the high-priesthood of Annas and Caiaphas, the word of God came unto John the son of Zacharias."

Elsewhere Luke dates the promise of the birth of John the Baptist "in the days of Herod, king of Judea" (1:5), and Matthew places the birth of Jesus "in the days of Herod the king" (2:1), this Herod being identified (2:22) as the father of Archelaus. In order to explain these references to Syrian and Palestinian authorities and to give an understanding of the inner political situation in Palestine in the time of Jesus, it is necessary now to tell briefly a complex and fascinating story which has its beginnings in the days of the Maccabean War.

Licinius was defeated, and in 324 was executed at Constantine's command. Thus Constantine the Great emerged as sole ruler of the Roman Empire (323-337). After Constantine, his three sons divided the empire, but Constantine II (337-340) died in civil war against his brother Constans (337-350) and the latter was slain by the usurper Magnentius. The remaining son Constantius (337-361) had received the East, and now upon defeating Magnentius again united the whole empire under one authority. He was followed by Julian the Apostate (361-363), and Jovian (363-364). In 364 the empire was divided again, Valentinian I (364-375) taking the West and Valens (364-378) the East. The later emperors in the West were Gratian (367-383) and Valentinian II (375-392), Theodosius I (394-395), Honorius (395-423), Joannes (424), Valentinian III (425-455), Maximus (455), Avitus (455-456), Majorian (457-461), Libius Severus (461-465), Anthemius (467-472), Olybrius (472), Glycerius (473), Julius Nepos (473-475), and Romulus Augustulus (475-476). The last named king was deposed by the Teutonic invaders in 476 and replaced by Odoacer as the first barbarian ruler of Italy. Thus the Roman Empire in the West came to an end. In the East the emperors who followed Valens included Theodosius I the Great (379-395), who also ruled the West for a time, Arcadius (395-408), Theodosius II (408-450), Marcian (450-457), Leo I (457-474), Leo II (474), Zeno (474-491), Anastasius I (491-518), Justin I (518-527), Justinian I the Great (527-565), and a long line of further rulers who occupied the throne until Constantinople fell to the Crusaders in 1204 and became the seat of a Latin Empire.

2. THE TIME OF THE MACCABEES, c.168-63 B.C.

It was an old priest Mattathias and his five sons who led the revolt against Antiochus IV Epiphanes (p. 208).[1] Of these sons, Judas, called Maccabeus, or the Hammer (c.165-c.161 B.C.), became the great general and gave his name to the struggle, while his brother Simon eventually ruled (c.142-c.135) as prince and high priest over a small independent kingdom. The dynasty thus founded was known as the Hasmonean, from Asamonaeus the father of Mattathias.[2] In the succession of rulers Simon was followed by his son John Hyrcanus (c.135-c.105), and his grandson Aristobulus I (c.105-c.104), who assumed the title of king. Under the latter's brother, Alexander Jannaeus (c.104-c.78), the Jewish kingdom attained its greatest extent, reaching to limits practically the same as those of the kingdom of David. The title of king was stamped proudly in Hebrew and Greek upon the coins of Alexander Jannaeus.

But the sons of Jannaeus, Hyrcanus II and Aristobulus II, quarreled for the throne and both appealed to the Romans for help. Pompey had already (64 B.C.) made Syria a Roman province and was near at hand in Damascus. When Aristobulus lost the confidence of the Romans and his adherents entrenched themselves in the temple, Pompey besieged Jerusalem. The city fell after three months (63 B.C.) and Pompey outraged the Jews by entering the Holy of Holies. Aristobulus II was taken prisoner to Rome, and the elder brother, Hyrcanus II (63-40 B.C.), was established as high priest and ethnarch. From that time on the Jews were subject to the Romans.[3]

[1] The history of the Maccabean struggle is narrated in a generally trustworthy way in I Maccabees.
[2] Josephus, *War.* i, i, 3.
[3] ibid., i, vii, 4; *Ant.* xiv, iv.

3. PALESTINE UNDER HERODIAN AND ROMAN RULE, 63 B.C.-A.D. 70

WHEN Pompey was defeated and Julius Caesar was established as master in Rome, Hyrcanus II and his friend Antipater, the Idumean, attached themselves to Caesar's party and rendered him such services as to secure for Judea freedom both from taxes and from the obligation of military service. Antipater, who already, it seems, had attained the position of procurator of Judea,[1] was confirmed in this office by Caesar. He soon appointed his two sons, Phasael and Herod, governors of Jerusalem and Galilee respectively.

Phasael ended his life by suicide when Antigonus (40-37 B.C.), son of Aristobulus II and last of the Hasmonean rulers, captured Jerusalem with Parthian help. For Herod there was a greater future. In Rome he gained the favor of Mark Antony and Octavian, who at that time divided the Roman world between themselves, and was given by the Senate the rank of king of Judea (40 B.C.). By 37 B.C. Herod was able to besiege and take Jerusalem. Antigonus was beheaded by the Romans, and Herod assumed the Jewish crown, meanwhile having strengthened his claim by marrying the Hasmonean princess, Mariamne. When Mark Antony was defeated and Octavian emerged as the sole emperor of the Roman Empire, Herod knew how to continue in his favor and even to gain by imperial favor the doubling of his own territory.

HEROD THE GREAT

Herod "the Great"[2] ruled for nearly 40 years (40-4 B.C.) with much energy and success, but was always hated by the Jews as a half-foreigner[3] and a friend of the Romans. Moreover, he had little real interest in Judaism and was instrumental in spreading Greek culture throughout the land. The love of Herod for pagan civilization was reflected in most of his numerous building activities.[4] Temples dedicated to pagan gods and emperor worship, halls and theaters in the Greek style, palaces, castles and baths were constructed throughout the land. On the site of ancient Samaria he built a new city, named

[1] *Ant.* xiv, viii, 1.
[2] This title is applied once to Herod by Josephus, *Ant.* xviii, v, 4.
[3] As an Idumean he was called a "half-Jew" by Josephus, *Ant.* xiv, xv, 2. The Idumeans, or Edomites, living in southern Palestine had been conquered and compelled to accept Judaism by John Hyrcanus (*Ant.* xiii, ix, 1).
[4] *War.* i, xxi.

Sebaste, in honor of the Emperor Augustus.[5] On the coast, on the site of the ancient Straton's Tower, he built a new city and port which he named Caesarea and which later was to be the capital of the country.

But the most magnificent single piece of building done by Herod was carried out in strict conformity with Jewish principles. This was the restoration of the temple in Jerusalem,[6] which was begun in 20-19 B.C. Only priests were allowed to build the temple proper, and Herod himself refrained from entering the inner temple, whose precincts should be trodden by none but priests. The temple proper was built in one year and six months, but other building work was long continued, and was finished only in the time of the procurator Albinus (A.D. 62-64), a few years before the temple's final destruction.

THE SONS OF HEROD

A few days before his death in 4 B.C., the aged Herod rewrote his will providing for the division of his kingdom among his sons. Of the various sons of Herod's ten legal marriages several had perished in intrigues or had been put to death by their father's orders, including Alexander and Aristobulus, the sons of Mariamne (who also was slain), and Antipater, who was executed five days before Herod died. Three younger sons were to inherit the kingdom. Philip, the son of Cleopatra of Jerusalem, became tetrarch of Gaulanitis, Trachonitis, Batanea and Panias (Paneas), regions north and east of the Sea of Galilee and mostly inhabited by pagans.[7] Over this territory Philip reigned well for 30 years. At the sources of the Jordan he rebuilt the city of Panias and gave it the name Caesarea in honor of the emperor.[8] To distinguish it from Caesarea on the coast it was called Caesarea Philippi (Matthew 16:13; Mark 8:27). Also he raised the village of Bethsaida, which was situated at the lake of Gennesareth, to the dignity of a city, both by the number of inhabitants it contained and by its size, and named it Julias after the daughter of the emperor.[9]

[5] The Latin title Augustus was rendered in Greek by Σεβαστός. cf. Dio Cassius (A.D. c.150-c.235), *Roman History.* LIII, xvi, 8. tr. E. Cary, LCL (1914-27), VI, p.235.

[6] *War.* I, xxi, 1; *Ant.* xv, xi.

[7] *War.* I, xxxiii, 8; *Ant.* XVII, viii, 1.

[8] *War.* II, ix, 1; *Ant.* XVIII, ii, 1.

[9] *Ant.* XVIII, ii, 1; cf. *War.* II, ix, 1. Julias was the daughter of Augustus, but was banished in 2 B.C. Since Philip hardly would have named a city for her after that event, Julias must have been built before 2 B.C.

Herod Antipas, the younger son of Malthace, became tetrarch of Galilee and Perea (4 B.C.-A.D. 39). He built a splendid capital for himself at a beautiful site on the western shore of the Sea of Galilee, and named it Tiberias in honor of Tiberius who was then on the Roman throne. Antipas brought trouble upon himself through putting away his first wife, the daughter of King Aretas of Nabatea, to marry Herodias, whom he alienated from his half-brother, Herod.[10] Thereafter Antipas was defeated in war by Aretas, and when he sought the king's title from Caligula was banished instead to Lyons in Gaul, whither Herodias followed him. Meanwhile his tetrarchy and that of Philip, together with the title of king, were conferred on the brother of Herodias, Herod Agrippa I.

Archelaus, the older son of Malthace, received the principal part of Herod's territory—Judea, Samaria and Idumea—and was intended by Herod to have the title of king but actually was given only that of ethnarch (4 B.C.-A.D. 6). Insurrection was spreading throughout the land, however, and the rule of Archelaus was violent and incompetent. When he was deposed and banished to Vienne in Gaul in A.D. 6, his territory was put directly under Roman rule.[11]

THE PROCURATORS

Authority over the former dominions of Archelaus was placed in the hands of a governor of the equestrian order, whose title was that of procurator, and who could receive help in case of need from the legate who governed the province of Syria.[12] The residence of the

---

[10] Herodias was a granddaughter of Herod the Great, her father being Aristobulus, the son of Mariamne, who was executed in 7 B.C. Mark 6:17; Matthew 14:3 (contrast Luke 3:19) call Herodias the wife of Philip, meaning doubtless the tetrarch of Trachonitis. Josephus (*Ant.* XVIII, v, 4) states that Herodias was married to Herod, the son of Herod the Great and the second Mariamne, the high priest's daughter. Also Josephus says that Herodias' daughter, Salome, was married to Philip, the tetrarch of Trachonitis. The relationships may have been confused in the Gospels, or it is barely possible that this Herod bore the surname Philip.

[11] *War.* II, viii, 1; *Ant.* XVII, xiii; XVIII, i, 1.

[12] In 27 B.C. Augustus divided the provinces of the Roman Empire into imperial and senatorial. (1) The imperial provinces, which the emperor continued to hold, were those which were most difficult to manage and which required the presence of a strong military force. They in turn were divided, with the exception of some which were administered by simple knights, into two classes: those administered by men who had been consuls, and those administered by men who had been praetors. The governors were nominated by the emperor, were directly responsible to him, and held office for a term the length of which depended on the emperor's pleasure. The governors of both consular and praetorian provinces were called *legati Augusti* (or *Caesaris*) *pro praetore*. (2) The provinces which were given over to the senate were those which did not require the presence of an army but only of a small garrison

procurator was at Caesarea, but on occasions when special oversight was necessary he would live for a time in Jerusalem.

The first procurator of Judea was Coponius (probably A.D. 6-9), and his immediate successors were Marcus Ambivius (probably A.D. 9-12), Annius Rufus (probably A.D. 12-15), Valerius Gratus (A.D. 15-26), Pontius Pilate (A.D. 26-36), Marcellus (A.D. 36-37) and Marullus (A.D. 37-41).

Of them all the most famous and perhaps the most ruthless was Pontius Pilate. Pilate was appointed to office through Sejanus, the anti-Semitic prime minister of Tiberius, and he gave offense to the Jews in many ways. His soldiers carried into the Holy City standards bearing the likeness of the emperor, which violated Jewish principles and provoked a determined and successful protest. Again, he took money from the temple treasury to build an aqueduct to Jerusalem, and mercilessly beat down the crowds which gathered to make petition against this act. Later he put inscribed shields in Herod's palace, which were taken down only when the Jews appealed to Tiberius. Yet another and otherwise unknown act of violence is referred to in Luke 13:1, where Pilate is said to have mingled the blood of certain Galileans with that of their animal sacrifices. Finally he slaughtered and imprisoned a multitude of Samaritans who had gathered at Mount Gerizim to search for some sacred vessels which were believed to have been buried there since the time of Moses. The Samaritans complained to Vitellius, the legate in Syria, and Pilate was replaced by Marcellus. Agrippa I charged against Pilate, according to a letter quoted by Philo, "corruptibility, violence, robberies, ill-treatment of the people, grievances, continuous executions without even the form of a trial, endless and intolerable cruelties," yet it must be admitted that the position of a Roman governor in Judea was very difficult, and no doubt it was to Pilate's credit that he retained office for as long as ten years.[13]

sufficient for the purpose of maintaining order. They were also divided into those administered by men who had been consuls and those administered by men who had been praetors. The governors of the senatorial provinces were appointed for a year at a time, were responsible to the senate, and were called proconsuls. (3) Certain other possessions were regarded as domains of the emperor and were placed under governors of the equestrian order responsible to the emperor. Their title was that of praefect or procurator, and the title procurator soon became the prevailing one. Judea thus belonged to the third and more exceptional class of provinces. Dio, *Roman History*. LIII, xii-xv; Strabo, *Geography*. XVII, iii, 25.

[13] Josephus, *Ant.* XVIII, iii, 1f.; iv, 1f.; *War*. II, ix, 2-4; Philo (c.20 B.C.-A.D. c.54), *Legatio ad Gaium* 38. ed. L. Cohn and P. Wendland VI (1915), p.210.

Of the Lysanias who is mentioned by Luke (3:1) as tetrarch of Abilene, little is known. The capital of the tetrarchy was at Abila, not far from Damascus, and an inscription of the time of Tiberius has been found there naming Lysanias as tetrarch.[14]

The legates who ruled Syria at the end of the old era and the beginning of the new were Titius (c.10 B.C.), C. Sentius Saturninus (9-6 B.C.), P. Quintilius Varus (6-4 B.C.), P. Sulpicius Quirinius (?) (3-2 B.C.), C. Caesar (?) (1 B.C.-A.D. 4), L. Volusius Saturninus (A.D. 4-5) and P. Sulpicius Quirinius (A.D. 6-9).[15]

Luke's reference to the census which was taken at the time of the birth of Jesus, and which was the first enrolment made when Quirinius was in command of Syria (2:2), constitutes an unsolved problem. We know from Josephus that Quirinius conducted a census in Syria in the thirty-seventh year of Caesar's victory over Antony at Actium,[16] or in the year beginning September 2, A.D. 6, but this is too late to be brought into connection with the birth of Jesus which took place while Herod the Great (d. 4 B.C.) was still king of Judea (Luke 1:5; Matthew 2:1). While Quirinius may also have held the governorship of Syria briefly in 3-2 B.C. this fact is not certain,[17] and at all events this date too is after the death of Herod the Great. It is true that Quirinius was in the East earlier than this, for he served as commander in the Homanadensian War in 10-7 B.C. (pp. 263f., n. 35). It may be supposed, therefore, that sometime during the last years of Herod's reign he was connected with a census in Syria and Palestine, but this is a hypothesis for which evidence outside of the New Testament is lacking at present.

As to the taking of such an enrolment in general, it is known from discoveries among the Egyptian papyri that a Roman census was taken regularly every fourteen years, and an edict of A.D. 104 says: "Since the census is approaching, it is necessary to command all who for any reason are out of their own districts to return to their own home, in order to perform the usual business of the taxation. . . ."[18] Thus the situation presupposed in Luke 2:3 is entirely plausible.

[14] *Corpus Inscriptionum Graecarum.* (1828-77), III, No.4521. This younger Lysanias to whom Luke refers and who undoubtedly existed, is not to be confused with an older Lysanias who ruled at nearby Chalcis, 40-36 B.C.

[15] Erich Klostermann, *Das Lukasevangelium* (*Handbuch zum Neuen Testament.* 5 [2d ed. 1929]), p.33.

[16] *Ant.* XVIII, ii, 1.   [17] CAH X, p.878.

[18] Adolf Deissmann, *Licht vom Osten, das Neue Testament und die neuentdeckten Texte der hellenistisch-römischen Welt.* 4th ed. 1923, p.231.

In A.D. 41 Claudius added Judea and Samaria to the possessions of Herod Agrippa I (A.D. 41-44) who, until the time of his death three years later,[19] ruled over the entire territory of Herod the Great. At later times, some portions of the country, including the former tetrarchy of Philip and parts of Galilee and Perea, were given to his son, Agrippa II (A.D. 50-100). But most of the country after the time of the death of Herod Agrippa I was ruled by procurators. They included Cuspius Fadus (A.D. 44-?), Tiberius Alexander (A.D. ?-48), Ventidius Cumanus (A.D. 48-52), Felix (A.D. c.52-c.60), Porcius Festus (A.D. c.60-62), Albinus (A.D. 62-64) and Gessius Florus (A.D. 64-66), and their cumulative cruelties drove the Jews to the great war (A.D. 66-73) which was climaxed with the destruction of Jerusalem in A.D. 70.

THE HIGH PRIESTS

Our brief outline of the history suggested by Luke's references may be completed by noting that from the time of Herod the Great to the destruction of Jerusalem, twenty-eight high priests exercised spiritual authority in Palestine.[20] The two to whom Luke (3:2) refers are Annas and Caiaphas. While Annas was actually high priest only in A.D. 6-15, he continued to be a dominant influence in the days when his sons Eleazar, Jonathan, Theophilus, Matthias and Ananos, and his son-in-law Caiaphas (A.D. 18-36) held that position.

[19] Acts 12:20-23; *Ant.* xix, viii, 2; Eusebius, *Church History.* ii, x. tr. Arthur Cushman McGiffert, NPNFss i, pp.111f.

[20] *Ant.* xx, x. The collation of Josephus' various notices of them gives the following list of 28 names (Emil Schürer, *A History of the Jewish People in the Time of Jesus Christ* [1896] ii, i, pp.197-202): Appointed by Herod (37-4 B.C.): Ananel (37-36 B.C.), Aristobulus (35 B.C.), Jesus the son of Phabes, Simon (the father-in-law of Herod the Great), Matthias (5-4 B.C.), Joseph, Joazar (4 B.C.); appointed by Archelaus (4 B.C.-A.D. 6): Eleazar, Jesus the son of Sie; appointed by Quirinius (A.D. 6): Annas or Ananos (A.D. 6-15), *Ant.* xviii, ii, 1f.; Luke 3:2; John 18:13, 24; Acts 4:6; appointed by Valerius Gratus (A.D. 15-26): Ishmael (A.D. c.15-c.16), Eleazar the son of Annas (A.D. c.16-c.17), Simon the son of Kamithos (A.D. c.17-c.18), Joseph called Caiaphas, the son-in-law of Annas (A.D. c.18-36), *Ant.* xviii, ii, 2; iv, 3; Matthew 26:3, 57; Luke 3:2; John 11:49; 18:13f., 24, 28; Acts 4:6; appointed by Vitellius (A.D. 35-39): Jonathan the son of Annas (A.D. 36-37), Theophilos the son of Annas (A.D. 37-40); appointed by Agrippa I (A.D. 41-44): Simon Kantheras, Matthias the son of Annas (A.D. c.43), Elionaios; appointed by Herod of Chalcis (A.D. 44-48): Joseph, Ananias (A.D. c.47-c.59), *Ant.* xx, v, 2; vi, 2; ix, 2-4; *War.* ii, xii, 6; xvii, 6, 9; Acts 23:2; 24:1; appointed by Agrippa II (A.D. 50-100): Ishmael (A.D. c.59-c.61), Joseph Kabi (A.D. 61-62), Ananos the son of Annas or Ananos (A.D. 62 for only three months), Jesus the son of Damnaios (A.D. c.62-c.63), Jesus the son of Gamaliel (A.D. c.63-c.65), Matthias the son of Theophilus; appointed by the people during the war (A.D. 67-68): Phannias.

4. SACRED WAYS AND SITES

"HERE everything is historical," is the way Dr. Gustaf Dalman always answered the question as to whether this or that place in Palestine was historical.[1] As one seeks to know the Palestine of Jesus' day it is often the country itself rather than any specific object which speaks most clearly. Its hills, lakes and rivers, its sky, sun and springtime flowers, must be much the same as they were in Jesus' day. Also, in many ways the life of the people, their villages, activities and customs, remain little changed. One still sees the women at the village well, the sower going forth to sow, and the shepherd leading his sheep, exactly as it is said in John 10:4, "He goeth before them, and the sheep follow him" (Fig. 101). But it is possible also to make many positive identifications of sacred places and to discover many tangible remains from the Palestinian world in which Jesus walked.

BETHLEHEM

Bethlehem is about six miles south and slightly west of Jerusalem, in the hill-country of Judea. It is situated on the two summits and intermediate saddle of a ridge some 2,500 feet in elevation. The terraced hillsides and fertile valleys justify the ancient name, Bethlehem, "House of Bread," and the modern name, Beit Lahm, "House of Flesh," but the city still remains small, having fewer than 10,000 inhabitants. Its whole claim to greatness is that it was the city of David and the birthplace of Jesus Christ (I Samuel 16:4-13; Matthew 2:1; Luke 2:4).

Three and one-half miles southeast of Bethlehem are the remains of the Herodium. This was a stronghold of Herod the Great, which he erected on an unusual, conical and artificially heightened hill. Two hundred steps of polished stones once led up to the circular towers of the fort on the summit, which contained richly furnished apartments for the king.[2] Here, at his desert watch-tower, Herod the Great at last was buried.[3] Today the hill is known as Frank Mountain and still has on its summit the ruins of Herod's towers.

Yet much farther southeast, on the western bank of the Dead Sea, was Masada, the "Mountain Stronghold." On a rock which rose high and steep on all sides, was a fortress which had existed from the time

---

[1] *Sacred Sites and Ways.* 1935, p.13.
[2] *War.* I, xiii, 8; xxi, 10; *Ant.* xiv, xiii, 9; xv, ix, 4.
[3] *War.* I, xxxiii, 9; *Ant.* xvii, viii, 3.

of Jonathan the high priest and had been fortified anew in the greatest strength by Herod the Great.[4] This was the very last stronghold of the Jews to fall to the Romans in the great war. Here the Sicarii[5] under Eleazar held out during a prolonged siege. When hope was gone, the besieged put one another to death rather than fall into the hands of their enemies. The fortress, blazing in flames, and containing only the multitude of the slain, was entered by the Romans in April, A.D. 73.[6]

NAZARETH

Nazareth lies high on a sharp slope in the Galilean hills. Its altitude is about 1,150 feet. From the summit above the village one looks south across the extensive plain of Esdraelon, west to Mount Carmel on the Mediterranean coast, east to near-by Mount Tabor,[7] and far north to snow-capped Mount Hermon (Psalm 89:12):

> The north and the south, thou hast created them:
> Tabor and Hermon rejoice in thy name.

The village itself has at present seven or eight thousand inhabitants. Stores, blacksmith shops where the sickles characteristic of Nazareth are made, and carpenter shops open directly on the steep and narrow streets. At the base of the hill is Mary's Well (Ain Maryam) as it has been called since A.D. 1100, the only source of water in the village. To it Mary must have come, just as the women of Nazareth do today with their water pitchers balanced gracefully on their heads.

Nazareth is now on the main highway which runs north and south through Palestine and stands also at the junction of that road with the branch which runs west to Haifa. Anciently the caravan road from Damascus to Egypt crossed the plain of Jezreel some six miles south of Nazareth, as does the Damascus-Haifa railroad of today, while a branch road to Akka passed at the same distance north of Nazareth. Also the main road from Sepphoris to Jerusalem ran south directly through Nazareth, while a branch from it ran through Japha

---

[4] *War.* vii, viii, 3.

[5] These fanatical patriots received their name from the short daggers (*sicae*) which they carried (*War.* ii, xiii, 3; *Ant.* xx, viii, 10).

[6] *War.* vii, ix.

[7] The Gospel according to the Hebrews made Mount Tabor the mountain of Temptation (M. R. James, *The Apocryphal New Testament* [1942], p.2), while in the fourth century A.D. it was believed to be the mount of the Transfiguration and in the sixth century three churches were built on its summit in memory of the three tabernacles (Mark 9:5 = Matthew 17:4 = Luke 9:33).

98. Pompey

99. Caesar Augustus

100. The Young Tiberius

101. A Palestinian Shepherd with his Sheep

102. The Jordan River

103. Plowing on the Hills above the Sea of Galilee

104. The Synagogue at Capernaum

105. The Synagogue Inscription of Theodotus

106. A Portion of the "Fourth Map of Asia" in Ptolemy's *Geography*

107. Herod's Towers at the West Gate of Samaria

108. The Garden of Gethsemane

109 Jerusalem from the Air

111. Warning Inscription from Herod's Temple

110. The Wailing Wall

112. Titus, the Conqueror of the Jews

113. Relief on the Arch of Titus at Rome

to join the Damascus-Egypt road by way of Megiddo or Legio (el-Lejjun). Yet a third route south led from Nazareth through Endor and by way of Jericho to Jerusalem. Thus Nazareth was by no means a small out-of-the-way place hidden in a corner of the land, but was on or near important thoroughfares carrying extensive traffic.

Japha, only one and one-half miles southwest of Nazareth, was an important village at that time and Sepphoris, or Zippori, Galilee's largest city, was but three miles distant to the north. Neither Japha[8] nor Sepphoris is mentioned in the New Testament, but Josephus refers to both places frequently. Japha was one of the strongholds of the country. On one occasion it was occupied by Josephus that he might guard from there the roads of Galilee to the south,[9] and another time it stoutly resisted the armies of Trajan.[10] The remains of a synagogue of the Roman period have been found there.[11]

Sepphoris was "the largest city in Galilee."[12] In the time of Alexander Jannaeus it was so strong that his enemy, Ptolemy Lathyrus, was unable to conquer it.[13] A royal palace was established there in the days of Herod the Great, and in the insurrection which followed his death the revolutionary leader Judas made Sepphoris a main center of rebellion.[14] Then Varus came with the Syrian legions and, assisted by Aretas, took Sepphoris, made its inhabitants slaves and burned the city.[15] Herod Antipas walled the city and rebuilt it so splendidly that it became the ornament of all Galilee.[16] It probably was Galilee's capital until the founding of Tiberias. Having learned from its earlier experience the futility of revolution against Rome, Sepphoris did not join in the uprising of A.D. 66, and, by taking a stand for peace with the Romans, received a Roman garrison for its protection.[17] The remains of a fort and of a theater, both probably built by Herod Antipas, were unearthed at Sepphoris in 1931 by an expedition of the University of Michigan.[18]

Thus Jesus grew to manhood in a village which was close to some of the most stirring events of those times.[19]

[8] It was the Japhia of Joshua 19:12.   [9] *Life of Josephus.* 52, cf. 45.
[10] *War.* III, vii, 31.
[11] L. H. Vincent in *Revue Biblique.* 1921, pp.434-438.
[12] *Life.* 45.   [13] *Ant.* XIII, xii, 5.   [14] *Ant.* XVII, x, 5.
[15] *Ant.* XVII, x, 9.   [16] *Ant.* XVIII, ii, 1.
[17] *War.* II, xviii, 11; III, ii, 4; iv, 1; *Life.* 8,22.25,45,65,67,74.
[18] Leroy Waterman, *Preliminary Report of the University of Michigan Excavations at Sepphoris, Palestine, in 1931.* 1937, pp.28f.
[19] cf. S. J. Case, *Jesus, A New Biography.* 1927, pp.202-212.

THE JORDAN

The Jordan River, in whose vicinity John the Baptist preached and in which Jesus was baptized, flows down through a flat, semi-desert valley, but the river itself is lined by rich foliage (Fig. 102). Locusts and wild honey (cf. Matthew 3:4) are still found and used on occasion by the Bedouins for food. Church tradition long has identified the site of Bethabara[20] where Jesus was baptized with the ford called Mahadet Hajleh where the main roads from Judea to southern Perea and from Jerusalem to Beth Haram cross the Jordan. This identification is not certain but some such location is probable.

THE SEA OF GALILEE

When Jesus left Nazareth and dwelt in Capernaum (Matthew 4:13) he left the highlands and took up his abode on the shores of a lake[21] lying some 686 feet below sea level. For the most part high plateaus surround the lake and slope steeply down to it. Viewed from the heights in the springtime, the Galilean lake seems the most beautiful place in Palestine, its blue surface set in the green frame of the hills. Flowers are then profuse and the radiant Syrian sunlight floods everything. One understands how Professor Adolf Deissmann could say in his *Licht vom Osten* that when a beam of the eastern sun falls into the darkness of a room "it begins to dawn, to glitter and to move; the one beam seems to double itself, to multiply itself ten-fold," and one appreciates his admonition, "Take then this single beam with you, as your own, beyond the Alps to your study: if you have ancient texts to decipher, the beam will make stone and potsherd speak . . . and, if the honor is vouchsafed you to study the holy Scriptures, the beam will awaken for you apostles and evangelists, will show you, yet more luminous than before, the sacred figure of the Saviour from the East, to whose worship and discipleship the church is pledged."[22]

Narrow strips of land along the lake are very fertile, but back up on the stony hills cultivation is difficult and everything which has

---

[20] John 1:28 RVm; cf. Origen, *Commentary on John.* VI, 24 (ANF IX, p.370); Baedeker, *Palestine and Syria*, p.131.

[21] It was called "The Sea of Galilee" (Matthew 4:18; 15:29; Mark 1:16; 7:31; John 6:1); "The Sea of Tiberias" (John 6:1; 21:1); "The Lake of Gennesaret" (Luke 5:1); "The Water of Gennesaret" (I Maccabees 11:67); and "The Lake of Chennereth" (Eusebius, *Onomasticon* see under *Chennereth*, Χενερέθ, ed. Joannes Clericus. 1707, p.55).

[22] *Licht vom Osten*, p.v. tr. Jack Finegan.

no deep roots withers beneath the blazing sun of summer. Fig. 103 which shows present-day plowing being done on these hills might almost serve as an illustration of the "rocky ground" in Jesus' parable of the soils (Mark 4:5 = Matthew 13:5 = Luke 8:6).

In visiting the chief sites on the Sea of Galilee, the pilgrim both in ancient and in modern times arrives at them most naturally in the order, Tiberias, Magdala, Capernaum and Bethsaida.[23]

TIBERIAS

Josephus says that the capital city, Tiberias, which Herod Antipas built (p. 217), was on the lake of Gennesareth in the best part of Galilee.[24] Since Josephus mentions Tiberias just following his notice of the coming of Pontius Pilate as procurator of Judea, the city may have been built around A.D. 26. Josephus also relates that Herod Antipas had to remove many sepulchers in order to make room for his city. This kept strict Jews from settling there at first, and therefore the tetrarch had to secure inhabitants by bringing in foreigners and beggars. After the fall of Jerusalem, however, Tiberias became a chief seat of Jewish learning and in the second century the Sanhedrin, which had been moved from Jerusalem to Jamnia and then to Sepphoris, was established there. Despite its undoubted importance and magnificence at the time, Tiberias is mentioned only once in the New Testament (John 6:23).[25] Today the Arabs call the town Tabariya, and some ruins of the ancient city and its castle are still to be seen.

MAGDALA

Magdala was three miles north of Tiberias, at the southern end of the Plain of Ginnesar or Gennesaret, and is known today as Mejdel. This is doubtless the place from which Mary Magdalene (Matthew 27:56, etc.) came, and if Magadan (Matthew 15:39) and Dalmanutha (Mark 8:10) are to be traced to Magdal and Magdal Nuna or Nunaiya ("Magdal of fish") then they can be identified with the same place. If this is the city which Josephus called by its Greek name Tarichaeae, it had a population of 40,000 in his day.[26]

[23] This was the route of the pilgrim Theodosius, A.D. c.530 (P. Geyer, *Itinera Hierosolymitana*. 1898, pp.137f.), cf. Petrus diaconus (Geyer, p.112) and Arculf (Geyer, p.273).

[24] *Ant.* XVIII, ii, 3.

[25] John also (6:1; 21:1) calls the Sea of Galilee the Sea of Tiberias.

[26] *War.* II, xxi, 4.

CAPERNAUM

The city on the lake which was of most importance in the ministry of Jesus was Capernaum. Insofar as Jesus had any fixed headquarters during his ministry in Galilee they were at Capernaum. The Gospels frequently mention his presence there[27] and Matthew calls it "his own city" (9:1; cf. Mark 2:1). Special reference is made to his teaching there on the sabbath day in the synagogue (Mark 1:21 = Luke 4:31), a building which was erected for the Jews by a sympathetic and generous Roman centurion (Luke 7:5). Finally Jesus pronounced a terrible woe against the city for its refusal to repent (Matthew 11:23 = Luke 10:15).

The site of Capernaum is doubtless that known today as Tell Hum,[28] where the most extensive ruins on the northwestern side of the lake are to be found. This location agrees with the geographical implications of an incident in which Josephus, suffering an accident near the Jordan and the city of Julias, was carried back to Capernaum for safety.[29] The other site whose identification with Capernaum has been considered seriously is Khan Minyeh, farther south along the shore beyond the springs known as Ain et-Tabgha and anciently called "Seven Springs."[30] But when the pilgrim Theodosius (A.D. c.530) came from Magdala to Capernaum he reached "Seven Springs" before arriving at Capernaum.[31] This he would have done if Capernaum were at Tell Hum but not if it were at Khan Minyeh.

The most important ruin at Capernaum is that of its famous synagogue.[32] This was explored by German archeologists and then excavated and restored (Fig. 104) by members of the Franciscan order on whose property the ruins stand. The synagogue was an imposing structure, built of white limestone, facing southward toward the lake and toward Jerusalem. In general, ancient synagogues in Palestine were built with this orientation toward Jerusalem, which in the case of those in northern Palestine was toward the south. This corresponded with the practice of offering prayer toward Jerusalem,

[27] Matthew 8:5 = Luke 7:1; Matthew 4:13; 17:24; Mark 2:1; 9:33; Luke 4:23.
[28] The name may come from the fact that in later centuries the Jews made pilgrimages there to visit the grave of the prophet Nahum, or Rabbi Tanhum (Tanchuma).
[29] *Life.* 72.
[30] The present name is a corruption of the Greek Heptapegon (ἑπτάπηγον i.e. Χωρίον), "seven springs."
[31] Geyer, *Itinera Hierosolymitana*, p.138.
[32] H. Kohl and C. Watzinger, *Antike Synagogen in Galiläa.* 1916, pp.4-41; E. L. Sukenik, *Ancient Synagogues in Palestine and Greece.* 1934, pp.7-21.

which is reflected both in the Old Testament (I Kings 8:38, 44, 48; Daniel 6:10) and in rabbinical teaching, according to which Rabbi Hanna said to Rabbi Ashi, "Ye who are located on the north side of Palestine must recite your prayers towards the south (so that you shall face Jerusalem)."[33]

On the side toward the lake the Capernaum synagogue had three doors and a large window. The interior was more than 70 feet long and 50 feet wide, with a colonnade built around the three sides other than that at the entrance. Above was an upper floor, probably intended for women. There was also a colonnaded court on the eastern side. Individual parts of the synagogue were gifts from various persons, and one fragment of a pillar still carries an inscription with the name of its donor, Zebida bar Jochanan, which is practically "Zebedee the son of John."

Ornamentation of the synagogue included figures of palm trees, vines, eagles, lions, centaurs and boys carrying garlands. The attitude of the Jews toward such pictorial representations of living beings has varied greatly. Sometimes the letter of the law in Exodus 20:4 and Deuteronomy 5:8 was held to absolutely prohibit all such representations. The strenuous opposition of the Jews to the acts of Pilate in bringing standards with the likeness of the emperor into Jerusalem and in placing even inscribed shields in Herod's palace has already been noted (p. 218). Also in 4 B.C. the Jews at Jerusalem pulled down the golden eagle which Herod had put on the temple,[34] and in A.D. 66 Josephus was instructed to press for the destruction of the palace of Herod Antipas at Tiberias because it contained representations of animals.[35] In this connection Josephus expressly says that Jewish law forbade the making of such figures. But again the law was held to prohibit only the making of images for purposes of worship, and in this case animal and human motifs could be employed with perfect propriety. R. Eleazar b. R. Zadok, for example, who was well acquainted with Jerusalem before its destruction, said, "In Jerusalem there were faces of all creatures except men." Obviously the Capernaum synagogue represents in its decoration the more liberal policy.[36]

The synagogue at Tell Hum has been believed to belong to the

[33] *Baba Bathra.* 25b (RBT 7 [v, XIII], p.77).
[34] *War.* I, xxxiii, 2f.; *Ant.* XVII, vi, 2.
[35] *Life.* 12.
[36] Sukenik, *Ancient Synagogues,* pp.61-64.

time before A.D. 70,[37] but is more probably to be dated around A.D. 200 or later, since all the earlier Jewish synagogues appear to have been destroyed by Titus during the Jewish war and by Hadrian after the second century rebellion of Bar Cochba.[38] Even so it is probable that the Capernaum synagogue stands on the site and follows the plan of an earlier synagogue or of earlier synagogues, and therefore may be safely regarded as a reconstruction of the one in which Jesus himself taught.

A number of other synagogues have been found in Galilee, but probably none of them is earlier than the third century A.D., while the famous synagogue of Beth Alpha, near Khirbet Beit Ilfa in the Valley of Jezreel, with its remarkable mosaic floor, belongs to the sixth century.[39]

An interesting inscription (Fig. 105) was discovered at Jerusalem, however, which undoubtedly is to be dated before A.D. 70.[40] It records the building of a synagogue by a certain Theodotus, whose family had had the honor of holding the office of ruler of the synagogue for three generations. Indeed the cornerstone had been laid already by the father and the grandfather of Theodotus, together with the elders (presbyters) of the synagogue and Simonides who doubtless had given some special gift toward the building. The enterprise, as Theodotus carried it to completion, included not only the erection of the synagogue proper but also the construction of a guest house and apartments for pilgrims from afar, together with arrangements for water for the ritual washings. The inscription reads: "Theodotus, son of Vettenos, priest and ruler of the synagogue,[41] son of a ruler of the synagogue, grandson of a ruler of the synagogue, built the synagogue for the reading of the law and for the teaching of the commandments;[42] furthermore, the hospice and the chambers, and the water installation for lodging of needy strangers. The foundation stone thereof had been laid by his fathers, and the elders, and Simonides."

[37] B. Meistermann, *Capharnaüm et Bethsaïde.* 1921, p.289; and *Guide to the Holy Land.* 1923, p.552; G. Orfali, *Capharnaüm et ses Ruines.* 1922, pp.74-86.
[38] Kohl and Watzinger, *Antike Synagogen in Galiläa*, p.218.
[39] E. L. Sukenik, *The Ancient Synagogue of Beth Alpha.* 1932.
[40] Deissmann, *Licht vom Osten*, pp.379f.; cf. Herbert G. May in BA VII, 1 (Feb. 1944), p.11.
[41] cf. Mark 5:35, etc.
[42] cf. Luke 4:16-21; Acts 13:15.

CHORAZIN AND BETHSAIDA

Linked with Capernaum in the memorable woe which Jesus pronounced (Matthew 11:21-23 = Luke 10:13-15), and therefore presumably in the same general area, were two other cities, Chorazin and Bethsaida. Slightly less than two miles away in the hills above Tell Hum is a site called Kerazeh which doubtless is to be identified with ancient Chorazin. Again, the most impressive feature of the ruins is a synagogue, which was richly ornamented with sculptures showing animals, centaurs fighting with lions, and representations of grape-gathering and grape-pressing.[43]

The Bethsaida of the New Testament was probably the Bethsaida which Philip rebuilt and renamed Julias (p. 216). This city was just east of the Jordan near where the river flows into the Sea of Galilee,[44] and is probably to be identified with the rocky hill now known as et-Tell. This site is only about two and one-half miles distant from Capernaum across the lake, and Bethsaida might even be regarded loosely as belonging to Galilee. This would account for John's reference (12:21) to "Bethsaida of Galilee." Ptolemy also reckoned that Julias belonged to Galilee,[45] and in a similar way mention was sometimes made of "Judea beyond the Jordan."[46]

CAESAREA PHILIPPI

It was in the neighborhood of Philip's other city, Caesarea (p. 216), that Peter's confession was made (Mark 8:27 = Matthew 16:13). Caesarea Philippi was some distance north of the Sea of Galilee on a plateau at the southern foothills of Mount Hermon. At this place a strong stream of water issues from a cave (Mugharet Ras en-Neba)

---

[43] Kohl and Watzinger, *Antike Synagogen*, pp.41-58; Sukenik, *Ancient Synagogues*, pp.21-24.

[44] Josephus describes Julias as being "in lower Gaulanitis" (*War*. II, ix, 1) and says that "below the town of Julias" the river Jordan "cuts across the Lake of Gennesar" (*War*. III, x, 7; cf. *Life*. 72).

[45] *Geography*. v, 15. ed. Stevenson, p.128.

[46] Matthew 19:1. The fact that Luke 9:10 speaks of Jesus and the disciples going "apart to a city called Bethsaida" while in the Marcan parallel at the close of the section (6:45) the disciples are sent "unto the other side to Bethsaida" has led to the hypothesis that there was a second Bethsaida on the western side of the lake, but it is probable instead that there is confusion in the topographical references at this point. cf. C. C. McCown in *Journal of the Palestine Oriental Society*. 10 (1930), pp.32-58. The extreme skepticism of *Formgeschichte* concerning *Situationsangaben* (Rudolf Bultmann, *Die Geschichte der synoptischen Tradition*. 2d ed. 1931, pp.67-69, 257f.,355,365,379f.,389f.), however, would lead one to expect such confusions far oftener than they actually occur.

in the hillside and is a main source of the river Jordan. Although the cave is filled now with fallen stone, it was described impressively by Josephus: "At this spot a mountain rears its summit to an immense height aloft; at the base of the cliff is an opening into an overgrown cavern; within this, plunging down to an immeasurable depth, is a yawning chasm, enclosing a volume of still water, the bottom of which no sounding-line has been found long enough to reach."[47] The cave was sacred to Pan and hence the place originally bore the name Panias (modern Banias). Herod the Great adorned the site with "a most beautiful temple of the whitest stone," dedicated to Caesar Augustus, and Philip transformed the place into a town of some size.

THE DECAPOLIS

The "Decapolis" which is mentioned on two or three occasions in the Gospels (Matthew 4:25; Mark 5:20; 7:31) was a kind of confederacy, at first consisting of ten towns, as the name suggests. These were Hellenistic towns which had been subjugated by Alexander Jannaeus and then set free from Jewish authority by Pompey. Thereafter they were subject to the legate of Syria but enjoyed a considerable degree of autonomy. According to Pliny (A.D. 23-79) the ten cities which comprised the league were Damascus, Philadelphia, Raphana, Scythopolis, Gadara, Hippo, Dion, Pella, Galasa and Canatha.[48] Ptolemy, a portion of whose map of Palestine and Syria is reproduced in Fig. 106, lists eighteen "towns in Coelesyria and Decapolis": Heliopolis, Abila which is called Lysinia, Saana, Ina, Damascus, Samulis, Abida, Hippus, Capitolias, Gadara, Adra, Scythopolis, Gerasa, Pella, Dium, Gadora, Philadelphia, Canatha.[49]

Scythopolis was at the point where the plain of Esdraelon joins the valley of the Jordan. This was the site of Old Testament Beth-shean (p. 142), the name of which survives in the designation of the present-day village at that place as Beisan. A large stone amphitheater still remains there from the time of the Hellenistic city. Aside from Scythopolis, all of the towns of the Decapolis lay in the country east of the Jordan. Hippos (Kalat el-Husn),[50] Dion, Raphana and Canatha (Kanawat) were east of the Sea of Galilee. Gadara is identified

---

[47] War. i, xxi, 3; Ant. xv, x, 3.
[48] Natural History. v, 16. tr. H. Rackham, LCL (1938-), ii, p.277.
[49] Geography. v, 14. ed. Stevenson, p.127.
[50] Hippos was the Susitha of the rabbis, and the latter name survives in Susiyeh, a little distance to the southeast.

with the ruins of Umm Qeis, some five miles southeast of the Sea of Galilee, beyond the river Yarmuk. The ruins of the city's theater, cut out of the black rock, are still to be seen.

Gerasa lay yet farther south, some fifty miles from the Sea of Galilee, on one of the tributaries of the Jabbok. The site is known today as Jerash. Excavations conducted at Gerasa by Yale University and the British School of Archaeology in Jerusalem in 1928-1930 and by Yale University and the American Schools of Oriental Research in 1930-1931 and 1933-1934, have revealed that in the early centuries of the Christian era Gerasa was one of the most brilliant cities of Transjordan. The city was adorned with fine colonnaded streets, a circular forum, and beautiful temples and theaters. South of the city an impressive triumphal arch carried an inscription welcoming Hadrian on his visit to Gerasa in A.D. 130,[51] and most of the architectural remains are somewhat later than the New Testament period.

In Mark's narrative of the demoniac, and the swine which rushed into the sea, the scene is laid in "the country of the Gerasenes" (Mark 5:1 = Luke 8:26). The reference, however, can hardly be to Gerasa, which was so far distant. Matthew (8:28) states that it was in "the country of the Gadarenes," and the reference to Gadara may be correct if that city's territory can be supposed to have extended to the shores of the lake. Otherwise, however, there is no evidence that Gadara's territory crossed the Yarmuk. According to some texts, Luke (8:26, 37 RVm) spoke of "the country of the Gergesenes," and this makes it possible to suppose that somewhere on "the other side of the sea" (Mark 5:1 = Matthew 8:28; cf. Luke 8:26) there was a place called Gergesa, in whose vicinity the event took place. It has been suggested that this Gergesa is represented by the present Kersa, a small place on the eastern shore just below the Wadi es-Semak. In this neighborhood the hills do plunge steeply to the lake, as is presupposed in the Gospel narrative (Mark 5:13 = Matthew 8:32 = Luke 8:33).

Pella (Fahl) was midway between Gadara and Gerasa, across the Jordan somewhat south of Scythopolis. Pella was the city to which the Christians fled from Jerusalem in A.D. 68 and again in A.D. 135. Philadelphia lay south of Gerasa and was the southernmost of the cities of the Decapolis. Formerly it was known as Amman,[52] having

---

[51] C. H. Kraeling, ed., *Gerasa, City of the Decapolis.* 1938, p.401, Inscr. No.58.
[52] Eusebius, *Onomasticon*, see under *Amman*, 'Αμμάν. ed. Clericus, p.15.

been the chief city of the Ammonites. It was the Rabbah of the Old Testament (Deuteronomy 3:11; Joshua 13:25; II Samuel 11:1, etc.). The Hellenistic city at this site was built by Ptolemy II Philadelphus, and named for him. Both at Pella and at Philadelphia extensive ruins are still to be seen.

SAMARIA

The direct route from Galilee to Jerusalem ran through the land of Samaria, and Josephus says that it was the custom of the Galileans, when they came to the Holy City at the festivals, to journey through the country of the Samaritans.[53] By that route, which was the shortest and quickest, one could reach Jerusalem in three days' time.[54] Journeys by Jesus through the country of the Samaritans are noted in Luke 9:52 and John 4:4 (cf. Luke 17:11).

When the city of Samaria fell to Sargon II, 27,290 of its people were carried off captive (p. 175). Doubtless these constituted the flower of the population, and those who remained behind were the poorest people. Then "the king of Assyria brought men from Babylon, and from Cuthah, and from Avva, and from Hamath and Sepharvaim, and placed them in the cities of Samaria" (II Kings 17:24) to take the place of those who had been deported. The descendants of the remnant of Israelites and the newly introduced foreigners constituted a mixed race which was looked upon with suspicion by the exiles who returned to Jerusalem. Any participation by the Samaritans in the rebuilding of the temple was spurned by the Jews (Ezra 4:3; Nehemiah 2:20), and Nehemiah expelled from Jerusalem the grandson of Eliashib, the high priest, because he was married to the daughter of Sanballat the Samaritan leader (Nehemiah 13:28). Eliashib's grandson was probably the Manasseh under whom the Samaritans set up their own rival priesthood and built their own temple on Mount Gerizim.[55]

The breach between the two groups was never healed. During the weak rule of the high priest Onias II (d. c.198 B.C.) the Samaritans carried off Jews into slavery,[56] and later John Hyrcanus made an expedition into Samaria and destroyed the Gerizim temple (c.128 B.C.).[57] In the time of unrest after the deposition of Archelaus (A.D.

---

[53] *Ant.* xx, vi, 1.   [54] *Life.* 52.

[55] Josephus (*Ant.* xi, vii-viii) would make Manasseh the great-grandson of Eliashib, and place the schism in the time of Alexander the Great and Jaddua the high priest (332 B.C.), but that is probably one hundred years too late.

[56] *Ant.* xii, iv, 1.   [57] *Ant.* xiii, ix, 1; x, 2.

6) the Samaritans defiled the Jerusalem temple by throwing in dead men's bodies at night.[58] Later a number of Galilean pilgrims were killed at Ginea (Jenin) as they started to cross Samaria on their way to Jerusalem. Thereupon a virtual civil war broke out which had to be appealed to Claudius Caesar (A.D. 51).[59]

The metropolis and chief center of the Samaritans was at Shechem,[60] between Mounts Gerizim and Ebal and on the most direct route from Galilee to Jerusalem. It was rebuilt as Flavia Neapolis in A.D. 72, and is today the village of Nablus, still inhabited by the remnant of the Samaritans. The village of Sychar which figures in John 4:5 has sometimes been identified with Shechem itself but is more probably to be found in the present-day village of Askar at the southeastern foot of Mount Ebal.[61]

"Jacob's Well" (John 4:6) is believed to be the well beside the main road, one and three-quarters miles southeast of Nablus and three-quarters of a mile southwest of Askar, but there are other wells in the neighborhood. This well, however, is near the crossing of the main north-south road with an important road running from the Jordan to the Mediterranean, and has been pointed to as Jacob's well by church tradition steadily since ancient times. From the well one looks directly up at the 3,000-foot summit of Mount Gerizim, concerning which the Samaritan woman said, "Our fathers worshipped in this mountain" (John 4:20).

The ancient city of Samaria itself was at this time a Hellenistic rather than a Samaritan city. Alexander the Great planted Macedonian colonists there (331 B.C.), and after many vicissitudes the city was bestowed upon Herod the Great by Augustus.[62] Herod rebuilt and greatly enlarged Samaria, honoring the Emperor Augustus both with the city's new name, Sebaste (p. 216), and with its temple dedicated to him.[63] This temple, which has been excavated, was approached by a massive stairway leading up to a large platform surrounded by pillars, behind which was the temple itself. At the foot of the stairway was an altar, near which the excavators found a fallen statue of Augustus.[64] Particularly impressive were the strong

---

[58] *Ant.* xviii, ii, 2.   [59] *Ant.* xx, vi; *War.* ii, xii.   [60] *Ant.* xi, viii, 6.

[61] Walter Bauer, *Das Johannesevangelium* (*Handbuch zum neuen Testament.* 6 [3d ed. 1933]), p.66.

[62] *Ant.* xv, vii, 3; *War.* i, xx, 3.   [63] *Ant.* xv, viii, 5; *War.* i, xxi, 2.

[64] Reisner, Fisher and Lyon, *Harvard Excavations at Samaria.* i, pp.48-50; Crowfoot, Kenyon and Sukenik, *The Buildings at Samaria*, pp.123-127.

fortifications which Herod the Great erected at Samaria. An example of his work is to be seen in the great round towers flanking the west gate and shown in Fig. 107.[65]

In the early months of the Jewish revolt (A.D. 66) Sebaste was captured and burned by the rebels. Afterward, in the time about A.D. 180 to 230, Sebaste enjoyed a period of prosperity and was adorned with fine classical buildings, a columned street and a Corinthian stadium.[66] In later times the Christian world was interested in Sebaste chiefly because it was supposed to be the place where John the Baptist was buried. Two shrines were dedicated to him here. One was at an old family burial place which dates probably from the second or third century and is in the eastern end of the city under the present mosque. It was identified as the tomb of John at least by the time of Julian the Apostate, for in an anti-Christian riot which took place at Sebaste during his reign the pagans demolished the tomb and scattered the ashes. The second memorial to the Baptist was at a high place south of the summit of the hill, where Herodias was supposed to have hidden John's head, and where eventually a Christian basilica was built.[67]

PEREA

If one did not wish to pass through Samaria, two other routes were possible from Galilee to Jerusalem. A western road ran down the coastal plain in the territory of the city of Caesarea, and then roads ascended to Jerusalem from east of Antipatris and from Lydda. Or one could take an eastern route by following down the valley of the Jordan River. From Capernaum such a route led through Tiberias and on south past Scythopolis, where there was a regularly used ford across the Jordan. Or it was possible to go around the eastern side of the lake and come south in the neighborhood of Hippos, Gadara and Pella.

Beyond Pella one entered Perea proper. This land, Galilee and Judea, were reckoned by the Jews as the three Jewish provinces, for Samaria was excluded from such dignity.[68] Josephus says that the length

---

[65] Watzinger, *Denkmäler Palästinas.* II (1935), p.52; Crowfoot, Kenyon and Sukenik, *The Buildings at Samaria*, pp.39-41.

[66] Crowfoot, Kenyon and Sukenik, *The Buildings at Samaria*, pp.35-37.

[67] ibid., pp.37-39.

[68] *Baba Bathra.* III, 2 (RBT 7, p.100), "There are three lands concerning the law of *hazakah*: The land of Judea, the land on the other side of the Jordan, and of Galilee."

of Perea was from Pella to Machaerus,[69] that is from the Jabbok to the Arnon, and the breadth from Gerasa and Philadelphia to the Jordan,[70] although sometimes the name Perea was used loosely to include the region on north to the Yarmuk.[71] The actual name "Perea" is not used in the Gospels, where the usual designation for this country is "beyond the Jordan" (Mark 3:8 = Matthew 4:25, etc.).

Mark seems to indicate that the Perean route was taken by Jesus on his last journey to Jerusalem. He came "beyond the Jordan" (Mark 10:1 = Matthew 19:1), went "on the way, going up to Jerusalem" (Mark 10:32 = Matthew 20:17), and arrived at last at Jericho (Mark 10:46 = Luke 18:35; cf. Matthew 20:29). Opposite Jericho the Jordan was forded regularly either at Ghoraniyeh (Roraniyeh) or at Hajleh (p. 224).

FROM JERICHO TO JERUSALEM

Jericho itself, in New Testament times, had spread out far to the south of the hill on which the Old Testament city stood. The celebrated palm and balsam district of Jericho was given by Antony to Cleopatra,[72] but restored to Herod the Great by Augustus.[73] Here Herod built a citadel called Cyprus,[74] a theater,[75] an amphitheater[76] and a hippodrome in which he planned to have the leading Jews murdered at the moment of his own death so that he would not lack for mourning.[77] The palace at Jericho in which Herod died afterward was burned down by Simon, a former slave of the king's, and then magnificently rebuilt by Archelaus.[78]

From Jericho to Jerusalem (cf. Luke 10:30) is a distance of some 17 miles. Approaching the Holy City, the Jericho road swings over the shoulder of the Mount of Olives. From the summit of the Mount of Olives one can look back across the entire eastern countryside of Judea. A tawny wilderness of hills drops away to the white Jordan Valley with its ribbon of green vegetation, and to the dull blue

[69] Machaerus was a fortress on a mountain east of the Dead Sea. Alexander Jannaeus was the first to fortify the place, and Herod greatly enlarged and strengthened it, also building there a magnificent palace (*War.* vii, vi, 2). From Herod the Great it passed into the hands of Herod Antipas together with Perea in which it was situated. It was here, according to Josephus (*Ant.* xviii, v, 5) that Herod Antipas imprisoned and beheaded John the Baptist (cf. Mark 6:17-29 = Matthew 14:3-12 = Luke 3:19f.).
[70] *War.* iii, iii, 3.
[71] *War.* iv, vii, 3, calls Gadara, which was near the Yarmuk, the capital of Perea.
[72] *War.* i, xviii, 5.
[73] *Ant.* xv, vii, 3; *War.* i, xx, 3.
[74] *Ant.* xvi, v, 2; *War.* i, xxi, 4, 9.
[75] *Ant.* xvii, vi, 3.
[76] *Ant.* xvii, viii, 2; *War.* i, xxxiii, 8.
[77] *Ant.* xvii, vi, 5; *War.* i, xxxiii, 6.
[78] *Ant.* xvii, x, 6; xiii, 1.

surface of the Dead Sea, some 1,275 feet below sea level, with the high wall of the mountains of Moab in the background. The arrival of Jesus and his disciples is introduced with the words: "And when they draw nigh unto Jerusalem, unto Bethphage and Bethany, at the mount of Olives. . . ." (Mark 11:1 = Matthew 21:1 = Luke 19:29). The exact location of Bethphage is unknown, but references to Beth Page in rabbinic literature point to its close connection with Jerusalem.[79] Bethany was doubtless on the east side of the Mount of Olives in the vicinity of the present village of el-Azariyeh, whose Arabic name preserves the tradition of the connection of Lazarus with Bethany (John 11:1).[80]

Gethsemane was apparently on the western slope of the Mount of Olives, just across the brook Kidron from the city of Jerusalem (Mark 14:26, 32 = Matthew 26:30, 36 = Luke 22:39; John 18:1). The precise location of the "enclosed piece of ground" (Mark 14:32 = Matthew 26:36, RVm) that was Gethsemane can hardly be determined now with certainty, since Josephus states that during the siege of Jerusalem Titus cut down all the trees and desolated the pleasant gardens for many miles round about Jerusalem.[81] The location of the beautiful little "Garden of Gethsemane" (Fig. 108) which belongs to the Franciscans corresponds very well to the general probabilities in the situation, however, and at least we can be certain that it was somewhere on the slope of this very hill that Jesus prayed.

JERUSALEM

From the western "descent" (Luke 19:37) of the Mount of Olives one looks directly across the Kidron Valley upon the Holy City. The city lies upon hills, 2,500 feet above sea level, yet in a sort of basin surrounded by somewhat higher ground. The present city, with a population of 25,000 inside its walls and 65,000 more outside, is built largely to the northwest of the ancient city. Nevertheless it is possible to recover a fairly accurate picture of the city of Jesus' time.

The site of Jerusalem (cf. p. 149) is a quadrilateral plateau, marked out on the east by the valley of the brook Kidron (II Samuel

[79] Dalman, *Sacred Sites and Ways*, p.252.

[80] The "tomb of Lazarus" has been shown at this place at least from the time of the Bordeaux Pilgrim, A.D. 333 (*Itinerary from Bordeaux to Jerusalem*, tr. A. Stewart, Palestine Pilgrims' Text Society. 1887, p.25). Even if it is not genuine, its location doubtless corresponded with accurate knowledge of the position of Bethany.

[81] *War.* v, xii, 4; vi, i, 1.

15:23, etc.; John 18:1),[82] now known as the Wadi Sitti Maryam or "Valley of St. Mary," and on the west and south by the Valley of Hinnom (Wadi er-Rababi).[83] The steep walls of these valleys provided the city with naturally strong defenses on their respective sides but left the north and northwest sides vulnerable. The situation of Jerusalem is shown clearly in the aerial photograph reproduced in Fig. 109. In the immediate foreground are the slopes of the Mount of Olives and the Valley of the Kidron, at the left is the Valley of Hinnom and at the right are the new northern suburbs. The prominent open area within the city walls is the Haram esh-Sherif where formerly the temple stood.

Within the city area there was a secondary valley, the Tyropoeon,[84] which runs southward parallel to the Kidron Valley. Jerusalem has been destroyed and rebuilt so repeatedly that over much of the ancient city 40 to 70 feet of debris has accumulated, and the Tyropoeon Valley today is largely filled up and remains only as a shallow depression called el-Wad. Formerly, however, it divided Jerusalem into two clearly defined parts. The broader and higher hill on the western side of the Tyropoeon Valley was the site of the Upper City, which Josephus called the Upper Market. The lower eastern hill, which sloped down from the Temple area, was called Acra and was the site of the Lower City.[85] The Temple area itself was the "third hill" of Josephus, and northward of the Temple was the "fourth hill," where the growing city was spreading out. This last and newest part was called, according to Josephus, Bezetha (probably meaning "House of Olives") and also New Town.

[82] Eusebius, *Onomasticon*, see under *Cedron*, Κεδρών. ed. Clericus, p.52.

[83] The name Valley of Jehoshaphat (cf. Joel 3:2, 12) has been applied to both the Valley of the Kidron and the Valley of Hinnom. The Bordeaux Pilgrim, A.D. 333 (tr. Stewart, p.24), said, "Also as one goes from Jerusalem to the gate which is to the eastward, in order to ascend the Mount of Olives, is the valley called that of Josaphat," thus evidently referring to the Kidron Valley. Eusebius, however, states that this name was applied to the Valley of Hinnom (*Onomasticon*, see under Vallis Ennom, Φάραγξ 'Εννόμ. ed. Clericus, p.157).

[84] Josephus (*War*. v, iv, 1) called it "the Valley of the Cheesemakers" (Φάραγξ τῶν τυροποιῶν) and it is from this designation that the name Tyropoeon is derived.

[85] *War*. v, iv, 1. According to Josephus' description, the Acra originally was higher than the Temple area and separated from it by a broad valley. The Hasmoneans cut down the height of Acra and filled in the intervening valley. Whether or not this tradition as to the earlier situation is correct, the hill doubtless was lower and the valley filled up in the time of Josephus, for he would have seen these facts with his own eyes. Josephus' error in locating the stronghold of David on the western instead of the eastern hill has already been noted (p.150 n.59).

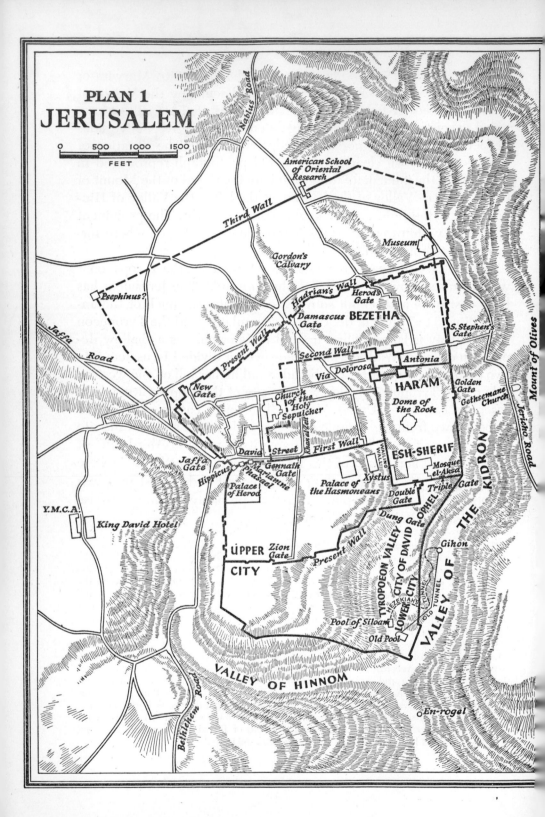

PLAN 1
JERUSALEM

0 500 1000 1500
FEET

American School
of Oriental
Research

Nablus Road

Third Wall

Museum

Gordon's
Calvary

Hadrian's Wall

Herod's
Gate

Psephinus?

Damascus
Gate

BEZETHA

S. Stephen's
Gate

Jaffa

Road

Present Wall

Second Wall

Via Dolorosa

Antonia

HARAM

New
Gate

Church
of the
Holy
Sepulcher

Dome of
the Rock

Golden
Gate

Gethsemane
Church

Jericho Road

Mount of Olives

First Wall

ESH-SHERIF

Jaffa
Gate

David Street

Khan ez Zeit

WAILING WALL

Hippicus

Mariamne
Phasael

Gennath
Gate

Mosque
el-Aksa

Palace of
the Hasmoneans

Xystus

Palace
of Herod

Double
Gate

Triple Gate

Y.M.C.A.

King David Hotel

Dung Gate

OPHEL

UPPER

Zion
Gate

Present Wall

CITY OF DAVID

CITY

Gihon

HEZEKIAH'S TUNNEL

OLD TUNNEL

TYROPOEON VALLEY

LOWER CITY

VALLEY OF THE KIDRON

Pool of Siloam

Old Pool

Bethlehem Road

VALLEY OF HINNOM

En-rogel

In his description of Jerusalem, Josephus mentions three walls which were in existence in his time.[86] Of these, two had been restored by permission of Julius Caesar[87] and hence encompassed the city in the days of Jesus, while the third was begun by Herod Agrippa I. The latter desisted from finishing this wall, fearing that Claudius suspected him of intention to rebel, and the third wall was only completed by the Jews between A.D. 66 and 70. The first and most ancient wall ran from the side of the Temple area west to the three imposing towers named Hippicus, Phasael and Mariamne. From there the wall ran south and then east along the edge of the Valley of Hinnom. Then it ran north and northeast, past the Pool of Siloam, and joined the Temple area at its southeast corner. From there the old wall was the same as the outer wall of the Temple. It ran north along the hill high above the Kidron Valley, and then, beyond the "Golden Gate," swung west to Antonia, the fortress which overlooked the Temple area at its northwest corner. From there it ran south along the western side of the Temple area to the point from which we described its beginning. The line of this wall from the Temple to Herod's citadel was probably just south of and parallel to the present David and Temple Streets, which are in the very heart of the modern city. The southern reaches of the wall as we have described it are now south of the present city wall and in less densely inhabited areas where some excavation has been possible. Portions of the south and east walls and of the gates at the southwest and southeast corners of the ancient city have been uncovered.

"The second wall started," according to Josephus, "from the gate in the first wall which they called Gennath, and, enclosing only the northern district of the town, went up as far as Antonia." This wall apparently started north from the First Wall at a point some distance east of Herod's three great towers, for if the junction of the Second Wall had been at Hippicus, Phasael and Mariamne these surely would have been mentioned instead of the otherwise never-mentioned Gate of Gennath, or Garden Gate. The latter gate was therefore presumably in the First Wall somewhere east of Hippicus, Phasael and Mariamne.[88] In this case the Second Wall may have

---

[86] *War.* v, iv, 2.   [87] *Ant.* xiv, x, 5.

[88] Dalman, *Sacred Sites and Ways*, p.375. A. T. Olmstead (*Jesus in the Light of History*, p.73 and Plan of Jerusalem) places the Gate of Gennath and the beginning of the Second Wall at the Tower of Hippicus. But immediately after stating that the second wall took its beginning at the Gate of Gennath, Josephus says that "The third

swung north just east of the present Church of the Holy Sepulcher, and then have turned eastward and run to Antonia. If this is a correct interpretation, the Second Wall was some distance inside the present northern wall of Jerusalem, which swings west far outside the Church of the Holy Sepulcher and runs east at a considerable distance north of the Temple area. As a matter of fact it is indicated now that the present north wall of Jerusalem corresponds to the north wall of the Roman colony of Aelia Capitolina founded by Hadrian in the second century (p. 250).

If the foregoing interpretation is correct, the site of the present Church of the Holy Sepulcher (p. 433) was in the time of Jesus outside the wall of Jerusalem, as the New Testament requires when it states that Jesus was crucified "without the gate" (Hebrews 13: 12). The Church of the Holy Sepulcher is, of course, far inside the present northern city wall, and if that wall were to be identified with the Second Wall of Josephus then it would be necessary to seek the site of the crucifixion outside of it. It is far more probable, however, that the Second Wall ran inside the present location of the Church of the Holy Sepulcher and that the line of the present northern city wall only represents the wall built long after the time of Jesus by Hadrian. It is not necessary, therefore, to turn to a hill north of the present city wall known as "Gordon's Calvary" as the site of the crucifixion. The latter identification was suggested in 1842 by Otto Thenius, a German pastor from Dresden, to whom the hill in question seemed to have the appearance of a skull (cf. Mark 15:22 = Matthew 27:33 = Luke 23:33; John 19:17). Forty years later this view was adopted by General Charles G. Gordon and since has enjoyed a wide popular acceptance, the hill in question continuing to be known by Gordon's name.[89] A near-by rock-hewn tomb, known as the "Garden Tomb," may be as late as the third or fourth century A.D.

The Third Wall, which was built by Herod Agrippa I more than a decade after the death of Jesus, had its beginning, according to Josephus, at the familiar tower of Hippicus. Evidently it ran far north

[wall] began at the tower Hippicus" (*War.* v, iv, 2), which makes it improbable that the Gate of Gennath and the Tower of Hippicus were at the same point. Olmstead (pp.72,239) agrees, however, that the course of the Second Wall was such that the present site of the Church of the Holy Sepulcher lay in the time of Jesus outside the city wall.

[89] *Palästinajahrbuch des deutschen evangelischen Instituts für Altertumswissenschaft des heiligen Landes zu Jerusalem.* 9 (1913), pp.100f.

and then east, for it enclosed Bezetha, the newly-built part of the city north of the tower of Antonia and the Temple area, into which the city's increasing population had been overflowing, and which hitherto had been quite unprotected by a city wall. Finally it ran south or southeast and joined the Old or First Wall at the Valley of Kidron, that is at the northeast corner of the Temple area. The line of the present northern wall of Jerusalem would seem to fulfill these conditions, but discoveries have shown that Agrippa's "Third Wall" must have stood yet considerably farther north. Explorations carried out by Professors E. L. Sukenik and L. A. Mayer of the Hebrew University at Jerusalem traced considerable sections of a wall which ran north to a point near the present Swedish School, then east to the American School of Oriental Research, and finally southeast toward the Temple area.[90] A tower of this wall was found beneath the tennis court of the American School of Oriental Research in 1940,[91] and certain other portions of it have been found even more recently.[92] Since these remains fit the description of Josephus, and since there was no "Fourth Wall" as far as we know, doubtless this was the Third Wall built by Agrippa.

Josephus described the towers Hippicus, Phasael and Mariamne as "for magnitude, beauty and strength without their equal in the world."[93] In reality Hippicus was 80 cubits (117 feet),[94] Phasael 90 cubits (131 feet) and Mariamne 50 cubits (73 feet) in height. The bases were of solid masonry and above were rooms, battlements and turrets. The three towers were named respectively for Herod's friend Hippicus, his brother Phasael (p. 215), and his wife Mariamne whom he murdered (p. 216). The towers doubtless stood in the neighborhood of the present Jaffa Gate, Hippicus and Phasael probably being represented by the northwest and northeast towers respectively of the present citadel (cf. p. 150 n.59).

Herod's palace adjoined the three towers.[95] It was entirely walled about, to a height of 30 cubits (44 feet), the walls on the north and west being the same as the old city walls. Josephus professed his inability to describe it for its magnificence, but alluded to its "immense banqueting-halls and bedchambers for a hundred guests," and

[90] Sukenik and Mayer, *The Third Wall of Jerusalem.* 1930.
[91] BASOR 83 (Oct. 1941), pp.5-7.   [92] BASOR 89 (Feb. 1943), pp.18-21.
[93] *War.* v, iv, 3.
[94] The cubit was approximately 17½ inches.
[95] *War.* v, iv, 4.

its grounds with canals and groves of various trees. In the days of the Roman procurators this building became their residence and seat of government when in Jerusalem,[96] which would suggest an identification of the Praetorium of Pilate (Mark 15:16) with Herod's former palace. Later tradition, however, located the Praetorium in the fortress Antonia. This fortress, which stood at the northwest corner of the Temple area, was rebuilt by Herod the Great and renamed Antonia in honor of Mark Antony, who at that time was still in power in the East.[97] It stood on a precipice nearly 75 feet high, and had four strong towers, themselves 75 or 100 feet high, at its four corners. Within, it was fitted up with the magnificence of a palace, and Josephus says a Roman cohort was always stationed there.[98]

The central court of the Castle of Antonia has been excavated and underneath the so-called Ecce Homo arch which may belong to the time of Herod Agrippa I,[99] an earlier pavement has been brought to light consisting of huge slabs of stone three feet square and a foot or more thick. If Pilate was residing at the Castle of Antonia at the time when Jesus was brought before him, as he might well have been in order to be in close proximity to the Temple at the Passover season, then Antonia was the "Praetorium" and this courtyard pavement may have been the very Pavement that was called Gabbatha (John 19:13).[100] In that event the traditional Via Dolorosa[101] or "Way of Sorrows" which runs from here to the Church of the Holy Sepulcher may preserve the true general direction of the last journey of Jesus from the Judgment Hall to Golgotha.

At the eastern side of the Upper City and overlooking the Temple area across from its southwestern corner was a building that had been the palace of the Hasmoneans.[102] From it Herod Agrippa II enjoyed looking down into the Temple and observing what was done there. The priests obstructed his view by building a high wall which, when the affair was appealed to Nero, was allowed to stand.[103] On the lower

[96] *War.* II, xiv, 8; xv, 5.
[97] *Ant.* xv, viii, 5; xi, 4; Tacitus (A.D. c.55-c.117), *Histories.* v, 11. tr. C. H. Moore, LCL (1925-31) II, p.195.
[98] *War.* v, v, 8.   [99] Watzinger, *Denkmäler Palästinas.* II, pp.57f.
[100] Millar Burrows in BA I, 3 (Sept. 1938), pp.17f.
[101] The first pilgrim to speak of treading "the way on which Christ walked carrying the Cross," and to describe its stations, was the preaching friar Ricoldus de Monte Crucis who visited Jerusalem in A.D. 1294. J. C. M. Laurent, *Peregrinatores Medii Aevi Quatuor.* 2d ed. 1873, p.112.
[102] Perhaps this is where Herod Antipas resided when in Jerusalem (Luke 23:7).
[103] *Ant.* xx, viii, 11.

slopes of the western hill, between Agrippa's palace and the Temple area, was the Xystus, apparently a sort of open-air gymnasium. From here a viaduct led across the Tyropoeon and thus gave direct connection between the Upper City and the Temple area.[104] Remnants of the arches of two ancient bridges communicating between the Upper City and the Temple may still be recognized at the western wall of the Temple area. One, near the southwestern corner of the Temple area, is known as Robinson's Arch, and the other farther to the north, as Wilson's Arch.[105]

THE TEMPLE

The sanctuary itself was naturally the chief center of interest in Jerusalem. The Herodian temple[106] is described by Josephus[107] and also by the Mishnic tractate Middoth ("Measurements"), which belongs to the second century A.D. and is to be found in the section Kodashim ("Holiness") of the Babylonian Talmud.[108] These are the chief written sources which are available for the archeologist who endeavors to recover a picture of the Temple in the time of Jesus. In general they are good guides, but there is a tendency on the part of Josephus toward vagueness and exaggeration, and on the part of the author of Middoth toward ignoring things which were distinctively heathen.[109]

"In the fifteenth year of his reign," relates Josephus, Herod "restored the Temple and by erecting new foundation-walls enlarged the surrounding area to double its former extent."[110] This increase in the area available for the Temple and its courts must have been accomplished by building up the hill itself. Today there is to be seen underneath the southeastern corner of the Haram esh-Sherif an extensive system of vaults popularly known as "Solomon's Stables." In their present form these probably were constructed at a date later

---

[104] *War.* II, xvi, 3; VI, vi, 2.

[105] Sir Charles William Wilson and Capt. R. E. Warren, *The Recovery of Jerusalem.* 1871, pp.58,72-85.

[106] cf. above pp.150f. for the First Temple of Solomon, and p.163 for the Second Temple of Zerubbabel.

[107] *Ant.* xv, xi; *War.* v, v; cf. *Against Apion.* I, 22, where Josephus gives a quotation descriptive of the Temple from Hecataeus of Abdera (c.300 B.C.).

[108] L. Goldschmidt, ed., *Der Babylonische Talmud.* IX (1935), pp.675-689; cf. JE VIII, pp.545f.

[109] Hollis, *The Archaeology of Herod's Temple, with a Commentary on the Tractate 'Middoth,'* p.105.

[110] *War.* I, xxi, 1.

than that of Herod. They preserve, however, ancient materials and traces of old work which may indicate the kind of efforts Herod made to build up a larger court for the Temple. At its outermost "pinnacle" (cf. Matthew 4:5 = Luke 4:9), the Temple enclosure was lifted 170 feet above the gorge of the Kidron until, as Josephus said, "one who looked down grew dizzy."[111]

The limits of the Temple area as established by Herod the Great probably were the same as the present limits of the Haram esh-Sherif on the east, south and west. On the north, however, the area now has been extended considerably farther than the limits of Herod's day. The Noble Sanctuary now includes part of the place where the Castle of Antonia then stood, and also extends over the fillings of what was then a ravine running diagonally into the Kidron Valley.[112] The northern limit in Herod's time was probably along a line joining the east wall at a point not far north of the present Golden Gate (p. 245).

Whereas Solomon had built a wall on the east side of the sanctuary area but left the other sides exposed,[113] Herod the Great completed the enclosure of the Temple hill with lofty walls on all sides. Remains of the typical Herodian masonry, which employed very large stones carefully fitted together, still are to be seen in portions of the wall around the Haram esh-Sherif, notably including the "Wailing Wall" (Fig. 110). Above ground this wall probably has been reconstructed and the stones are not fitted together as carefully now as they were formerly, but otherwise it must appear much as it did in New Testament times. The nine lowest courses of stone consist of huge blocks, as was characteristic of Herodian masonry, the largest one being 16½ feet long and 13 feet wide. Above are 15 courses of smaller stones. The practice of the Jews, to lament the destruction of the Temple, is attested as long ago as the time of the Bordeaux Pilgrim (A.D. 333). He mentions two statues of Hadrian which had been erected at the place where the Temple stood and says that "not far from the statues there is a perforated stone, to which the Jews come every year and anoint it, bewail themselves with groans, rend their garments, and so depart."[114] What is meant by the "perforated stone" is uncertain but it may have been the sacred Rock

[111] *Ant.* xv, xi, 5.
[112] Today the measurements of the area, outside the walls, are south side 929 feet, north side 1,041 feet, east side 1,556 feet, west side 1,596 feet.
[113] *War.* v, v, 1.   [114] Tr. Stewart, p.22.

(p. 151) itself. Today it is the Herodian wall just described which is the wailing place of the Jews.

The outer court of the Temple area[115] was entered on the west by four gates, according to Josephus,[116] two of which were doubtless at the points indicated by Robinson's Arch and Wilson's Arch. Gates. on the other sides are mentioned in the tractate Middoth. On the south were the two gates of "Chuldah,"[117] whose location is probably represented by the Double Gate and Triple Gate now walled up in the southern wall of the Temple area at a point some 35 feet below the present level of the Haram.[118] Ramps probably led from these gates up to the level of the court. On the east was the Shushan Gate, which probably was somewhat south of the present Golden Gate, a structure of the fourth or fifth century.[119] This is the gate which has been blocked up since A.D. 810 by the Arabs who fear that one day a conqueror will enter by it.[120] Finally, on the north was one gate, called Todi,[121] while in the northwest there were also steps to the Tower of Antonia. These last were the steps that the chief captain together with the soldiers and centurions "ran down" into the Temple on the occasion of the riot over Paul, and from which the apostle made his address to the people (Acts 21:32, 40).

Upon entering the outer court one found its walls lined with porticoes, or cloisters of double rows of marble columns, roofed with carved cedar. The east porticoes were said by Josephus to be the work of Solomon, and probably did at least survive from some earlier time, for they were in need of repair in the time of Herod Agrippa II.[122] This was probably the Solomon's Porch of the New Testament (John 10:23; Acts 3:11; 5:12). On the south, where the

---

[115] In the Gospels, "the temple" ($τὸ$ $ἱερόν$) ordinarily means the entire area (Mark 11:11; 13:1, 3, etc.), although occasionally it refers to some particular part. "The sanctuary" ($ὁ$ $ναός$) was the temple edifice itself, including the Holy Place and the Holy of Holies with the veil between them (Mark 15:38, etc.).

[116] *Ant.* xv, xi, 5; *Middoth.* I, 3 mentions only one, perhaps the principal one, on the west, named "Qiponos."

[117] Josephus says only (*Ant.* xv, xi, 5), "the fourth front of the temple, which was southward, had indeed itself gates in its middle."

[118] The "Single Gate" in the same wall is believed to be much later.

[119] This has been thought to be the Gate Beautiful of Acts 3:2, 10, $ὡραία$ ("beautiful") having been taken over as *aurea* ("golden") in Latin, but more probably the Beautiful Gate was the one at the east entrance to the court of the women, which was distinguished by folding doors of Corinthian brass (*War.* v, v, 3).

[120] cf. Ezekiel 44:1f., which says that the east gate of the sanctuary should be shut because by it the Lord had entered in.

[121] Josephus refers to it incidentally in *War.* vi, iv, 1.

[122] *Ant.* xx, ix, 7.

El-Aksa mosque now is, were the royal porticoes, or Stoa Basilica, with 162 columns, each of such size that three men could just reach around it. These were arranged in four rows which formed three aisles.

Since even Gentiles were allowed access to this outer court, it is commonly designated the Court of the Gentiles. Within it was an inner court, set apart by a stone partition, beyond which none but Jews might pass. This was described by Josephus as follows: "Proceeding . . . toward the second court of the Temple, one found it surrounded by a stone balustrade, three cubits [about 4½ feet] high and of exquisite workmanship; in this at regular intervals stood slabs giving warning, some in Greek, others in Latin characters, of the law of purification, to wit, that no foreigner was permitted to enter the holy place, for so the second enclosure of the Temple was called."[123] One of these stone slabs of warning was found at Jerusalem by M. Clermont-Ganneau in 1871 and is now in the Museum of the Ancient Orient at Istanbul, while part of another such inscription was discovered more recently.[124] The first-mentioned inscription is shown in Fig. 111. It is carved in a limestone block some 23 inches high, 34 inches long and 15 inches thick. The letters are over 1½ inches in height. The inscription reads: "No foreigner[125] may enter within the balustrade and enclosure around the Sanctuary. Whoever is caught will render himself liable to the death penalty which will inevitably follow." In Acts 21:28f. Paul apparently was believed to have taken Trophimus beyond this barrier, and there may also be a side reference to it in Ephesians 2:14 where Paul speaks of "the middle wall of partition."

Within the wall beyond which Gentiles could not go were several courts together with their walls, gates and terraces. The Women's Court represented the limit beyond which women might not go.[126] Farther on was the Court of Israel or Men's Court, and then the

---

[123] *War.* v, v, 2; cf. vi, ii, 4; *Ant.* xv, xi, 5. This is probably the same wall that is called the Soreg in *Middoth.* ii, 3, although the Soreg is described as only "ten handbreadths in height." Since in the Hebrew system one handbreadth equaled one-sixth of a cubit this would have been just about 30 inches in height. Perhaps there was at first only a low stone barrier on which the warning tablets were erected, and later the higher and exquisitely worked stone trellis was added which Josephus describes.

[124] *The Quarterly of the Department of Antiquities in Palestine.* 6 (1938), pp.1-3.

[125] The same word appears in Luke 17:18 where it is translated "stranger," or "alien."

[126] *War.* v, v, 2; *Ant.* xv, xi, 5; *Middoth.* ii, 5.

Court of the Priests.[127] In the Priests' Court and in front of the temple edifice itself was the altar upon which sacrifices and burnt-offerings were made.[128] It is not certain whether the altar stood upon the sacred Rock (es-Sakhra) or in front of it, but the former seems somewhat more probable (p. 151).

The sanctuary or temple edifice itself stood within this inmost court and was approached by a flight of twelve steps.[129] It was built of white stones, to each of which Josephus assigns the enormous size of approximately 35 feet by 12 feet by 18 feet.[130] In front its height and its breadth were equal, each being 100 cubits (nearly 150 feet) according to Josephus, and it was covered all over with gold (cf. Matthew 23:16), so that it reflected the rising sun with fiery splendor.[131] Within, it was divided into two parts, the first of which was the Holy Place (cf. Exodus 26:33). In the Holy Place were the seven-armed lampstand, the table of shew-bread and the altar of incense. The second and most sacred part of the sanctuary was the Holy of Holies. "The innermost recess measured twenty cubits," says Josephus, "and was screened in like manner from the outer portion by a veil. In this stood nothing whatever: unapproachable, inviolable, invisible to all, it was called the Holy of Holy."[132] It was entered only once a year by the high priest on the Day of Atonement.[133]

The orientation of the Temple edifice was toward the east,[134] as was in accordance with general oriental practice, and the Holy of Holies arose above or more probably, as we have seen (p. 151), behind the ancient and sacred Rock.

The entire appearance of Herod's Temple must have been very impressive. Even Tacitus described it as "a temple of immense

---

[127] *Middoth.* II, 7. [128] *Ant.* xv, xi, 5. [129] *War.* v, v, 4.
[130] *Ant.* xv, xi, 3. [131] *War.* v, v, 4f.
[132] *War.* v, v, 5; cf. Tacitus (*Hist.* v, 9) who says that after Pompey's conquest of Jerusalem and entry into the Temple (63 B.C.) "it was a matter of common knowledge that there were no representations of the gods within, but that the place was empty and the secret shrine contained nothing."
[133] Leviticus 16; *Tract Yomah.* RBT 3 (VI), pp.72f.
[134] cf. *The Letter of Aristeas.* 88. tr. H. St. J. Thackeray (1917), p.41: "The Temple looks towards the east, and its back is turned westwards." Precise measurements indicate that the east wall of the enclosure runs slightly toward the northwest, and is exactly at right angles to the line of direction between the sacred Rock and the summit of the Mount of Olives. But the eastern boundary of the "Platform of the Rock" runs due north and south and the inner courts and temple edifice probably had their eastern lines parallel with this.

wealth,"[135] and the exclamation of one of the disciples of Jesus is recorded in the Gospels, "Teacher, behold, what manner of stones and what manner of buildings!" (Mark 13:1). Indeed the city as a whole must have presented the incoming visitor with a magnificent panorama. The Mount of Olives then as now would have provided the best point of view. From it one would have seen the Temple directly in the foreground, where the Dome now rises over the sacred Rock. Surrounded by sumptuous colonnades, its courts rose one within the other and each higher than the last to the inner Sanctuary itself, whose marble and golden façade gleamed and glittered "like a snow-clad mountain."[136] At the northwestern corner of the Temple arose the powerful mass of the fortress Antonia, and beyond it, outside the wall, extended the villas of the northern suburb. To the south an uninterrupted sequence of houses and palaces fell away to the Pool of Siloam at the foot of the hill of Ophel. In the background on the western hill were ranged other populous quarters, crowned on the horizon by the imposing silhouette of Herod's Palace and Towers. "At no period of its history could the Sanctuary and City have presented a more inspiring aspect. The rhythm and harmony of Graeco-Roman art, so beautifully rendered against the oriental sky, restrained the louder tendencies of Herod himself, while infusing order and taste into the traditional chaos of the city."[137] The pride of the rabbis was not unjustified when they said, "He who has not seen Jerusalem in its beauty, has not seen a beautiful great city in his whole life; and who has not seen the building of the Second [i.e. Herod's] Temple, has not seen a handsome building in his life."[138]

[135] *Hist.* v, 8.
[136] *War.* v, v, 6.
[137] J. Garstang in Sir J. A. Hammerton, ed., *Wonders of the Past.* 1937, p.584.
[138] *Tract Succah.* v, 2. RBT 4 (VII), p.77; cf. *Baba Bathra.* I, 1. RBT 7, p.6, "It was said that he who had not seen the new Temple of Herod had not in all his life, seen a fine building."

5. THE LATER HISTORY OF JERUSALEM

BUT when the disciples were amazed at the splendor of the Temple, Jesus said, "Seest thou these great buildings? There shall not be left here one stone upon another which shall not be thrown down" (Mark 13:2 = Matthew 24:2 = Luke 21:6). His prophecy was fulfilled swiftly. In A.D. 66 the Jewish war broke out, an "utterly hopeless, and therefore unreasonable and disastrous struggle."[1] In A.D. 70, shortly before the Passover, Titus[2] (Fig. 112) and the Roman armies surrounded Jerusalem. A long and terrible siege ensued. Battering rams hammered against the walls, earthworks surrounded the city, and when the starving poor people slipped out to look for food the Romans caught and crucified them in sight of the city. Finally late in the summer Jerusalem fell, its beautiful temple was burned and its people were slaughtered indiscriminately.[3] The city was razed to the ground and when Titus departed only Herod's towers—Hippicus, Phasael and Mariamne—and a portion of the wall were left standing.

In Rome the following year Titus celebrated his triumph, together with his father Vespasian. The triumphal procession was adorned by 700 of the most handsome Jewish prisoners and by abundant spoils of war. Speaking of the spoils, Josephus said, "Conspicuous above all stood out those captured in the temple at Jerusalem. These consisted of a golden table, many talents in weight, and a lampstand, likewise made of gold. . . . After these, and last of all the spoils, was carried a copy of the Jewish Law."[4] On the Arch of Titus, which was completed and dedicated *divo Tito*, "to the deified Titus,"[5] only after the death of the emperor (A.D. 81), was carved a

---

[1] Schürer, A *History of the Jewish People in the Time of Jesus Christ*. I, ii. p.209.

[2] The war against the Jews was begun by Vespasian but when he assumed the throne at Rome in A.D. 68 his son Titus took over the command of the Roman army in the Jewish war. Eventually Titus himself became emperor (A.D. 79-81).

[3] Rabbinic tradition (*Taanith*. IV RBT 4 [VIII], pp.80,86f.) held that Herod's Temple was destroyed on the 9th day of Ab, even as the First Temple had been before it. II Kings 25:8f. and Jeremiah 52:12f. were interpreted by them as meaning that Nebuchadnezzar's men entered the Temple on the 7th day, ate and did damage in it also on the 8th and 9th and set it on fire toward the evening of the 9th, after which it continued to burn all day on the 10th. Josephus (*War*. VI, iv, 5) represents the same tradition that the Temple was burned by the Romans on the identical day that it was formerly burned by the king of Babylon, although he specifies the 10th instead of the 9th day of Lous or Ab. The month of Ab corresponded to our July-August.

[4] *War*. VII, v, 5.

[5] M. da Firenze, *Itinerarium Urbis Romae*. 1931, p.141.

representation of this event. It is in the form of a bas-relief (Fig. 113) on the passage of the arcade and shows a part of the triumphal procession. Roman soldiers, without weapons and crowned with laurels, are carrying the sacred furniture which was captured in the Temple. This included the seven-armed lampstand and the table of shew-bread upon which the sacred trumpets are resting. Tablets fastened on staves are also to be seen, but the Law or Pentateuch mentioned by Josephus does not appear. In the relief on the other side of the passage Titus is shown, crowned by Victory, standing in a car drawn by four horses and conducted by a woman representing the city of Rome. In the relief under the vault the conqueror of the Jews appears once again, sitting on an eagle. The arch and the relief can be seen to this day in the city of Rome, a melancholy memorial to the Temple that is no more. The tradition still prevails there that no Jew ever passed beneath the arch.[6]

The Jewish national state and its central religious organization were now destroyed.[7] Judea was henceforth a Roman province separate from Syria and ruled directly by Roman governors residing at Caesarea. At Jerusalem, which had been razed to the ground, the Emperor Hadrian (A.D. 117-138) founded a new heathen city named Aelia Capitolina.[8] This provoked one more fanatical and useless rebellion. It flamed out when Timeius Rufus was governor of Judea (A.D. 132). It was led by Bar Cochba, "Son of a Star," in whom Rabbi Akiba saw the Messianic fulfillment of the prophecy in Numbers 24:17. The suppression of the rebellion was only completed by Julius Severus, who was sent to Judea from his governorship in Britain for that task. Bethar,[9] the last stronghold of Bar Cochba and his followers, fell to Julius Severus in A.D. 135, and the final struggle of the Jews to regain independence was over.[10]

[6] JE XII, p.164.

[7] The Sanhedrin disappeared and the daily sacrifice was no more. Even the Jewish temple-tax was paid into the temple of Jupiter Capitolinus (p.291) in Rome (*War.* VII, vi, 6). But the Law still existed and the study of it was pursued more zealously than ever. The most notable center of rabbinical scholarship at this time was at Jamnia (p.225).

[8] *Colonia Aelia Capitolina.* It was called Aelia after Hadrian's family name, and Capitolina after the Capitoline Jupiter. cf. Ptolemy, *Geography.* v, 15. ed. Stevenson, p.128: "Hierosolyma which now is called Aelia Capitolia."

[9] Or Beth-ther. Probably the modern Bettir, some three hours southwest of Jerusalem. The rabbis said that like the Temple it too fell on the 9th of Ab (*Taanith.* IV; cf. p.249 n.3).

[10] Eusebius, *Ch. Hist.* IV, vi; Dio, *Roman History.* LXIX, 12-14.

With the suppression of the rebellion, Hadrian, who was devoted to the erection of magnificent buildings and cities, was free to proceed energetically with the building of Aelia Capitolina. A Roman legion had continued to be garrisoned here since the time of Titus, and Greeks were now introduced in lieu of the Jews who were forbidden to enter the territory under pain of death. The city was divided into seven quarters, and many fine public edifices were built or rebuilt, including two baths, a theater and the hippodrome. Two chief sanctuaries were established. On the site of the former Jewish temple of Jehovah, a temple of Jupiter Capitolinus was erected.[11] In it Jupiter, Juno and Minerva were represented and probably there was also a statue of Hadrian himself, while in the court in front of the temple there was a statue of the emperor on horseback. On the place where, according to Christian tradition, the sepulcher of Christ had been, a high terrace was constructed and a sanctuary of Venus (Aphrodite) erected.[12] On coins of the time it is represented as a round building with a dome. Within was a marble statue of the goddess.[13]

In A.D. 325 Jerusalem was made a Christian city by Constantine. The city was captured by the Neo-Persians under Chosroes II in A.D. 614, by the Arab Caliph Omar in A.D. 638, and by the Seljuk Turks in A.D. 1072. The crusader Godfrey de Bouillon took the city in A.D. 1099 and it was the seat of the Latin kingdom of Jerusalem until A.D. 1187, when it fell to Saladin. It was taken by the Ottoman Turks in A.D. 1517 and was entered by General Sir E. H. Allenby in December, 1917.

[11] Dio, *Roman History.* LXIX, 12.
[12] Eusebius, *Life of Constantine.* III, 26 (NPNFSS I, p.527).
[13] Watzinger, *Denkmäler Palästinas.* II, pp.79f.

VI

Following Paul the Traveler

1. THE DECLINE AND DISAPPEARANCE
OF JEWISH CHRISTIANITY

THE fall of Jerusalem in A.D. 70 marked the end of the Jewish
national state and the centralized religious organization of
Judaism. It also sealed the fate of Jewish Christianity. The
church at Jerusalem had already seen Stephen stoned (Acts 7:59),
James the son of Zebedee beheaded (Acts 12:2) and James the
brother of the Lord thrown from the pinnacle of the Temple, stoned
and beaten to death with a club.[1] Then at the time of the Jewish war
a revelation was received by the church to leave Jerusalem and
migrate to Pella in Transjordan (p. 231).[2] This was a Gentile city,
hated by the Jews and laid waste by them at the beginning of the
war,[3] but it offered refuge to the Christians. Jewish Christianity
survived here for a time, as did different kinds of Jewish sects which
also, for various reasons, had taken refuge east of the Jordan, and
Christian bishops of Pella are mentioned as late as the fifth and
sixth centuries A.D.[4] But the land east of the Jordan was apart from
the main streams in which the history of the future was to flow.
In the isolation of its lonely deserts Jewish Christianity sank quietly
into oblivion.[5]

[1] Eusebius, *Ch. Hist.* II, xxiii.   [2] *Ch. Hist.* III, v, 2f.
[3] Josephus, *War.* II, xviii, 1.
[4] M. LeQuien, *Oriens Christianus.* (1740) III, pp.698f.
[5] Karl Pieper, *Die Kirche Palästinas bis zum Jahre 135.* 1938, p.58. Inscriptions on
stone ossuaries recently found near Jerusalem are believed to date from before A.D. 70
and to contain lamentations by Jewish disciples on the crucifixion of Jesus. If this
interpretation proves correct, we owe to Jewish Christians what may be the oldest
archeological record of Christianity. *The New York Times*, Oct. 3, 1945, p.3.

2. THE WORK OF PAUL

THE wider world was to be won by that true and universal Christianity which found no room for distinctions of Jew or Greek but saw all as one man in Christ Jesus (Galatians 3:28). It was Paul who recognized most clearly this universal character of Christianity and labored most effectively to put it into practice by launching a world-wide mission.

TARSUS

To follow the footsteps of Paul one must go far afield from Palestine. Tarsus of Cilicia is named in the book of Acts (9:11; 21:39; 22:3; cf. 9:30; 11:25) as the home of Paul. Tarsus was a meeting place of East and West. The two chief trade routes from the East, one coming from the Euphrates over the Amanus Pass and the other coming from Antioch by the Syrian Gates, united fifty miles east of Tarsus and entered the city as a single road. This road then ran northward toward the mountain wall of the Taurus thirty miles away. The road over these mountains is 70 or 80 miles in length. The actual pass, one hundred yards in length, is known as the Cilician Gates,[1] and is a place where dark cliffs narrow to a mere slit, at the bottom of which is a torrent. Engineering work done here, probably as long ago as 1000 B.C., opened the way to central Asia Minor and the West.

Tarsus itself was situated in the Cilician Plain. The "cold and swift" Cydnus River[2] flowed directly through the heart of the city, entered some miles beyond it a lake called Rhegma, and flowed on to the Mediterranean ten miles away. Shipping came at that time all the way up the river to the city,[3] and thus it was an important port as well as a center on the land route.

The history of Tarsus goes back to Hittite times, and the city is mentioned on the Black Obelisk of Shalmaneser III as one of the cities captured by him.[4] Xenophon (c.400 B.C.) found Tarsus "a large and prosperous city,"[5] and II Maccabees 4:30f. mentions an insurrection there which Antiochus IV Epiphanes hastened to quiet (c.170 B.C.). In the time of the Seleucids, Tarsus became strongly

---

[1] Pliny, *Natural History.* v, 22.
[2] Strabo, *Geography* XIV, v, 12; cf. Plutarch, *Life of Alexander.* XIX.
[3] Plutarch, *Life of Antony.* XXVI.
[4] ARAB I, §583.
[5] *Anabasis.* I, ii, 23. tr. C. L. Brownson, LCL (1921-22) I, p.263.

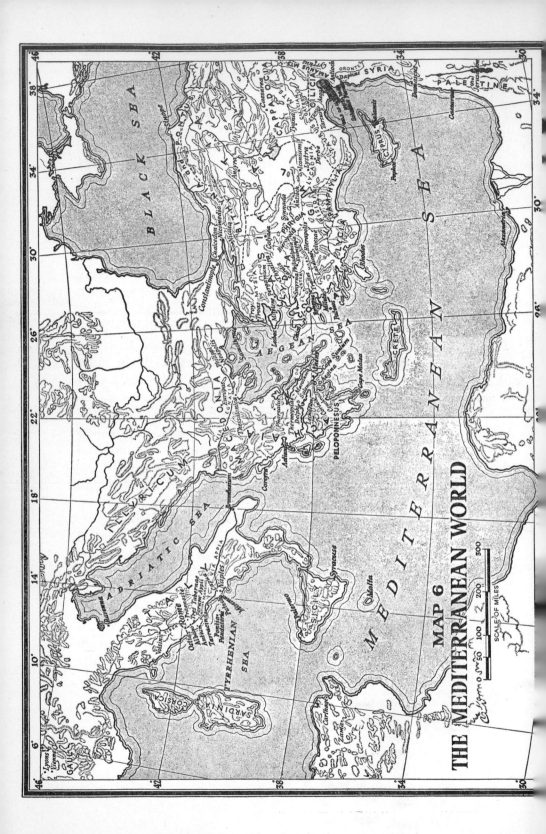

THE MEDITERRANEAN WORLD

MAP 6

SCALE OF MILES

50 0 100 200 300

Hellenized, and in 64 B.C. Pompey made Cilicia a Roman province with Tarsus as the residence of the Roman governor. From the time of Antony and Augustus on it was a free city, densely populated and wealthy. Tarsus was also an intellectual center with a famed university. Strabo said, "The people at Tarsus have devoted themselves so eagerly, not only to philosophy, but also to the whole round of education in general, that they have surpassed Athens, Alexandria, or any other place that can be named where there have been schools and lectures of philosophers."[6] The most famous philosopher of Tarsus was the Stoic, Athenodorus, who was the teacher of the Emperor Augustus.

The ancient and splendid city of Paul is represented by the modern and relatively unprepossessing Tersoos, a place of some 20,000 inhabitants. Beneath the grounds of the American Tarsus College there are enormous vaults which may have belonged to the hippodrome of Roman times, and at the southeastern edge of the town is the large mound of Gözlü Kule where excavations were conducted, beginning in 1934, by Bryn Mawr College.[7] A native factory of about the middle of the second century A.D. was unearthed. Apparently it had catered to the needs of the hippodrome and the theater, for it made terra-cotta figures of victorious charioteers and horsemen, lamps representing chariot races and gladiatorial combats, and theatrical masks. Here and elsewhere in the digging numerous representations of deities came to light, including Artemis, Athena, Apollo, Serapis, Isis, Aphrodite, Zeus and Hermes. In the lower levels of the mound the excavators penetrated to remains of Hittite and Babylonian times.

Another link with the past is the trade of tent-making which is still carried on, as it was in the time of Paul (Acts 18:3). Goats living on the Taurus Mountains where the snow lies until May, grow magnificent coats whose hair has long been famous for strength and durability. This is spun into thread and woven into a tough fabric which anciently was known from the name of the province as *cilicium*. This fabric, in turn, is made into tents and other necessities.

DAMASCUS

The conversion of Paul to the faith which once he persecuted is

6 *Geography.* XIV, v, 13.
7 Hetty Goldman in AJA 39 (1935), pp.526-549; 41 (1937), pp.262-286.

intimately connected with the city of Damascus (Galatians 1:17; II Corinthians 11:32; Acts 9:1-25; 22:5-16; 26:12-20). Damascus lies in a fertile plain east of the Anti-Lebanon range, with snowy Mount Hermon filling the western horizon. The river el-Barada, "the Cool," runs through the heart of the city, while el-A'waj descends from the eastern slopes of Mount Hermon to water the southeastern plain. The Barada is doubtless the Abanah and the A'waj may be the Pharpar of II Kings 5:12, which Naaman thought "better than all the waters of Israel." So fertile is the oasis in which Damascus stands that the Arabian poets compared it with Paradise. The scene is indeed one of beauty with the white roofs, the domes, and the minarets of the city standing out against the green of the environing orchards.

Damascus is mentioned in Genesis (14:15; 15:2) as a city which was in existence in the days of Abraham, and in the fifteenth century B.C. was one of the places controlled by Thutmose III. After Alexander the Great, Damascus was possessed first by the Ptolemies and then by the Seleucids. Around 85 B.C. Antiochus XII was killed in battle with the king of the Nabateans, and Damascus came under the control of the latter.[8] The Nabateans were a people who had established themselves beyond the Dead Sea in the district of Petra, the ancient home of the Edomites, and the Nabatean king who conquered Antiochus XII was Aretas III (c.85-c.60 B.C.). In 64 B.C. Damascus was taken by the Romans under Metellus,[9] and thenceforward presumably belonged to the Roman province of Syria which was constituted soon afterward. At the time when Paul fled from Damascus, however, the city is stated to have been under a governor of Aretas the king (II Corinthians 11:32). This must have been the Nabatean king, Aretas IV, whose original name was Aeneas and who reigned from 9 B.C. to A.D. 40. He is also known to us for his defeat of Herod Antipas in revenge for the divorce of his daughter by the latter (p. 217). Apparently, therefore, Damascus had been returned to the control of Aretas IV at the time to which II Corinthians refers. Some confirmation of this fact may be seen in the coins of Damascus, on which the image of Tiberius appears down to A.D. 34. Then in the time of Caligula (A.D. 37-41) and Claudius (A.D. 41-54) no Damascus coins are known which have the image of the

---

[8] Josephus, *Ant.* XIII, xv, 1f.; *War.* I, iv, 7f.
[9] *Ant.* XIV, ii, 3; *War.* I, vi, 2.

Roman emperor. But coins of Nero begin again in A.D. 62. In the interval Damascus may have belonged to the Nabatean king.[10]

Today Damascus has a population of somewhat less than 200,000 and is an oriental city of narrow, crooked streets and numerous mosques, with a certain occidental veneer in the form of tramcars, telegraph wires and radios. The East Gate (Bab esh-Sherqi) of the city probably dates from Roman times. It was a threefold archway, but two of the three arches are now walled up. The street which runs directly west from this gate through the city is still called Derb el-Mustaqim ("Straight Street") or Suq et-Tawileh ("Long Bazaar") and probably preserves the line of "the street which is called Straight" of Acts 9:11 (Fig. 114).

ANTIOCH IN SYRIA

The Syrian city of Antioch played an important part in early Christian history. It was there that "the disciples were called Christians first" (Acts 11:26), and it was from there that Paul and Barnabas were sent out for wider missionary work (Acts 13:1-3).

Antioch lies on the Orontes River, about 20 miles from the Mediterranean, at the foot of Mount Silpius. Much information concerning the history and topography of the city is to be derived from the *Chronicle* of John Malalas (A.D. c.491-c.578), a Byzantine monk who was born and spent most of his life in Antioch. He relates that Seleucus I Nicator wished to build many cities and made a beginning at the sea of Syria. On the seashore at the trading place of Pieria he founded a city which he called Seleucia after his own name. Then "he built Antioch after the name of his son, Antiochus, surnamed Soter." John Malalas also says that Seleucus planted cypresses in Heraclea, which is now called Daphne, and states that "this same city was built outside a grove by the temple of Athena."[11]

Under Antiochus I Soter, Antioch became the capital of the western part of the Seleucid Empire. This king also added a second quarter to the city on its eastern side. Later a third quarter was built by Seleucus II Callinicus on an island in the river; and a fourth was built by Antiochus IV Epiphanes on the slopes of Mount Silpius. Strabo says, "Antiocheia is . . . a Tetrapolis, since it consists

[10] Schürer, *A History of the Jewish People in the Time of Jesus Christ.* I, ii, pp.357f.
[11] Matthew Spinka, *Chronicle of John Malalas, Books VIII-XVIII, translated from the Church Slavonic.* (1940) VIII, i-ii (pp.13-15).

of four parts; and each of the four settlements is fortified both by a common wall and by a wall of its own."[12]

Antioch fell into the hands of Tigranes of Armenia around 83 B.C., but about twenty years later was taken from him by the Romans and made a free city and the capital of the Roman province of Syria. It was further beautified by the Roman emperors, including Augustus and Tiberius, and Herod the Great paved one of its broad streets and erected colonnades along it.[13] Perhaps this was in appreciation of the very good relations which existed there between the Gentiles and the Jewish inhabitants, for in Antioch Jews were accorded the right of citizenship and "privileges equal to those of the Macedonians and Greeks who were the inhabitants."[14]

Josephus called Antioch the third city of the Roman Empire, only Rome and Alexandria taking precedence.[15] The city was known as "the Beautiful,"[16] but the reputation of its moral life was not good and Juvenal (A.D. c.60-c.140) described the flooding of Rome with the superstition and immorality of the East as a flowing of the Orontes into the Tiber.[17]

In comparison with its former splendor, the modern city of Antakiyeh with some 35,000 inhabitants, presents a very poor appearance. Since the present town covers but a fraction of the area of the ancient city, however, excellent opportunity exists for archeological work, and excavations have been conducted here beginning in 1932 by Princeton University with the cooperation of the Baltimore Museum of Art, the Worcester Art Museum and the Musées Nationaux de France.[18]

Although the excavations at Antioch, like those at many other places, were terminated by the outbreak of the Second World War, numerous important finds were made. The island on which one of the principal districts of the city was built had disappeared from sight with the silting up of one of the channels of the Orontes, but

---

[12] *Geography.* XVI, ii, 4.

[13] Josephus, *War.* I, xxi, 11; *Ant.* XVI, v, 3.

[14] *Ant.* XII, iii, 1.   [15] *War.* III, ii, 4.

[16] Athenaeus (end of 2d cent. A.D.), *The Deipnosophists.* I, 20. tr. B. Gulick, LCL (1927-41) I, p.87; cf. the oration in praise of Antioch delivered probably in A.D. 360 by Libanius, a native of that city (Leo Hugi, *Der Antiochikos des Libanios* [1919]).

[17] *Satire.* III, 62. tr. G. G. Ramsay, LCL (1918), p.37.

[18] *Antioch on-the-Orontes, Publications of the Committee for the Excavation of Antioch and Its Vicinity.* I: *The Excavations of 1932,* ed. G. W. Elderkin. 1934; II: *The Excavations 1933-1936,* ed. Richard Stillwell. 1938; III: *The Excavations 1937-1939,* ed. R. Stillwell. 1941.

it was found again, and the wall which Justinian threw around the city in the sixth century was traced. Two ancient cemeteries of the second century A.D. were discovered, and the acropolis of the city was found to be on Mount Stauris instead of on Mount Silpius as was formerly supposed. The location was plotted of the two principal streets of the city, which had been famous in antiquity for their colonnades. The circus, which was one of the largest and most important in the Roman Empire, was found and excavated. It is believed to have been erected originally in the first century B.C. Other discoveries included baths, Roman villas, and a Byzantine stadium belonging to the fifth and sixth centuries.

Commanding the lower Orontes and looming above the sea south of the Gulf of Alexandretta is the mountain called Musa Dagh. The major portion of Antioch's seaport city, Seleucia Pieria, was built on a long, sloping spur of this mountain, and the city's walls ran on down to enclose the harbor, an area which now is largely marshland. Among the structures studied at Seleucia Pieria were the market gate, houses, the Doric temple of Hellenistic times, and the memorial church which will be referred to later along with the church at Kaoussie also near Antioch (pp. 446-450).

The suburb of Daphne was on a plateau lying four or five miles southwest of Antioch and rising more than 300 feet above the average level of the city. There are springs on the plateau, and the system of aqueducts by which their waters were carried to Antioch has been traced and studied. Beautiful pleasure villas were at Daphne, and there was a fine theater which was built in a splendid natural bowl formed by encircling hillsides on the slope of the plateau overlooking the valley of the Orontes. The theater was constructed probably around the end of the first century A.D.

Many sculptured pieces have been found, but doubtless the most spectacular finds at Antioch and its suburbs have been the numerous floor mosaics, many of which have been uncovered fortuitously or by the operation of natural forces. These extend in date from around A.D. 100 to the sixth century, and provide an unequaled wealth of material for the study of Greco-Roman mosaic art. One mosaic, which decorated the floor of the triclinium of a house belonging to the end of the first century A.D., portrays the judgment of Paris, and a drinking contest between Heracles and Dionysus, with the latter the victor. Other subjects include Oceanus and Thalassa in the midst of the fishes of the sea, landscapes and hunting scenes, and an illustrated calendar in which the months of the year are personified as little figures carrying fruits and other symbols of the months.[19]

CYPRUS

The destination of Paul and Barnabas, when they were first sent out by the church at Antioch, was near-by Cyprus (Acts 13:4), one of the largest islands in the Mediterranean. The first appearance of Cyprus in history is when it was captured by Thutmose III of Egypt.[20] Later the island was colonized by the Phoenicians and the Greeks. About 58 B.C. it was taken from Ptolemy Auletes by Rome and later made a separate province.[21] In 22 B.C. it was transferred to the senate, and its governor therefore had the title of proconsul (cf. pp. 217f. n.12). Acts 13:7 names a certain Sergius Paulus as proconsul when Paul came, and an inscription of the year A.D. 55 has been found at Paphos with the words "in the time of the proconsul Paulus."[22]

THE CITIES OF GALATIA

From Cyprus, Paul and Barnabas went to the mainland of Asia Minor. According to Acts (13:14, 51; 14:6) they preached there in Antioch of Pisidia, Iconium of Phrygia, and Lystra and Derbe of Lycaonia.

Pisidian Antioch[23] was another of the some sixteen Antiochs founded by Seleucus I Nicator, and it was made a free city by the Romans about 189 B.C. and a Roman colony by Augustus before 11 B.C. Antioch was in the extreme northeast of the district of Pisidia

---

[19] In connection with Antioch, the so-called "Chalice of Antioch" must be mentioned which is reported to have been found by natives at or near this city. It consists of an inner plain silver cup held in an outer openwork gilded shell and set on a solid silver base. The openwork holder is decorated with vines, birds and animals, and twelve seated human figures. The last are divided into two groups, in each of which five persons are placed about one central figure. Evidently the central figure in each of the two groups is Christ and the others are his apostles. A first century date has been advocated vigorously for this remarkable object, with the additional suggestion that the inner cup is nothing other than the Holy Grail (Gustavus A. Eisen, *The Great Chalice of Antioch*. 1933), but on the other hand the authenticity of the chalice has been called in question (C. R. Morey in *Art Studies, Medieval, Renaissance and Modern* 3 [1925], pp.73-80), and the most that can be said is that it may be a piece of early Christian silver from the fourth or fifth century (H. Harvard Arnason in BA IV, 4 [Dec. 1941], pp.49-64; V, 1 [Feb. 1942], pp. 10-16).

[20] ARE II, §493, 511 (Isy = Cyprus).

[21] Strabo, *Geography*. XIV, vi, 6.

[22] Stephen L. Caiger, *Archaeology and the New Testament*. 1939, p.119.

[23] Ptolemy, *Geography*. V, 4. ed. Stevenson, p.116: *Antiochia Pisidiae*.

and on the frontier of the district of Phrygia. The Pisidians and the Phrygians were peoples of less high civilization but Antioch itself was a thoroughly Hellenized and Romanized city.

The site of Antioch was on the lower slopes of a majestic mountain now called Sultan Dagh, and on the right bank of the Anthius River. The place was discovered in 1833 by Francis V. J. Arundell, British chaplain at Smyrna, and is near the modern Turkish town of Yalovach. The ruins show that Antioch was a strongly fortified city, and the remains of the Roman aqueduct which brought water from the foothills of the Sultan Dagh still are to be seen.[24] The principal temple was dedicated to the god Men and was studied by Sir William Ramsay just before the First World War. The great altar and many engraved tablets were uncovered, and the underlying soil was found to be full of the bones of sacrificial animals. An inscription was found which referred to a "Lucius Sergius Paullus the younger," whom Ramsay believed to be the son of Sergius Paulus, proconsul of Cyprus.[25]

Later, more intensive excavations were conducted by the University of Michigan,[26] and the most important remains of the Roman city founded by Augustus were brought to light. The city enjoyed two fine squares, the upper known as the Augusta Platea or Square of Augustus and the lower as the Tiberia Platea or Square of Tiberius. The two were connected by a broad flight of steps, at the top of which stood the three triumphal archways of the propylaea erected in honor of Augustus. The archways were adorned with many relief sculptures and probably were once surmounted with statues in the round as well. The reliefs in the spandrels of the arches portrayed captive Pisidians and commemorated the victories of Augustus on land, while a frieze with Poseidon, Tritons, dolphins and other marine symbols celebrated his triumphs at sea, especially at Actium.

On the Square of Augustus stood the great temple, which was not Hellenistic as Ramsay believed but also belonged to the age of Augustus. A wonderful frieze of bulls' heads adorned the temple, the heads being connected by garlands of leaves and all kinds of fruits realistically rendered. The bull's head was the symbol of Men,

[24] W. M. Ramsay, *The Cities of St. Paul.* 1907. Plate facing p.252.

[25] W. M. Ramsay, *The Bearing of Recent Discovery on the Trustworthiness of the New Testament.* 4th ed. 1920, pp.150f.

[26] David M. Robinson in AJA 28 (1924), pp.435-444.

who was the local god upon whom the prosperity of agriculture was believed to depend. As the god who bestowed all blessings upon the people, it was not difficult also to identify him with the Roman emperor Augustus.

Both the architecture and the sculpture of these first century structures were very impressive. "Nowhere else in the Roman empire has yet been discovered a better combination of superb realistic sculpture with excellent solid architecture in excellent vertical and horizontal rhythm," says David M. Robinson. "Greek refinement and restraint seem here to be combined with Roman luxuriance, Greek simplicity with Roman complexity, Greek beauty with Roman realism and massiveness."[27]

Another monumental structure at Pisidian Antioch was a triple gateway built into the city wall. It bore an inscription, in bronze letters which are preserved, of G(aius) Jul(ius) Asp(er), consul in A.D. 212, and was adorned with sculptures, but of a quality inferior to those of the propylaea and the temple. Other discoveries included numerous terra-cotta pipes through which the spring water brought by the aqueduct was distributed throughout the city; playing-boards, incised with circles and rectangles, where the Romans spent their idle hours in various games; and a Latin edict of Domitian's praetorian legate L. Antistius Rusticus which prescribed measures for preventing profiteering, controlling the price of grain after a severe winter and ensuring sufficient seed for the next season. Also there was a Christian basilica at Antioch which was more than 200 feet long, and which dates, according to an inscription, in the time of Optimus, who was bishop of Antioch in the last quarter of the fourth century.

Iconium was 60 miles distant from Antioch to the southeast, on the frontier between Phrygia and Lycaonia. Therefore it was sometimes considered as the last city of Phrygia,[28] and was sometimes spoken of as belonging to the neighboring district of Lycaonia.[29] In Acts 14:6 it is regarded as belonging to Phrygia, for it is implied that in fleeing from Iconium to Lystra and Derbe Paul went from Phrygia to Lycaonia.[30]

The ancient Iconium is now known as Konia, and is a relatively

[27] Robinson in *The Art Bulletin* 9 (Sept. 1926-June 1927), p.6.
[28] Xenophon, *Anabasis*. I, ii, 19.   [29] Strabo, *Geography*. XII, vi, 1.
[30] W. M. Ramsay, *A Historical Commentary on St. Paul's Epistle to the Galatians.* 1900, p.215.

modern Turkish city of some 47,000 inhabitants. It is in a plain watered by streams from the Pisidian mountains, and near by are twin conical hills known as the peaks of St. Philip and St. Thecla. Thecla was the young woman of Iconium who was associated with the apostle Paul in the apocryphal Acts of Paul. The latter is the work which contains the famous description of Paul as "a man of little stature, thin-haired upon the head, crooked in the legs, of good state of body, with eyebrows joining, and nose somewhat hooked, full of grace: for sometimes he appeared like a man, and sometimes he had the face of an angel."[31]

Lystra and Derbe were in the region of Lycaonia, and in the first century the common people still spoke the native Lycaonian language as is indicated in Acts 14:11. Lystra was some 25 miles from Iconium, and its site was discovered in 1885 by J. R. Sitlington Sterrett. It was identified by an altar still standing in its original position. This was a stone, about three and one-half feet high and twelve inches thick, with a clearly cut Latin inscription (Fig. 115). The inscription gave the usual Roman spelling of the city's name, Lustra, and indicated that it was a Roman colony.[32] Derbe was situated some distance southeast of Lystra, and its site is believed to be represented by the large mound known as Gudelisin, which also was first observed by Professor Sterrett.[33]

In New Testament times all four of these cities—Antioch, Iconium, Lystra and Derbe—were included in the Roman province of Galatia. The Roman province took its name from the smaller northern district of Galatia proper which it included. This ethnographical district of Galatia proper was named from three Gallic tribes which entered Asia Minor around 278-277 B.C. and settled permanently in this region. In 64 B.C. they became a client state of the Roman Empire, and in the following years were able to extend their territory to include the whole center of Asia Minor. Amyntas, their last native king, ruled over Galatia, Phrygia-towards-Pisidia, Pisidia, Lycaonia and part of Pamphylia.[34] Upon the death of Amyntas in 25 B.C. this kingdom was bequeathed to the Romans,[35] and became the Roman

[31] James, *The Apocryphal New Testament*, p.273.
[32] Sterrett, *An Epigraphical Journey in Asia Minor*. 1888; Ramsay, *A Historical Commentary on St. Paul's Epistle to the Galatians*, p.224.
[33] Ramsay, *The Cities of St. Paul*, p.452 n.18.
[34] CAH, p.69.
[35] King Amyntas was taken prisoner and put to death by the brigand tribes of the Taurus known as Homanadenses. Augustus ultimately avenged the death of his subject

province of Galatia. The new province at first included the entire kingdom of Amyntas, but it was somewhat reduced in size in 20 B.C.[36] Thereafter, however, it continued to comprise Galatia proper, Pisidia and western Lycaonia.[37] Thus Antioch, Iconium, Lystra and Derbe were all within the boundaries of the Roman province of Galatia.[38]

Paul's letter addressed "unto the churches of Galatia" (Galatians 1:2) presumably went, therefore, to the churches of Antioch, Iconium, Lystra and Derbe, which he himself had founded. To address them as "churches of Galatia," meaning the Roman province of Galatia, was entirely correct.[39] Those who insist on confining the word "Galatia" to its strict ethnographical meaning, on the other hand, believe that the letter was intended for otherwise unknown Christian churches in north Galatia proper.[40] This is less probable, and the first time that the existence of a Christian congregation at Ancyra is even mentioned is in A.D. 192.[41] Ancyra was the chief city of north Galatia and the capital of the entire province. The real greatness of this place dated from the time when Constantinople became the Roman metropolis and the location of Ancyra gave it a lasting importance. Today it is the modern Angora or Ankara, the capital of Turkey. Its most important monument is the Augusteum, a white marble temple which the council of the three Galatian tribes erected to Rome and Augustus during the lifetime of Augustus. On its walls is carved a long Latin inscription narrating the public life and work of the emperor. The original which is now lost was composed in a dignified style by Augustus himself and was completed in A.D. 14, to be engraved on bronze tablets in front of his mausoleum in Rome. Fragments of other copies of the

king by sending out Publius Sulpicius Quirinius as consul to "pacify" the Homanadensians, which was done with characteristically cruel Roman thoroughness in the years 10-7 B.C. This was the Quirinius who later was governor of Syria (p. 219). CAH X, pp.271f.

[36] Eastern Lycaonia, together with Cilicia Tracheia, was transferred to the rule of the king of Cappadocia.

[37] CAH X, p.261.

[38] Ramsay, The Cities of St. Paul, pp.262f.,343,401.

[39] Ramsay, A Historical Commentary on St. Paul's Epistle to the Galatians; and in HDB II, pp.81-89; Edgar J. Goodspeed, The Story of the New Testament. 1916, p.9; Frederic Rendall in The Expositor's Greek Testament. III, p.128.

[40] Paul W. Schmiedel in T. K. Cheyne and J. Sutherland Black, eds., Encyclopaedia Biblica. 1899-1903, cols.1592-1616; James Moffatt, An Introduction to the Literature of the New Testament. 3d ed. 1918, pp.90-101; and in EB IX, p.972.

[41] EB I, p.893.

same text have been found also at Pisidian Antioch and at Apollonia.[42]

EPHESUS

Ephesus was the city of Asia Minor where Paul worked for the longest time (Acts 19:1-20:1). The earliest inhabitants of Ephesus were of Asiatic origin, and about the seventh century B.C. the Ionian Greeks settled there. In the sixth century B.C. the city fell to Croesus of Lydia and then to Cyrus of Persia. Around 334 B.C. Ephesus came under the control of Alexander the Great, and later was held by the Seleucids of Syria. When the Romans defeated Antiochus III the Great about 190 B.C. they handed over Ephesus to Eumenes II (c.197-c.159 B.C.), king of Pergamum. It was Eumenes II who built the great Altar of Zeus at Pergamum which was reconstructed so splendidly in the Berlin Museum. This great structure was erected in celebration of the victory of Eumenes over the Gauls around 180 B.C. and is adorned with a frieze of magnificent sculptures depicting the combat of gods and giants. The remains of the Temple of Rome and Augustus have also been discovered at Pergamum. This temple was founded in 29 B.C. and was the first in the empire to be dedicated to the cult of Roman emperor worship, with which Christianity was to come into such serious conflict. Either the Altar of Zeus or the Temple of Rome and Augustus was probably the "Satan's throne" of Revelation 2:13.[43]

About 133 B.C. the last king of Pergamum, Attalus III Philometor, bequeathed Ephesus, together with the rest of the Pergamenian kingdom, to the Romans and thereafter it continued subject to them. At first Pergamum remained the capital of the Roman province of Asia, but eventually this honor passed to Ephesus. Whether it had become the capital in the time of Paul is uncertain. At any rate Ephesus was "the largest emporium in Asia this side of the Taurus,"[44] and ranked along with Antioch in Syria and Alexandria in Egypt as one of the three great cities of the eastern Mediterranean. This prominence it owed very largely to its favorable geographical location, for it was on the main line of communication between Rome and the Orient in general. The city was situated within three miles of the sea, on the left bank of the river Cayster.

[42] *Res Gestae Divi Augusti*. tr. F. W. Shipley, LCL (1924).
[43] *Altertümer von Pergamon*. 10 vols. 1912-37; Hans Erich Stier, *Aus der Welt des Pergamonaltars*. 1932.
[44] Strabo, *Geography*. XIV, i, 24.

At that time this river was navigable as far up as the city, although attention was required to keep the city harbor and the channel of the Cayster free from silt. A breakwater was built under the Pergamenian king Attalus Philadelphus (c.159-c.138 B.C.), with the intention of contributing to this end but unfortunately it had the opposite result and made the harbor shallower. Around A.D. 65 the governor of Asia took further measures to improve the connection between harbor and sea.[45] In later centuries the engineering work necessary to maintain the harbor was neglected, and now the mouth of the river has been silted up badly and the harbor reduced to a marsh.

From Ephesus, the Cayster Valley offered the shortest route to Pisidian Antioch and the East. The way was relatively steep, but nevertheless was often preferred by travelers on foot because of its shorter distance. It was probably the route taken by Paul in Acts 19:1. The longer but more level route on which the heavier traffic moved, crossed a 600-foot pass to the south of Ephesus and then followed the Maeander Valley eastward by Laodicea even as the modern railroad does.

The railroad station nearest to the site of Ephesus today is the small village of Ayasoluk, or Seljuk as the Turks now call it. Ayasoluk is a corruption of Agios Theologos, as St. John "the Theologian" was called, to whom Justinian dedicated here a fine church.[46] The houses of Ayasoluk mostly are made of stones brought from the ruins of Ephesus, a mile or two away to the southwest.

Ephesus was particularly famous for the worship of Artemis and the Artemision or temple of this goddess was accounted one of the seven wonders of the ancient world. The goddess originally had been a Lydian deity of character similar to the Phrygian Cybele and the Phoenician Astarte. The Greek colonists in Ephesus identified her with their own Artemis, who was known to the Romans as Diana. The first systematic exploration of Ephesus was carried out by the English architect, J. T. Wood, whose chief purpose was to find the famous temple of Artemis. The search was begun on May 2, 1863, and after the most persistent endeavor the temple wall was discovered on May 2, 1869. The clue which led to the discovery was

---

[45] Tacitus, *Annals*. XVI, 23. tr. J. Jackson, LCL (1931-37) IV, p.373.
[46] Procopius (A.D. c.490-c.562), *Buildings*. V, i, 4-6. tr. H. B. Dewing, LCL VII (1940), pp.317-319.

a Roman inscription which was found in the course of clearing the theater and which dates in the time of Trajan, that is about 50 years after the time of Paul. This inscription described a number of gold and silver images of Artemis (cf. Acts 19:24), weighing from three to seven pounds each, which were to be presented to the goddess and placed in her temple. According to the inscription, an endowment was provided for the care and cleaning of the images, and instruction given that when they were carried from the temple to the theater for the birthday anniversary of the goddess the procession was to enter the city by the Magnesian Gate and leave it afterward by the Coressian Gate. By finding the site of the two city gates mentioned and then following the road from the Magnesian Gate, Wood finally discovered the temple, which stood more than a mile northeast of the city proper.[47]

Wood continued his work until 1874, and in 1904-1905 further excavations were made and the entire history of the temple studied by David G. Hogarth on behalf of the British Museum.[48] In the meantime in 1896 the Austrian Archaeological Institute began its thorough and long-continued excavations at Ephesus, the results of which have appeared in a series of impressive publications.[49]

It is believed that the earliest beginnings of the Artemision go back to a time around the end of the eighth century B.C. At that time only a small shrine was in existence, being little more than an enclosure containing a platform, a sacred tree and an altar, and perhaps later a wooden image. In the centuries immediately following this shrine was reconstructed at least twice. Later these primitive structures were replaced by a much larger and more splendid temple which was probably begun about 550 B.C., and to which Croesus, the famous king of Lydia, contributed some beautiful columns.[50] The building work continued for 120 years,[51] and the final dedication was around 430 B.C. Herodotus speaks of this temple as standing in his day, and tradition has it that it was burned in 356 B.C. on the night in which Alexander the Great was born.

[47] J. T. Wood, *Modern Discoveries on the Site of Ancient Ephesus*. 1890, pp.37-41,84.

[48] Hogarth, *Excavations at Ephesus, The Archaic Artemisia*. 1908; and in EB VIII, pp.641-644.

[49] *Forschungen in Ephesos, veröffentlicht vom Österreichischen archaeologischen Institute*. 4 vols. 1906-37.

[50] Herodotus. I, 92; A. S. Murray in *The Journal of Hellenic Studies*. 10 (1889), p.9.

[51] Pliny, *Natural History*. xxxvi, 14.

This temple, in turn, was succeeded by what is known as the Hellenistic temple, the plans for which were drawn by Dinocrates, the famous architect of Alexandria. This structure was begun probably before 350 B.C. and work was continuing on it when Alexander came to Ephesus in 334 B.C. and offered to pay the cost of its completion. It stood on a large platform nearly 240 feet wide and over 400 feet long. The temple itself was more than 160 feet wide and 340 feet long and boasted 100 columns over 55 feet high. This Hellenistic temple endured until A.D. 262, when it was sacked and burned by the Goths. The altar foundations have been discovered, behind which no doubt stood the statue of the goddess. The roof was covered with large white marble tiles, and the building was adorned with sculpture, painting and gold. The cry, "Great is Artemis of Ephesus" (Acts 19:28, 34) was fully justified, therefore, by what we know of the external splendor of the cult center.[52] Yet today the site of the temple of Diana which was built originally on marshy soil[53] has become but a stagnant pond, inhabited by myriads of frogs, and is permanently flooded.

The theater of Ephesus is also of special interest as having been the scene of the tumult which was aroused by the work of Paul (Acts 19:29). The site of the theater, which is shown in Fig. 116, was in the hollow of a hill from which one looked out over the busiest parts of the city. The theater had an imposing façade with aediculae and niches and was adorned with fine statuary. While the existing remains represent a reconstruction carried out after the period of Paul, the plan of the structure is probably essentially the same as that of the apostle's time.

Another important feature of ancient Ephesus was the agora or marketplace. This was a great rectangular, colonnaded area entered by magnificent gateways and surrounded by halls and chambers. Near by was the library, built with fine columns and with its walls recessed with niches for bookcases. Other buildings which have been excavated include gymnasia, baths and burial monuments. One of the city's finest streets ran directly from the theater to the river harbor, being nearly one half mile long and about 35 feet

[52] cf. W. M. Ramsay, *The Church in the Roman Empire before A.D. 170.* 1912, pp.135-139.
[53] Pliny, *Natural History.* XXXVI, 14.

wide, and lined with halls on either side. Also at the harbor there were monumental gateways.

Later Christian times are represented not only by the remains of Justinian's Church of St. John already mentioned (p. 266), but also by the very interesting ruins of the double Church of the Virgin Mary, where the Council of Ephesus was held in A.D. 431. This church was built probably around A.D. 350 on the foundations of a pagan building more than 800 feet long, probably a school, which had been destroyed in the preceding century. There is an extensive Christian catacomb at Ephesus, too, which dates from the fifth and sixth centuries, and is connected with the legend of the Seven Sleepers of Ephesus. According to the story, these were seven Christian youths at Ephesus who took refuge in a cave outside the city during the persecution under Decius (A.D. 250). By the emperor's command they were sealed up in the cave, but instead of perishing they fell into a sleep from which they were awakened nearly 200 years later when some stones happened to be removed from the entrance. Thereupon the youths reaffirmed their Christian faith before Theodosius II (A.D. 408-450) and Bishop Maximus, and then died.

PHILIPPI

After making the memorable crossing from Troas to what we now know as Europe, Paul preached in Philippi, the first city of that district of Macedonia and a Roman colony (Acts 16:12). This city was founded in the middle of the fourth century B.C. by Philip of Macedon. "In earlier times Philippi was called Crenides," says Strabo, "and was only a small settlement, but it was enlarged after the defeat of Brutus and Cassius."[54] This Battle of Philippi took place in 42 B.C. and to celebrate their victory Antony and Octavian made the city a Roman colony, its name, Colonia Julia Philippensis, honoring the victory of the cause of Julius Caesar. The first citizens appear to have been veterans of this battle, and after the Battle of Actium in 31 B.C. dispossessed adherents of the defeated Antony also were settled here. The victory of Augustus over Antony and Cleopatra was commemorated by the additional title Augusta, so that the full name of the city became Colonia Augusta Julia Philippensis.

The territory of the colony included Neapolis (the modern

[54] *Geography.* VII, fr. 41.

Kavalla), the seaport at which Paul landed (Acts 16:11), some nine miles distant on the coast. From Neapolis the Via Egnatia, the main overland route from Asia to Rome, ran over Mount Symbolum and directly into Philippi where it passed the whole length of the city's forum, and where the marks of wagon and chariot wheels can still be seen scored to a depth of three and four inches.

The once proud Roman colony is known today as Felibedjik, or "Little Philippi," and its ruins cover many acres of ground (Fig. 117). Excavations were conducted here between 1914 and 1938 by the École Française d'Athènes, which have provided much information concerning the city.[55] The forum, which has been uncovered completely, was a rectangular area over 300 feet long and 150 feet wide. It was entered through five porticoes on three sides, and had on its north side a rectangular podium to which steps gave access on both sides. This was evidently the tribunal from which orators spoke and magistrates dispensed justice. The forum was overlooked by temples at either end, and otherwise surrounded with public buildings. Most of these ruins date from a rebuilding in the second century, but it is probable that the plan of the forum was not radically different in Paul's day. Incidentally, the Roman rain-gutters are so well preserved that they still carry off water.

Other features of Philippi which have been studied by the French archeologists include the acropolis, the Roman baths, the theater dating originally perhaps from the fourth century B.C. and rebuilt in the second century A.D., and the Christian churches whose ruins belong to a much later date.

While most of the extant remains at Philippi belong to a period considerably after that of Paul, one important structure has been identified which is believed to date from the time of the apostle and even to figure in the account of his work given in Acts. This is a colonial archway whose ruins are to the west of the city. It probably was constructed at the time the Roman colony of Philippi was established, and it served to symbolize the dignity and privileges of the city. Also, it may have marked the line of the pomerium

---

[55] *Bulletin de correspondance hellénique.* 44 (1920), pp.406f.; 45 (1921), pp.543-547; 46 (1922), pp.527-531; 47 (1923), pp.534-536; 48 (1924), p.501; 49 (1925), p.462; 52 (1928), pp.492f.; 54 (1930), pp.502-506; 55 (1931), pp. 499-502; 57 (1933), pp.279-285; 58 (1934), pp.257-261; 59 (1935), pp.285-291; 60 (1936), pp.478-480; 61 (1937), pp.463-468; 62 (1938), pp.1-3; Paul Collart, *Philippes ville de Macédoine depuis ses origines jusqu'à la fin de l'époque romaine.* 2 vols. 1937.

within which foreign deities were not permitted. As the Via Egnatia left Philippi and headed west it ran beneath this arch and then, at a distance of a little over one mile from the city, it crossed the river Ganga or Gangites.[56] It seems natural to conclude, therefore, that the "gate" mentioned in Acts 16:13 was this very archway, that the Jews met beyond it because this was required by law, and that the "river side" where Paul spoke to the assembled women was on the edge of the Gangites.[57]

THESSALONICA

From Philippi Paul proceeded to Thessalonica, 70 miles distant along the Via Egnatia. According to Strabo, this city was founded by Cassander (c.315 B.C.) and named after his wife Thessalonica, the sister of Alexander the Great.[58] Because of its support of Antony and Octavian in the Battle of Philippi, it was rewarded by being made a free city (*civitas libera*). In the time of Strabo, Thessalonica was the most populous city in Macedonia.[59]

Thessalonica is now the modern city of Salonika, an important seaport with a population of about 237,000. It enjoys a picturesque location at the head of the Gulf of Salonika and has mountains piled behind it. The course of the Via Egnatia is still represented by the main street of the city on which there also stands the Arch of Galerius (A.D. 305-311). At its western entrance to the city, the Via Egnatia was spanned until 1876 by another Roman arch called the Vardar Gate. This was of special interest since it carried an inscription, now in the British Museum, beginning, "In the time of the Politarchs. . . ." It is probably to be dated somewhere between 30 B.C. and A.D. 143, while several other Thessalonian inscriptions, including one definitely dated in the reign of Augustus, also mention Politarchs. This is of importance since in the Greek of Acts 17:6 the rulers of Thessalonica are called Politarchs. The term is otherwise unknown in extant Greek literature, but Luke's accuracy in the matter is entirely vindicated by the inscriptions.[60]

[56] Appian (2d cent. A.D.), *Roman History, The Civil Wars.* IV, xiii, 106. tr. Horace White, LCL (1912-13) IV, p.319; Hirschfeld in Pauly's *Real-Encyclopädie der classischen Altertumswissenschaft,* ed. Georg Wissowa and Wilhelm Kroll. I (1894), col.2191.

[57] Collart, *Philippes ville de Macédoine,* pp.319-322,458-460.

[58] *Geography.* VII, fr. 21.   [59] *Geography.* VII, vii, 4.

[60] Ernest DeWitt Burton in *The American Journal of Theology.* 2 (1898), pp.598-632.

ATHENS

When Paul came to Athens (Acts 17:15) he was in one of the world's most famous centers of philosophy, architecture and art, a city in whose ruins are still to be seen today some of the most beautiful things ever made by man. Systematic study of the topography of ancient Athens was begun in the seventeenth century by the French consuls Giraud and Chataignier and by the Capuchin monks, while toward the end of the century descriptions of Greece and Athens were published by the French physician Jacques Spon[61] and the Englishman Sir George Wheeler.[62] The most important studies of the next century were made by James Stuart and Nicholas Revett, who spent three years at Athens (1751-1754) and published four large volumes on *The Antiquities of Athens* (3d ed. 1885). In the nineteenth century the work of W. M. Leake[63] introduced the period of modern research. The scientific investigations of modern times, in which Greek archeologists and the Greek government as well as at least six foreign archeological schools have participated, have made available a wealth of information concerning ancient Athens. Although the multitudinous details cannot be considered here, it is of much interest to be able to glimpse, little dimmed by time, the beauty of "the city of the violet-crown," in which the culture of the ancient world reached its greatest height and where the apostle Paul once stood though but briefly.

The remarkable and precipitous rocky hill (512 feet high) known as the Acropolis was occupied by man as early as Neolithic times. In the seventh century B.C. the city of Athens emerged from obscurity and in the wars with Persia after 500 B.C. became the natural leader of Greece. Under the administration of Pericles around 443-429 B.C. Athens reached its golden age. The friend of Pericles, the sculptor Phidias (d. c.432 B.C.), superintended the adornment of the city with a magnificent array of temples, public buildings and works of art. From the spoils of Marathon, Phidias made a colossal bronze statue of Athena Promachos, the goddess who fights in front, which was erected on the Acropolis and towered so high that mariners rounding the promontory of Sunium could see the sunlight flashing on her spear and helmet.[64] Then the incomparable Parthenon was built and

[61] *Voyage d'Italie, de Dalmatie, de Grèce et du Levant.* 1678.
[62] *Journey into Greece.* 1682.   [63] *The Topography of Athens.* 2d ed. 1841.
[64] Pausanias, *Description of Greece.* I, xxviii, 2. tr. W. H. S. Jones, LCL (1918-35) I, p.147.

a great gold and ivory statue of Athena by Phidias erected within (c.438 B.C.). Later came the completion of the stately entrance, the Propylaea, and of the beautiful temples, the Erechtheum and the shrine of Athena Nike, the goddess of victory. Of the Parthenon-crowned Acropolis J. P. Mahaffy wrote, "There is no ruin all the world over which combines so much striking beauty, so distinct a type, so vast a volume of history, so great a pageant of immortal memories. . . . All the Old World's culture culminated in Greece—all Greece in Athens—all Athens in its Acropolis—all the Acropolis in the Parthenon."[65]

Along the southern base of the Acropolis ran the colonnaded precinct of Asclepius, the god of healing. Just to the east and partly hollowed out from the declivity of the Acropolis was the lovely Theater of Dionysus. The earlier wooden structures of this theater were replaced by stone under the administration of Lycurgus around 337-323 B.C. Farther east was the Odeum of Pericles where musical contests were held, and beyond was the small circular Monument of Lysicrates, dedicated about 335 B.C. Southeast of the Acropolis stood the colossal temple of Olympian Zeus (Fig. 118). Measuring 354 feet by 135 feet at its base and towering to a height of over 90 feet, this was the largest temple in Greece and one of the largest in the ancient world. Begun by the Athenian ruler Pisistratus about 530 B.C., it stood unfinished for several centuries. Then the work was resumed by Antiochus IV Epiphanes, king of Syria, who employed the Roman architect Cossutius on the project. Even then the temple was not finished entirely, and it remained for the Emperor Hadrian to complete certain details, probably including the interior colonnades and the roof. For the most part the extant remains probably represent the work of Cossutius.[66]

After the sacred precinct of the Acropolis, the most important part of ancient Athens was the agora or marketplace which was the center of the city's civic and commercial life. According to the book of Acts (17:17) it was "in the agora" as well as in the Jewish synagogue that Paul "reasoned . . . every day with them that met him." The agora was a considerable distance to the north of the west end of the Acropolis and covered a large area. The western portion of this region is recog-

[65] *Rambles and Studies in Greece.* 1878, p.83. For the buildings of the Acropolis see Nicolas Balanos, *Les monuments de l'Acropole, relèvement et conservation.* 1936.
[66] Charles H. Weller, *Athens and Its Monuments.* 1924, pp.161-165.

nized as having been the Hellenic agora, while the space to the east represents an enlargement of the marketplace probably financed by Julius Caesar and Augustus and hence known as the Roman agora. Early agora excavations were conducted by the Greek Archaeological Society, and by the German Archaeological Institute under Professor Wilhelm Dörpfeld. Then between 1931 and 1940 very large-scale excavations, which involved the moving of around 250,000 tons of earth, were undertaken in the western or specifically Greek section of the agora by the American School of Classical Studies at Athens under the leadership of T. Leslie Shear.[67]

On the eastern side of the Greek agora stood a colonnaded portico known as the Stoa of Attalos, which, together with the near-by so-called Stoa of the Giants, had been uncovered by the Greek Archaeological Society. Along the south side ran two large parallel stoas and on the west were a number of important buildings all of which have been unearthed by the American archeologists. The structures excavated on the west side of the agora include from north to south the Stoa of Zeus Eleutherios, the last name having been applied to Zeus because he delivered the Athenians from the Persian menace; the Temple of Apollo Patroos (the Father); the Sanctuary of the Mother of the Gods; the Bouleuterion, where the Athenian Council of Five Hundred assembled; and the circular Tholos, where the executive sections of the Council were maintained. Other buildings found in the agora are the Temple of Ares, the Odeum or Music Hall in which poets and musicians contended for prizes, and the Library dedicated to Trajan and located just south of the Stoa of Attalos.

Overlooking the agora from the west is the hill called Kolonos Agoraios, on which are the well preserved ruins of a temple now identified as that of Hephaistos, the god of fire and metal-working. To the east in the region of the Roman agora are the ruins of numerous shops and arcades, and just beyond is the Horologium popularly called the Tower of the Winds. The latter was an octagonal marble structure with sun dials on the exterior and probably a water-clock on the inside. It served as a public timepiece for the city of Athens and therefore was near the chief trading center. Like the Roman

[67] Shear in *Hesperia*. 2 (1933), pp.96-109,451-474; 4 (1935), pp.311-339,340-370; 5 (1936), pp.1-42; 6 (1937), pp.333-381; 7 (1938), pp.311-362; 8 (1939), pp.201-246; 9 (1940), pp.261-307; 10 (1941), pp.1-8.

agora, the Horologium was probably constructed in the second half of the first century B.C.[68]

In view of the address by Paul reported in Acts 17:22-31, special interest attaches to the Areopagus. Areopagus or Hill of Ares is the name of a bare, rocky hill, about 377 feet high, immediately northwest of the Acropolis and separated from it by a narrow declivity now largely filled in. Steps cut in the rock lead to the top where rough, rock-hewn benches, forming three sides of a square, can still be seen. In ancient times this was the meeting place of the Areopagus court. This court or council was composed of city fathers and in early times had supreme authority in both political and religious matters. In the time of Pericles the council became largely a criminal court, but in Roman times was charged again with the care of religion and of education. From its place of assembly the court itself was called the Areopagus, and in Acts 17:34 we find one of its members referred to as an Areopagite. The word Areopagus in Acts 17:19, 22 might be interpreted, therefore, either as referring to the hill or (v. 19 RVm) to the court. In either case, however, it remains probable that the place of Paul's speech was on this hill, since it was the customary meeting place of the court.[69]

It is true that the Areopagus court seems to have met at times in the Stoa Basileios or Royal Stoa, and if this happened to be the case when Paul was in Athens then the place of his address would have to be sought in this stoa. The stoa in question is identified by some with the already mentioned Stoa of Zeus Eleutherios at the northwest corner of the agora as now excavated,[70] but is believed by others to have lain yet farther north. The point cannot be decided at present since the excavations did not reach the northern limits of the agora. As a matter of fact, work in this northern region may be long delayed because of the presence of an important modern street and also of a railway line.[71]

In his Areopagus address Paul is reported (Acts 17:23) to have referred to an altar with the inscription, "To an unknown god," or

[68] Henry S. Robinson in AJA 47 (1943), pp.291-305.
[69] Walther Judeich, *Topographie von Athen* (in Walter Otto, ed., *Handbuch der Altertumswissenschaft.* III, ii, 2, 2d ed. 1931), p.299.
[70] Homer A. Thompson in *Hesperia.* 6 (1937), pp.5-77. Wilhelm Dörpfeld (*Alt-Athen und seine Agora* [Heft 2, 1939], pp.146-167) thinks that the Stoa Basileios was the building immediately south of the Stoa of Zeus which the Americans called the Temple of Apollo Patroos.
[71] T. Leslie Shear in *Hesperia.* 4 (1935), p.354; 6 (1937), p.360.

"To the unknown god."[72] Not far from the time when Paul was in Athens, the city was visited by Apollonius of Tyana. This remarkable wandering Neo-Pythagorean philosopher, whose career parallels that of Paul's in some regards, was born at Tyana in Cappadocia, around the beginning of the Christian era, and died at Ephesus, probably in A.D. 98. After studying in Tarsus and in the temple of Asclepius at Aegae on the Gulf of Iskanderun, he traveled into all parts of the known world, at one time enduring trial and imprisonment in Rome. The last ten years of his life were spent in Greece. The biography of Apollonius was written by Flavius Philostratus (A.D. c.170-c.245) at the request of Julia Domna, the wife of the Emperor Severus, but not published until after her death in A.D. 217. Philostratus was able to draw upon a collection of letters by Apollonius and upon a travel journal by the Assyrian Damis, the disciple and companion of Apollonius. Nevertheless he added large amounts of legendary and miraculous material so that the *Life* resembles an historical novel. The biography is of interest to us, however, because it contains a remark of Apollonius to the effect that it is a proof of wisdom "to speak well of all the gods, especially at Athens, where altars are set up in honour even of unknown gods."[73]

Another remarkable traveler who visited Athens at a somewhat later date than Apollonius was the geographer Pausanias. Born in Lydia, he had already traveled in Palestine and Egypt before he came to Greece. He visited Athens in the period between A.D. 143 and 159 and then devoted the first 30 chapters of his *Description of Greece* to an extensive and accurate topographical account of Athens as he saw it. He says that on the road from the Phaleron Bay harbor to the city he had noticed "altars of the gods named Unknown, and of heroes,"[74] and also mentions "an altar of Unknown Gods"[75] at Olympia.

Although no such altar now remains at Athens, a comparable one was discovered in 1909 at Pergamum in the sacred precincts of the temple of Demeter (Fig. 119). A corner of the stone is broken and a portion of the inscription is lost but it is probably to be read:

[72] The article is absent in the Greek, but since this is common in inscriptions, either translation is permissible.

[73] ἀγνώστων δαιμόνων βωμοί. Philostratus, *The Life of Apollonius of Tyana*. VI, 3. tr. F. C. Conybeare, LCL (1912) II, p.13.

[74] βωμοὶ δὲ θεῶν τε ὀνομαζομένων Ἀγνώστων καὶ ἡρώων. I, i, 4.

[75] Ἀγνώστων θεῶν βωμός. V, xiv, 8.

To unknown gods,
Capito,
torch-bearer.[76]

A somewhat similar altar stands on the Palatine Hill at Rome and dates from about 100 B.C. Its inscription begins, *Sei deo sei deivae sac[rum]*, "Sacred to a god or goddess."[77]

After the time of Paul the Emperor Hadrian (A.D. 117-138) added to the city of Athens with lavish benefactions. About A.D. 143 a wealthy Roman resident, Herodes Atticus, rebuilt the old stadium, making it into an immense marble structure which would accommodate 44,000 spectators. The same man also later built a theater at the southwestern base of the Acropolis, known as the Odeum, in memory of his wife. In Byzantine times Athens sank into the position of a provincial town and was robbed of many of its works of art. The Athena Promachos and the Athena Parthenos were taken away to adorn Constantinople, and other spoliation took place when the church of Hagia Sophia was rebuilt in the sixth century. The Parthenon, the Erechtheum, and other temples, however, were converted into Christian churches and thus preserved throughout the Middle Ages. When the Acropolis was taken by the Turks in 1458 the Parthenon was transformed into a mosque, and a minaret was built at its southwestern corner. The Turkish commandant used the Propylaea as a residence and employed the Erechtheum for his harem. In 1687 the Venetians bombarded the Acropolis where the Turks were entrenched, and a bomb from a mortar struck the Parthenon and blew up a powder magazine in it, damaging the building severely.[78] The Turks remained in possession of the Acropolis until 1833, when Athens became the capital of the independent kingdom of Greece. At that time it was only a village of 5,000 inhabitants but in the twentieth century it became a city of over 450,000 people.

Eventually philosophers like Justin Martyr (A.D. c.100-c.165) were to recognize that in Christ the true Word had become manifest, only

[76] Adolf Deissmann, *Paul*. tr. William E. Wilson. 2d ed. 1926, pp.288-291.

[77] Hammerton, *Wonders of the Past*. I, p.524. Although it is possible to give exact literary and epigraphic attestation only to the plural form "to unknown gods," it would have been quite possible even in a polytheistic environment for someone to have felt a sense of gratitude "to *an* unknown god." Therefore it is unnecessary to argue with E. Norden (*Agnostos Theos* [1913], p.121) that the author of the Areopagus address first changed the plural form to the singular in order to obtain the text for a monotheistic sermon.

[78] Theodor E. Mommsen in AJA 45 (1941), pp.544-556.

fragments of which had been laid hold of by the search and speculation of Socrates and the other thinkers of the past, and thus the Greek tradition was to be brought into relation to the Christian message.[79] But the sophisticated Athenians (cf. Acts 17:21) of Paul's time gave little serious attention to his message, and Paul apparently went on soon to Corinth, convinced that "the wisdom of this world is foolishness with God" (I Corinthians 3:19), and seeking hearers to whom the foolishness of the preaching would seem a wisdom greater than that of men (cf. I Corinthians 1:21, 25).

CORINTH

In going from Athens to Corinth (Acts 18:1) Paul was moving from the intellectual center of Greece to its most splendid commercial city. Whereas Athens was situated on the Greek mainland near the southern end of the great plain of Attica, Corinth was just across the narrow isthmus which connects central Greece with the Peloponnesus. This isthmus was a natural meeting place for trade from East and West. Ships from Asia Minor, Syria and Egypt put in to the port of Cenchreae (cf. Romans 16:1) on the eastern side of the isthmus, while those of Italy, Sicily and Spain docked at Lechaeum, the harbor on the western side. The distance between these two ports was less than ten miles, and while the cargoes of the larger vessels were transshipped, the smaller boats were hauled across bodily on a sort of tramway. Otherwise, the circumnavigation of stormy Cape Malea,[80] requiring a detour of 200 miles, was necessary. Naturally enough the desirability of cutting a canal across the isthmus was recognized by many men including Alexander the Great, Julius Caesar and Nero. In A.D. 66 Nero went so far as to dig the first dirt of such a canal with a golden spade, and to set at the task of excavating it 6,000 young Jews recently captured by Vespasian in the Jewish War which had just begun. But this and all the other similar projects of antiquity were abandoned[81] and it was not until A.D. 1881-1893 that the present canal was cut. This canal runs straight across

[79] *Apology.* II, 10 (ANF I, p.191); cf. Paul Elmer More, *Christ the Word.* 1927, pp.9-11.
[80] cf. Strabo, *Geography.* VIII, vi, 20: "But when you double Malea, forget your home."
[81] Philostratus (*Life of Apollonius.* IV, 24) records the report that Nero stopped the work of cutting the canal "because Egyptian men of science explained to him the nature of the seas, and declared that the sea above Lechaeum would flood and obliterate the island of Aegina."

the isthmus at its narrowest point and is four miles in length. It is crossed by the 170-foot-high iron bridge of the Athens and Corinth railway. Situated but one and one-half miles south of this isthmus and commanding the ports on either side of it, the city of Corinth obviously was destined for commercial greatness. Pindar called the Isthmus of Corinth "the bridge of the sea,"[82] and Strabo summed up the situation accurately when he said, "Corinth is called 'wealthy' because of its commerce, since it is situated on the Isthmus and is master of two harbors, of which the one leads straight to Asia, and the other to Italy; and it makes easy the exchange of merchandise from both countries that are so far distant from each other."[83]

The site of Corinth was occupied as anciently as in the Neolithic and Chalcolithic ages,[84] and in Greek mythology the city was the home of Medea, Sisyphus and Bellerophon. From early times the distinctive cult associated with Corinth was that of the worship of Aphrodite. In the eighth and seventh centuries B.C. Corinth established colonies at Syracuse and Corcyra, and under the tyrants Cypselus (c.657-c.629 B.C.) and Periander (c.629-c.585 B.C.) rose to great prominence and prosperity. She dominated extensive trade routes, and Corinthian bronze and pottery were exported widely over the Mediterranean. About 146 B.C. Corinth warred with Rome and upon defeat was completely destroyed, probably because of commercial jealousy. The inhabitants were sold into slavery and for one hundred years the site of the city lay desolate. Then in 46 B.C. Julius Caesar refounded the city as the Colonia Laus Julia Corinthiensis, and peopled it with Italian freedmen and dispossessed Greeks.[85] Its commercial prosperity was recovered rapidly, and Augustus made Corinth the capital of Achaia and seat of its proconsul (cf. Acts 18:12). After the time of Paul, Hadrian beautified the city with public works. In the Middle Ages it continued to be a flourishing place until captured by the Sicilians in 1406 and the Turks in 1458. In 1858 the ancient city suffered a terrible earthquake and the survivors built New Corinth on a new site three and one-half miles

[82] Pindar (c.522-c.448 B.C.), *The Nemean Odes*. VI, 40. tr. Sir John Sandys, LCL (1915), p.373.

[83] *Geography*. VIII, vi, 20.

[84] John G. O'Neill, *Ancient Corinth, with a Topographical Sketch of the Corinthia*, Part I *From the Earliest Times to 404 B.C.* 1930, pp.60f.; Saul S. Weinberg in *Hesperia*. 6 (1937), pp.487-524.

[85] Strabo, *Geography*. VIII, iv, 8; vi, 23; XVII, iii, 15.

northeast of the old city. This city, too, was almost wholly destroyed by earthquake in 1928, but was rebuilt and thereafter attained a population of some 10,000.

The excavation of ancient Corinth has been conducted over a period of many years, beginning in 1896, by the American School of Classical Studies at Athens.[86] The city spreads out over two terraces, one about 100 feet higher than the other, while in the southwestern background a towering mountain, Acro Corinth,[87] rises 1,500 feet above the city and 1,886 feet above the sea. In the center of the city was a large agora or marketplace, surrounded with colonnades and monuments. On the north side the road from Lechaeum entered the agora through a stately gateway or propylaea. Just east of this was the famous fountain of Pirene, and from the eastern side of the marketplace the road to Cenchreae departed. West of the Lechaeum road and north of the marketplace, on a low hill was the temple of Apollo. It was built probably in the sixth century B.C.,[88] and seven of its fine Doric columns still stand. A corner of this temple is shown in Fig. 120, with Acro Corinth looming in the background. Some distance away to the northwest was the theater of Corinth, built in the Greek Period and repaired under the Romans. On the summit of Acro Corinth was a temple of Aphrodite.

Among the shops opening onto the agora at Corinth were ones which had clearly been used for the sale of meat and other foodstuffs. Interestingly enough, each was provided with a well connecting with a subterranean channel through which flowed fresh water. Evidently this arrangement provided the shops not only with a source of water but also with a means of cooling perishable products.[89] An inscription found there, belonging to the last years of Augustus or to the reign of Tiberius, calls one of these shops a "market," using in the Latin exactly the same word which Paul employs in the Greek in I Corin-

[86] See various volumes of *Corinth, Results of Excavations Conducted by the American School of Classical Studies at Athens*, especially I, 1 Harold N. Fowler and Richard Stillwell, *Introduction, Topography, Architecture*. 1932; I, 2 R. Stillwell, Robert L. Scranton and Sarah E. Freeman, *Architecture*. 1941; also AJA 34 (1930), pp.403-454; 37 (1933), pp.554-572; 39 (1935), pp.53-75; 40 (1936), pp.21-45,466-484; 41 (1937), pp.539-552; 42 (1938), pp.362-370; 43 (1939), pp.255-267,592-600.
[87] Strabo, *Geography*. VIII, iv, 8; vi, 21.
[88] Benjamin Powell in AJA 9 (1905), pp.44-63; Saul S. Weinberg in *Hesperia*. 8 (1939), pp.191-199.
[89] Oscar Broneer in *The Lutheran Companion*. Nov. 12, 1942, p.1306.

thians 10:25.[90] Another Corinth inscription mentions a certain Erastus, but it remains uncertain if he is to be identified with the Erastus named as a friend of Paul's in Romans 16:23, II Timothy 4:20 and Acts 19:22.[91]

On the Lechaeum road in Corinth, at the foot of the marble steps leading to the propylaea, a stone was found in 1898 which once formed the lintel over a doorway. It bears an inscription in Greek and although the stone is broken at the right and damaged at the left the inscription clearly reads "Synagogue of the Hebrews."[92] The inscription is usually dated somewhere between 100 B.C. and A.D. 200.[93] Consequently it may once have stood over the entrance to the synagogue in which Paul preached (Acts 18:4), or have marked a later building on the same site. The letters, which are two and one-half to three and one-half inches high, are poorly cut and suggest that the synagogue was not wealthy. This would accord with Paul's characterization of the Corinthian Christians in his letter to them (I Corinthians 1:26). Since the stone is of considerable weight it may be presumed that it was found not far from the place where the synagogue stood, and if this is correct then the synagogue was on or near the road to Lechaeum and not far from the marketplace. The west side of the Lechaeum road was lined with colonnades and shops close under the hill where the temple of Apollo stood, and the more probable location of the synagogue was therefore on the east side of the street. This area was in the main a residential district, as the many remaining house walls indicate, and consequently the house of Titus Justus could easily have been hard by (Acts 18:7).

In the agora one of the prominent features is an elevated platform which once served as an outdoor speaker's platform. It is mentioned in an inscription by the Latin name *rostra* which is the equivalent of the Greek word by which the tribunal or "judgment-seat"[94] at Corinth is referred to in Acts 18:12-17, and is doubtless to be identified with the very place where Paul stood before Gallio. In the photograph reproduced in Fig. 121 the marketplace is viewed from the east and the ruins of the rostra appear just to the left of the center of

[90] Macellum, μάκελλον. H. J. Cadbury in JBL 53 (1934), pp.134-141; Gerhard Kittel, ed., *Theologisches Wörterbuch zum Neuen Testament*. (1933-), IV, pp.373f.
[91] H. J. Cadbury in JBL 50 (1931), pp.42-58.
[92] First published by Benjamin Powell in AJA 7 (1903), pp.60f.
[93] Deissmann, *Licht vom Osten*, p.12 n.8.
[94] τὸ βῆμα.

the picture. In the distance at the extreme left are the slopes of Acro Corinth and at the right is the temple of Apollo.

The Gallio who was proconsul of Achaia when Paul was in Corinth (Acts 18:12) was the elder brother of the philosopher Seneca and is mentioned by Tacitus[95] and Dio Cassius.[96] An important inscription has been found which makes it possible to date Gallio's arrival in Corinth as proconsul quite accurately. It was discovered at Delphi, which was on the other side of the Gulf of Corinth some six miles inland. The inscription begins: "Tiberius Claudius Caesar Augustus Germanicus, Pontifex Maximus, of tribunican authority for the 12th time, imperator the 26th time, father of the country, consul for the 5th time, honorable, greets the city of the Delphians." The emperor then goes on to say that he has long been well disposed to the city of Delphi, and that he has observed the religious ceremonies of the Pythian Apollo that were held there. The actual business with which the communication deals is lost in the broken places in the inscription, but it is possible to make out further along the words, "as Lucius Junius Gallio, my friend, and the proconsul of Achaia wrote. . . ." This inscription therefore provides testimony to the fact that Gallio did serve as proconsul of Achaia. Furthermore, at the time the emperor's letter was written to Delphi, Gallio had evidently been in office long enough to have given Claudius information of importance concerning the Delphians. Since the reference to the 12th tribunican year and the 26th imperatorship of Claudius dates this communication between January and August of the year A.D. 52, Gallio must have arrived in Corinth not later than the year 51. Dio Cassius reports a decree of Claudius that new officials should start for their provinces by the first day of June,[97] and therefore Gallio must have entered upon his proconsulship in Corinth in the summer, probably around July 1, in A.D. 51. The impression given by the book of Acts is that Gallio had arrived in Corinth only shortly before the time when the Jews brought Paul into his presence. Since at that time the apostle had been in the city a year and six months (Acts 18:11), we can date Paul's arrival in Corinth with considerable confidence at the beginning of the year 50.[98]

ROME

Already upon his last visit to Achaia Paul was purposing to go to

[95] *Annals.* xv, 73.
[96] *Roman History.* LXI, xxxv, 2.
[97] *Roman History.* LVII, xiv, 5.
[98] Deissmann, *Paul*, pp.265-283.

Rome (Romans 15:23-28; Acts 19:21). That intention was achieved, though hardly in the way he might have wished, when the apostle was led into Rome as a prisoner in the charge of Julius the centurion (Acts 27:1; 28:16). Nero (Fig. 122) was then on the throne (A.D. 54-68), the city was approaching the height of its imperial greatness, and Martial (A.D. c.40-c.102) was soon to hail the proud capital of the world as "Rome, goddess of earth and of the nations, that has no peer and no second."[99] We shall seek to gain a swift glimpse of the city as it was when Paul entered it, in the midst of Nero's reign and before the great fire of A.D. 64. For the purpose of such an inquiry there is available an immense wealth of notices in ancient literature, inscriptions, and archeological monuments, all of which have been the object of intensive study by scholars of many nations, by the Roman Catholic Church and by the Italian government.

Approaching Rome, Paul's feet must have trod "the worn and well-known track of Appia, queen of the long roads."[100] The Via Appia was built from Rome to Capua by the censor Appius Claudius Caecus in about 312 B.C. and later was extended, until by around 244 B.C. it reached Brundisium (modern Brindisi), the important harbor 350 miles away on the southeastern coast. Paul, who had landed at Puteoli (Acts 28:13), the modern Puzzuoli, on the northern shore of the Bay of Naples, would have reached the Via Appia at Capua, some 20 miles away. From Capua it was 132 miles to Rome. At Tarracina (modern Terracina) the Via Appia touched the coast. From there it ran for the final 56 miles almost as straight as an arrow across the Pontine Marshes and the Alban Hills to Rome. The Market of Appius (Acts 28:15) or Forum Appii, where the first of "the brethren" met Paul, was a post station 43 miles from Rome and mentioned by Horace (65-8 B.C.) as the usual halt at the end of the first day's journey from Rome.[101] The Three Taverns (Acts 28:15) or Tres Tabernae was a village nearly 10 miles farther on and is mentioned by Cicero (106-43 B.C.) as the point where a branch road from Antium joined the Appian Way.[102]

[99] *Terrarum dea gentiumque Roma,*
   Cui par est nihil et nihil secundum.
Epigrams. XII, viii, 1f. tr. W. C. A. Ker, LCL (1925-27) II, p.325.
[100] Statius (A.D. c.45-c.96), *Silvae.* II, ii, 12. tr. J. H. Mozley, LCL (1928) I, p.97.
[101] I, v, 3-6. tr. H. R. Fairclough, LCL (1926), p.65.
[102] *Letters to Atticus.* II, xii. tr. E. O. Winstedt, LCL (1913-19) I, p.143.

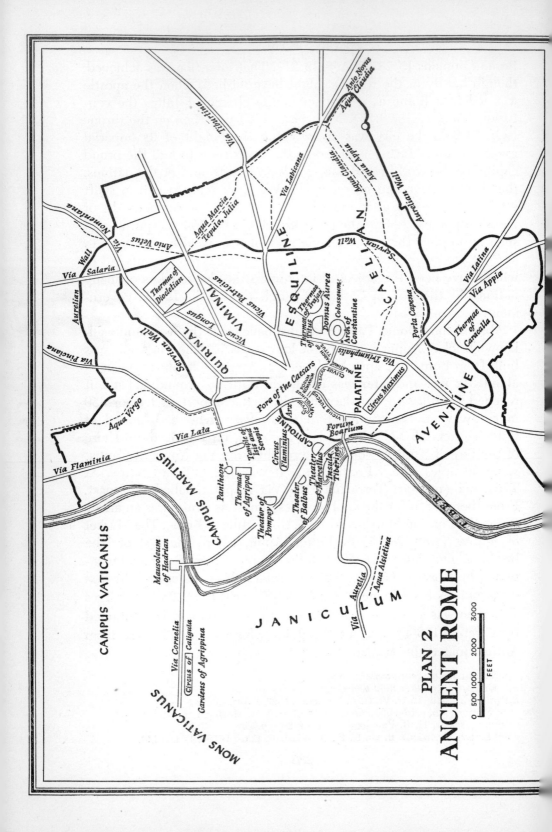

PLAN 2
ANCIENT ROME

0 500 1000 2000 3000
FEET

Aqua Claudia
Anio Novus
Aqua Appia
Aqua Claudia
Via Labicana
Via Tiburtina
Via Nomentana
Aurelian Wall
Via Latina
Via Appia
Via Salaria
Aqua Marcia
Tepula, Julia
Anio Vetus
Wall
Servian Wall
Thermae of
Diocletian
ESQUILINE
CAELIAN
Vicus Patricius
Vicus Longus
VIMINAL
Thermae of Trajan
Domus Aurea
Colosseum
Arch of Constantine
Thermae of Titus
Porta Capena
Thermae of
Caracalla
Aurelian Wall
Via Pinciana
QUIRINAL
Servian Wall
Fora of the Caesars
Via Triumphalis
PALATINE
Circus Maximus
AVENTINE
Aqua Virgo
Via Lata
Via Flaminia
Pantheon
Thermae of Agrippa
Temple of Isis and Serapis
Circus Flaminius
CAMPUS MARTIUS
Theater of Pompey
Theater of Balbus
Theater of Marcellus
Insula Tiberina
Forum Boarium
CAPITOLIUM
Arx
Clivus Argentarius
Clivus Capitolinus
Vicus Tuscus
TIBER
Mausoleum of Hadrian
CAMPUS VATICANUS
MONS VATICANUS
Via Cornelia
Circus of Caligula
Gardens of Agrippina
JANICULUM
Via Aurelia
Aqua Alsietina

Nearing Rome, the Via Appia crossed what is known as the Campagna di Roma, the low plain surrounding the city. Near-by ran the great aqueduct Claudia which was completed by the Emperor Claudius in A.D. 50 (Fig. 123). The water which it brought from more than 40 miles away was carried across the Campagna on arches 110 feet high, the remains of which are yet very impressive.[103] This was but one of eight or nine conduits and aqueducts which at that time brought water to Rome from distant springs and rivers.[104] Of them Sextus Julius Frontinus, their keeper at the close of the first century A.D., remarked, "With such an array of indispensable structures carrying so many waters, compare, if you will, the idle Pyramids or the useless though famous works of the Greeks!"[105]

On the Campagna, the Via Appia began to penetrate the suburbs of the city. The plain was dotted with houses, gardens and magnificent villas. Nearing the city the houses naturally became closer together and smaller in size. Deep within the city of the first century A.D. was the old Servian Wall, through which the Via Appia entered by the Porta Capena. This ancient wall is named for King Servius Tullius (c.578-c.534 B.C.) but was actually built by order of the republican Senate between 378 and 352 B.C. After the Punic Wars of the third and second centuries B.C. it was allowed to fall into decay and the city spread far beyond its limits. Some portions of it still exist, and the remains of the Porta Capena have been found near where the Via di San Gregorio now unites with the Via di Porta San Sebastiano. In the third century A.D. the approach of the barbarians led to the building of a new wall. It was begun by the Emperor Aurelian (A.D. 270-275) and completed by the Emperor Probus (A.D. 276-282). Restored by later emperors and popes, the Aurelian Wall

---

[103] cf. Pliny, *Natural History.* XXXVI, xxiv.

[104] (1) The first, the Appia, was constructed about 312 B.C. by Appius Claudius Caecus, who also built the Via Appia. It was a ten-mile covered tunnel from springs east of the city. (2) The Anio Vetus, built around 272 B.C., brought water 41 miles from the river Anio in the Apennines. (3) The Marcia was built about 145 B.C. by Marcius the praetor. It was 58 miles long, the last seven miles being on arches high enough to carry the flow to the summit of the Capitol. (4) The Tepula of around 127 B.C. was small and short. (5) The Julia and (6) the Virgo were built by Agrippa in 33 B.C. and 20 B.C. respectively. (7) The Alsietina was constructed by Augustus. (8) The Claudia was started by Caligula in A.D. 36 and finished by Claudius. An archway of the Claudia was made by Aurelian into one of the gates of his city wall, and is now the Porta Maggiore. (9) The Anio Novus also was begun by Caligula but only completed in A.D. 86. Esther B. Van Deman, *The Building of the Roman Aqueducts.* 1934; Thomas Ashby, *The Aqueducts of Ancient Rome.* 1935.

[105] *The Aqueducts of Rome.* I, 16. tr. C. E. Bennett, LCL (1925), pp.357-359.

still surrounds the city on the left bank of the Tiber. The wall on the right bank of the Tiber dates mainly from the time of Pope Urban VIII (1623-1644).[106]

The main part of the city, which was attained when one reached the Porta Capena, was built upon a famous group of seven hills (cf. Revelation 17:9), past which the Tiber River sweeps in three great curves. Standing at the Porta Capena, the Aventine hill was on the left, the Caelian on the right and the Palatine directly ahead. Beyond the Palatine was the Capitoline, which rises near the inner curve of the Tiber and the island in the river. Ranged north of the Caelian hill were the Esquiline, Viminal and Quirinal hills. The plain west of the Quirinal and enclosed in the outward curve of the Tiber was the Campus Martius. Across the Tiber, on its right or western bank, was the commanding height of the hill of Janiculum, and beyond it at the northwestern end of Rome the Ager Vaticanus or Vatican district. The latter included a low eminence known as Mons Vaticanus and a plain beside the river called the Campus Vaticanus.

The Via Appia and the other highroads which led into Rome, such as the Via Ostiensis and Via Latina on the south, the Via Labicana and Via Tiburtina on the east, and the Via Nomentana, Via Salaria, Via Pinciana and Via Flaminia on the north, were good thoroughfares, 15 to 20 feet in width. In many cases these highways continued directly into the heart of the city in the form of fine avenues, and frequently the streets of modern Rome follow their lines exactly. The Via Flaminia, for example, which was constructed by the Roman statesman Caius Flaminius Nepos about 200 B.C., continued as the Via Lata directly to the foot of the Capitoline hill. It is represented by the splendid central avenue of modern Rome, the Corso Umberto Primo, beneath which at a depth of 15 or 20 feet the lava paving blocks of the ancient street are still found.[107]

Within the old Republican Wall and on the Seven Hills, however, many of the streets were narrow, steep and crooked. They were usually called *vici*, as for example the Vicus Longus and the Vicus Patricius. In cases where they made steep ascents and descents they were frequently known as *clivi*, as for example the Clivus Capitolinus and the Clivus Palatinus. It was required that they be at least nine

---

[106] I. A. Richmond, *The City Wall of Imperial Rome*. 1930; G. Säflund, *Le mura di Roma reppublicana*. 1932.
[107] Rodolfo Lanciani, *Ancient and Modern Rome*. 1925, p.145.

115. Inscription at Lystra

114. Straight Street in Damascus

116. The Theater at Ephesus

117. Air View of Philippi

118. The Temple of Zeus, with the Acropolis in the Background

119. The Altar to Unknown Gods at Pergamum

120. Ruins of the Temple of Apollo at Corinth, with Acro Corinth in the Background

121. The Agora at Corinth

122. Nero

123. The Appian Way and the Claudian Aqueduct

124. Caricature of the Crucifixion

125. The Roman Forum

198. The Pyramid of Cestius and the Gate of St. Paul

and one-half feet wide to allow for projecting balconies. In many parts of the inner city they formed an inextricably tangled labyrinth. It was said that if they could have been straightened out and laid end to end they would have reached for more than 60 miles.[108] They were often defiled by refuse and were quite unlighted by night. By day they were jammed with pedestrians, horsemen, litters and carrying chairs, and by night they were filled with the noise of transport carts of all sorts, such wheeled vehicles being permitted within the city only between dusk and dawn.[109]

In the residential districts the dwellings were of two chief types. The *domus* was the home of the wealthy. It spread out horizontally in a series of halls, and had its doors and windows opening on its interior courts. The *insula* was the residence of the masses. It was an apartment house, filling a square or block, and rising vertically to surprising heights. Augustus found it necessary to place a limit of 70 feet on the height of structures on the public streets,[110] but this still allowed apartment houses of three, four, five and six stories to be common. In external appearance these apartment houses, the finest of which were adorned with balconies and brightened with window gardens, would have seemed quite modern. Their conveniences within were strictly limited, however. Light and heat were inadequate. Water from the aqueducts seems to have been conveyed only to the ground floors, which alone were connected with Rome's excellent network of sewers.[111] Often, too, builders and landlords sought to increase their profits by cheap construction and poor repair even though the lives of the renters were imperiled by the frequent collapses of the buildings which ensued. In his satire on life at Rome Juvenal cried, "Who at cool Praeneste, or at Volsinii amid its leafy hills, was ever afraid of his house tumbling down? . . . But here we inhabit a city propped up for the most part by slats: for that is how the landlord patches up the cracks in the old wall,

---

[108] Pliny, *Natural History.* III, ix, 67.

[109] A. Grenier in Ch. Daremberg and Edmond Saglio, eds. *Dictionnaire des antiquités grecques et romaines d'après les textes et les monuments.* (1877-1919), v, cols.861-863.

[110] Strabo, *Geography.* v, iii, 7.

[111] The central collector for the system of sewers was the Cloaca Maxima, the mouth of which still can be seen opening into the Tiber, and which was in use until very recently. Pliny, *Natural History.* XXXVI, xxiv.

bidding the inmates sleep at ease under a roof ready to tumble about their ears."[112]

Thus Rome was a teeming metropolitan center at the time when Paul came to it. The population of the city in the first century A.D. has usually been estimated at about 1,200,000, or substantially the same as the modern population which in January 1939 was 1,284,600. In 1941, however, the discovery of an inscription at Ostia was announced with statistics indicating that in A.D. 14, the year of the death of Tiberius, the city of Rome had a population of 4,100,000 inhabitants.[113] Statistics from 250 years after the time of Paul list 1,797 *domus* and 46,602 *insulae*, or blocks of apartment houses, in the city.[114]

The great city was fortunate in the possession of many parks and gardens. It has been calculated that one-eighth of the total area of the city was given over to parks and open spaces, whereas in modern London, for example, only one-tenth of the total area is so used.[115] In the Campus Martius numerous garden porticoes were to be found, many of which had been built by Augustus and his wealthy friends. These were large parallelograms of green enclosed by a colonnade. For the enjoyment of the public, the twelve largest of these porticoes protected an area of 28,000 square yards from sun and rain. Under such shelter it was possible to walk all the way from the Forum Boarium, which was between the Palatine hill and the Tiber, to the opposite end of the city where Hadrian's mausoleum was built. There were imperial gardens also in the Vatican district. The elder Agrippina, the wife of Germanicus (15 B.C.-A.D. 19), possessed a villa on the north slope of the Janiculum, and her son Caligula built his famous Circus in the plain beneath. To the east were the gardens of Domitia, Nero's aunt. After her death the entire district became a single domain, known as Horti Neronis or Nero's Gardens.

The buildings erected for purposes of amusement and recreation were among the most impressive structures in Rome. These included not only circuses but also theaters, amphitheaters, and baths, which were frequented avidly by a populace whose leisure time included

---

[112] *Satire.* III, 190-196.   [113] AJA 45 (1941), p.438.

[114] These figures are from the *Regionaries*, which are two descriptions of Rome, one called the *Curiosum* and the other the *Notitia*, and both deriving from a lost original which probably was compiled in the reign of Constantine between A.D. 312 and 315. Jérôme Carcopino, *Daily Life in Ancient Rome.* 1940, pp.23,287f.

[115] A. G. Mackinnon, *The Rome of Saint Paul.* 1930, p.168.

no less than 159 holidays in the year. Ninety-three of these holidays were devoted to games and performances held at public expense.[116] The games par excellence at Rome in the time of Paul were the chariot races of the circus.[117] The characteristic plan of the circus was a long rectangle rounded off at one end into a semicircle, and with a low wall called the spina or "backbone" running lengthwise in the center. Of them all the Circus Maximus[118] was the oldest and largest. It was situated in the hollow between the Aventine and the Palatine, and Paul must have seen it soon after passing through the Porta Capena. This circus had been used for centuries, but was greatly enlarged and improved by Caesar in 46 B.C., and later was adorned with the obelisk of Ramesses II which Augustus brought from Heliopolis and which today is to be seen in the Piazza del Popolo. The Circus was 1,800 feet in length and seated 150,000 spectators.[119] After enlargements by Nero it seated 250,000.[120] The walls of the Circus Maximus have now disappeared almost entirely, but the form is still distinctly traceable. The Circus Flaminius[121] was built about 221 B.C. by the censor Caius Flaminius Nepos who also constructed the Via Flaminia (p. 286). It stood on the site of the present Palazzo Caetani, and was 1,300 feet in length. The Circus of Caligula[122] (A.D. 37-41) was built on the west side of the Tiber in the Ager Vaticanus as was mentioned above (p. 288). It was intended as a private course for chariot-racing and was relatively small in size, being about 600 feet long. On the spina Caligula erected an obelisk which he brought from Heliopolis, this being a monolith of red granite without hieroglyphics. The circus in the Vatican was a favorite place for the sports and orgies of Claudius (A.D. 41-54) and Nero (A.D. 54-68), and is often known as the Circus of Nero.

The theaters to which Romans went at that time to enjoy plays included the Theater of Pompey (55 B.C.) seating about 10,000,[123] the Theater of Balbus (13 B.C.) seating around 7,700,[124] and the yet

---

[116] Carcopino, *Daily Life in Ancient Rome*, p.205.

[117] cf. Juvenal, *Satire*. x, 77-81, "The public has long since cast off its cares; the people . . . now . . . longs eagerly for just two things—Bread and Circuses!"

[118] PATD, pp.114-120.

[119] Dionysius of Halicarnassus (c.54-c.7 B.C.), *Roman Antiquities*. III, lxviii, 2f. tr. E. Cary, LCL (1937-) II, pp.241-243.

[120] Pliny, *Natural History*. XXXVI, xxiv.

[121] PATD, pp.111-113.   [122] PATD, pp.113f.,370f.   [123] PATD, pp.515-517.

[124] PATD, p.513.

well preserved Theater of Marcellus (11 B.C.) accommodating some 14,000.[125]

The chief development of the amphitheater, to whose cruel spectacles the Romans became so addicted, came after the time of Paul. One permanent amphitheater had been built in the southern part of the Campus Martius in 29 B.C., and was standing when Paul came to Rome.[126] The great Flavian amphitheater or Colosseum[127] in which the gladiators were to be sent to their work of mutual massacre and the Christians were to be thrown to the wild beasts, was not yet built. It was first begun by Vespasian, on a site which had formerly been occupied by an artificial lake at Nero's palace (p. 292), and was completed by Titus and decorated by Diocletian. A tremendous elliptical structure, measuring nearly one-third of a mile in circumference and built of hard travertine stone, the Colosseum has survived the centuries to loom up still in Rome in gloomy grandeur. In its midst now rises a cross, in memory of the Christian martyrs who died there and in silent protest against the barbarism which cost so many lives before the spirit of Christianity abolished it.[128]

More in accord with the Greek spirit, although a distinctively Roman development, were the *thermae* or baths. These were public institutions where the ideal of "a sound mind in a sound body"[129] was cherished and where gymnasium, bath and library provided for exercise, cleanliness and culture. In 33 B.C. when Augustus' son-in-law Agrippa was aedile there were already 170 public baths in Rome, and by Pliny's time he found them to be so numerous that he gave up trying to count them.[130] Remains of the Thermae which Agrippa built during his aedileship are still to be seen in the Campus Martius,[131] which is where the Thermae of Nero[132] also were erected. The most famous baths and those whose ruins are most impressive today, however, were built after the time of Paul. These included the Thermae of Titus[133] now destroyed, the Thermae of Trajan[134]

---

[125] PATD, pp.513-515.   [126] PATD, p.11.   [127] PATD, pp.6-11.
[128] Carcopino, *Daily Life in Ancient Rome*, pp.244-247. Gladiatorial combats were stopped by the Emperor Honorius in A.D. 404 (Theodoret, *Ecclesiastical History*. v, 26 [NPNFSS III, p.151]).
[129] Juvenal, *Satire*. x, 356.   [130] *Natural History*. XXXVI, xxiv.
[131] Karl Baedeker, *Rome and Central Italy*. 16th ed. 1930, p.280.
[132] cf. Martial, *Epigrams*. VII, xxxiv, 4f.:
    What was worse than Nero?
    What is better than Nero's warm baths?
[133] PATD, pp.533f.   [134] PATD, pp.534-536.

on the Esquiline just southeast of the present church of San Pietro in Vincoli, the magnificent Thermae of Caracalla[135] on the Via Appia outside the Porta Capena, the extensive Thermae of Diocletian[136] which loom up so impressively as one emerges from the railway station in Rome and which today house the National Roman Museum, the Church of Saint Mary of the Angels and the Oratory of Saint Bernard, and the Thermae of Constantine[137] on the Quirinal.

In the very midst of the city were the Capitoline and Palatine hills, with the Forum lying in the valley between. The outstanding feature of the Capitoline hill was the great temple of Jupiter[138] on the southwestern summit. This temple was originally built by Tarquinius Superbus, the last of the kings, and was dedicated in 509 B.C., the first year of the Republic. It was burned down in 83 B.C., rebuilt, burned again in A.D. 69, and finally reconstructed most splendidly by Domitian. The marble fragments which have been found in excavation of its ruins are probably from the time of Domitian, but even in Paul's time the temple of the chief god of the Romans must have been very impressive. The northern summit of the Capitoline hill was the citadel (Arx) of early Rome and the site later of the temple of Juno Moneta (the Warner). The Arx and north slope of the Capitol are occupied now by the enormous Monument of Victor Emmanuel II, while the site of the temple of Juno is taken by the church of Santa Maria in Aracoeli. On the side of the Capitoline, commanding the Forum, was the Tabularium, erected after the fire of 83 B.C. to provide a fireproof hall of records for the state. It was probably the first attempt at such a building which was to be absolutely impervious to the accidents of the elements, and its walls are well preserved although much rebuilt in the Palazzo del Senatore, which is the modern council chamber of Rome.

The Palatine hill was the residence of the Roman emperor. Augustus, Tiberius and Caligula all built there until the imperial palace covered a large part of the hill. The house of Livia, the wife of Augustus, still remains on the hill, its walls containing excellent murals. Also the substructures of the palace of Tiberius (Domus Tiberiana) are to be seen occupying a large part of the northwest

---

[135] PATD, pp.520-524. They were begun by Septimus Severus in A.D. 206, inaugurated by Antoninus Caracalla before being finished, and finally completed by Severus Alexander between 222 and 235.

[136] PATD, pp.527-530.   [137] PATD, pp.525f.   [138] PATD, pp.297-302.

corner of the Palatine. The ruins which are in the center of the hill are usually called the Domus Augustiana but actually are mostly a reconstruction by Domitian. These structures now appear as great masses of brickwork with arched roofs, but in Paul's day they were splendidly encased in marble and presented a magnificent appearance.[139] The Palatine itself could not content the extravagant Nero, however, and so he built a palace extending from the Palatine to the Esquiline, northeast of where the Colosseum now stands. Shortly after its completion this building was burned in the great fire of A.D. 64 and upon being rebuilt received the name Golden House (Domus Aurea). Suetonius described it as follows: "Its vestibule was large enough to contain a colossal statue of the emperor a hundred and twenty feet high; and it was so extensive that it had a triple colonnade a mile long. There was a pond too, like a sea, surrounded with buildings to represent cities, besides tracts of country, varied by tilled fields, vineyards, pastures and woods, with great numbers of wild and domestic animals. In the rest of the house all parts were overlaid with gold and adorned with gems and mother-of-pearl."[140]

On the southwest side of the Palatine, near the Circus Maximus, was a building now known as the Paedagogium, which probably belonged to the offices of the imperial palace. Some of its rooms are thought to have been used as prisons. The walls are still covered with rudely scratched drawings and inscriptions, such as are called graffiti. One of these, which was discovered by Garrucci in 1856 and is now in the Museo Kircheriano in Rome, is the famous "caricature of the crucifixion" (Fig. 124). This crude graffito shows a man's body with an ass's head, on a cross. The feet are supported on a platform and the outstretched arms fastened to the transverse bar of the cross. To the left is a smaller figure of a boy or young man with one hand raised in an attitude of adoration. The inscription reads, "Alexamenos worships his god." Presumably this represents the mockery to which some young Christian in the imperial palace was subjected. This graffito is to be dated perhaps 150 years after Paul was in Rome, or at the beginning of the third century, but it shows vividly how the word of the cross was foolishness to many (I Corinthians 1:18).

[139] Augustus boasted of Rome that "he had found it built of brick and left it in marble." Suetonius (A.D. c.100), *Augustus* 28. tr. J. C. Rolfe, LCL (1914) I, p.167.
[140] *Nero*, 31.

The Palatine was the site not only of the imperial palace but also of at least two important temples. One was the Temple of Apollo, which was erected by Augustus, and whose identification among the ruins on the Palatine is now difficult. The other was the Temple of the Magna Mater, or Cybele, the great mother deity of the Phrygians. This goddess, in the form of a meteoric stone, was brought to Rome in response to an oracle in 204 B.C. when Hannibal was threatening the city.[141] Another temple where an imported oriental religion was already entrenched in Rome was that of Isis and Serapis. The sanctuary of these Egyptian gods was on the Campus Martius not far from the famous Pantheon,[142] and was erected probably about A.D. 39. It was a vast structure, the central part being 420 feet long, and approached by a long colonnaded court lined with lions and sphinxes. The site of the temple is now occupied by part of the Church of Sant' Ignazio, a section of the Collegio Romano, the apse of the Church of Santa Maria sopra Minerva and the Via del Piè di Marmo. The famous sculptures of the Nile (now in the Vatican Museum) and the Tiber (now in the Louvre in Paris) probably belonged to this temple, as did several obelisks including those now in front of the Pantheon (Piazza della Rotonda), Santa Maria sopra Minerva (Piazza della Minerva), and the Railway Station (Piazza delle Terme).

If Julius the centurion led Paul the prisoner directly to the Forum, the party would have skirted the eastern edge of the Palatine and then have begun to tread the Via Sacra at the point where the Arch of Constantine later was built and now stands. From there the Via Sacra ascended to the summit of the Velia, a low hill running across between the Palatine and Esquiline where the Arch of Titus was to be erected not many years afterward (p. 249), and then traversed the great Forum area along its longitudinal axis from southeast to northwest. In front of where the Basilica of Constantine later was to stand the street was lined with the elegant shops of goldsmiths, bronze-workers, jewelers and dealers in oriental pearls. Beyond were

[141] Livy (59 B.C.-A.D. 17), *History of Rome.* xxix, 10-14. tr. Cyrus Edmonds, *Bohn's Classical Library.* iii (1878), pp.1244-1250; cf. Samuel Dill, *Roman Society from Nero to Marcus Aurelius.* 1925, p.548.

[142] The best preserved ancient edifice in Rome today, the Pantheon ("all-holy"), originally was built by Agrippa, the son-in-law of Augustus, and was given its present circular form and beautiful dome by Hadrian. It was made into the church Sancta Maria ad Martyres in A.D. 609 when 28 wagon-loads of the bones of the martyrs were brought there from the catacombs, and is now known as Santa Maria Rotonda.

the Palace of the Vestal Virgins (Atrium Vestae) with many of its walls and a few of its statues remaining today, the Temple of Vesta (Aedes Vestae) in which the sacred fire was kept ever alight, and the Regia, an office building with historical lists of the Roman magistrates carved on its marble walls (Fasti Consulares). Then came the Triumphal Arch of Augustus (19 B.C.), of which only the foundations now exist, and on its left the Temple of Castor and Pollux and on its right the Temple of Julius Caesar. The temple to the twin gods, Castor and Pollux, is the most prominent ruin in the Forum today, and if, as is probable, the three beautiful columns which are still standing belong to a reconstruction in the reign of Augustus,[143] they were seen by the eyes of the apostle Paul. The Templum Divi Juli, of which only the concrete substructures now remain, was erected by Augustus to the deified Julius Caesar and dedicated in 29 B.C. Thus the worship of the deceased emperor was established in Rome in the same year in which in the province of Asia the worship of the living emperor was instituted (p. 265). By the time Paul was in Rome a temple to Augustus had also been erected there. This Templum Divi Augusti was founded by Tiberius and completed by Caligula, later (after Nero's fire) being restored magnificently by Domitian. It has often been identified with ruins lying south of the Temple of Castor and Pollux on the Vicus Tuscus, but this is uncertain. Later than the time of Paul but of interest because of the excellent preservation of its portico is the Temple of Faustina not far northeast of the Temple of Julius Caesar and now incorporated in the church of San Lorenzo in Miranda. It was dedicated by Antoninus Pius in A.D. 141 to his deified wife, the elder Faustina, and then was given an additional dedication to the emperor himself after his own death. Ten beautiful columns of the portico are still standing, and above them is the inscription, the first line of which was added after the death of Antoninus:

> "To the deified Antoninus and
> to the deified Faustina by the decree of the Senate."[144]

Finally one reached the Forum Romanum proper, the center of the ancient city and in Paul's day the center of the world. New fora

---

[143] Baedeker, *Rome and Central Italy*, p.331.
[144] *Divo Antonio et
divae Faustinae ex S.C.*
The initials S.C. are the customary abbreviation for *Senatus consulto*.

had already been erected in the larger plain to the north, the Forum
Julium, begun by Caesar and completed by Augustus, and the Forum
of Augustus; and yet others would be constructed, the Forum of
Vespasian, the Forum Transitorium begun by Domitian and finished
by Nerva, and the magnificent Forum of Trajan with Trajan's
marvelous Column, which still stands.[145] But nothing could replace
the original Forum in the affections of the city, and the glorious traditions connected with it were commemorated with columns, statues,
bronzes, marbles and other works of art. Just to the northwest of the
Forum, beyond the rostra or orators' platform and near where the
Arch of Severus (A.D. 203) now stands, was the Umbilicus Urbis
Romae, the ideal center of the city. Just to the southwest of the
Forum, near the Arch of Tiberius (A.D. 16) and in front of the Temple
of Saturn, was the Miliarium Aureum, a gilded column erected by
Augustus and giving the names and distances of the chief towns to
which highroads radiated from Rome. These included points no less
distant than Londinium (ancient London) on the west and Jerusalem on the east. When Paul, the world-minded, reached here he
had indeed reached the center from which the gospel he preached
might spread to the uttermost parts of the earth.

A general view of this central part of ancient Rome is shown
in Fig. 125. The eight columns standing in the left foreground belong
to the Temple of Saturn which was dedicated originally around 497
B.C. and restored about 44 B.C. Beside and below them is the Forum
Romanum proper and glimpsed through the last two of the eight
columns is the portico of the Temple of Faustina. Beyond the trees
in the right foreground and only partially hidden by them are the
three columns of the Temple of Castor and Pollux. Just to the left
of these columns and much farther beyond them is the Arch of Titus,
while on the horizon appears the Colosseum.

On either side of the Forum stood great basilicas, or quadrangular
courts surrounded by colonnades and containing court chambers and
public shops. On the north was the Basilica Aemilia, built originally
around 179 B.C. by the censors Aemilius Lepidus and Fulvius Nobilior
and reconstructed about 54 B.C. by Aemilius Paullus. In the latter

---

[145] The Column is adorned with a spiral frieze over 650 feet in length, depicting
military campaigns of Trajan. The emperor's ashes were deposited in the base upon
his death in A.D. 117. His bronze statue which once stood on the summit, was replaced
by a statue of Saint Peter in the sixteenth century.

year on the other side of the Forum, Julius Caesar began the Basilica Julia, which he dedicated in 46 B.C. although it was not altogether completed until A.D. 12. Both of these vast and splendid structures, of which extensive remains are yet to be seen, are of interest in connection with Paul. It was probably within the colonnaded courts of the Basilica Julia that Paul eventually heard the sentence of death pronounced upon him. It was from the Basilica of Aemilius Paullus that the Roman prefect Probianus in A.D. 386 took 24 beautiful columns of Phrygian marble to adorn the Church of Saint Paul which was being erected outside the walls of the city—an event of which the condemned prisoner little could have dreamed.[146]

A short distance northwest of the Forum Romanum and beneath the present church of San Giuseppe de' Falegnami is the prison known as the Carcer Mamertinus. Built in the side of the Capitoline hill, it has an upper vaulted chamber, and a lower chamber or dungeon originally accessible only through a hole in its ceiling. The lower chamber was probably an old springhouse and hence was called Tullianum from the early Latin word *tullius*, meaning "spring." This was where noted prisoners like Jugurtha, the Catilinarian conspirators, and Vercingetorix were kept before execution. In telling of the execution of Catiline's confederates, the Roman historian Sallust (86-34 B.C.) describes the Tullianum almost exactly as it now exists: "In the prison . . . there is a place called the Tullianum, about twelve feet below the surface of the ground. It is enclosed on all sides by walls, and above it is a chamber with a vaulted roof of stone. Neglect, darkness, and stench make it hideous and fearsome to behold."[147]

[146] Mackinnon, *The Rome of Saint Paul*, pp.33f.
[147] *The War with Catiline*. LV, 3f. tr. J. C. Rolfe, LCL (1921), p.115.

3. THE MARTYRDOM OF PAUL AND PETER

According to tradition which goes back at least to the fifth century, the Mamertine prison is the place where both Paul and Peter were confined before their execution under Nero.[1] Whether this is correct or not is difficult to determine, but the fact is certain that the two great apostles suffered martyrdom in Rome under Nero. In the case of Paul, the last statement of the book of Acts is that he abode two whole years in his own hired dwelling in Rome, preaching freely to all who came to him (Acts 28:30f.). Whether his martyrdom followed at the close of these two years, as the further silence of Acts might seem to imply,[2] cannot now be said with certainty. Perhaps he was set free at the expiration of that period and enabled to achieve his cherished purpose of preaching in Spain (Romans 15:24, 28), before eventually suffering death in Rome.[3] In the case of Peter there is a veiled reference to his death in John 21:18: "when thou shalt be old, thou shalt stretch forth thy hands, and another shall gird thee, and carry thee whither thou wouldest not."

Then, before the end of the first century we find a writer at Rome referring at some length to the impressive example set by Peter and Paul in their martyrdom. The passage is to be found in a letter which Clement, the bishop of Rome (A.D. c.88-c.97), wrote to the Corinthians around A.D. 95. Since there was disharmony in the Corinthian church which had its roots in envy and jealousy, Clement pictured the evil results which had followed upon such attitudes both in ancient and in recent times. As a recent illustration, he cited the persecution and martyrdom of Peter and Paul. Clement said:[4]

"But to leave the ancient examples, let us come to the champions who lived nearest our times; let us take the noble examples of our generation.

---

[1] A. S. Barnes, *The Martyrdom of St. Peter and St. Paul.* 1933, p.67.

[2] cf. B. W. Bacon (*The American Journal of Theology.* 22 [1918], p.15), "But as to Paul the reader is *not* really left in ignorance. His fate *is* made known, but made known with that chaste reticence which the Greek poets employ when they only report through others the tragedies enacted behind the scenes. In the great Farewell Discourse of Acts 20:17-38 the martyr takes his leave. In Acts 28:17-31 the tragedy itself is veiled behind the triumph of the cause."

[3] I Clement 5, which is quoted more fully just below, gives support to this view for it speaks of Paul as "having come to the farthest bounds of the West," which to one writing in Rome as Clement did surely would have meant Spain. The Muratorian Fragment (middle of the 2d century A.D.) also refers to "the departure of Paul from the city (i.e. Rome) on his journey to Spain" (Joseph C. Ayer, *A Source Book for Ancient Church History.* 1913, p.118).

[4] I Clement, 5f. (Ayer, *A Source Book for Ancient Church History,* pp.7f.).

On account of jealousy and envy the greatest and most righteous pillars of the church were persecuted, and contended even unto death. Let us set before our eyes the good Apostles: Peter, who on account of unrighteous jealousy endured not one nor two, but many sufferings, and so having borne his testimony, went to his deserved place of glory. On account of jealousy and strife Paul pointed out the prize of endurance. After he had been seven times in bonds, had been driven into exile, had been stoned, had been a preacher in the East and in the West, he received the noble reward of his faith; having taught righteousness unto the whole world, and having come to the farthest bounds of the West, and having borne witness before rulers, he thus departed from the world and went unto the holy place, having become a notable pattern of patient endurance."

Clement then proceeded immediately to group with Peter and Paul a large number of Christians, including both men and women, who were persecuted fiendishly and put to death:

"Unto these men who lived lives of holiness was gathered a vast multitude of the elect, who by many indignities and tortures, being the victims of jealousy, set the finest examples among us. On account of jealousy women, when they had been persecuted as Danaïds and Dircae,[5] and had suffered cruel and unholy insults, safely reached the goal in the race of faith and received a noble reward, feeble though they were in body."

That is an unmistakable reference to the persecution of the Christians at Rome by Nero, as it is more fully known to us through the Roman historian Tacitus (A.D. c.55-c.117). Although Tacitus was not an eyewitness of the persecution, he had very good opportunities for obtaining accurate information and his account is regarded as entirely trustworthy. In the fifteenth book of his *Annals* he tells of the terrible conflagration which broke out at Rome on the eighteenth day of July in the year 64. Raging for six days and driven by the wind, the fire swept irresistibly through the labyrinth of Roman streets and when finally it was stopped only four of the city's fourteen districts were standing entire.[6] Whether the fire started accidentally or was set deliberately by Nero,[7] public suspicion turned upon the emperor as its instigator. Thereupon Nero cast the blame

---

[5] That is, they were forced to play the part of the daughters of Danaüs who, according to Greek mythology, suffered in the underworld, and of Dirce who was tied by the hair to a wild bull and dragged to death.

[6] Tacitus, *Annals*. xv, 38, 40.

[7] Suetonius (*Nero*, 38) states that the city was set on fire openly by Nero, who pretended to be disgusted with the ugliness of Rome's old buildings and the narrow and crooked streets.

upon the hated Christians and subjected them to the most atrocious tortures. This persecution is described vividly by Tacitus:

"Nero put in his own place as culprits, and punished with most ingenious cruelty, men whom the common people hated for their shameful crimes and called Christians. Christ, from whom the name was derived, had been put to death in the reign of Tiberius by the procurator Pontius Pilate. The deadly superstition, having been checked for awhile, began to break out again, not only throughout Judea, where this mischief first arose, but also at Rome, where from all sides all things scandalous and shameful meet and become fashionable. Therefore, at the beginning, some were seized who made confessions; then, on their information, a vast multitude was convicted, not so much of arson as of hatred of the human race. And they were not only put to death, but subjected to insults, in that they were either dressed up in the skins of wild beasts and perished by the cruel mangling of dogs, or else put on crosses to be set on fire, and, as day declined, to be burned, being used as light by night. Nero had thrown open his gardens for that spectacle, and gave a circus play, mingling with the people dressed in a charioteer's costume or driving in a chariot. From this arose, however, toward men who were, indeed, criminals and deserving extreme penalties, sympathy, on the ground that they were destroyed not for the public good, but to satisfy the cruelty of an individual."[8]

This description by Tacitus agrees remarkably well with the intimations of Clement's letter and fills out the details of the indignities and tortures heaped upon the Christians at Nero's circus play. Both accounts evidently refer to the same events, and the close agreement between Tacitus and Clement is strong reason for regarding the year 64 as the date of the death of the two great apostles.

Around A.D. 200 Tertullian likewise refers to the death of Peter and Paul as having taken place at Rome under Nero and correctly interprets John 21:18 as a reference to Peter's crucifixion: "At Rome Nero was the first who stained with blood the rising faith. Then is Peter girt by another, when he is made fast to the cross. Then does Paul obtain a birth suited to Roman citizenship, when in Rome he springs to life again ennobled by martyrdom."[9] On another occasion Tertullian incidentally indicates the manner of both martyrdoms by comparing the death of Peter to that of Jesus and the death of Paul to that of John the Baptist:[10] "How happy is its church, on which apostles poured forth all their doctrine along with their blood! Where

---

[8] *Annals.* xv, 44. [9] *Scorpiace.* 15 (ANF III, p.648).
[10] *On Prescription against Heretics.* 36 (ANF III, p.260).

Peter endures a passion like his Lord's![11] where Paul wins his crown in a death like John's!"[12]

Also Eusebius relates in his *Church History* that Peter and Paul suffered martyrdom at about the same time in Rome under Nero. The *Church History* was published in A.D. 326, but Eusebius derived his information in this regard from authorities who had lived much earlier. He cites Caius, who probably lived in Rome in the time of Pope Zephyrinus about A.D. 199-217, and Dionysius, who was bishop of Corinth at the same time that Soter was bishop of Rome around A.D. 166-174. The entire passage, with the quotations from the two earlier sources, is as follows:[13]

"When the government of Nero was now firmly established, he began to plunge into unholy pursuits, and armed himself even against the religion of the God of the universe. . . . He was the first of the emperors who showed himself an enemy of the divine religion. The Roman Tertul-

[11] The martyrdom of Peter is narrated with apocryphal elaboration in the Acts of Peter (James, *The Apocryphal New Testament,* pp.333f.), which is probably to be dated around A.D. 200-220. In this work is found the famous and beautiful *"Domine quo vadis?"* legend, according to which Peter was warned to leave Rome and went forth but met Jesus coming into the city. "And as he went forth out of the city, he saw the Lord entering into Rome. And when he saw him, he said: Lord whither goest thou here? And the Lord said unto him: I go into Rome to be crucified. And Peter said unto him: Lord, art thou being crucified again? He said unto him: Yea, Peter, I am being crucified again. And Peter came to himself: and having beheld the Lord ascending up into heaven, he returned to Rome, rejoicing, and glorifying the Lord, for that he said: I am being crucified: the which was about to befall Peter." When Peter was crucified he insisted that it should be "with the head downward and not otherwise" and so it was done. Eusebius also states, on the authority of Origen, that Peter was crucified head-downward (see below, n.13).

[12] Mark 6:27. That Paul should have been put to death by the sword was to be expected since he was a Roman citizen (Acts 16:37; 22:27f.; 23:27). Both crucifixion and condemnation *ad bestias* appear to have been methods of execution usually reserved for persons of lower standing than Roman citizens. D. W. Riddle (*Paul, Man of Conflict.* 1940, pp.140f.) suggests the possibility that Paul was thrown to the wild beasts, since Ignatius (A.D. c.110-c.117) who was to die that way (Romans 4. ANF I, p.75) said that he wanted to "be found in (*literally* under) the footsteps of Paul" (Ephesians 12. ANF I, p.55). Ignatius, however, well may have been referring simply to the fact of martyrdom, since in another place he hopes that by fighting with beasts at Rome he "may indeed become the disciple of Jesus" (Ephesians 1 [ANF I, p.49]). Riddle regards the ascription of Roman citizenship to Paul by Acts as a tendentious and therefore unreliable statement, but that Saul who bore the eminent Roman cognomen Paul actually was a Roman citizen is entirely probable.

[13] *Ch. Hist.* II, xxv; cf. III, i, where Eusebius says, "Peter appears to have preached in Pontus, Galatia, Bithynia, Cappadocia, and Asia to the Jews of the dispersion. And at last, having come to Rome, he was crucified head-downwards; for he had requested that he might suffer in this way. What do we need to say concerning Paul, who preached the Gospel of Christ from Jerusalem to Illyricum, and afterwards suffered martyrdom in Rome under Nero? These facts are related by Origen in the third volume of his Commentary on Genesis."

lian is likewise a witness of this. He writes as follows: 'Examine your records. There you will find that Nero was the first that persecuted this doctrine, particularly then when after subduing all the east, he exercised his cruelty against all at Rome. We glory in having such a man the leader in our punishment. For whoever knows him can understand that nothing was condemned by Nero unless it was something of great excellence.' Thus publicly announcing himself as the first among God's chief enemies, he was led on to the slaughter of the apostles. It is, therefore, recorded that Paul was beheaded in Rome itself, and that Peter likewise was crucified under Nero. This account of Peter and Paul is substantiated by the fact that their names are preserved in the cemeteries of that place even to the present day. It is confirmed likewise by Caius, a member of the Church, who arose under Zephyrinus, bishop of Rome. He, in a published disputation with Proclus, the leader of the Phrygian heresy, speaks as follows concerning the places where the sacred corpses of the aforesaid apostles are laid: 'But I can show the trophies of the apostles. For if you will go to the Vatican or to the Ostian way, you will find the trophies of those who laid the foundations of this church.' And that they both suffered martyrdom at the same time is stated by Dionysius, bishop of Corinth, in his epistle to the Romans, in the following words: 'You have thus by such an admonition bound together the planting of Peter and of Paul at Rome and Corinth. For both of them planted and likewise taught us in our Corinth.[14] And they taught together in like manner in Italy, and suffered martyrdom at the same time.' "[15]

This passage in Eusebius is of particular interest because of the quotation which it contains from Caius. As a presbyter in the Roman church at the beginning of the third century, he was involved in a disputation with Proclus, the leader of the sect of the Montanists. As is evident from a later passage in the *Church History,* Proclus had supported his position by an appeal to the existence of the tombs of Philip and his four daughters at Hierapolis in Asia.[16] This

[14] The mention of a "Cephas" party at Corinth in I Corinthians 1:12 makes it probable that Peter did work there as Dionysius states.

[15] "At the same time" (κατὰ τὸν αὐτὸν καιρόν. ed. E. Schwartz, *Kleine Ausgabe.* 3d ed. 1922, p.73), allows some margin and does not necessarily imply on the very same day. In his *Chronicon* (ed. Scaliger. 1606, p.192, cf. p.162) Eusebius places the deaths of Peter and Paul together in the fourteenth year of Nero, which would be A.D. 67-68. But in the very same connection Eusebius describes Nero's persecution of the Christians in Rome and assigns it likewise to Nero's fourteenth year. It must be concluded, therefore, that Eusebius made an error as to the date of the Neronian persecution, which is definitely known to have taken place in the summer of A.D. 64. It should be noted that a date around A.D. 67 for the martyrdom of Peter and Paul does have the support of a statement by Jerome that Seneca (c.4 B.C.-A.D. 65) died two years before the apostles (Orazio Marucchi, *Pietro e Paolo a Roma.* 4th ed. 1934, p.21), but since this involves separating their death by several years from the fire and persecution of A.D. 64 it seems less probable.

[16] A city about five miles north of Laodicea, and mentioned in Colossians 4:13.

latter passage reads: "And in the Dialogue of Caius which we mentioned a little above, Proclus, against whom he directed his disputation, in agreement with what has been quoted, speaks thus concerning the death of Philip and his daughters: 'After him there were four prophetesses, the daughters of Philip, at Hierapolis in Asia. Their tomb is there and the tomb of their father.' "[17]

Over against the claims of Proclus, Caius appealed to the existence in Rome of the glorious last resting places of Peter and Paul, who had taught there and laid the foundations of the Roman church. "But," said he in reply to Proclus, "I can show the trophies of the apostles.[18] For if you will go to the Vatican or to the Ostian way, you will find the trophies of those who laid the foundations of this church." The Greek word "trophy" which is used here, originally meant the memorial of a victory which was raised on the field of battle. Thus, for example, the armor or weapons of the defeated enemy might be fixed to a tree or upright post, with an accompanying inscription and dedication. In similar fashion when a Christian hero fell on the field of martyrdom, his grave appropriately enough might be referred to as a "trophy."

The Vatican, to which Caius referred as the place of the tomb of Peter, was the Ager Vaticanus, where "Nero's Circus" and "Nero's Gardens" were (pp. 288f.), and where so many other Christians also perished in Nero's frightful exhibition of cruelty (p. 299). There on the outskirts of Nero's Circus, as near as possible to the place of his triumph in death, was the grave of Peter. According to the first chapter of the Liber Pontificalis[19] the exact location was between the Via Aurelia and the Via Triumphalis, near a temple of Cybele which by popular error was later called a shrine of Apollo.

The Ostian Way, to which Caius referred as the place of the tomb of Paul, was the ancient Via Ostiensis. This road led from Rome to the port city of Ostia, some fourteen miles distant at the mouth of the Tiber.[20] It departed from the southern side of Rome at a point some distance west of the Via Appia by which Paul had

[17] Ch. Hist. III, xxxi.

[18] Ch. Hist. II, xxv, 7: ἐγὼ δὲ τὰ τρόπαια τῶν ἀποστόλων ἔχω δεῖξαι. ed. Schwartz, p.73.

[19] The Liber Pontificalis is a series of biographies of the popes and was compiled in the text in which we have it in the seventh century from earlier papal annals. While a considerable part is obviously legendary it also contains much valuable historical material. Louis Duchesne, Le liber pontificalis, texte, introduction et commentaire. 2 vols. 1886-92; LLP, pp.ix-x.

[20] The city derived its name from the ostium or mouth of the river.

first entered the city. As Paul was led forth to die his eyes must have fallen upon one monument which still stands today upon the Via Ostiense. This is the Pyramid of Cestius at the present Porta San Paolo (Fig. 126). It was a tomb which was erected in Egyptian pyramidal form for a certain Caius Cestius Epulo who died before 12 B.C. One hundred and sixteen feet high and covered with marble slabs, the pyramid was enclosed by Aurelian within his city wall but extricated in 1660 by Pope Alexander VII, and looms up today exactly as it did when Paul passed. The last resting place of the great apostle was some one and one-quarter miles farther out the Via Ostiensis.[21]

Thus, as Caius is witness, the graves of Peter and of Paul at the Vatican and on the Ostian Way respectively, were perfectly well-known martyr-memorials in Rome around A.D. 200. Nor could these graves have been recent inventions of pious credulity as if they first had been arbitrarily "discovered" say around A.D. 170. By that time the Christian custom of burial in the catacombs was fully established, and if one had wished to invent the graves of Peter and of Paul it would have been most natural to place them in or near some of these recognized Christian cemeteries where undisturbed veneration of the holy places would have been possible. Instead both graves are remote from all Christian cemeteries and in fact lie amidst pagan cemeteries of the first and second centuries. This fact has been established by recent excavations which have revealed pagan columbaria in the immediate neighborhood of the graves of both Peter and Paul. No one would have "invented" the holy graves in such unholy surroundings.[22]

[21] The place of Paul's execution is believed to have been yet another one and one-quarter miles out on the Via Laurentina at the Abbey of the Three Fountains (Abbadia delle Tre Fontane). There are three springs here which anciently were known as the Aquae Salviae, and according to the apocryphal Acts of Peter and Paul (R. A. Lipsius and M. Bonnet, *Acta Apostolorum Apocrypha.* i [1891], p.214) Paul was beheaded at a place of this name and under a pine tree. The late legend that when the apostle's head struck the earth it bounced three times and at each place one of the springs welled forth, is of course as worthless as the other story that when his head was struck off, milk came forth (Carl Schmidt, ed., *Praxeis Paulou: Acta Pauli.* 1936, pp.68f.). But the location of the execution at this place also has the authority of Pope Gregory I the Great (A.D. 590-604) and may be not incorrect. The old abbey which stood here was virtually abandoned for a long time owing to malaria but around 1867 was entrusted to French Trappist monks. It is an interesting fact that when the Trappists were doing some digging in connection with one of their buildings in 1875 they unearthed a mass of coins of Nero together with several fossilized pine-cones. R. Lanciani, *Wanderings through Ancient Roman Churches.* 1924, p.169.

[22] Hans Lietzmann, *Petrus und Paulus in Rom.* 2d ed. 1927, pp.246f.

In the light of history it is eminently fitting that Peter's grave should be hard by Nero's Circus to proclaim that the tyrant's triumph was transient but the apostle's was everlasting. And it is likewise appropriate that Paul who had traveled so far for Christ should be buried at last beside a highway as if to signify that his strong heart was still eager for the preaching of the gospel in distant places. Both graves are truly trophies of victory.

VII

Manuscripts Found in the Sand

As EXTENSIVELY as Paul himself traveled, his letters traveled even farther. Occasionally his correspondence was addressed to cities and churches where his face had never been seen (cf. Colossians 2:1), and some of his letters were passed on from one church to another (Colossians 4:16). Moreover, within twenty-five years after his death, copies of his letters were gathered from the various churches to which he had sent them, and published as a collection.[1] From A.D. 90 on these collected letters of Paul were known widely, and their language and ideas were reflected frequently in other Christian writings.[2] In II Peter 3:16 this collection is referred to and is already regarded as "scripture."

Joined eventually with the other writings of the canonical New Testament, the letters of Paul have become known down through the centuries and around the world. The influence of a single one of them, that to the Romans, for example, has been nothing less than world-transforming. The conversion of Augustine came when he took up "the volume of the Apostles" and read Romans 13:13-14.[3] The sudden enlightenment of Martin Luther came when he was reading the epistle to the Romans in his monastery cell. The decisive experience in the life of John Wesley came from hearing Luther's

---

[1] E. J. Goodspeed (*Christianity Goes to Press*. 1940, pp.49-62) thinks that the collection was made first at Ephesus, possibly by Onesimus, who had been the slave of Philemon and around A.D. 110 became bishop of Ephesus.

[2] A. E. Barnett (*Paul Becomes a Literary Influence*. 1940) finds that Pauline influence was strong in I Peter, Hebrews, I Clement, the Johannine writings, Ignatius and Polycarp; that it subsided, perhaps due to an anti-Marcionite reaction, in James, Jude, Hermas, Barnabas, the Didache, II Clement, the Martyrdom of Polycarp and the Apology of Aristides; and that it revived again in II Peter, Tatian's Address to the Greeks, Justin, Melito, Athenagoras and the Pastoral Epistles.

[3] *Confessions*. VIII, 12 (NPNF I, p.127).

[305]

preface to the Commentary on Romans read in a little meeting in Aldersgate Street, London. Twentieth century theology has been influenced by the endeavor of Karl Barth to see modern life through the lens of Paul's conception of faith, and the writing by Barth of his first book on *The Epistle to the Romans*.[4] Certainly this single writing of Paul's has been a *Schicksalsbrief*, a "letter of destiny," in the history of Christianity. It will be convenient to illustrate the bearing of modern discovery on the text of the New Testament by following this letter through a number of its earliest and most important copies.

First, however, a brief survey must be made of the writing materials and practices of the early Christian centuries.

[4] *Der Römerbrief.* 1919. tr. Edwyn C. Hoskyns, 1933.

1. THE WRITING MATERIAL OF
THE ANCIENT WORLD

THE common writing material of the ancient world was papyrus, from which the modern word "paper" is derived.[1] Papyrus first came into use in Egypt, where the representation of scribes writing on rolls of papyrus is found from very ancient times.[2] The statuette of a scribe shown in Fig. 127 comes from the Third Dynasty and may be the earliest such figure that has ever been found. The scribe is seated cross-legged and holds upon his lap a roll of papyrus. The unrolled portion of the papyrus is grasped by the left hand and the free end of the roll lying across the lap is held down by the right hand which is in a position to write. The expression upon the face is that of one waiting to take dictation. Similar examples are to be found in the statue of Henka the scribe (Fourth Dynasty) in the Berlin Museum, in that of the Scribe Accroupi (Fifth Dynasty) in the Louvre at Paris, and in that of Harmhab (Eighteenth-Nineteenth Dynasties) already mentioned (p. 102, Fig. 48). Another interesting representation is that of the limestone relief carving from the Eighteenth Dynasty shown in Fig. 128. Here four scribes are standing and bending forward attentively, each with his papyrus roll and pen.

The oldest actual specimen of a papyrus manuscript yet discovered dates from the Fifth Dynasty,[3] and from that ancient time papyrus continued in use on down through the Greek and Roman Periods and well into the days after the occupation of Egypt by the Arabs in A.D. 641. Extant papyri are written not only in the language of ancient Egypt, but also in Greek,[4] Latin,[5] Hebrew,[6]

[1] Greek, πάπυρος; Latin, papyrus; German, Papier; French, papier; English, paper.
[2] Reference has already been made to the early development of writing in Mesopotamia (p.22), Egypt (pp.73f.) and Sinai-Palestine (pp.126f.,139).
[3] F. G. Kenyon, The Palaeography of Greek Papyri. 1899, p.14. The statement of the Roman antiquarian, Varro (c.116-c.27 B.C.), which is quoted by Pliny (Natural History. XIII, 11) that the use of papyrus for writing was discovered first in the time of Alexander the Great is entirely incorrect and was doubted by Pliny himself (XIII, 13).
[4] Greek was the official language of Egypt from the founding of the Ptolemaic Dynasty until the Arab invasion, and by far the largest number of extant papyri are written in Greek.
[5] Latin was used chiefly for military and legal business and in private correspondence between Roman officials, and papyri written in this language are not numerous.
[6] Hebrew papyri are rare. There is a small fragment in the Cambridge University Library, known as the Nash Papyrus, written probably in the second century B.C.,

Aramaic,[7] Coptic[8] and Arabic.[9] Thus, this amazing writing material was in continuous and demonstrable use in Egypt for a period of three or four thousand years.[10]

From Egypt the use of papyrus spread to many other lands. In Palestine it was certainly in common use in the sixth century B.C., as is shown by the clay seal of Gedaliah found at Lachish on the back of which is the impression of the papyrus document to which it was originally attached (p. 161). Doubtless papyrus was also employed much earlier than this in Palestine, and the paucity of epigraphic material discovered there is probably due to the general use of papyrus instead of ostraca or stone. Under Palestine's relatively damp and unfavorable climatic conditions the papyri would perish rapidly. In Mesopotamia the use of papyrus is attested by fragments of this material which were discovered at Dura-Europos and which date in the third century B.C.[11]

Among the Greeks papyrus was in use at least in the fifth century B.C.[12] and probably much earlier. In the century and a half after the birth of Christ it was the usual writing material, and it continued to be employed as late as the sixth and seventh centuries A.D. The Romans were using papyrus in the third century B.C. and continued to employ it until the seventh century A.D. Thus, as Caspar René Gregory has said of the period in which the New Testament was written, papyrus "was the common writing material, the paper, of that day, whether at Alexandria or at Antioch or at Rome. If a man put a handbill up at Rome, he wrote it on a big piece of coarse papyrus. If he wrote a delicate note to his wife or his mother, he wrote it on a little piece of fine papyrus. Papyrus was their paper."[13]

---

and containing the Ten Commandments and the Shema (Deuteronomy 6:4ff.). Norbert Peters, *Die älteste Abschrift der zehn Gebote, der Papyrus Nash.* 1905; W. F. Albright in JBL 56 (1937), pp.145-176.

[7] The best known Aramaic papyri are those from Elephantine which already have been mentioned (p.201).

[8] The Copts were the native Egyptians, descended from the ancient inhabitants of the land, and large numbers of Coptic papyri have been found.

[9] C. H. Becker, *Papyri Schott-Reinhardt.* i (1906). After the Arab conquest Greek continued for some time to be employed officially alongside Arabic and then gradually died out.

[10] Wilhelm Schubart, *Das alte Ägypten und seine Papyrus.* 1921, p.6.

[11] C. B. Welles in *Münchener Beiträge zur Papyrusforschung und antiken Rechtsgeschichte.* 19 (1934), pp.379-399.

[12] Herodotus. v, 58.

[13] *Canon and Text of the New Testament.* 1907, p.317.

THE PAPYRUS PLANT

Papyrus derived its name from the plant from which it was made. This was a reed or sedge called papyrus[14] which grew abundantly in Egypt and was also found in adjoining lands.[15] The papyrus plant appears frequently in Egyptian art, from the earliest times. A particularly delightful example is the wall painting representing a wildcat in a papyrus thicket (Fig. 129) from the famous tomb of Khnumhotep (Twelfth Dynasty) at Beni Hasan (p. 83). Another scene, in the tomb of Puyemre (Eighteenth Dynasty), shows the papyrus plant being harvested and split for papermaking (Fig. 130).

THE MANUFACTURE OF PAPYRUS

The process of making writing material from the papyrus plant has been described, although not with complete clarity, by Pliny in his *Natural History:*[16]

"Papyrus grows either in the marshes of Egypt, or in the sluggish waters of the river Nile, when they have overflowed and are lying stagnant, in pools that do not exceed a couple of cubits [about three feet] in depth. The root lies obliquely, and is about the thickness of one's arm; the section of the stalk is triangular, and it tapers gracefully upwards towards the extremity, being not more than ten cubits [about fifteen feet] at most in height. . . ."[17]

"Paper is made from the papyrus, by splitting it with a needle into very thin leaves, due care being taken that they should be as broad as possible. That of the first quality is taken from the center of the plant, and so in regular succession, according to the order of division. . . .

"All these various kinds of paper are made upon a table, moistened with Nile water; a liquid which, when in a muddy state, has the peculiar qualities of glue. This table being first inclined, the leaves of papyrus are laid upon it lengthwise, as long, indeed, as the papyrus will admit of, the jagged edges being cut off at either end; after which a cross layer is placed over it, . . . When this is done, the leaves are pressed together, and then dried in the sun; after which they are united to one another, the best sheets being always taken first, and the inferior ones added afterwards. There are never more than twenty of these sheets to a roll."

In other words, single sheets of paper were made out of thin vertical and horizontal strips of papyrus glued together, and a number

[14] Linnaeus, *Cyperus papyrus.*
[15] Strabo, *Geography.* XVII, i, 15. The plant now is practically extinct in Lower Egypt, but is found in Nubia, Ethiopia, Palestine and at Syracuse in Sicily.
[16] XIII, 11f.
[17] cf. Theophrastus (c.372-c.287 B.C.), *Enquiry into Plants.* IV, viii, 3. tr. A. Hort, LCL (1916) I, pp.347-349.

of such sheets were glued together, side by side, to form a continuous roll. The single sheet[18] was, of course, made in a variety of sizes, and papyri are extant varying in height from less than 2 inches to over 15 inches. A sheet of average size probably ran about 9 to 11 inches in height and 6 to 9 inches in width. A single such sheet would suffice for a brief letter or other document. New Testament writings such as Philemon and II and III John probably each occupied a single sheet.[19]

THE PAPYRUS ROLL

When Pliny said that a papyrus roll never consisted of more than 20 of these sheets, he must have been referring to the length of the papyrus rolls as they were customarily placed on the market. With individual sheets not usually running over 9 inches in width, a roll such as Pliny refers to, composed of 20 sheets, would have attained a length of 15 feet at the maximum. Of course if the work of an individual writer did not extend to this length he could cut off a portion, or if it was of greater length he could glue a second roll onto the first. A normal Greek literary roll probably did not exceed 35 feet, but Egyptian ceremonial copies of the Book of the Dead were often 50 or 100 feet in length. The longest papyrus known is a panegyrical chronicle of the reign of Ramesses II called the Harris Papyrus, which is 133 feet in length and 17 inches in height.[20] An average roll in New Testament times, however, would have been probably 30 or 35 feet in length, and when rolled up upon itself would have appeared as a cylinder perhaps 10 inches in height and one or one and one-half inches in diameter. A book such as the Gospel According to Luke would have filled an ordinary papyrus roll 31 or 32 feet long, while the book of Acts by the same author would have required a second such roll. Doubtless this is one of the reasons why Luke-Acts was issued in two volumes (Acts 1:1). Likewise, Paul's ten collected church letters would probably have filled two papyrus rolls. The papyrus roll (Greenfield Papyrus) shown in Fig. 131 is considerably larger than the average since it

---

[18] The sheet was called a κόλλημα because the strips of papyrus of which it was made up were glued together (κολλᾶν). Papyrus which was prepared for writing but not yet written upon was called χάρτης as in II John 12. W. H. P. Hatch, *The Principal Uncial Manuscripts of the New Testament.* 1939, p.6 n.29,30.

[19] F. G. Kenyon, *Books and Readers in Ancient Greece and Rome.* 1932, pp.49f.

[20] ARE IV, §151-412.

measures 19 inches in height. Other and smaller rolls both open and sealed are shown in Fig. 132.

A sheet or roll of papyrus was ordinarily written on only one side, that where the papyrus fibers ran in the horizontal direction naturally being preferable (recto). The other side (verso) where the component strips ran vertically, could also be used, however, and a roll written on both front and back is called an opisthograph. It is a book of this sort that is described in Revelation 5:1, "a roll with writing on both sides, sealed with seven seals." The text was written in a column or series of columns (σελίδες), each of which was usually two or three inches wide. In the case of a roll, these columns were not correlated with the sheets of papyrus and the writing frequently ran over the juncture of two sheets. Except in the more elegant books the margins were not large and the columns were close together.

PEN AND INK

Writing was done with a reed pen (κάλαμος) such as is mentioned in III John 13. A pen of this sort was made from a thoroughly dried reed stalk, the end of which was sharpened to a point and split into two parts. The ink was known as μέλαν and is referred to in II Corinthians 3:3, II John 12, and III John 13. Two kinds were in common use, one made from lampblack, gum and water, and the other from nutgalls, green vitriol and water. The former was very black and unfading, the latter turned in the course of time into a handsome rusty brown color.[21]

BIBLIA

Papyrus rolls of the sort just described constituted the regular form of books throughout the first century A.D. The book of Revelation, which was probably written during the reign of Domitian A.D. 81-96, expressly speaks of itself as a papyrus roll four times in 22:18f. The Greek word that is used here is *biblion* (βιβλίον), which was the regular term for a papyrus scroll. This is the diminutive form of the Greek word *biblos* (βίβλος) which, in turn, was derived from the name (βύβλος or βίβλος) of the pith of the papyrus stalk. In the plural, papyrus rolls were called βιβλία (II Timothy 4:13) and hence the early Christians came to refer to the books which made up the New Testament as τὰ βιβλία,[22] that is, "the scrolls" or "the books"

---

[21] Hatch, *The Principal Uncial Manuscripts of the New Testament*, pp.13-15.
[22] II Clement 14:2.

par excellence. In the Latin form, *biblia,* this plural noun came to be regarded as a singular form, and so eventually our word "Bible" emerged.

THE PAPYRUS CODEX

The papyrus roll was relatively inconvenient to use. The reader had to employ both hands, unrolling it with one hand and rolling it up with the other as the reading proceeded. Moreover, there was no simple way to give a reference to a specific passage within a longer roll, and to find a given section might necessitate unrolling it to the very end. Consequently, it was inevitable and desirable that the roll should be superseded by a more usable form. This was found in the codex, where the leaves of the manuscript were fastened together as in a modern book. The Latin word *caudex* or *codex* originally meant the trunk of a tree, and then a block of wood split up into leaves or tablets. Such tablets often were smeared with wax and written upon (cf. Isaiah 8:1; 30:8; Luke 1:63), and hence the word codex came to denote a book whose leaves were not rolled together but laid one upon another.[23]

The exact date of the introduction of this form for the making of papyrus books is not known, but it was certainly in use among the Christians of the second century A.D. If the codex form was not actually a Christian invention, it was, at any rate, most promptly employed and generally used by the Christians. Whereas the roll continued in practically universal use for works of pagan literature during the second and third centuries A.D., the majority of Christian works were already in codex form.[24] The convenience of this form for books as much used for reference as those of the New Testament is obvious. The earliest fragment of a manuscript of a New Testament book that is now known, is the Papyrus Rylands Gk. 457, a tiny piece of a papyrus leaf of the Gospel According to John. It was discovered in 1935 in the John Rylands Library in Manchester among papyri which had been acquired in Egypt by B. P. Grenfell in 1920. The fragment is written on both sides, as may be seen in Fig. 133 where the recto is shown at the left and the verso at the right, and once was a part of a leafbook or codex. According to its style of handwriting it is dated in the first half of the second cen-

[23] George Milligan, *The New Testament and Its Transmission.* 1932, p.15.
[24] F. G. Kenyon, *The Text of the Greek Bible.* 1937, p.18.

tury A.D.[25] From that time on, the codex was in general use for Christian writings, and eventually it became the universal form for the publication of books.

These ancient codices were bound like modern books in quires. A sheet of papyrus was folded once in the middle, thus forming two leaves of equal size. By fastening together a number of such two-leaf quires a codex could be produced. Or, a more extensive quire could be made by laying from three to six sheets one upon another, these forming, when folded, six to twelve leaves. In making such a quire it was customary to place alternately uppermost the recto side and the verso side of the papyrus sheets, so that when the book was opened a recto page would face a recto page, and a verso a verso. By binding together a number of such quires, large codices could be produced very satisfactorily, and the multiple-quire book was the ultimate development in form.

The adoption of the codex led gradually to a change in the style of columns employed. In the roll form of book it had been convenient to write in narrow columns of short lines. With the codex it became desirable to write in wider columns of longer lines. Eventually the prevailing practice was that of having only one or two columns on each page.[26]

LEATHER, PARCHMENT AND VELLUM

Because of its relative fragility in climates less favorable than that of Egypt, papyrus was finally superseded by a more durable material. This was parchment, or vellum. Its development roots back in the use of leather, which was a familiar writing material in the Mediterranean lands from ancient times. In Egypt, for example, the victory of Thutmose III at Megiddo "was recorded upon a roll of leather in the temple of Amun."[27] According to Herodotus, the Greeks of Ionia had formerly, when papyrus was scarce, written on the skins of goats and sheep, a custom which was continued by the barbarians in his own day.[28]

A number of facts suggest that the Hebrews employed leather as a writing material at an early time.[29] When Jeremiah dictated his

[25] C. H. Roberts, *An Unpublished Fragment of the Fourth Gospel in the John Rylands Library*. 1935, p.16. Actual size of fragment is 3.5 x 2.3 inches.

[26] Hatch, *The Principal Uncial Manuscripts of the New Testament*, pp.17-19.

[27] ARE II, §433.   [28] v, 58.

[29] L. Löw, *Graphische Requisiten und Erzeugnisse bei den Juden*. (1870-71) I, p.114.

prophecies to his secretary Baruch (Jeremiah 36:4), they were probably written upon a roll of leather, since King Jehoiakim later used a knife to cut the roll in pieces when he wanted to burn it (Jeremiah 36:23).[30] In the Talmud, we find that the Law was written upon the hides of cattle,[31] and this doubtless reflects an ancient tradition. The Letter of Aristeas and Josephus say that the copy of the Law which was sent from Jerusalem to Egypt for the making of the Septuagint translation, was written on leather (διφθέραι).[32]

The invention of parchment was a special development from the ancient use of skins for writing. Whereas leather is tanned, parchment is made by soaking the skin in limewater, scraping off the hair on the one side and the flesh on the other, stretching and drying in a frame, and rubbing with chalk and pumice stone, thus producing a fine material capable of receiving writing on both sides. The skins of sheep, goats and other animals are used for parchment, but the finest kind of all is prepared from calfskins. This is properly called "vellum,"[33] but the name vellum is now used also less discriminatingly to include the other kinds of skins as well, when prepared with particular care to receive writing. The chief marks of vellum are its semitransparent fineness and the striking beauty of its polish.[34]

The Latin expression for parchment was *membrana*, while the Greeks continued to employ the term διφθέρα, meaning leather, or borrowed the word μεμβράνα from the Romans. The word περγαμηνή, *pergamena*, or "parchment,"[35] appears first in an edict of Diocletian in A.D. 301, and apparently is derived from the city of Pergamum in Asia Minor. According to Pliny,[36] Varro stated that parchment was invented at Pergamum. His story was that rivalry existed between King Eumenes II (c.197-c.159 B.C.) of Pergamum and King Ptolemy of Egypt over their respective libraries. Since Ptolemy feared that the library at Pergamum might come to surpass the library of Alexandria, he endeavored to retard the literary progress of the rival

---

[30] The knife employed was a "scribe's knife" (LXX [III, p.328], τῷ ξυρῷ τοῦ γραμματέως), such as a scribe employed for making erasures on leather. For the roll form in the Old Testament cf. Psalm 40:7; Ezekiel 2:9; Zechariah 5:1; the pen is mentioned in Jeremiah 8:8; Psalm 45:1; and ink in Jeremiah 36:18.

[31] *Maccoth.* 5. RBT 9 (XVII), p.28.

[32] *Letter of Aristeas.* 3, 176. ed. H. G. Meecham. 1935, pp.5,25,174; Josephus, *Ant.* XII, ii, 11.

[33] French, *vélin*; from Latin *vitellus*, diminutive of *vitulus*, a calf.

[34] G. Peignot, *Essai sur l'histoire du parchemin et du vélin.* 1812, p.28.

[35] cf. German, *Pergament*; French, *parchemin*.

[36] *Natural History.* XIII, 21.

city by prohibiting the export of papyrus from Egypt. Consequently, the people of Pergamum were driven to the invention of parchment. This account can hardly be historical, but it is doubtless true that a high quality of parchment was developed at Pergamum and that the city was famous for its manufacture and export.[37]

THE VICTORY OF VELLUM

Parchment or vellum came only slowly into general use. It is mentioned occasionally by Roman writers of the first century B.C. and the first century A.D.,[38] but at that time was still regarded generally as inferior to papyrus, being employed chiefly for notebooks and for rough drafts or inferior copies of literary works.[39] In an interesting passage in II Timothy 4:13 a request is made for the bringing of "the books, especially the parchments" (τὰ βιβλία, μάλιστα τὰς μεμβράνας). The "books" must have been papyrus rolls, while the "parchments" probably were vellum rolls of the Old Testament.[40] A fragment now in the British Museum shows that an oration of Demosthenes was copied on vellum, probably in the second century A.D.,[41] while a vellum fragment of Tatian's Diatessaron has been found at Dura-Europos, a town which was destroyed about A.D. 256.[42] There are also some vellum fragments of the *Iliad*[43] and the *Odyssey*[44] which are believed to have been written at least by around A.D. 300.

It was in the fourth century A.D. that vellum definitely superseded papyrus in importance. The famous library of Origen (d. A.D. c.254) and Pamphilus (d. A.D. 309) at Caesarea had fallen into decay and about the middle of the fourth century was restored by two priests, Acacius and Euzoius, who replaced its damaged papyrus rolls with

[37] Theodor Birt, *Kritik und Hermeneutik nebst Abriss des antiken Buchwesens* (*Handbuch der klassischen Altertumswissenschaft.* 1913), p.280.

[38] Cicero, *Letters to Atticus.* XIII, xxiv; Horace II, iii, 2; Martial, *Epigrams.* XIV, 7.

[39] Quintillian, A.D. c.35-c.100 (*Institutio Oratoria.* x, iii, 31, tr. H. E. Butler, LCL [1921-22], IV, p.109) preferred to write on wax rather than parchment, because the latter "although of assistance to the eye, delays the hand and interrupts the stream of thought owing to the frequency with which the pen has to be supplied with ink."

[40] Mackinnon (*The Rome of St. Paul*, pp.87,146) thinks that Paul's mention of parchment implies that he used this material for his own letters which he knew to be of permanent value. The "occasional" character of Paul's correspondence, however, renders this supposition unlikely.

[41] Kenyon, *The Palaeography of Greek Papyri*, p.113.

[42] C. H. Kraeling, *A Greek Fragment of Tatian's Diatessaron from Dura.* 1935.

[43] Sir E. M. Thompson, *An Introduction to Greek and Latin Palaeography.* 1912, pp.198f.,201.

[44] A. S. Hunt, *Catalogue of the Greek Papyri in the John Rylands Library.* I (1911), p.91.

copies written on vellum.[45] In A.D. 332 the Emperor Constantine instructed Eusebius to have fifty vellum manuscripts of the Bible prepared for the churches in his new capital, Constantinople. The emperor's letter to Eusebius read in part: "I have thought it expedient to instruct your Prudence to order fifty copies of the sacred Scriptures, the provision and use of which you know to be most needful for the instruction of the Church, to be written on prepared parchment in a legible manner, and in a convenient, portable form, by professional transcribers thoroughly practiced in their art."[46]

"Such were the emperor's commands," reports Eusebius, "which were followed by the immediate execution of the work itself, which we sent him in magnificent and elaborately bound volumes of a threefold and fourfold form."[47] Furthermore, two great vellum codices of the Bible, copied doubtless in the fourth century A.D., are still extant, Codex Vaticanus and Codex Sinaiticus. These facts indicate the triumph of vellum in the fourth century, from which time on it remained the chief writing material until the general establishment of the use of paper in the fourteenth century.

The codex form, which had proved so convenient in the case of papyrus manuscripts, was naturally retained when vellum was introduced. The quires were built up on a principle similar to that which had been employed in the papyrus codex, in that the flesh side of each sheet of vellum was laid upon the flesh side of another, and the hair side upon a hair side. Thus when the codex was opened the pages which faced each other were of similar kind. In order to guide the writing, lines were drawn on the hair side with a sharp instrument and allowed to show through on the flesh side.

STYLES OF HANDWRITING

In the Roman period papyrus manuscripts of a literary character generally were written in a relatively handsome, regular "bookhand," while other documents and letters were often written in a non-literary script of "cursive" type. In the latter case the letters were characterized by their roundness and relative continuity of forma-

[45] F. G. Kenyon in HDB IV, p.947.

[46] *Life of Constantine.* IV, 36 (πεντήκοντα σωμάτια ἐν διφθέραις).

[47] ibid. IV, 37. The expression "threefold and fourfold" (τρισσὰ καὶ τετρασσά) probably means "having three columns and four columns" and indicates that the pages were written respectively in three columns and in four columns. J. H. Ropes in F. J. Foakes Jackson and Kirsopp Lake, *The Beginnings of Christianity Part I The Acts of the Apostles.* III (1926), p.xxxvii.

tion, the pen being carried on to some extent from one character to another. The literary and non-literary scripts were sometimes used side by side, and their forms also varied a great deal from one period to another, occasionally almost approximating one another and again diverging widely. The appearance of any given manuscript depended, of course, largely upon the skill and neatness of the individual who wrote it, and at all times there was both poor writing and good.[48]

Since Paul's writings were genuine letters they were probably written originally in the non-literary script. The letters, however, were apparently dictated to Christian helpers who were practiced in the art of penmanship. This is shown in Romans 16:22, where the scribe interjects, "I Tertius, who write the letter, salute you in the Lord," and also is indicated by Paul's custom of adding the closing part of the letter in his own handwriting (II Thessalonians 3:17). In Galatians 6:11 Paul refers to his own writing as being with "large letters." Probably this means that as a man more accustomed to manual labor (cf. I Thessalonians 2:9; Acts 18:3) than to the fine art of penmanship, Paul made relatively large, stiff, square characters which contrasted with the flowing cursive script of his scribe. It may be presumed, therefore, that the main body of a Pauline letter was written originally in a relatively careful and practiced hand of the non-literary type. When the New Testament writings came to be regarded as literature, however, they were naturally copied in the literary bookhand. This style of handwriting developed into the handsome form which is found in the vellum codices and to which the term "uncial" is customarily applied. "Uncial characters" are mentioned by Jerome[49] (A.D. c.340-420) in connection with elegant manuscripts of his time, and since the Latin word *uncia* means "the twelfth part" it is thought that an uncial character may have been one occupying about one-twelfth of a line.[50] This would fit the case of Codex Sinaiticus, for example, where there are approximately twelve letters per line. The New Testament codices from the fourth to the ninth centuries were written in uncial characters.

The uncial style of writing was quite slow and cumbersome, however, and the need was felt for a script which could be written

[48] H. Idris Bell in EB XVII, p.97; Wilhelm Schubart, *Griechische Palaeographie* (in Walter Otto, ed., *Handbuch der Altertumswissenschaft.* I, iv, 1. 1925), p.19.
[49] *Preface to Job* (NPNFSS VI, p.492).
[50] Hatch, *The Principal Uncial Manuscripts of the New Testament*, p.22 n.5.

more easily and swiftly and yet be of sufficient legibility and beauty to be employed appropriately for literary and sacred writings. The rapid non-literary cursive script which we met with in Roman times had continued in use in various forms during the Byzantine Period (A.D. c.300-c.650) but did not have the dignity demanded by the Bible and works of literature. From it there was developed, however, a truly calligraphic script which could still be written at a relatively high speed. This is known as minuscule script and is characterized by smaller, differently formed letters, many of which are connected without the raising of the pen. Coming into use in the ninth century, the minuscule hand gradually superseded the uncial characters and thereafter was never supplanted but continued in use as long as books were copied by hand. Thus, numerically speaking, the great mass of New Testament manuscripts are minuscules.[51]

By careful study of these various styles of handwriting and the many intermediate changes of form which they underwent, paleographers are able to establish at least approximate dates for manuscripts upon the basis of the character of the writing which they display.[52]

PUNCTUATION

In the first century, manuscripts were usually written practically without punctuation and with the words following each other in an unbroken succession of letters, as if one should begin to copy Paul's Letter to the Romans in the English in this manner:

PAULASERVANTOFJESUSCHRISTCALLEDTO

BEANAPOSTLESEPARATEDUNTOTHEGOSPE

LOFGODWHICHHEPROMISEDAFORETHROU

GHHISPROPHETSINTHEHOLYSCRIPTURES

Those who were accustomed to such writing could read it rapidly, but even so the possibility of error and misunderstanding was present owing to the absence of punctuation and the lack of division between words. There was, therefore, a gradual increase in the employment of punctuation marks and other aids to the reader.

In the second century papyrus fragment of the Gospel According to John the words sometimes appear to be slightly separated, but there is still no punctuation, although a diaeresis is usually placed over the initial letter Iota. In the Chester Beatty Papyri of the Let-

---

[51] F. G. Kenyon, *Handbook to the Textual Criticism of the New Testament.* 2d ed. 1912, p.124.

[52] cf. Thompson, *An Introduction to Greek and Latin Palaeography,* pp.144-147.

127. Statuette of an Early Egyptian Scribe

128. Four Scribes with Pens and Rolls

129. Wildcat in a Papyrus Thicket

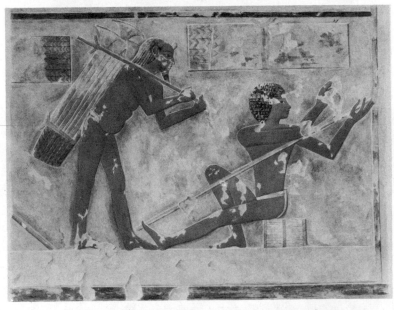

130. Gathering and Splitting Papyrus for Papermaking

131. Papyrus Roll before Opening

132. Papyrus Rolls Open and Sealed

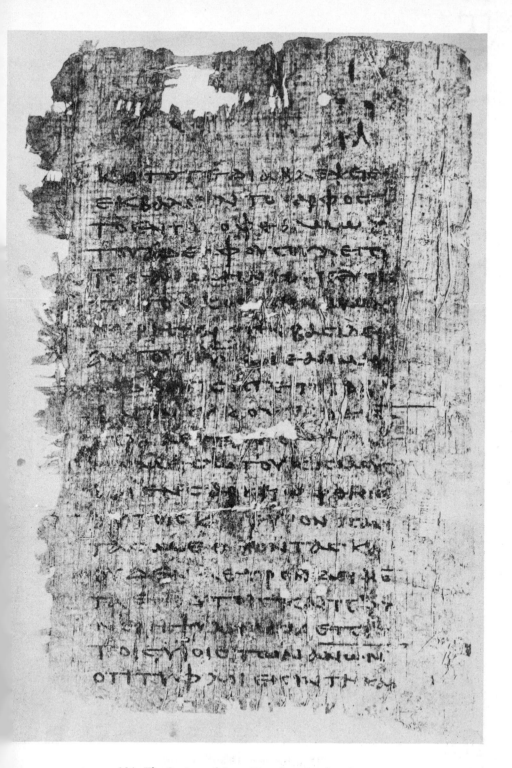

134. The Sayings of Jesus Found at Oxyrhynchus

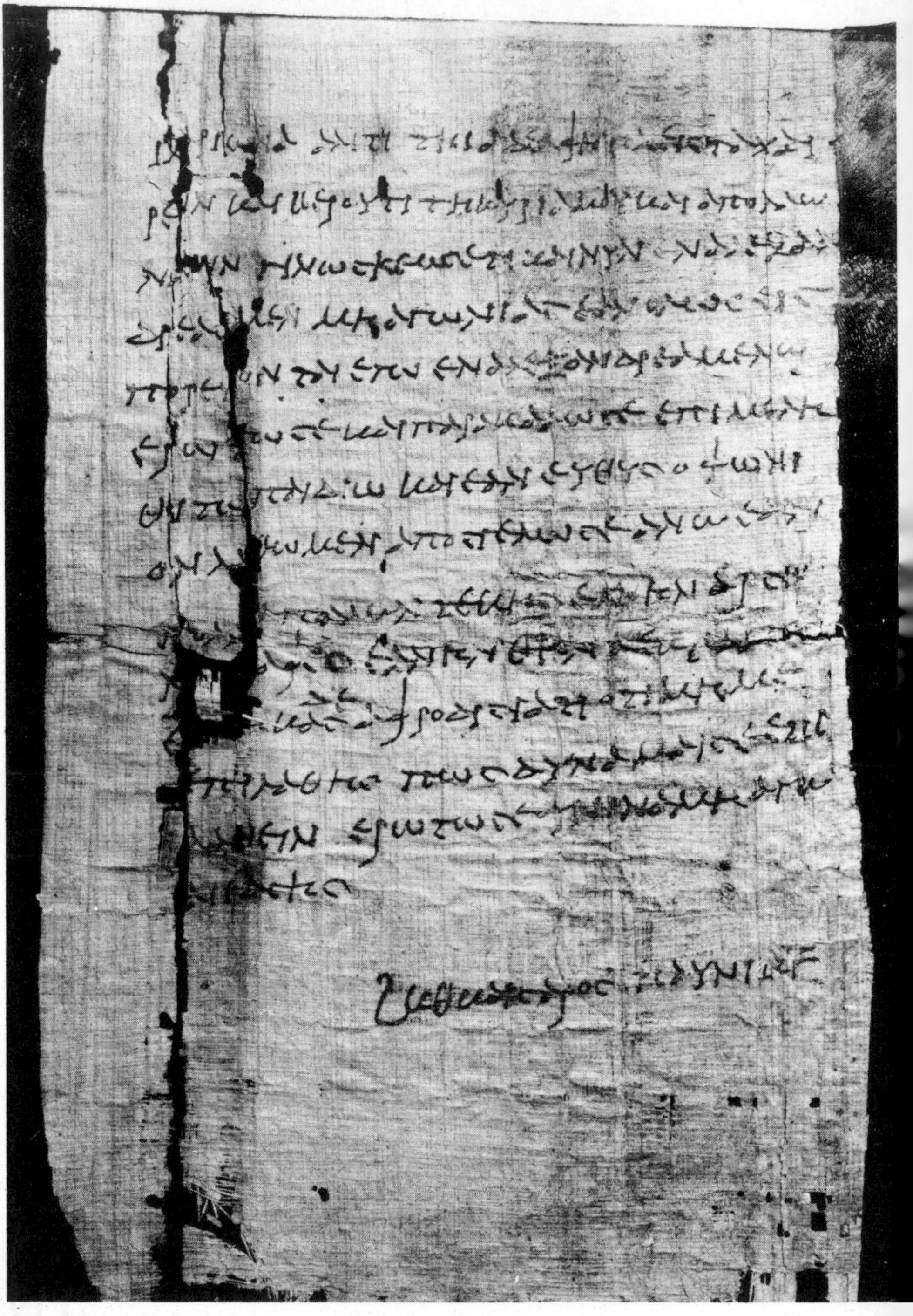

135. Letter from Hilarion to Alis

137. Letter from Irene to a Family in Mourning

136. Letter from Mystarion to Stotoëtis

139. Letter from a Prodigal Son to his Mother

139. Letter from an Avian to Epimachus

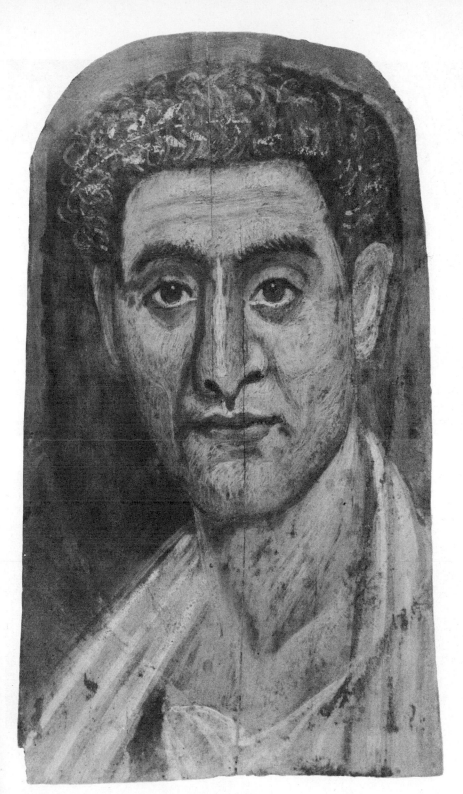

140. Portrait of Demetris

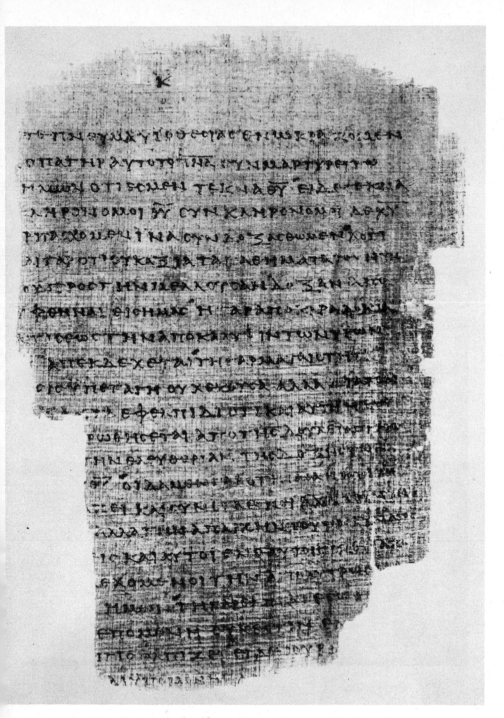

143. A Page from the Chester Beatty Papyrus of Paul's Letters

144 A Papyrus Fragment with the Opening of Paul's Letter to the Romans

145. The First Page of the Letter to the Romans in Codex Vaticanus

116. The Monastery of Saint Catherine at Mount Sinai

147. The Appearance of Codex Sinaiticus before Binding

148. The First Page of the Letter to the Romans in Codex Sinaiticus

149. The First Page of the Letter to the Romans in Codex Alexandrinus

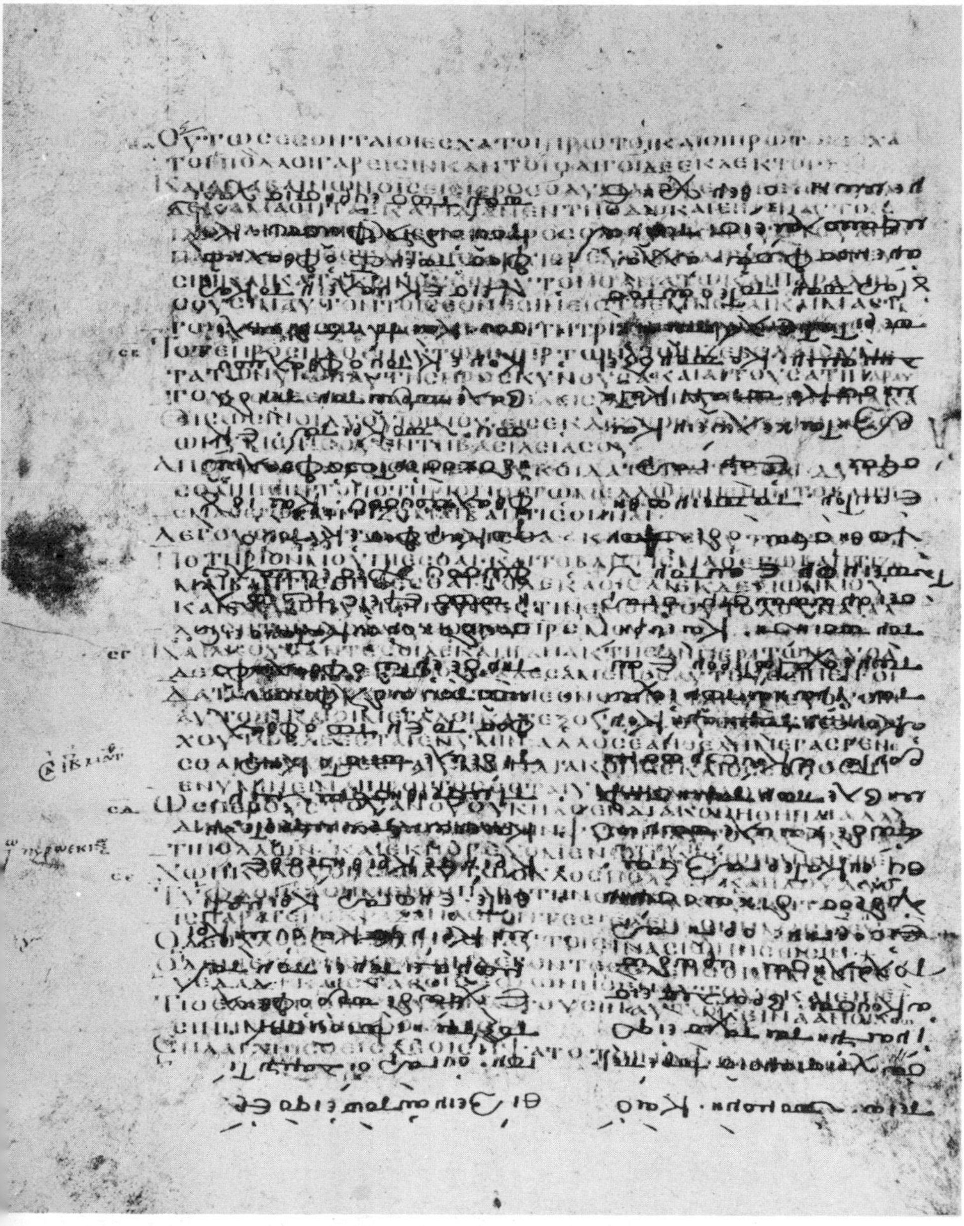

150. A Page in Codex Ephraemi Rescriptus

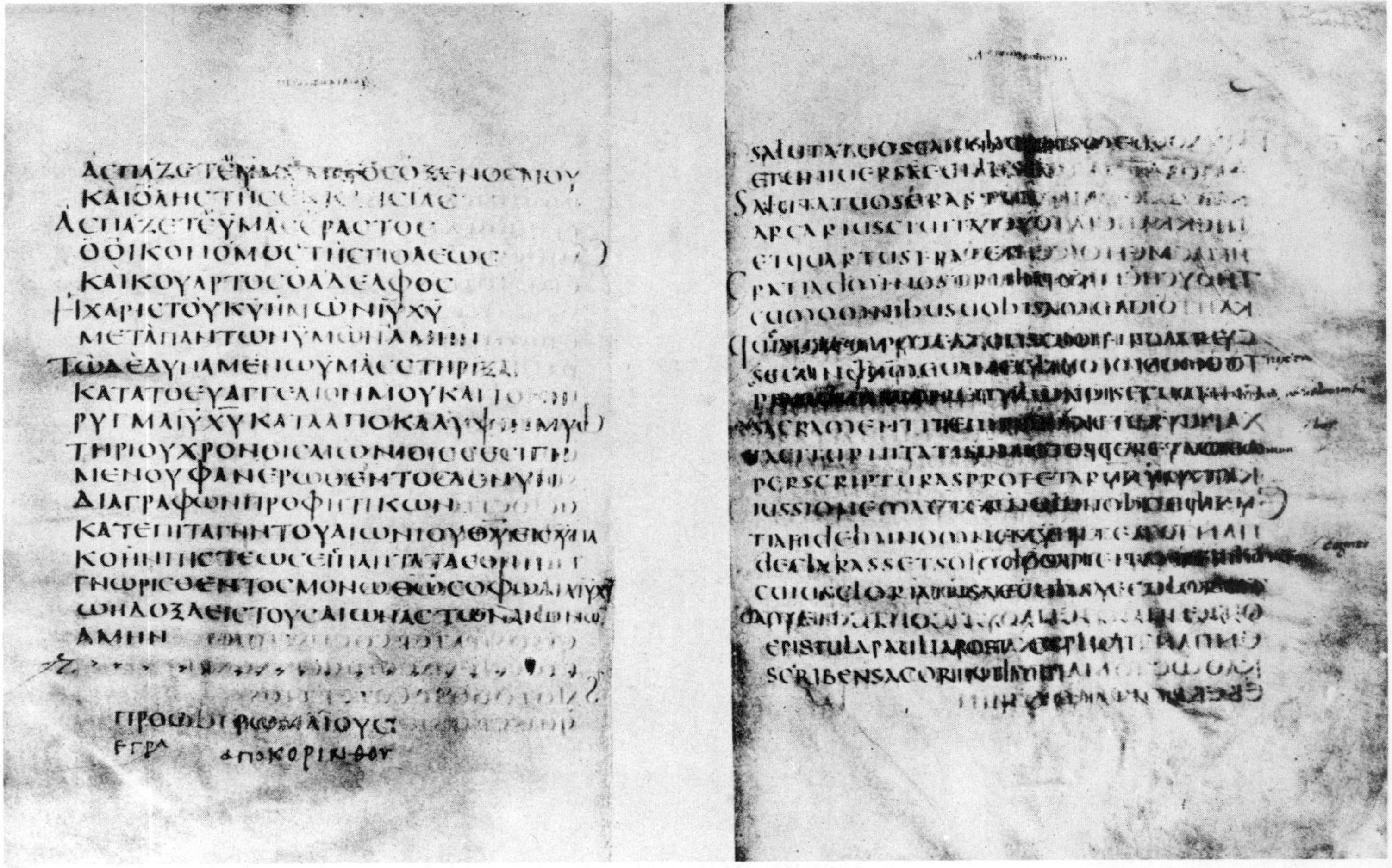

151 A Double Page in Codex Claromontanus

+ ΠΡΟΣ ΡΩΜΑΙΟΥΣ +

152. The First Page of Romans in a Minuscule Manuscript Written in A.D. 1045

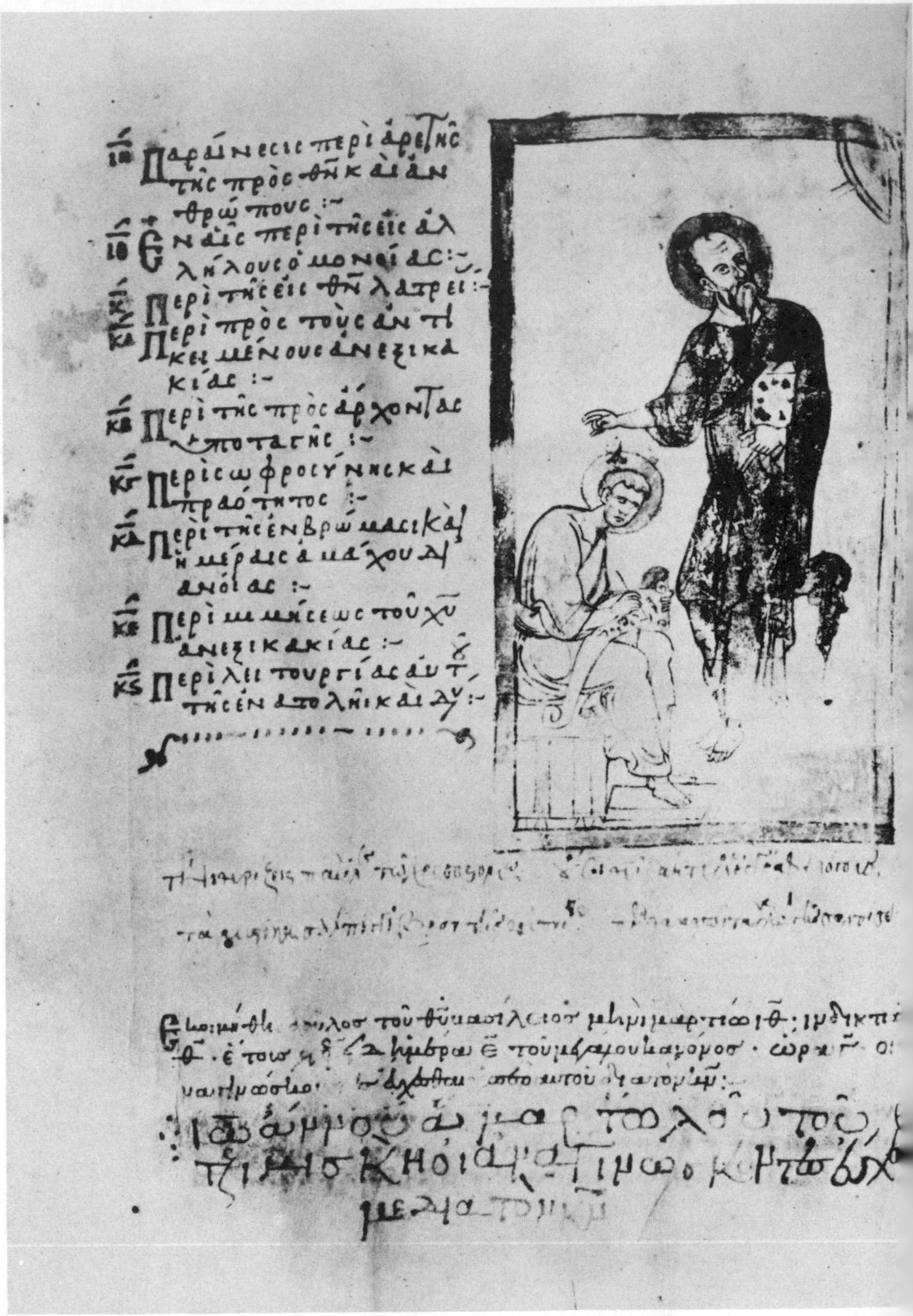

153. An Illustration in the Minuscule Manuscript of A.D. 1045

ters of Paul there are occasional slight intervals between words to mark pauses in sense, initial Iota and Upsilon are marked with a diaeresis, and Greek breathings and accents are employed. Also a single point is occasionally used to mark a division in the text. Such use of a point or dot became more frequent in later centuries and high, middle and low points were differentiated to indicate respectively what would now be signified by a period, a comma and a semicolon. Eventually a comma proper, a colon, and a question mark written like a modern semicolon, as well as some other marks came to be employed.

Brief headings to the various books are found as early as the Chester Beatty Papyri of Paul's Letters, where there are also subscriptions giving the number of stichoi (στίχοι) contained, the latter being syllable lines of a standard number of syllables.[53] Later the superscriptions and subscriptions of the New Testament books were expanded to contain more data of a traditional character concerning their origin.

The convenience of the readers was served further by the development of systems of chapter division. The oldest such system known to us is that which is employed in Codex Vaticanus where the Gospels are divided into a large number of sections and where the chapters into which Paul's letters are divided are numbered continuously throughout as if all the letters formed one book. In Codex Alexandrinus there are chapters (κεφάλαια) with summary headings (τίτλοι) describing their contents.[54] On the basis of earlier work by Ammonius of Alexandria, Eusebius of Caesarea divided the Gospels into sections (the "Ammonian Sections") and prepared tables (the "Eusebian Canons") of parallel and independent passages,[55] while the so-called "Euthalian Apparatus" supplied tables of chapters, tables of Old Testament quotations and other introductory materials for Acts and the Epistles.[56] The system of chapter divisions now found in the New Testament was the work of Cardinal Hugo de S. Caro in 1238, while the modern verses were introduced by Robert Étienne (Stephanus) in 1551.

[53] J. Rendel Harris, *Stichometry*. 1893; and in NSH XI, pp.91-94.
[54] Kirsopp Lake, *The Text of the New Testament*. 6th ed. rev. by Silva New, 1928, pp.55f.
[55] These tables as well as the letter of Eusebius to Carpian in which he describes the plan of his work are printed regularly in the preface to Nestle's *Novum Testamentum Graece*. 16th ed. 1936.
[56] Ernst von Dobschütz in NSH IV, p.215.

NOMINA SACRA

Another interesting feature of the biblical manuscripts is the employment of abbreviations for the sacred names (*nomina sacra*) and for certain other words. Instead of writing in full the word Lord (κύριος), for example, the scribe would save time and space by writing only the first and last letters and drawing a line above them thus $\overline{\text{KC}}$. Similarly the word God (θεός) was contracted to $\overline{\text{ΘC}}$, Jesus (Ἰησοῦς) was written as $\overline{\text{IC}}$, or sometimes as $\overline{\text{IHC}}$ or $\overline{\text{IH}}$, and Christ (Χριστός) appeared as $\overline{\text{XC}}$ or $\overline{\text{XPC}}$. Among other words which were abbreviated were Father (πατήρ)—$\overline{\text{ΠP}}$ or $\overline{\text{ΠHP}}$; Son (υἱός)—$\overline{\text{YC}}$; Spirit (πνεῦμα)—$\overline{\text{ΠNA}}$; man (ἄνθρωπος)—$\overline{\text{ANC}}$ or $\overline{\text{ANOC}}$; and cross (σταυρός) —$\overline{\text{CTC}}$, $\overline{\text{CPC}}$ or $\overline{\text{CTPC}}$.

Such abbreviations appear in the fragments of an unknown Gospel dating probably around the middle of the second century A.D. (p.325), in the Chester Beatty Papyri of Paul's Letters belonging to around A.D. 200 (p. 334), and in many other manuscripts down to the latest times.[57] It is probable that the practice of making contractions of this type was borrowed by the Christians from the Jews. When the Jews translated the Tetragrammaton YHWH into Greek they represented the holy name by Lord or God, written in the abbreviated form $\overline{\text{KC}}$ or $\overline{\text{ΘC}}$. The Christians naturally adopted this practice and extended it to the specifically Christian names and to other words as well.[58]

[57] Gregory, *Canon and Text of the New Testament*, p.335. No sacred names appear on the tiny second century fragment of the Gospel According to John (p.312; Fig. 133), so it cannot be told whether abbreviations were employed in this manuscript. The earliest literary attestation of the abbreviation IH for the name of Jesus appears around A.D. 130 in the *Letter of Barnabas* (9 [ANF I, p.143]).

[58] Ludwig Traube, *Nomina Sacra, Versuch einer Geschichte der christlichen Kürzung.* 1907, p.31. Gunnar Rudberg (in *Skrifter utgifna af Kungl. Humanistiska Vetenskaps-Samfundet i Uppsala.* 17 [1915], No. 3) proposes the less plausible theory that the practice was taken over from the use of short forms of the names of the Roman emperors.

2. THE MODERN DISCOVERY
OF ANCIENT PAPYRI

Now we may turn to the story of the actual recovery of ancient manuscripts, and first of all those written on papyrus. The first papyri to reach Europe, so far as is known, were one Greek and two Latin fragments which were given to the library at Basel about the end of the sixteenth century by the theologian Johann Jakob Grynaeus. In 1752 the charred remains of a library of Greek philosophical works were found in the ruins of Herculaneum, and in 1778 an unknown European dealer in antiquities purchased a papyrus roll from Egyptian peasants, who had already burned 50 other ancient rolls because they enjoyed the aromatic odor![1] Since that first discovery, Egypt has proved to be an almost inexhaustible storehouse of ancient papyri. In its dry climate and buried beneath its drifted sands the fragile papyri have resisted the ravages of time as effectively, and endured as indestructibly, as the pyramids.

During the nineteenth century an increasing number of papyri found their way to the museums of Europe, as the *fellahin* of Egypt awakened to the fact that they could obtain money for these ancient fragments. Many papyri were found accidentally by natives digging in the ancient mounds for *sebakh,* or nitrous earth which is used for fertilizer. Others were unearthed by Egyptian antique dealers and also by illicit plunderers. In 1877 a great mass of papyri was discovered in the site of Arsinoë, which earlier was Crocodilopolis, in the Fayum, but probably half of it was lost through the carelessness of the natives.[2]

Before the end of the nineteenth century, however, the Fayum became the scene of truly scientific and highly rewarding work in the recovery of papyri. This district, in which such important finds have been made, is a sunken oasis in the Libyan desert west of the Nile, its capital, Medinet el-Fayum, being about 80 miles south-southwest of Cairo. In ancient times the famous Lake of Moeris[3] occupied a large part of this depression and still is represented by the Birket Qarun. The Egyptian name for this lake was *Shei,* "the lake," and

[1] Deissmann, *Licht vom Osten,* p.23; Ulrich Wilcken, *Die griechischen Papyrusurkunden,* p.10.

[2] James Baikie, *Egyptian Papyri and Papyrus Hunting.* 1925, pp.230f.

[3] Herodotus. II, 149; Strabo, *Geography.* XVII, i, 35.

later *Piom*, "the sea," whence the name Fayum is derived. The capital and most important city of the district was situated on this lake, and was a center of worship of the crocodile god, Sebek. The city was known to the Greeks as Crocodilopolis, or Arsinoë,[4] and its ruins are represented by mounds north of the present capital, Medinet el-Fayum. There were other towns and villages in the district, and just south of the oasis was the important city of Oxyrhynchus, the modern Behnesa. It was only about ten miles from the Nile, and on the chief canal (Bahr Yusef) which brought water to the Fayum. In ancient times Oxyrhynchus was the capital of the Oxyrhynchite nome, and in the fourth and fifth centuries A.D. was famous for the number of its churches and monasteries, Christianity apparently having found a place there at a relatively early date.

In the winter of 1889-1890, Professor Flinders Petrie excavated a Ptolemaic cemetery at Gurob, near the mouth of the Fayum, and found a quantity of papyrus manuscripts which had been used as cartonnage in making the inner coffins of mummies. Professor Petrie, of course, fully realized the value of such finds and patiently recovered from their unusual place of preservation all the papyri possible. Then, in the winter of 1895-1896, the Egypt Exploration Fund sent out under the leadership of Drs. B. P. Grenfell, A. S. Hunt and D. G. Hogarth the first expedition definitely undertaken for the discovery of papyri. The work which was done that year, and continued by Grenfell and Hunt during a number of subsequent seasons, was amazingly successful.[5]

At Tebtunis papyri were found in a resting place even stranger than the human mummy cases at Gurob. Here, there was a crocodile cemetery in which sacred crocodiles had been buried ceremonially. One after another of the mummified crocodiles was turned up, until finally a workman, who was hoping for far better finds, in disgust smashed one of the burials in pieces. It broke open, revealing that the crocodile had been wrapped in the same kind of papyrus cartonnage as the Gurob mummies, and in several instances papyrus rolls were found stuffed into the animals' mouths or other cavities in their bodies.

THE OXYRHYNCHUS SAYINGS OF JESUS

Of all the sites, however, Oxyrhynchus was the most rewarding.

[4] Strabo, *Geography*. XVII, i, 38.
[5] Grenfell, Hunt and Hogarth, *Fayum Towns and Their Papyri*. 1900.

On January 11, 1897, Grenfell and Hunt began to dig in the rubbish mounds of the ancient town which had stood at this place, and on the second day unearthed a tattered papyrus leaf, nearly four by six inches in size, of which the verso is shown in Fig. 134.[6] In the upper right-hand corner of the verso was a numeral which was clearly a page number and showed that this leaf had been a part of a papyrus codex. In the case of this particular leaf the verso had been uppermost in the codex. The first indication of the character of the contents of the leaf came with the recognition of the word κάρφος, or "mote," which at once reminded Dr. Hunt of Jesus' saying concerning the mote and the beam (Matthew 7:3-5 = Luke 6:41f.). When the entire fragment was read it was found that it actually did contain a series of sayings of Jesus as follows:

". . . and then shalt thou see clearly to cast out the mote that is in thy brother's eye.

"Jesus saith, Except ye fast to the world, ye shall in no wise find the kingdom of God; and except you make the sabbath a real sabbath, ye shall not see the Father.

"Jesus saith, I stood in the midst of the world, and in the flesh was I seen of them, and I found all men drunken, and none found I athirst among them, and my soul grieveth over the sons of men, because they are blind in their heart, and see not.

". . . poverty.

"[Jesus saith,] Wherever there are two, they are not without God, and wherever there is one alone, I say, I am with him. Raise the stone, and there thou shalt find me, cleave the wood, and there am I.

"Jesus saith, A prophet is not acceptable in his own country, neither doth a physician work cures upon them that know him.

"Jesus saith, A city built upon the top of a high hill and established, can neither fall nor be hid.

"Jesus saith, Thou hearest with one ear [but the other ear thou hast closed]."

This papyrus is probably to be dated in the third century A.D., and shows the kind of collection of Jesus' sayings that was being read by Christians in Egypt at that time. A second fragment containing sayings of Jesus was found by Grenfell and Hunt at Oxyrhynchus in 1903.[7] It was a piece of a papyrus roll, which was probably written slightly later in the third century than the fragment first found. In it the words of Jesus have lost yet more of their

[6] Grenfell and Hunt, *Sayings of Our Lord.* 1897.
[7] Grenfell, L. W. Drexel and Hunt, *New Sayings of Jesus and Fragment of a Lost Gospel.* 1904.

original freshness and simplicity, and have taken on still more of the complexity of the later age.

All together, Grenfell and Hunt recovered from the sands of Egypt many thousands of manuscripts and fragments of papyrus, while other workers who followed them have made many important additions to the vast mass of material now available for papyrological research.

OTHER EARLY CHRISTIAN PAPYRI

Among the more recent discoveries of early Christian papyri, aside from the papyri of Paul's letters which will be described later (pp. 332-339), may be mentioned a fragment of a Testimony book and some portions of an unknown Gospel. Not long after the finding of the fragment of the Gospel According to John in the John Rylands Library (p. 312), there was discovered in a large group of papyri which had been purchased for the same library by Dr. J. Rendel Harris in 1917, a part of a double leaf of a papyrus codex, written in a hand of probably the fourth century, and containing verses from different parts of the Septuagint.[8] Two other fragments belonging to the same codex are in Oslo. The Old Testament texts used include portions of the "Messianic" passages in the fifty-second and fifty-third chapters of Isaiah, and in general are such as could be applied to Christ and Christianity.[9] It is believed, therefore, that the work represented by these surviving fragments originally comprised a collection of "prophetic" passages from the Old Testament which could be used as witnesses to the truth of Christianity.[10]

The fragments of an unknown Gospel were found in a collection

---

[8] C. H. Roberts, *Two Biblical Papyri in the John Rylands Library*, Manchester. 1936, pp.47-62.

[9] The combined texts contain quotations from the following verses: Isaiah 42:3f.; 66:18f.; 52:15; 53:1-3, 6f., 11f.; Genesis 26:13f.; II Chronicles 1:12; Deuteronomy 29:8 (9), 11 (12).

[10] Such works are otherwise known, as for example in the collection of *Testimonies against the Jews* made by Cyprian about A.D. 248, and consisting of extensive quotations from the Old Testament arranged under various headings (*Treatise*. XII. ANF V, pp.507-557). J. Rendel Harris even believed that such an assemblage of "testimonies" directed against the Jews was the first Christian book to be written and that its influence could be traced throughout the New Testament as well as in the church fathers (J. R. Harris and V. Burch, *Testimonies*. 2 vols. 1916-20; cf. D. Plooij in *Verhandelingen der Koninklijke Akademie van Wetenschappen te Amsterdam, Afdeeling Letterkunde, Nieuwe Reeks Deel*. XXXII, 2 [1932]). This remains only a hypothesis, as far as deriving proof from the new discovery is concerned, since the Testimony papyrus is late in date and not evidently polemical in character.

of papyri purchased from a dealer around 1935.[11] The pieces in question are two imperfect leaves and a scrap of a third from a papyrus codex dating probably not later than the middle of the second century. They contain an account of four different incidents, a dispute between Christ and the rulers of the people who attempt to stone him, the healing of a leper, a question about paying dues to kings, and a miracle of some sort on the bank of the Jordan. The first and last of these episodes are not recorded in the canonical Gospels, but the other two are clearly the same as happenings narrated in the Synoptic Gospels. On the whole, however, the language of these papyri is far more akin to that of the Gospel According to John than to that of the Synoptic Gospels. It is believed, therefore, that the unknown Gospel of which these portions still exist, was written by an early second century author who was well acquainted with the Gospel According to John and perhaps also knew one or more of the Synoptic Gospels, but who also had access to other sources now lost. It may be noted that the writer employed abbreviations for Lord ($\overline{KC}$), God ($\overline{\Theta C}$), Jesus ($\overline{IH}$), prophets ($\overline{\Pi PO\Phi AC}$ for προφήτας) and some other words.

EARLY PAPYRUS LETTERS

Since it is our purpose to pay particular attention to manuscripts of the letters of Paul, it will be of special interest to notice the numerous pagan letters on papyrus which we have from years not far distant from the time when Paul's letters were penned. On June 17, 1 B.C., an Egyptian laborer Hilarion, who had gone to Alexandria to work, wrote a short letter to his wife Alis, who had remained at home in Oxyrhynchus. The letter (Fig. 135) sounds amazingly modern at most points, yet reflects the pagan custom of exposure of children. It reads:

"Hilarion to Alis his sister, heartiest greetings, and to my lady Berous and to Apollonarion. Know that we are still even now in Alexandria. Do not worry if when all the others return I remain in Alexandria. I beg and beseech of you to take care of the little child. And as soon as we receive wages I will send them to you. If—good luck to you!—you bear a child,

[11] H. Idris Bell and T. C. Skeat, *Fragments of an Unknown Gospel and Other Early Christian Papyri.* 1935, pp.1-41; H. Idris Bell, *Recent Discoveries of Biblical Papyri.* 1937, pp.17-20.

if it is a boy, let it live; if it is a girl, expose it. You told Aphrodisias, 'Do not forget me.' How can I forget you? I beg you, therefore, not to worry."[12]

At the bottom is the date, "In the 29th year of Caesar, Pauni 23," corresponding to June 17, 1 B.C.,[13] and on the back side is the address: "Hilarion to Alis, deliver." The greeting of Alis as "sister" may be only a tender form of address but perhaps is to be taken literally since marriages of brother and sister were not uncommon in Egypt. Berous, who is courteously called "lady"[14] may have been the mother of Alis, and Apollonarion perhaps was the child of Alis and Hilarion. On the whole the letter is written rather crudely and contains a number of grammatical errors, such as the use of the accusative when the dative is required,[15] which are not shown in the translation above.

On September 13, A.D. 50, an Egyptian olive planter named Mystarion sent a letter (Fig. 136) to a chief priest named Stotoëtis in order to introduce a certain Blastus who was to perform an errand and return quickly:

"Mystarion to his own Stotoëtis many greetings. I have sent unto you[16] my Blastus for forked sticks for my olive-gardens. See then that you do not stay him. For you know how I need him every hour.

"Farewell

"In the year 11 of Tiberius Claudius Caesar Augustus Germanicus Imperator in the month Sebastos 15."[17]

The address was written on the back: "To Stotoëtis, chief priest, at the island. . . ." This note was penned at the very time when the first of Paul's letters were being written and is an example of letters of introduction such as Paul himself mentions and writes (I Corinthians 16:3; II Corinthians 3:1; Romans 16:1). But the letter of Mystarion is of special interest because the closing "Farewell" and the lengthy date are written in a hand different from the careful scribal hand in which the body of the letter and the address on the back are penned. Evidently Mystarion himself took the pen

[12] Grenfell and Hunt, The Oxyrhynchus Papyri. (1898-) IV, No. 744; Wilhelm Schubart, Ein Jahrtausend am Nil. 2d ed. 1923, pp.65f.
[13] For the months see the table in George Milligan, Selections from the Greek Papyri. 1910, p.xviii.
[14] The same polite form of address is found in II John 1 and 5.
[15] In line 8 of the Greek text.
[16] The grammar is exactly the same as in I Corinthians 4:17 and similar passages.
[17] Fritz Krebs, Ägyptische Urkunden aus den Königlichen Museen zu Berlin, Griechische Urkunden. I, No.37.

at the close to add a final personal touch, just as Paul said he did in every letter (II Thessalonians 3:17; cf. Galatians 6:11; I Corinthians 16:21; Colossians 4:18).

The timeless woes of human life are reflected poignantly in a tiny[18] second century letter (Fig. 137) from Irene to Philo and Taonnophris, a married couple who have lost a son in death. Irene, who is evidently a friend of the sorrowing mother (since the latter is named before the father in the salutation), and who has already gone through the experience of losing her own loved one Didymas, writes to the bereaved parents as follows:

"Irene to Taonnophris and Philo, good cheer.
"I am as much in grief and weep over the blessed one as I wept for Didymas. And everything that was fitting I did and so did all of mine, Epaphroditus and Thermuthion and Philion and Apollonius and Plantas. But truly there is nothing anyone can do in the face of such things. Do you therefore comfort one another.
"Farewell. Athyr 1."[19]

The letter is addressed on the back, "To Taonnophris and Philo."[20]

In the second century a young man named Apion from the small Egyptian town of Philadelphia in the Fayum entered the Roman navy and sailed to Misenum, the naval harbor near Naples. When the voyage became stormy and dangerous Apion was in peril but he prayed to the lord Serapis and was delivered. Upon reaching port he received three pieces of gold as pay, was given a new Roman name, Antonis Maximus, in keeping with his new Roman service, and was assigned to the company Athenonica. Like a modern youth in the service he had his picture made in his new uniform to send home, and then he wrote the following letter (Fig. 138) to his father:

"Apion to Epimachus his father and lord, many greetings. Before all things I pray that you are in health and that you prosper and fare well continually together with my sister and her daughter and my brother. I thank the lord Serapis that, when I was in peril in the sea, he saved me immediately. When I came to Miseni[21] I received as journey-money from the Caesar three pieces of gold. And it is well with me. I beseech you therefore, my lord father, to write me a little letter, firstly of your health,

[18] The actual size of the papyrus is about three inches square.
[19] The date is equivalent to October 28.
[20] *Oxyrhynchus Papyri*. I, No.115; Milligan, *Selections from the Greek Papyri*, pp.95f.
[21] This is the plural form of the name of the harbor generally called Misenum.

secondly of that of my brother and sister, thirdly that I may look upon your handwriting with reverence, because you have taught me well and I therefore hope to advance rapidly, if the gods will. Salute Capito much and my brother and sister and Serenilla and my friends. I am sending you by Euctemon a little picture of me. Moreover my name is Antonis[22] Maximus. Fare you well, I pray.

"Centuria Athenonica."[23]

The companions of Apion wanted him to include their greetings and since there still was room along the side of the papyrus sheet Apion added: "There salute you Serenus the son of Agathus Daemon, and . . . the son of . . . and Turbo the son of Gallonius and D . . . nas the son of. . . ." The letter was to go by military post to the garrison of the Apamenians in Egypt and through the office of the paymaster of that company be forwarded to the father. This address was written on the back, "To Philadelphia for Epimachus from Apion his son," with the instruction, "Give this to the first cohort of the Apamenians to Julianus . . . the Liblarios, from Apion so that he may send it to Epimachus his father." The lines of address and instruction were divided in the middle by two heavy X-marks which indicate the place for tying up the letter.

Not only does the letter of Apion sound as if it could have been written in the twentieth century instead of the second, but it contains a number of expressions similar to ones found in New Testament letters. "I pray that you are in health" is the same polite and standard formula of greeting that appears in III John 2. Apion's word of thanks to the lord Serapis, the Egyptian god whose worship was widespread throughout the Roman Empire, reminds one of Paul's almost constant habit of beginning his letters with thanks to God (I Thessalonians 1:2; II Thessalonians 1:3; I Corinthians 1:4; Romans 1:8; Philippians 1:3; Colossians 1:3; Philemon 4; cf. Ephesians 1:3,16). The phrase "in peril in the sea" is nearly identical with Paul's words in II Corinthians 11:26, although the Roman soldier's grammar is not quite as excellent as Paul's. Likewise "Salute Capito much" is very similar to the form of greeting in I Corinthians 16:19.

Interestingly enough we have a second letter from the same Apion

[22] Antonis is a short form of the name Antonius.
[23] Paul Viereck, *Ägyptische Urkunden aus den Königlichen Museen zu Berlin.* II, No. 423.

to his sister, written probably years later when his father was dead and he himself had children of his own.

Also filled with human interest is another second century letter, which a prodigal son wrote to his mother (Fig. 139). Addressed on the back, "To . . . his mother from Antonius Longus her son," the pathetic epistle reads:

"Antonis Longus to Nilus his mother many greetings. Continually I pray for your health. Supplication on your behalf I direct each day to the lord Serapis. I wish you to know that I had no hope that you would come up to the metropolis. On this account neither did I enter into the city. But I was ashamed to come to Karanis,[24] because I am going about in rags. I write to you that I am naked. I beseech you, mother, be reconciled to me. But I know what I have brought upon myself. Punished I have been every way. I know that I have sinned. I hear from Postumus[25] who met you in the Arsinoïte nome, and unseasonably related all to you. Do you not know that I would rather be a cripple than be conscious that I am still owing anyone an obol? . . . come yourself . . . I have heard that . . . I beseech you . . . I almost . . . I beseech you . . . I will . . . not . . . do otherwise."[26]

Not only is the grammar here similar to that of the New Testament at several points, including the expressions, "I wish you to know" (cf. Philippians 1:12) and "I beseech you" (Philemon 10, etc.), but the youth himself was almost a living example of the lost son in the parable told by Jesus.

Many other letters and documents of all sorts could be cited from these very same times, including a letter saying "Do not lose heart about the rent, for you will certainly get it,"[27] a letter regarding funeral expenses, a boy's letter, an invitation to dinner, a public notice, a contract of apprenticeship, a report of a lawsuit, a marriage contract, a deed of divorce, a deed of adoption, a warrant for arrest, a tax receipt, a census return, a lease of a perfumery business, a will, a magical incantation and many others.[28] But already it is clear that the papyri have cast a flood of light upon the daily and amaz-

---

[24] A village in the Fayum, and probably the home of the writer.

[25] The reading of the name is not certain.

[26] Krebs, *Ägyptische Urkunden aus den Königlichen Museen zu Berlin.* III, No. 846; Milligan, *Selections from the Greek Papyri*, pp.93-95.

[27] C. M. Cobern, *The New Archaeological Discoveries and their Bearing upon the New Testament and upon the Life and Times of the Primitive Church.* 9th ed. 1929, pp.93f.

[28] See Milligan, *Selections from the Greek Papyri*; A. S. Hunt and C. C. Edgar, *Select Papyri.* 2 vols. LCL (1932-34); E. J. Goodspeed and E. C. Colwell, *A Greek Papyrus Reader.* 1935.

ingly modern life of the ancient world, as well as affording the possibility of a new understanding of the writings of the New Testament.

The longer papyrus letters generally have an opening address or greeting, a thanksgiving and prayer, special contents, and closing salutations and valediction. These are exactly the main features which in a more elaborate form are found in the letters of Paul.[29] Even more important is the fact that the language of the papyri is similar to that of the New Testament. Both the grammar and the vocabulary of the New Testament are strikingly different from classical Greek. Out of approximately 5,000 words in the vocabulary of the Greek New Testament, more than 500 formerly had to be classified as "biblical" words since they were unknown except in the Bible,[30] and the language was regarded by some as standing quite by itself as "New Testament Greek." Others tried to explain it as "Hebraic Greek," while one German scholar even called it "a language of the Holy Ghost."[31] A new understanding of its character was found by Adolf Deissmann, then Privatdozent at Marburg and later Professor of New Testament at *Friedrich-Wilhelms-Universität* at Berlin. When looking at a volume in the University Library at Heidelberg, containing transcripts from the papyrological collections at Berlin, he suddenly recognized that the Greek which he was reading was similar to that with which he was familiar in the New Testament. This proved to be a clue to the solution of the problem, and now it is widely recognized that the language in which the New Testament was written was not the formal language of literature, in which an attempt was made to imitate the classical authors of the past, nor a special kind of "biblical" language, but rather the non-literary language of everyday life, the *Koine* or Common Greek, which was spoken by the ordinary men and women of the Greco-Roman world. The New Testament was written, not in the language of books, but in the language of life, and it spoke with bold and unpretending vigor directly to the life of its day. The knowledge that

[29] G. Milligan, *The New Testament Documents, their Origin and Early History.* 1913, p.93.
[30] Deissmann, *Licht vom Osten*, p.60.
[31] R. Rothe, *Zur Dogmatik.* 1863, p.238, quoted by J. H. Moulton and G. Milligan, *The Vocabulary of the Greek Testament Illustrated from the Papyri and Other Non-literary Sources.* 1930, p.xi.

this was so makes possible a translation that speaks with the same straightforward simplicity and effectiveness to our day.[32]

In connection with the intimate glimpses afforded by the papyri into the daily life of the first centuries A.D., it may be noted that we also possess many excellent portraits of the people of that time. Like the papyri, these, too, come largely from the Fayum. As we have seen (p. 101), it was the custom in ancient Egypt to place a portrait mask over the face of the mummy, and under the influence of this practice the Greek settlers in Egypt were in the habit of having portraits painted from life and then upon death bound over the face of the mummy. Many of these paintings have been found from Roman times when they were executed with a high degree of technical skill. It is evident that they are realistic portraits, and give a vivid representation of actual features and character.[33] The painting reproduced in Fig. 140 shows the portrait of a certain Demetris, which was painted when he was about 50 years of age and then placed on his mummy when he died at the age of 89. The painting dates probably from the first half of the second century A.D. The portrait of a young woman shown in Fig. 141 probably comes also from the second century, and the painting of a small child, the daughter of a woman named Aline, reproduced in Fig. 142 dates from around A.D. 100. Not far different from these must have been the people of Paul's own day.

[32] E. J. Goodspeed, Preface to *The New Testament, An American Translation*. 1923.
[33] W. M. F. Petrie, *The Hawara Portfolio: Paintings of the Roman Age*. 1913; John D. Cooney, *Late Egyptian and Coptic Art, An Introduction to the Collections in the Brooklyn Museum*. 1943, p.8.

3. MANUSCRIPTS OF PAUL'S LETTERS

IT IS our purpose now to turn to Paul's Letter to the Romans and to follow it through some of the most important copies in which it has been transmitted across the centuries. The original copy doubtless was dictated by the apostle to a scribe who penned it upon a roll of papyrus in a careful non-literary hand, while Paul himself may have added a personal note in his own handwriting. When the letter was completed it must have been carried by messenger to Rome and there read many times in Christian gatherings. Eventually the autograph copy wore out and, like all the other originals of the New Testament writings, is now lost to us. But before this happened the Roman church made another copy of the letter, while yet more copies may have been made for other churches or Christians who wished to have them. Before the end of the first century all of Paul's letters were brought together (p. 305) and from that time on they were regularly copied as a collection.

THE CHESTER BEATTY PAPYRUS OF PAUL'S LETTERS

Our oldest copy of Paul's letters has been discovered only recently. It is a papyrus codex found in a group of papyrus manuscripts, the existence of which first became known in 1931. The entire assemblage comprises no less than eleven codices, which date from the second to the fourth century and presumably represent the library of some early Christian church. The codices contain parts of nine Old Testament and fifteen New Testament books as well as the Book of Enoch and a homily by Melito of Sardis. They were found and marketed by native diggers and dealers in Egypt and the greater part of the collection was purchased by Mr. A. Chester Beatty of London while some portions of it were acquired by the University of Michigan and other individuals.

The part of the entire collection with which we are concerned here is a codex of the letters of Paul, to which E. von Dobschütz has given the number $\mathfrak{p}^{46}$, and which is dated by U. Wilcken around A.D. 200.[1] We now have, therefore, a copy of Paul's letters which is 150 years older than the oldest manuscript known hitherto, and one which is removed from the time of the origin of the Pauline collection by little more than a century, and from the time of the composition of the originals by 150 years in round numbers.

[1] *Archiv für Papyrusforschung.* 11 (1935), p.113.

Eighty-six leaves of this notable codex survive, of which 30 belong to the University of Michigan[2] and the remainder to Mr. A. Chester Beatty.[3] Seven leaves are missing at the beginning, which implies that an equal number are lost at the end, while four other leaves near the beginning and end also are missing. Thus the original codex must have consisted of 104 leaves. It was formed by laying 52 sheets of papyrus one upon another, each having the recto side uppermost, and then folding the entire stack in the middle.[4] None of the extant leaves is preserved perfectly, but most of them have lost only a few lines at the bottom. The maximum size of the present leaves is approximately 9 by 6 inches, and the original column of writing was normally around 8 inches high by 4¾ inches wide.

The codex contains the letters of Paul in the following order: Romans, Hebrews, I and II Corinthians, Ephesians, Galatians, Philippians, Colossians, I Thessalonians. The last leaf which is extant contains the conclusion of I Thessalonians, but, as was pointed out just above, seven leaves have been lost from the end of the codex. Of these the first two doubtless contained II Thessalonians, with which book the codex seems to have closed. It is believed that the remaining five leaves were left blank, for ten more leaves instead of five would have been required if I and II Timothy, Titus and Philemon had been included.[5] If this is true, then it appears that at this time the standard Pauline collection included his church letters but not the four letters to individual persons. The place of Hebrews immediately following Romans is almost unique but is in agreement with Egyptian opinion which at that time ascribed Hebrews to Paul.[6] At the same time the Muratorian Canon, representing the usage of Rome about A.D. 200, does not include Hebrews among Paul's letters,[7] and the doubt of its Pauline authorship relegated it

---

[2] H. A. Sanders, *A Third Century Papyrus Codex of the Epistles of Paul.* 1935.

[3] The entire manuscript is edited by Frederic G. Kenyon, *The Chester Beatty Biblical Papyri.* Fasciculus III. Text 1934, Supplement Text 1936, Supplement Plates 1937.

[4] Consequently in the first half of the manuscript the verso side of the leaf precedes the recto, and in the second half the recto precedes the verso. The change comes at folio 53.

[5] Frederic Kenyon, *Our Bible and the Ancient Manuscripts.* 1940, p.126 n.1.

[6] Clement of Alexandria (A.D. c.200) said that Hebrews was the work of Paul (Eusebius, *Ch. Hist.* VI, xiv) and repeatedly quoted it as Pauline (e.g. *Stromata.* IV, 16, 20 [ANF II, pp.427f.,432]).

[7] *The Muratorian Fragment* (Ayer, *A Source Book for Ancient Church History,* p.119); E. J. Goodspeed, *The Formation of The New Testament.* 1926, pp.187f.

afterward to a place following II Thessalonians,[8] and finally, when the Pastorals and Philemon were accepted fully, to a place on the borderland between the Pauline epistles and James. Aside from the inclusion of Hebrews, and also the reversal of the order of Galatians and Ephesians, the Chester Beatty Papyrus lists Paul's church letters in exactly the order which became accepted generally and is used now in our printed Bibles. The principle of arrangement seems to be in the order of length, with letters which have the same address placed together.

Since the first seven leaves of the manuscript have been lost, Romans 1:1-5:17 is missing. Folio 8 contains Romans 5:17-6:14 but more than half of the leaf is broken away. Folios 9 and 10 again are missing, but beginning with folio 11 (Romans 8:15ff.) the remainder of Romans is substantially preserved. Folio 11 verso, containing Romans 8:15-25, is reproduced in Fig. 143. The text is broken away slightly at the left, but the missing words or portions of words are easily restored. At the bottom of the page four lines have been lost. The scribe wrote a large, flowing hand of calligraphic character, with the individual letters upright and square in formation and well spaced. Another hand put in the page numeration, the Greek letter κ at the top of this page being equivalent to number 20. Probably this latter hand is responsible also for the rather thick oblique stroke above the line which marks the ends of clauses as in lines 3, 5, 8, 10, 15, 20 and 22. The original scribe occasionally used a high dot for punctuation, as in line 3, and generally marked initial Upsilon and Iota with a diaeresis, as in lines 1, 5, 11 and 23.[9] The scribe also abbreviated some words including the sacred names. The following examples appear on this page: "Spirit" ($\overline{\text{ΠΝΑ}}$), line 2; "of God" ($\overline{\text{ΘΥ}}$), lines 3, 4, 15; and "of Christ" ($\overline{\text{ΧΥ}}$), line 4.

The text of this page reads as follows, the translation and punctuation being made in the style of the American Standard Version for convenience in comparison.

> Ye received the spirit of adoption, whereby we cry,
> Abba, Father. The Spirit itself beareth witness with
> our spirit, that we are children of God: and if children,

[8] This is the position it has in Codex Sinaiticus. Hebrews also follows Thessalonians in the present arrangement of Codex Vaticanus, but the paragraph numbers indicate that in an older division of this manuscript Hebrews stood between Galatians and Ephesians. Gregory, *Canon and Text of the New Testament*, pp.336,344.

[9] Medial Iota also has the diaeresis in line 9.

then heirs of God and joint-heirs with Christ;
if so be that we suffer, that we may be glorified with him. For
I reckon that the sufferings of this present time are not worthy
to be compared with the glory which shall
be revealed to us-ward. For the earnest expectation
of the creation waiteth for the revealing of the sons
of God. For the creation was subjected to vanity,
not of its own will but by reason of him who
subjected it, in hope that the creation itself also shall be delivered from the bondage of
corruption into the liberty of the glory of the
children of God. For we know that the whole creation
groaneth and travaileth in pain together until now.
And not only so, but we who have
the first-fruits of the Spirit also ourselves groan within ourselves, waiting for the redemption
of our body. For in hope were we saved:
but hope that is seen is not hope:
for who hopeth for that which he seeth? But if we hope for
that which we see not, then do we with patience wait for it.

Even a rapid reading of the above passage indicates that the
Chester Beatty Papyrus of the Letters of Paul presents substantially the same text with which we are familiar in the best modern
versions of the Bible. Indeed this very fact is the most significant
thing about the manuscript. Here is our oldest copy of Paul's letters,
and it emphatically confirms the accuracy and soundness of the
general textual tradition.[10]

When manuscripts are copied many times, however, mistakes and
alterations both unintentional and intentional creep in. Intentional
alterations which are found include the simplification of a difficult
passage, the addition of a lacking word or a desired quotation, and
even changes made for dogmatic reasons. Far more frequent are
unintentional alterations, which include writing a word once when
it should be repeated, writing a word twice when it should appear
only once, omitting a word or line when the eye skips to a second
word or line ending similarly, and other errors of like kind. It is
not surprising that such mistakes occurred in the laborious copying
by hand of ancient manuscripts, for the same types of errors are
perfectly familiar to modern stenographers, and even appear in

[10] Hans Lietzmann, *Zur Würdigung des Chester-Beatty-Papyrus der Paulusbriefe*
(*Sitzungsbericht der Preussischen Akademie der Wissenschaften Phil.-Hist. Kl.* 1934.
xxv), pp.3f.

printed books whose proofs have been carefully examined and re-examined. Thus, an edition of the English Bible printed in 1653 omitted the word "not" in I Corinthians 6:9 and made the passage read, "Or know ye not that the unrighteous shall inherit the kingdom of God?" The famous "Printer's Bible" gave Psalm 119:161 in the form "Printers have persecuted me without a cause" instead of "Princes have persecuted me without a cause," and an edition printed in 1717 became known as the "Vinegar Bible" because it misprinted "Vinegar" for "Vineyard" in the headline to the twentieth chapter of Luke. It is no wonder, therefore, that Irenaeus (A.D. c.180) thought it necessary to add the following note at the close of one of his writings: "I adjure thee who mayest copy this book, by our Lord Jesus Christ, and by his glorious advent when he comes to judge the living and the dead, to compare what thou shalt write, and correct it carefully by this manuscript, and also to write this adjuration, and place it in the copy."[11]

Rufinus (A.D. c.345-c.410) included an even longer adjuration and entreaty in the prologue to his translation of Origen's *De Principiis:*

"And, verily, in the presence of God the Father, and of the Son, and of the Holy Spirit, I adjure and beseech every one, who may either transcribe or read these books, by his belief in the kingdom to come, by the mystery of the resurrection from the dead, and by that everlasting fire prepared for the devil and his angels, that, as he would not possess for an eternal inheritance that place where there is weeping and gnashing of teeth, and where their fire is not quenched and their worm dieth not, he add nothing to Scripture, and take nothing away from it, and make no insertion or alteration, but that he compare his transcript with the copies from which he made it, and make the emendations and distinctions according to the letter, and not have his manuscript incorrect or indistinct, lest the difficulty of ascertaining the sense, from the indistinctness of the copy, should cause greater difficulties to the readers."[12]

And in his Preface to the Vulgate Translation of the Four Gospels (A.D. 383), Jerome spoke of "the mistakes introduced by inaccurate translators, and the blundering alterations of confident but ignorant critics, and further, all that has been inserted or altered by sleepy copyists."[13]

As a very early manuscript, the Chester Beatty Papyrus of Paul's letters is free from many alterations which appear in later codices.

11 Irenaeus, *On the Ogdoad;* quoted by Eusebius, *Ch. Hist.* v, xx.
12 ANF IV, p.238; cf. Revelation 22:18f.
13 NPNFSS VI, p.488.

An instance of this may be seen in line 12 of the page reproduced in Fig. 143. Here in Romans 8:20f. it is probable that Paul wrote exactly as the papyrus reads, "by reason of him who subjected it, in hope that[14] the creation itself also shall be delivered. . . ." Codex Vaticanus, Codex Alexandrinus and Codex Ephraemi rescriptus all agree that this is the correct reading. But in Codex Sinaiticus, Codex Claromontanus and Codex Boernerianus a slight alteration is found whereby the sentence is made to read, "by reason of him who subjected it, in hope, because[15] the creation itself also shall be delivered. . . ." At many other points also the Chester Beatty Papyrus clearly preserves what Paul wrote originally. In Romans 6:8 he wrote, "But if we died with Christ, we believe that we shall also live with him." Later scribes changed the last word "him" into "the Christ" in order to remove any possible ambiguity, but the papyrus preserves the original "him."[16] In Romans 9:31 Paul wrote "but Israel, following after a law of righteousness, did not arrive at the law,"[17] just as the papyrus has it. But some scribe thought that Paul should have used the same phrase in both parts of his sentence, and so changed the conclusion to read "did not arrive at the law of righteousness,"[18] and this appears in the mass of the later manuscripts. In Romans 10:15 Paul wrote, "How beautiful are the feet of them that bring glad tidings of good things!" and that is the way the Chester Beatty Papyrus has it.[19] This was a quotation, however, from Isaiah 52:7 and later manuscripts added from the Septuagint, "How beautiful are the feet of them that bring glad tidings of peace,[20] of them that bring glad tidings of good things."

In a number of instances, however, alterations have already crept into the text of the Chester Beatty Papyrus. Examples may be seen in lines 17-20 and 22 of the page illustrated in Fig. 143. In Romans 8:23 Paul wrote originally, "but also ourselves, who have the first-fruits of the Spirit, we also ourselves groan within ourselves, waiting for the adoption, the redemption of our body."[21] This was an involved and complicated sentence, as many of Paul's sentences are.

---

[14] ἐφ᾽ ἐλπίδι ὅτι.   [15] ἐφ᾽ ἐλπίδι διότι.

[16] αὐτῷ P46 SABC sa bo; τῷ Χριστῷ DG Latt.

[17] νόμον P46 SAB sa bo DG.   [18] νόμον δικαιοσύνης Latt Koine.

[19] P46 SABC sa bo.

[20] + τῶν εὐαγγελιζομένων εἰρήνην DG Latt.

[21] ἀλλὰ καὶ αὐτοὶ τὴν ἀπαρχὴν τοῦ πνεύματος ἔχοντες ἡμεῖς καὶ αὐτοὶ ἐν ἑαυτοῖς στενάζομεν υἱοθεσίαν ἀπεκδεχόμενοι, τὴν ἀπολύτρωσιν τοῦ σώματος ἡμῶν SAC.

In the papyrus the first "also ourselves" was omitted and so was the word "adoption" with the result that the sentence emerged in simplified form but with Paul's tumultuous manner of speech and richness of thought considerably modified: "but we who have the first-fruits of the Spirit also ourselves groan within ourselves, waiting for the redemption of our body." Codex Claromontanus and Codex Boernerianus later did the same as the papyrus in the omission of the word "adoption," but handled the first part of the sentence differently: "but also ourselves, who have the first-fruits of the Spirit, ourselves groan within ourselves, waiting for the redemption of our body." Codex Vaticanus, on the other hand, did nothing but omit the original "we."

In Romans 8:24 the Chester Beatty Papyrus again seems to have slightly changed and simplified an originally more complex Pauline sentence. The papyrus reads, "for who hopeth for that which he seeth?"[22] Other forms in which the sentence is found are: "for what a man seeth, why doth he hope for?"[23] "for what a man seeth, why doth he yet hope for?"[24] "for who yet waiteth for that which he seeth?"[25] and "for what a man seeth, why doth he yet wait for?"[26] Of these the last is probably the original form since it is more probable that a scribe would change the verb "wait for" into "hope for" which appears so frequently in the rest of the passage, than that someone would invent the new expression "wait for."

Elsewhere in the papyrus appear errors, changes in words and attempted corrections. For example there is a grammatical error in Romans 6:13 made through carelessness,[27] a word changed in 9:27 to make a quotation agree more exactly with the Septuagint,[28] and an omission of two words in 11:17 in order to simplify Paul's grammar where three genitives follow one another in unbroken succession.[29]

Thus, although the Chester Beatty Papyrus is free from many alterations which appear in later manuscripts, it shows how changes

---

22 ὃ γὰρ βλέπει τίς ἐλπίζει P46 B.   23 ὃ γὰρ βλέπει τις, τί ἐλπίζει DG Latt.

24 ὃ γὰρ βλέπει τις, τί καὶ ἐλπίζει C Koine.

25 ὃ γὰρ βλέπει τις καὶ ὑπομένει S.   26 ὃ γὰρ βλέπει τις, τί καὶ ὑπομένει A.

27 ζῶντες P46 DG instead of ζῶντας.

28 κατάλιμμα P46 DG instead of ὑπόλειμμα SAB.

29 τῆς ῥίζης τῆς πιότητος τῆς ἐλαίας ("of the root of the fatness of the olive tree") SBC; "of the root" is omitted by P46 DG; another attempt to make the sentence more readable is represented by the addition of "and" in A Koine, "of the root and of the fatness of the olive tree."

and errors had already been introduced. Doubtless this papyrus is typical of many other codices which were in existence in the third century A.D., no two of which were exactly alike and in each of which numerous variations were to be found.

OTHER EARLY PAPYRI OF PAUL'S LETTERS

While the future may hold other great discoveries comparable to that of the Chester Beatty Papyrus, at present other copies of Paul's letters on papyrus exist only in small widely scattered fragments. These include, from the third century: $\mathfrak{p}^{32}$ now in Manchester (P. Ryl. Gk. 5) and containing a portion of Titus; $\mathfrak{p}^{30}$ now in Ghent (Bibliothèque Universitaire, Pap. 61) and containing fragments of I-II Thessalonians; $\mathfrak{p}^{27}$ (Oxyrhynchus Papyri No. 1355) now in the Cathedral Library at Worcester and containing a bit of Romans; from the fourth century: $\mathfrak{p}^{13}$ (Oxyrhynchus Papyri No. 657) now in the British Museum at London and containing parts of Hebrews; $\mathfrak{p}^{10}$ (Oxyrhynchus Papyri No. 209) now in the Harvard University Semitic Museum at Cambridge, Massachusetts, and containing the first paragraph of Romans; $\mathfrak{p}^{15}$ (Oxyrhynchus Papyri No. 1008) now in Cairo and containing a portion of I Corinthians; and from the fifth century: $\mathfrak{p}^{11}$ now in Leningrad and also containing parts of I Corinthians.[30]

$\mathfrak{p}^{13}$ and $\mathfrak{p}^{10}$ merit special mention. $\mathfrak{p}^{13}$ was written originally in the third century as a papyrus roll with an epitome of Livy. In the latter part of that century or early in the fourth century it was re-used, the back having the Epistle to the Hebrews written on it, of which portions of chapters 2-5 and 10-12 still survive. $\mathfrak{p}^{10}$ (Fig. 144) comes from Oxyrhynchus in the early fourth century and was believed by Dr. Adolf Deissmann[31] to have served as an amulet for one Aurelios Paulos who is named in the cursive writing on the sheet. At the top, Romans 1:1-7 is copied in eleven lines of rough, large letters. The following divine names are all abbreviated: Christ Jesus (line 1), God (lines 2, 9, 10), Son (line 3), Son of God (line 5), Spirit (line 5), Jesus Christ (lines 6, 8), Lord (line 6), Father (line 10) and Lord Christ Jesus (lines 10-11). $\mathfrak{p}^{10}$ and Codex Vaticanus are the chief witnesses for the characteristic Pauline "Christ Jesus" (instead of "Jesus Christ") in verse 1, while $\mathfrak{p}^{10}$ is quite alone in the

---

[30] Nestle, *Greek New Testament.* 16th ed. 1936, p.31.
[31] *Licht vom Osten,* p.203 n.4.

same order in verse 7 (lines 10-11) and in reading "the name of Jesus Christ" instead of "his name" in verse 5 (line 8).

Although most of these papyri exist only in fragments, they doubtless give us a much more realistic impression of how Paul's letters appeared originally than do the relatively elegant vellum manuscripts of which we shall speak now.

THE EGYPTIAN TEXT

It is readily understandable that the existence of many different manuscripts, each with its own alterations in the text, led to the desire for a better, more nearly standard text, freed from as many as possible of these changes and errors, and it is a plausible hypothesis that in the fourth century the scholars at Alexandria brought together a number of the better manuscripts, such as the Chester Beatty Papyrus, and endeavored to strike out their variants and thus arrive at a good average text.[32] At any rate the next few manuscripts to be mentioned form a sort of family whose text well might have arisen in this very way. In each of these several manuscripts there are still individual corrections, changes and errors, but the group has such decided similarities that it is commonly referred to as representing the Egyptian or Alexandrian text. Since this characteristic text may go back to the Egyptian bishop and martyr Hesychius (d. A.D. c.311),[33] whose work on the text of the gospels is mentioned by Jerome,[34] it is also called the Hesychian recension (𝕳). Four great vellum Bibles, written in uncial characters, constitute the chief witnesses to the Egyptian text. These are Codex Vaticanus, Codex Sinaiticus, Codex Alexandrinus and Codex Ephraemi Syri rescriptus.

CODEX VATICANUS

Codex Vaticanus, technically designated as B, is a fine parchment codex containing almost the entire Greek Bible. It was already in the possession of the Vatican Library at Rome before the first catalogue of that library was made in 1475. Napoleon carried the manuscript to Paris as a prize of war, and it remained there from

[32] Lietzmann, *Zur Würdigung des Chester-Beatty-Papyrus der Paulusbriefe*, p.10.
[33] Eusebius, *Ch. Hist.* VIII, xiii.
[34] Preface to the Vulgate Translation of the Four Gospels, addressed to Pope Damasus, A.D. 383 (NPNFSS VI, p.488); cf. Hans Lietzmann, *Einführung in die Text-geschichte der Paulusbriefe* (in *An die Römer, Handbuch zum neuen Testament*. 8 [3d ed. 1928]), p.13.

1809 until it was returned to Rome in 1815. While at Paris the manuscript was studied by Leonhard Hug, a Roman Catholic professor from Tübingen, and its great age and true value were recognized for the first time. In 1843 Constantine Tischendorf was able to study the manuscript in Rome, but only under very restricted circumstances, and full and accurate knowledge was not available to the scholars of the world until a complete photographic facsimile was published in Rome in 1889-1890.

The codex must have originally contained about 820 leaves, of which 759 are preserved, 142 of these belonging to the New Testament. Each leaf measures about 10½ by 10 inches, and there are three columns of text to the page with 42 lines to a column. The writing is in perfectly simple and unadorned uncials, smaller letters sometimes being crowded in at the ends of lines. The words are written continuously without separation. There is almost no punctuation, although initial Iota and Upsilon are marked with a diaeresis and sacred names are abbreviated. Old Testament quotations are marked with a horizontal caret (>). One scribe copied the entire New Testament, although a different scribe wrote the Old Testament. Two correctors have made corrections in the manuscript, one being almost contemporary with the original scribes, and the other being as late as the tenth or eleventh century. The later corrector retraced the pale letters, omitting only the letters and words which he believed to be incorrect, and also added the breathings and accents. The style of handwriting and almost complete absence of ornamentation indicate a date for Codex Vaticanus in the middle of the fourth century A.D., and the place of writing may have been in Alexandria.[35]

When we read Paul's letters in this manuscript, therefore, we are perusing a copy which was made, in round numbers, 150 years later than the Chester Beatty Papyrus and 300 years after the originals. The opening page of Paul's Letter to the Romans, with its simple title, "To the Romans," is reproduced in Fig. 145.

CODEX SINAITICUS

Codex Sinaiticus (S)[36] derives its name from Mount Sinai where

[35] Lake, *The Text of the New Testament*, pp.14f.
[36] Tischendorf named the manuscript Aleph (א) but since this is the only important manuscript for which a Hebrew letter has been proposed, Professor Hans Lietzmann (*Einführung in die Textgeschichte der Paulusbriefe*, p.6) has introduced S as a more

it was found in the Monastery of Saint Catherine (Fig. 146). The traditional region of Mount Sinai (cf. p. 129) was one of the places sought out by hermits and anchorites upon the inception of the Christian monastic movement in the third and fourth centuries. These hermits settled in the caves of Jebel Serbal, and eventually churches and convents were built in the neighboring valley of Pharan (now the Wadi Feiran), which became the seat of the Bishop of Pharan. Other hermits established themselves 25 miles away at a place where a bush was shown as the Burning Bush of Exodus 3:2-4. This was in a desolate valley of nearly 4,000 feet altitude at the foot of Jebel Musa and near-by Jebel Catherine. It is believed that St. Helena built a church here to enshrine the Burning Bush and also a tower of refuge for the hermits who were under attack by Arab raids. Such interest on the part of Helena is not improbable since we know that she visited Jerusalem about A.D. 327 and was interested in the erection of churches in the Holy Land (p. 438). About A.D. 460 the region was visited by the Spanish nun and pilgrim Etheria. She was received at a certain monastery and energetically climbed various mountains including a middle one to which the name of Sinai was especially attached, but whether this was at Jebel Serbal or Jebel Musa is difficult to make out. Her travel journal reads:

"We reached the mountain late on the sabbath, and arriving at a certain monastery, the monks who dwelt there received us very kindly, showing us every kindness; there is also a church and a priest there. We stayed there that night, and early on the Lord's Day, together with the priest and the monks who dwelt there, we began the ascent of the mountains one by one. These mountains are ascended with infinite toil, for you cannot go up gently by a spiral track, as we say snail-shell wise, but you climb straight up the whole way, as if up a wall, and you must come straight down each mountain until you reach the very foot of the middle one, which is specially called Sinai."[37]

In A.D. 530, since the attacks of the Arabs were continuing, the Emperor Justinian built a massive wall around St. Helena's church and tower. At about this time the Church of the Burning Bush was rebuilt on a larger scale and renamed the Church of the Transfigura-

appropriate and convenient designation. Otherwise S is attached only to unimportant manuscripts.
[37] *The Pilgrimage of Etheria.* tr. M. L. McClure and C. L. Feltoe in *Translations of Christian Literature.* Series III Liturgical Texts, pp.3f.

tion. When the settlement at Pharan broke up under Arab raids the Bishop of Pharan took refuge in the Monastery of the Burning Bush, and after A.D. 630 his successors had the title of Bishop of Sinai. The Archbishop of Sinai now resides in Cairo. Saint Catherine, by whose name the Monastery of the Burning Bush later became known, was a martyr in Alexandria under the Roman ruler Maximinus (A.D. 305-313). According to legend her body was transported by angels to Mount Sinai, where some five centuries later her bones were discovered and where, at least in part, they are still preserved. Curiously enough, the monastery enclosure now includes also a mosque with a square minaret which rises beside the bell tower of the church. The story told concerning this is that centuries ago a Turkish general was marching against the monastery with troops which were thirsting for the conquest. He was met by a deputation of monks and dissuaded from his purpose, but fearing that his troops could not be restrained, he advised the hasty erection of the mosque. When the troops arrived the minaret appeared beside the church tower, and the Mohammedans spared the place where it appeared that their Prophet was known.[38]

Such is the story of the famous monastery in which one of the greatest manuscript discoveries of all time was made. The discoverer was the unrivaled critic and decipherer of ancient manuscripts, Dr. Constantine Tischendorf. He told the story of the great discovery in his own words as follows:

"It was at the foot of Mount Sinai, in the Convent of St. Catherine, that I discovered the pearl of all my researches. In visiting the library of the monastery, in the month of May, 1844, I perceived in the middle of the great hall a large and wide basket full of old parchments; and the librarian, who was a man of information, told me that two heaps of paper like these, mouldered by time, had been already committed to the flames. What was my surprise to find amid this heap of papers a considerable number of sheets of a copy of the Old Testament in Greek, which seemed to me to be one of the most ancient that I had ever seen. The authorities of the convent allowed me to possess myself of a third of these parchments, or about forty-three sheets, all the more readily as they were destined for the fire."[39]

Tischendorf was allowed to take the 43 leaves to Leipzig where

[38] H. V. Morton, *Through Lands of the Bible*. 1938, p.347.
[39] *Codex Sinaiticus, the Ancient Biblical Manuscript now in the British Museum, Tischendorf's Story and Argument Related by Himself*. 8th ed. 1934, pp.23f. The quotations from this book are made by permission of the Lutterworth Press, Redhill, Surrey, England.

he edited them under the title *Codex Friderico Augustanus* (1846) in acknowledgment of the patronage of the king of Saxony. In 1853 Tischendorf returned to Sinai but could find nothing more of the manuscript. Once again in 1859 he came back, this time with the approval of the emperor of Russia for systematic researches in the East, but still there was no trace of the great treasure. He was on the point of leaving when the steward of the convent invited him to his cell. Tischendorf relates that the monk "took down from the corner of the room a bulky kind of volume, wrapped up in a red cloth, and laid it before me. I unrolled the cover, and discovered, to my great surprise, not only those very fragments which, fifteen years before, I had taken out of the basket, but also other parts of the Old Testament, the New Testament complete, and, in addition, the Epistle of Barnabas and a part of the Pastor of Hermas."[40]

After complex transactions it became possible for Tischendorf to place the great manuscript in the hands of the emperor of Russia and for himself to prepare a facsimile edition of it. Payment of some $6,750 was made to the monks by the emperor for the manuscript. Acclaim came to Tischendorf from throughout the Christian world for his notable discovery. Relating the recognitions which he received, Tischendorf said:

"The two most celebrated universities of England, Cambridge and Oxford, desired to show me honour by conferring on me their highest academic degree. 'I would rather,' said an old man—himself of the highest distinction for learning—'I would rather have discovered this Sinaitic manuscript than the Koh-i-noor of the Queen of England.'

"But that which I think more highly of than all these flattering distinctions is the fact that Providence has given to our age, in which attacks on Christianity are so common, the Sinaitic Bible, to be to us a full and clear light as to what is the real text of God's Word written, and to assist us in defending the truth by establishing its authentic form."[41]

Codex Sinaiticus remained in Leningrad until it was purchased from the Soviet government by the British Museum for some $500,000. When the valuable manuscript arrived at the British Museum December 27, 1933, its appearance was still much as when Tischendorf first saw it at Sinai, a large pile of loose quires and leaves, lacking both beginning and end and having no covers or binding (Fig. 147). It has been carefully bound by the British Museum in two volumes, Old Testament and New Testament.

[40] ibid., p.26. [41] ibid., pp.31f.

Whereas originally the Sinaitic manuscript probably had at least 730 leaves, only 390 (including those at Leipzig) remain today—242 in the Old Testament and 148 in the New Testament. The leaves are about 15 inches high by 13½ or 14 inches broad, and the text is written in four columns to the page, with 48 lines to the column. The words are written continuously without separation and there are no accents or breathings, although high and middle points and colon are used for punctuation, initial Iota and Upsilon have the diaeresis and sacred names are abbreviated. The codex was written by three scribes, known as A, B and D, of whom Scribe A wrote almost all of the New Testament. The three hands are very much alike, but they show individual peculiarities, particularly in the matter of spelling; it is largely on the basis of spelling that the three are differentiated. Many corrections have been made in the manuscript not only by the original scribes but also by a series of correctors from the fourth to the twelfth century.[42] No less than 14,800 places are enumerated in Tischendorf's edition where some alteration has been made to the text.[43] The dignified simplicity of the elegant capital letters in which the manuscript was originally written is comparable to that of Codex Vaticanus, and both manuscripts were probably written at about the same time around A.D. 350, the Vatican manuscript being perhaps a little the older of the two.[44] The place where the Codex Sinaiticus was written is uncertain but at least there is nothing to contradict an Egyptian origin although Caesarea or Palestine are also regarded as possibilities. Since Codex Vaticanus and Codex Sinaiticus are written in three and four columns respectively it has sometimes been believed that they are two of the 50 vellum Bibles ordered by Constantine from Eusebius of Caesarea in A.D. 332 (p. 316), but there is no further proof for this supposition. The first page of Paul's Letter to the Romans in Codex Sinaiticus is shown in Fig. 148.

CODEX ALEXANDRINUS

Codex Alexandrinus (A) was the second of the three great Greek codices to become known, and was the first manuscript to be designated with a capital letter, a style which was followed later to

[42] H. J. M. Milne and T. C. Skeat, *Scribes and Correctors of the Codex Sinaiticus.* 1938, pp.22f.,40-50.
[43] Milne and Skeat, *The Codex Sinaiticus and the Codex Alexandrinus.* 1938, p.19.
[44] Schubart, *Griechische Palaeographie*, p.155.

denote the other uncial manuscripts of the New Testament. Codex Alexandrinus was given by Cyril Lucar, patriarch of Constantinople, to Sir Thomas Roe, the English ambassador to the Sublime Porte, to be presented to the king of England, and is first mentioned in a letter by Roe dated January 20, 1624 (i.e. January 30, 1625) as "an autographall bible intire, written by the hand of Tecla the proto-martyr of the Greekes, that liued in the tyme of St. Paul; and he doth auerr yt to be true and authenticall, of his owne writing, and the greatest antiquitye of the Greeke church."[45] The codex arrived in England in 1628 and was placed in the Royal Library, which in 1757 was incorporated in the British Museum.

Cyril Lucar had been patriarch of Alexandria before assuming the same position in Constantinople in 1620, and probably brought the codex with him from Alexandria when he came to Constantinople. The earlier Alexandrian location of the manuscript is also indicated by an Arabic note written at the bottom of the first page of Genesis: "Made an inalienable gift to the Patriarchal Cell in the City of Alexandria. Whosoever shall remove it thence shall be accursed and cut off. Written by Athanasius the humble."

This Athanasius who calls himself "the humble" was probably the Melchite patriarch who died in A.D. 1308. Another Arabic note of the thirteenth or fourteenth century is written at the back of the Table of Books and gives the tradition alluded to in Sir Thomas Roe's letter that the manuscript was written by the martyr Thecla, but this is probably only a legend. The close connection of the codex with Alexandria makes it probable that that city was its place of origin. In point of time Codex Alexandrinus was presumably somewhat later than the Vatican and Sinaitic manuscripts, generally being ascribed to the first half of the fifth century.[46]

The manuscript originally contained perhaps 820 leaves, of which 773 are extant, 630 in the Old Testament and 143 in the New Testament. The vellum leaves measure approximately 12⅝ by 10⅜ inches. The quires were of 8 leaves, numbered in Greek characters in the center of the top margin of each first page. A fourteenth century Arabic numeration is written in the lower outer corner of the verso of the leaves, while Patrick Young, librarian to Charles I, made the modern ink foliation and chapter notation. The text is written in

45 Milne and Skeat, *The Codex Sinaiticus and the Codex Alexandrinus*, p.28.
46 ibid., p.31.

two columns per page with from 46 to 52 lines to the column. The words are written continuously without separation and there are no accents and only rare breathings. High and middle points are used, initial Iota and Upsilon have the diaeresis, sacred names are abbreviated, and Old Testament quotations are marked.

While in general this manuscript still has the air of simplicity which is characteristic of the oldest uncials, a small amount of ornamentation has been introduced. At the beginning of each book a few lines are written in red, and the paragraphs are marked by larger letters set in the margin. It is not necessarily the first letter of the first word of the new paragraph which is thus enlarged. Rather, the new paragraph begins in the line wherever it may happen to fall, and then the first letter which strikes the next line is placed in the margin. Also, there are panel-shaped tailpieces or colophons at the end of the various books. Two scribes are distinguishable in the Old Testament, and the first of these seems also to be responsible for the New Testament, except perhaps in Luke 1 to I Corinthians 10:8 where a smoother, lighter hand may indicate the work of yet a third scribe.[47] There are also many corrections, but most of them are of an early date. The appearance of the opening page of Romans in Codex Alexandrinus is shown in Fig. 149.

CODEX EPHRAEMI RESCRIPTUS

Codex Ephraemi Syri rescriptus (C) was in the possession of Cardinal Ridolfi of Florence, a member of the de' Medici family, in the sixteenth century, and later in the same century through Catherine de' Medici, wife of Henry II of France, was brought to Paris, where it is now in the Bibliothèque Nationale.

The codex is what is technically known as a palimpsest, or rewritten manuscript. Originally it was written in the fifth century as a manuscript of the Greek Bible. In the twelfth century, when vellum was scarce, the original writing was erased and many of the sheets were used over again to receive a Greek translation of the discourses of Ephraem Syrus, the latter having been a prominent theologian of the Syrian church in the fourth century A.D. The underlying writing was not destroyed entirely, however, although it did appear impossible that it could ever be read again. Several attempts to make it out, including one in which chemical reagents were em-

47 ibid., p.32.

ployed, had failed or met with very limited success, when the task was undertaken by Tischendorf. In 1840 the man who was to study the Vatican manuscript in 1843 and to discover the Sinaitic treasure in 1844 had just habilitated as a Privatdozent in the theological faculty at Leipzig. During 1841-1842 he attempted the decipherment of the famous palimpsest and was able in 1843 to publish a complete edition of the New Testament.[48] Today it has been found possible to use ultra-violet rays to read such manuscripts, but this device was not available to Tischendorf.

Only 209 leaves remain of the original codex, but of these 145 are in the New Testament and portions of every New Testament book except II Thessalonians and II John are contained. The leaves measure 12½ by 9½ inches and the text is written in a single column of 40 to 46 lines to the page. The words are written continuously without separation and there are no accents or breathings but high and middle points are employed. Two correctors, perhaps of the sixth and of the ninth centuries respectively, have worked on the manuscript, the second of whom inserted a cross after the high point. The original writing is generally believed to belong to the fifth century, and perhaps to be a little later than Codex Alexandrinus. A page from Codex Ephraemi rescriptus (Matthew 20:16-34) is shown in Fig. 150.

Such are the four great uncial manuscripts which, together with the Sahidic (sa) and Bohairic (bo) versions,[49] and church fathers like Clement of Alexandria and Origen, are the chief witnesses to the Egyptian text.[50] With this type of text the Chester Beatty Papyrus is most often in agreement,[51] as is shown in the examples cited above (p. 337), although sometimes the papyrus goes its own way and sometimes agrees with the Western text. On the whole the Egyptian text is the best and most dependable which we have, but nevertheless it has to be compared constantly with as many other early manuscripts as possible.

[48] C. Tischendorf, *Codex Ephraemi Syri rescriptus sive fragmenta Novi Testamenti*. 1843.

[49] These are third and fourth century translations into the native Egyptian language known as Coptic, Sahidic being the dialect spoken 'in Upper Egypt and Bohairic that spoken in Lower Egypt.

[50] It should be noted that in the Gospels the text of Codex Alexandrinus is Byzantine.

[51] The preponderance of agreement is with B and next with SAC. Kenyon, *The Chester Beatty Biblical Papyri*. Fasc. III. Suppl. Text, pp.xvi-xvii.

THE WESTERN TEXT

Of other ancient witnesses an important group is formed by those sources which represent the so-called Western text. The name "Western" (𝔚) was applied originally to this text family because it was found in the Latin church fathers and versions and in D, but it should be understood that it is a technical and not a geographical designation and includes not only manuscripts written in the West but also ones written in the East like the Old Syriac versions.[52]

The two most important manuscripts which represent this family are Codex Claromontanus and Codex Boernerianus, both of which give the text in Latin as well as in Greek.

CODEX CLAROMONTANUS

Codex Claromontanus (D[p])[53] is a sixth century vellum manuscript of the letters of Paul (including Hebrews), which was acquired between 1565 and 1582 by Théodore de Bèze (Beza), Calvin's follower at Geneva. Beza stated that the manuscript was found in a convent at Clermont-en-Beauvaisis, and thence its name is derived. Louis XIV bought the codex in 1656 and it is now in the Bibliothèque Nationale, Paris.[54] The manuscript comprises 533 leaves, each measuring 9¾ by 7¾ inches and having wide margins. The Greek text is written in a single column on the left-hand page and the corresponding Latin on the right-hand. There are 21 lines to the page, the lines being divided according to pauses in the sense and the first letter of a new section being thrust into the margin. The words are written continuously without separation and there is no punctuation. Initial Iota and Upsilon have the diaeresis but the accents and breathings have been added by one of the

---

[52] Lake, *The Text of the New Testament*, pp.65,68. The Old Syriac versions include the so-called Curetonian and Sinaitic, both of which give texts of the Gospels. The former consists of fragments of a fifth century Syriac manuscript brought in 1842 from the monastery of S. Maria Deipara in the Nitrian desert, and recognized in 1847 and published in 1858 by Dr. Cureton. The latter is found in palimpsest leaves of a fifth century Syriac manuscript discovered in 1892 in the monastery of Saint Catherine at Mount Sinai by Mrs. Lewis and Mrs. Gibson.

[53] C. Tischendorf, *Codex Claromontanus sive Epistulae Pauli omnes Graece et Latine.* 1852.

[54] It is not to be confused with Codex Bezae (D), a bilingual manuscript of the Gospels and Acts, which also was once owned by Beza and is now in the University Library at Cambridge. See *Codex Bezae Cantabrigiensis Quattuor Evangelia et Actus Apostolorum complectens Graece et Latine Sumptibus Academiae phototypice repraesentatus.* 1899.

numerous later correctors. The first three lines of each letter are written in red, and so are the quotations from the Old Testament. The Greek and Latin columns of the manuscript do not always agree, and the Latin translation was not just made from this Greek· text but doubtless is one of the Latin translations already in existence before Jerome. A double page from this manuscript (Romans 16:23-27) is shown in Fig. 151.

Codex Boernerianus (G)[55] came into the possession of Professor Christian Friedrich Börner in 1705 and is now in the Royal Library at Dresden. It is also a bilingual manuscript, but in this case the Latin is written interlinearly above the Greek. In addition to these two bilingual codices, the Old Latin versions of the New Testament are known from the Latin church fathers and particularly from two commentaries, one found in the works of Ambrose (A.D. c.340-397) but written by an unknown author of the time of Pope Damasus (A.D. 366-384), and the other written by Pelagius (c.400). A revision of the Old Latin versions was carried out by Jerome, at the suggestion of Damasus, and is known as the Vulgate.

The Western type of text is very old and was the basis for Marcion's revision of Paul's letters before A.D. 150. Nevertheless, when judged by inner criteria, it is found to contain numerous alterations. Quotations are supplemented according to the Septuagint, corrections are made which result in a smoother style or clearer sense, and unintentional alterations are introduced through mistakes in copying. In general the Western text is characterized by many interpolations, and hence was regarded by Westcott and Hort as of greatest weight in its omissions. That is, its omissions are not omissions so much as non-interpolations.

THE KOINE OR BYZANTINE TEXT

The long process of textual revision, in which yet other families of text, such as the Caesarean, can be distinguished in more intensive study, led at last to the Koine (𝕶) or Common Text which came to be adopted generally in the Byzantine church. It is represented by three ninth century uncial manuscripts, Codex Angelicus (L), Codex Porphyrianus (P) and Codex Mosquensis (K), and by the great mass of minuscule manuscripts which belong to this and

[55] *Der Codex Boernerianus der Briefe des Apostels Paulus . . . in Lichtdruck Nachgebildet.* 1909.

following centuries, as well as by the Peshitto[56] and Gothic[57] versions and the writings of church fathers like Chrysostom (A.D. c.390), Basil of Caesarea in Cappadocia (d. A.D. 380) and Ephraem Syrus (d. A.D. 373). A sample page of one of the many minuscule manuscripts is shown in Fig. 152. This particular manuscript is now in Paris and is known as Cod. Gr. 223. It contains the Pauline Epistles and Acts with Commentary, and is dated explicitly in the year 1045. On another page of the same manuscript is an illustration showing the apostle Paul dictating to his secretary (Fig. 153).

The Koine is now clearly recognized as a late and secondary text. Interpolations and corrections are numerous in it. Often it combines Egyptian and Western readings and thus retains them both. For example in Romans 1:29 the Egyptian text reads "wickedness, covetousness, maliciousness," although these three words stand in different order in different manuscripts.[58] The Western text changed "wickedness" into "fornication," these two words having a very similar appearance in the Greek.[59] The Byzantine text then combined the Egyptian and Western readings and the result was a list including "fornication, wickedness, covetousness, maliciousness."[60]

THE DEPENDABILITY OF THE NEW TESTAMENT TEXT

At first, European translations of the New Testament were based simply upon the Latin Vulgate. Then men sought to go back to the Greek text, but only manuscripts of the less accurate Koine type were available. This was still the case when the Authorized Version was made under King James (1611), for the value of Codex Vaticanus was not yet realized at that time nor was Codex Sinaiticus even discovered. The scholars who made the Revised Version had the advantage of the use of these great manuscripts, and therefore that translation is more accurate than former ones could be. But every scrap of biblical parchment or papyrus recovered from the sands of the past adds to the vast amount of material available for the work of textual criticism, and the task of painstaking com-

---

[56] Peshitto means "Simple" Version and is a Syriac recension prepared by Bishop Rabbula of Edessa A.D. c.420.

[57] A translation by Bishop Ulfilas A.D. c.350.

[58] πονηρίᾳ πλεονεξίᾳ κακίᾳ B; πονηρίᾳ κακίᾳ πλεονεξίᾳ SA; κακίᾳ πονηρίᾳ πλεονεξίᾳ C bo sa.

[59] κακίᾳ πορνείᾳ πλεονεξίᾳ DG.

[60] πορνείᾳ πονηρίᾳ πλεονεξίᾳ κακίᾳ L; πορνείᾳ πονηρίᾳ κακίᾳ πλεονεξίᾳ Peshitto. Lietzmann, An die Römer, pp.13,35.

parison of all the witnesses to the original text is an unending labor.

The total number of New Testament manuscripts is very impressive. We have now some 170 papyrus manuscripts and fragments (including fragments of vellum found with papyri and ostraca), over 200 uncial manuscripts and fragments, and over 2,400 minuscule manuscripts.[61] No other Greek book has anything like this amount of testimony to its text. It is true that there are numerous textual variations among these different New Testament manuscripts, but the majority of them are of a relatively minor character, as has appeared in the examples given in this chapter. As a matter of fact, it has been estimated by careful students that there are substantial variations in hardly more than a thousandth part of the entire text.[62]

The close relationship in time between the oldest New Testament manuscripts and the original texts is also nothing less than amazing. The proximity of the Chester Beatty Papyri of the Letters of Paul to the time when the apostle wrote those letters, or for that matter the closeness of Codex Vaticanus and Codex Sinaiticus to the period of the composition of the New Testament, can be appreciated properly only by contrast with the situation prevailing in regard to the rest of the literature of the Greco-Roman world. For our knowledge of the writings of most of the classical authors we are dependent upon manuscripts the oldest of which belong to a time between the ninth and eleventh centuries A.D., or in other words are a thousand years removed from their originals.[63] Thus it is that the certainty with which the text of the New Testament is established exceeds that of any other ancient book. The words which Paul sent to Rome have crossed the further miles and centuries to us substantially unchanged in form and certainly undiminished in power.

[61] Kenyon, *Our Bible and the Ancient Manuscripts*, pp.105-107.
[62] Gregory, *Canon and Text of the New Testament*, p.528.
[63] Hans Lietzmann in *Die Antike, Zeitschrift für Kunst und Kultur des klassischen Altertums.* 11 (1935), pp.142-146.

VIII

Exploring the Catacombs and Studying the Sarcophagi

LESS than one hundred years after Paul wrote his Letter to the Romans, or by the middle of the second century A.D., the Christians of Rome are known to us through their remarkable places of burial, the catacombs.

Cremation was the normal practice of pagan Rome in the first century A.D.,[1] and the cinerary urns were placed in the niches of vaults constructed for this purpose and known as columbaria. Not until the time of Hadrian (A.D. 117-138) did cremation give way to inhumation among the pagan population of Rome. Then their interments were made in and beneath the columbaria and also in sarcophagi. But from the first the Christians seem to have found the burning of the bodies of the deceased abhorrent and no trace of early Christian cremation has been found. Rather, the first Christians followed the practice of the Jews who were living in Rome and buried their dead in underground sepulchral chambers and galleries.

[1] A. D. Nock in *Harvard Theological Review.* 25 (1932), p. 232.

1. THE CHARACTER OF THE CATACOMBS

THE development of such subterranean burial places was specially favored at Rome by the underlying geological formation. The great plain surrounding the city is composed of materials of volcanic origin. There is sand (*pozzolana*), there is stone (*tufa litoide*), and there is granular tufa (*tufa granolare*). The sand is too soft to permit excavations unless the walls are faced with brick, and the stone is so hard that it is quarried for building purposes, but the granular tufa is relatively easy to cut, yet is strong and holds up satisfactorily. Also, it is porous and drains well. The existence of this tufa facilitated the digging of the catacombs.[1] The actual excavation was done by a sort of guild of workers known as *fossores* or "diggers." Their title appears in inscriptions on their own tombs in the catacombs and they are depicted in the wall paintings, holding pick and spade, the tools of the trade.[2]

The characteristic form of a catacomb is that of a network of interconnected corridors and chambers containing burial niches in the walls. The corridors are usually approximately three feet in width and have a normal height of a little over six feet. This corresponds to a man's height, with a bit of additional room for the *fossor* to swing his pick. In their simplest form the graves were square-cornered, horizontal recesses, known as *loculi*, cut in the walls of the galleries and chambers. The corpses were laid here wound in wrappings, in accordance with Jewish custom, and the openings were closed with bricks or marble slabs. A more elaborate form of grave was that known as an *arcosolium*, where a semicircular recess was cut in the wall, and the body was placed in a coffin-like space closed from above by a horizontal slab.

When additional space was needed for more graves the corridor was often deepened. By digging the floor of the gallery some three feet deeper two more rows of graves could be accommodated, and this process was sometimes continued until there were as many as a dozen tiers of graves one below the other. As a moment's consideration of the work involved will indicate, this was an entirely feasible procedure, but to have attempted to *heighten* the corridor would have necessitated extremely awkward manipulation of pick and

[1] cf. G. de Angelis D'Ossat, *La Geologia delle Catacombe Romane.* 1938-.
[2] L. von Sybel, *Christliche Antike, Einführung in die altchristliche Kunst.* I (1906), p.102.

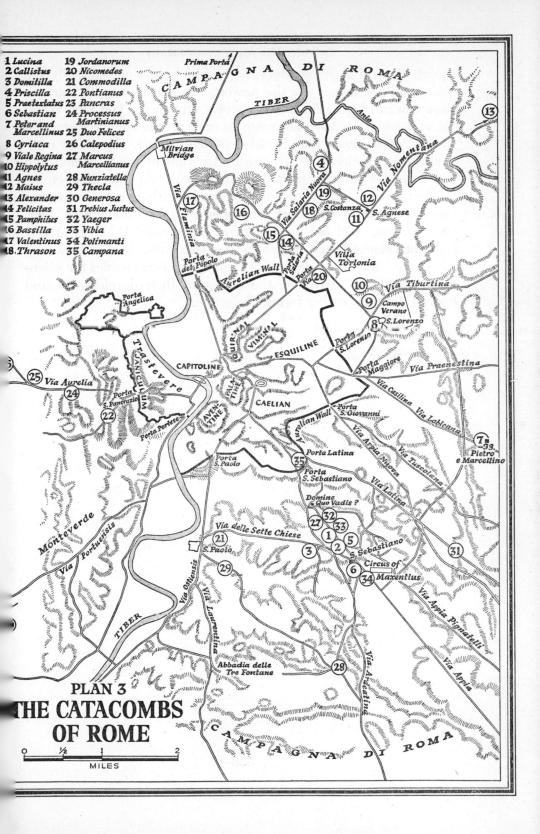

1 Lucina
2 Callistus
3 Domilla
4 Priscilla
5 Praetextatus
6 Sebastian
7 Peter and Marcellinus
8 Cyriaca
9 Viale Regina
10 Hippolytus
11 Agnes
12 Maius
13 Alexander
14 Felicitas
15 Pamphilus
16 Bassilla
17 Valentinus
18 Thrason

19 Jordanorum
20 Nicomedes
21 Commodilla
22 Pontianus
23 Pancras
24 Processus Martinianus
25 Duo Felices
26 Calepodius
27 Marcus Marcellianus
28 Nunziatella
29 Thecla
30 Generosa
31 Trebius Justus
32 Yaeger
33 Vibia
34 Polimanti
35 Campana

PLAN 3

THE CATACOMBS OF ROME

0   ½   1   2
MILES

shovel. Thus in such corridors the highest graves are normally the oldest and the lowest are the newest. Also entire second, third or more stories of galleries and chambers often were laid out. While the uppermost corridors are some 20 or 25 feet below the surface of the earth, the lowest may be 40 or 50 feet deeper. The oldest catacombs seem to have been excavated within privately owned and therefore relatively small and limited areas and thus characteristically assumed a sort of gridiron pattern. When later catacombs were excavated in more extensive properties owned by the church, their corridors branched out and out almost endlessly. Whereas at first sight the catacombs now appear to be inextricably tangled networks, an appreciation of the process of their excavation enables the scientific investigator to retrace the course of their development and understand their earlier forms.

2. THE REDISCOVERY OF THE CATACOMBS

THE rediscovery of the catacombs at Rome dates from 1578 when some workmen accidentally happened upon one of the long-lost subterranean cemeteries. The pioneer investigation of the catacombs was undertaken by Antonio Bosio, who devoted thirty-six years to the task, and whose *Roma Sotterranea* was published in 1632, three years after his own death. Not until the nineteenth century was Bosio's work worthily resumed, most notably by Giovanni Battista de Rossi (d. 1894).[1] He was assisted by his brother, Michele Stefano de Rossi, who had the knowledge of a geologist and an engineer, and was followed in the work by his pupils, Josef Wilpert[2] and Orazio Marucchi.[3] More recently Professor Paul Styger[4] has applied the most rigorously scientific techniques to a fresh investigation of the catacombs, with results necessitating many revisions of the earlier conclusions.

[1] *La Roma Sotterranea Cristiana.* 1864-77.
[2] *Die Malereien der Katakomben Roms.* 1903.
[3] *Le Catacombe Romane, opera postuma.* 1932.
[4] SRK.

3. THE JEWISH CATACOMBS

BEFORE proceeding to describe the oldest and most important Christian catacombs, a word should be said about the Jewish catacombs. It was noted above that the Christians were probably following a Jewish custom in adopting catacombs for burial places, and some half-dozen ancient Jewish cemeteries of this sort have been found in Rome.

The beginnings of the Jewish community in Rome, like those of the later Christian community, are little known. In 161 B.C. an embassy of Judas Maccabeus came to Rome seeking assurances of support in the struggle against the Seleucids, and in 139 B.C. Simon, the last of the sons of Mattathias, renewed relations with Rome and obtained ratification of a treaty between Rome and the now independent Jewish state. In the same year that the embassy of Simon was received in honor by the Roman Senate and sent away with the promise of friendship, Hispalus, the praetor peregrinus, who was the magistrate having jurisdiction in cases involving foreigners, banished the Chaldeans and the Jews from Rome and Italy within a period of ten days. But the Jews returned, and in the first half of the first century A.D. the Jewish population of Rome is estimated at about twenty thousand.[1]

It was always the custom of the Jews to practice inhumation, and in Palestine many graves were hewn in the native rock. At Rome the soft tufa formation made it easily possible to dig more extensive corridors and halls to receive the graves. The oldest catacomb of the Jews now known was discovered by Bosio in 1602 but was lost to knowledge again and rediscovered only in 1904. The other Jewish catacombs have also become known only since the middle of the nineteenth century and later. The oldest Jewish catacomb just mentioned lies near Monteverde, before the Porta Portese in Trastevere, and burials were probably begun there in the first century A.D.[2] One of the inscriptions of this catacomb, probably belonging to the second century, is shown in Fig. 154. It reads, simply and pathetically, "Here lies Leontia, 20 years old." The seven-armed candlestick is a characteristic mark in all the Jewish catacombs.

Two other Jewish catacombs are on the Via Appia before the

[1] Hermann Vogelstein, *Rome* (1940. tr. from rev. ed. of *Geschichte der Juden in Rom*), pp.9f.,17.
[2] N. Müller, *Die jüdische Katakombe am Monteverde zu Rom, der älteste bisher bekannt gewordene jüdische Friedhof des Abendlandes*. 1912, p.120.

Porta San Sebastiano, one in the Vigna Randanini and the other in the Vigna Cimarra. A fourth is on the Via Appia Pignatelli, a fifth under the Via Labicana east of the Esquiline and the sixth, most recently discovered, is in the Villa Torlonia (onetime residence of Benito Mussolini), before the Porta Pia in the northeast part of the city.

Numerous rooms in the catacomb of the Villa Torlonia are adorned with paintings, and as usual the ruling motif is the seven-armed lampstand. One of the frescoes is reproduced in Fig. 155. On the right is the scroll of the Law, on the left the ethrog and in the middle the seven-armed candlestick. The scroll of the Law is rolled around a rod whose knobs are indicated by heavy points. A small triangular piece of parchment is to be seen above at the right. In reality this was glued to the roll and contained the title of the work. The perspective is primitive and shows both ends of the roll at once. The ethrog is a citron, which was used along with the lulab or festive palm-branch in the Feast of Tabernacles, and hence was a symbol of Judaism.[3] The seven-armed candlestick likewise was a notable symbol of the Jewish religion. The prototype was the golden lampstand in the temple at Jerusalem which Titus carried off in triumph (pp. 249f.) but similar candlesticks burned also in the synagogues and in the homes of the Jews at the reading of the Law and at other religious ceremonies. So instead of seeking in the symbol of the seven-armed candlestick some mysterious astral-eschatological significance as certain scholars have done, it is correct to interpret it far more simply. Wherever it appears it signifies, "Here a Jew worships his God," and when it is found upon graves it means, "He was a faithful Jew."[4]

[3] This was in accordance with Leviticus 23:40, the citron being held to be "the fruit of goodly trees" (cf. JE v, pp.261f.).

[4] Hermann W. Beyer and Hans Lietzmann, *Die jüdische Katakombe der Villa Torlonia in Rom.* 1930, p.18.

4. THE CHRISTIAN CATACOMBS

THE great development of catacombs, however, was carried out by the Christians. Michele Stefano de Rossi estimated that the catacombs known in 1867 covered a surface area of 615 acres and, basing his calculations upon the average development of the galleries under a given area, he computed that the total length of their corridors was over 500 miles.[1] Today 35 or more separate Christian catacombs are known at Rome (see Plan 3). They are for the most part in a circle outside the city, some three miles from its center, the reason being that Roman law prohibited burial or cremation within the walls and forbade dwelling in the neighborhood of a sepulchral monument. Like the pagan tombs which were built along all the public roads leading out from Rome, so the catacombs also were chiefly on the main roads like the Via Appia and others.

According to Professor Styger's researches into their origins, the oldest of the catacombs belong to a time around the middle of the second century.[2] Although no Christian catacombs earlier than this have been found, it is possible that such did exist. The catacombs of the middle of the second century manifest a fully developed system of construction which not only reflects Jewish models but suggests that the Christians themselves had learned by actual experience in earlier excavations. If such earlier catacombs did exist they of course had to be outside the Wall of Servius, but could still have been considerably nearer the center of the city than the later ones were. The city was growing rapidly at that time and seldom, if ever, was there more building done here than in the first half of the second century, particularly in the reign of Hadrian. The areas of suburban extension on all sides are clearly shown by the line which the Aurelian Wall had to follow in A.D. 270-275. This rapid suburban development must constantly have pushed the burial zone farther out from the center of the city to where it is represented by the now known catacombs. If there were earlier catacombs it may be that they had to be abandoned and were destroyed as the city grew. The four oldest catacombs now known are those of Lucina, Callistus, Domitilla and Priscilla, all of which belonged originally to the middle of the second century.

[1] Karl Baedeker, *Central Italy and Rome.* 15th ed. 1909, p.453.
[2] SRK, p.319.

THE CRYPTS OF LUCINA

On the edge of the Via Appia, a little more than a mile outside the Porta San Sebastiano, are the impressive remains of a tomb which probably belonged to some prominent Roman of the first century. Connected with the monument was a piece of ground beneath which, at about the end of Hadrian's reign (A.D. 117-138), a Christian cemetery was excavated. Whether the owner of the tomb had himself become a Christian, or simply had allowed his Christian slaves and freedmen to make their burials on his property, remains unknown. The first excavation consisted of entrance steps leading down to a long passageway about six feet in height, from which two other passageways branched off. From this earliest period only empty loculi remain, perhaps fifty in number.

A decade or two later the subterranean cemetery was extended by the digging of steps to a passageway at a deeper level and also by the excavation of several chambers opening off from the original passageways. Paintings, datable to about the middle of the second century,[3] remain in some of these chambers. The finest is the ceiling painting in the chamber known as "Y" (Fig. 156), in which the motifs in part are still those of classical Roman interior decoration. The field is divided by lines into circles and sections, while the figures are represented in an almost statuary way and with an exaggerated thinness. The representations include little winged persons, women with arms uplifted in prayer, and the Good Shepherd who carries a lamb upon his shoulders. In the center stands Daniel between two lions.

Toward the end of the second century additional room was gained in the cemetery by deepening the passageways, and early in the third century other extensive work was done on a series of galleries at a lower level. At about the end of the third century, the remains of Pope Cornelius, who had died in exile in 253, were buried in one of the chambers. Later accounts state that this was done by a certain Saint Lucina (p. 363), but since several persons of the same name are mentioned in sixth century legends it is difficult to establish for

[3] Here and elsewhere in this chapter the dates that are given for the Christian catacombs at Rome and also for their paintings, are those of Styger. The paintings are dated somewhat later by Fritz Wirth who believes that no Christian catacomb paintings in Rome are earlier than the third century A.D. (*Römische Wandmalerei vom Untergang Pompejis bis ans Ende des dritten Jahrhunderts.* 1934, p.226). Wirth ascribes the ceiling painting in the Lucina catacomb which is mentioned in the text above, to a time around A.D. 220 (ibid., pp.168f.).

certain any historical facts concerning the woman whose name the area has come to bear.[4]

THE CATACOMB OF CALLISTUS

Somewhat farther back in the same field in which the Crypts of Lucina were located, another Christian cemetery was begun at about the middle of the second century. The area in which it was excavated may have belonged to the church by purchase or gift. Two main corridors, each entered by its own steps, were driven lengthwise along the two longer sides of this area. Later these were connected at the far end of the field by a cross corridor, and additional cross galleries began to give the whole a sort of gridiron plan. At first the place was known simply as Coemeterium or "sleeping chamber," which was the name generally applied by the early Christians to their burial places. Pope Zephyrinus (c.198-c.217) placed the cemetery under the administration of Callistus, who at that time was a priest and was to become the next pope (c.217-c.222). This is narrated by Hippolytus, who states that Zephyrinus entrusted Callistus with the management of the clergy and "appointed him over the cemetery."[5] A notable extension of the cemetery was carried out under the leadership of Callistus, and thereafter the catacomb retained his name although he had not been its founder nor was buried there himself. The old passageways were deepened at this time, new cross corridors were made and a number of larger burial chambers were excavated.

Of these the most important was a large double chamber which became a burial place for the Roman popes and hence is known as the Crypt of the Popes (Fig. 157). Up to this time most of the popes had been buried, like Peter himself, in the Vatican. The Liber Pontificalis lists fourteen men who headed the Roman church between Peter and Zephyrinus and indicates burial at the Vatican for all but two of them. The two exceptions are Clement I, who is said to have been buried in Greece, and Alexander who is stated to have been buried on the Via Nomentana. Otherwise the typical statement concerning each of these popes is, "He also was buried near the body of the blessed Peter in the Vatican." But for Zephyrinus and his successors the burial notices in the Liber Pontificalis run as follows:

---

[4] SRK, pp.21-33.
[5] *The Refutation of All Heresies* (*Philosophumena*). IX, vii (ANF V, p.130).

Zephyrinus (d. c.217) "He also was buried in his own cemetery near the cemetery of Calistus on the Via Appia."

Callistus I (d. c.222) "in the cemetery of Calipodius on the Via Aurelia at the third milestone"

Urbanus I (d. 230) "in the cemetery of Pretextatus on the Via Appia"

Pontianus (d. 235) "in the cemetery of Calistus on the Via Appia"

Anteros (d. 236) "in the cemetery of Calistus on the Via Appia"

Fabianus (d. 250) "in the cemetery of Calistus on the Via Appia"

Cornelius (d. 253) "And his body was taken up at night by the blessed Lucina and the clergy and was buried in a crypt in her own garden, near the cemetery of Calistus on the Via Appia."

Lucius (d. 254) "in the cemetery of Calistus on the Via Appia"

Stephen I (d. 257) "in the cemetery of Calistus on the Via Appia"

Xystus II (d. 258) "in the cemetery of Calistus on the Via Appia"

Dionysius (d. 268) "in the cemetery of Calistus on the Via Appia"

Felix I (d. 274) in the cemetery of Callistus (according to earlier lists)[6]

Eutychianus (d. 283) "in the cemetery of Calistus on the Via Appia"

Gaius (d. 296) "in the cemetery of Calistus on the Via Appia"

Marcellinus (d. 304) "on the Via Salaria in the cemetery of Priscilla"

Marcellus (d. 309) "in the cemetery of Priscilla on the Via Salaria"

Eusebius (d. c.310) "in the cemetery of Calistus on the Via Appia"

Miltiades (d. 314) "in the cemetery of Calistus on the Via Appia"

Sylvester (d. 335) "in the cemetery of Priscilla on the Via Salaria, three miles from the city of Rome."

Of these popes who are stated by the Liber Pontificalis to have been buried "in the cemetery of Calistus," at least some found their last resting place in the simple niches of the double chamber under consideration. This is certain for Pontianus, Anteros, Fabianus, Lucius and Eutychianus, whose grave inscriptions have been found there and who are mentioned in prayers scratched on the walls by pious visitors of ancient times, and it is probable for Stephen I, Xystus II, Dionysius and Felix I, although their actual epitaphs are now lost. Several of these popes were martyrs, including Xystus II who perished on August 6, 258 in Valerian's persecution, when he and four deacons were taken by surprise in the catacomb and killed.

[6] LLP, p.33 n.1; SRK, p.48.

The papal crypt was enlarged in later times, and the wall between the two halves of the double chamber gave way to two simple marble columns, but the original plan is still clearly recognizable. Pope Damasus (366-384), who everywhere was zealous to honor the martyrs, placed one of his monumental inscriptions here. As is well known, these inscriptions were composed in poetic style by Damasus, lettered by his secretary and artist Furius Dionysius Filocalus, and placed in a large number of Rome's most venerated tombs. While most of the originals have perished, the text of many of them is preserved in copies which were made by pilgrims.[7] The marble slab which bore the inscription of Damasus in the crypt of the popes was broken into over one hundred fragments, but has been restored and replaced in its original location as may be seen in Fig. 157. The inscription reads: "Here if you inquire, lies crowded together a throng of the righteous, the venerable tombs hold the bodies of the saints, their lofty spirits the palace of heaven took to itself. Here the companions of Xystus who bore trophies from the enemy; here a number of the leaders who ministered at the altars of Christ; here is placed the priest who lived in long peace; here the holy confessors whom Greece sent; here young men and boys, old men and their pure descendants, who chose to keep their virgin modesty. Here, I confess, I Damasus wished to deposit my body, but I feared to disturb the holy ashes of the righteous."[8]

It was probably in the fourth century that the further chamber beyond the Crypt of the Popes was excavated; it is known as the Tomb of Cecilia. By the middle of that century it was adorned with marble and mosaic work. Having been damaged perhaps at the time of the Goths (410) and Vandals (455), it was restored toward the end of the fifth century and some of the mosaics were replaced by paintings. The name of the chamber is connected with Saint Cecilia, whose remains are said to have been discovered by Pope Paschal I (817-824). She is represented, along with Pope Urban (222-230) and with Christ, in the frescoes of the main wall, which are dated by their style in the ninth century. At the same time pilgrims have scratched on the walls their appeals to the famous martyr and saint. Definite information concerning Saint Cecilia is no longer available, however, since the existing late fifth century account of her life is full of con-

---

[7] C. M. Kaufmann, *Handbuch der altchristlichen Epigraphik*. 1917, pp.338-365.
[8] Walter Lowrie, *Monuments of the Early Church*. 1901, pp.74f.

tradictions and improbabilities, and the date of her martyrdom is unknown.

Under the administration of Callistus the entire cemetery increased greatly in size, many of the common Christians of Rome as well as the clergy and martyrs no doubt now being buried there. On the other side of the main corridor from the papal crypt, three large chambers were excavated in the time of Callistus, and to these yet three more were later added. The six chambers have received the name of Sacrament Chapels since, when first discovered, their frescoes were believed to be symbolical representations of the sacraments of baptism, the Eucharist, confirmation and confession.[9] Actually, it is probable that these chambers served not only as burial places but also as rooms in which the survivors held meals in honor of the deceased. Therefore they were adorned especially with numerous paintings for which place was found on the ceilings and on the walls between the graves. The paintings of the first chamber are now destroyed almost completely, but those which remain in the other rooms include the following subjects: the Fossor, the Woman with Arms Uplifted in Prayer, the Shepherd, a Meal Participated in by Seven Persons, Abraham's Sacrifice of Isaac, Moses' Miracle of Bringing Water from the Rock, Jonah, the Baptism of Jesus, the Healing of the Paralytic, and the Resurrection of Lazarus.

The first three chambers are believed to belong to the time of Callistus, and the style of the paintings which remain in them is in agreement with a date at the beginning of the third century. In the middle of the second century the classical tradition still prevailed and tall figures stood in statuary repose, with all details carefully worked out, but here the forms are relatively coarse, the faces are but masks, and details, such as the number of fingers, are neglected.[10]

THE CATACOMB OF DOMITILLA

The Catacomb of Domitilla is some distance from that of Callistus on the Via delle Sette Chiese where anciently ran the Via Ardeatina. It has been known as Coemeterium Domitillae at least since the seventh century and doubtless since its origin. The Domitilla whose name it preserves was probably the Flavia Domitilla who is described

[9] J. Wilpert, *Die Malereien der Sacramentskapellen in der Katakombe des hl. Callistus.* 1897.

[10] SRK, pp.34-62; cf. G. B. de Rossi, *La Roma Sotterranea Cristiana.* II (1867); E. Josi, *Il Cimiterio di Callisto.* 1933.

in Dio's *Roman History* as a relative of the Emperor Domitian and wife of the consul Flavius Clemens. In A.D. 95 both she and her husband were condemned on account of "atheism" and inclination toward Judaism, these being familiar charges against the early Christians, and while he was beheaded she was banished to the island of Pandateria in the Tyrrhenian Sea. Dio's statement is: "And the same year Domitian slew, along with many others, Flavius Clemens the consul, although he was a cousin and had to wife Flavia Domitilla, who was also a relative of the emperor's. The charge brought against them both was that of atheism, a charge on which many others who drifted into Jewish ways were condemned. Some of these were put to death, and the rest were at least deprived of their property. Domitilla was merely banished to Pandateria."[11]

Substantially the same account is recorded by Eusebius, although he probably is wrong in calling Domitilla the niece instead of the wife of Flavius Clemens. He also names a different but nearby island, Pontia, as the place of Domitilla's exile, and explicitly describes her as a Christian although he does not mention Flavius Clemens as also having been a Christian martyr. The statement of Eusebius is: "In the fifteenth year of Domitian Flavia Domitilla, daughter of a sister of Flavius Clemens, who at that time was one of the consuls of Rome, was exiled with many others to the island of Pontia in consequence of testimony borne to Christ."[12] Jerome also tells how at the end of the fourth century the widow Paula visited "the island of Pontia ennobled long since as the place of exile of the illustrious lady Flavia Domitilla who under the Emperor Domitian was banished because she confessed herself a Christian," and saw "the cells in which this lady passed the period of her long martyrdom."[13]

It does not appear, however, that the catacomb was constructed in the time of Domitilla herself. Without doubt this area of ground belonged to her, and two heathen inscriptions were found near by which indicated that burials had been made there by the permission of Flavia Domitilla. Evidently she had made a gift of her property or a portion of it for burial purposes, and since the burials there were pagan she must not yet have been converted to Christianity. The pagan possessors of the property developed it into an extensive place of burial. This is indicated by the ruins of columbaria

[11] *Rom. Hist.* LXVII, xiv, 1f.   [12] *Ch. Hist.* III, xviii.
[13] *Letter 108 to Eustochium* (NPNFSS VI, p.197).

and of an enclosing wall which still exist there, and it is probable that pagan burials continued to be made until around A.D. 140. Up to this time it is extremely unlikely that a Christian catacomb would have been excavated beneath ground while pagan rites and ceremonies were conducted overhead. Meanwhile the area continued to be known by the name of Domitilla. Then shortly before the middle of the second century the owners of the property appear to have accepted Christianity. At any rate the pagan burials ceased above ground and beneath the surface a Christian catacomb came into existence. Whose name should it bear if not that of the earlier owner of the property, Flavia Domitilla, who now long since had become a Christian and a glorious martyr?

The origin of the Christian cemetery only shortly before the middle of the second century is indicated not only by the continuation of pagan burials above ground until about that date, but also by the oldest frescoes in the catacomb itself. These are comparable in style to those in the crypts of Lucina and like them evidently belong to a time near the middle of the second century. They are to be found in a region of the catacomb which is generally known as the Hypogeum of the Flavians. This name was given because of the belief that the catacomb was established sometime in the relatively quiet period between Nero and Domitian and was the burial place of members of the Flavian house. This was the view presented originally by G. B. de Rossi, but no Flavian inscriptions have been discovered in the Hypogeum, and Professor Paul Styger finds no historical argument which justifies the first century date.[14]

Another portion of the catacomb whose origins probably go back to the same period at the middle of the second century as the Hypogeum of the Flavians, is the so-called Region of the Aurelians. This area is relatively distinct and is marked by corridors of unusual height. Evidently its owners limited themselves to their own definite area and kept digging their passageways deeper as more burial space was required.

Between these two regions is yet a smaller area where a third group of the owners of the property made their burials. It is a subterranean room containing a number of burial places in the floor and two niches designed to receive sarcophagi. One sarcophagus still remains *in situ*, and De Rossi saw a second of similar type standing there when the

[14] SRK, p.78.

place was first discovered in 1854, but the latter has since been purloined. The sarcophagus which remains is of the tub-shaped kind, adorned with rippled marks and lions' heads, which is ascribed to the time of the Antonines in the middle of the second century. Since there is nothing distinctively Christian about this sarcophagus and since Roman custom did change to inhumation in the immediately preceding time of Hadrian, it is possible that it was a pagan who was buried here. But even if that is the case, the subterranean room must have become a Christian burial place very soon afterward, that is around the middle of the century, when the portions of the same property on either side were so employed, for Christians and pagans would not have shared an almost common cemetery. Later the upper part of this subterranean room was destroyed by the building of a basilica directly above it. This was the Basilica of Saint Petronilla, which was in use from the fifth to the eighth centuries, and the area which we have described beneath it is known as the Hypogeum under the Basilica.

The hypothesis that the property of Domitilla was made available to a group of pagans for a burial ground in the first century, and that about the middle of the second century their heirs accepted Christianity and established the three underground burial places just described, is substantiated by the inscriptions found in the debris in these regions. These are both Christian and pagan in character, and it is presumable that the heathen inscriptions belonged originally to the heathen burial area within the enclosing wall above ground. The older Flavian inscriptions are almost entirely pagan, but the inscriptions from the time of the Antonines are not only pagan but also frequently Christian. It was, therefore, at this time that Christianity was being accepted by those to whom the former property of Domitilla belonged.

Two other areas of the cemetery of Domitilla have often been regarded as of great antiquity, but more recent research places them at the end of the third century or in the fourth century. These are the region with the painted chamber at the foot of the great stairway by the Tor Marancia, and the region of the grave of Ampliatus. These sections are outside the old wall which surrounded the original pagan burial area, and eventually many other areas were excavated in yet other directions also. Evidently in its later development the catacomb could be extended quite freely and was not limited to a precisely defined area. Thus there developed in the fourth century a vast system of subterranean galleries and rooms, connecting with the three most ancient regions and branching off in all directions. To the entire mighty complex the name of Domitilla continued to belong.[15]

THE CATACOMB OF PRISCILLA

The Catacomb of Priscilla is on the other side of Rome from the catacombs thus far described, on the Via Salaria Nuova. Its extent and complexity surpass anything met hitherto, but three chief component parts of the entire cemetery can be clearly distinguished. Evidently these three areas originally were separate, privately owned burial places.

The first is the so-called Hypogeum of the Acilians, which was excavated and studied by De Rossi in 1880, and which lies beneath the Basilica di San Silvestro. It has been believed that this was the burial place of Manius Acilius Glabrio who was consul in the year 91, and in 95 was condemned to death by Domitian on account of Christian faith at the same time that Domitilla was exiled and Titus Flavius Clemens was executed. No trace of his grave has been found, however, and on the contrary the style of the oldest painting here is that of the middle of the second century. The Priscilla whose name the entire catacomb preserves may well have been a member of the same senatorial family. The catacomb bore her name at least from the fifth century and probably from the beginning. A third century inscription found in the debris mentions a certain Priscilla in connection with a Manius Acilius, both of whom are called "most illustrious." Perhaps the connection of the original Priscilla with this catacomb is comparable to that of Domitilla with the cemetery previously considered.

The Hypogeum is entered by a subterranean stairway, which leads to a wide corridor running first to the northwest and then to the southwest. This corridor originally was vaulted, and traces of the paintings which adorned its walls still remain. The schematic division of field by red, green and brown lines and the classical elegance of birds and flowers which are still recognizable in these paintings indicate a date around the middle of the second century. In later years the Hypogeum was extended to include a number of further passageways and rooms.

[15] SRK, pp.63-99.

The stairway which leads down to the Hypogeum also gives access to a complex of corridors in a near-by area. These are laid out on a regular plan of the gridiron type as in Lucina and Callistus, and probably also belong to the middle of the second century. While in the Hypogeum there are sarcophagus niches for relatively well-to-do persons, the corridors here have only simple loculi and presumably served for the poor. On the graves were marked the anchor, the palm and the dove.

A second major area of the catacomb likewise belongs in its origin to the middle of the second century. This is known as the Region of the Cryptoporticus and includes the famous Cappella Greca. Here again a common entrance gives access on the one hand to a large hall with chambers and niches for rich graves and on the other hand to an unadorned corridor whose simple arcosolia and loculi were for the poor. The most important and best preserved room is the so-called Cappella Greca (Fig. 158) which opens off from the large hall just mentioned. The "Greek Chapel" is a relatively small room around the sides of which runs a masonry bench with two simple graves underneath it. It has been believed that this room was intended for the celebration of the Eucharist in solemn church assembly, but since not more than ten people could find comfortable seats in it at once it may have served only for the holding of meals in honor of the dead. A neighboring room, which has a water drain of lead piping, has been interpreted wrongly as a baptistery,[16] but was probably the place where these meals were prepared.

The Cappella Greca is adorned with the greatest series of early Christian paintings which is preserved in any single room of the catacombs. In general the elegance of the tall, statuary figures, the conscientious reproduction of the features, the exact treatment of the garments and the plastic handling of light and shade represent a style comparable to that in the oldest paintings of the Crypts of Lucina on the Via Appia and of the Hypogeum of the Flavians on the Via Ardeatina and indicate a date around the middle of the second century. This date is confirmed by the coiffure of the half-veiled woman

---

[16] If the drain pipe had been shut off water could have stood in this room only to a depth of about four inches. Moreover, it is unlikely that the Roman Christians were baptized in the catacombs at all. The *Teaching of the Twelve Apostles* (7 [ANF VII, p.379]), written about the beginning of the second century, calls for baptism in running water, and at Rome this was probably in the Tiber where, according to Tertullian (*On Baptism* 4 [ANF III, p.671]), Peter himself baptized.

in the painting of the meal scene which will be mentioned in a moment. She wears the braid of hair on the crown of the head in the same way as that worn by the Empress Faustina, wife of Antoninus Pius (138-161), as seen on some well-known coins bearing her likeness, while the daughter, Faustina Junior, wife of Marcus Aurelius (161-180) changed the style.

On the wall at the end of the chamber is painted a meal scene, showing seven persons provided with fish and baskets full of bread to eat (Fig. 159). Elsewhere in the chamber are a number of biblical scenes, including Noah in the Ark, Abraham's Sacrifice, the Miracle of the Water in the Wilderness, the Three Youths in the Fiery Furnace, Daniel between the Lions, the Story of Susanna, the Adoration of the Magi, the Healing of the Paralytic and the Resurrection of Lazarus.

The painting of the Resurrection of Lazarus is now almost effaced but it is still possible to recognize that on one side is depicted a small building containing a mummy and on the other, the sister of Lazarus standing with arms upraised. In the middle Christ is shown, facing toward the tomb and with the right hand uplifted in a gesture of speech. He is represented in the Roman type, and is dressed in tunic and pallium, the left hand holding the garment. He is youthful and beardless, with short hair and large eyes. The left portion of this picture, showing Christ in the center and the sister of Lazarus at the left, is reproduced in Fig. 160. Although it is now only barely recognizable, this picture is of great interest since it is the oldest representation of Jesus that is preserved anywhere.

In part the Region of the Cryptoporticus lies in an area where there had been a sand quarry. The third major region of the Catacomb of Priscilla arose in farther reaches of this abandoned quarry whose subterranean galleries could be readily employed to receive Christian graves. In general this part of the cemetery (Fig. 161) is simple and little adorned and appears to have served largely for the burial of the poorer Christians. A date around the end of the second or beginning of the third century is probable for the origin of this burial place. Some of the graves have bricks with which they were originally closed, still remaining in place, and stamps on these indicate a time under the Severan house of emperors.

In the neighborhood of some stamped bricks of this date, and at the end of one of the quarry galleries there are a number of badly damaged paintings. They are grouped around the highest loculus on the right wall of the corridor and all were produced at the same time. On the ceiling in painted stucco relief are two shepherds with lambs, represented amidst olive trees. One of these pictures, with the Good Shepherd standing between two lambs and carrying another on his shoulders, is reproduced in Fig. 163. To the right, on the ceiling, is a painting (Fig. 162) showing a mother, seated and holding her child, and with a star above her head. Standing beside her is a man dressed in a pallium, holding a roll in his left hand and pointing upward with his right hand. This is believed to be a representation of Isaiah prophesying the birth of the Messiah (Isaiah 7:14), with the fulfillment of the prophecy indicated at the same time in the Madonna. On the wall of the corridor to the left of the loculus are three figures of the deceased, a man, a woman and a child, with up-lifted arms, while at the right is another standing figure of a man together with traces of a feminine figure.

When compared first with the earliest frescoes in Lucina and Domitilla, and then with the later ones in the Callistus chambers, these are clearly seen to be comparable to the latter. The tall, ele-gant form of the figures in the paintings of classical style does not appear here. Rather the figures are relatively heavy and executed without close attention to detail. A date at the end of the second or beginning of the third century is probable. Thus of the three main areas of the catacomb the two older arose about the middle of the second century, while the newer was established at the end of the second century or beginning of the third. All three evi-dently were at first private property. Around the middle of the third century they appear to have been used no more. Then, approximately in the time of Constantine, they again came into use, this time as church property, and were connected with one another and further extended.[17]

THE CATACOMB OF PRAETEXTATUS

On an ancient road to the left of the Via Appia and not far from the cemetery of Callistus lies a catacomb which preserves the name of an otherwise unknown founder, Praetextatus. Of the eight distinct areas which are recognizable within the entire complex, the first is known as the Region of the Scala maggiore. It is characterized by the

[17] SRK, pp.100-145.

large stairway leading down to a long corridor, with which are connected two chambers and seven branch corridors. The main chamber is adorned with frescoes which represent the scene at Jacob's Well, the Healing of the Woman with an Issue of Blood, the Resurrection of Lazarus and another incident which may be an illustration of Similitude VIII in the Shepherd of Hermas. The style of these paintings seems to be midway between that of the oldest frescoes in Lucina, Domitilla and Priscilla and the early third century paintings in Callistus, and a date toward the end of the second century is indicated. The first excavation probably was done a decade or so before the time of the paintings.

A second area is called the Spelunca Magna in the pilgrim itineraries of the eighth century. This means literally "large cave" but the pilgrims used *spelunca* practically as a synonym for "cemetery." A long corridor some six and one-half feet in height was later deepened to more than eleven feet and elegant burial chambers were established on either side of it. The original excavation here belongs to the middle of the third century, while the later chambers, including the so-called crypt of Januarius, are dated by the style of their frescoes in the middle of the fourth century.

Adjoining the Spelunca Magna is a third area which is designated as the Region Cocorum from a graffito which seems to refer to a collective burial place of cooks and bakers. The frequently encountered abbreviation of *Christos* known as the Christ-monogram or the Constantinian monogram indicates a fourth century date.[18] At the foot of the entrance to the Spelunca Magna a stairway leads to a fourth area at a lower level, whose numerous chambers likewise seem to belong to the middle of the fourth century. A few steps from the entrance to the Spelunca Magna is another stairway which leads down to a system of subterranean corridors which is laid out in an unusually orderly fashion. This is the Region of the Scala minore and constitutes the fifth area of the cemetery. It belongs to the fourth century.

[18] This is the symbol (☧) which Constantine is said to have seen in a dream or vision, and to have inscribed on the shields of his soldiers or to have fashioned as a labarum or imperial standard, before his victory at the Milvian bridge (p.212 n.2), and which appears thereafter with frequency on his coins and those of his sons, and in Christian inscriptions. Lactantius (A.D. c.260-c.325), *Of the Manner in Which the Persecutors Died.* 44 (ANF VII, p.318); Eusebius, *Life of Constantine.* I, 28-31; Max Sulzberger in *Byzantion, Revue Internationale des Études Byzantines.* 2 (1925), pp.393-448.

The sixth area is excavated at an intermediate level and still bears dates from the year A.D. 384. Also to the late fourth century belongs the seventh area which lies beneath the Via Appia Pignatelli. Its corridors are crowded with loculi of the poorest appearance. The eighth region is that where the great arcosolium grave of Celerina was found, with its late fourth century paintings representing the story of Susanna and portraying saints including Liberius and Xystus II.

Thus in the catacomb of Praetextatus the origins of the Region of the Scala maggiore go back into the late second century and of the Spelunca Magna into the middle of the third. The other complexes which were connected with these regions later, belong to the fourth century.[19]

THE CATACOMB OF SEBASTIAN

The cemetery of Sebastian is in a valley on the Via Appia. This depression was so marked as to give to the region the name Catacumbas, "by the hollow." The Emperor Maxentius (A.D. 306-312) built a circus near by, and a notice in the Roman city calendar of A.D. 354 which states that this circus was built *in catacumbas*, meaning "in the place which is called Catacumbas," is the earliest appearance of the term. The Christian cemetery at this place originally was known, therefore, as Coemeterium Catacumbas, and only later received the name of Saint Sebastian. By a natural misunderstanding the name "catacombs" now has come to be applied generally to all subterranean burial places of the early Christians throughout Rome and elsewhere in Italy and other lands.

Excavations begun here in 1915 beneath the Church of San Sebastiano have led to the most significant discoveries. At the lowest level to which the digging penetrated, a heathen necropolis was unearthed. No less than sixteen pagan columbaria were found in the precincts of the basilica alone. These were rectangular brick structures dating, according to the style of their inscriptions, stucco paintings and mosaics, in the first and second centuries. Their walls held niches for the urns of cremation. As the custom changed to inhumation, burials were made in the earth beneath, with clay pipes leading down through the floor into the graves for the usual oblations of wine. At the beginning of the second century, three two-story mausoleums were built near by. One of these was constructed to accommodate urns for ashes but the other two were intended exclusively for

[19] SRK, pp.146-174.

inhumation. When the first one came into the possession of a certain M. Clodius Hermes, who is known from an inscription at the door, he had the niches for the urns walled in and new frescoes painted. These showed a deceased person being led by Hermes, the conductor of souls, into the presence of Hades, the ruler of the underworld. In the course of the second century the necropolis grew also through the building of assembly rooms for holding meals in memory of the dead. Nowhere at this lowest level was any trace of a Christian monument found. The necropolis was exclusively pagan.

Then the property came into the possession of Christians. Perhaps this was by purchase or gift, but more probably the owners themselves were converted to Christianity at this time. At any rate, about the middle of the third century the heathen necropolis was entirely filled in, rooms for Christian use were built above it, and a Christian catacomb came into existence beneath ground. The level at which the Christian rooms were found in the excavations was above that of the pagan necropolis but still some six feet beneath the floor of the church. The first room now called the Triclia, was supported at the back against an old basalt wall, which probably was the enclosing wall of the heathen necropolis, and at one end rested upon the first century columbaria. At the front, on the slope of the hill, pillars supported a roof and provided an open loggia. Masonry benches ran around the sides of the room. At one corner was a small spring, in the slime of whose drain were found remains of food, bones of fish, chicken and hare, and bits of broken glass. A fresco showed a bright garden scene, with a reed hedge, vine leaves and fluttering birds.

The most important discovery was that of the numerous graffiti which had been scratched on the walls of the room by those who visited it (Fig. 164). A great part of the wall with these rough inscriptions is still preserved in its original position, while broken pieces lay on the floor and could be pieced together again. The graffiti are written in both Greek and Latin and in capital as well as in cursive letters. Most of them are short prayers to Paul and Peter for remembrance and intercession, like the following:

PAULE ET PETRE PETITE
PRO VICTORE

PAUL AND PETER PRAY
FOR VICTOR

Others mention *refrigeria* or "refreshments" in honor of the apostles. These were meals held according to ancient custom at famous graves in remembrance of venerated saints. One such inscription reads:

PETRO ET PAULO
TOMIUS COELIUS
REFRIGERIUM FECI

TO PETER AND PAUL
I TOMIUS COELIUS
MADE A REFRIGERIUM

In all, the names of the two great apostles are scratched on the wall more than one hundred times.[20] A second room was of somewhat similar character, and also had the names of the apostles, *Petre Paule*, scratched at least once on a brick column.

The style of the painting and the paleographical character of the graffiti point to a date around the middle of the third century for the origin of these rooms. Since not a single visitor scratched on the wall a so-called Constantinian monogram, such as is met at every turn on fourth century monuments, the Triclia cannot have continued in use long after the year 313. Soon after this date, and certainly within the first half of the fourth century, the two rooms, as well as other buildings on this part of the hill, were largely destroyed as the site was leveled up for the building there of a great three-aisled church, the "Basilica of the Apostles." Since the technique of the construction of its walls is similar to that of the near-by Circus of Maxentius (306-312), the basilica must belong to Constantinian times.

The character of the rooms which were frequented so eagerly from the middle of the third to the early part of the fourth century, and which then disappeared so completely beneath the basilica until their recent discovery, is indubitable. They constituted a memorial gathering place, where the Christians honored the memory of Paul and Peter. In the so-called Triclia, common meals were held in remembrance of the two great apostles and the visitors scratched innumerable prayers to them on the walls.[21]

All the evidence points, therefore, to the fact that at this time the

[20] As far as the order of the two names is concerned, they are written "Paul and Peter" or "Peter and Paul" without any apparent preference. Lanciani, *Wanderings through Ancient Roman Churches*, p.89.
[21] SRK, pp.331-345.

bones of Peter and of Paul actually rested here. This is confirmed by an inscription of Pope Damasus I, who as we know was eager to adorn the graves of the martyrs with precious marbles and poetic inscriptions composed by himself. While the original of the inscription in question has perished, it is known from several medieval manuscripts and from a partial thirteenth century copy which stands in the Church of Saint Sebastian, presumably in its original place. This is near the entrance to the crypt of Sebastian, which as we shall see was in the immediate vicinity of the resting place of Peter and Paul. The inscription reads:

> Hic habitasse prium sanctos cognoscere debes,
> Nomina quisque Petri pariter Paulique requiris,
> Discipulos Oriens misit, quod sponte fatemur—
> Sanguinis ob meritum, Christumque per astra secuti
> Aetherios petiere sinus regnaque piorum—
> Roma suos potius meruit defendere cives.
> Haec Damasus vestras referat nova sidera laudes.

> You should know that the saints formerly dwelt here,
> if you are seeking the names of Peter and Paul. The
> Orient sent the disciples, as we freely admit, but on
> account of their bloody martyrdom—they followed
> Christ through the stars and reached the heavenly
> bosom and the realm of the pious—Rome rather has
> won the right to claim them as citizens. This
> Damasus records to your praise, ye new stars.[22]

The inscription of Damasus is in complete agreement with the evidence of the graffiti in the Triclia. Writing in the latter half of the fourth century, Damasus declares that Peter and Paul "formerly dwelt here," which is a poetic way of saying "were formerly buried here." At a time from the middle of the third to the early part of the fourth century, Christians came here in numbers to hold meals in honor of Paul and Peter and to scratch prayers to the two great saints on the walls.

We have seen already that around A.D. 200 Caius pointed to the graves of Peter and of Paul at the Vatican and on the Ostian Way respectively as well-known martyr memorials, and we have con-

---

[22] Lietzmann, *Petrus und Paulus in Rom*, pp.145f.; Walter Lowrie, SS. *Peter and Paul in Rome*. 1940, pp.87f. A misunderstanding of this inscription appears to have given rise to the fifth century legend of an attempt by men from the Orient to carry off the bodies of Peter and Paul (Lipsius and Bonnet, *Acta Apostolorum Apocrypha*, I, pp.220f.).

cluded that the tradition of the apostles' original interment near the respective places of their martyrdoms is entirely trustworthy (p. 303). It must be concluded, therefore, that at the middle of the third century their remains were transferred temporarily to the Via Appia. As a matter of fact there is further evidence that this was the case. This evidence is to be found in the fourth century Church Calendar for the City of Rome. The latter document constituted a sort of yearbook for the inhabitants of Rome, which was edited in A.D. 354 by Furius Dionysius Filocalus, the calligrapher who later was in the service of Pope Damasus and carried out the making of the latter's poetical inscriptions in honor of the martyrs.[23] The portion of the Calendar with which we are concerned is the Depositio Martyrum. This is a list of the dates of the various festivals which were held in honor of the martyrs during the church year, together with an indication of the places where these observances were celebrated. The notation for June 29 reads:

> III KAL. IUL.   Petri in Catacumbas
> et Pauli Ostense Tusco et Basso cons.[24]

A more complete and correct text of the same notice is found in the Martyrologium Hieronymianum as follows:

> Romae Via Aurelia natale[25] sanctorum apostolorum
> Petri et Pauli, Petri in Vaticano, Pauli vero
> in via Ostensi, utrumque in Catacumbas, passi
> sub Nerone, Basso et Tusco consulibus.

Thus, according to sources from the middle of the fourth century, at that time the church festivals in honor of the martyrdom of Peter and Paul were celebrated at three different places. The festival in honor of Peter was held at the Vatican, that in remembrance of Paul on the Ostian Way, and a celebration in honor of both of them was held in Catacumbas. What is signified by "Basso et Tusco consulibus"? This is the consular date indicating the year 258. In that year Valerian's brief but terrible persecution of the Christians was raging, when, among other acts of violence which were committed, on August 6 Pope Xystus II and four deacons were taken by surprise in a catacomb and killed (p. 363). We conclude naturally that fear was felt for the safety of the bones of the two great apostles hitherto rest-

23 J. P. Kirsch, *Aus den römischen Katakomben*. 1926, p.15.
24 Hans Lietzmann, ed., *The Three Oldest Martyrologies*. 1904, p.4.
25 It is the "birthday" of the heavenly life of the saints that is celebrated.

ing at their relatively exposed locations in the Vatican district and on the Ostian Way, and that on June 29, 258, they were transferred to the greater safety of the subterranean cemetery *ad Catacumbas*. More than half a century later, under Constantine, the churches of Saint Peter and Saint Paul were built at the Vatican and on the Ostian Way and then the remains of the two apostles were returned to rest permanently in their original graves. But the names of Peter and Paul continued to be remembered *in Catacumbas* as well as *in Vaticano* and *in via Ostensi*.[26]

The temporary presence of the remains of Paul and Peter *ad Catacumbas* greatly accelerated the development of an extensive Christian cemetery at this place. Many of the faithful wished to find their last rest in proximity to the spot thus hallowed by the two great saints. So there developed a vast network of subterranean corridors and chambers, constituting one of Rome's largest catacombs. Wide areas of these subterranean complexes continued to be visited by pilgrims throughout the Middle Ages as in the case of no other catacomb, but today a great part is filled up and forgotten beneath the surrounding hills. In corridors so long trampled by pilgrim feet it is not to be expected that many monuments should remain and as a matter of fact only a few traces of frescoes are to be seen and a few inscriptions with dates in the latter part of the fourth century.

The name by which the entire catacomb is known is that of Sebastian, the saint and martyr. The Roman city calendar of A.D. 354 lists the festival *Sebastiani in Catacumbas* on the date XIII KAL. FEB. or January 10.[27] According to the fifth century *Acts of Saint Sebastian* he was shot with arrows in the Colosseum as a victim of the great persecution by Diocletian and then was buried *ad Catacumbas in initio cryptae iuxta vestigia apostolorum*, "at Catacumbas in the entrance of the crypt near the vestiges of the apostles."[28] Actually the present crypt of Sebastian is found in immediate proximity to

[26] Lietzmann, *Petrus und Paulus in Rom*, p.126; cf. Kirsch, *Aus den römischen Katakomben*, p.36; Lowrie, *SS. Peter and Paul in Rome*, pp.91f. Styger believes that if not both of the apostles at least Peter originally was buried on the Via Appia and only later interred near-by the place of his martyrdom. But he is then able to give no more convincing explanation of the reference to the year 258 in the Calendar of Filocalus than that it signifies that the two apostles began to be honored *in Catacumbas* around the middle of the third century (SRK, p.346). Why not until then if one or both were buried here in A.D. 64, and why is the precise year 258 specified?
[27] Lietzmann, ed., *The Three Oldest Martyrologies*, p.4.
[28] Lietzmann, *Petrus und Paulus in Rom*, p.169.

the memorial of the apostles at the entrance to the catacomb. The grave was originally in the wall of a simple corridor, and later the opposite wall was removed to provide more room for the numerous visitors. Probably in the time of Constantine, a basilica was built above ground. It was known as the Church of the Apostles and later as the Church of Saint Sebastian.[29] The martyr's grave continued to be accessible by steep steps leading down from within the church. At the beginning of the fifth century two priests, Proclinus and Ursus, rebuilt the crypt of Sebastian, giving it strong brick walls and a new monumental entrance, as well as placing the holy relics in an altar at the same place where the original grave had been.[30]

THE CATACOMB OF PETER AND MARCELLINUS

The Catacomb of Peter and Marcellinus lies on the Via Casilina, as the ancient Via Labicana now is known, and is one of the most extensive complexes of subterranean Rome. It is also notable since no other cemetery possesses so many chambers adorned with frescoes. Before it received the name of Peter and Marcellinus it was known simply by a place-designation as Inter duas Lauros, "Between the two Laurels" (p. 428). Three great stairways lead down to as many regions, which were originally independent of one another but developed so extensively as eventually to interconnect. The first stairway led down from the Via Labicana at right angles to the main corridor, from which side corridors ran off at regular intervals. Several chambers were excavated in connection with these corridors, and the paintings in the first of them are in the style of the fourth century.

The last corridor attained special significance when the remains of two martyrs (Peter, an exorcist, and Marcellinus, a priest[31]) were interred there in simple wall graves. This took place perhaps in the time of the peace of the church, since at the time of their death under Diocletian in A.D. 304 the two martyrs were buried at the place of their beheading on the Via Cornelia. Since many persons now wished to find a last resting place in the catacomb near the revered saints, numerous burial chambers were laid out in the vicinity. They are adorned with paintings in the style of the ad-

[29] San Sebastiano was rebuilt in the form it has today in 1612.

[30] SRK, pp.177-184; cf. F. Farnari, S. Sebastiano "extra moenia." 1934.

[31] Not to be confused with Pope Marcellinus (296-304), who also died later in the same year in the persecution of Diocletian and was buried in the cemetery of Priscilla on the Via Salaria.

vanced fourth century. The excavation in the immediate neighborhood became so extensive that a small, subterranean basilica had to be built for the protection of the graves of the martyrs. Later a Constantinian basilica was built above ground and became the center of a cemetery lying in the open air.

The second stairway led down to another extensive region with numerous chambers. The paintings here belong to the fourth century and include frequent representations of a meal scene. The third stairway gave access to yet a third region of more limited extent. Its most important chamber contains a fresco of the advanced fourth century. Thus this catacomb appears to have undergone its most important development during the later years of that century.[32]

[32] SRK, pp.198-205.

5. THE ART OF THE CATACOMBS

IN DESCRIBING the above Roman catacombs some of the more important paintings on their walls have been mentioned. A brief summary of the development of Christian art in the catacombs can now be given. In the first place, early Christian art did not hesitate to borrow from representations already familiar in pagan art. Christianity was not hostile to ancient culture except where faith or moral principles were endangered. Just as Clement of Alexandria around A.D. 200 held that a Christian should not employ for his signet ring any idolatrous, warlike or licentious symbol but rather such seals as a dove, a fish, a ship, a lyre or an anchor,[1] so too the artists of the catacombs freely employed such figures in a decorative way and even gave some of them deeper Christian meaning. The little winged persons, which we noted in the Crypts of Lucina (p. 361) and which are known as Erotes or Amoretti, might have seemed less acceptable since actually they came from pagan tombs where they had represented departed souls. But such signification had long since been forgotten and they were employed in a purely decorative way and without offense to Christian taste, along with butterflies, birds and flowers.

Other representations were interpreted to convey deeper Christian meanings. The fish had already appeared in pagan art, but the Christians soon discovered that in the Greek language the five letters constituting the word "fish" were the initial letters of the phrase "Jesus Christ, the Son of God, the Saviour."[2] Writing about A.D. 200 *On Baptism*, Tertullian said, "But we, little fishes, after the example of our FISH Jesus Christ, are born in water,"[3] while Augustine (A.D. c.425) said that in the word fish "Christ is mystically understood, because he was able to live, that is, to exist, without sin in the abyss of this mortality as in the depth of waters."[4] Thus the fish might stand symbolically for the name of Christ. In the catacomb of Priscilla there is an inscription reading "ALEXANDER IN," after which a fish is shown, completing the phrase "Alexander in Christ."[5] Or fishes

[1] *The Instructor.* III, 11 (ANF II, p.285).
[2] ΙΧΘΥΣ—'Ιησοῦς Χριστὸς Θεοῦ Υἱὸς Σωτήρ.
[3] *On Bapt.* I (ANF III, p.669).
[4] *The City of God.* XVIII, 23 (NPNF II, p.373).
[5] Orazio Marucchi, *The Evidence of the Catacombs for the Doctrines and Organization of the Primitive Church.* 1929, p.32.

156. Painting on the Ceiling of Chamber "Y" in the Crypts of Lucina

154. Inscription and Seven-armed Candlestick
in the Jewish Catacomb at Monteverde

155. Fresco in the Jewish Catacomb of Villa Torlonia

157. The Crypt of the Popes in the Catacomb of Callistus

158. The Cappella Greca in the Catacomb of Priscilla

159. The Meal Scene in the Cappella Greca

160. The Oldest Picture of Christ, a Fresco in the Cappella Greca

161. Burial Niches in the Catacomb of Prœcilla

162. The Prophet and the Madonna

163. The Good Shepherd as Painted in the Catacomb of Priscilla

164. Graffiti Invoking Peter and Paul

165. Grave Inscription of Licinia Amias

166. The Deceased Offering Prayer in the Garden of Paradise,
a Painting in the Catacomb of Callistus

57. Statuette of the Good Shepherd

168. Noah in the Ark, a Painting in the Catacomb of Peter and Marcellinus

169. Wall Paintings in the Catacomb of Domitilla

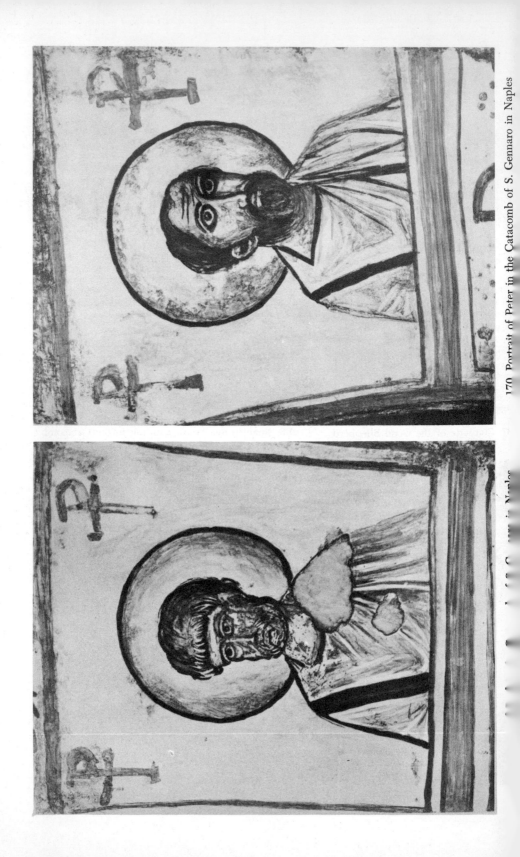

170 Portrait of Peter in the Catacomb of S. Gennaro in Naples

ERRATUM

The legends beneath Figs. 170 and 171 are reversed: Peter is on the left, Paul on the right.

172. Early Christian Sarcophagus of the "Philosopher" Type

173. Sarcophagus with the Story of Jonah

174. Sarcophagus of the Latin Frieze Type

175. A "City-Gate" Sarcophagus

176. A "Bethesda" Sarcophagus

177. The Sarcophagus of Junius Bassus

might stand for the Christians themselves. A grave inscription of Licinia Amias from around A.D. 200 (Fig. 165) has the word "Fish" followed by "of the living," which must mean "Jesus Christ, the Son of God, the Saviour of the living," and is adorned with two fishes, which may represent the Christians who are "the living."[6] The initials D.M. which appear on this inscription stand for *Dis Manibus*, meaning "To the spirits of the world of the dead."[7] These initials appeared regularly on pagan graves, and were frequently employed by Christians simply as a conventional form and without further thought of their original meaning.

The representations of a woman with arms uplifted in prayer and of a shepherd with a lamb on his shoulders were also familiar in Hellenistic art. But these figures recur with great frequency in the Christian art of the catacombs from this time on and are invested with special significance. The woman with hands lifted up in prayer is known as an orant[8] and reflects the Hellenistic tendency to personify abstract ideas.[9] Here in the catacombs the orant becomes a distinctive Christian figure, a personification of prayer for salvation and a symbol of Christian devotion. Since such figures occasionally are shown amidst the garden of paradise, and have the names of the departed written nearby, it is clear that they might also be regarded as symbolical representations of the deceased who offer prayer to God in the blessedness of heaven (Fig. 166).[10]

The sight of a shepherd carrying a sheep on his shoulders is familiar in the Middle East today, and the representation of a subject of this type is found not only in Greco-Roman times as for example in Hermes Criophorus, the protector of flocks who carries a ram on his shoulders, but also much more anciently. In Assyria and Syria, reliefs have been found from the eighth and tenth centuries B.C. which portray a man bearing a gazelle upon his shoulders, while the statue from Mari of a man carrying a kid in his arms is as early as the third millennium B.C. (p. 46; Fig. 21). These older figures, to be sure, represent worshipers bringing animals for sacrifice, but at least by the time of the ram-bearing Hermes of Greece and perhaps much

---

[6] F. J. Dölger, *Ichthys, das Fischsymbol in frühchristlicher Zeit.* i (1910), pp.159-177.

[7] René Cagnat, *Cours d'épigraphie latine.* 4th ed. 1914, p.424.

[8] C. M. Kaufmann, *Handbuch der christlichen Archäologie.* 3d ed. 1922, p.272.

[9] Charles R. Morey, *Early Christian Art.* 1942, p.63.

[10] H. Leclercq in *Dictionnaire d'Archéologie chrétienne et de liturgie.* ii, col. 2472.

earlier the thought of the Good Shepherd was introduced.[11] In Christian art the type was conceived anew and filled with Christian meaning.[12] The Good Shepherd now is none other than Christ himself (John 10:11) who carries the lost sheep back to the fold (Luke 15:5f.). The particular appropriateness of such a picture in the catacombs is seen in the conception preserved in a later Latin liturgy: "Lord, let these who are asleep, when they are redeemed from death, freed from guilt, reconciled to the Father, and brought home on the shoulders of the Good Shepherd, enjoy everlasting blessedness in the train of the eternal king and in the company of the saints."[13] The famous marble statuette of the Good Shepherd (Fig. 167), usually dated in the third century and now in the Lateran Museum in Rome, also once may have stood in a cemeterial crypt. It shows the Shepherd as a young and beardless man whose curly hair falls upon his shoulders. He wears a tucked-up tunic and high stockings, and has a basket slung on a strap. He carries the lost sheep gently on his shoulders holding its front feet in one hand and the rear feet in the other.[14]

The juxtaposition of the orant and the Good Shepherd is found as early as in the painting in the Lucina crypt (p. 361; Fig. 156) and recurs frequently thereafter in Christian art. The significance of placing these two symbols in connection with each other is unmistakable. The Christian prayer for deliverance in time of need and death is answered by the Good Shepherd who carries the soul safely home to its fatherland in paradise.[15]

The famous inscription of Abercius[16] casts light on the place held by the Shepherd and the Fish in Christian thought at the end of the second century. Abercius was a Christian of Hieropolis,[17] a small town in Phrygia between Eumenia and Synnada, who at the age of 72

[11] A. Parrot in *Mélanges Syriens offerts a Monsieur René Dussaud.* I (1939), pp.171-182; G. Ernest Wright in BA II, 4 (Dec. 1939), pp. 44-48; also for prehistoric antecedents in Egypt see Valentine Muller in JNES 3 (1944), pp.87-90.

[12] Pierre Maranget, *Jésus-Christ dans les peintures des catacombes.* 1932, p.41; J. Wilpert, *Principienfragen der christlichen Archäologie.* 1889, p.15.

[13] Hans Lietzmann, *Geschichte der alten Kirche.* II (1936), p.138.

[14] O. Marucchi, *I Monumenti del Museo Cristiano Pio-Lateranense riprodotti in atlante di XCVI tavole, con testo illustrativo.* 1910, p.13.

[15] cf. Cyprian (A.D. c.200-258), *Treatise VII On the Mortality.* 26 (ANF V, p.475): "We regard paradise as our country."

[16] Dölger, *Ichthys.* II (1922), pp.454-507; *Die Eucharistie nach Inschriften frühchristlicher Zeit.* 1922, pp.10-42.

[17] He is probably to be identified with the Avircius Marcellus to whom an anti-Montanist work was dedicated in that region around A.D. 183 (Eusebius, *Ch. Hist.* V, xvi, 3).

composed an epitaph relating his visit to Rome and return by way of Syria and Mesopotamia. He said:

"I, a citizen of an elect city, in my lifetime have erected this monument, to have where to place my body when time shall require it.

"My name is Abercius, a disciple of the holy Shepherd who feeds his sheep upon the hills and plains, whose eyes are large and all-seeing, who taught me the sure learning of life, and sent me to Rome to see the imperial majesty and the queen clad in a golden robe and with golden shoes. There I saw a people who had the gleaming seal. I saw also the plains of Syria and all cities, Nisibis, beyond the Euphrates. Everywhere I had a companion, for Paul sat in the chariot with me; everywhere Faith was my guide, and gave me everywhere for food the Fish from the spring, the great, the pure, which the spotless Virgin caught and ever puts before the friends to eat; she has also delicious wine, and she offers wine mixed with water together with bread. I, Abercius, dictated this to be written in my presence, and in fact in the seventy-second year of my life. Let every fellow believer who understands this pray for Abercius.

"No man may lay another in my grave; but if it be done, he must pay to the Roman treasury two thousand gold pieces, and to my dear native city Hieropolis a thousand gold pieces."

The language of Abercius is poetic but he expects fellow Christians to understand. Rome is referred to as "the imperial majesty and the queen clad in a golden robe," in fashion somewhat similar to the symbolism employed in Revelation (17:3-5, 9, 18). The Christians are the people with the "gleaming seal." Abercius had Paul for a companion in the sense that he carried the Pauline letters with him. Even so he describes Christ now as the great Shepherd who cares for his flock upon the hills and plains, and again as the Fish from the spring, caught by the holy Virgin. He says that the Virgin places the Fish before the friends to eat, and offers them wine and bread. The inner meaning of this last language is that the Christians everywhere partake of Christ in the observance of the Lord's Supper. It will be remembered that meal scenes are frequently represented in the catacombs with fish and bread, and sometimes wine, for food. It is not certain whether these scenes depict the meals that were held in honor of the dead, as was also done in pagan custom,[18] or represent the Lord's Supper itself. Perhaps the loaves and fishes reflect the Feeding of the Five Thousand, which was regarded as the prototype of the Lord's Supper because of the interpretation given to it in John 6:54, "He that eateth my flesh and drinketh my blood hath

[18] Morey, *Early Christian Art*, p.64.

eternal life; and I will raise him up at the last day."[19] At any rate the words of Abercius, combining the Fish with the bread and wine, give some support to the interpretation of the meal scenes of the catacombs in a eucharistic sense.

In the second place, not only pagan but also Jewish art seems to have made its contribution to the Christian art of the catacombs. Some seven Old Testament scenes appear repeatedly among the oldest paintings in Lucina, Domitilla and Priscilla (middle of the second century), and Callistus and Praetextatus (end of the second and beginning of the third century). These seven subjects are: Noah in the Ark, Abraham's Sacrifice of Isaac, Moses' Miracle of Water in the Wilderness, the Story of Jonah, the Three Youths in the Fiery Furnace, Daniel in the Lion's Den, and, from the Old Testament Apocrypha, the Story of Susanna.[20] It is now known that the Jews used paintings and other artistic representations in their catacombs (p. 359) and synagogues (p. 405) and some of those that have been found reveal the same subjects that appear in the Christian catacombs at Rome. In the synagogue at Dura one of the wall paintings depicts Abraham's Sacrifice of Isaac, in a third-century Palestinian synagogue the floor mosaic shows Daniel between the Lions, and around A.D. 200 the city of Apamea in Phrygia, under the influence of the Jews who lived there, stamped on some of its coins the same type of portrayal of Noah in the Ark that is familiar in the Christian catacombs. Thus it is probable that at least some of the Christian representations of Old Testament events were taken over from the realm of Jewish art.[21]

In the third place, the Christian artists went on to develop their own representations of New Testament subjects. Perhaps this was done first for the decoration of the walls of Christian houses and cult-rooms,[22] and from there the paintings were copied in the catacombs. At any rate some half-dozen New Testament scenes appear repeatedly in the oldest Roman catacombs. These are: the Visit of the Magi, the Baptism of Jesus, the Healing of the Paralytic, the Healing of the Woman with an Issue of Blood, the Samaritan Woman at the Well, and the Resurrection of Lazarus.[23]

[19] Lietzmann, *Geschichte der alten Kirche.* II, p.141.
[20] SRK, p.356.
[21] Lietzmann, *Geschichte der alten Kirche.* II, p.140.
[22] cf. the house church at Dura, see below pp.407f.
[23] SRK, p.356.

These thirteen scenes which have now been mentioned—seven from the Old Testament and six from the New Testament—not only appear frequently in the five oldest Christian cemeteries at Rome but also are repeated over and over again in all the later catacombs. The Old Testament picture of Noah in the Ark reproduced in Fig. 168 is from the Catacomb of Peter and Marcellinus, while the paintings in Fig. 169 are from the Catacomb of Domitilla and include three of the New Testament scenes, the Raising of Lazarus, the Coming of the Magi, and the Walking of the Paralytic with his Bed, as well as a representation of the Bringing of Water from the Rock. Ultra-symbolic interpretations have been advanced for all these subjects, but actually their leading motif is the simple theme of deliverance. As the early Christians faced tribulation and death, their courage was increased by the remembrance of God's mighty deeds in the past on behalf of his children. The wonderful deliverances which had taken place were types of the resurrection to which Christian faith looked forward with confidence. This conception which shines through the earliest art of the catacombs is preserved also in written sources. Thus, for example, in the *Constitutions of the Holy Apostles*, a work belonging probably to the fourth century, the author urges that martyrdom be faced with equanimity because of the certainty of the resurrection, and says: "Now he that brought Jonah in the space of three days, alive and unhurt, out of the belly of the whale, and the three children out of the furnace of Babylon, and Daniel out of the mouth of the lions, does not lack power to raise us up also."[24] Even so, in the prayer for a departing soul which is still in use today in the Roman Catholic Church the words are found: "Deliver, O Lord! the soul of Thy servant, as Thou didst deliver Noah in the flood . . . Isaac from the sacrificing hand of his father . . . Daniel from the lion's den . . . the three children from the fiery furnace . . . Susanna from her false accusers."[25]

From the time of Constantine and the peace of the church on, a large number of other subjects are found among the paintings in the catacombs. More than sixty new scenes appear, including pictures from the Old Testament like those of Job, Adam and Eve, and Moses before Pharaoh; representations from the Gospels like the Annuncia-

[24] v, i, 7 (ANF VII, p.440).
[25] P. Griffith, compiler, *The Priest's New Ritual, revised in accord with the latest Vatican Edition of the Roman Ritual.* 1939, pp.138-140.

tion to Mary, the Entry into Jerusalem, and the Women at the Tomb; events from the Book of Acts like the Sin of Ananias and Sapphira, and the Raising of Tabitha; and stories from the New Testament Apocrypha like Peter's Miracle of the Water (pp. 395f.), and the Healing of Petronilla. In contrast to the constantly repeated thirteen scenes of older times, these new subjects appear far less frequently, over half of them being found but a single time. It is probable that they were copied from the new paintings and mosaics which were being developed to adorn the numerous new churches of Constantinian times.[26]

[26] SRK, pp.357-360.

6. THE INSCRIPTIONS IN THE CATACOMBS

AN additional word should be said about the inscriptions in the catacombs. In the Jewish catacombs at Rome most of the inscriptions are in Greek and some in Latin. Inscriptions in Hebrew are rare, except for the single word Shalom, meaning peace or rest. Very frequently found are the Greek words, "May his [or her] sleep be in peace."[1]

The Christian inscriptions are also more often in Greek than in Latin and thus may indicate the humble and foreign extraction of those on whose graves they are written.[2] The following are typical inscriptions in the Christian catacombs:

> Victorina, in peace and in Christ.
>
> Julia, in peace with the saints.
>
> Thou wilt live in God.
>
> Mayest thou live in the Lord Jesus.
>
> Mayest thou live in the Holy Spirit.
>
> Thou wilt live forever.
>
> May God give thee life.

An epitaph on the grave of a little child reads:

> To Paul, my son, in peace. May the spirit of all the saints receive thee. He lived two years.

Some inscriptions refer to the life beyond as a *refrigerium* or refreshment:

> May God refresh thy spirit.

Some contain a prayer on behalf of the departed one:

> Demetris and Leontia, to their daughter, Sirita. Jesu, be mindful of our child.

Others request the prayers of the departed:

> In thy prayers pray for us, for we know that thou dwellest in Christ.[3]

---

[1] G. M. Bevan, *Early Christians of Rome, their Words and Pictures.* 1927, p. 24.
[2] Morey, *Early Christian Art*, p.60.
[3] Bevan, *Early Christians of Rome, their Words and Pictures*, pp.28-32.

Not only paintings and inscriptions are found in the catacombs but also many small objects which were left at the graves. These include lamps, pitchers, vases, plates, and the interesting "gold-glasses" within whose glass bottoms medallions made of gold leaf were sealed.[4]

[4] Oskar Beyer, *Die Katakombenwelt, Grundriss, Ursprung und Idee der Kunst in der römischen Christengemeinde.* 1927, pp.106-112.

7. CATACOMBS IN OTHER CITIES AND LANDS

NUMEROUS catacombs are to be found elsewhere in Italy and in other places including Sicily, Malta, North Africa, Egypt and Palestine.[1] As a single example we may mention the catacombs at Naples. Six early Christian catacombs exist here whose origins are in the second and third centuries and whose use continued for many centuries thereafter. They are adorned with many paintings, and the development of their art is traceable through several periods. In the first period, in the second and third centuries, it may be seen clearly that the Christian art has arisen out of the decorative painting of the ancient world. Flowers, birds and leaping animals like antelopes and panthers are represented, while also such a biblical subject as that of Adam and Eve makes its appearance. In the second period, in the fourth century, the influence of the Roman catacomb art is felt strongly, and the painters at Naples copied Roman models to represent the Story of Jonah, Moses Striking Water from the Rock, and other familiar subjects. Only in the third period, from the fifth to the eighth centuries did the Christian art of Naples achieve independent significance and attain its high point. Examples of the portraits characteristic of this period may be seen in two fifth century paintings of Peter and Paul. The two apostles are decidedly different in type, Peter (Fig. 170) with his broader face, curling hair and short beard, and Paul (Fig. 171) with his bald head, lofty brow, long nose and straight beard. Peter's expression is distrustful or almost sullen, and may reflect the influence of monasticism, while in the companion picture of Paul a Christian thinker and philosopher is depicted.[2]

[1] See Leclercq in *Dictionnaire d'Archéologie chrétienne et de liturgie.* II, cols. 2442-2450.

[2] Hans Achelis, *Die Katakomben von Neapel.* 1936.

8. THE LATER HISTORY OF THE ROMAN CATACOMBS

A BRIEF word may be said concerning the later history of the catacombs at Rome. During the third century the persecuted Christians frequently sought refuge in the catacombs and many even suffered martyrdom within them.[1] In that century and the next the veneration of the martyrs who were buried in the catacombs became very important and we have already noted (pp. 364, 377) the contributions of Pope Damasus to the beautification of the crypts now so eagerly visited by pilgrims. With the peace of the church under Constantine it became possible to build cemeterial churches above the catacombs and to erect other churches elsewhere. From this time on it became gradually customary to bury the dead no longer in the subterranean rooms of the catacombs but in graves and sarcophagi in and around these churches. As the burials in surface cemeteries became more and more numerous, the catacombs fell into disuse. With the sack of Rome by Alaric in A.D. 410, interments in them ceased entirely. The tombs of the martyrs were still visited after that and kept in repair, but other sections of the catacombs were neglected and often became inaccessible. When the Goths besieged Rome in 537 and the Lombards in 755 the catacombs suffered much destruction and the crypts of the martyrs were damaged badly. The popes of the eighth and ninth centuries found it necessary to bring the bones of the martyrs from their graves in the catacombs to safer resting places in the churches inside the city. Where there are basilicas still standing outside the city today, however, these churches were always kept in use and the remains of the martyrs buried there did not have to be removed.[2] But after the remains of the martyrs were removed from the crypts at the catacombs, the catacombs fell into complete ruin. Their entrances were choked with dirt, the grass of the Campagna covered them and their very existence was forgotten until their accidental rediscovery in 1578.

[1] In his edict of A.D. 257, Valerian forbade the Christians to hold assemblies or to enter into the catacombs (Eusebius, *Ch. Hist.* VII, xi, 10) but in A.D. 261 Gallienus again allowed the Christians to use their places of worship inclusive of the cemeteries (*Ch. Hist.* VII, xiii).

[2] Kirsch, *Aus den römischen Katakomben*, pp.10-12.

9. EARLY CHRISTIAN SARCOPHAGI

OCCASIONALLY in the catacombs and far more frequently in and around the churches above ground there are found the sculptured stone coffins which are known as sarcophagi.[1] These constitute relatively elaborate tombs and reflect the existence of a wealthier group of believers than some of the poor who buried their dead in the humble niches of the catacombs.[2]

The employment of sarcophagi for pagan burials has already been alluded to (pp. 353, 367f.), and it may be presumed that when Christians first began to use such tombs they were procured directly from the workshops of those who served the population as a whole. In such cases the sarcophagi would not exhibit any marks distinctive of Christianity, but would be adorned like the pagan coffins with lines, animal heads, scenes from the sea and the chase, and other subjects. Themes repugnant to Christian principles, of course, would be avoided in the selection of the sarcophagi.[3]

SARCOPHAGI OF THE THIRD CENTURY

But the time soon came when Christianity developed its own plastic art, and sculptured sarcophagi appear which are unmistakably Christian productions. According to the researches of Friedrich Gerke, the oldest of these are to be dated around the middle of the third century A.D.[4] It was probably at about this time, and particularly under the influence of the philosopher Plotinus who worked in Rome from 244 until 270, that a distinctive type of pagan sarcophagus arose in whose sculptures the deceased was represented in the role of a philosopher with his book.[5] When, therefore, a number of Christian sarcophagi display this very theme, it is a natural conclusion that they are to be dated at about the same time. In the case of the latter productions, however, the orant and the Good Shepherd are characteristically added in the sculptures to show that the content of the true philosophy is the Christian message of immortality.

[1] James C. Stout in *Papers of the American Society of Church History.* Second series. 8 (1928), pp.1-15.
[2] Morey, *Early Christian Art*, p.67.
[3] O. Marucchi, *Manual of Christian Archaeology.* tr. from 4th Italian edition by Hubert Vecchierello, 1935, pp.330f.
[4] F. Gerke, *Die christlichen Sarkophage der vorkonstantinischen Zeit.* 1940, p.316.
[5] Gerhart Rodenwaldt in *Jahrbuch des Deutschen Archäologischen Instituts.* 51 (1936), pp.101-105.

A Christian sarcophagus of the "philosopher" type, which was found in the Via Salaria in Rome and now is in the Lateran Museum, is shown in Fig. 172. This sarcophagus is of the tub-shaped kind and is adorned at the corners with figures of rams. Two trees serve to divide the sculptures on the front into three groups. At the left sits the deceased man in the guise of a philosopher accompanied by two friends. At the right is his wife, with whom are two companions. Of these, however, the one in front appears as an orant who gazes toward the Good Shepherd in the center. The Shepherd in turn looks toward the orant, and in this unmistakable juxtaposition of the two figures the motif familiar in the catacombs (p. 384) appears again.[6] The prayer for deliverance from death is answered by the Good Shepherd. This theme holds the place of focal importance in the composition and toward this central truth of Christian philosophy the attention of the believers is directed.[7]

In the latter part of the third century another distinctive type of Christian sarcophagus makes its appearance. General symbolism here gives way to specifically biblical composition. The motif in the sculptures is still that of deliverance from death, but the idea now is conveyed through the portrayal of events from the Bible. Obviously the influence of the art of the catacombs continues to be effective, and the stories which are represented include such familiar ones as those of Jonah, Daniel, and the Fiery Furnace.

Of the prominent class of sarcophagi which portray the history of Jonah, an outstanding example now in the Lateran Museum is shown in Fig. 173. Against a unified background of sea and rocky coast, the story of Jonah is unfolded in three consecutive parts. At the left Jonah is being cast out of the ship and received into the mouth of the sea monster. In the scene immediately adjacent the sea monster is shown again, throwing up Jonah on the rocks of the coast. The picture is enlivened at this point with representations of the flora and fauna of the seacoast, including reeds and trees, the snail, the lizard, the crab and the heron. An angler is drawing a fish from the ocean, and a shepherd is seen with his sheep before a massive sheep stall. The third part of the dramatic history of Jonah is represented just above the seacoast, where Jonah rests beneath the shade of the gourd. Al-

[6] The heads of both the orant and the Good Shepherd are modern restorations, but sufficient traces of the original heads remain to show clearly that they were represented as gazing at each other.

[7] Gerke, *Die christlichen Sarkophage der vorkonstantinischen Zeit.* pp.246-299.

though most of the front of the sarcophagus is occupied by this detailed and extensive portrayal of the story of Jonah, some room remains in which other biblical subjects are introduced. On a bit of open sea between the monster and the coast, Noah floats in his ark, and in an upper panel we see from left to right the Resurrection of Lazarus, the Water Miracle of Moses, and what is probably yet a further scene from the life of Moses.[8]

SARCOPHAGI OF THE FOURTH CENTURY
THE LATIN FRIEZE STYLE

The greatest number of early Christian sarcophagi belong to the fourth century, and in this period it is possible clearly to distinguish two main groups among them, namely those of the frieze type and those of the columnar style. In the case of the frieze group the entire front of the sarcophagus is occupied with a continuous series of figures. Such a style of arrangement was customary in the pagan sarcophagus art of the Latin West during the second and third centuries and doubtless provided the pattern for the Christian sculptors. The Christian sarcophagi display a basic difference, however, in that the façade is made to carry not a single unified representation but a half-dozen or more separate scenes crowded together in undivided succession. The purpose clearly is to tell as many stories as possible in the space at hand. The subjects chosen are largely biblical scenes such as were already represented in conveniently abbreviated form in the art of the catacombs.[9]

A sarcophagus executed in the Latin frieze style and now in the Lateran Museum is shown in Fig. 174. Placed side by side upon its front are the representations of no less than nine different events. At the left is the Fall of Man, with Adam and Eve standing on either side of the tree and the Lord laying his hand on Adam's shoulder. Continuing to the right we see the Miracle of the Wine at Cana, the Healing of the Blind, and a Resurrection scene which may represent one of the miracles of Christ or Ezekiel's vision of the valley of dry bones (Ezekiel 37:1-14). In the center Christ is prophesying the Denial of Peter, at whose feet the symbolic cock appears. Farther to the right we find the Healing of the Paralytic, the Sacrifice of Isaac, the Arrest of Peter, and Peter Smiting the Rock to bring water to

[8] ibid., pp.38-46.
[9] Alexander C. Soper in *The Art Bulletin.* 19 (1937), pp.148-202.

baptize his jailers. The last scene is similar to that of Moses' Miracle of Water in the Wilderness, but is believed to be derived from some apocryphal incident in the life of Peter.

THE ASIATIC COLUMNAR STYLE

In contrast with the crowded and indiscriminate arrangement of the sculptures of the Latin frieze sarcophagi, a far more orderly composition is exhibited by the so-called columnar sarcophagi. The latter are characterized by the placing of the various figures in an architectural framework which is usually made up of columns and arches. This type of arrangement is known in the pagan sarcophagi of the second and third centuries, and seems to have originated in Asia Minor. The Christian sarcophagi of the columnar group are regarded, therefore, as standing under the direct influence of this Asiatic style, and it is believed that many of them, although made in the West, were executed by Asiatic artisans.[10]

Since the columnar sarcophagi constitute a numerous group, the general style may be illustrated by two examples in each of which a characteristic modification appears. Fig. 175 shows a sarcophagus which was discovered in the foundation of St. Peter's Church in Rome and is now in the Louvre. Its Asiatic style is unmistakable, and in this case the columns and arches are so arranged as to give the appearance of a series of city-gates. Sarcophagi of this type commonly are spoken of as belonging to the "city-gate" group.[11] We see that in the present case the entire front of the sarcophagus is given over to a single scene, that of the Mission of the Apostles. Christ stands upon the mount, surrounded by the Twelve, and with the two donors of the sarcophagus represented as small figures at his feet. While many of the heads were broken and have been restored, that of Christ is original and shows him as bearded. Christ is giving the scroll of the new law to Peter, who carries a jeweled cross and heads the apostles from the right. Paul occupies the corresponding position on the left.

The sarcophagus shown in Fig. 176, and now in the Lateran Museum, displays the architectural features of the Asiatic style and by virtue of the appearance of the gate of Jerusalem at the extreme right is allied with the "city-gate" sarcophagi. A special modification

[10] Marion Lawrence in *The Art Bulletin.* 13 (1931), pp.535f.; 14 (1932), pp.103-185.
[11] ibid., 10 (Sept. 1927-June 1928), pp.1-45.

occurs here, however, in the introduction, near the center, of a double-register scene portraying the Healing of the Paralytic at the Pool of Bethesda. In the lower register, the paralytic lies upon his bed; in the upper, at the command of Christ, he walks away with his bed upon his back. Sarcophagi having this central scene as an identifying feature are commonly designated as belonging to the "Bethesda" type.[12] The other representations which appear on the sarcophagus illustrated include at the left the Healing of Two Blind Men, and the Healing of the Woman with an Issue of Blood, and at the right the Triumphal Entry of Christ into Jerusalem.

THE SARCOPHAGUS OF JUNIUS BASSUS

The influence of the eastern tradition in the West led in many cases to a mingling of the Asiatic and the Latin styles, and some of the resultant productions were very fine. For a single example we may turn to the sarcophagus of Junius Bassus (Fig. 177), which is believed to have been the work of a Latin artist using various Asiatic models.[13] This magnificent stone coffin, which was found in the Church of St. Peter in 1595, was the tomb of a prefect of Rome who died in A.D. 359. This is indicated by the following inscription upon the sarcophagus: "Junius Bassus, a most illustrious man, who lived forty-two years and two months, and when he was in office as prefect of the city and after he had received baptism went to God on the 25th day of August in the year in which Eusebius and Hypatius were consuls." On the top of the sarcophagus may be scenes from the life of Junius Bassus, which are now difficult to make out, on the ends are representations from ancient nature mythology, but on the front are wholly Christian scenes. Here there are two rows of sculptures, each row in turn being divided by columns into niches in which the various scenes are found. In the upper row the scenes are from left to right (1) Abraham's Sacrifice, (2) the Arrest of Peter, (3) Christ Enthroned above Caelus[14] and bestowing upon Peter and Paul their missions and (4) Christ Led before Pilate. In the lower row are (1) Job, (2) Adam and Eve, (3) Christ's Entry into Jerusalem, (4) Daniel between the Lions,[15] and (5) Paul Led to Execution. In be-

[12] ibid., 14 (1932), p.121.　　　　[13] ibid., 14 (1932), p.133.

[14] The god who in Roman art spreads out the veil of the sky, as on the breastplate of Augustus (cf. Fig. 99 and p.212).

[15] The figure of Daniel in the middle is a modern restoration. The lions are accompanied by men holding rods.

tween, in the spandrels of the lower colonnade, lambs play the parts in scenes representing the Three Hebrews in the Fiery Furnace, Peter's Miracle of Water, the Baptism of Christ, the Multiplication of Loaves and Fishes, Moses Receiving the Law, and the Resurrection of Lazarus. The plan of the main sculptures is clear if we may consider that when they were carried out the niches of Abraham and Paul became reversed. Thinking of Abraham as belonging to the lower register we find there a series of Old Testament scenes, with Christ in the center, riding triumphantly through the world of human sin and suffering. Placing Paul in the upper series, we have there the theme of the passion in which Christ is followed in death by his two apostles. On the right, Christ walks slowly between two soldiers toward the judgment place, while Pilate sits upon the magistrate's chair and a servant prepares to pour the water for the symbolic washing of his hands. On the left, Peter stands between two soldiers, calmly awaiting the end, and Paul, in the other niche, bows his head as the officer draws the sword while reeds indicate the marshes of the Tiber where his execution was fulfilled. In the center the heavenly Christ is upon his throne of eternal victory and over the entire sarcophagus there is a calm peace, the peace which the early Christians wished for their deceased when they carved the words *in pace*.[16]

[16] Friedrich Gerke, *Der Sarkophag des Junius Bassus*. 1936.

IX

The Story of Ancient Churches

THE meeting places of the early Christians were in private homes. At Jerusalem the first disciples, being Jews, continued for a time to frequent the Temple (cf. Acts 3:1), but it was doomed to destruction in A.D. 70. In the Gentile world Paul at first went regularly to the synagogue to preach, but Christianity could not remain long within its confines (cf. Acts 13:5,14,45f., etc.). Having, therefore, no other meeting place of their own, the disciples perforce assembled in private houses. Wherever some Christian had the room and desire to invite his fellow believers to gather in his home for worship, there a "house church" arose.

The use of private homes for Christian assemblage is reflected clearly in various New Testament passages. An upper room in a private house in Jerusalem was used by Jesus and the twelve for the Last Supper (Mark 14:15), and the apostles later stayed in an upstairs room (Acts 1:13) in that city, while the house of Mary the mother of John Mark was a place where they gathered for prayer (Acts 12:12). Even so it is said that Saul "laid waste the church, entering into every house, and dragging men and women committed them to prison" (Acts 8:3). When he himself as a Christian preacher was ejected from a synagogue, he frequently went to private homes instead. Paul's experience at Corinth may well have been typical of that which happened at many other places. He preached in the synagogue every Sabbath but his assertion that Jesus was the Christ met with contradiction and abuse, so finally he left the synagogue "and went into the house of a certain man named Titus Justus, one that worshipped God, whose house joined hard to the synagogue" (Acts 18:7). At Philippi, Lydia, who as a seller of purple may have been relatively well-to-do, made her house available for Paul and perhaps also for Christian meetings (Acts 16:14f.). At Troas the

Christian gathering took place in an upper chamber (Acts 20:8), and at Caesarea the house of Philip the evangelist may have been the Christian center (Acts 21:8). At Rome Paul lived in his own rented house, and preached in it (Acts 28:30f.).

The references in Paul's letters are even more explicit. "Aquila and Prisca salute you . . . with the church that is in their house" (I Corinthians 16:19). "Salute Prisca and Aquila . . . and the church that is in their house" (Romans 16:3,5; cf. 14f.). "Salute . . . Nympha, and the church that is in her house" (Colossians 4:15). "Paul . . . to Philemon . . . and to the church in thy house" (Philemon 1f.).

Eusebius mentions a tradition that up to the time of Hadrian's siege there existed in Jerusalem a very large Christian church which was constructed by the Jews.[1] Nothing else is known about this church, but it may have been a large assembly room in the house where the heads of the church lived.[2] In the account of the *Martyrdom of Justin Martyr* (d. A.D. c.165) it is related that Rusticus, the prefect of Rome, asked Justin in what place he had his followers assemble, and Justin replied that he lived with a certain Martinus, and that those who wished came there to him to hear his teaching.[3] Similarly, in the *Recognitions of Clement*[4] it is narrated that when Peter was in Tripoli large numbers of people wished to hear him preach. Upon his asking where there was a suitable place for discussion, a certain Maro offered his house saying, "I have a very spacious hall which can hold more than five hundred men, and there is also a garden within the house." "Then Peter said: 'Show me the hall, or the garden.' And when he had seen the hall, he went in to see the garden also; and suddenly the whole multitude, as if some one had called them, rushed into the house, and thence broke through into the garden where Peter was already standing, selecting a fit place for discussion."[5]

[1] *Demonstratio Evangelica.* III, v, 108. ed. G. Dindorf, *Eusebii Caesariensis Opera.* (1867) III, p.188.

[2] J. W. Crowfoot, *Early Churches in Palestine.* 1941, p.1.

[3] *Martyrdom.* 2 (ANF I, p.305).

[4] A fictional work of the early fourth century, probably based upon an earlier and lost Clement romance of A.D. c.260, which describes a journey of Clement of Rome to Palestine where he met and talked at length with Peter and marvelously had his own long lost parents and brothers restored to him (hence the name, *Recognitions*). E. J. Goodspeed, *A History of Early Christian Literature.* 1942, p.127.

[5] *Rec.* IV, 6 (ANF VIII, p.136).

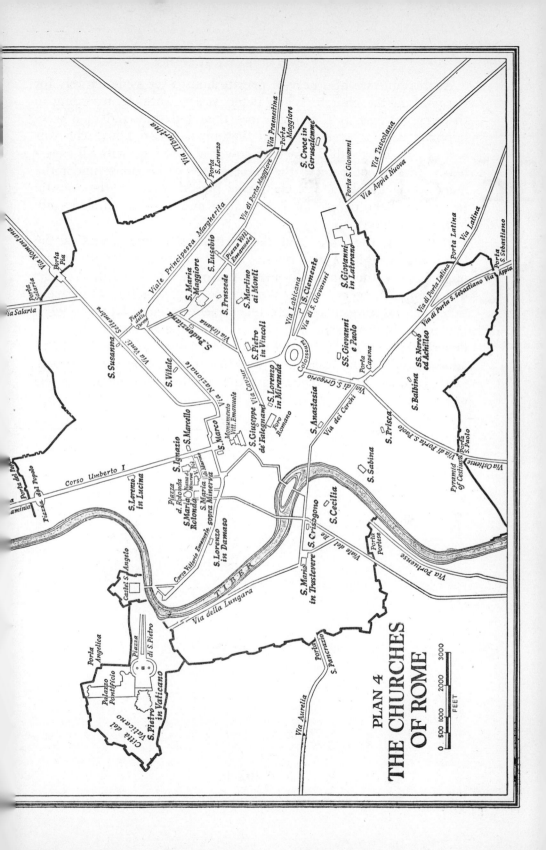

PLAN 4

THE CHURCHES
OF ROME

0 500 1000 2000 3000
FEET

Via Tiburtina

Via Praenestina

Porta Maggiore

Via Tuscolana

S. Croce in Gerusalemme

Via Appia Nuova

Porta S. Giovanni

Via di Porta Maggiore

Porta S. Lorenzo

Via Lorenzo

Viale Principessa Margherita

S. Eusebio

Piazza Vitt. Emanuele

S. Maria Maggiore

S. Prassede

S. Martino ai Monti

Via Labicana

S. Clemente

S. Giovanni in Laterano

Via di Porta Latina

Porta Latina

Via Latina

Porta S. Sebastiano

Via S. Sebastiano

Via Appia

Via di Porta S. Sebastiano

Porta Pia

Via Nomentana

Porta Salaria

Via Salaria

S. Susanna

Via Settembre

S. Vitale

Via Nazionale

Piazza delle Terme

S. Pudenziana

Via Urbana

S. Pietro in Vincoli

S. Lorenzo in Miranda

Colosseo

Via S. Giovanni

Via di S. Gregorio

SS. Giovanni e Paolo

Porta Capena

SS. Nereo ed Achilleo

S. Balbina

Via di Porta Latina

Via Cavour

S. Giuseppe de' Falegnami

Monumento Vitt. Emanuele

S. Marco

Foro Romano

S. Anastasia

Via dei Cerchi

S. Prisca

S. Sabina

Via di Porta S. Paolo

Pyramid of Cestius

Via Ostiense

Porta S. Paolo

S. Ignazio

S. Marcello

Piazza d. Rotonda

S. Maria Rotonda

S. Maria sopra Minerva

S. Lorenzo in Lucina

Corso Umberto I

Porta del Popolo

Piazza del Popolo

Porta Flaminia

Corso Vittorio Emanuele

S. Lorenzo in Damaso

S. Crisogono

S. Cecilia

Viale del Re

Porta Portese

Via Portuense

Castel S. Angelo

Via della Lungara

S. Maria in Trastevere

Porta

S. Pancrazio

Via Aurelia

T I B E R

Porta Angelica

Piazza di S. Pietro

Palazzo Pontificio

Città del Vaticano

S. Pietro in Vaticano

At this time we also hear of private houses set aside entirely for the work of the church. When Peter was in Antioch, according to the *Recognitions of Clement,* more than ten thousand men were baptized within seven days and thereupon "Theophilus, who was more exalted than all the men of power in that city, with all eagerness of desire consecrated the great palace of his house under the name of a church, and a chair was placed in it for the Apostle Peter by all the people; and the whole multitude assembled daily to hear the word."[6]

It is clear, therefore, that the earliest gathering places of the Christians were in private houses. Having no temple or synagogue of their own, they naturally made use of available rooms in their own homes. When concealment was necessary, as in time of persecution, such meeting places were inconspicuous and relatively secret. When conditions warranted, parts or even the whole of such residences might be dedicated entirely to church use and equipped and adorned for this purpose. Such were the meeting places of the early Christians, as we may reconstruct the situation from literary references.

[6] *Rec.* x, 71 (ANF VIII, p.210).

1. DURA-EUROPOS

It is of great interest, therefore, that such an actual house church of the early Christians has now been discovered. We must tell the story of it in some detail. The city of Dura-Europos lies in the Syrian desert on an immemorial caravan route beside the Euphrates. Here, on the site of an earlier settlement known by the Aramaic name of Dura, there was established around 300 B.C. a Seleucid fortress. This took place in the early part of the reign of Seleucus I Nicator, and although the colony was actually established by the king's governor general, Nicanor, Seleucus Nicator was regarded as the founder. Hence the place was renamed Europos after Europos in Macedon, the native city of Seleucus. In the second half of the second century B.C. Dura-Europos became a part of the Parthian Empire and in the years of Partho-Roman peace rose to be an important agricultural and caravan city. Although it remained a Parthian city at this time, the prestige of Rome was high in Dura; also the influence of the famous city of Palmyra[1] nearly 150 miles to the west, situated in an oasis in the Syrian desert, was strongly felt. In the second century A.D. there was war between Parthia and Rome, and Dura was taken by the Romans and made a part of the province of Syria. The ancient fortress received a Roman garrison in A.D. 167 and was maintained as an important stronghold on the Euphrates frontier of the Roman Empire.

Yet the end was not far distant. It came in the third century when the Sassanian kings took the offensive against the Roman Empire. The troops of Ardashir (224-241) nearly captured Dura-Europos in A.D. 238, and the final siege came soon after 256. The exact date of the fall of Dura is unknown but it was probably just after the famous battle of Edessa (between 258 and 260), where the Roman emperor Valerian was taken prisoner (p.198) by the Sassanian king Shapur I (241-272). Dura was probably occupied for a short time by the Persians and then abandoned. It reverted swiftly to the desert, and on the expedition in which he was to die

---

[1] Palmyra is the Greek and Latin name of the city which is called Tadmar in the inscriptions of Tiglath-pileser I (ARAB I, §287, 308). It is mentioned in II Chronicles 8:4 where Solomon is said to have built "Tadmor in the wilderness." But this passage is evidently based upon I Kings 9:18 which says that Solomon built "Tamar in the wilderness," a city in Judah (Ezekiel 47:19; 48:28). The Chronicler must have altered the name to Tadmor to increase the extent of Solomon's kingdom and heighten the glory of his achievements.

fighting against Shapur II (310-379) the Emperor Julian (361-363) hunted lions among its ruins. It was reserved for modern archeologists to rescue the city from oblivion.[2]

The first intimation of what might be waiting beneath the desert sand came by chance in 1921. The British army was operating against the Arabs, and in the course of digging trenches in the ruins of Dura some notable temple paintings came to light.[3] Since 1928 a series of archeological expeditions has been conducted at Dura by Yale University and the French Academy of Inscriptions and Letters under the general supervision of M. I. Rostovtzeff.[4] The house church with which we are concerned here was found in the season of 1931-1932, and the Jewish synagogue which also is to be mentioned came to light in 1932-1933.

THE SYNAGOGUE

As a striking air view (Fig. 178) made in 1932 shows, the city was surrounded by a wall against which the desert sand is now heaped heavily. The main gate of the city was on the west side where the wall faces the desert (at the left side of the photograph). A little distance north of this gate, with the city wall at its back and a street in front, was the synagogue. This building was originally a private residence, and may have served as an informal synagogue even before being rebuilt. Later it was enlarged and made into a formal house of worship, this being under the presbytership of Samuel the priest, as an inscription states, and "in the year 556 which is the second year of Philip Caesar." The date is given in the Seleucid era (p.207) and corresponds to A.D. 245. Some years later this building was replaced by a new synagogue, which seems to have been opened for services in about 253, although at that time it was not yet entirely finished. The completion of the synagogue probably was in 255, when the frescoes were added. This was only a very few years before the destruction of Dura.[5]

One entered the synagogue through a courtyard on the east and came into a room of approximately 25 by 40 feet in size, along whose walls were benches for the worshipers. The orientation was

[2] M. I. Rostovtzeff, *Dura-Europos and its Art.* 1938, pp.10-30.

[3] J. H. Breasted, *Oriental Forerunners of Byzantine Painting, First-Century Wall Paintings from the Fortress of Dura on the Middle Euphrates.* 1924.

[4] Rostovtzeff, ed., *The Excavations at Dura-Europos.* 1929-.

[5] AJA 47 (1943), p.335.

toward the west, and in the middle of the west wall was a niche where the Ark of the Law was placed during the services. The walls were adorned from top to bottom with paintings, many of which are well preserved and have been removed to Damascus. Around the niche just mentioned are a representation of the shrine in which the Law was kept, a seven-branched candlestick, an ethrog and lulab on the left and a picture of Abraham's Sacrifice of Isaac on the right. Abraham stands with his back to the viewer, holding a knife in his right hand. Isaac is bound on the altar, but a hand symbolizes the intervention of God and a ram is waiting by the bush behind Abraham. Other wall paintings include scenes from the life of Moses, the Exodus, the Return of the Ark, Ezekiel's Vision of the Valley of Dry Bones, the Story of Job and other subjects.[6]

The painting of the Return of the Ark (I Samuel 5f.) shows five lords of the Philistines sending away the ark upon a cart drawn by two oxen, while the Philistine temple stands in the background (Fig. 179). Strewn upon the ground are holy vessels, musical instruments, and the broken images not of Dagon but of the principal Palmyrene gods which were worshiped in Dura.[7] In the picture of the story of Job one of the friends rides to visit the afflicted man, and it is at first surprising to note that the friend is represented in kingly splendor. The explanation is found in a midrash which evidently was familiar to the Jews of Dura and which states explicitly that the three friends of Job were kings. A careful comparison of the Vision of Ezekiel, the Finding of Moses and the Visit to Job in these paintings, and in corresponding miniature paintings in later Christian illustrated manuscripts, has shown that both must go back to an earlier and common Jewish source.[8] Thus again the dependence of early Christian art upon Jewish art is suggested.

THE CHRISTIAN CHURCH

The Christian church was on the same street as the synagogue but to the south of the main city gate. Like the synagogue, it had

[6] Comte du Mesnil du Buisson in *L'Illustration*. 185 (July 1933), pp.454-457; Marcel Aubert in *Gazette des Beaux-Arts*. 6e période. 20 (1938), pp.1-24; Sukenik, *Ancient Synagogues in Palestine and Greece*, pp.82-85.

[7] Comte du Mesnil du Buisson in *Gazette des Beaux-Arts*. 6e période. 14 (1935 2e semestre), pp.25-203; Lietzmann, *Geschichte der alten Kirche*. II, pp.35f.

[8] Gitta Wodtke in *Zeitschrift für die neutestamentliche Wissenschaft und die Kunde der älteren Kirche*. 34 (1935), pp.51-62.

once been a private house. Probably this house belonged to a citizen of some means and standing for it was somewhat larger than the average home at Dura. Otherwise, however, it conformed in its original plan exactly to the customary arrangement of a private residence at Dura. From the street one entered by a little vestibule which turned into an inner paved court. Around this court was a series of rooms, while a covered stairway led to the flat roof which was over fifteen feet high. When the house was being built, or soon afterward, someone pressed into the plaster a graffito which supplies the date of the building, the year A.D. 232-233.

One of the rooms in the house was used, probably from the first, as a Christian chapel. A few years later two other rooms were thrown together to provide a larger meeting place, accommodating about one hundred people and having an elevated rostrum at one end for the speaker. From this time on the larger part of the building, or perhaps all of it, was employed openly and entirely as a church.[9] Of its Christian use there can be no doubt. Three graffiti read, "One God in heaven," "Remind Christ of Proclus among yourselves" (TON XN IN YMEIN MNHCKECΘ[E . . .]OKΛOY), and "Remind Christ of the humble Siseos" (TON XPIC[10] MNHC-KETE CICEON TON TAΠINON), the two latter being requests that Proclus and Siseos should be remembered by the congregation in prayer. The greatest interest attaches to the small room known as the chapel. At its west end is a niche set against the wall with an arched roof resting on pillars. This contains a sunken receptacle which may have been a baptismal font.[11] Like the baptistery in the later church at Kaoussie (p. 447), this was too small to have permitted the practice of immersion, and if it was really a baptistery it must be assumed that the rite was performed by affusion. Since the more general custom among the early Christians was that of im-

[9] *Preliminary Report of Fifth Season of Work October 1931-March 1932 of the Excavations at Dura-Europos conducted by Yale University and the French Academy of Inscriptions and Letters*, pp.237-252 "The Christian Church" by C. Hopkins.

[10] The abbreviation XPIC is unusual (*Preliminary Report of Fifth Season of Work*, p.285), but for a parallel see M. Avi-Yonah, *Abbreviations in Greek Inscriptions (The Near East, 200 B.C.-A.D. 1100)* in *The Quarterly of the Department of Antiquities in Palestine* Supplement to vol. 9 (1940), p.112.

[11] C. Hopkins in *Preliminary Report of Fifth Season of Work*, pp.249-252; Rostovtzeff, *Dura-Europos and its Art*, p.131.

mersion,[12] other explanations have been sought such as that this was the tomb of a martyr.[13]

The chapel was decorated with wall paintings in a fashion very similar to that of the synagogue.[14] At the back of the niche just mentioned are two paintings, the lower depicting Adam and Eve, the upper showing the Good Shepherd. Adam and Eve stand with the tree between them as in similar representations in the West. The Good Shepherd carries a huge ram on his shoulders in the manner with which we are familiar, but whereas in Rome he usually stands in a symmetrical composition between his sheep, here he stands behind his flock. The placing of these two scenes together evidently is meant to show that through Adam came death but through Christ came salvation.

The south wall of the chapel is broken by two doors which give access to the room. Between these two doors and under an arched niche is a painting of David and Goliath, the two characters being identified by their names which are written on in Greek. Goliath is misspelled Golitha. While this scene could be regarded as representing the familiar theme of deliverance (cf. I Samuel 17:37), it does not otherwise occur frequently in early Christian art. At the west end of the same wall the Samaritan woman is shown grasping a rope with both hands to raise a pail from the mouth of a well. Doubtless for lack of space the figure of Christ does not appear. The coiffure of the Samaritan woman is like that of Julia Soaemias who was killed at the same time as her son Elagabalus in A.D. 222, and confirms a date early in the third century for these paintings. In the upper register on the same wall was another scene now so badly damaged that only the traces of a garden can be recognized.

The pictures on the north wall were placed most conspicuously opposite the two entrances to the chapel. In the lower register is a scene showing a structure which has been called a huge sarcophagus and beside which are at least three women. This has been interpreted as a representation of the women at the sepulcher of Christ (cf. Mark 16:1).[15] The coiffure of the two women whose heads

[12] cf. Tertullian, *On Baptism*. 7 (ANF III, p.672); Kenneth Scott Latourette, *A History of the Expansion of Christianity*. I (1937), p.259.

[13] P. V. C. Baur in *Preliminary Report of Fifth Season of Work*, p.255.

[14] *Preliminary Report of Fifth Season of Work*, pp.254-283 "The Paintings in the Christian Chapel" by P. V. C. Baur.

[15] It has also been suggested that the same painting may have been continued on

still appear in the painting is the same as that used by Julia Mamaea and Orbiana, the mother and wife respectively of the Emperor Severus Alexander (222-235). In the upper register on the north wall are two scenes. On the right is the Miracle of the Lake (Matthew 14:24-31). In a ship which is plowing through the water are seated several men. They look out to sea with gestures of astonishment at two figures walking on the water. Peter is sinking. Christ is walking toward him with outstretched hand which Peter is about to grasp. Christ is clad in a tunic, but the head and shoulders of the figure are destroyed. The figure of Peter, who is shown with beard and thick curly hair, is well preserved and of much interest since it is the earliest representation of that apostle now known.

To the left of the foregoing scene and with no line of demarcation, is the picture (Fig. 180) of the Healing of the Paralytic (Mark 2:1-12). The sick man lies at full length on his left side on a small bed. The bed has a coverlet with red fringes and the man is dressed in a yellow tunic outlined in brown. Above the bed stands Jesus, clothed in tunic and mantle, and in the act of reaching out his right hand toward the paralytic. The second act in the drama is shown at one side. The sick man, now healed, is walking away. He has turned his bed upside down and is carrying it upon his back, holding it by the crisscross lacing. In the West the Healing of the Paralytic is a subject frequently employed, as we have seen (p. 386), but the first part of the scene with Christ standing over the bed is usually omitted and only the sequel shown in which the man walks away with his bed. Also in the West the bed is carried with its legs hanging down. The illustration at Dura is of special interest because the picture of Christ is one of the two oldest such representations now known. The almost destroyed painting of Christ in the Catacomb of Priscilla at Rome (p.371 and Fig. 160) probably belongs, as we have seen, to the middle of the second century. The painting at Dura is dated even more definitely in the first part of the third century. In both pictures Christ is shown as a young and beardless man with short hair and wearing the ordinary costume of the day. These and similar portrayals are the earliest type of Christ as far as is now known in early Christian art.[16] Later in the third century

the east wall of the room, and that it may have portrayed the parable of the Wise and Foolish Virgins (Joseph Pijoan in *The Art Bulletin*. 19 [1937], pp.592-595).

[16] cf. L. von Sybel, *Christliche Antike*. I, pp.225,229,233.

Christ appears still as youthful but with long, curly hair, and from the fourth century on the more familiar bearded type appears.

Such was the gathering place of the Christians in Dura and similar to this, doubtless, were many other house churches throughout the Roman Empire during the early centuries of Christianity's life.

2. EARLY CHURCHES AT ROME

AT THE same time that the Christians of Dura were meeting in the house church just described, many Christians in Rome were assembling in private buildings which had been transferred to the church for the purpose of public worship. In Rome almost all of these later disappeared beneath new buildings by which they were replaced, but for centuries each of these churches continued to be designated by the name or *titulus* of its former owner and founder. For this reason they are called "title churches." Of the 25 churches which are known to have had this designation, 18 are earlier than Constantine and the majority of these probably go back at least as far as to the middle of the third century or to around the time of the Dura house church.[1]

SAN CLEMENTE

As an example of one of these title churches in Rome we may turn to San Clemente, which according to tradition was built on the site originally occupied by the house of Clement I who suffered martyrdom around A.D. 100. San Clemente is now on the modern Via di San Giovanni, running from the Colosseum to the Lateran, but once stood in the middle of an *insula* or block of buildings, fronting on a public road and with more distant streets on the other three sides. From the Via di San Giovanni one descends a few steps to the level of the present church. This is a structure which was consecrated in 1108 by Pope Paschal II and has been restored frequently since. It is a building oriented on an east-west axis, with a nave ending in a semicircular apse, and flanked by two side aisles likewise terminating in apses. In front is an atrium of oblong shape, surrounded by colonnaded porticoes.

Beneath this church Prior Mulhooly (d. 1880) discovered in 1852 a second and older basilica. Like the church above, it was divided by rows of columns into a nave and two aisles. The nave ended in an apse, and in front of the church was an atrium. This lower church was a grander structure than the building afterward superimposed, its nave being as wide as the upper church's nave and right aisle combined. This lower church was probably constructed around A.D. 390.

[1] Lietzmann, *Geschichte der alten Kirche.* II, p.256.

In turn, beneath this church are the remains of still older Roman buildings. The Roman structure under the main section of the lower church was a rectangular edifice, constructed of heavy tufa blocks, and probably was a part of some public building. It is believed to date from the end of the first or beginning of the second century. Behind this public building and separated from it only by a narrow passage, a large private house was built. The latter is to be dated probably not before the middle of the second century. At a later time, perhaps in the second quarter of the third century, the inner courtyard of this house was transformed into a Mithraeum, or chapel in which Mithras was worshiped.[2]

In approximately the third quarter of the third century, a new brick house was erected above the tufa edifice. It was a large building and contained an extensive hall on the ground floor. This hall was divided by rows of supports in a longitudinal direction, and opened in a series of wide apertures on both sides onto the exterior level. Later this last house was transformed into the existing lower basilica, in which a portion of the adjoining building, where the Mithraeum had been, was also incorporated. This rebuilding involved piercing the west wall of the house with the large hall and constructing an apse which projected into the neighboring house, adding a narthex and atrium at the east end, and erecting two rows of columns in the interior, thus making a nave and two aisles.

The complicated architectural history just outlined is of much interest because it enables us to show clearly that the fourth-century basilica of San Clemente was preceded by a third-century house in which there was a large ground-floor hall appropriate for public gatherings. It is very probable, therefore, that the third-century building was the *titulus* of the Christian community before the lower basilica came into being. Whether the house and hall were constructed by the Christians from the very beginning or only purchased by them to serve as a place of meeting, remains uncertain. But at any rate in this hall, which evidently was arranged for relatively large Christian gatherings, we see an important transitional stage between the simple homes in which the earlier believers met and the large basilicas in which the later Christians were privileged to worship.[3]

[2] At Ostia, the remains of seven such Mithraea have been found (Baedeker, *Rome.* 16th ed., p.540).

[3] Richard Krautheimer, *Corpus Basilicarum Christianarum Romae.* i, 2 (1937), pp.117-136; E. Junyent, *Il titolo di San Clemente in Roma.* 1932, p.23 Fig. 1.

3. YEARS OF PERSECUTION AND
YEARS OF PEACE

IN THE same period in which the hall church just described was in use in Rome, many other buildings were probably being erected throughout the empire for Christian assembly. Christianity underwent bitter persecutions in the time of Decius (A.D. 250) and Valerian (A.D. 257-258), but in A.D. 261 the Emperor Gallienus granted toleration in an edict which permitted the Christians again to use their places of worship and their cemeteries and provided that no one should molest them.[1] The final and terrible persecution of Diocletian (A.D. 303) was yet to come, but in the more than forty years intervening Christianity attracted great masses of people, and for their accommodation in services of worship it was necessary to erect buildings specifically planned as churches. This situation is explicitly indicated by Eusebius in the following words: "But how can anyone describe those vast assemblies, and the multitude that crowded together in every city, and the famous gatherings in the houses of prayer; by reason of which not being satisfied with the ancient buildings they erected from the foundation large churches in all the cities?"[2] In connection with an isolated case of martyrdom which took place at this same time, Eusebius incidentally mentions "the church" at Caesarea.[3]

DIOCLETIAN

Over these churches which sprang up during the relatively peaceful last four decades of the third century, a devastating storm was soon to break. This was the great persecution of Diocletian, who ruled in the East as Augustus, Galerius Caesar being his subordinate colleague and Nicomedia his capital. It was largely at the instigation of Galerius that the blow was planned. At dawn on February 23, 303, officers appeared before the Christian church in Nicomedia. The gates were forced open, the church pillaged and the Bibles burned. The church was situated on rising ground within view of the imperial palace where Diocletian and Galerius were standing, watching. Galerius wished to have the building set on fire, but Diocletian feared that the fire might spread to other parts of the city, so the Praetorian Guards were sent with axes and other instruments of

---

[1] Eusebius, *Ch. Hist.* VII, xiii (cf. above p.392 n.1).
[2] *Ch. Hist.* VIII, i, 5.   [3] *Ch. Hist.* VII, xv, 4.

iron, "and having been let loose everywhere, they in a few hours levelled that very lofty edifice to the ground."[4] On the next day an edict went out which was published everywhere. It not only deprived the Christians of all legal rights and called for the burning of the Scriptures but also commanded that the churches should be leveled to the ground.[5] Eusebius was living in Caesarea at this time and gives an eyewitness account of the persecution as it was carried out in Palestine. "We saw with our own eyes the houses of prayer thrown down to the very foundations,"[6] he says, and goes on to tell of the burning of Bibles and the torturing and slaying of martyrs.[7]

How many churches were destroyed before Galerius terminated the persecutions with an edict signed on his deathbed we do not know. Doubtless they were many. If, perchance, some did not fall before the storm they were ultimately replaced by later structures so that they, too, disappeared from sight. Of all the church buildings whose existence we infer in the latter years of the third century, scarcely a trace now survives.[8]

CONSTANTINE

It is first from the time of the Emperor Constantine and the true peace of the church that abundant and material evidence remains concerning early Christian churches. When Constantine and his eastern colleague, Licinius, issued the Edict of Milan in A.D. 313, full legal standing was granted to Christianity, and all confiscated church buildings and properties were returned. The churches which had been destroyed were now rebuilt and new ones were erected, all on a grander scale than had been known hitherto. "We saw," says Eusebius, "every place which shortly before had been desolated by the impieties of the tyrants reviving as if from a long and death-fraught pestilence, and temples again rising from their foundations

[4] This account is given by Lactantius, who was a teacher of rhetoric in Nicomedia at this time and therefore an eyewitness. It is found in his book entitled *Of the Manner in Which the Persecutors Died* (12), in which he shows the evil end to which all of the emperors came, from Nero on, who persecuted the Christians.

[5] Lactantius, *Of the Manner in Which the Persecutors Died.* 13; Eusebius, *Ch. Hist.* VIII, ii, 4 = *Martyrs of Palestine*, Intro.

[6] *Ch. Hist.* VIII, ii, 1.

[7] *Martyrs of Palestine* (a separate work, later appended to Bk. VIII of the *Church History*).

[8] Lietzmann, *Geschichte der alten Kirche.* III (1938), p.43.

to an immense height, and receiving a splendor far greater than that of the old ones which had been destroyed."[9]

THE CATHEDRAL AT TYRE

On the rubbish-covered site of an earlier church at Tyre, a new and elegant cathedral was erected, at the dedication of which around A.D. 316 Eusebius himself delivered an oration. From this address we can gain some idea of the church. The area in which it stood was enclosed by a wall and the main entrance was through a vestibule on the east. Between the outer entrance and the church building proper was a colonnaded court open to the sky with a fountain in the middle. Triple doors gave access to the church itself, which was paved with marble and roofed with cedar. Adjacent to the church were additional rooms and buildings, probably including a baptistery.[10]

THE "BASILICA"

The church at Tyre was evidently built on the plan characteristic of most of the great churches of the fourth and fifth centuries and to which the name basilica is given. The word "basilica" refers literally to a kingly hall,[11] and was therefore applied to a building of grandeur, but came to have a meaning almost as broad as our simple word, hall. Greek and Roman law courts, markets and meeting halls all were occasionally known by this term basilica (cf. p.295).[12] But the private houses of the Greeks and Romans[13] and the synagogues of the Jews[14] also often exhibited the rectangular, colonnaded form which is the chief characteristic of the basilica and, as we have seen, it is most probably out of such backgrounds that Christian meeting places were developed.

In its most distinctive Christian development the basilica had some or all of the following features. It might stand, as at Tyre, in an area surrounded by a wall or *peribolos*. Also as at Tyre, the entrance was often through a colonnaded court or *atrium*, which protected the worshipers from the noise of the streets and contained the fountain (*cantharus*) where the hands were washed symbolically before entering.[15] The basilica proper was a long, rectangular

---

[9] *Ch. Hist.* x, ii, 1.   [10] *Ch. Hist.* x, iv, 37-45.   [11] βασιλική i.e. στοά.
[12] Sartell Prentice, *The Heritage of the Cathedral*. 1936, pp.19-28.
[13] Lowrie, *Monuments of the Early Church*, pp.97-101.
[14] Kohl and Watzinger, *Antike Synagogen in Galiläa*, p.219.
[15] Lowrie, *Monuments of the Early Church*, p.179.

178. Air View of Dura-Europos

180. The Healing of the Paralytic

181. Constantine, the First Christian Emperor

183. Canopy over the Altar in St. Peter's

184. The Church of St. Paul outside the Walls, Rome

185. Interior of St. Paul's outside the Walls

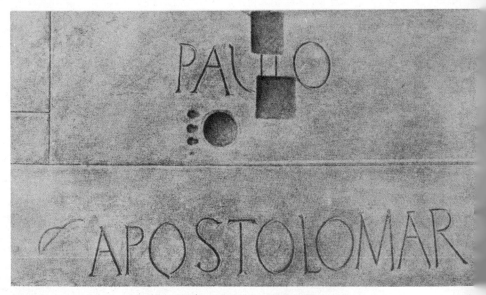

186. The **Marble** Slab over the Tomb of Paul

187. Apse Mosaic in Santa Pudenziana

188. The Taking of Jericho

189. Jerusalem as Represented on the Madeba Mosaic Map

190. The Church of the Holy Sepulcher, Jerusalem

191. The Church of the Nativity, Bethlehem

192. Interior of the Church of the Nativity

193. Early Mosaic in the Church of the Nativity

195. Mosaic in the Church of the Prophets,
Apostles and Martyrs at Gerasa

194. Mosaic in the Church of the Loaves
and Fishes at et-Tabgha

196. Air View of the Ruins of the Church at Kaoussie

197. Ruins of the Martyrion at Seleucia Pieria

198. Mosaic in the Martyrion at Seleucia Pieria

199. The West Door of the Church of St. Simeon Stylites

201. A Flask of St. Menas

202. The Baptistery at the Church of St. Menas

200. The Crypt in the Church of St. Menas

203. The Church of Hagia Sophia at Istanbul

204. Interior of Hagia Sophia

hall, which might be entered through a vestibule or *narthex*. The main, longitudinal area within the basilica was known as the *nave*, a word probably derived from the Latin word for ship (*navis*), to which the church was often likened. On each side of the nave were one or two rows of columns, which formed side aisles. These aisles had relatively low roofs, while the roof of the nave was much higher. The part of the nave which rises clear of the lower roofs of the side aisles is known as the *clerestory* and its walls were pierced with windows for lighting the central part of the basilica's interior. The nave and aisles were the parts occupied by the laity, and movable seats or benches were presumably provided for them here. At its far end the nave opened into the *apse*, which was a semi-circular recess, usually covered by a half dome. Between the nave and apse there might be a *transept* or cross aisle. If the latter projected beyond the side aisles it gave the church the form of a cross. The great arch above the half dome of the apse is known as the triumphal arch, and where there was a transept another trium-phal arch might separate it from the nave. The part of the church formed by the transept and apse was reserved for the clergy and might be called the *presbyterium*. Low screens sometimes sepa-rated it from the rest of the church. They were known in Latin as *cancelli* and later the presbyterium itself was called the *chancel*. There might also be a row of columns standing in front of the presbyterium for adornment. The altar, usually a relatively simple table of wood or stone, stood in the center of the transept or in the apse. If the church was built above the grave of a martyr the altar if possible was placed directly above the holy tomb, and in case this lay at some depth beneath the ground was connected with it by a vertical shaft. To the chamber around the tomb, and the shaft connecting it with the altar, the name *confessio* is applied. The altar might be further dignified by a *ciborium*, or roof erected over it on four columns. The clergy sat behind the altar, on benches running around the wall of the semicircular apse. In the center and raised above the presbyters' seats was the *cathedra*, or official chair in which the bishop sat and from which he preached.[16] An *ambon* or pulpit in the nave was used for the scripture reading, and some-

---

[16] The famous statue of Hippolytus (d. after A.D. 235), which was probably made soon after his death and is now in the Lateran Museum, shows this Roman church leader seated upon such a chair.

times the sermon was preached from it, too, in order for the speaker to be nearer the people. The baptistery was usually a small, separate building in the center of which was a round or octagonal pool (*fons* or *piscina*), entered by a flight of steps, for the act of immersion. Other structures, too, might be grouped around the church, including chapels, hospices, baths, hospitals or schools.

In exterior appearance the basilica ordinarily was very plain, although it was decorated occasionally with mosaic on the façade or, as in Syria, was developed impressively with single and double towers. Within, however, the basilica was often richly adorned. A marble incrustation (*opus sectile*) was frequently applied to the lower portion of the walls, while on the upper walls of the nave, on the triumphal arch and in the half dome of the apse were often placed the most beautiful representations in mosaic. This was fitting, since the essential purpose of the basilica was fulfilled in its interior. There the congregation felt itself a unity, and the thoughts of all were led forward to the place where the Lord's table stood and where the gospel was preached.

A mention of such a basilica and a description of the worship of the Christians within it, is found in the *Apostolic Constitutions,* written about A.D. 380. It compares the church to a ship and reads in part as follows:

"Let the building be long, with its head to the east,[17] with its vestries on both sides at the east end, and so it will be like a ship. In the middle let the bishop's throne be placed, and on each side of him let the presbytery sit down; and let the deacons stand near at hand, with closely girt garments, for they are like the mariners and managers of the ship. In accordance with their arrangement, let the laity sit on the other side, with all quietness and good order. And let the women sit by themselves, they also keeping silence. In the middle, let the reader stand upon some high place: let him read the books of Moses . . . and the Epistles of Paul . . . and the Gospels. . . . In the next place, let the presbyters one by one, not all together, exhort the people, and the bishop in the last place, as being the commander. Let the porters stand at the entrances of the men and give heed to them, while the deaconesses stand at those of the women, like shipmen. . . . But if anyone be found sitting out of his place, let him be rebuked by the deacon, as a manager of the foreship, and removed into the place proper for him; for the church is not only like a ship, but also like a sheepfold. For as the shepherds place all the brute

---

[17] This rule calling for the orientation of the apse toward the east, was frequently but by no means always followed.

creatures distinctly . . . so is it to be in the church. Let the young men sit by themselves, if there be a place for them, but if not let them stand upright. Let those already advanced in years sit in order and let the children stand beside their mothers and fathers. Let the younger women also sit by themselves if there be a place for them but if not let them stand behind the elder women. Let those women who are married and have children be placed by themselves, while the virgins and the widows and the elderwomen stand or sit before all the rest. Let the deacon be the disposer of the places, that every one of those that comes in may go to his proper place and not sit at the entrance. In like manner let the deacon oversee the people that nobody may whisper nor slumber nor laugh nor nod, for all ought in the church to stand wisely and soberly and attentively, having their attention fixed upon the word of the Lord. After this, let all rise up with one consent and looking towards the east, after the catechumens and penitents are gone out, pray to God eastward. . . . As to the deacons, after the prayer is over, let some of them attend upon the oblation of the eucharist, ministering to the Lord's body with fear. Let others of them watch the multitude and keep them silent. But let that deacon who is at the high priest's hand say to the people, Let no one have any quarrel against another; let no one come in hypocrisy. Then let the men give the men, and the women give the women, the Lord's kiss. . . . After this let the deacon pray for the whole church, for the whole world. . . . Let the bishop pray for the people. . . . After this let the sacrifice follow, the people standing and praying silently; and when the oblation has been made, let every rank by itself partake of the Lord's body and precious blood in order, and approach with reverence and holy fear, as tc the body of their king. Let the women approach with their heads covered, as is becoming the order of women; but let the door be watched, lest any unbeliever, or one not yet initiated, come in."[18]

[18] II, 57 (ANF VII, pp.421f.); cf. E. II. Short, *A History of Religious Architecture.* 1936, p.65.

4. CHURCHES IN ROME

THE BASILICAS OF CONSTANTINE

THE most famous basilicas of the fourth century were built by Constantine, who after his victory over Licinius and the death of the latter in A.D. 324 and until his own death in A.D. 337 was sole ruler of the Roman Empire. His political and military position was so secure that he could personally devote much time and interest to religious matters, including the building of great churches. A letter which he directed at this time to all the bishops in the various provinces has been preserved by Eusebius in which the emperor urged "all to be zealous in their attention to the buildings of the churches, and either to repair or enlarge those which at present exist, or, in cases of necessity, to erect new ones."[1] The bishops were authorized to request whatever was needful for the work from the provincial governors, to whom corresponding instructions were sent. "In every province," states Eusebius, "he [Constantine] raised new churches on a far more imposing scale than those which had existed before his time."[2] The personal appearance of this benefactor of early Christianity is seen in Fig. 181, this being the head of a colossal statue which once stood in the Basilica of Constantine in the Roman Forum.

A list of the churches which Constantine erected in Rome is given in the Liber Pontificalis. This list forms a part of the biography of Sylvester who was pope (314-335) at the time of Constantine's reign. Since Sylvester was the thirty-fourth Head of the Roman Church, his biography constitutes Chapter 34 of the Liber Pontificalis. While the text of the Liber Pontificalis dates from the seventh century (p.302 n.19), the notices which are numerous from the time of Sylvester on, concerning churches built or repaired and gifts offered for them, must often have been copied directly from memoranda and records in the papal archives. In particular the list of Constantine's churches and donations gives evidence of genuineness although there is some corruption in the text, as for example where the proper names occasionally become unintelligible.[3]

THE CHURCH OF ST. PETER

The holiest sites upon which churches could be erected at Rome were the graves of Peter and Paul, and the Liber Pontificalis records

---

[1] *Life of Constantine.* II, 46.   [2] ibid., III, 47.   [3] LLP, pp.xvii-xviii.

that Constantine founded basilicas at both of these places. The location of the graves at the Vatican and on the Ostian Way has been discussed already, and also the temporary transfer of the remains to Catacumbas in A.D. 258 (pp.301-303, 376-379). Peace having come to the church, these remains could be returned to their original resting places and suitable memorials erected in the form of fine basilicas. Concerning the first of these two buildings the Liber Pontificalis records:

"At the same time Constantine Augustus built by the request of Silvester, the bishop, the basilica of blessed Peter, the apostle, in the shrine of Apollo, and laid there the coffin with the body of the holy Peter; the coffin itself he enclosed on all sides with bronze, which is unchangeable: at the head 5 feet, at the feet 5 feet, at the right side 5 feet, at the left side 5 feet, underneath 5 feet and overhead 5 feet: thus he enclosed the body of blessed Peter, the apostle, and laid it away.

"And above he set porphyry columns for adornment and other spiral columns which he brought from Greece.

"He made also a vaulted roof in the basilica, gleaming with polished gold, and over the body of the blessed Peter, above the bronze which enclosed it, he set a cross of purest gold weighing 150 lbs. . . . and upon it were inscribed these words: 'CONSTANTINE AUGUSTUS AND HELENA AUGUSTA THIS HOUSE SHINING WITH LIKE ROYAL SPLENDOR A COURT SURROUNDS,' inscribed in enamelled letters upon the cross."

A list follows of the precious vessels and revenues which Constantine bestowed upon the church.[4]

Constantine's basilica stood until it was destroyed by the popes of the Renaissance to make way for the present Church of St. Peter. In those intervening centuries it was altered somewhat and much added to, but seems basically to have preserved its original structure. Thus, while practically nothing now remains of Constantine's original church its essential character can be surmised from sketches and descriptions of the building as it stood in the Middle Ages. A flight of steps led up to a propylaeum which gave access to a large atrium. This court was surrounded by colonnades and had a fountain in the center. The basilica was entered by five doors and divided into nave and two aisles on either side. The columns in the church had been taken from ancient monuments and their bases, shafts and capitals were varied in size and style. The Constantinian origin of the building was shown plainly when the apse

[4] LLP, pp.53f.

was finally demolished, for the emperor's stamp was on its bricks. The mosaic which at that time still was on the triumphal arch, showing Constantine offering a model of the church to Christ, probably also dated from the original basilica.[5] On the arch, Constantine's inscription addressed to Christ read: "Because, led by thee, the world rises triumphant to the stars, Constantine, victorious, built this hall for thee."[6]

In order to erect the basilica, Constantine destroyed what remained of the Circus of Caligula. As a matter of fact the grave of Peter was so close to the Circus that it was possible to employ portions of the Circus as foundations for the church. The south wall and the two southernmost rows of columns of the church were built upon the three parallel walls which previously formed the north side of the Circus. The fact that the walls of the church were placed not on the exact center of the walls of the Circus but slightly to one side doubtless contributed largely to the ultimate collapse of the Constantinian basilica.[7] It is also noteworthy that the utilization of the Circus walls for foundations led to an orientation of the church in which the grave of Peter came within the apse of the church but was not exactly in the center as it should have been if the place had been only a free invention.[8]

In the course of the fourth and fifth centuries a baptistery was added in the right arm of the transept, the atrium was paved, a mosaic was placed on the façade[9] and the church was connected with Hadrian's mausoleum and bridge by an arcaded boulevard. Many subsidiary buildings grew up around the basilica and eventually an entire suburb surrounded it. In the barbarian invasions Alaric king of the Goths (410) and Genseric king of the Vandals (455) ordered that the church of St. Peter should be spared, and it also escaped damage in the siege by the Lombards (756). But in the Saracen invasion in 846 it suffered damage and, after that, Pope Leo IV (847-855) built for its protection the so-called Leonine Wall around the basilica and the Vatican hill.

[5] A. L. Frothingham, *The Monuments of Christian Rome*. 1908, pp 25-27.
[6] E. Diehl, *Inscriptiones latinae christianae veteres*. I (1925), No. 1752.
[7] PATD, pp.113f.
[8] Lietzmann, *Petrus und Paulus in Rom*, pp.206f.
[9] Repair or decoration of the basilica by Leo I (440-461) is mentioned in the Liber Pontificalis (see below p.423) and the mosaic on the façade is known to have borne a dedicatory inscription concerning a restoration by the praetorian prefect Marinianus and his wife Anastasia at Leo's request.

By the time of Pope Nicholas V (1447-1455) Constantine's basilica was leaning badly to one side and generally falling into ruin. It was decided that the old church would have to be torn down and a new one built upon its site. The new structure was designed by Bramante and the first stone laid in 1506. The work was carried forward in following years under the direction of Raphael (1514) and Michelangelo (1546). Dedication was in 1626.

As it stands today the Basilica di San Pietro in Vaticano is the largest church in the world. Its interior is 609 feet in length and its area is about 163,200 square feet. The great dome, which is its crowning glory, is 138 feet in diameter and rises to a height of 405 feet. At an early time the subterranean tomb of Peter was made inaccessible to protect it from marauders and when the old basilica was demolished and the new one built the tomb was not molested. Bramante's plan, indeed, called for moving the tomb in order to give the new church a different orientation, but Pope Julius II (1503-1513) refused to allow this to be done. In 1594, when the present high altar was being built, the bottom of the shaft leading to the grave was laid open and Pope Clement VIII and three cardinals saw a cross of gold lying upon the tomb. But the pope immediately ordered the shaft to be filled up again and it has never since been opened.[10] Through one unblocked opening, Hartmann Grisar was able in 1895 to catch a glimpse of the ancient marble slab which covered the tomb, it then being broken in half but still in place.[11]

In front of the church, in the center of the piazza, stands the great obelisk which Caligula brought from Heliopolis to adorn the *spina* of his Circus. The original location of the obelisk in the Circus is still marked by a stone in the small Piazza del Circo Neroniano, just south of St. Peter's. The obelisk was moved to its present site by Xystus V in 1586. The two semicircular colonnades which now beautify the sides of the elliptical piazza were erected by Bernini in 1657-1663 (Fig. 182).

Bernini also designed (1633) the imposing *baldacchino* or bronze canopy which rises to a height of 95 feet over the high altar in St. Peter's. It will be remembered (p.419) that above the tomb of Peter, Constantine set porphyry columns and other spiral columns. Apparently the porphyry columns supported the ciborium above the altar, while the spiral columns formed a colonnade separating the

[10] LLP, p.53 n.3.   [11] E. Pucci in EB XXIII, p.5.

confessio from the nave. Several of the spiral columns still exist, some now adorning the upper niches in the four huge piers that support the dome of St. Peter's, and one being preserved in the side chapel known as the Cappella della Pieta. These served Bernini as models for the great gilded spiral columns which support the present ciborium over the high altar (Fig. 183).

THE CHURCH OF ST. PAUL OUTSIDE THE WALLS

The Liber Pontificalis states that the basilica over the grave of Paul, now known as San Paolo fuori le Mura, was also founded by Constantine. One manuscript, however, adds the name of his son, the Emperor Constantius (337-361), who probably carried this church to completion. The statement in the Liber Pontificalis is: "At the same time Constantine Augustus and Lord Constantius Augustus built the basilica of blessed Paul, the apostle, at the bidding of Silvester the bishop, and laid his body away there in bronze and enclosed it, as he did the body of the blessed Peter. . . . Moreover he placed a golden cross over the tomb of blessed Paul, the apostle, weighing 150 lbs." Gifts and revenues devoted to the church also are listed, as in the case of the basilica of St. Peter.[12]

The Constantinian basilica of St. Paul was only a small structure. This seems surprising in comparison with the large church built in honor of Peter, but the explanation is to be found in the character of the available site. The grave of Paul lay between the Via Ostiensis and another small paved street, the Via Valentiniana, which joined it at a sharp angle somewhat to the south. Only the area in the angle between these two streets was available for the basilica, unless the streets were to be destroyed. Also, the site was unfavorable because it stood far distant from the city residences of most of the Christians and because it was in a low-lying area frequently overflowed by the Tiber River. Nevertheless the basilica was erected here. Certainly the location was not invented, but only accepted because it was the actual place of Paul's grave.[13]

In 384 the three emperors, Valentinian II, Theodosius I the Great, and his son Arcadius, issued a decree which moved the inconvenient side street far enough away so that space was gained to accommodate a truly monumental church, and in 386 a letter

[12] LLP, pp.57f.
[13] Lietzmann, *Petrus und Paulus in Rom*, pp.220f.

to Sallust, the prefect of Rome, ordered the construction of the new basilica. The work was completed under the Emperor Honorius (395-423) the younger son of Theodosius, and dedicated by Pope Siricius (384-399), the latter's name and the date 390 still existing on a column of the church.[14] The orientation of the new structure was the reverse of the old, so that the main entrance was from the bank of the Tiber and the apse faced to the east. The church extended across the disused Via Valentiniana and was so much greater than the Constantinian basilica that its transept alone was larger than the entire old church. It was so arranged, however, that the grave of Paul was not changed and the altar and *confessio* remained on their original site.

The basilica of the three emperors stood until destroyed by a great fire in 1823. It was probably damaged by Genseric and the Vandals in 455 and may have been struck by lightning about the same time, since the Liber Pontificalis says that the roof was rebuilt "after the fire from God" by Pope Leo I the Great (440-461): "He replaced all the consecrated silver vessels in all the parish churches after the Vandal devastation. . . . He repaired the basilica of blessed Peter,[15] the apostle, and restored the vaulting of blessed Paul after the fire from God."[16]

Pope Symmachus (498-514) is credited with extensive works of restoration and beautification: "Also in the church of blessed Paul, the apostle, he rebuilt the apse of the basilica, which was falling into ruin, and he embellished it with a picture behind the confession and he made a vaulting and a transept; and over the confession he erected a silver image of the Saviour and the 12 apostles, which weighed 120 lbs.; and before the doors of the basilica he rebuilt steps into the atrium and a fountain; and behind the apse he brought down water and built there a bath from the foundation."[17] Although the Lombards devastated the environs of Rome during the siege of 756, they spared St. Paul's. The Saracens did more damage and may even have rifled the tomb of the apostle Paul. Afterward Pope John VIII (872-882) followed the example of Leo IV at the Vatican (p. 420) and surrounded the basilica of St. Paul and the

[14] Frothingham, *Monuments of Christian Rome*, p.48.
[15] Another text reads, "He made the vaulting and decorated the basilica of blessed Peter."
[16] LLP, p.100.
[17] LLP, p.121.

suburb that had grown up around it with a strong battlemented wall. He called the suburb Johannipolis.

Immediately after the terrible fire of 1823, Leo XII began the work of building a new church. The transept of the modern structure was consecrated in 1840 and the entire church in 1854. The square forecourt, lined with granite columns, was added in 1890-1929. In plan and dimensions the new basilica closely followed its predecessor. The main entrance is by the western façade (Fig. 184), which faces toward the Tiber, and the interior is arranged with nave, double aisles and transept. Eighty columns of polished gray granite support the ceiling of the nave, which is coffered instead of being open as formerly. The large dimensions of the interior, 394 feet in length and 75 feet in height, and the rich ornamentation combine to produce a very imposing effect (Fig. 185).

The mosaics on the triumphal arch of the basilica of the three emperors were executed in 440-461 by order of the Empress Galla Placidia, sister of the Emperor Honorius, but were damaged badly in the great fire, and the present mosaics are an entirely modern restoration. The mosaic inscription states that the basilica was begun by Theodosius and finished by Honorius and that it was restored and decorated by Placidia under Pope Leo. The mosaics in the apse date from around 1218 and also had to be restored completely after the fire.

When the present church was being constructed there was seen at the bottom of the shaft under the high altar a marble slab with an inscription in letters characteristic of the time of Constantine: PAULO APOSTOLO MARTYRI (Fig. 186). The circular hole seen in the slab was the *billicum* or opening of a little well which led into the tomb, through which it was customary to lower objects to touch the coffin beneath. The two square holes may have been connected with some obscure medieval ceremony.[18]

While exceedingly little from Constantinian and earlier times now remains at the sites of the churches of Paul and Peter, the chain of archeological evidence is such that the last resting places of the two great apostles may confidently be sought beneath the extensive hall of the three emperors and the soaring dome of Bramante and Michelangelo.

[18] Barnes, *Martyrdom of St. Peter and St. Paul*, p.148.

SAN GIOVANNI IN LATERANO

In addition to the basilicas of Peter and Paul, five more churches were built in Rome by Constantine. As a matter of fact, in the Liber Pontificalis one of these stands at the head of the list of all the basilicas erected by Constantine, being mentioned even before St. Peter's and St. Paul's. This is "the Constantinian basilica" as the Liber Pontificalis calls it,[19] or St. John Lateran (San Giovanni in Laterano) as it is now known. A palace belonging to the senator Plautius Lateranus was confiscated by Nero and thus became imperial property. A portion of it was given by the Emperor Maximian (286-305) to his daughter Fausta, who was married to Constantine in 307. Fausta lived there until she was put to death in 326, and the place became known as the Domus Faustae, or House of Fausta. In 313 a church council under Pope Miltiades met "in the house of Fausta in the Lateran,"[20] and after Fausta's death Constantine gave the palace to Pope Sylvester I as a residence. It continued to be the official residence of the popes for nearly a thousand years. It was burned down in 1308 and the present Palazzo del Laterano was not erected until 1586. In 1843 Gregory XVI made this palace into the Museum Gregorianum Lateranense.

According to tradition, the basilica which Constantine built at the Lateran was dedicated in 324. It was destroyed by an earthquake and reerected by Pope Sergius III (904-911), at that time being dedicated to John the Baptist. After being burned down twice in the fourteenth century it was rebuilt by Urban V (1362-1370) and Gregory XI (1370-1378) and repeatedly altered and modernized at various later times. The interior appears today chiefly in the form given to it by Borromini in the seventeenth century, and the principal façade is the work of Alessandro Galilei in the eighteenth century. Many important church councils have been held here and, as the papal cathedral, the basilica bears the inscription "the mother and head of all the churches of the city and the world." But of the building of Constantine nothing remains.[21]

SANTA CROCE IN GERUSALEMME

"At the same time," continues the Liber Pontificalis after record-

[19] LLP, p.47.   [20] LLP, p.47 n.1.

[21] The Altar of the Sacrament in the south transept of the present church has four antique columns of gilded bronze which are said to have belonged to the original basilica. Baedeker, *Rome*, p.384.

ing the founding of St. Peter's and St. Paul's, "Constantine Augustus constructed a basilica in the Sessorian palace, where he also placed and enclosed in gold and jewels some of the wood of the holy cross of our Lord Jesus Christ, and he dedicated the church under the name by which it is called even to this day, Hierusalem."[22] The Sessorian palace was the residence of Constantine's mother, the Empress Helena, and two inscriptions in her honor have been discovered there. While Helena's pilgrimage to the Holy Land is a well known fact, Eusebius says nothing of her discovery of the actual cross of Christ[23] and the accounts of that happening given about the middle of the fifth century by Socrates[24] and Sozomen[25] are certainly legendary in character. The existence of the cross and the sending of pieces of its wood throughout the world were believed in, however, by Cyril of Jerusalem around A.D. 348.[26] It is evident, therefore, that the Sessorian palace hall was transformed into a basilica and named in honor of the discovery of the cross at Jerusalem. The present church, Santa Croce in Gerusalemme, has been rebuilt and restored but still shows traces of once having been a private hall.

SANT' AGNESE FUORI LE MURA

"At the same time," continues the Liber Pontificalis concerning Constantine, "he built the basilica of the holy martyr Agnes at the request of Constantia,[27] his daughter, and a baptistery in the same place, where both his sister, Constantia, and the daughter of Augustus were baptized by Silvester the bishop."[28] St. Agnes was a famous martyr who is mentioned by Jerome[29] and whose place of burial was outside the city on the Via Nomentana, where the catacomb is located which now bears her name. The basilica which Constantine erected in honor of St. Agnes was carried beneath the level of the ground in order to bring its altar immediately over the holy tomb. Rebuilt by Pope Honorius I (625-638) and restored again in the fifteenth and nineteenth centuries, the present Church of St. Agnes outside the Walls (Sant' Agnese fuori le Mura) still lies at a low

---

[22] LLP, p.58.   [23] *Life of Constantine.* III, 26, 42.
[24] *Church History.* I, 17 (NPNFSS II, p.21).
[25] *Church History.* II, 1 (NPNFSS II, p.258).
[26] *Catechetical Lectures.* IV, 10; X, 19; XIII, 4 (NPNFSS VII, pp.21,63,83).
[27] Actually the name of Constantine's daughter was Constantina, while his sister was named Constantia.
[28] LLP, p.60.
[29] *Letter 130 to Demetrias.* 5 (NPNFSS VI, p.262).

level, being reached by a descending stairway of 45 steps, and still retains many characteristics of an early Christian basilica.

SANTA COSTANZA

Near by is a circular, domed building which is known now as the Church of Santa Costanza. No doubt it represents the baptistery mentioned by the Liber Pontificalis in connection with the basilica of Agnes, although its original character seems to have been that of a mausoleum. Probably it was used later as a baptistery, the font perhaps having been located in the central space under the dome. The funerary character of the building is shown by the niches in the wall intended to receive sarcophagi, and by the one sarcophagus actually found here and now kept in the Vatican Museum. Despite the statement in the Liber Pontificalis, the structure may not have been erected by Constantine himself, since his daughter for whom it was intended as a mausoleum survived him by seventeen years. A date in the time of the Emperor Constans (337-350) is possible. At any rate this is doubtless the place to which reference is made by the Roman historian Ammianus Marcellinus (c.330-c.395) when he says that in A.D. 360 the body of Helena, another daughter of Constantine, was sent to Rome to be buried on the Via Nomentana where her sister Constantina already lay.[30]

Fine fourth century mosaics still survive in the low vault of the circular aisle which runs around the interior of Santa Costanza. These include naturalistic representations of flowers, fruit, birds and sheep, and an interesting vintage scene in which cupids pluck the grapes, carry them to vats and trample out the juice. As in the catacombs, so here in the realm of mosaics, we find the earliest Christian art making free use of the materials of the Roman antique tradition.[31]

SAN LORENZO FUORI LE MURA

The Liber Pontificalis continues: "At the same time Constantine Augustus built the basilica of blessed Lawrence, the martyr, on the Via Tiburtina in the Ager Veranus over the buried crypt, and he made stairs of ascent and of descent to the body of the holy martyr Lawrence. In that place he erected an apse and adorned it with porphyry and the spot over the tomb he enclosed with silver and

[30] xxi, 1, 5. tr. J. C. Rolfe, LCL (1935-39) II, p.93.
[31] E. W. Anthony, *A History of Mosaics.* 1935, p.63; H. H. Powers, *The Art of Mosaic.* 1938, p.79.

beautified it with railings of purest silver, which weighed 1000 lbs."[32] Lawrence was the famous martyr who was put to death over a slow fire in the Valerian persecution of 258. The Constantinian basilica was located so that the altar came over the martyr's crypt to which a stairway gave access. The passage in the Liber Pontificalis is specially interesting since it is one of the earliest descriptions of such a *confessio*.

In 578 Pope Pelagius II rebuilt the church, his work evidently being thorough since the Liber Pontificalis says that "he built from its foundations a basilica over the body of blessed Lawrence."[33] He is also responsible for the mosaic which in restored form is still to be seen on the arch, with Christ in the center, Peter, Lawrence and Pelagius (with a model of the basilica) on his right side, Paul, Stephen and Hippolytus on his left, and the cities of Jerusalem and Bethlehem beneath. These are the earliest mosaics in Rome to show Byzantine influence, Christ being seated on the globe of the world as in San Vitale at Ravenna, and Peter being placed in accordance with Byzantine tradition at Christ's right side instead of at the left as was the Roman tradition from the fourth to the thirteenth century.

A complete reorientation and remodeling of this church took place under Honorius III (1216-1227). He turned the nave into a choir with a crypt beneath it, added the present nave at a level ten feet higher on the opposite side of the triumphal arch, thus leaving the mosaics of Pelagius facing the choir, and transferred the entrance to the opposite end of the church. The present San Lorenzo in Agro Verano,[34] or San Lorenzo fuori le Mura, is therefore a basilica far different from that originally built by Constantine.

SANTI PIETRO E MARCELLINO

"At the same time Constantine Augustus built a basilica to the blessed martyrs Marcellinus, the priest, and Peter, the exorcist, at Inter duas Lauros; also a mausoleum where his mother, Helena Augusta, was buried on the Via Lavicana, at the 3rd milestone."[35] The catacomb which still bears the name of these two martyrs has been mentioned (p. 380) but the basilica which Constantine built in their honor has disappeared completely. The remains of the octagonal, domed mausoleum of Constantine's mother still stand, how-

[32] LLP, pp.61f.   [33] LLP, p.168.
[34] The Campo Verano is now the chief cemetery of modern Rome.
[35] LLP, p.63.

ever, and the huge porphyry sarcophagus which was found here is preserved in the Vatican Museum near the sarcophagus from the mausoleum of Constantina. A small church called Santi Pietro e Marcellino has been fitted up in the mausoleum of Helena, which otherwise now is known as the Torre Pignattára. The latter name comes from the *pignatte* or earthenware vessels which were used in the construction of the vaulting for the sake of lightness, as was customary in the late imperial period.

This completes the list of churches erected in Rome by Constantine as given by the Liber Pontificalis. Outside of Rome the same source ascribes to him the building of basilicas at Ostia, Albano, Capua and Naples,[36] but does not mention the ones he founded in more distant places like Palestine. Before turning to some of the basilicas erected by Constantine in lands outside of Italy a few other Roman churches will be mentioned briefly.

THE "TITLE CHURCHES"

At this time the so-called "title churches" (p. 410) formed the majority of the Roman churches and provided the basis of administrative organization, since they were the seats of the presbyters. The priests were divided among the title churches and had responsibility for the corresponding sections of the Roman church members, namely those who lived in that part of the city. The cardinal priests are still assigned to these churches and are titularly in charge of them.[37] By the fifth century the list of title churches numbered 25 and included those known today as Santi Giovanni e Paolo, San Clemente, Santi Pietro e Marcellino, San Pietro in Vincoli, San Martino ai Monti, Santa Prassede, Santa Pudenziana, Sant' Eusebio, San Vitale, Santa Susanna, San Marcello, San Lorenzo in Lucina, San Lorenzo in Damaso, San Marco, Santa Anastasia, Santi Nereo ed Achilleo, Santa Balbina, Santa Sabina, Santa Prisca, Santa Maria in Trastevere, Santa Cecilia and San Crisogono, as well as the churches of Xysti, of Aemilianae and of Cyriaci whose identifications are not certain.[38] Of the foregoing, San Clemente and Santi Pietro e Marcellino have already been noted; and of the remainder we shall discuss only Santa Pudenziana and Santa Sabina.

[36] LLP, pp.66f.,69f.
[37] J. P. Kirsch, *Die römischen Titelkirchen.* 1918, p.1.
[38] These churches are listed by Frothingham (*Monuments of Christian Rome*, pp.39f.) according to the fourteen *regiones* of ancient Rome.

SANTA PUDENZIANA

The church of Santa Pudenziana is mentioned in an epitaph of
A.D. 384 and was rebuilt by Pope Siricius (384-399) who changed it
from a hall church into a three aisled basilica. The date of its original
founding is unknown but tradition ascribes it to Pius I (c.142-c.154).
To his biography as given by the Liber Pontificalis the following
sentences are added in certain eleventh century manuscripts: "He
by request of the blessed Praxedis dedicated a church in the baths
of Novatus in the Vicus Patricius[39] to the honor of her sister, the holy
Pudentiana, where also he offered many gifts and frequently he ministered, offering sacrifice to the Lord. Moreover he erected a font of
baptism and with his own hand he blessed and dedicated it and many
who gathered to the faith he baptized in the name of the Trinity."[40]
Pudentiana and Praxedis[41] were the daughters of Pudens, but
whether he is to be identified with the Pudens of II Timothy 4:21
is questionable.

Santa Pudenziana is most famous for the mosaic in its apse which
probably dates from the time of Pope Siricius. The mosaic was restored somewhat at the end of the eighth century under Pope Hadrian I (772-795) and was heavily trimmed around the curved margin when the apse was narrowed in 1588. Also a portion of the lower
part was removed later by the erection of the *baldacchino* and in
1831 the right side was largely done over. Nevertheless it remains
the earliest and most beautiful apse mosaic in existence and is characterized by a solemn and triumphant grandeur (Fig. 187). In the
center Christ arrayed in a tunic of gold is seated upon a throne and
holds an open book in his hand bearing the inscription "The Lord,
Guardian of the Church of Pudentiana." Originally the twelve tunic-
clothed apostles were to be seen on either side of Christ, but the
outermost figure on each side was lost when the apse was narrowed.
Peter stands at the right[42] and Paul[43] at the left. Behind each of
the two great apostles stands a woman clothed in gold, holding over
his head a laurel crown. These women are believed to represent the

[39] The Vicus Patricius was near the modern Via Urbana, on which Santa Pudenziana
now is located.

[40] LLP, p.15 n.3.

[41] To whom the church of Santa Prassede is dedicated.

[42] That is, at the right as seen by the viewer, or at the left hand of Christ. This was
the position which was customary in the Roman tradition (p.428).

[43] The opening words of Matthew appear on the open book in Paul's hand but the
inscription is a modern restoration.

Jewish Church (Ecclesia ex Circumcisione) and the Gentile Church (Ecclesia ex Gentibus) respectively. The background is formed by a portico above which in the center looms the rock of Calvary, surmounted by a great jeweled cross.[44] At the right appears a structure which is probably to be identified with the Church of the Nativity at Bethlehem, while the one at the left probably represents the Church of the Holy Sepulcher in Jerusalem. Above in the clouds are the winged symbols of the four evangelists, now appearing for one of the earliest times in art: the man (angel), lion, ox and eagle (cf. Ezekiel 10:14; Revelation 4:7) representing respectively Matthew, Mark, Luke and John.[45]

SANTA SABINA

The church of Santa Sabina was erected by the priest Peter under the pontificate of Celestine I (422-432) as is evident from the dedicatory *titulus* inscription in mosaic which still is in place over the door of the entrance wall. The church was restored in the thirteenth, fifteenth, sixteenth and twentieth centuries, but with its 24 marble columns and open roof the essential structure is still that of an early Christian basilica. Originally, however, it was almost entirely covered within with mosaics, of which all are now lost except the mosaic inscription over the door. On either side of the mosaic inscription is the figure of a woman, the one at the left being shown as a woman of Palestine and labeled Ecclesia ex Circumcisione and the one at the right being represented as a Roman matron and labeled Ecclesia ex Gentibus.[46]

Santa Sabina is most famous for its great cypress doors whose carvings also belong to the time of the origin of the church around 430. Of their original 28 panels only 18 are left. Eight large panels give scenes from the life of Moses and other Old Testament subjects, while ten small ones are mostly devoted to scenes of the passion of Christ and his appearances after the resurrection. It is thought that the original plan of the door provided a parallelism between the events of the Old Testament and those of the New.[47] The crucifixion appears for perhaps the first time in Christian art.[48]

[44] The style of the cross seems later than that of the rest of the composition and it may be due to Hadrian's restoration.

[45] Anthony, *A History of Mosaics*, pp.66-68; cf. Thomas Albert Stafford, *Christian Symbolism in the Evangelical Churches.* 1942, p.101.

[46] Anthony, *A History of Mosaics*, p.76.   [47] Morey, *Early Christian Art*, p.138.

[48] Lowrie, *Monuments of the Early Church*, p.273.

SANTA MARIA MAGGIORE

Our survey of some of the most interesting early Christian churches in Rome may be concluded with mention of Santa Maria Maggiore, which is neither a Constantinian basilica nor a title church but the largest of the eighty churches in the city dedicated to the Virgin, being exceeded in size only by St. Peter's, St. Paul's and St. John Lateran. It was built by Pope Liberius (352-366), who probably remodeled an already existing palace, and sometimes was known as the Basilica Liberiana. The Liber Pontificalis states in the biography of this pontiff: "He built the basilica of his own name near the Macellum of Libia."[49] The latter is equivalent to "the market of Livia." This basilica was rebuilt by Xystus III (432-440), concerning whom the Liber Pontificalis says, "He built the basilica of the holy Mary, which was called by the ancients the basilica of Liberius, near the Macellum of Lybia."[50]

Santa Maria Maggiore is most famous for its glorious mosaics. Those of the triumphal arch go back to Xystus III, whose inscription still may be read on them: XYSTUS EPISCOPUS PLEBI DEI, "Bishop Xystus to the People of God."[51] The mosaics of the nave, like its ancient marble columns, may go back to Liberius but more probably also belong to the period of Xystus III.[52]

Of the 42 original panels of nave mosaics, 27 remain. These give a remarkable series of Old Testament pictures of which the Taking of Jericho is shown in Fig. 188. The procession of the ark and trumpeters is shown in the lower panel of the picture, and in the upper the Israelite warriors surround the city whose walls already are falling down. In antique perspective, the man and building which actually are within the city are shown on top of the walls. On the triumphal arch in Santa Maria Maggiore are beautiful scenes relating to the infancy of Christ.

[49] LLP, p.77. [50] LLP, p.94.
[51] A. Schuchert, S. *Maria Maggiore zu Rom*. I, *Die Gründungsgeschichte der Basilika und die ursprüngliche Apsisanlage*. 1939, p.55.
[52] Morey, *Early Christian Art*, p.146; Anthony, *A History of Mosaics*, p.76.

5. CHURCHES IN PALESTINE

THE most sacred sites in all the world on which to erect Christian churches of course were to be found in the Holy Land. Concerning the basilicas which Constantine and his family erected there, we are informed by Eusebius, whose writings are substantially contemporary.[1]

THE CHURCH OF THE HOLY SEPULCHER

For nearly two hundred years a pagan sanctuary (p. 251) had stood over the sepulcher of Christ at Jerusalem. But at the command of Constantine this temple and its idols were thrown down and the polluted surface soil carried away. In the course of this work the tomb of Christ came to light again and the emperor forthwith wrote to Macarius, the bishop of Jerusalem, instructing him to erect there at imperial expense a basilica[2] which should surpass in beauty all others everywhere.[3] This church was dedicated in A.D. 335 and is described in considerable detail by Eusebius.[4] Following his description in reverse order, we find that the propylaea or main entrances opened off from the middle of the chief market street of the city, and "afforded to passers-by on the outside a view of the interior which could not fail to inspire astonishment." Beyond and several feet above the level of the street was the first court or atrium which was entered by three doorways, surrounded by porticoes and left open to the sky. Passing through this one came to the basilica proper, later called the Martyrium, to which access was gained by three doors at the eastern end. Its walls were made of accurately fitted stones, while the roof was covered with lead as a protection against the winter rains. Within, the church was floored with marble slabs of various colors and on each side of the nave were double aisles with galleries above. The ceiling was finished with sculptured panel work like a great sea, "and, being overlaid throughout with the purest gold,

---

[1] cf. Paul Mickley, *Die Konstantin-Kirchen im Heiligen Lande, Eusebius-Texte übersetzt und erläutert.* 1923. *The Life of Constantine*, in which much of the relevant material is found, was finished after the death of Constantine (337), since it records that event (IV, 64), but cannot have been written much later, since Eusebius himself died in 340.

[2] Constantine's express designation of the building as a "basilica" is the first appearance of this term in literature in reference to a Christian church (Watzinger, *Denkmäler Palästinas.* II, pp.117f.).

[3] Eusebius, *Life of Constantine.* III, 26-32.

[4] ibid., III, 33-40.

caused the entire building to glitter as it were with rays of light." The crowning part of the basilica was what Eusebius calls the Hemisphere. This was at the western end and rose to the very summit of the church, being encircled by twelve columns whose capitals were adorned with large silver bowls presented by the emperor himself.

Beyond the basilica was a second atrium or open court. This was paved with finely polished stone and enclosed with colonnades on three sides. Yet farther to the west was the rock tomb itself. As the place where once the angel had announced the resurrection, this was the chief part of the entire work and was "beautified with rare columns and profusely enriched with the most splendid decorations of every kind." So much is related by Eusebius.

A brief description of the site and church is given also in the itinerary of the famous Bordeaux Pilgrim who visited Jerusalem in A.D. 333. It reads: "On the left hand[5] is the little hill of Golgotha where the Lord was crucified. About a stone's throw from thence is a vault wherein his body was laid, and rose again on the third day. There, at present, by the command of the Emperor Constantine, has been built a basilica, that is to say, a church of wondrous beauty, having at the side reservoirs from which water is raised, and a bath behind in which infants are baptized."[6]

It is evident from these passages that Constantine's architects sought to develop a plan which would be related to two chief points, the rock of Calvary and the tomb itself. The structures which they built were axially on a line which ran from east to west between the market street and the site of the tomb. This left the rock of Calvary just to the south of the main axis. Therefore the second court was colonnaded on three sides, as Eusebius described it, but left open on the south to face directly upon the rock of Calvary. This rock was probably brought to a regular shape by quarrying away superfluous portions of its slopes, and stood in the open air, surrounded by a grille and rising twelve or fifteen feet above the ground. West of the rock of Calvary there was a dip in the ground and then a rise. In the upward slope, "about a stone's throw" from Calvary, was the

---

[5] The description is given from the point of view of one "walking towards the gate of Neapolis." Flavia Neapolis (now corrupted into Nabulus or Nablus) was the name given to the ancient city of Shechem in honor of the Flavian emperor Vespasian, when it was rebuilt after his conquest of the country (p.233). The Gate of Neapolis was therefore in the north wall of Jerusalem.

[6] *The Bordeaux Pilgrim.* tr. Stewart, pp.23f.

rock-cut tomb which had been the sepulcher of Christ. Here, too, unimportant portions of the rock round about appear to have been cut away and the sepulcher left standing up prominently from a rock floor. The sacred monument then was enclosed by a round, domed building with a circle of columns on the inside. In the middle stood the tomb itself, probably surrounded by a grille and covered with a pointed roof. This building became known as the Anastasis because it commemorated the place of the resurrection. Somewhere near at hand must have been the baptistery mentioned by the Bordeaux Pilgrim.[7]

Of these Constantinian structures only a few fragmentary portions remain today. They include a part of the wall of the first court, now embodied in the Russian and Coptic buildings at this place, and a segment of the outer wall of the Anastasis which still forms a part of the wall of the present Rotunda above the sepulcher. Perhaps also the lower courses of masonry in the present chapel of St. John just south of the Rotunda once belonged to the Constantinian baptistery.

Our knowledge of the original Church of the Holy Sepulcher rests primarily, therefore, upon the contemporary accounts of Eusebius and the Bordeaux Pilgrim and upon the fragments of Constantinian masonry which still stand. Confirmation of the general picture which we have drawn is to be found in the writings of Cyril of Jerusalem. Cyril was probably born around A.D. 315 and seems to have grown up in or near the city of which later he was bishop. About A.D. 348 he delivered a famous series of catechetical lectures in the Constantinian basilica itself. In the course of these he referred repeatedly to Golgotha or Calvary, speaking of it sometimes as near the place in which he and his listeners were assembled,[8] and sometimes as standing up above them in their sight.[9] Again he asked his hearers if they saw the spot of Golgotha, and they answered with a shout of praise.[10] A second group of lectures for those newly baptized was held in the "Holy Place of the Resurrection" or the Anastasis itself.[11]

In addition we have one or two very important representations of the Church of the Holy Sepulcher in early Christian art. The fourth century mosaic in the apse of Santa Pudenziana in Rome (Fig. 187; pp. 430f.), portrays Christ seated in front of a great rock surmounted

---

[7] E. T. Richmond in W. Harvey, *Church of the Holy Sepulchre, Jerusalem.* 1935, p.vi; Crowfoot, *Early Churches in Palestine*, pp.19f.
[8] *Catechetical Lecture.* XIII, 4 (NPNFSS VII, p.83).
[9] ibid., x, 19.　　　　　[10] ibid., XIII, 23.　　　　　[11] ibid., XVIII, 33.

by a tall jeweled cross. It is probable that this scene is based upon one of the ceremonies at Jerusalem in which the bishop sat upon a throne in front of the rock of Calvary, surrounded by the deacons. The arcade in the background may then depict the second atrium itself and the buildings at the left be the Anastasis and other structures of Constantine.[12] The other representation of the church is in the famous mosaic map at Madeba. Madeba is an ancient site across the Jordan and some fifty miles south of Gerasa. About 1880 it was occupied by Christians from Kerak, who in the course of building operations uncovered a number of churches and floor mosaics. One of the mosaics, dating from the end of the sixth century, gives a map of Palestine. On this map the sea is shown in deep green, plains in light brown and mountains in dark brown, while place locations are named in Greek letters. Portions of the mosaic are destroyed, but the Jerusalem area is well preserved (Fig. 189) and the city is shown in such detail that even individual buildings can be distinguished. Jerusalem appears as a large oval, with its chief, colonnaded street running from north to south through the heart of the city. On the entire map the directions are recognizable without any doubt, since the street just mentioned parallels the course of the Jordan River and the Dead Sea seen in the distance. The basic outline of the Christian city is still that of Hadrian's colony. At the north end of the main street (left side in our reproduction) is the gate from which the Roman road led to Neapolis and Caesarea. Remains of this gate still exist beneath the present Damascus Gate in Jerusalem. Behind it the mosaic shows an open place and a memorial column on which once stood a statue of Hadrian. The colonnaded street ran through the city to the Roman gate at the south. This was called the middle market street by Eusebius and is identical with the present Khan al-Zeit. A row of columns has been found which probably represents a late Byzantine reconstruction of the western colonnade of this street. The mosaic shows a second colonnaded street running from the plaza at the north gate diagonally to the northwest corner of the temple area and then parallel to the west wall of the temple. The city must have had a main east-west street also but only small, short streets running in this direction are shown on the map. The interior of the city is filled with churchly buildings. Most prominent is the Church of the Holy Sepulcher at a point perpendicular to the middle

[12] Crowfoot, *Early Churches in Palestine*, p.19.

of the chief market street. The mosaic clearly shows the flights of steps leading up to the first atrium, the three entrance doors, the roof of the basilica and the dome of the Anastasis.[13]

Not long after the time when the Madeba mosaic map was made, the Constantinian Church of the Holy Sepulcher was destroyed by the Persians. This took place in A.D. 614, and afterward Modestus, who was patriarch, carried out a reconstruction in far simpler style but on the same general lines as those of Constantine's work. Thereafter many vicissitudes were in store, including earthquake, fire, pillage and general neglect. In 935 a mosque was built on the site of the atrium of the church, and in 1009 the church itself was destroyed by the Fatimid Caliph al-Hakim but later rebuilt by the Byzantine emperor Constantine IX Monomachus (1042-1054). The Crusaders, who captured Jerusalem in 1099, found Constantine Monomachus's timber-domed rotunda above the Holy Sepulcher, the tomb itself being surrounded by a circular colonnade of columns and piers. To the east was the court, with the rock of Calvary on its southern side standing to the height "of a lance." Constantine's basilica was in ruins, but its crypt, known by the name of St. Helena, still existed. The Crusaders designed and built a church which covered beneath its roof both the rock of Calvary and the court which formerly adjoined it. This church was connected with the rotunda by a triumphal arch, and with the crypt of St. Helena, now made into a chapel, by a stairway. The basilica of the Crusaders still stands, although eight centuries of neglect have damaged it badly. Constantine Monomachus's dome over the Anastasis was repaired around 1719, then destroyed by fire in 1808. Thereafter the Greeks were authorized by Sultan Mahmud II to repair the church, and they constructed certain walls which obscured the interior arrangement of the rotunda, built a new edicule over the sepulcher, replaced the doors of the main entrance by new ones, and erected a new dome which lasted for about fifty years. The latter was again rebuilt in 1863-1868, but in recent times the general condition of the whole church has become so questionable as to demand a thoroughgoing investigation of its structural weaknesses and a comprehensive plan for works of restoration and preservation.[14]

[13] Watzinger, *Denkmäler Palästinas*. II, pp.81f.
[14] William Harvey, *Church of the Holy Sepulchre, Jerusalem, Structural Survey, Final Report*. 1935, pp.vii-xv.

Thus the handiwork of man over a period of more than nineteen centuries is represented by the existing Church of the Holy Sepulcher. The earliest examples are the traces of the original sepulcher that still survive, as well as another ancient rock tomb still to be seen in the western part of the rotunda, just south of the present Jacobite Chapel. The most recent are the works of repair carried out in the twentieth century. The history and traditions of the centuries are such that we may with confidence seek beneath the roof of this structure the true place of Golgotha and the sepulcher of Christ.[15]

A photograph of the main south front of the church is shown in Fig. 190. On the left of the open court are several chapels, including the chapel of St. John, and the bell tower which was built about 1170. The façade of the church is divided into two stories and there are two doors with corresponding windows above. One of the portals is now walled up, as are many of the windows of the church. This is the main entrance and leads directly ahead into the western end of the south aisle of the Crusaders' church which, as will be remembered, was located where the second atrium was in Constantinian times. The chapel of St. Helena, where once Constantine's basilica stood, is descended to by steps leading out from the eastern end of this church. The dome which appears prominently in this picture rises above the western part of the Crusaders' church, while the large dome of the rotunda of the sepulcher is hidden behind the bell tower.

THE CHURCH OF THE NATIVITY

At Bethlehem the Church of the Nativity was built under the leadership of Helena, the mother of Constantine. Not long before her death, which occurred around A.D. 327 at the age of eighty years, this venerable lady visited the Holy Land in person. Eusebius tells how she dedicated a church "at the grotto which had been the scene of the Saviour's birth," and explains, "For he who was 'God with us' had submitted to be born even in a cave of the earth, and the place of his nativity was called Bethlehem by the Hebrews." The sacred cave was beautified with all possible splendor, and the emperor joined his mother in costly offerings.[16]

[15] Joachim Jeremias in ΑΓΓΕΛΟΣ, *Archiv für neutestamentliche Zeitgeschichte und Kulturkunde.* 1926, p.33; H. T. F. Duckworth, *The Church of the Holy Sepulchre.* 1922, p.11.

[16] Eusebius, *Life of Constantine.* III, 41-43; cf. Socrates, *Ch. Hist.* I, 17; Sozomen, *Ch. Hist.* II, 2.

While the gospel narrative of the birth of Jesus relates only that Mary "laid him in a manger, because there was no room for them in the inn" (Luke 2:7), it is not surprising that this place should have been a cave, since until today caves frequently are employed in Palestine to house both animals and men. The cave is mentioned between A.D. 155 and 160 by Justin Martyr, who says: "when the child was born in Bethlehem, since Joseph could not find a lodging in that village, he took up his quarters in a certain cave near the village."[17] Again in A.D. 246-248, Origen writes: "Corresponding to the narrative in the Gospel regarding his birth, there is shown at Bethlehem the cave where he was born, and the manger in the cave where he was wrapped in swaddling clothes. And this sight is greatly talked of in surrounding places, even among the enemies of the faith, it being said that in this cave was born that Jesus who is worshipped and reverenced by the Christians."[18]

As a matter of fact, this cave was evidently identified as the birthplace of Christ long before the time of Hadrian, for that emperor defiled it with pagan worship just as he did the site of the Holy Sepulcher in Jerusalem. This is related by Jerome, who himself lived at Bethlehem from 386 until his death in 420:[19]

"From the time of Hadrian to the reign of Constantine—a period of about one hundred and eighty years—the spot which had witnessed the resurrection was occupied by a figure of Jupiter; while on the rock where the cross had stood, a marble statue of Venus was set up by the heathen and became an object of worship. The original persecutors, indeed, supposed that by polluting our holy places they would deprive us of our faith in the passion and in the resurrection. Even my own Bethlehem, as it now is, that most venerable spot in the whole world of which the psalmist sings: 'the truth hath sprung out of the earth,'[20] was overshadowed by a grove of Tammuz, that is of Adonis; and in the very cave where the infant Christ had uttered his earliest cry lamentation was made for the paramour of Venus."[21]

The church which was erected over this sacred site by Helena and Constantine is mentioned in A.D. 333 by the Bordeaux Pilgrim. Speak-

[17] *Dialogue with Trypho.* 78 (ANF I, p.237).
[18] *Against Celsus.* I, 51 (ANF IV, p.418).
[19] *Letter 58 to Paulinus.* 3 (NPNFSS VI, p.120).   [20] Psalm 85:11.
[21] Tammuz, or Adonis as the Greeks called him, was a god who died and rose annually with the death and rebirth of vegetation. He was the lover of Venus (Aphrodite), and her lamentations over his tragic death and descent to the underworld were echoed in the liturgical wailings of his worshipers (cf. Ezekiel 8:14). HERE XII, pp.187,191.

ing of Bethlehem, he says, "There a basilica has been built by order of Constantine."[22] Under the Emperor Justinian (527-565), the original Constantinian basilica was demolished and a larger church constructed. This fact is stated in a document written at the beginning of the tenth century by Eutychius, the patriarch of Alexandria. Eutychius says that the Emperor Justinian ordered his legate to pull down the church at Bethlehem, which was a small building, and to erect another of such size and beauty that not even the temple at Jerusalem might vie with it in beauty. The legate arrived, had the church at Bethlehem destroyed, and built the church as it stands now. When he had finished his work he returned to the emperor, who proceeded to question him as to the way in which he had carried out his commands. But when he described the building the emperor became very angry. "I gave you money," he said, "and you have pocketed it all, but the building you have erected is badly put together, the church is quite dark, and the result is not at all what I intended or according to the plan I told you to follow." And straightway he ordered him to be punished.[23]

Justinian's church, much dilapidated, still stands in Bethlehem. It was spared by the Persians in 614, because they saw on the exterior a mosaic of the adoration of the Magi in which the latter were clothed in Persian dress. The Moslems held the church in veneration and it escaped the general destruction of Palestinian churches ordered in 1009 by the Fatimid Caliph al-Hakim. Baldwin I was crowned king here at Christmas in 1101, and during the period of the Latin kingdom (twelfth century) the church was invested with splendid mosaic decoration. Since that time, however, earthquake, fire and neglect have reduced it to a sad state of deterioration.[24]

The Church of the Nativity is on the promontory upon which the southeastern part of the village of Bethlehem is now built. The western front and principal entrance of the church are shown in Fig. 191. The large open area paved with stone is where the atrium of the Constantinian basilica must have been. A modern graveyard now encroaches from the north and the buildings of the Armenian Convent project prominently at the right. The narthex was formerly

[22] The Bordeaux Pilgrim. tr. Stewart, p.27.
[23] Annales (Jacques Paul Migne, Patrologiae cursus completus . . . Series Graeca. 111 [1863], col.1070, 159f.).
[24] E. T. Richmond in William Harvey, Structural Survey of the Church of the Nativity, Bethlehem. 1935, pp.v-xv.

entered through three doors, but these have now been blocked save for a small low rectangular opening in the central door, which remains as the chief public entrance. Within (Fig. 192)[25] the nave is still flanked by Justinian's columns, which form double aisles on either side. Beneath the central area where the transept crosses the main axis of the church, and descended to by steps on either side of the chancel, is the grotto of the Nativity.

The church as described hitherto is essentially that of Justinian. Is anything known of the Constantinian basilica? In 1934 Mr. William Harvey discovered the remains of the church of Helena and Constantine beneath the floor of the present church. Only limited excavations were possible, but the essential nature of the original church was determined.[26] The general plan was similar to that of the Church of the Holy Sepulcher. As at Jerusalem the structures were set out axially, but in this case ran from west to east. First there was the atrium. Then three doors gave access to the basilica at its western end. The north and south walls of the basilica stood on the same lines as the existing side walls of the present church, and the interior was divided practically as now into nave and four aisles. At its eastern end the basilica connected directly with an octagonal building which stood above the subterranean cave of the Nativity. Steps arranged on an octagonal plan surrounded the circular mouth of a shaft about twelve feet across, through which it was possible to look down into the grotto itself. The roof of the cave was broken through to make this view possible from the Octagon above.

The floors of the aisles, the nave and the passage around the shrine in the Octagon, were paved with patterned mosaics. Considerable fragments of these remain, and being probably of Constantinian time are the earliest floor mosaics which have been found in a Palestinian church. Since they were to be trodden underfoot no religious scenes were represented, but geometrical designs, swastikas, acanthus leaves, flowers, fruits and birds constituted the decorations. A small panel on the north side of the Octagon where no one ordi-

[25] The cross wall shown at the head of the nave in this photograph has now been removed.

[26] W. Harvey, *Structural Survey of the Church of the Nativity, Bethlehem,* pp.20-30; and in *Palestine Exploration Fund Quarterly Statement.* 1936, pp.28-32; E. T. Richmond in *The Quarterly of the Department of Antiquities in Palestine.* 6 (1938), pp.63-66; Crowfoot, *Early Churches in Palestine,* pp.22-30,119-121.

narily would walk, had the Greek word "Fish" (IXΘΥC) in the center (Fig. 193).

An almost contemporary picture of this church is probably to be seen in the apse mosaic of Santa Pudenziana, Rome (Fig. 187). Whereas Jerusalem appears at our left in the mosaic, Bethlehem is seen at our right. In the extreme corner is a high entranceway, to the left of which a long low building represents the atrium of the Church of the Nativity. Adjoining this is a somewhat taller building which is the basilica and immediately to the left of it is the yet loftier Octagon.

THE CHURCH ON THE MOUNT OF OLIVES

Yet another Palestinian church was founded by Helena and likewise enriched by Constantine. The statement of Eusebius concerning it is: "And further, the mother of the emperor raised a stately structure on the Mount of Olives also, in memory of his ascent to heaven who is the Saviour of mankind, erecting a sacred church and temple on the very summit of the mount. And indeed authentic history informs us that in this very cave the Saviour imparted his secret revelations to his disciples. And here also the emperor testified his reverence for the King of kings, by diverse and costly offerings."[27] The Bordeaux Pilgrim writes: "From thence you ascend to the Mount of Olives, where before the Passion, the Lord taught his disciples. There by the orders of Constantine a basilica of wondrous beauty has been built."[28]

Evidently the basilica was built near the place on the Mount of Olives where fourth century tradition believed the ascension had taken place (cf. Acts 1:9, 12) and directly over a cave in which it was said Jesus had taught his disciples. The Bordeaux Pilgrim says that these teachings were delivered before the Passion, and perhaps the discourse on the last things was in mind which was described in the gospels as given on the Mount of Olives (Mark 13:3 = Matthew 24:3). Eusebius, however, speaks of the teachings as "secret revelations" which makes one think of the apocryphal teachings which Christ was supposed to have given on the Mount of Olives in the period between the resurrection and the ascension.[29]

However confused some of these traditions may have been, it is

[27] *Life of Constantine.* III, 43.   [28] Tr. Stewart, pp.24f.
[29] See e.g. *The Gospel of Bartholomew.* 4:1 (James, *The Apocryphal New Testament,* p.173).

certain that a Constantinian basilica did stand over a cave on the Mount of Olives directly across from the Holy City and just south of the summit of the ridge of the Mount. Since the name of the Mount of Olives was Eleona ('Ελαιών, Luke 21:37), the basilica was known as "the church of Eleona," or simply Eleona for short. Although hardly more than a few stones of its walls and small patches of its mosaic floor have survived, the Dominicans have been able to trace the ground plan from the foundation trenches cut in the solid rock, and to establish a very probable reconstruction of its original character.[30]

According to these investigations, it appears that one approached the basilica through a fine portico with six columns, which gave access to a colonnaded atrium under which was a large cistern. At the farther end of the atrium several steps led up to the level of the basilica itself. The length of the basilica proper was about 100 feet, this being a little longer than the one at Bethlehem and probably a little shorter than the one in front of the Anastasis. It was divided by two rows of columns into a nave and two side aisles, and the nave terminated in a semicircular apse, on the north side of which was an additional small chamber. The famous cave itself, which was transformed into a crypt, lay beneath the eastern end of the nave and the apse.

The church was destroyed by the Persians in 614, somewhat restored by Modestus, and finally quite ruined. During the Middle Ages two chapels were built on the site, one called the Pater to mark the place where Jesus was supposed to have taught the Pater Noster or Lord's Prayer, and the other named the Credo to commemorate the place where the Apostles were said to have written the Creed. These were destroyed also, and the present Church of the Creed and Church of the Lord's Prayer date only from 1868 when the site was purchased by the Princesse de la Tour d'Auvergne. The east end of the Constantinian basilica and the cave crypt lie directly under the second of these present-day structures.

[30] Hugues Vincent and F. M. Abel, Jérusalem, recherches de topographie, d'archéologie et d'histoire. II (1914), pp.337-360,383f. A different reconstruction and a later date have been proposed by E. Weigand (in Zeitschrift des Deutschen Palästina-Vereins. 46 [1923], pp.212-220) and Watzinger (Denkmäler Palästinas. II, p.127), but probably are not to be accepted (see Vincent in Revue Biblique. 21 [1924], pp.310f.; 45 [1936], p.419; Crowfoot, Early Churches in Palestine, pp.30-34).

THE CHURCH AT MAMRE

Not only Constantine's mother, Helena, but also his mother-in-law, Eutropia, joined him in interest in the erection of churches in the Holy Land. Eutropia visited the famous oaks of Mamre (Genesis 18:1) and found the place defiled by heathen idols and sacrifices. When she informed Constantine of the situation the emperor straightway wrote a letter, preserved in full by Eusebius, to Macarius of Jerusalem and the other bishops in Palestine, informing them of his desire that the pagan altar should be demolished and replaced by a church.[31] At this place, which is nearly two miles north of Hebron on the east side of the road to Jerusalem,[32] there is a large enclosure now known as the Haram Ramet el-Khalil. Part of the walls seem to date from the time of Herod and part from the time of Hadrian. At the east side are the ruins of a church which has been partially excavated by Father Mader. It was a small basilica with a long narthex and the apse "inscribed," or built within the rectangle of the church. While the church was restored, perhaps by Modestus, the present ruins doubtless represent the site and plan of the Constantinian basilica.[33]

THE CHURCH OF THE LOAVES AND FISHES
AT ET-TABGHA

Many other churches were built in Palestine during the following centuries, but to them only the briefest allusion here is possible. Most of them were basilical in plan, long buildings with a nave and two aisles. The finest floor mosaics are in the Church of the Loaves and Fishes at et-Tabgha (p. 226), the place where fourth century tradition located the feeding of the five thousand (Mark 6:30-44). This church was built above an earlier small chapel on the same site and must be at least as late as the end of the fourth or beginning of the fifth century. The best preserved mosaic is that in the left or north transept (Fig. 194), with its wonderful pictures of birds and plants. Amidst lotus, papyrus and other plants, ducks are nestling, cormorants flapping their wings, and a flamingo is fighting with a snake.[34]

[31] *Life of Constantine.* III, 51-53.
[32] Sozomen, *Ch. Hist.* II, 4.
[33] A. E. Mader in *Rivista di archeologia cristiana.* 6 (1929), pp.249-312; and in *Revue Biblique.* 39 (1930), pp.84-117.
[34] A. M. Schneider, *Die Brotvermehrungskirche von et-tâbga am Genesarethsee und ihre Mosaiken.* 1934.

The Palestinian city of Roman times whose ruins are best preserved today is Gerasa (p. 231) in Transjordan. This city was rebuilt in the second century A.D., shattered by earthquakes in the eighth, and left deserted for most of the next thousand years. A number of early Christian churches have been investigated there. The first is known as the cathedral and is a three-aisled basilica with an inscribed apse. It faced upon a paved court in the middle of which was a fountain reported to run with wine annually on the anniversary of the miracle at Cana in Galilee. The church and the miracle are referred to in A.D. 375 by Epiphanius, bishop of Constantia (Salamis) in Cyprus, and the excavators date the church around A.D. 365.[35] In 494 a second basilica, dedicated to the martyr Theodore, was founded on the other side of the fountain court, and with the addition of a baptistery block, baths and other structures the Christian precinct became a very impressive complex. Yet other churches at Gerasa include: the one dedicated to the Prophets, Apostles and Martyrs, which was built (464-465) in the form of a Latin cross and contains interesting floor mosaics (Fig. 195); the basilica built by a certain Procopius (526-527); the round church of St. John the Baptist with the basilicas of St. George and SS. Cosmas and Damianus on either side of it (529-533); the Synagogue which was rebuilt as a church (530-531); the basilica of SS. Peter and Paul (c.540); the Propylaea church (565); and the basilica containing the name of Bishop Genesius (611).

[35] Kraeling ed., *Gerasa, City of the Decapolis*, pp.212-219.

6. CHURCHES IN SYRIA

THE work of Constantine in the erection of churches was also extended to Syria, according to Eusebius. At Heliopolis (Baalbek), a city whose hitherto exclusively pagan character is emphasized by Eusebius and attested by its world famous ruins of temples and altars, the emperor built "a church of great size and magnificence," and at the same time made arrangements concerning its clergy and provision for the necessities of the poor.[1] At Antioch likewise he erected another church which was "of unparalleled size and beauty." "The entire building," Eusebius continues, "was encompassed by an enclosure of great extent, within which the church itself rose to a vast elevation, being of an octagonal form, and surrounded on all sides by many chambers, courts, and upper and lower apartments; the whole richly adorned with a profusion of gold, brass, and other materials of the most costly kind."[2]

THE CHURCH OF ST. BABYLAS AT KAOUSSIE

While we are dependent upon Eusebius for our knowledge of the Constantinian church at Antioch, excavations in the vicinity of that important site have disclosed two other important early Christian churches. The first of these was found to the north of the city, on the way to the village of Kaoussie, on the right bank of the Orontes River.[3] As may be seen in the air view in Fig. 196, the plan of the church is essentially that of a cross with four equal arms oriented to the four points of the compass. While the walls have been destroyed their foundations remain, together with extensive portions of the mosaics with which the floors were adorned, and thus a good idea of the original structure can be obtained.

The four radiating arms or naves of the church are almost equal in their dimensions, each being about 36 feet wide and 82 feet long. Of the mosaics with which their floors were covered, those in the north, west and south naves display a similar pattern of continuous geometric designs. Each of these three floor mosaics is accompanied by an inscription containing substantially the same statement. The one in the north nave reads, "In the time of our most holy bishop

---

[1] *Life of Constantine*. III, 58. For Baalbek see Theodor Wiegand, *Baalbek, Ergebnisse der Ausgrabungen und Untersuchungen in den Jahren 1898 bis 1905.* 4 vols. 1921-25.

[2] *Life of Constantine*. III, 50.

[3] Jean Lassus in *Antioch on-the-Orontes. II: The Excavations 1933-1936*, pp.5-44.

Flavian,[4] and in the time of the most pious Eusebius the steward and presbyter, Dorys the presbyter in fulfillment of a vow completed the mosaic of this hall too. In the month of March of the year 435 [A.D. 387]." The mosaics in the east nave are of a different character, being divided into large areas each with its own style of decoration including triangles, circles and other figures. Any inscription which was here unfortunately is lost.

From all four of the naves attention clearly was directed toward the center of the church. Here the four halls opened into a central room which was about 55 feet square. Above, the roofs of the naves abutted upon the presumably yet higher roof of this room. In the center of the room was a raised platform, and beneath the floor were two tombs. One was a tomb of bricks, the other was like a monolithic sarcophagus with a horizontal division in the middle so that it could accommodate two bodies.

The *simple et grandiose* plan of this church, as its excavators call it, was not seriously altered by later additions. Among the smaller structures which were annexed to the main halls the most important was a baptistery. This was entered from the north nave through a hall designated by a mosaic inscription as a Pistikon (ΠΕΙCΤΙΚΟΥ), perhaps the place where the catechumen recited the confession of faith before being baptized. The inscription is dated under Theodotus who was bishop of Antioch in A.D. 420-429. In the baptistery the baptismal basin was large enough to receive the candidate into the water but not large enough to provide for his immersion, so the ceremony must have been carried out by affusion.

As the inscription of Dorys shows, the mosaics which he placed in the main church were completed in A.D. 387. An interesting bit of history enables us with considerable probability to date the original construction of the church a few years earlier and to identify its name.[5] Babylas, bishop of Antioch, suffered martyrdom in A.D. 250 under Decius. His remains presumably were interred first at Antioch, afterward were transferred to Daphne, and finally were brought back to Antioch. In a discourse concerning Babylas, Chrysostom[6] refers to the return of the body to Antioch, and says, "You indeed gave him

---

[4] Flavian was bishop of Antioch in A.D. 381-404 (NSH IV, p.327).

[5] Glanville Downey in *Antioch on-the-Orontes. II: The Excavations 1933-1936*, pp.45-48.

[6] *De Sancto Hieromartyre Babyla.* 3 (Migne, *Patrologiae cursus completus . . . Series Graeca.* 50 [1859], col.533).

back to the band of fellow enthusiasts; but the grace of God did not suffer him to remain there forever, but again removed him beyond the river, so that much of the countryside was filled with the sweet odor of the martyr." In connection with this burial of the saint beyond the river, Chrysostom continues, "And he was not destined when he went there to remain alone, but he soon received a neighbor and fellow lodger (γείτονα καὶ ὁμόσκηνον), one of similar life; and he had shared the same office with him."

This second person, Chrysostom says, had been responsible for the construction of the church in which the martyr and he himself were buried. While the church was being built, he had visited it every day and even participated in the actual labor of its erection. This must have been Meletius, the bishop of Antioch, who died in Constantinople in A.D. 381 during the meeting of the ecumenical council over which he presided, and whose remains, according to Sozomen, "were . . . conveyed to Antioch, and deposited near the tomb of Babylas the martyr."[7] Meletius therefore seems to have been buried at Antioch about A.D. 381 in a church in the construction of which he had been instrumental and in a tomb which was in immediate proximity to the interred martyr Babylas. Since Meletius had a stormy career and was most secure in his position as bishop of Antioch in about A.D. 379 and following, it is probable that he began the construction of the church only within the year or so preceding his death.

The identification of the church at Kaoussie with the one which figures in the foregoing account is most probable. Since its main floor mosaics were completed in A.D. 387, the church itself could very well have been built about A.D. 380 by Meletius. In the center of the church, moreover, was a sarcophagus which had once received two bodies. Very possibly this was the place where Babylas received as a "neighbor and fellow lodger" the man who had held the same office that he had, namely Meletius the bishop of Antioch. If these coordinations between the history as known from literary sources and the material findings revealed in the excavations are correct, the church at Kaoussie was constructed and received the remains of the famous martyr Babylas about A.D. 380; Meletius, the builder, was buried there in 381; and the adornment with many of its fine mosaics followed in 387. Its proper name is the Church of St. Babylas.

[7] Sozomen, *Ch. Hist.* VII, 10; cf. NSH VII, p.288.

THE MARTYRION AT SELEUCIA PIERIA

The second church newly discovered in the same vicinity is at Seleucia Pieria, the seaport of Antioch. It seems to have been a memorial church, and commonly is referred to as the Martyrion.[8] According to the style of its mosaics and architecture it is dated tentatively in the last quarter of the fifth century A.D. It is believed to have been destroyed by earthquakes in A.D. 526 and 528 and to have been rebuilt soon after that time.

In its original plan the structure comprised a central quatrefoil, with an ambulatory around it, and a chancel projecting on the east side. The outlines of the quatrefoil and ambulatory appear clearly in Fig. 197, which is a view of the ruins looking north.

The floor of the ambulatory was adorned with a rich mosaic pavement which undoubtedly belonged to the first construction of the building. A portion of the mosaic in the north ambulatory is shown in its original place in Fig. 198. The border is of the type known as rinceau, and shows a continuous stalk of grapevine running in regular undulations, together with bunches of grapes, birds and fowls. The main field represents a veritable paradise of natural wild life, and shows animals, birds, trees, flowers and bits of landscape. Among the animals identified by the excavators are a lonely giraffe, a zebra startled by a large crane, inquisitive horses, fleet gazelles, a childishly irritable elephant, ferocious lions, sheep, goats, a hyena and other beasts. The birds in the field and border include an eagle flapping its wings, a gallinule scratching its head, peacocks, flamingoes, cranes, ducks and geese. Pomegranate, pear, fir and pine trees, date palms, plants and flowers add to the beauty of the scene.

The Martyrion was also adorned with an important series of sculptured marble revetments. The fragments recovered fall into two groups, one of which is composed of incised drawings believed to date in the fifth century, the other made up of low plastic reliefs thought to belong to the end of the fifth century or first half of the sixth. The bas-reliefs represent Old Testament subjects exclusively, including Daniel, Moses before the Burning Bush, Samson Fighting with a Lion, and others. The incised reliefs show not only Old Testament scenes such as Joseph in Prison, and Saul Fighting the Amalekites, but also New Testament pictures including the Adoration

---

[8] W. A. Campbell in *Antioch on-the-Orontes. III: The Excavations 1937-1939*, pp.35-54.

of the Magi, the Rich Man and Lazarus, the Feeding of the Multitude, and various scenes of healing, and furthermore include figures like Constantine and St. Simeon Stylites. Thus these reliefs include a very comprehensive selection of themes and afford a glimpse of the richness of Christian iconography at this time.[9]

THE CHURCH OF ST. SIMEON STYLITES

In the interior of Syria there were many early Christian churches which were lost to knowledge until, in the second half of the nineteenth century, a number of them were rediscovered and described by the Marquis de Vogüé.[10] More intensive studies have been made since by American and German scholars.[11] The churches date in the time from the fourth to the seventh centuries. On the whole it may be said that it was characteristic of the architecture revealed here to retain the basic form of the basilica but to place a new emphasis upon the development and decoration of the exterior. Single and double towers were employed to achieve an impressive façade, which was often adorned further with an open loggia above a broadly arched entrance.

Of all the Syrian churches the greatest was that of Qalat Siman, the Church of St. Simeon Stylites,[12] which was on a hilly plateau some forty miles northeast of Antioch. Simeon, in whose honor it was built, was born in northern Syria around A.D. 390, and became the first and most famous saint to practice living on top of a pillar. At the age of thirty and after having experimented with numerous other austerities, he built a pillar six feet high and made his home on its

[9] Kurt Weitzmann in *Antioch on-the-Orontes. III: The Excavations 1937-1939*, pp.135-149.

[10] C. J. Melchior de Vogüé, *Syrie Centrale*. 2 vols. 1865-77.

[11] *The Publications of an American Archaeological Expedition to Syria in 1899-1900. II: Architecture and Other Arts*, by Howard Crosby Butler. 1903; *Publications of the Princeton Archaeological Expeditions to Syria in 1904-5 and 1909. II: Architecture. A. Southern Syria*. 1919, *B. Northern Syria*. 1920, by H. C. Butler; H. C. Butler, *Early Churches in Syria, Fourth to Seventh Centuries*. ed. E. Baldwin Smith, 1929; Hermann W. Beyer, *Der syrische Kirchenbau*. 1925.

[12] De Vogüé, *Syrie Centrale*, pp.141-152 and Planches 139-148; Butler in *The Publications of an American Archaeological Expedition to Syria in 1899-1900*. II, pp.184-190; in *Publications of the Princeton Archaeological Expeditions to Syria in 1904-5 and 1909. II: B.*, pp.261-284; and in *Early Churches in Syria, Fourth to Seventh Centuries*, pp.97-110; Beyer, *Der syrische Kirchenbau*, pp.60-71; Daniel Krencker, *Die Wallfahrtskirche des Simeon Stylites in Kal'at Sim'ân I Bericht über Untersuchungen und Grabungen im Frühjahr 1938 ausgeführt im Auftrag des Deutschen Archäologischen Instituts (Abhandlungen der Preussischen Akademie der Wissenschaften*. 1938. Phil.-hist. Kl. 4 [1939]).

summit. He increased the height of the pillar gradually until after
ten years it was sixty feet high. Here, protected from falling as we
may suppose by a railing and possibly reached by a ladder up which
his disciples brought his food, he lived without ever coming down
until his death in 459.

The church built in memory of the saint is believed to have been
erected shortly after his death, probably between A.D. 460 and 490.
The extensive and impressive ruins of this structure which still stand
(Fig. 199) provide a good indication of its character. The ground
plan was similar to that of the Church of St. Babylas at Kaoussie, in
that four rectangular halls were arranged to radiate from a central
area, thus forming a cross. In St. Simeon's church the focal point of
interest was the column on which the saint had dwelt. This pillar,
a piece of which remains today, was left standing in its original
position and the memorial edifice was built around it. Each of the
four halls which extended out from this center was divided by columns into a nave and two side aisles, and the eastern hall ended in a
magnificent triple apse. The central area where the four arms of the
cross met was arranged as an octagon and, according to the latest
research, was roofed with a soaring wooden cupola or dome.[13]

Hitherto it has been widely believed that the central octagon was
left as an unroofed court open to the sky. The chief support for this
opinion is a passage in which the church historian Evagrius (b. A.D.
c.536) describes the edifice as he saw it upon a visit to the site
around A.D. 560. He writes: "The temple is constructed in the form
of a cross, adorned with colonnades on the four sides. Opposite the
colonnades are arranged handsome columns of polished stone, sus-
taining a roof of considerable elevation; while the center is occupied
by an unroofed court of the most excellent workmanship, where
stands the pillar, of forty cubits, on which the incarnate angel upon
earth spent his heavenly life."[14] Since Evagrius explicitly describes
the central area as an unroofed or open air court (αὐλὴ ὑπαιθρίος), this
must be accepted as the state of the church at the time of his visit.
The probability is, however, not that it had been built that way
originally, but that by the time Evagrius came the dome had been
destroyed by fire or earthquake. When it proved too difficult to

[13] Krencker, *Die Wallfahrtskirche des Simeon Stylites in Kal'at Sim'ân.* I, pp.20f.
[14] *Church History.* I, 14 (*Bohn's Ecclesiastical Library.* 1854, pp.275f.).

rebuild, the central room was left from that time on as an open court.

In the year 979 some further building work was done at Qalat Siman, as is indicated by an inscription which was found written in Greek and in Syrian. The Syrian form of the inscription gives the date in the Seleucid era as 1290, which refers to the year extending from October 7, 978, to October 6, 979. The Greek inscription actually uses the Christian era ($\kappa\alpha\tau\grave{\alpha}$ $\overline{\mathrm{X}[\nu]}$), a system of reckoning which in this time occurs but seldom.[15]

Around Qalat Siman were grouped monasteries, and at the foot of the western hill was a town whose ruins show what elaborate accommodations were necessary to care for the large numbers of pilgrims who for centuries came to the place made memorable by the saint whom Evagrius called an "aerial martyr."[16]

[15] A slightly earlier example from the year 834 ($\dot{\alpha}\pi\grave{o}$ $\delta\grave{\epsilon}$ $\mathrm{X}\rho\iota\sigma\tau o[\hat{v}]$ $\check{\epsilon}\tau o\upsilon s$ $\omega[\lambda]\delta$) is found in *Corpus Inscriptionum Graecarum*. iv, No.8680.

[16] *Church History*. i, 13.

7. CHURCHES IN EGYPT

THE CHURCH OF ST. MENAS

FOR a single example of early Christian churches in Egypt we turn to the remarkable ruined city of St. Menas, Karm Abu Mina, the "vineyard of Menas." According to the legendary lives of this saint, he was an Egyptian born of Christian parents in answer to a prayer of the mother addressed to an ikon of the Virgin. Since a voice seemed to answer this prayer with "Amen," the child was named Amen, or Menas. Growing up, he became a soldier and was on duty at Cotyaea in Phrygia when Diocletian's persecution broke out. Here, around A.D. 295, Menas bravely confessed his faith in Christ and suffered martyrdom. When his fellow soldiers were sent back from Phrygia to the Mareotis district in Egypt they took his corpse with them. They were threatened en route by terrible sea monsters, but fire went forth from the corpse and drove the creatures back. Arriving safely in Egypt, they buried the body of Menas beside the Lake of Mareotis where he had been born. When the troops were moved again they placed the bones of the saint on a camel to carry with them, but the camel refused to move. When another camel did likewise, it was interpreted as a sign and the bones were interred permanently at the place where the camels had stood. The grave would have been forgotten, save that one day a sick sheep drank from the near-by spring and was miraculously healed. Other wonderful healings, not only of animals but also of men, began to take place, and so many pilgrims were attracted there that a church was built above the martyr's tomb and an entire pilgrim city sprang up. Almost everyone who came carried away in a little flask some of the water from the spring or some oil from the lamp which hung in the church and burned day and night. Wherever the water or oil was carried miraculous healings took place.

As remarkable as are the legends attaching to the name of St. Menas, almost more remarkable still are the actual churches and city which were built at his grave, lost for nearly 1000 years and rediscovered at the beginning of the twentieth century. The Lake of Mareotis dried up in the Middle Ages and, although during the siege of Alexandria in 1801 the British cut through the dunes at Abusir and let in the sea, the ruins of the city of St. Menas lie now in a barren wilderness. The site, which is thirty miles or more southwest of

Alexandria, was rediscovered and excavated by Carl Maria Kaufmann in 1905-1907.[1]

The Burial Church of St. Menas seems to have been consecrated under the Emperor Theodosius I the Great (379-395) although the first building work above the martyr's grave may have been done by Athanasius (c.298-373) with the help and interest of Constantine himself. The Burial Church was a basilica, 125 feet long and 74 feet wide, with nave and aisles each terminating in an apse. It was so arranged that the altar came directly above the martyr's crypt which lay some 26 feet below. Not only did this *confessio* enable the holy tomb to be viewed from the room above but also there was provided a great marble stairway at one side which led directly down into the crypt. On the wall opposite the point at which the stairway enters the crypt the place can still be seen where a large marble plate was once affixed, doubtless bearing the famous representation of Menas with two camels bowing down to him. A photograph of the crypt is shown in Fig. 200. The picture is taken from a little chapel on the west of the crypt and looks toward the cryptoporticus which was built later to connect with the basilica of Arcadius. The recess which once held the Menas relief is on the south wall at the immediate right and is approximately three-quarters life size. While this relief no longer exists, it doubtless was the prototype of the picture of Menas between the camels which is stamped on so many of the flasks which were carried away from here by pilgrims. One of these flasks is shown in Fig. 201.

The basilica just described was oriented from west to east. Under the Emperor Arcadius (395-408), in order to accommodate the increasing masses of people a much larger basilica was built on at the eastern end of the first church. A large transept, 164 feet long and 66 feet wide gave the latter structure the form of a cross. At the same time a monumental baptistery church was erected at the western end of the first church. This was a square structure, which was turned into an octagon by the niches in the corners. In the center of its marble pavement was the deep marble tank, entered by steps from each side, in which the immersions were conducted (Fig. 202).

[1] C. M. Kaufmann, *Die Ausgrabung der Menasheiligtümer in der Mareotiswüste.* 1906; *Zweiter Bericht über die Ausgrabung der Menasheiligtümer in der Mareotiswüste.* 1907; *Die Menasstadt.* 1910; *Die heilige Stadt der Wüste.* 4th ed. 1924; Leclercq in *Dictionnaire d'archéologie chrétienne et de liturgie.* xi, cols. 324-397.

Notably under the eastern Emperor Zeno (474-491) this place developed into a great pilgrim city, and yet other basilicas, baths and guesthouses were erected. Also there was a flourishing pottery industry which produced lamps, statuettes, plates, vases and flasks for the pilgrims. Eventually came decline. In the seventh and eighth centuries, the Melchites and Jacobites[2] contended for possession of the sanctuary and in the ninth century a Melchite architect was permitted to carry away the church's marble pillars. Later in the ninth century the place was despoiled by the Moslems and thereafter it became the prey of marauding Bedouins. The Church of St. Menas was seen around A.D. 1000 by an anonymous Arab traveler, but from then until its rediscovery by Kaufmann in 1905 it remained lost beneath the sands of the Mareotic Desert.

[2] The Melchites were Egyptian Christians who accepted the decrees of the Council of Chalcedon (A.D. 451) which were directed against the Jacobites and others. The Jacobites took their name from Jacob Baradai, bishop of Edessa (d. 578), the reorganizer of Syrian Monophysitism.

8. CHURCHES IN CONSTANTINOPLE

AFTER the defeat and death of Licinius (324), Constantine lived almost continuously in the East and in A.D. 330 officially founded his new capital, Constantinople, which formerly had been the city of Byzantium.[1] New Rome, as Constantinople was also called, was intended to be a wholly Christian city and therefore was adorned not only with a hippodrome, baths, fountains and porticoes, but also with numerous houses of prayer and memorials of martyrs. A little distance away on the Bosporus was a sanctuary of the Archangel Michael.[2]

THE CHURCH OF ALL THE APOSTLES

At least two churches were founded by Constantine within the city.[3] One of these was dedicated to All the Apostles and intended by Constantine to be his own last resting place.[4] According to Eusebius, the building was carried to a vast height and had a great dome. From foundation to roof it was encased with slabs of various colored marbles while the roof was of brass adorned with gold.[5] This church was reconstructed by Justinian the Great (527-565),[6] but upon the fall of Constantinople to the Turks in 1453 was torn down and replaced by the Mosque of Sultan Mohammed II the Conqueror.[7] The Church of All the Apostles was resembled closely by Justinian's Church of St. John at Ephesus[8] and also is believed to have served as a model for St. Mark's at Venice.

[1] In Nicomedia of Bithynia, which had served as capital and under Diocletian had been the chief city of the East, Constantine erected a magnificent and stately church as "a memorial of his victory over his own enemies and the adversaries of God" (Eusebius, *Life of Constantine.* III, 50).

[2] Sozomen, *Ch. Hist.* II, 3; Eusebius, *Life of Constantine.* III, 48.

[3] That Constantine later gave encouragement at least toward the building of yet other churches is indicated by his letter to Eusebius (*Life of Constantine.* IV, 36), in which the emperor mentions the need for an increased number of churches in Constantinople to accommodate the growing mass of Christians, and places an order for fifty fine copies of the Bible to be placed in these churches (cf. p.316).

[4] Eusebius, *Life of Constantine.* IV, 70; Socrates, *Ch. Hist.* I, 40.

[5] *Life of Constantine.* IV, 58-60.

[6] Procopius, *Buildings.* I, iv, 9-16. Procopius stated (ibid., I, iv, 19) that the church was built by the Emperor Constantius but the explanation of this difference from Eusebius is doubtless that it was begun by Constantine and completed after his death by his son.

[7] A. Van Millingen, *Byzantine Churches in Constantinople.* 1912, pp.3,175; Ernest Mamboury, *Constantinople.* 1925, p.355.

[8] Procopius, *Buildings.* v, i, 6.

THE CHURCH OF ST. EIRENE

The second church had already been in existence as a Christian sanctuary in the old town of Byzantium, but was considerably enlarged and adorned by Constantine. He dedicated it to holy peace —Eirene—in honor of the peace which he had brought to the world after eighteen years of civil war.[9] In this Constantine followed the example of Augustus who likewise had symbolized the calm and quiet he brought to a torn world by the dedication of an altar at Rome, the Ara Pacis, to the imperial peace. Constantine's church stood for two centuries and then was burned to the ground in the fire of A.D. 532. It was restored by Justinian the Great,[10] but again damaged by fire in 564 and seriously injured by the violent earthquake of 740. The church still stands but has been used by the Turks as an armory and a museum. The present walls of the main body of the building probably date from the new structure erected by Justinian after 532, and the narthex and some other portions represent the same emperor's repairs after 564. The apse and upper part of the church including the dome probably belong to the reconstruction after the earthquake and may have been carried out by the Emperor Leo III the Isaurian (717-740) or by his son and successor Constantine V Copronymus (740-775).[11]

The essential plan of St. Eirene as it now exists is that of the basilica, with atrium, narthex, nave, side aisles and apse. But a great dome is placed above the nave, even as Eusebius mentioned a dome as a prominent feature of the lost Church of All the Apostles. The combination of a domed superstructure with the earlier ground plan of the basilica became the characteristic theme of Byzantine church buildings. The culminating example of the domed basilica type was to appear in Justinian's church of Hagia Sophia in Constantinople.

THE CHURCH OF HAGIA SOPHIA

The first foundations of the famous Church of Hagia Sophia,[12] or "Holy Wisdom," are believed by some to have been laid by Constantine,[13] but the church historian Socrates states only that it was

[9] Socrates, *Ch. Hist.* I, 16; II, 16.   [10] Procopius, *Buildings.* I, ii, 13.
[11] Walter S. George, *The Church of Saint Eirene at Constantinople.* 1912; Van Millingen, *Byzantine Churches in Constantinople,* pp.101f.
[12] Emerson H. Swift, *Hagia Sophia.* 1940; William Emerson and Robert L. Van Nice in AJA 47 (1943), pp.403-436.
[13] A. Van Millingen, *Byzantine Constantinople.* 1899, p.36.

built by Constantine's son and successor, Constantius II (337-361) and consecrated in A.D. 360.[14] It was known as "The Great Church"[15] and was dedicated to the Immortal Wisdom of Christ. The structure of Constantius was of the basilican type, with atrium, narthex, and nave flanked by side aisles marked off with rows of columns. Its roof was of wood, except for the half dome of the apse. This church was burned to the ground in A.D. 404, restored, and again burned down in A.D. 532. Then it was rebuilt in magnificence by Justinian, with Anthemius of Tralles and Isidorus of Miletus as his master builders. Dedication was in A.D. 537. Earthquake damage in 553 and 557 was repaired by Justinian and the dome somewhat raised by Isidorus the younger, nephew of the other Isidorus. Since that time the Great Church has survived the vicissitudes of the centuries, little changed. The huge exterior buttresses were added by the Emperor Andronicus II Palaeologus (1282-1328), and the four minarets were erected after the Mohammedans made the church into "the great mosque of Hagia Sophia" (Fig. 203). In 1931 the Turkish Government issued an order enabling the Byzantine Institute to begin to lay bare and study the ancient mosaics with which the church was adorned.[16] In 1934 the use of the building for a mosque was terminated and it was announced that it would be preserved henceforth as a museum and monument of Byzantine art.

A contemporary description of Hagia Sophia as it appeared in the time of Justinian was given by Procopius of Caesarea, who wrote extensively concerning that emperor's reign and particularly his widespread and notable building achievements.[17] "The church," wrote Procopius, "has become a spectacle of marvellous beauty, overwhelming to those who see it, but to those who know it by hearsay altogether incredible. For it soars to a height to match the sky, and as if surging up from amongst the other buildings it stands on high and looks down upon the remainder of the city."[18] Impres-

[14] *Ch. Hist.* ii, 16, 43.

[15] Procopius, *Buildings.* i, i, 66. This title was sometimes applied to include both Hagia Sophia and St. Eirene, which stood close together and were regarded as forming one sanctuary.

[16] Thomas Whittemore, *The Mosaics of St. Sophia at Istanbul, Preliminary Report on the First Year's Work, 1931-1932, The Mosaics of the Narthex.* 1933; *Second Preliminary Report, Work Done in 1933 and 1934, The Mosaics of the Southern Vestibule.* 1936; and in AJA 42 (1938), pp.219-226; 46 (1942), pp.169-171 and Plates i-x.

[17] The treatise on the *Buildings* of Justinian was published in 560 or soon thereafter.

[18] *Buildings.* i, i, 27.

sive as was the exterior of the Great Church, the interior (Fig. 204) was more wonderful still. It was adorned with many colored marbles and bathed with an abundance of light until the visitor "might imagine that he had come upon a meadow with its flowers in full bloom."[19] The crowning glory was the huge golden dome which seemed not to rest upon solid masonry but to hang suspended from heaven.[20] In its misty vastness the Spirit of God seemed to descend, and whoever entered to pray felt "that He cannot be far away, but must especially love to dwell in this place which He has chosen."[21] Such was the culminating achievement in the Byzantine development of the basilica.

The mysticism of the East was matched by the aspiration of the West. In the West the path of future development led through the modifications of Romanesque style[22] to the Gothic,[23] whose soaring loftiness is the soul's upward reach toward God. But basic to both Gothic and Byzantine adaptations was the essential structural form and meaning of the early Christian basilica which they preserved. This was the place where Jesus Christ was remembered and His gospel preached. In Him the natural upreach of religion and the answering presence of the Spirit of God meet in central historical reality.

[19] *Buildings.* I, i, 59.   [20] *Buildings.* I, i, 46.   [21] *Buildings.* I, i, 61.

[22] Romanesque means Roman-like and describes the architectural style which prevailed in the West from the fall of Rome (A.D. 476) down to the rise of Gothic. Here the basic basilican idea was modified chiefly through the increasing use of the rounded arch.

[23] Gothic architecture, which developed in Western Europe after A.D. 1100, was an outgrowth of Romanesque but particularly characterized by the use of the pointed arch.

INDEX OF SCRIPTURAL REFERENCES

GENERAL INDEX

All references are to pages, except where Figures, Maps or Plans are specifically indicated.

Light from the Ancient Past

This is a connected account of the background of the Bible and of early Christianity as known through the discoveries of archeology, covering the period 5000 B.C. to A.D. 500. Lucidly written and copiously illustrated, it can be read with delight by the general reader as well as by students of Near East civilization, ancient art, and Hebrew-Christian archeology.

Mr. Finegan traces the history and civilization of the lands in which the Hebrew and Christian religions arose, showing how Biblical history fits into this wider history, and describing and evaluating the Hebrew and Christian monuments which remain from ancient times. His work is founded upon the ancient sources, both literary and monumental, and in the fascinating section on Early Christianity he makes interesting research contributions of his own.

Light from the Ancient Past is notable for its compactness, its sense of continuity and variety of interest. While it was written primarily to illuminate and vivify the history of the Hebrew-Christian religion, it also contains much material relative to other ancient religions, to the history of thought and the development of culture, and to the evolution of art and architecture.

The author is an American scholar who received his Lic. theol. degree *magna cum laude* from the University of Berlin in 1934. He is a minister of the Disciples of Christ and director of religious activities at Iowa State College in Ames.